THE NATIONAL UNDERWRITER COMPANY

a division of ALM Media, LLC

2019 FIELD GUIDE: ESTATE & RETIREMENT PLANNING, BUSINESS PLANNING & EMPLOYEE BENEFITS

Randy L. Zipse, J.D., AEP® (Distinguished)
Donald F. Cady, J.D., LL.M., CLU®, Author Emeritus

This easy-to-use, practical reference is designed to provide quick summaries of the key concepts, tested techniques, expert analyses, and authoritative guidance to support your estate, business, retirement, and employee benefits planning.

2019 Field Guide: Estate & Retirement Planning, Business Planning & Employee Benefits includes over 100 presentation tools and practical illustrations, enabling you to communicate key concepts clearly to your clients to help them gain the understanding they need. It covers a broad range of information on almost any financial advisory topic, including:

- Estate tax planning concepts, charts, rates, exemptions, and 2019 inflation adjusted numbers (if they were available from the IRS at time of printing. Those that were not yet released are marked as projected)
- Life insurance concepts and creative ways to use it in retirement and estate planning
- Detailed employee benefits discussion for both employees and employers
- Trust planning, including saving for college, special needs and charities
- Social Security planning to maximize benefits
- Practical information on doing retirement and estate planning with blended families
- End-of-life directives
- Powers of attorney
- Small business succession planning
- Reference tables, such as mortality tables, 2019 income tax rates, RMD rates, and present and future valuation tables

With over 200 re-written pages to cover the 2017 Tax Reform Act, the 2019 edition features the following additional topics:

- Trust decanting
- Disability buy out plans

- Domestic partners
- Dynasty trust
- Stock options
- Opportunity zones under the Tax Reform Act
- Qualified business income deduction under the Tax Reform Act
- Updated content on C Corporations and S Corporations

This guide is the perfect resource for quick answers and overviews of unfamiliar topics, including citations to more information for those doing deeper research. Any type of financial advisor will find this handbook a valuable tool, such as insurance producers, CFPs, CPAs, Lawyers, and more!

Related Titles Also Available:

- *Tax Facts*
- *Social Security & Medicare Facts*
- *The Tools & Techniques of Trust Planning*
- *The Tools & Techniques of Estate Planning*
- *The Tools & Techniques of Estate Planning for Modern Families*
- *The Advisor's Guide to Annuities*

For customer service questions or to place orders for any of our products, please call 1-800-543-0874 or email customerservice@nuco.com.

2019 FIELD GUIDE

ESTATE & RETIREMENT PLANNING, BUSINESS PLANNING & EMPLOYEE BENEFITS

• Illustrated Sales Tools & Concepts
• Planning Pointers and Charts • Terms & Concepts
• Checklists • Statistics • Tables

Randy L. Zipse, J.D., AEP® (Distinguished)
Donald F. Cady, J.D., LL.M., CLU®, Author Emeritus

ISBN: 978-1-949506-31-0
ISSN: 1053-4407

The National Underwriter Company
a division of ALM Media, LLC
4147 Olympic Blvd., Suite 225, Erlanger, KY 41018

Printed in U. S. A.

ABOUT THE NATIONAL UNDERWRITER COMPANY

a division of ALM Media, LLC

For over 110 years, The National Underwriter Company, *a division of ALM Media, LLC* has been the first in line with the targeted tax, insurance, and financial planning information you need to make critical business decisions. Boasting nearly a century of expert experience, our reputable Editors are dedicated to putting accurate and relevant information right at your fingertips. With *Tax Facts*, *Tools & Techniques*, *Field Guide*, *FC&S®*, *FC&S Legal* and other resources available in print, eBook, CD, and online, you can be assured that as the industry evolves National Underwriter will be at the forefront with the thorough and easy-to-use resources you rely on for success.

Update Service Notification

This National Underwriter Company publication is regularly updated to include coverage of developments and changes that affect the content. If you did not purchase this publication directly from The National Underwriter Company, *a division of ALM Media, LLC* and you want to receive these important updates sent on a 30-day review basis and billed separately, please contact us at (800) 543-0874. Or you can mail your request with your name, company, address, and the title of the book to:

The National Underwriter Company
a division of ALM Media, LLC
4157 Olympic Boulevard
Suite 225
Erlanger, KY 41018

If you purchased this publication from The National Underwriter Company, *a division of ALM Media, LLC*, directly, you have already been registered for the update service.

Contact Information

To order any National Underwriter Company title, please

- call 1-800-543-0874, 8-6 ET Monday – Thursday and 8 to 5 ET Friday
- online bookstore at www.nationalunderwriter.com, or
- mail to Orders Department, The National Underwriter Company, *a division of ALM Media, LLC*, 4157 Olympic Blvd., Ste. 225, Erlanger, KY 41018

ABOUT THE AUTHORS

Randy L. Zipse, J.D., AEP (Distinguished) is currently Vice President, Advanced Markets for Global Atlantic Financial Group and has worked in the life insurance industry for the past twenty years where he has managed advanced markets departments for major life insurance carriers and independent distribution organizations.

Mr. Zipse has written numerous articles on trust taxation, estate planning, and business succession planning which have appeared in the *Journal of Financial Service Professionals*, *Broker World*, *Estate Planning, Life Insurance Selling*, and *National Underwriter*. He is the author of National Underwriter's *Field Guide*. He is also a co-author with Stephan R. Leimberg of *Tools and Techniques of Charitable Planning* and a member of the *Tax Facts* Editorial Advisory Board. Mr. Zipse is a frequent lecturer at industry meetings, including such major events as the AALU, Forum 400, Million Dollar Round Table, New York University Tax Institute, University of Miami Heckerling Tax Institute, Hawaii Tax Institute, and the Annual Harris M. Plaisted Conference.

Prior to entering the life insurance industry, he worked as an attorney in private practice. Mr. Zipse has been associated with several large firms, including Jones Day Reavis & Pogue and Gardere & Wynne – both in Dallas, Texas. As a private practice attorney, Mr. Zipse concentrated on estate planning, deferred compensation, business succession planning, and charitable planning. Prior to becoming an attorney, Mr. Zipse worked as a CPA with Deloitte Haskins & Sells.

An honors graduate of the University of Northern Iowa (B.A. in accounting), Mr. Zipse subsequently received his J.D. from Drake University College of Law (Order of the Coif, class rank number one), and is a member of the Iowa, Texas and Missouri Bars.

AUTHOR EMERITUS

Donald F. Cady conceived and developed the *Field Guide to Estate Planning, Business Planning & Employee Benefits* in 1989 and updated it annually for twenty-five years, when Randy L. Zipse was named the successor author. Mr. Cady continues as author of the *Field Guide to Financial Planning*, which is cowritten with Michael Kitces, MSFS, MTAX, CFP®, CLU, ChFC, RHU, REBC, CASL.

Mr. Cady is an attorney and a Chartered Life Underwriter. He is a graduate of St. Lawrence University with a B.A. in Economics, where he received the Wall Street Journal Award for excellence in that subject. He received his J.D. degree from Columbia University School of Law, holds the degree of LL.M. (Taxation) from Emory University School of Law, and is a member of the New York Bar.

He is an independent consultant working with The National Underwriter Company in providing support materials and services to the financial planning industry. In addition to this publication, he is the author of *Field Guide Online*[1], the web version of this book.

For twenty years Mr. Cady was with the Aetna Life Insurance & Annuity Company in various advanced underwriting positions. Prior to this, he was a member of the U.S. Army Judge Advocate Generals Corps, with tours of duty in both Vietnam and Europe. He and his wife live in Fort Myers Beach, Florida.

Mr. Cady has been a frequent speaker on the subjects of estate planning, business planning, and employee benefits, before business and professional organizations, estate planning associations, life underwriter's meetings and various civic groups. Through these appearances, together with his work with agents, their clients, and advisers, Mr. Cady has shared the frustrations of trying to effectively explain and communicate planning concepts and techniques to both student and laymen. The two *Field Guide* publications represent his response to that challenge.

CONTRIBUTING AUTHORS

Kristopher C. Stegall, CFP®, TEP, is Vice President, International Insurance at NFP Corporation. Kris is an expert in research, analysis and case design for the international marketplace. He is experienced in developing comprehensive solutions to address unique or complex goals related to wealth planning, business planning and specialized risk management. His knowledge enables him to navigate potential jurisdictional issues while evaluating a client's short and long-term needs. The result is holistic case consultation on a global scale for multinational individuals, families and businesses. At NFP, Kris manages worldwide market intelligence as it pertains to solicitation, taxation and country-specific issues. Utilizing NFP's direct access to carriers, case managers, product resources and underwriters, Kris provides a seamless experience from start to finish for the insurance advisor. Prior to joining NFP in 2007, Kris served as the operations lead for national and global organizations looking to increase profitability and ensure cost efficiencies. He earned his bachelor's in mathematics from Texas State University. Kris is a Certified Financial Planner™ and a full member of The Society of Trust and Estate Practitioners.

Mel Warshaw is the General Counsel of Financial Architects Partners. His primary responsibility is to deepen the company's relationship with advisors including trusts and estates lawyers, CPAs, family offices, corporate trustees and trust companies involved in complex life insurance programs undertaken for super affluent individuals and families. He has been a frequent speaker at industry forums, including the 2012 University of Miami Heckerling Institute, the University of Santa Clara Kasner Estate Planning Symposium and many regional bar association events.

Mel is currently a member of the editorial advisory board on insurance for Trusts & Estates magazine. Mel is the past chair of both the American Bar Association (ABA), Real Property Trusts & Estates Section (RPTE) Task Force on Policy Valuation and the ABA RPTE Life Insurance and Financial Planning Committee.

Mel has published numerous articles in *Trust & Estates* magazine, *Estate Planning Journal* and other publications. His recent articles include topics such as cost of insurance increases, investor control in private placement life insurance, life insurance as an asset class and use of life insurance by non-residents.

Prior to joining the company, Mel was a senior wealth advisor at JP Morgan Private Bank in Boston, MA and Greenwich, CT. From 1997-2004 Mel was the head of the Boston office Private Client Department and a partner in the international law firm of McDermott, Will & Emery. Previously, from 1981 until 1997, he was a partner in the Boston, MA law firm of Burns & Levinson. From 1977 to 1981, Mel was as an attorney in the General Counsel's office of the Internal Revenue Service in Washington, D.C.

Mr. Warshaw earned his LL.M. in Taxation from Georgetown University Law Center in 1980, his J.D. from St. Louis University School of Law in 1975, and his B.A. with Honors from University of Rochester in 1972.

ACKNOWLEDGEMENT

The author would like to thank Kevin Blanton and Marc Teitelbaum for their work as contributing editors in the past.

MANAGING EDITOR

Richard H. Cline, J.D., is the Manager, Tax and Insurance Content for the Practical Insights Division at the National Underwriter Company, an ALM Media Company. He is responsible for both the print and online versions of Tax Facts as well as developing new tax products for our customers.

Richard joined the company in 2013 but has over twenty-five years of tax editing and publishing experience. Prior to joining our team, Richard worked for Lexis-Nexis, CCH, Inc., and PricewaterhouseCoopers.

He has a B.S. degree from Franklin and Marshall College in Lancaster, Pennsylvania, and earned his law degree from Tulane University in New Orleans, Louisiana.

EDITORIAL SERVICES

Connie L. Jump, Senior Manager, Editorial Operations

Patti O'Leary, Senior Editorial Assistant

Emily Brunner, Editorial Assistant

[1] *Field Guide Online* is a trademark of The National Underwriter Company.

TABLE OF CONTENTS

Page

Page

BUSINESS PLANNING

EMPLOYEE BENEFITS

Page

REFERENCE MATERIALS

Page

Page

Page

Page

Page

Page

INTRODUCTION

The Purpose Of This Book

This book is intended to provide you with a ready means of identifying and understanding the concepts and techniques used in estate, business, and employee benefit planning. Recognizing that we live in a world of visual communication, numerous drawings and charts have been included to assist you in identifying and understanding many of the concepts which are most frequently encountered when working with clients and other professionals. It can serve as a desktop reference source, a classroom training aid, or, carried in your briefcase, as a resource to be shared with your client or his advisors. However, it is not intended to be a replacement for competent legal or tax counsel; only qualified professionals can provide such advice.

In recent years, maybe more so than in recent memory, tax reform and tax policy has been front and center in American politics. On December 22, 2017, President Donald Trump signed into legislation the Tax Cuts and Jobs Act of 2017. This legislation, that passed on nearly an entirely partisan basis, fundamentally changes the taxation of American business. It permanently reduces the C corporation tax rate to a flat 21 percent. It makes significant changes to pass-through taxation for S corporations, LLCs, and partnerships – including a 20 percent reduction in taxable income for many such entities. Individual tax changes are much less significant – but not insignificant for many taxpayers. Some individuals will see reductions in their taxes because of a reduction in marginal tax rates, but others will see increased taxes because of the elimination of many itemized deductions, including a cap on the deduction for state and local taxes. While the corporate tax changes are permanent, the individual changes will sunset at the end of 2025, unless extended by a future Congress and President. As a result of this significant change in tax law – much of the this book has been modified. We hope that this book can help advisors begin the process of understanding what this legislation means for their clients.

Organization

The Field Guide has been organized into three sections, dealing with the subjects of estate and retirement planning, business planning, and employee benefits. Each section is in turn divided into units typically consisting of a chart and accompanying text. Following most of the charts you will find a section entitled "Information Required For Analysis & Proposal." This is the minimum information you must obtain in order to prepare an analysis and proposal for your client. Also included are cross references to *Tax Facts on Insurance & Employee Benefits* or *Social Security & Medicare Facts*, and the footnotes. Following the charts, you will find references that support the subjects of estate planning, business planning, and employee benefits. Terms & Concepts contains expanded discussions of the materials previously referred to in the text and footnotes.

In using this book, first refer to the chart and read the accompanying text. Also, be sure to read the footnotes; they will provide you with a better understanding of the subject matter and references to additional materials.

Cross References To Tax Facts On Insurance & Employee Benefits

No attempt is made to provide either an exhaustive technical analysis or extensive citations to legal authority (Internal Revenue Code sections, regulations, case law, revenue rulings, and private letter rulings). For these purposes, you are encouraged to refer to the appropriate questions in the 2019 edition of *Tax Facts on Insurance & Employee Benefits*, published by The National Underwriter Company in two volumes. The cross references contain the question number followed by a brief description of the material covered (e.g., "**Q 322**. Valuation of closely held business interest for federal estate tax purposes when there is a purchase agreement").

Where appropriate, there are also cross references to the 2019 edition of *Tax Facts on Investments* and the 2019 edition of *Social Security & Medicare Facts*, also published by The National Underwriter Company.

All of these publications are updated online as needed and are available for purchase at www.Nationalunderwriter.com.

TABLE OF CONTENTS

POINTERS

After more than a decade of confusion Congress finally acted to bring greater certainty to the estate tax law. Under the American Taxpayer Relief Act of 2012 (ATRA) reunification of the estate and gift tax regimes, the $5 million exemptions for estate taxes, gift taxes, and generation-skipping transfer taxes became permanent and are no longer subject to periodic sunsets. Beginning in 2013 the top estate tax rate was increased from 35 percent to 40 percent. The ATRA permanently extended both indexing of the exemption and the portability provisions of the 2010 Tax Relief Act that allow any unused exemption to be passed to a surviving spouse without the need to re-title assets and establish complex wills and trusts (see the discussion of Portability on page 491).

Post ATRA, individuals will pay either no federal estate tax or an estate tax at the rate of 40 percent (see table on page 582). Subject to the federal estate tax, the top 2/10 of 1 percent of estates (i.e., the "Forty-Percenters") are multi-millionaires with estates over $11.4 million (projected in 2019) that will continue to grow at or above the rate of inflation ($22.8 million in 2019 (projected) in the case of a married couple).

However, despite the estate tax certainty supposedly brought by ATRA, Congress and President Trump once again brought uncertainty to estate and business planning by passing the Tax Cuts and Jobs Act of 2017 (2017 Tax Act). The 2017 Tax Act, at a scheduled cost of $1.5 Trillion, brings "permanent" change to corporate taxation through significant reductions in marginal rates and other significant changes. However, individual tax changes, including moderately lower marginal income tax brackets and a doubling of the estate tax exemption – are temporary with a scheduled "sunset" for December 31, 2025.

Even at the time of printing the 2019 edition of Field Guide, the GOP-led Congress and President Trump continue to discuss further tax cuts. The immediate future of additional tax reform will likely be dependent upon the 2018 mid-year elections and if the GOP remains in control of the House and Senate.

Estate Planning for the Zero-Percenters.

With the inflation-adjusted exemption AFTRA permanently (or so Congress said at the time) shielded these estates from the federal estate tax. For the Zero-Percenters federal estate taxes are no longer a consideration in estate planning.

Reconsider Gifts. Zero-Percenters should consider retaining assets in their estates in order to obtain a stepped-up basis for their heirs (i.e., there is no federal estate tax at death and the stepped-up basis will reduce the heir's income tax burden when assets are subsequently sold). The potential value of a stepped-up basis is enhanced by the recent increase in the maximum capital gains tax to 20 percent and the 3.8 percent Medicare tax on investment income (see page 635). However, for large estates over the AFTR exemption ($5 million indexed for inflation), consideration needs to also be made as to the benefit of utilizing the additional gift tax exemption created under the 2017 Tax Act (scheduled to sunset after 2025).

Review Trusts. Changed circumstances may indicate a need to consider either foregoing gifts to the trust, canceling the trust and distributing the funds, or revising the trust terms (see Decanting on page 334).

Asset Protection. In the past many estate tax avoidance techniques involved irrevocable trusts, limited liability companies, and family limited partnerships (see pages 98-101, 210, and 449). These vehicles should not be discontinued merely because the federal estate tax no longer threatens the estate. There is still a need for asset protection, income shifting, and wealth management. With the passage of ATRA it is clear that revenue-sharing by the federal government via the state death tax credit will not return. Estates will continue to be subject to state death taxes in those states that have decoupled from the federal estate tax (see the discussion of Decoupling on page 335 and on Domicile on page 136.

Estate Planning for the Forty-Percenters.

Despite temporary doubling of the estate and gift tax exemption included in the 2017 Tax Act, the Forty-Percenters should recognize there is a very likely possibility that their estates will be subject to some form of taxation at death. Currently, the estates of Forty-Percenters will be subject to a federal estate tax of 40 percent on amounts above the inflation-adjusted exemption (in 2019, $11.4 million for single individuals and $22.8 million for a married couple). They will also be subject to *state* death taxes in states that have decoupled from the federal estate tax. To raise revenues in the face of significantly increasing federal deficits, a future Congress could once again reduce that estate tax exemption, or replace the current estate and gift tax system with the current Congress. It is likely that it would be replaced by a capital gains tax at death or carry-over cost basis (passing the capital gains tax to their beneficiaries).

Reconsider the Bypass Trust. When assets are placed in a bypass trust future appreciation of those assets is taxed to the beneficiaries of the trust upon sale of the assets (see Trust Will chart on page 21 and QTIP Trust chart on page 31). However, if these assets are left outright to a surviving spouse, then upon the surviving spouse's death this appreciation will receive a stepped-up basis and upon subsequent sale the gain would be tax-free to the beneficiaries. Since with portability the estate tax exemption will not be lost, the first-to-die spouse should consider foregoing use of the bypass trust in order to obtain a stepped-up basis for subsequent appreciation (i.e., pass property to the surviving spouse, not to the trust). Irrevocable Life Insurance Trust (ILIT). The ILIT remains a very effective estate planning tool to provide funds for paying estate taxes (among other purposes) for the Forty-Percenters (see chart on page 55).

Estate Planning for All

The Nontax Reasons for Estate Planning. The primary objectives of most estate plans involve estate creation, support and care of a surviving family, and the orderly transfer of property during lifetime or at death, as well as planning to minimize state death taxes. This often involves providing for the care of minor children, support for disabled children and elderly parents, and protection of loved ones from creditors. For some individuals the motivation to plan their estates is found in a strong desire to assure the survival of a business, or to provide for their church or a charity.

Life Insurance. Are there enough life insurance proceeds, liquid assets, and other sources of income to maintain the current living standards of your client's surviving family? Unfortunately, all too many individuals remain underinsured. For those clients needing insurance to pay taxes, delaying the purchase of currently needed life insurance could be disastrous.

Coordination is important. It is often difficult, if not impossible; to design an effective estate plan without considering your client's employee benefit programs and business disposition plans. Effective planning cannot be achieved unless there is an awareness of the interplay between the various strategies and techniques of estate planning, business planning, and employee benefits. For example, the liquidity needs of a business owner's estate plan are directly influenced by whether the business is to be sold, continued, or liquidated (see chart on page 163).

Overall Rise of the Importance of Income Tax Planning in Estate Planning

Recent tax law changes have in many cases shifted the focus of such planning from estate and gift tax planning to income tax planning. This shift has occurred for several reasons.

First, as noted above, with the increase in the federal estate tax exemptions under ATRA and the 2017 Tax Act, fewer people and fewer estates are subject to the federal estate tax while income taxes remain applicable to a broad base of taxpayers.

Second, despite slightly lower (or temporary until sunset on December 31, 2025) marginal income tax rates for individuals, effective income tax rates actually increased for many people because of the loss of tax deductions. While ATRA established a new top rate for ordinary income of 39.6 percent for taxpayers at the highest income levels, it was reduced to 37 percent by the 2017 tax reform legislation. This rate applies to those with taxable income in excess of $510,300 for single individuals, $612,350 for married couples filing jointly, and only $12,750 for estates and trusts in 2019 (projected). In addition, the top long-term capital gain and qualified dividend tax rate remained at 20 percent for taxpayers in the above mentioned highest ordinary income tax bracket.

In addition, The Patient Protection and Affordable Care Act ("PPACA"), which was originally enacted in 2010, established a new 3.8 percent surtax on investment income which first became effective in 2013. For purposes of this tax, investment income includes interest, dividends, rent, royalties, capital gain and passive activity income. This additional tax applies to taxpayers with an adjusted gross income in excess of $200,000 for single individuals and $250,000 for married couples filing jointly. For estates and trusts, this tax applies to the lesser of (i) undistributed net investment income or (ii) the excess of adjusted gross income over the amount at which the top income tax bracket for trusts and estates begins $12,750 in 2019 (projected). Considering this additional 3.8 percent tax, for taxpayers in the highest bracket, their effective ordinary federal income tax rate (not considering state income tax rates) can be as high as 38.8 percent, and the top long term capital gain and qualified dividend tax rate is now effectively almost 24 percent.

ESTATE PLANNING MATRIX

In the traditional sense, estate planning means preparing for the orderly and efficient transfer of assets at death. Within this definition, the basic objectives of estate planning are set forth in the discussion of the Estate Funnel on page 10.

However, estate planning has also come to involve planning for the accumulation and distribution of an estate during lifetime as well as at death. It must also be recognized that comprehensive estate planning will often involve the concepts and techniques contained in the business planning and employee benefits chapters of this guide. For example, although additional estate liquidity would be provided from the sale of a business interest, estate taxes will be increased through inclusion of the proceeds of the sale in the taxable estate. Likewise, an effective estate plan should maximize employee benefits, while at the same time taking into consideration their impact upon the estate.

The following matrix should provide a better understanding of how the concepts and techniques, represented in the charts, can be used to solve estate planning problems.

PROBLEM	SOLUTION(S)	PAGE
Loss of Estate Value Through Estate Tax	TRUST WILL provides the opportunity to reduce estate taxes.	20
	QTIP TRUST provides opportunity to reduce taxes while controlling disposition of estate.	30
	GIFTS & SPLIT-GIFTS remove property from the estate.	50
	LIFE INSURANCE AS PROPERTY shows how life insurance can be excluded from the gross estate for federal tax purposes.	98
	LIFE INSURANCE TRUST can remove life insurance death proceeds from the estate.	54
	CHARITABLE REMAINDER TRUST can remove from estate taxable property that can be replaced by life insurance in a Wealth Replacement Trust.	58
	GRANTOR RETAINED ANNUITY TRUST allows a grantor to retain an annuity interest while at the same time reducing estate taxes.	62
Loss of Estate Value Through Estate Tax (continued)	GENERATION-SKIPPING TRANSFERS shows use of exemption in 2019 to transfer $11,400,000 (projected value) to grandchildren.	34
Estimating the Estate Tax	FEDERAL ESTATE TAX explains the calculations.	14

Payment of Estate Costs	LIFE INSURANCE PRODUCTS can be used to provide funds to pay these costs. Chart compares alternative plans and explains their basic characteristics and essential differences.	102
Distribution of Estate	SIMPLE WILL can provide for the distribution of estate assets, including specific bequests.	18
	TRUST WILL offers added tax savings and the post death management of assets.	20
	REVOCABLE LIVING TRUST (RLT) is a will substitute offering many advantages during lifetime and at death.	24
	POUR-OVER WILL functions as a "fail safe" device to transfer property at death into the RLT.	28
Replacement of Income:		
Upon Death	LIFE INSURANCE PRODUCTS can provide funds to replace lost income in case of death (one approach to determining the necessary funds is contained in the discussion of human life value)	102
Upon Disability	DIABILITY – THE LIVING DEATH demonstrates the need for proper planning before disability occurs.	248
Upon Retirement	DEFERRED ANNUITY can be used to accumulate funds on a tax-favored basis.	42
Insufficient Income or Assets for Custodial Care In Retirement	LONG-TERM CARE planning provides an understanding of the risk and cost of long-term care and how the risk can be managed.	114
Management of Assets and Orderly Payment of Income to Spouse and Children	LIFE INSURANCE TRUST provides for both asset management and ongoing payments.	54
	TRUST WILL with provisions for both asset management and payment of continuing income to beneficiaries.	20
	REVOCABLE LIVING TRUST can provide for management of assets both before and after death.	24
Guardianship of Children	SIMPLE WILL with provisions for appointment of guardian (TRUST WILL can also contain these same provisions).	18

THE ESTATE FUNNEL

The estate funnel helps to explain the types of property found in most estates, the problems often encountered in settling an estate, and the objectives of estate planning.

The property found in most estates generally falls into one of five categories:

Personal property, such as furniture, cars, jewelry, cash, bonds, savings, and other personal effects.

Real estate, such as a home, a vacation house, land, and rental property such as apartments or office buildings.[1]

Business interests, in the form of closely held corporations, partnerships, or sole proprietorships.

Life insurance, either group insurance or individual policies.

Government benefits, such as social security, disability, retirement, and survivor income benefits.

Unfortunately, at death there is often a great deal of CONFLICT. This occurs due to the differing and conflicting ways in which many of these assets pass to the family or other heirs. For example, personal property can pass by will, by state law if there is no will, by title, or by trust.[2] Real estate and business interests may also pass by all of these means, as well as by agreement. Generally life insurance passes by beneficiary designation, and government benefits by federal statute.

These conflicts, together with the generally slow probate process, can easily result in a DELAY of 1 to 2 years or more.[3]

Considerable EXPENSE may also be incurred during the estate settlement process. For example, existing debts must be paid. There are also medical expenses, funeral expenses, attorney fees, income taxes, and estate taxes. The final result is often a shrinkage of 30 percent or more by the time an estate is passed to the surviving family.[4]

The basic objectives of estate planning are to provide for the orderly and efficient accumulation, conservation, and distribution of an estate, while avoiding conflict, shortening delays, and reducing expenses.[5]

Footnotes on page 13

PEOPLE AT WORK - CAPITAL AT WORK

Personal Property | Real Estate | Business Interests | Life Insurance | Government Benefits

CONFLICT

Will • State Law • Title • Trust • Agreement
Beneficiary Designation • Federal Statute

DELAY

1 to 2 Years or More

EXPENSE

Debts • Medical & Funeral Expenses
Attorney Fees • Income & Estate Taxes

Shrinkage of 30% or More

Family

OBJECTIVES OF ESTATE PLANNING

Avoid Conflict • Shorten Delays • Reduce Expenses

INFORMATION REQUIRED FOR ANALYSIS & PROPOSAL

1. Names of client, spouse, and children.
2. Dates of birth.
3. For client and spouse – smoker/nonsmoker.
4. Type of wills (simple, exemption trust, marital share, etc.).
5. Trusts established.

Assets (determine how titled – individual, joint, etc.)

6. Personal and intangible property (fair market value and cost basis):

   liquid – cash, checking accounts, certificates of deposit, money market funds, mutual funds, municipal bonds, corporate bonds, annuities, options, etc.

   illiquid – contents of home, personal effects, jewelry, collections, cars, notes, leases, royalties, and tax sheltered investments.

   employee benefits – individual retirement accounts, HR-10 plans, tax deferred annuities, 401(k) plans, and vested deferred compensation and pension plan benefits (including beneficiary designations).
7. Real estate: home, vacation home, land, lots, commercial property, and investment property.
8. Business interests: corporations, partnerships, sole proprietorships, and farming operations.
9. Insurance: group and individual life insurance, disability and health coverage (including ownership and beneficiary designations).
10. Government benefits: social security disability payments, survivor benefits, and retirement payments.

Liabilities

11. Short-term debt: bills payable, loans, notes, consumer debt.
12. Long-term debt: home mortgage and home equity loans.

Obligations and Objectives

13. Debt to be paid at death (including final expenses).
14. Charitable bequests.
15. Monthly income required by surviving family.
16. Monthly income required by spouse after children are grown.
17. Cost for children's education (per year).
18. Monthly income in case of long-term disability or retirement.

Special Circumstances

19. Support for ex-spouse or children from prior marriage.
20. Support for other dependents.
21. Citizenship of client and spouse, if not U.S.

Footnotes

1 Where more than one person owns real estate or certain types of personal property, the form of ownership determines how the property is passed upon death. The form of ownership also determines the extent to which the property is includable in the gross estate for federal estate tax purposes:

a. Where the property is owned in a **tenancy in common**, each tenant – or co-owner – has a fractional, divisible interest in the property. Upon the death of a co-owner, his fractional interest is probate property and passes by will or by state intestacy laws. Each surviving co-tenant retains his proportionate interest in the property. The fair market value of the decedent's fractional interest is includable in the federal gross estate.

b. Where the property is owned in **joint tenancy with right of survivorship**, each joint tenant has an undivided interest in the entire property. The survivorship right is the key characteristic: upon the death of a joint tenant, the decedent's interest passes by operation of law to the surviving tenant or tenants. The decedent's interest is not a probate asset and therefore cannot be disposed of by will or intestacy law. For federal estate tax purposes, joint tenancy with right of survivorship does not necessarily prevent all or any of the property from inclusion in the federal gross estate upon the death of a joint owner. However, a joint-and-survivorship property interest created *between spouses* after 1976 is considered to be a "qualified joint interest." As such, only *one-half* of the value is included in the gross estate for federal tax purposes. All other joint-and-survivorship property is *fully* includable in the gross estate of the first owner to die, except to the extent that the decedent's estate can demonstrate that the survivor contributed to the purchase price. However, jointly owned property obtained through gift or inheritance is included in proportion to the decedent's ownership interest.

c. Some states recognize a **tenancy by the entirety**. Generally, this form of ownership parallels joint-and-survivorship property except that it may be created by husband and wife only.

d. In **community property** states each spouse is considered to own an undivided one-half interest in such property during the marriage, and each spouse is free to dispose of his or her share of community property upon death. One-half of the fair market value of community property is includable in the decedent spouse's estate. See the expanded discussion of community property on pages 317-318.

2 The unlimited marital deduction allows jointly owned property to pass to a surviving spouse free of the federal gift or estate tax. However, having virtually all property in joint title with right of survivorship can defeat the potential estate tax advantages of the Trust Will (chart, page 21). When property is jointly owned, it passes by law directly to the surviving spouse and therefore cannot pass into the non-marital, or "B" trust. Such over qualification of the unlimited marital deduction means that the property may be subject to taxation upon the subsequent death of the surviving spouse. Furthermore, there may be certain income tax disadvantages to having property jointly owned if and when the surviving spouse sells the property. See page 555 for an expanded discussion of stepped-up basis.

3 See page 500 for a discussion of the probate process.

4 See page 299 for a discussion of asset protection techniques.

5 During the fact-finding phase of estate planning it is important to obtain for review numerous client documents (see page 583). See also, Survivor Checklist on page 602.

FEDERAL ESTATE TAX

One of the potential expenses of settling larger estates is the federal estate tax.[1] It is a continuous lien on your client's property, but its foreclosure date is yet to be determined. Proper planning involves anticipating and reducing the estate tax liability wherever possible as well as providing for payment of the tax. Unlike other expenses of settling an estate, it can be particularly burdensome in that it is generally due and payable *in cash* 9 months after death.[2]

The estate tax computation is not difficult, and in many ways resembles the calculations involved in determining income tax. When we file our income tax return each year, the calculations involve terms such as gross income, taxable income, deductions, and credits.

When an *estate* tax return is filed, we are likewise dealing with terms such as gross estate, adjusted gross estate, taxable estate, deductions, and credits.

Generally, the **gross estate** includes *all* property of any description and wherever located, to the extent the decedent had any interest in the property at the time of death.[3] It may even include property previously given away or over which the decedent had no control at the time of his death.

To illustrate, assume that in 2019 we have an unmarried individual with an estate totaling $8,000,000. In determining the adjusted gross estate, we can subtract the decedent's debts, such as loans, notes, and mortgages, plus the debts of the estate, such as funeral and administrative expenses. If these debts totaled $500,000, then the **adjusted gross estate** would be $14,500,000. For this discussion, assume that the taxable estate is also $14,500,000[4] With a taxable estate of $14,500,000 the **tentative tax** would be $5,800,800.

However, in 2019 there is an **estate tax unified credit** available which can offset up to $4,505,800 (projected value) of the tentative tax. Generally, the unified credit allows an individual to pass $11,400,000 (projected) of property free of federal estate taxes upon death.[5]

After taking advantage of the credit, the estate will still owe a tax of $1,240,000, which means that the amount of the original estate remaining for the children or other heirs has been reduced to $13,260,000.

In addition to federal estate taxes, eighteen states and the District of Columbia have either a state inheritance or estate tax.[6]

Footnotes on page 17

GROSS ESTATE

$15,000,000

ADJUSTED GROSS ESTATE

(Taxable Estate)

$14,500,000

BENEFIT OF UNIFIED CREDIT

$4,417,700 (projected)

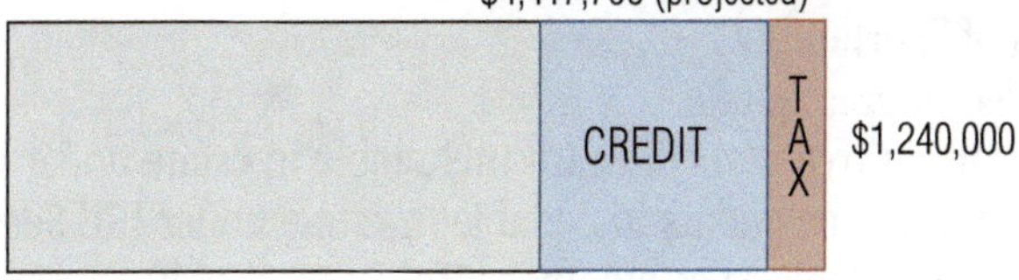

REMAINING

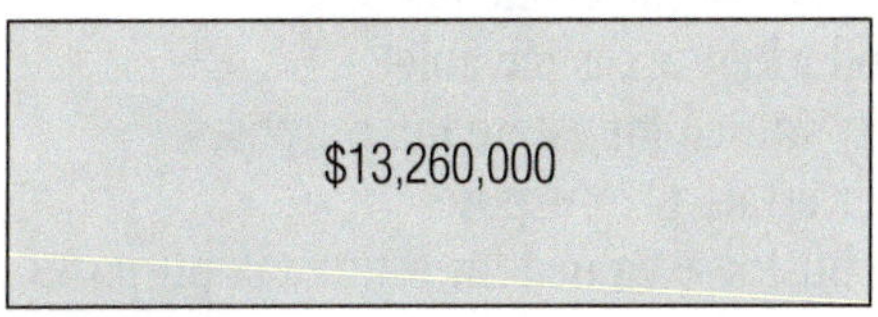

INFORMATION REQUIRED FOR ANALYSIS & PROPOSAL

Current listing and values of all property to include:

1. Cash.
2. Liquid assets (stocks, bonds).
3. Real estate (home, land, rental property).
4. Personal property (household goods, collections, and jewelry).
5. Business interests (closely held stock, partnership interests, and sole proprietorships).
6. Life insurance owned or insurance payable to estate (group insurance and individual policies).
7. Employee benefits (IRA, HR-10, 403(b) plan, pension/profit sharing, and 401(k) plan).
8. Current debts (short-term and long-term).
9. Prior taxable gifts made after December 31, 1976.

Note: A copy of the client's latest personal financial statement should disclose most of this information. Be sure to determine how the assets are titled (separate, joint ownership with spouse, community property, etc.). A copy of wills and trusts should also be obtained. See also pages 12 and 583.

CROSS REFERENCES TO TAX FACTS ON INSURANCE & EMPLOYEE BENEFITS, VOL. 1 (2019)

Q 746. Taxation of income in respect of a decedent.
Q 829. Overview of estate tax.
Q 833. Explanation of "portability."
Q 834. Items included in gross estate.
Q 837. Gifts made within three years of death includable in estate under IRC Section 2035.
Q 841. Annuities or annuity payments includable in estate under IRC Section 2039.
Q 842. Joint interests includable in estate under IRC Section 2040.
Q 844. Powers of appointment includable in estate under IRC Section 2041.
Q 847. Life insurance proceeds includable in estate under IRC Section 2042.
Q 858. Deductions which are allowed.
Q 871. Credits that may be taken against the estate tax.
Q 877. Who must file a return and when tax is payable.
Q 926. How is investment property valued for estate tax purposes.
Q 935. Mutual funds valuation for estate tax purposes
Q 937. Interests in a closely-held business valued for estate tax purposes

Footnotes

1 This chart illustrates the changes made to the estate tax exemption so that only estates valued at over $10,000,000 (as indexed for inflation) are subject to federal estate taxes and the top estate rate beginning in 2013 is 40 percent. See Estate Tax Pointers on page 5.

2 If certain strict conditions are met, payment of the *federal* estate tax can be deferred (see page 336). However, this does not mean that payment of applicable state inheritance and estate taxes can be similarly postponed (see page 138). A federal estate tax return (Form 706), if required, must be filed, and the tax paid, by the executor within nine months after death. The *penalty* for failure to file a timely return is 5 percent of the tax for each month the return is past due, up to a maximum of 25 percent. A detailed listing of these penalties is on page 484.

3 The gross estate also includes "income in respect of a decedent" (IRD), which refers to those amounts to which a decedent was entitled as gross income, but which were not includable in the taxable income for the year of death. IRD is subject to income taxation in the hands of the person who receives it. For an expanded discussion see page 403.

4 For purposes of illustration, this chart assumes there is no surviving spouse and that the adjusted gross estate is equal to the taxable estate. In the usual calculation sequence, debts (including funeral expenses), administrative expenses, and losses during administration are subtracted from the gross estate (as reduced by exclusions) to arrive at the adjusted gross estate. Charitable and marital deductions are then subtracted from the adjusted gross estate to determine the taxable estate. The principal deduction in this latter step has always been the marital deduction. Since it has been assumed that there is no surviving spouse, there can be no marital deduction, and therefore the adjusted gross estate is equal to the taxable estate. In community property states, the assumption of "no surviving spouse" means that all property is assumed to be separately owned.

5 This $11,400,000 (projected, $10,000,000 as indexed for inflation) is known either as the "applicable exclusion amount" or the "basic exclusion amount." When there is a surviving spouse, the "applicable exclusion amount" includes the $11,400,000 basic exclusion amount, plus the deceased spousal unused exclusion amount (i.e., the unused exclusion of the last deceased spouse). In 2019 the basic exclusion amount of $11,400,000 reflects indexing for post-2017 inflation. In the past this exemption has been variously referred to as the "exemption equivalent," "estate tax exemption equivalent," "unified credit equivalent," and "unified credit exemption equivalent." The 2017 Tax Act temporarily doubles this applicable exclusion amount while continuing to index the underlying $5,000,000 exemption for inflation.

6 Connecticut, Delaware, DC, Hawaii, Illinois, Maine, Massachusetts, Minnesota, New York, Oregon, Rhode Island, Vermont, and Washington have a state estate tax. Iowa, Kentucky, Nebraska, and Pennsylvania have an inheritance tax, New Jersey and Maryland have both. Over the past decade states have been regularly adjusting their estate and inheritance tax exemptions and rates. It's important to know the individual state rules for your state of residence.

SIMPLE WILL

Everyone should have a will. By having a will, we can be sure that property goes to *whom* we want, and in the *amounts* we want, rather than as provided under a state's intestacy laws.

Although there are various types of wills, the most common is the *simple* will.[1] A typical simple will provides for: (1) payment of just debts and expenses; (2) appointment of an executor or executrix; (3) specific bequests; (4) transfer of the entire estate to the surviving spouse; (5) if there is no surviving spouse, then transfer of the estate to children or other heirs; and (6) appointment of a guardian or guardians for minor children and their property.

UPON THE FIRST DEATH, the simple will generally passes *all* property to the surviving spouse. No matter how large the estate, **no taxes** will be paid on this transfer. This is possible because of the unlimited marital deduction.

UPON THE SECOND DEATH, provided the estate does not exceed $11,400,000 ($10,000,000 as indexed for inflation in 2019 (projected)), the estate will not be subject to federal estate taxes.[2]

For the individual who has a relatively small estate, the simple will is usually adequate. However, this most basic of wills does not take advantage of the opportunity to place assets in trust, provide for the continued management of estate assets for a surviving spouse, and assure that the estate will eventually pass to children upon the death of the surviving spouse.

---

[1] Some commentators have suggested that, because it passes all property to the surviving spouse, the simple will should be called the "I love you" will. Without a will, property passes according to state law (see Intestate's Will, page 585 and State Laws on Intestate Succession, pages 586-594).

[2] Each spouse has an estate tax exemption of $11,400,000 (projected, $10,000,000 as indexed for inflation). This is called the "basic exclusion amount." When there is a surviving spouse, the deceased spouse's unused basic exclusion may be added to the surviving spouse's basic exclusion (called the "applicable exclusion amount"). Without prior planning this enables a married couple to pass to their children up to $22,800,000 ($10,000,000 as indexed for inflation) free of federal estate taxes (2 × $11,400,000 = $22,800,000). However, the surviving spouse can only claim this unused exclusion if the executor of the deceased spouse's estate files an estate tax return making a deceased spousal unused exclusion amount (DSUEA) election. With portability of the exclusion between spouses, it is not necessary to establish an exemption trust or by-pass will in order to realize federal estate tax savings (see discussion on page 491). See also, footnotes 1 and 6 on page 17.

ESTATE

UPON THE FIRST DEATH

All Property To Spouse

↓

No Taxes

UPON THE SECOND DEATH

To Children

↓

TRUST WILL

A will creating a trust can provide for the continued management of estate assets for a surviving spouse and assure that the estate will eventually pass to children upon the death of the surviving spouse. With large estates a trust can freeze the value of property during the surviving spouse's lifetime so that future appreciation will not be subject to federal estate taxes upon the surviving spouse's death.[1]

UPON THE FIRST DEATH, with the typical trust will, the estate is divided into *two* parts, with one part placed in a family or nonmarital trust ("B" trust in the chart).[2] No taxes are paid on this since the amount is equal to or less than the applicable exclusion amount (i.e., the amount in 2019 that each individual can pass tax-free to the next generation).[3]

Unless there is a disclaimer, the remaining estate is passed to the surviving spouse.[4] This qualifies for the unlimited marital deduction and can be passed free of federal estate taxes.[5] Although it is sometimes given outright, this portion of the estate is often placed in trust, which is referred to as either the "A" trust or the "marital deduction" trust.[6] If the property is placed in trust, the spouse should be given a life estate with a power of appointment or a QTIP interest.[7]

The surviving spouse can also be given a right to *all income* from the "B" trust, as well as the right to demand, each year, either $5,000 or 5 percent of the trust corpus, whichever amount is larger. Property subject to a $5,000 or 5 percent demand right held at death is subject to taxation in the surviving spouse's estate only to the extent of the demand right.

UPON THE SECOND DEATH in 2019, unless the surviving spouse's estate exceeds $11,400,000 (projected, $10,000,000 as indexed for inflation), the estate will not be subject to federal estate taxation.[8] The amount previously placed in the "B" trust passes tax-free to the children under the terms previously established in that trust. Since the surviving spouse has no power to control the disposition of property placed in this trust, it is not included in the surviving spouse's estate.

Footnotes on page 23

ESTATE

UPON THE FIRST DEATH

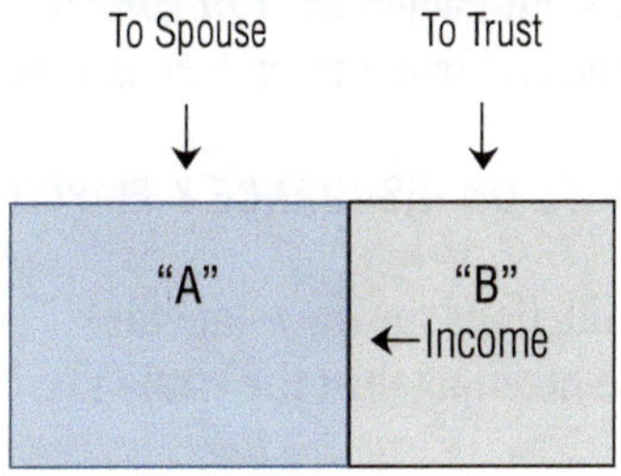

UPON THE SECOND DEATH

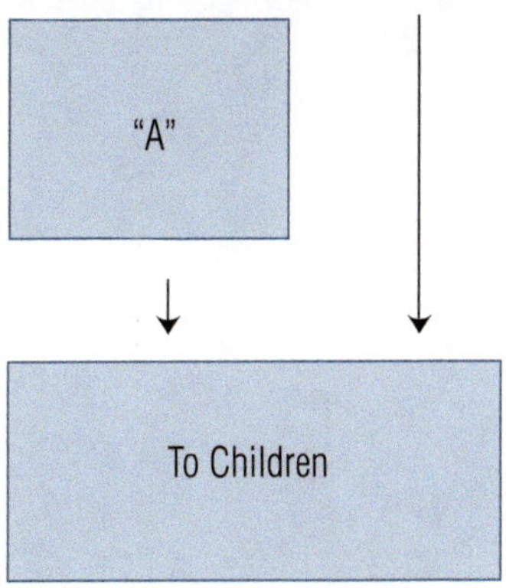

INFORMATION REQUIRED FOR ANALYSIS & PROPOSAL

Attorney Drafting Will Must Know

1. Spouse's name.
2. Spouse's citizenship.
3. Children's names.
4. Name of executor/executrix.
5. Ages of minor children.
6. Names and ages of other beneficiaries.
7. Trustee after testator's death.
8. To whom, in what amounts, and when trust *income* is to be paid.
9. To whom, in what amounts, and when trust *corpus* is to be paid.

CROSS REFERENCES TO TAX FACTS ON INSURANCE & EMPLOYEE BENEFITS, VOL. 1 (2019)

Q 857. Description of the deductions for the estate tax.
Q 871. Credits which may be taken against the estate tax.

Footnotes

[1] See footnote 6 on page 17 for an explanation of terms "applicable exclusion amount" and "basic exclusion amount" and page 491 for a discussion of the portability of the unused exclusion between spouses. Portability of the unused exclusion amount serves a similar function as a "family" trust in many estates, but proper planning will depend on the particulars of the individual estates, such as whether the estate ultimately faces some estate taxation.

[2] This is often referred to as a *limited* trust will, in that the amount placed in the "B" trust is limited to the applicable exclusion amount, $11,400,000 ($10,000,000 as indexed for inflation in 2019 (projected)) if no lifetime taxable gifts were made (see footnote 6, page 17). This trust is also referred to as an exemption, bypass, unified credit, credit shelter, credit amount, or credit equivalent bypass trust. If most property is held by a husband and wife in joint title with right of survivorship, the "A" trust could be *overqualified* and there may not be $11,400,000 of other property available to place in the "B" trust. In contrast, when a tax-driven formula is used to determine the amount going to the "B" trust, it may become overfunded (e.g., when a will directs that the amount to the "B" trust shall be the maximum amount that can be passed without paying an estate tax). In contrast to the Trust Will, see the Marital Plan Will, page 536.

[3] In large estates in 2019 the $11,400,000 (projected $10,000,000 as indexed for inflation) generation skipping transfer tax (GSTT) exemption can be used when there is a desire to pass property to grandchildren while avoiding estate or gift taxation at the children's generation (see chart, page 35).

[4] There may be occasions when it is desired to give the surviving spouse the opportunity to take more, or less, property than would be received under the typical trust will. This can be accomplished with the use of disclaimers, which are more fully explained on page 346.

[5] There may be circumstances in which the testator will *not* wish to take advantage of the unlimited marital deduction. For example, by taking full advantage of the marital deduction, the business asset will continue to appreciate in the estate of the surviving spouse. This potential appreciation would be eliminated by passing the business to the children or other heirs upon the first death. However, the cost to do this is the early payment of estate taxes on business values in excess of $11,400,000 (projected, $10,000,000 as indexed for inflation). Of course, considerations other than financial ones may influence the ultimate decision (e.g., adult children working in the family business have a strong desire to take over operation and full ownership of the business, rather than to receive the business upon the ultimate death of the surviving parent). Generally, the marital deduction is unavailable when the surviving spouse is not a United States citizen unless the transfer is to a qualified domestic trust (see expanded discussions, pages 473 and 509). For an expanded discussion of the marital deduction, see page 459. In fact, with estate taxes at least temporarily eliminated for most family business owners, non-tax considerations should be a bigger than ever consideration when planning.

[6] One type of marital deduction trust is also referred to as a "power of appointment" trust, in that the surviving spouse is given a general power of appointment over the trust during lifetime or at death. For a discussion of the power of appointment trust, see page 493.

[7] Refer to page 31 for a chart illustrating the use of a qualified terminable interest property trust. Also, see page 493 for a discussion of powers of appointment.

[8] In 2019, the combined estates of husband and wife would have to exceed $22,800,000 (projected $20,000,000 as indexed for inflation) before there would they would be subject to the federal estate tax. However, the estates could be subject to state death taxes (see page 138).

REVOCABLE LIVING TRUST

The revocable living trust (RLT) is a ***will substitute*** that can accomplish many estate planning objectives. It is an agreement established during the grantor's lifetime that may be amended or revoked at any time prior to the grantor's disability or death. The primary advantages of the RLT include: (1) providing for the management of grantor's assets upon his mental or physical disability thus avoiding conservatorship proceeding; (2) reducing costs and time delays by avoiding probate; (3) reducing the chances of a successful challenge or election against a will; (4) maintaining confidentiality by not having to file a public will; and (5) avoiding ancillary administration of out-of-state assets.[1]

Two additional documents are typically executed together with the RLT:[2]

- The **durable power of attorney** authorizes the power-holder to act for the grantor when the grantor is disabled.[3]
- The **pour-over will** functions as a "fail safe" device to transfer at death any remaining probate assets into the RLT, to undergo minimal probate as a means of clearing the estate of creditor claims, and to appoint guardians of any minor children.[4]

DURING LIFETIME. The grantor establishes the RLT and typically names himself as the sole trustee. Following creation of the trust the grantor retitles and transfers his property to the trust.[5] Because the grantor maintains full control over trust assets there are no income, gift, or estate tax consequences.[6]

UPON DISABILITY. If the grantor becomes disabled due to legal incompetency or physical incapacity, a designated successor trustee steps in to manage the grantor's financial affairs.[7] Disability is determined under trust provisions providing a standard of incapacity (e.g., certification by two physicians that the grantor is unable to manage his financial affairs). Also, during the grantor's disability, the holder of the durable power of attorney is authorized to transfer additional grantor-owned assets to the trust.

UPON DEATH. The RLT becomes irrevocable when the grantor dies. Under the grantor's pour-over will, any probate assets not previously transferred to the RLT during lifetime are transferred to the RLT as part of the grantor's residuary estate. Assets held in trust are then disposed of according to the terms of the trust. This can include an outright distribution to the trust beneficiaries, or the trust may contain provisions establishing separate tax-savings subtrusts similar to the marital and family trusts under the exemption trust will.[8]

Although the RLT is not for everyone, it clearly offers substantial benefits for many individuals. The utility of a funded revocable trust increases with the grantor's age, when there is an increased likelihood of incompetency or incapacity and the need for asset management.[9]

Footnotes on page 27

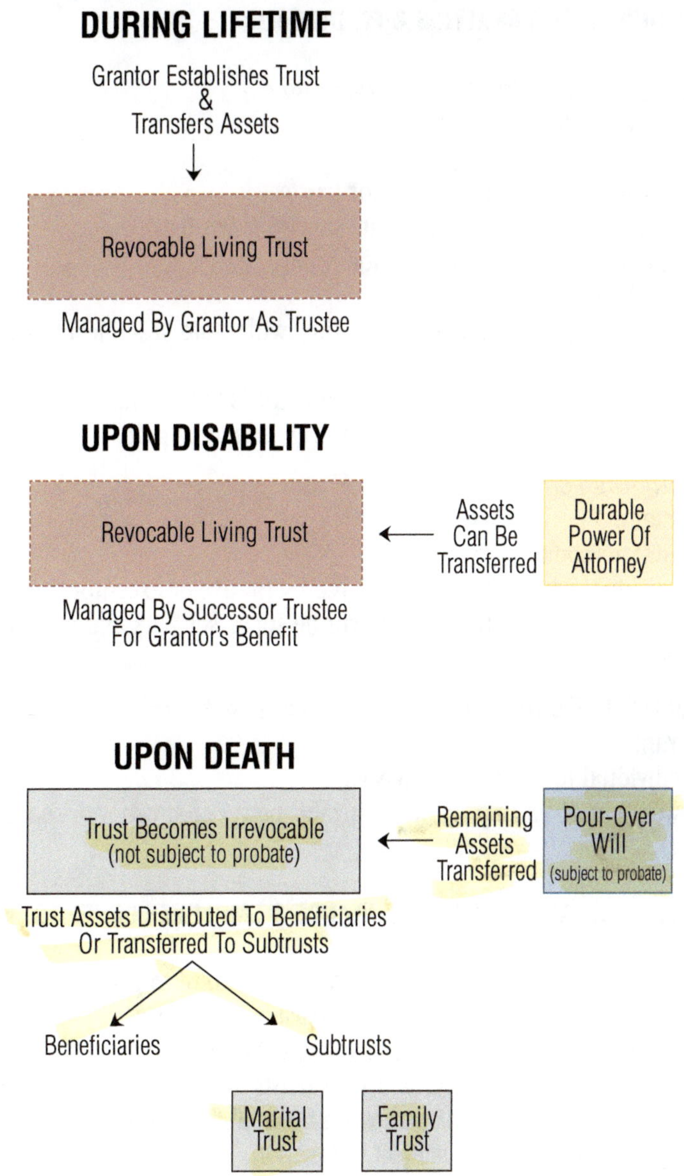
DURING LIFETIME
Grantor Establishes Trust & Transfers Assets
Revocable Living Trust
Managed By Grantor As Trustee
UPON DISABILITY
Revocable Living Trust
Assets Can Be Transferred
Durable Power Of Attorney
Managed By Successor Trustee For Grantor's Benefit
UPON DEATH
Trust Becomes Irrevocable (not subject to probate)
Remaining Assets Transferred
Pour-Over Will (subject to probate)
Trust Assets Distributed To Beneficiaries Or Transferred To Subtrusts
Beneficiaries
Subtrusts
Marital Trust
Family Trust

INFORMATION REQUIRED FOR ANALYSIS & PROPOSAL

Attorney Drafting Trust Instrument Must Know

1. Name of trust grantor.
2. Name of trust grantor's spouse.
3. Name of individual who will be successor trustee.
4. Name of institution that will be alternate successor trustee.
5. Name of beneficiaries other than grantor.
6. Ages of minor beneficiaries.
7. Approximate size of grantor's gross estate (i.e., will estate be subject to federal estate taxes or state death taxes).
8. To who, in what amounts, and when trust income is to be paid.
9. To who, in what amounts, and when trust *corpus* is to be paid.

Attorney Drafting Pour-Over Will Must Know

1. Name of testator.
2. Name of testator's spouse.
3. Name of individual who will be personal representative or executor.
4. Name of individual or institution who will be successor personal representative or alternate executor.

Attorney Drafting Durable Power Of Attorney Must Know

1. Name of grantor.
2. Name of individual to be given the power.
3. Type of power to be given (e.g., *general* durable power of attorney or *special* durable power of attorney).

CROSS REFERENCES TO TAX FACTS ON INSURANCE & EMPLOYEE BENEFITS, VOL. 1 (2019)

Q 149. When income of funded life insurance trust is taxed to grantor.
Q 150. When income is taxable to trust or to trust beneficiaries.
Q 834. Items that are included in a decedent's gross estate.
Q 868. Computation of federal income tax for trusts and estates for non-U.S. citizens.
Q 869. Description of the estate tax deduction for qualified family owned businesses.
Q 903. Types of transfers that are subject to taxation.

Footnotes

[1] There is disagreement among commentators regarding the contestability of the RLT. Clearly, wills are subject to being challenged. Likewise, a trust can be attacked under contract law based on fraud, forgery, lack of mental capacity, and duress. However, it seems reasonable that once a RLT has been in existence and administered by the grantor for a number of years, it would be less vulnerable to a *successful* attack than a will that comes into being upon the testator's death. It has also been suggested that the perceived privacy or confidentiality advantage is of limited value, since most individuals are not all that concerned that their probate records will be available for public scrutiny. It has also been observed that it is wise to evaluate the actual costs being avoided, since establishing and maintaining a RLT involves both time and expense; and in most jurisdictions attorneys' fees and probate costs are quite reasonable (most estates never actually pay executor fees, since the typical will provides for a waiver of fees and commissions if a family member is appointed to act as executor, as is common). It is true that with both RLTs and wills, assets must be collected and distributed, bills must be paid, and tax returns must be filed. In the final analysis, the undoubted benefit of having professionals who enthusiastically advocate the use of RLTs is that it motivates their clients to do sorely needed planning. The merits of the RLT should be carefully evaluated in light of individual circumstances and needs.

[2] Other documents that should be considered as part of a comprehensive estate plan include: (1) **revocable assignments** transferring property to the RLT that is not subject to precise titling (e.g., jewelry); (2) the **appointment of a health care representative** to act for the grantor in health care matters (e.g., to sign insurance forms); and (3) a **living will** stating that in case of a terminal illness or condition the grantor does not wish to be subject to procedures that serve only to prolong the dying process (see page 453). Although typically not binding on the executor or family – an informal list of personal property with the intended recipient can be a simple and often effective means of passing tangible personal property.

[3] The durable power of attorney is discussed on page 351.

[4] The RLT cannot be used to designate the guardian of a minor child. This must be done under a will that is subject to court approval. See Pour-Over Will chart on page 29.

[5] Although there is a fair amount of paperwork involved in transferring title to existing property, or putting new acquisitions in the name of a trust, it is likely that the grantor is better prepared to accomplish this task while alive and competent, than a conservator in case of disability or an executor in case of death. When done by the grantor, it facilitates management or transfer of assets upon the grantor's incompetency or death (and likely saves time and money). Even a partial transfer of assets to a RLT can reduce the size of an estate to the point where it qualifies for a summary probate and unsupervised administration. Before *real property* is transferred, it should be ascertained that the transfer would not cause acceleration of a note or mortgage, reassessment of the property for tax purposes, or loss of a real estate homestead exemption.

[6] Because the trust is revocable the assets are not removed from the grantor's estate, and since the grantor is considered the owner of the trust corpus, there are no income tax advantages (i.e., as a "grantor trust" all trust income is taxed to the grantor, see page 393). A transfer of property from the trust to someone other than the grantor would be subject to gift taxes (see chart, page 51). As long as the grantor is the trustee there is no requirement that a separate income tax return be filed. However, once a successor trustee takes over during disability a separate informational return must be filed. After title is transferred, the grantor would receive account statements reading: "John Q. Jones, as Trustee of the John Q. Jones Revocable Trust dated January 7, 2010."

[7] In those states (such as Florida) requiring executors or personal representatives to be state residents, the RLT can be used to facilitate the use of an out-of-state trustee.

[8] In and of itself, the RLT is not a tax-saving device. But the trust can offer estate tax benefits if it contains provisions similar to the Trust Will (see chart, page 21).

[9] With a young entrepreneur who is actively investing, buying and selling property, as a matter of convenience, property is often not transferred to the RLT. In these situations, the necessary transfers are made using the power of attorney and pour-over will.

POUR-OVER WILL

The "pour-over will" should be executed at the same time as the revocable living trust (RLT).[1] As a last will and testament, the essential functions of this document include:

- Providing for payment of obligations, expenses, and taxes not paid by the RLT (i.e., to clear the estate of creditor claims).
- Transferring tangible personal property.[2]
- Naming guardians of minor children.
- Functioning as a "fail-safe" device.

Generally the most important function of the pour-over will is in providing a fail-safe device. Assets not transferred (either intentionally or unintentionally) to the RLT prior to death will not be governed by the provisions of the RLT.[3] After death this clean-up feature sweeps these assets into the trust, thereby carrying out the grantor's intentions. Should the trust itself become invalid, or otherwise unavailable, the pour-over will can also direct distribution of all assets as would have been made under the trust.[4]

DURING LIFETIME. The grantor establishes a RLT and thereafter transfers property to the trust.[5] At the same time the grantor executes a pour-over will, the primary beneficiary of which is the RLT.

UPON DEATH. Any probate assets not transferred prior to death will become part of the grantor's probate estate and must *pass thru probate* before they can be transferred ("poured over") to the trust.[6] The assets are then distributed as provided for in the trust. However, provided the RLT has been diligently funded during the grantor's lifetime, it is possible that few, if any, assets will actually have to be transferred under the pour-over will (i.e., there will be a minimal probate for purpose of clearing the estate of the claims of creditors and the naming of guardians of minor children when both parents have died).

---

[1] The term "pour-over will" is not used in the legal document, but rather is merely used as an apt means of describing the process of transferring assets from the probate estate to the trust.

[2] The will may pass tangible personal property to a surviving spouse, make specific bequests to children and others, or make reference to distribution according to separate written and signed lists making gifts to named individuals.

[3] Unless passed by joint tenancy with rights of survivorship or beneficiary designation, these assets will likely be distributed through the probate process under the state intestacy statutes. See State Laws On Intestate Succession on pages 586-594.

[4] In the absence of both a trust and a pour-over will, the *entire* estate will be distributed through the probate process under the state intestacy statutes (e.g., in North Carolina with only one child, real property goes ½ to spouse and balance to child, with respect to personal property, spouse gets first $30,000 plus ½ of balance, with remainder to child, see page 591).

[5] See the Revocable Living Trust chart on page 25.

[6] Passing assets through probate can be both time-consuming and costly. See the discussion on page 500.

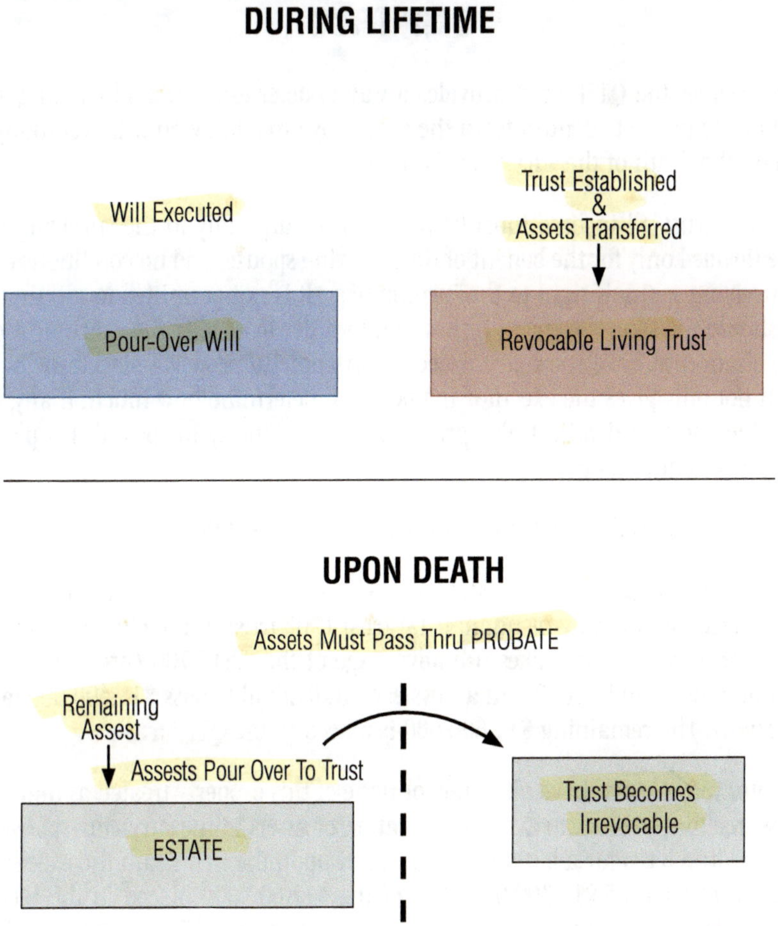
DURING LIFETIME
Will Executed
Trust Established
&
Assets Transferred
Pour-Over Will
Revocable Living Trust
UPON DEATH
Assets Must Pass Thru PROBATE
Remaining
Assest
Assests Pour Over To Trust
ESTATE
Trust Becomes
Irrevocable

QTIP TRUST

With large estates the QTIP trust provides a way to defer estate taxes by taking advantage of the marital deduction, yet "control from the grave" by directing who will eventually receive the property upon the death of the surviving spouse.[1]

Under such a trust all income must be paid at least annually to the surviving spouse.[2] The trust can be invaded only for the benefit of the surviving spouse, and no conditions can be placed upon the surviving spouse's right to the income (e.g., it is not permitted to terminate payments of income should the spouse remarry). However, in order to qualify the executor must make an irrevocable election to have the marital deduction apply to property placed in the trust.[3] This requirement not only gives the executor the power to determine how much, if any, of the estate will be taxed at the first death, it also provides great flexibility for post-death planning based upon changing circumstances.[4]

Our example assumes that in 2019 we have an estate of $23,000,000.[5]

UPON THE FIRST DEATH, the estate is divided into *two* parts, with one part equal to $11,400,000 placed in a family or nonmarital trust ("B" trust in the chart).[6] No taxes are paid on this amount since the trust takes full advantage of the 4,417,700 (projected) unified credit (i.e., the amount of credit in 2019 that allows each individual to pass $11,400,000 tax-free to the next generation). The remaining $11,600,000 is placed in the QTIP trust.[7]

The executor may elect to have all, some, or none of this property treated as marital deduction property. Assume that in order to avoid appreciation of assets in the surviving spouse's estate and obtain a stepped-up basis for additional assets taxed upon the first death the executor decides to make a partial election of $11,300,000 (i.e., of the $11,600,000 placed in the QTIP trust only $11,300,000 will be sheltered from estate taxes at the first death).[8] This means that $300,000, the "nonelected" property, will be taxed at the first death. Although $120,000 of estate taxes must be paid, the remaining $180,000 will now be excluded from the taxable estate of the surviving spouse (any appreciation of this property after the first death will also be excluded).[9] If authorized under the trust document or by state law, the executor can sever the QTIP trust into separate trusts.[10]

UPON THE SECOND DEATH, the estate subject to taxation is limited to $11,300,000 (the amount remaining in the trust for which estate taxes were deferred). After paying taxes of $4,520,000, there remains $6,780,000.[11] This amount, together with the $180,000 from the severed trust and the $11,400,000 from the "B" trust, are passed to the beneficiaries under the terms previously established in these trusts.[12]

Footnotes on page 33

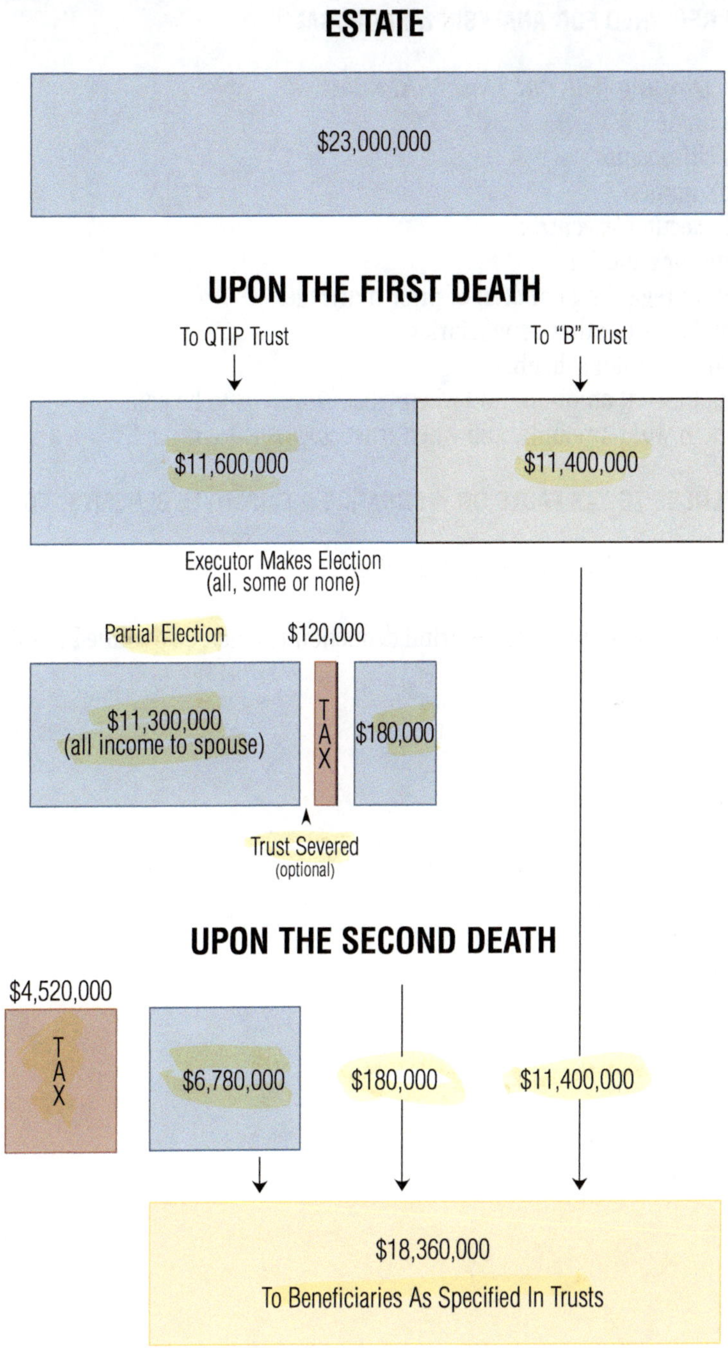
ESTATE
$23,000,000
UPON THE FIRST DEATH
To QTIP Trust
To "B" Trust
$11,600,000
$11,400,000
Executor Makes Election
(all, some or none)
Partial Election
$120,000
$11,300,000
(all income to spouse)
TAX
$180,000
Trust Severed
(optional)
UPON THE SECOND DEATH
$4,520,000
TAX
$6,780,000
$180,000
$11,400,000
$18,360,000
To Beneficiaries As Specified In Trusts

INFORMATION REQUIRED FOR ANALYSIS & PROPOSAL

Attorney Drafting Will And Trust Must Know

1. Spouse's name.
2. Spouse's citizenship
3. Children's names.
4. Name of executor/executrix.
5. Ages of minor children.
6. Information regarding children of prior marriages.
7. Names and ages of other beneficiaries.
8. Trustee after testator's death.
9. To whom, in what amounts, and when trust *income* is to be paid.
10. To whom, in what amounts, and when trust *corpus* is to be paid.

CROSS REFERENCES TO TAX FACTS ON INSURANCE & EMPLOYEE BENEFITS, VOL. 1 (2019)

Q 863. Description of the estate tax deduction.

Q 864. What is QTIP property?

Q 922. Description of the gift tax marital deduction (to include qualified terminable interest property).

Footnotes

[1] QTIP stands for "qualified terminable interest property." Assets placed in a QTIP trust are referred to as qualified terminable interest property. Under the Trust Will, to take advantage of the unlimited marital deduction the traditional "A" trust (marital trust) must give the surviving spouse the power to appoint, during lifetime or at death, all property placed in this trust in favor of the surviving spouse or the surviving spouse's estate (see chart, page 21). However, this arrangement is objectionable to some individuals, since control is lost over the eventual disposition of the property (e.g., a surviving widow could pass the property to her new husband or to her children by a prior marriage).

[2] Property placed in a QTIP trust must be income producing and the surviving spouse is typically given the power to force the trustee to make trust property productive. The spouse's *income* interest may be contingent upon the executor's election. Also, limited powers given to the spouse to invade the *corpus* of the QTIP trust may be contingent (e.g., upon the executor's election or upon the spouse not remarrying).

[3] This election by the executor *cannot* be mandated by the deceased prior to his death. It must be done on the estate tax return and cannot be revoked after the date for filing the return.

[4] For a discussion of the nontax reasons why a testator may *not* wish to take advantage of the marital deduction, see footnote 5, page 23.

[5] To simplify the example, the taxes are calculated assuming no debts, expenses, deductions, or prior taxable gifts, and no prior use of the unified credit.

[6] Funding of the "B" trust is limited to the applicable exclusion amount, $11,400,000 in 2019 (projected, see footnote 6, page 17, and footnote 2, page 23). For example, rather than using a tax-driven formula to allocate property to the "B" trust, a single QTIP type trust is established. This allows the surviving spouse to disclaim assets that then pass into either the marital trust or the "B" trust.

[7] This example shows the QTIP trust being used only with the "B" trust (family trust). When the "A" trust (marital trust) is also used, it provides the executor even greater flexibility in allocating assets between the QTIP trust and "A" trust (see chart, page 21).

[8] The taxpayer has made a decision that it is worth paying $120,000 of estate taxes in order to shift subsequent appreciation on the remaining $180,000 out of the surviving spouse's estate and obtain a stepped-up basis at the prior spouse's death.

[9] Liquidity for paying estate taxes at the first death might come from the tax-free death proceeds paid to an irrevocable Life Insurance Trust (see chart, page 47).

[10] The division of the QTIP trust must be done on a fractional or percentage basis to reflect the partial election. It is not necessary that each asset be divided pro rata between the severed trusts; so long as it is based upon the fair market value of all trust assets at the time of the division.

[11] The estate has a right of recovery for any taxes paid, unless waived by the deceased spouse (if there is no waiver, then the failure to recover is subject to gift taxes).

[12] Lifetime QTIP trusts can be used as an alternative to outright gifts.

GENERATION-SKIPPING TRANSFERS

The basic intent of the federal estate tax system is to tax property as it is passed from one generation to the next. The generation-skipping transfer (GST) tax is intended to prevent wealthy families from reducing estate taxes by skipping one or more generations (e.g., grandparents pass their estate to grandchildren in order to reduce or avoid estate taxes at children's deaths).

The GST tax is in *addition* to the normal estate or gift tax and is applied to the transfer of property to a person two or more generations younger than the transferor (e.g., from grandparent to grandchild).[1] The *maximum* estate tax rate, 40 percent in 2019, is used in calculating the GST tax.[2] However, there is an exemption which allows aggregate transfers of $11,400,000 (projected), during lifetime or at death, to be exempt from the GST tax ($22,800,000 total for both husband and wife).[3]

To illustrate, assume that Grandparents have an estate totaling $32,000,000. Assume also that their Children have substantial estates in their own right and the Grandparents desire to fully use their GST tax exemptions.

UPON THE FIRST GRANDPARENT'S DEATH. To take maximum advantage of the GST tax exemption in 2019, $11,400,000 could be passed to a GST tax-exempt irrevocable trust (the "B" trust). Discretionary distributions can be made to all family members from this trust.[4]

UPON THE SECOND GRANDPARENT'S DEATH. Again, in order to take maximum advantage of the GST tax exemption, an additional $11,400,000 could be passed to a GST tax-exempt irrevocable trust. After payment of $3,680,000 in federal estate taxes on a taxable estate of $9,200,000, $5,520,000 is passed to the GST tax-exempt irrevocable trust. In order to avoid any GST taxes, the remaining $5,520,000 is passed to the Children. Of the original $32,000,000 estate, estate taxes totaling $3,680,000 have been paid at the second death.[5]

Application of the GST tax can be quite complicated and its impact is substantial in larger estates. For taxpayers with estates that exceed the temporary $11,400,000 exemption created by the 2017 Tax Act, consideration should be given to utilizing the expanded gift and GST exemption while it is available. However, careful analysis by qualified counsel is essential if unexpected tax consequences are to be avoided.[6] By making life gifts to grandchildren using the GST exemption – taxpayers can avoid estate taxes at their deaths and at the death of their children. But, by making gifts while living – the recipient takes the current income tax basis (basis is not "stepped up" at death). For most taxpayers, holding assets until death may create a better tax result than making lifetime gifts. State laws differ on the length of time that property can remain in trust. See Dynasty Trust discussion on page 356 and 530.

Footnotes on page 37

GRANDPARENT'S ESTATE

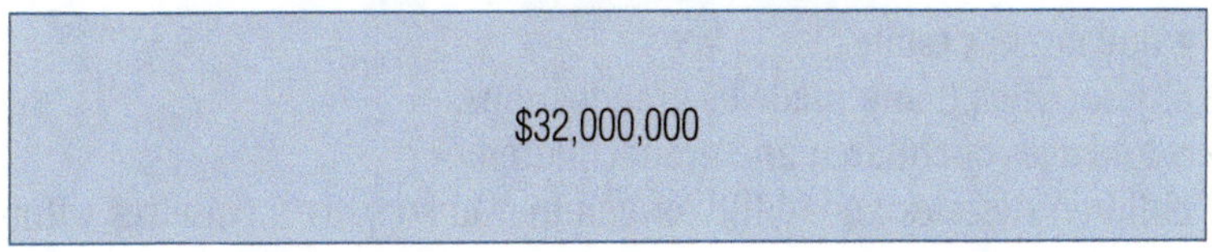

UPON THE FIRST GRANDPARENT'S DEATH

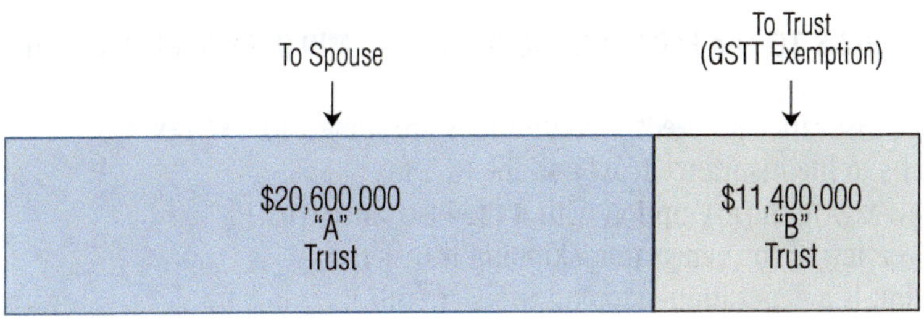

UPON THE SECOND GRANDPARENT'S DEATH

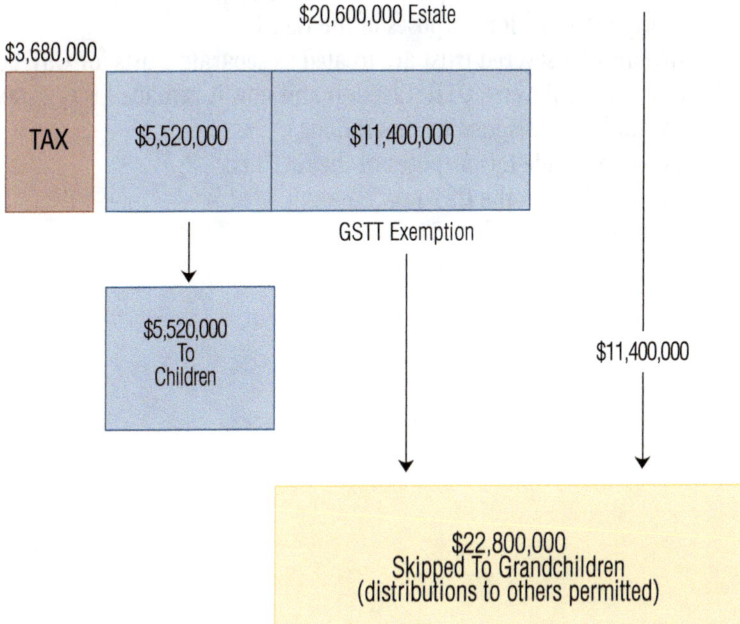

INFORMATION REQUIRED FOR ANALYSIS & PROPOSAL

1. Size of grandparent's estate.
2. Nature of prior gifts, if any, made by grandparents.
3. Numbers and ages of children and grandchildren.
4. Size of children's estates and ability of children to support themselves without inherited assets.
5. Existence of any predeceased family members.

See also information required for exemption trust wills on page 22.

CROSS REFERENCES TO TAX FACTS ON INSURANCE & EMPLOYEE BENEFITS, VOL. 1 (2019)

Q 103. Life insurance proceeds and annuities are subject to GST tax.
Q 104. Gifts to life insurance trust and the GST tax.
Q 105. Leveraging the exemption with a life insurance trust.
Q 884. Overview of the generation-skipping transfer tax.
Q 885. What is a generation-skipping transfer (GST).
Q 886. Determination of the GST tax and exemption.
Q 887. Application of the GST exemption in determining the GST tax.
Q 889. Use of the Inclusion Ratio for purposes of the GST tax.
Q 891. How property is valued for purposes of the GST tax.
Q 893. When portions of a severed trust are treated as separate trusts for GST tax purposes.
Q 895. Explanation of the Reverse QTIP Election and how it is made for GST tax purposes.
Q 897. How individuals are assigned to generations.
Q 898. Split gifts can be made for purposes of the GST tax.
Q 899. Credits allowed against the GST tax.
Q 900. Return requirements for the GST tax.
Q 901. Who is liable for paying the GST tax.

Footnotes

[1] Because grandchildren are two or more generations below the grandparent (transferor), they are known as *skip persons*, whereas children are known as *nonskip persons* (the transferor's spouse is also a nonskip person, since she is treated as being of the same generation as the transferor, whether she is or not). When the transfer is directly from one generation to a person two or more generations younger than the transferor it is referred to as a "direct skip" (e.g., in his will grandfather leaves property to grandchild). In the case of a direct skip, the GST tax is payable at the time of the transfer, not upon the death of the person in the skipped generation (e.g., the GST tax is payable upon the grandfather's death, not when the child dies). Any transfer is generally not subject to the GST tax if the person in the intervening generation (the child) is not alive at the time of the transfer to the skip person (the grandchild). The grandchild effectively moves up a generation upon the death of the child.

[2] The amount of tax is calculated by multiplying the "taxable amount" by the "applicable rate." The applicable rate is a product of the then effective maximum federal estate tax rate multiplied by the "inclusion ratio." The inclusion ratio, in turn, depends on the amount of GST exemption allocated to a specific transfer. For example, assume G transfers $11,400,000 to an irrevocable trust in 2019 (projected) and allocates $11,400,000 of GST exemption to the transfer. The applicable fraction is 11,400,000 ÷ 11,400,000, or 1. The inclusion ratio is 1 minus 1, or 0. The maximum estate tax rate, 40 percent, is multiplied by the inclusion ratio of 0, resulting in a 0 percent rate of GST tax for this irrevocable trust. Such a trust is commonly referred to as a GST tax-exempt trust. Under the Taxpayer Relief Act of 2010 the applicable rate in determining GST taxes for 2010 transfers was zero, meaning that in 2010 there was no GST tax.

[3] In 2019, the generation-skipping exemption is projected to be $11,400,000 (the same dollar amount as the estate tax applicable exclusion allowance). This exemption can be allocated on the gift tax return of the transferor, or on the estate tax return if claimed on a bequest. There is no GST tax imposed on direct skip gifts that qualify for the gift tax annual exclusion (see chart on page 51) or that are "qualified transfers." In general, qualified transfers are payments for the education or medical care of a skip person. In addition, a gift to a trust, which qualifies for the annual $15,000 gift tax exclusion, is generally GST tax-free (i.e., no allocation of GST exemption is required) if the trust is for the exclusive benefit of a skip person, and any remaining assets will be included in the skip person's gross estate.

[4] Depending on the type of transfer, the GSTT will be imposed at different times. Under the GSTT if the original transfer creates an interest in more than one party, at least one of whom is a skip person (the child) and one is a non-skip person (the grandchild), a tax will not be imposed until the non-skip person (the child) no longer has any interest in the trust. For example, in the chart on page 35 if income were paid to the child for life, with the remainder to the grandchild, the GSTT would not be imposed until the death of the child (i.e., upon the date of termination of the last remaining interest held by a non-skip person). This is an example of what is called a "taxable termination." Two other types of generation-skipping transfers are the "direct skip," where there is a transfer subject to gift or estate taxes, and the "taxable distribution," where there is any distribution from a trust to a skip person that is neither a direct skip nor a taxable termination. In the chart, allocation of the full $11,400,000 GST tax exemption eliminates the GST tax because the inclusion ratio is zero (1 – (11,400,000 ÷ 11,400,000) = 0). For further discussion, see footnote 2 above.

[5] This assumes that the Child's estate, often referred to as the "intervening generation's estate," would be subject to a maximum federal estate tax rate of 40 percent in 2019 (.40 × $11,400,000 = $4,560,000).

[6] Although a life insurance trust can be very effective in leveraging the GST tax exemption, application of the GST tax can be complicated. The GST tax generally applies to an irrevocable life insurance trust whenever grandchildren are trust beneficiaries. It is essential to maintain a zero inclusion ratio (see footnotes 2 and 4 above). To shelter such a trust from the GST tax, the exemption must be allocated by filing a timely gift tax return *after each gift* to the trust.

INSTALLMENT SALE & PRIVATE ANNUITY

Both the installment sale and the private annuity are used to transfer future appreciation through sale of property (e.g., a business interest) from one individual to another, in our example, from parent to child. There are, however, substantial differences in both the tax implications and resulting rights and obligations.[1]

INSTALLMENT SALE. The primary distinguishing characteristic of the installment sale, as compared to the private annuity, is the *fixed schedule* of payments made by the buyer. The parent (as seller) can spread a large gain and the resulting income tax liability over a number of years, while at the same time transferring future appreciation to the child (as purchaser).

The child's obligation to the parent may be *secured*, which also distinguishes the installment sale from the private annuity. With respect to the parent, each payment is divided into gain, interest income, and a nontaxable recovery of basis. If the parent dies, payments continue to the parent's estate.[2] Although the child's obligation could be cancelled by the parent's executor, or passed by will to the child, previously unreported gain would still be taxable to the estate.[3]

PRIVATE ANNUITY. The private annuity obligates the child to make payments for the *lifetime* of the parent, and the obligation may not be secured in any way. Unlike the installment sale, the parent must recognize the entire amount of the gain or loss at the time of the transaction, and the child cannot deduct any part of the payments.[4] Each payment is divided into interest income and a nontaxable recovery of basis. Because payments terminate at the parent's death, the annuity is considered to have no value and should escape taxation in the parent's estate.

In considering a private annuity, both parties must recognize that if the parent lives for many years, the child could end up paying more for the asset then would have been paid with an installment sale. The parent must also recognize that the expected income could be in jeopardy if the child were to die. However, providing for insurance on the child's life sufficient to meet the annuity obligation can usually eliminate this risk. For most taxpayers, the temporary gift and estate tax exemption increase to $11,200,000 (double that for husband and wife) does away with the tax need to transfer property other than by gift (or bequest). But, for parents who need the cash flow created by installment sales and private annuities – these planning tools remain important alternatives. The health (and anticipated life expectancy) of the parents as well as the amount of potential taxable gain are the two primary issues to consider when deciding between these planning options.

Footnotes on page 41

INSTALLMENT SALE

- May be secured
- Each payment is divided into gain, interest income, and a nontaxable recovery of basis
- Child deducts interest portion
- If parent dies, payments continue until obligation satisfied

PRIVATE ANNUITY

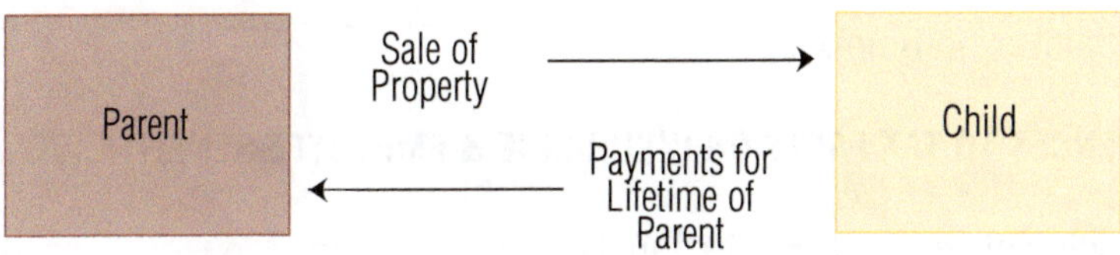

- May not be secured
- Each payment is divided into interest income and a nontaxable recovery of basis
- Child cannot deduct any part of payments
- When parent dies, payments terminate

INFORMATION REQUIRED FOR ANALYSIS & PROPOSAL

Installment Sale

1. Value of property to be sold.
2. Seller's cost basis in property.
3. Number of years payments are to be made.
4. Interest rate to be used.
5. Purchaser:
    a. Sex.
    b. Date of birth.
    c. Smoker/nonsmoker.

Private Annuity

1. Value of property.
2. Seller's cost basis in property.
3. Seller's date of birth.
4. Purchaser:
    a. Sex.
    b. Date of birth.
    c. Smoker/nonsmoker.

CROSS REFERENCES TO TAX FACTS ON INSURANCE & EMPLOYEE BENEFITS, VOL. 1 (2019)

Q 606. Taxation of payments received under private annuity.
Q 609. Tax consequences to obligor under private annuity.
Q 633. Usual private annuity results in nothing to be included in estate of annuitant (unless benefits payable to survivor).
Q 670. Nature and taxation of installment sale.

Footnotes

[1] The selection of either the installment sale or the private annuity depends upon a consideration of many factors, which include: the relative income and anticipated marginal tax brackets of the parties; the age of the seller; the need for flexibility in determining payments and tax consequences; the degree of trust between the parties; and the relationship between the parties (i.e., family members or disinterested third persons).

The tax implications can be compared by summarizing the breakdown of payments and tax allocations. The following calculations assume that real estate valued at $250,000 is transferred, with a cost basis to the seller of $100,000. The installment sale calculation assumes payments are made over a period of years approximating the seller's life expectancy under the Section 7520 mortality table (21.5 years) and uses 2.29 percent interest (the September, 2018 long-term applicable federal rate). The private annuity calculation uses 3.4 percent interest (the September 2018 Section 7520 applicable federal rate).

	21-Year Installment Sale	*Private Annuity to Male, Age 60*
Annual Payment	$16,078	$15,294
Taxation to Seller:		
Gain	7,143	n/a
Interest Income	4,173	4,963
Nontaxable Recovery of Basis	4,762	10,331
Taxation to Purchaser:		
Interest Expense	4,173	-0-
Nondeductible Capital Expenditure	11,905	15,294

Note that such comparisons are heavily influenced by the assumed interest rate and the duration of the installment sale, as well as the age of the seller, who is also the annuitant in the private annuity arrangement. See also, footnote 4 below regarding proposed regulations.

[2] Use of an installment sale to purchase part or all of a business, or other property interest, after the owner's death offers little or no tax advantage to the estate. Because of the stepped-up basis, the estate will usually have no taxable gain, and thus no tax reason to spread gain over a period of years. In fact, reliance on the installment sale could be to the detriment of the estate and the heirs if the purchaser fails to make the agreed payments. Provided the business owner is insurable, funding a buyout agreement with life insurance is generally far better than an installment sale. If an installment sale is used, life insurance on the purchaser's life will assure that, if the purchaser dies, funds are available to make the required payments.

[3] The cancellation of an obligation between "related" parties (i.e., parent and child) will result in the seller, or his estate, having to recognize gain in an amount equal to the difference between the fair market value of the obligation on the date of cancellation and the seller's basis in the obligation. Passing a note by will to the purchaser is treated as a cancellation. There is no stepped-up basis, since this is "income in respect of a decedent," or IRD (see footnote 4 on page 17, and page 403). See also the expanded discussion of Self-Cancelling Installment Notes (SCINs) on page 542.

[4] In October of 2006 the IRS issued proposed regulations that would require the entire amount of the gain, or loss, to be recognized at the time of the sale (i.e., the parents would be in the same position as if they had sold the property for cash and then purchased the annuity). The regulations are effective for exchanges made after October 18, 2006 (except the effective date is delayed until April 18, 2007, for exchanges involving an unsecured annuity contract issued by an individual, provided the property that is exchanged is not sold or disposed of for a two year period). Any gain to the parent will be a capital gain if the asset qualifies for capital gain treatment. Recovery of basis is spread equally over a period of years measured by the parent's life expectancy. After this period, each annuity payment will be entirely interest income.

DEFERRED ANNUITY

Although the fear of dying is certainly common, many people fear living too long as much or more than they fear death. As life expectancies have increased, the problems that come with old age have become more and more visable. While we have all seen the physical challenges that come with aging, most of us have also seen the financial struggles. Many Americans have provided financial assistance to aging parents or know someone who has had to help their parents. Further causing concern is the uncertainty around Social Security and the fact that few businesses offer traditional pensions like many of our parents and grandparents enjoyed. The fear of running out of retirement income, coupled with the fear of losing control which comes with financial problems, is one of the most serious issues facing people today. The fear of living too long requires advanced planning to assure sufficient funds are available during retirement years.[1]

Deferred annuities provide an opportunity to accumulate retirement funds on a tax-favored basis.[2] As a flexible cash accumulation vehicle, these annuities are available with either a *single* payment or *multiple* payments over a number of years. In either case, prior to the annuity starting date, the cash values of the annuity accumulate tax-deferred, with specific contractual guarantees and at competitive rates of interest.[3]

LIVE. For the annuitant who lives to retirement, the annuity can provide a guaranteed income for life. The actual amount of each payment will depend upon the values that have accumulated prior to retirement and the desired frequency of payments. When the deferred annuity matures, payments can be taken in a variety of ways, to include "full" annuity payments for the life of one person (the annuitant) or "reduced" annuity payments for the lives of the annuitant and another person (e.g., a joint and survivor annuity).

DIE. If the annuitant dies *prior* to the annuity starting date, accumulated values can be paid in a lump-sum or as an ongoing income to one or more beneficiaries. The specific amount and duration of ongoing payments depend on the particular settlement option selected.

QUIT. Should the annuitant decide to surrender the contract prior to the annuity starting date, accumulated values, minus applicable surrender charges, can be paid in a lump-sum, or applied towards a settlement option providing ongoing income payments. Before making a decision, the tax implications of each option should be carefully considered.[4]

Of course, the annuitant might die *after* the annuity starting date. To protect a surviving spouse, or other beneficiary, the annuitant can elect a settlement option providing somewhat reduced annuity payments in return for ongoing payments to a survivor. Other options are also available:

- Payments could be elected to begin prior to normal retirement age;
- Payments could be guaranteed for a minimum number of years;
- A life only annuity could be combined with a life insurance contract to protect a surviving spouse:
- Payments could be elected for a fixed number of years.[5]

Footnotes on page 45

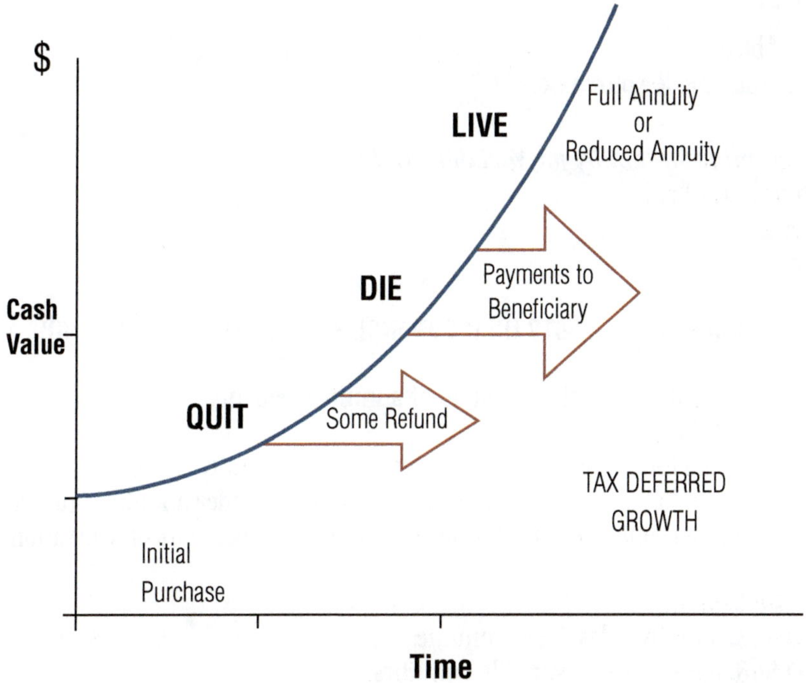
$
Cash
Value
LIVE
Full Annuity
or
Reduced Annuity
DIE
Payments to
Beneficiary
QUIT
Some Refund
TAX DEFERRED
GROWTH
Initial
Purchase
Time

INFORMATION REQUIRED FOR ANALYSIS & PROPOSAL

1. Name of annuitant.
2. Sex.
3. Date of birth.
4. Funds available for purchase.

To Determine Suitability for Variable Product

5. Attitude toward risk.
6. Income.
7. Net worth.

CROSS REFERENCES TO TAX FACTS ON INSURANCE & EMPLOYEE BENEFITS, VOL. 1 (2019)

Q 495. General rules governing taxation of annuity payments.
Q 498. Fixed deferred annuity
Q 520. Basic rule for taxing amounts received prior to annuity starting date.
Q 527. Penalties that apply to "premature" distributions under annuity contracts.
Q 594. Amount payable upon death prior to maturity subject to income taxation.

See Generally

Q 531-Q 552. Annuity rules: fixed annuities.
Q 553-Q 568. Annuity rules: variable annuities.
Q 585-Q 589. Gift tax annuity rules.
Q 623-Q 632. Estate tax annuity rules.

Footnotes

[1] The Penalty of Waiting table on page 639 gives the monthly deposit required to save $100,000 by age 65, assuming 6 percent interest. The table also shows the additional savings required if there is a delay of one or 5 years in starting to save for retirement. This same concept is illustrated another way in the table entitled Early Saver vs. Late Saver on page 640.

[2] Annuities are either immediate or deferred. *Immediate* annuities, by definition, are single-premium contracts that begin paying installments immediately. (Immediate annuities are also often referred to as "income annuities.") For example, an immediate monthly annuity would begin paying to the annuitant one month after the premium was paid and the contract issued. A *deferred* annuity is one in which payments to the annuitant are delayed to a specified future date more than one payment period in the future. See also, the Annuity Matrix, page 287.

[3] Deferred annuities are also available as *variable* annuities (see the expanded discussion on page 578). With the variable annuity, the cash accumulations reflect the performance of an underlying portfolio of investments such as stocks and bonds. While these investments can provide a hedge against inflation and an increased opportunity for growth, there is also the risk that investment performance will be poor and that an annuity's value will decrease or be lost (in contrast, see the discussion of the equity-indexed annuity on pages 366-367). As an alternative to annuitization, the guaranteed minimum withdrawal benefit ensures the owner of a minimum income stream (see page 396). Since it is a security, in order to sell variable annuities you must hold a valid federal securities license and state license where required. In addition, *a prospectus must be delivered* with or preceding a proposal to a prospect or client. This chart refers to a *nonqualified* annuity, which is purchased with after-tax dollars. A *qualified* annuity is described in the chart entitled 403(b) Plans, on page 273. An equity indexed annuity is an alternative to a variable annuity not requiring a securires license or prospectus. These provide a degree of growth potential (tied to an index with gains capped), but also provide downside protection against decreases in the index.

[4] An early withdrawal of funds from an annuity can cause serious tax consequences. For example, taxable interest is considered to be distributed first when there is a partial withdrawal from an annuity contract purchased after August 13, 1982. This means that with such a contract a tax-free return of the amount invested in the annuity cannot be received until all accrued interest earnings have been withdrawn. If amounts are invested after August 13, 1982 in a preexisting annuity contract, amounts withdrawn are treated first as return of pre-August 14, 1982 investment, then as income on pre-August 14, 1982 investment, then as income on investment made after August 13, 1982, and finally as return of post-August 13, 1982 investment. In addition, there is a 10-percent-penalty tax applied to all taxable withdrawals from the annuity, with certain specific exceptions: such as withdrawals made after age 59½, or on account of disability, or of earnings on investment made before August 14, 1982, or as part of a series of substantially equal payments for life and not modified before age 59½ or within 60 months if modified after age 59½.

[5] These settlement options are similar to those available with most life insurance cash values.

PENSION MAXIMIZATION

Upon retirement under a qualified pension plan, married workers and their spouses are often faced with making a difficult decision regarding the desired payout election.[1] Basically one of two elections may be made: (1) to take a reduced monthly income with a survivor income benefit providing for payments during the lifetimes of both the retiree and his spouse;[2] or (2) to take an increased monthly income for the lifetime of the retiree without provisions for a survivor income benefit. Although plans differ, typically when the survivor income benefit is elected there is a reduction of 25 to 30 percent.[3]

CURRENT PENSION PLAN. For example, assume that the election under the current pension plan involves a choice between a retirement benefit of $1,600 per month to both husband and wife, or $2,100 per month for the retiree only. This difference of $500 per month can be viewed as the "cost" of securing a survivor benefit for the retiree's spouse. The election must be made prior to retirement and under most plans it is irrevocable once retirement begins.[4]

The retiree and his spouse are faced with a dilemma! If the survivor income benefit is elected they will receive only $1,600 per month. And, if his spouse dies first, he will continue to receive only this reduced monthly income. On the other hand, if he elects to receive $2,100 per month and dies before his spouse, no further payments will be made to the surviving spouse.

PURCHASE OF LIFE INSURANCE can provide an alternative means of providing for the surviving spouse.[5] If life insurance is purchased upon retirement, it may be possible, depending upon the particular plan of insurance, for the increased monthly after-tax income to pay for this coverage.[6] However, it is generally better to obtain the insurance some years prior to retirement, when premiums are lower and the worker is more likely to be insurable.[7] In either case, the amount of insurance should be sufficient to provide an income in replacement of the survivor benefit that was not elected.[8]

Although life insurance can be an effective way to plan around the difference in benefits between life only and survivor benefits, it is important for the retiree and his or her spouse to carefully consider the options as well as specifics of the life insurance policy being considered. You generally have only one opportunity to make your pension election.

AFTER RETIREMENT the contract insuring the retiree provides great flexibility. If the *retiree* dies first, then the death benefit can be used to pay a lifetime annuity to the surviving spouse. If the *spouse* dies first, then accumulated cash values are available to the retiree.[9] By either terminating the contract, or placing it in a "paid-up" status, the retiree could then stop premium payments and retain his full retirement income of $2,100 per month.[10]

It is important, however, when working with qualfied plan assets to consider the possible impact of the Department of Labor (DOL) Fiduciary Rules. Although the recent DOL Fiduciary rules have been invalidated, there are still fiduciary standards that apply in the advisor-investor content. These rules are discussed on page 340.

Footnotes on page 49

CURRENT PENSION PLAN

AN ELECTION

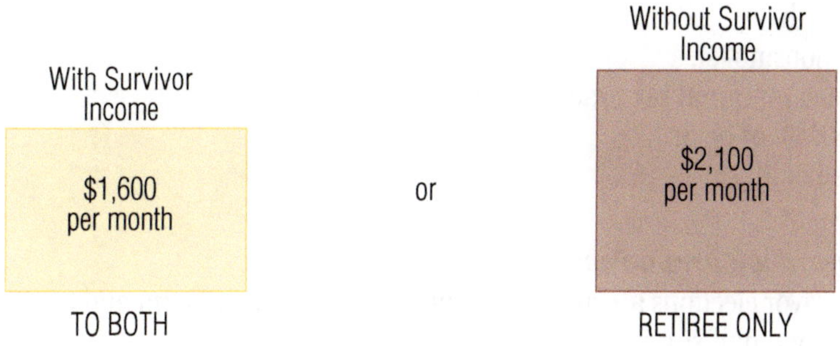

PURCHASE LIFE INSURANCE

Prior To Retirement or Upon Retirement

AFTER RETIREMENT

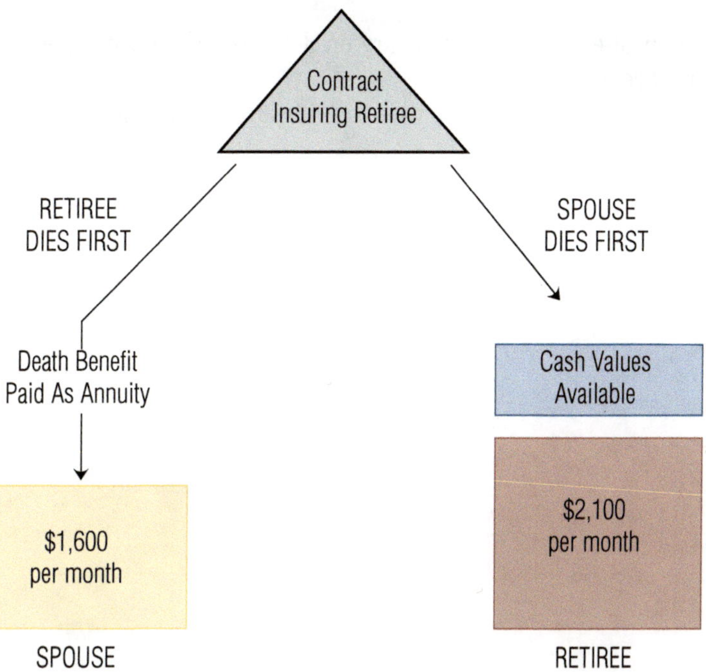

INFORMATION REQUIRED FOR ANALYSIS & PROPOSAL

1. Name.
2. Sex.
3. Date of birth.
4. Smoker/nonsmoker.
5. Anticipated marginal tax bracket during retirement.
6. Spouse's date of birth.
7. Spouse's health.

With Regard to Current Pension Plan

8. What survivor elections are available (joint and full survivor, joint and two-thirds survivor, joint and one-half survivor, etc.)?
9. What is the monthly dollar amount payable under the preferred survivor election?
10. What is the monthly dollar amount payable if no survivor income is elected (i.e., a straight-life annuity is paid to the retiree)?
11. Does the plan provide cost-of-living increases? If so, what annual rate of increase is anticipated?
12. Does the plan require surviving spouse election in order to maintain medical benefits?

CROSS REFERENCES TO TAX FACTS ON INSURANCE & EMPLOYEE BENEFITS, VOL. 2 (2019)

Q 3938. Taxation of employee's beneficiary on death benefit payments when employee dies after retirement.

Q 3939. Determining taxable income when term insurance provided.

Footnotes

[1] "Pension maximization" is also referred to as pension maximizer, pension expander, pension trap, pension predicament, and retirement dilemma.

[2] In the chart it is assumed that survivor payments will be in the same amount as those made while both the retiree and spouse are living. This option is known as a "joint and full survivor" annuity. Another option often made available is known as a "joint and two-thirds" annuity (e.g., $2,100 per month to both husband and wife, with $1,400 per month to the survivor). In order to protect surviving spouses, the law requires that qualified pension plans must provide as a minimum a joint and one-half annuity (e.g., $1,800 per month to both husband and wife, with $900 to the survivor). The retiree's *spouse must join* with the retiree in agreeing to waive the minimum joint and survivor annuity in order to obtain the increased benefit for the life of the retiree only.

[3] The reduction will depend upon the survivor option selected. For example, if a straight-life benefit pays $2,100 per month, a joint and full survivor benefit might pay $1,600 per month, whereas a joint and one-half survivor benefit might pay $1,800 per month to both retiree and spouse and $900 per month to the survivor. Typically these options are said to be "actuarially equivalent," in that at retirement they annuitize the value of the retiree's pension benefit according to actuarial tables.

[4] Occasionally a plan may provide for reinstatement of the retiree's full benefits upon the death of his spouse. However, such a "bounce-back" provision will not recapture benefits lost prior to the spouse's death.

[5] Pension maximization may be particularly useful to the retiree who is reluctant to accept a permanently reduced retirement income to assure a survivor income to his terminally ill spouse. However, as with any pension maximization proposal, it is *absolutely essential* to ascertain whether any medical benefits would be lost to the surviving spouse if no survivor option were elected.

[6] Note that the full increase in retirement income will not be available for making premium payments, since these payments must be made with after-tax retirement dollars. On the other hand, if the surviving spouse takes an annuity payout of the tax-free death benefits, less of each payment will be subject to income tax than post-retirement survivor benefits received under a noncontributory pension plan (i.e., less death benefits will be required to provide the surviving spouse a given after-tax income).

[7] When proposed some years prior to retirement, it is appropriate to consider the time value of money, since initial premium payments will come from other than additional after-tax retirement funds. However, the pension maximization concept can be particularly useful in demonstrating the need for ongoing insurance coverage after retirement. In fact, a discussion of the concept may *demonstrate the need for permanent insurance* to a breadwinner who is considering term insurance to meet a family income need (e.g., once children are grown the same insurance can be used to provide protection for a spouse during retirement, thus there is an ongoing but different need for permanent insurance).

[8] When a plan provides cost-of-living adjustments this potential for increasing survivor income would be lost by electing an option providing for no survivor income. However, to some degree this would be offset by the increased annuity payments available to his spouse from a level death benefit (i.e., the longer the retiree lives, the older the surviving spouse; the older the surviving spouse, the larger the annuity payments from a given death benefit). Availability of an *increasing* death benefit might more than make up for such cost-of-living adjustments.

[9] If taken as a lump-sum, cash values in excess of net premiums paid would be subject to income taxation. Alternatively, the retiree might obtain additional income by exercising a settlement option under the contract by receiving existing cash values as an annuity.

[10] Maintaining the policy or taking "paid-up" insurance would preserve the death benefit for children or other heirs.

GIFTS & SPLIT-GIFTS

For families that are potentially subject to estate taxes, lifetime giving is a very important part of estate planning, and can reduce the ultimate estate tax burden very substantially.[1] However, because of increased estate tax exemptions passed into law in recent years, fewer and fewer individuals have potentially taxable estates.

Property gifted during life has a "carry-over" basis meaning that any gain at the time of the gift passes to the recipient. Whereas, property held until death has a basis "step-up" with the recipient being assigned a cost basis equal to the date of death fair market value. For most families, the ability to "wash away" gains at death can be more important than transfer tax considerations.

INDIVIDUAL GIFTS. To illustrate, assume that a donor has money that is not needed for his own support. Under the federal gift tax provisions, an individual may give – under most circumstances – up to $15,000 per person, as indexed in 2019 for inflation, annually free of gift tax.[2] Thus, with three children the donor could give each of them $15,000 per year.[3] This per-donee exclusion is allowed each and every year, but it is *not cumulative* (i.e., exclusion unused in any year may not be "carried over" to the following year).

In order for the gift to be one that qualifies for the annual exclusion, it must be a *present interest gift*: the donee must be entitled to its immediate use and enjoyment.[4] If within the year the donor makes only present interest gifts, and gifts do not exceed a total of $15,000 per donee, the donor will *not* be required to file a gift tax return for that year and – under most circumstances – have no further income, gift, or estate tax consequences from the gift.[5] Likewise, the gift is not included in the donee's taxable income.

SPLIT-GIFTS. With split-gifts the spouse joins in making the gift, and this allows a married couple to increase their gifts to $30,000 per year to each donee. This can be done without tax consequences, provided it is a present interest gift. The funds could still be entirely either the husband's or the wife's, but by having a spouse join in making each gift, they are able to double the amount of their tax-free gifts. However, in order to claim the benefits of these provisions of the law, they must file a gift tax return.[6] Gift taxes, if any, are normally paid by the donor.[7] Split-gifts made to a trust of which one of the donors is a beneficiary face complicated limitations.

Present interest gifts that qualify for the annual exclusion are particularly attractive in reducing the donor's estate, since they will: (1) avoid the gift tax; and (2) likely be excluded from his estate for federal estate tax purposes no matter how soon death occurs after making the gift (e.g., the day after or even the moment after the gift is made).[8]

Footnotes on page 53

INDIVIDUAL GIFTS

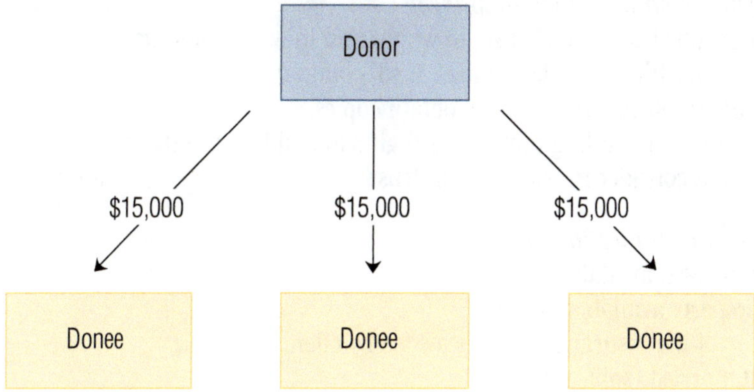

SPLIT-GIFTS

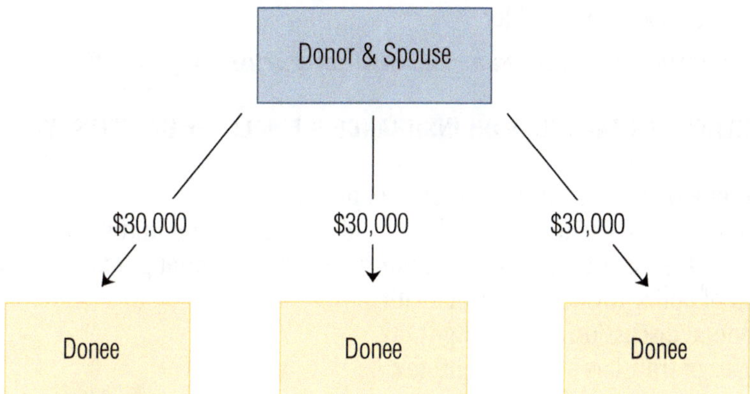

INFORMATION REQUIRED FOR ANALYSIS & PROPOSAL

To Determine Attitude Toward Making Gifts

1. Have prior gifts been made? If so, to whom and in what amounts?
2. Has client ever filed a gift tax return? If so, obtain copies.
3. Has client established trusts? If so, obtain copies.
4. Client's attitude regarding making cash gifts to children or others.
5. Would client consider making gifts in trust?

To Determine Ability To Make Gifts

6. Amount of cash available for gifts.
7. Other property available for gifts.
8. Inventory of life insurance policies owned by client or spouse.
9. Is client married (split-gifts)?

To Determine Benefits From Making Gifts

10. Numbers and ages of children and grandchildren.
11. Size of estate (i.e., to determine if currently subject to estate taxes).
12. Anticipated rate of estate growth.
13. Are client and spouse insurable?

See also information required for life insurance trusts on page 56.

CROSS REFERENCES TO TAX FACTS ON INSURANCE & EMPLOYEE BENEFITS, VOL. 1 (2019)

Q 119. Valuation of life insurance for gift tax purposes.
Q 218. Use of annual exclusion to make gifts of policies and premiums.
Q 222. Gift of life insurance policy to minor qualifies for annual gift tax exclusion.
Q 224. Gift of policy within 3 years of death.
Q 902. General discussion of federal gift tax.
Q 903. Types of transfers subject to gift tax.
Q 910. Valuation of net gifts (donee pays tax).
Q 911. Gift to minor generally qualifies for annual exclusion.
Q 914. "Split-gift" provisions.
Q 915. Gift tax exclusions.
Q 921. Gift tax marital deduction.
Q 924. Unified credit and how it is applied against gift tax.
Q 925. Filing of return and payment of tax.

Footnotes

1 Present interest gifts can be a highly effective estate planning tool without having to file a 4-page gift tax return (Form 709).

2 The $10,000 annual exclusion for gifts is indexed for inflation and was increased from $13,000 in 2012 to $14,000 in 2014-2017 and to $15,000 in 2018 (and 2019 projected). This cost-of-living adjustment is the percentage, if any, by which the Consumer Price Index (CPI) for the preceding calendar year exceeds the CPI for the base calendar year (for these purposes a CPI calendar year ends August 31). However, any increases are rounded down to the next lowest multiple of $1,000.

3 While gifts are generally discussed in a family setting, anyone can make gifts under these rules, whether the donor is a father, mother, child, distant relative, or even a benevolent stranger. In most states a gift to a minor under either the Uniform Transfers to Minors Act or the Uniform Gift to Minors Act will qualify as a present interest gift, even though the minor does not have legal capacity to make demands upon the custodian (see Minors and Life Insurance on page 469). The irrevocable life insurance trust offers an excellent means of taking advantage of the yearly opportunity to make present interest gifts through annual gifts to the trust for premium payments (see chart, page 55).

4 When a gift is made late in the year in the form of a check it should be deposited in time to clear the donor's bank by the end of the year, otherwise the gift might not be considered complete until the following year. Payments made directly for medical or educational bills are not considered gifts for gift tax purposes, and therefore are not subject to gift taxes (the funds should be paid to the provider of medical services or the educational institution, not to the donee). Gifts to a charity can qualify for the gift tax charitable deduction (see discussion regarding charitable gifts of life insurance, page 308, and charitable remainder trust chart, page 59).

5 Although the donee is not liable for income taxes upon receiving the gift, if the property is subsequently sold the donee would be liable for reporting and paying taxes on any gain realized from the sale. For the purpose of calculating gain, the donee's income tax basis is generally the same as the donor's basis in the property, often referred to as a "substituted" basis.

6 The gift tax return, Form 709, must be filed by the donor on or before April 15 following the close of the calendar year in which the donor makes the gift, except that an extension of time granted for filing the income tax return serves also as an extension of time for filing the gift tax return. In order to avoid having to file a gift tax return, one spouse could transfer funds to the other spouse, and thereafter each spouse could then make separate gifts to the trust. Only a husband and wife can take advantage of split-gifts; unmarried individuals may not. The election on the IRS Form 709 to split gifts applies to all gifts made by the married couple during the year reported by the return. The election to gift split applies to ALL gifts made by an individual in that calendar year (cannot be elected gift by gift or recipient by recipient).

7 Although the donor is the party having primary liability for payment of the gift tax, a gift can be made subject to a condition that the gift tax is paid by the donee (or by the trustee if the gift is in trust). The value of the gift is reduced by the amount of the tax. In effect, the amount of the gift tax paid by the donee reduces the value of the gift and the gift tax liability. This net gift technique can be useful when the donor desires to transfer large amounts of property, but does not have cash to pay the gift tax. However, the donor ends up in the same position whether she transfers $1,350,000 to a donee and the donee pays $350,000 in gift tax, or she transfers $1,000,000 to a donee and pays the $350,000 gift tax herself. If the donor gives property, the donor will have to recognize income to the extent any gift tax paid by the donee exceeds the donor's basis in the property.

8 One important exception is that proceeds of a life insurance policy *transferred* by gift from the insured within three years of the insured's death are brought back into the insured's estate.

LIFE INSURANCE TRUST

The trust is one of the most basic tools of estate planning. When made irrevocable and funded with life insurance, it accomplishes multiple objectives. For example, it can:

- Provide Creditor Protection
- Provide Income for a Family
- Provide Liquidity for Estate Settlement Costs
- Reduce Estate Taxes
- Avoid Probate Costs
- Provide for Management of Assets
- Maintain Confidentiality
- Take Advantage of Gift Tax Laws

DURING LIFETIME, it is possible for a grantor to establish a trust that will accomplish all of these objectives. The beneficiaries of such a trust are normally members of the grantor's family and likely to be estate beneficiaries.[1]

Once the trust is created, policies on the life of the grantor can be given to the trust. If no such policies are available, then the trustee would obtain the needed life insurance.[2] In either case, funds are given to the trust, which, in turn, pays the premiums to the insurance company.

In order to take full advantage of the gift tax annual exclusion, the beneficiaries must have a limited right to demand the value of any gifts made to the trust each year.[3] However, in order not to defeat the purpose of the trust, the beneficiaries should not exercise this right to demand. In this way, each year up to $15,000 per beneficiary, as indexed for inflation in 2019, can be given gift tax-free to the trust.[4]

UPON DEATH, the grantor's property passes to his estate. At the same time, the insurance company also pays a death benefit to the trust. If the trustee was the original applicant for and owner of the policies, or if the grantor lived at least 3 years following any gift of existing policies to the trust, the death benefit will be received free of federal (and, typically, state) estate taxes.[5]

There are two ways the trustee can provide the liquidity to pay estate settlement costs. Either the trust makes loans to the estate, or the estate sells assets to the trust. In any event, guided by specific will and trust provisions the beneficiaries can receive distributions of income and principal.[6]

Footnotes on page 57

DURING LIFETIME

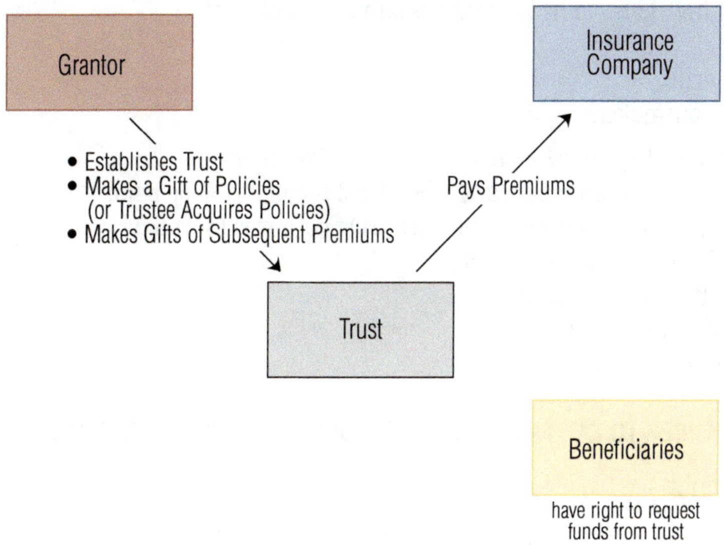

UPON DEATH

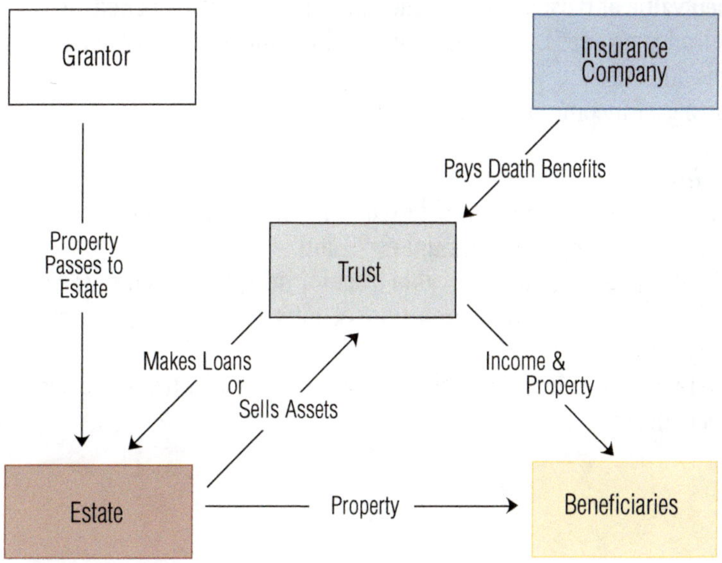

INFORMATION REQUIRED FOR ANALYSIS & PROPOSAL

1. Name of individual to be insured (usually trust grantor).
2. Sex.
3. Date of birth.
4. Smoker/nonsmoker.

Attorney Drafting Trust Instrument Must Also Know

5. To whom, in what amounts, and when trust income is to be paid.
6. To whom, in what amounts, and when trust corpus is to be paid.
7. Trustee during insured's lifetime.
8. Trustee after insured's death.
9. Names of beneficiaries.
10. Ages of minor beneficiaries.

CROSS REFERENCES TO TAX FACTS ON INSURANCE & EMPLOYEE BENEFITS, VOL. 1 (2019)

Income Tax

Q 150. When income taxable to trust or to trust beneficiaries.
Q 153. Death proceeds received by trust free of income taxes.

Estate Tax

Q 179. When proceeds either included or excluded from insured's estate.
Q 181. When value of trust assets included in estate of income beneficiary.
Q 182. Insurance proceeds included in insured's estate when trustee ***required*** to pay estate debts and taxes.
Q 183. Transfer of income-producing property to trust.

Gift Tax

Q 154. Value of gift when policy transferred to life insurance trust.
Q 159. Qualification for gift tax annual exclusion.
Q 160. Annual exclusion and irrevocable trust for minor beneficiary (Sec. 2503(c)).
Q 161. Qualification for annual exclusion of gifts to trust to pay premiums (Crummey rules).
Q 162. When lapse of withdrawal right can result in transfer from one beneficiary to another beneficiary.

Footnotes

[1] Just as the surviving spouse is often made a beneficiary of the family trust under the Trust Will ("B" trust on page 21), the surviving spouse can also be made a beneficiary and given "present interest" demand powers under the irrevocable life insurance trust (see footnote 4 below). This type of trust is typically referred to as a Spousal Access Trust or a Spousal Lifetime Access Trust ("SLAT").

[2] During the insured's lifetime the trustee is typically an individual other than the grantor who: (1) takes possession of the life insurance policies; (2) applies for a taxpayer identification number using IRS form SS-4, Application for Employer Identification Number; (3) opens a checking account; (4) receives funds placed in the trust; (5) notifies beneficiaries of their right to make demands of these funds; and (6) pays premiums as they come due. It is usually advisable for a corporate trustee to be named at the insured's death. The new trustee then administers the life insurance proceeds according to the trust provisions.

[3] With respect to a demand power, the IRS has taken the position that the annual exclusion is available only when the powerholder is a *primary* trust beneficiary who has a substantial economic interest in the trust (e.g., child of the insured who stands to receive distributions from the trust). However, the Tax Court has held that a powerholder who is a beneficiary with only a *contingent remainder interest* would also qualify for the annual exclusion (e.g., grandchild would only take under the trust if his parent, who is the primary beneficiary, were deceased). Some uncertainty remains as to how "remote" is too remote – thus making the powerholder's demand right illusory.

[4] The *right* to demand qualifies gifts for the annual exclusion as "present interest" gifts. Where there is more than one trust beneficiary this power is often limited to the greater of $5,000 or 5 percent of the trust corpus (often referred to as a "5-or-5" power). This right is considered a general power of appointment. When the beneficiary fails to exercise a general power of appointment, the "lapse" is deemed a non present interest gift from that beneficiary to the other trust beneficiaries to the extent that the property with respect to which the power lapsed exceeds the greater of $5,000 or 5 percent of the trust corpus. Such "gifts" *between beneficiaries* will result in an unnecessary utilization by the beneficiaries of their unified credit, or even payment of gift taxes. When premiums exceed $5,000 times the number of trust beneficiaries, one means of avoiding a lapse of the beneficiary's power of withdrawal is to use a *"hanging" Crummey power*. With this provision the beneficiary's entire power of withdrawal does not terminate within a specified period of time, but rather the beneficiary retains and accumulates his rights to demand gifts to the trust in excess of the "5-or-5" limit ($5,000, or 5 percent of the trust corpus, whichever is greater). Such accumulations of future rights of withdrawal (i.e., the hanging powers) give beneficiaries the right to demand distribution of prior gifts which exceeded the "5-or-5" limits. If in a future year the grantor makes no gifts to the trust, these accumulated powers lapse within the limits of the "5-or-5" power. The building up of substantial cash values would accelerate the lapse of these accumulated powers, since each beneficiary would have the right to demand the *greater of* $5,000, or 5 percent of the trust corpus (e.g., 5 percent of $150,000 in cash values is $7,500, and this is substantially more than $5,000). The *testamentary power of appointment* provides another means of avoiding the lapse of amounts in excess of $5,000 or 5 percent. Under such an arrangement, amounts exceeding $5,000 or 5 percent "partially lapse" to a limited testamentary power of appointment in favor of a designated class of beneficiaries (typically, the power holder's heirs). If the power is not exercised in the holder's will, then the amounts subject to the power vest in the trust. However, the amounts subject to this power are likely to be included in the holder's estate. The *cumulative power of appointment* is another technique used to avoid this problem (see page 320 for an additional discussion of present interest gifts).

[5] Provided the policy is purchased by another person, including a trustee, it now appears certain that, provided the proceeds are payable outside the estate, the death benefits of a life insurance contract will be excluded from the insured's estate no matter when death occurs (see the discussion on pages 374-375).

[6] There may also be provisions in both the trust and the grantor's will which provide for a merging of the trust and estate assets, with subsequent management of the combined assets for the beneficiaries. These are often referred to as "pour-over" provisions.

CHARITABLE REMAINDER TRUST

The charitable remainder trust enables an individual to make a substantial deferred gift to a favored charity while retaining a right to payments from the trust. Under the right circumstances use of such a trust offers multiple tax and nontax advantages, particularly to the individual who owns substantially appreciated property. These advantages include a charitable deduction resulting in reduced taxes, an increase in cash flow, avoidance of capital gains upon a sale of the appreciated property, the eventual reduction or elimination of estate taxes, and the satisfaction of knowing that property placed in the trust will eventually pass to charity. When combined with a wealth replacement trust, the full value of the estate can still be preserved for heirs.

DURING LIFETIME the grantor, after establishing a charitable remainder trust, gives property to the trust while retaining a right to payments from the trust.[1] A **unitrust** provides for the grantor to receive annually a fixed *percentage* of the trust value (valued annually), whereas an **annuity trust** provides for the grantor to receive annually a fixed *amount*.[2] Either type of trust could require that payments be made for the joint lives of the grantor and another person, such as the grantor's spouse.

At the time the property is given to the trust, the grantor can claim a current income tax deduction equal to the present value of the charity's remainder interest.[3] Upon receipt of the gift, the trustee will often sell the appreciated property and reinvest the proceeds in order to better provide the cash flow required to make the payments to the grantor. This sale by the trust is usually free of any capital gains tax.[4]

The tax savings and increased cash flow offered by the use of a charitable remainder trust will often enable the grantor to use some or all of these savings to fund a **wealth replacement trust** for the benefit of his or her heirs, thereby providing for the tax effective replacement of the property transferred to the charitable remainder trust. If the wealth replacement trust is established as an irrevocable life insurance trust it is often possible to gain gift tax advantages during the grantor's lifetime, while at death entirely avoiding inclusion of the life insurance proceeds in the estates of the grantor and the grantor's spouse.[5]

UPON DEATH the property placed in the charitable remainder trust passes to the designated charity. At the same time a tax-free death benefit is paid to the wealth replacement trust, which funds can then be held or distributed to the grantor's heirs pursuant to the terms of this trust.

Footnotes on page 61

DURING LIFETIME

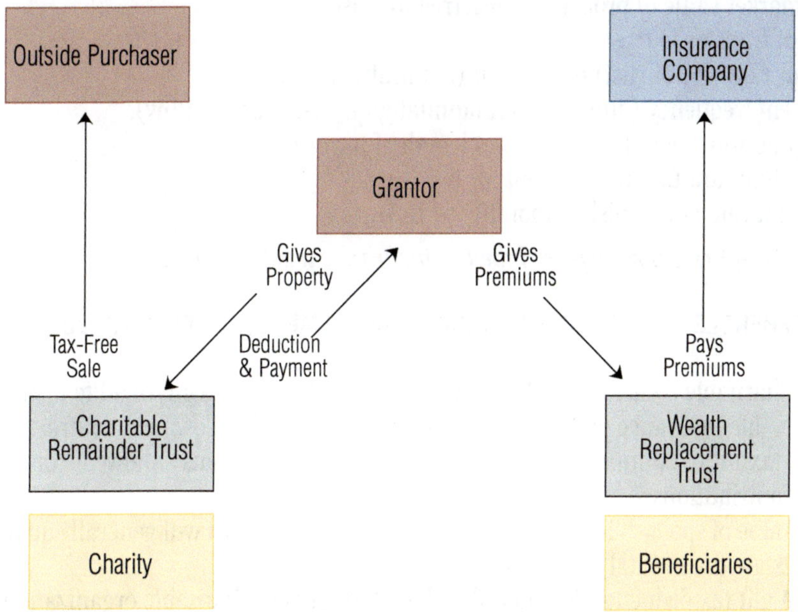

UPON DEATH

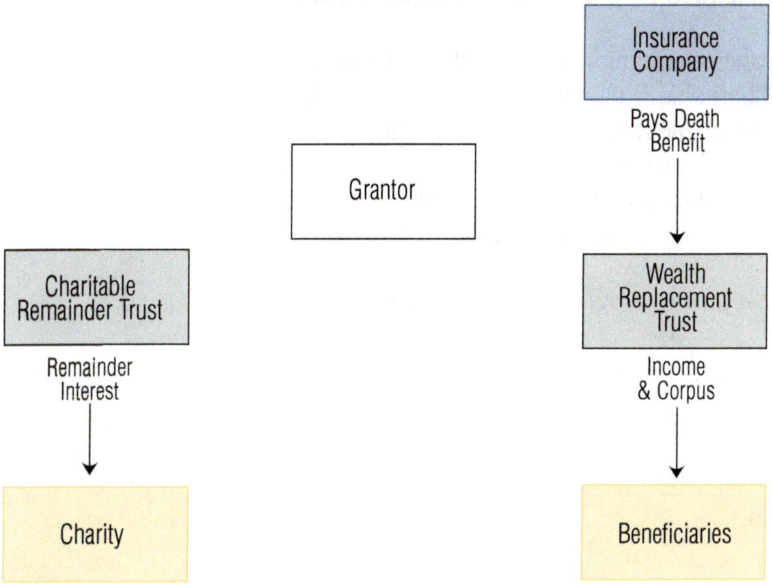

INFORMATION REQUIRED FOR ANALYSIS & PROPOSAL

1. Fair market value of property transferred to trust.
2. Date of transfer to trust.
3. Payout rate (if unitrust) or amount (if annuity trust).
4. Payment frequency (annually, semiannually, quarterly, or monthly).
5. Age of person whose life determines length of payments.
6. Age of joint annuitant (if payout for two lives).
7. Discount rate (as published monthly by IRS).

See also information required for life insurance trusts on page 56.

CROSS REFERENCES TO TAX FACTS ON INSURANCE & EMPLOYEE BENEFITS, VOL. 1 (2019)

Q 120. Charitable contribution deductions may be taken for the gift of a life insurance policy, life insurance premiums, maturing annuity, and endowment contract.
Q 739. Maximum annual limits on income tax deductions allowed for charitable contributions.
Q 857. Value of spouse's interest in a charitable remainder trust will generally qualify for the estate tax marital deduction.
Q 923. A gift tax deduction is generally allowed for gifts to charitable organizations.
Q 932. How remainder interests are valued.

CROSS REFERENCES TO TAX FACTS ON INVESTMENTS (2019)

Q 8073. When charitable deduction allowed for contributions to a charitable remainder trust.
Q 8074. Charitable remainder annuity trust defined.
Q 8075. Charitable remainder unitrust defined.
Q 8083. Pooled income fund defined.
Q 8085. Deduction for gift to charitable remainder annuity trust or unitrust.
Q 8086. Beneficiary subject to four-tier income tax treatment.

See also cross references to life insurance trusts on page 56.

Footnotes

[1] The term "grantor" is used to describe a person who establishes a trust, whereas the term "donor" is used to describe a person who makes a gift. For simplicity, only the term "grantor" has been used in describing the charitable remainder trust.

[2] Characteristics common to both unitrusts and annuity trusts are: (1) payments must be made at least annually and may not be less than 5 percent, nor more than 50 percent, of the net fair market value of the trust assets (determined when trust is created with an annuity; determined annually with a unitrust); (2) value of charity's remainder must be at least 10 percent of trust assets; (3) the trustee cannot be required to invest in specific assets (e.g., stock in a corporation or life insurance); and (4) payments may be for a term not greater than 20 years, or for the life or lives of the beneficiary(ies). Any individual beneficiary must be living when the trust is created.

[3] Selection of a payout rate can have a substantial impact upon the current income tax deduction (i.e., the present value of the charitable remainder interest). If the deduction is to be meaningful, the payout rate is usually limited to 7 percent or less. For example, assuming a $100,000 gift to a charitable remainder unitrust to be paid for the beneficiary's life, the following table illustrates the interrelationship of the beneficiary's age and the selected payment percentage:

Age of Beneficiary	Payout	Deduction
50	5%	25,943
	10%	9,413
60	5%	37,656
	10%	17,530
70	5%	51,905
	10%	30,197

[4] With gifts of long-term capital gain property, the full present value of the remainder interest is deductible if the property is intangibles or real estate. Tangible personal property is not appropriate.

Whether the deduction can be taken in a particular year depends upon the application of three percentage limitations that relate to the taxpayer's "contribution base" (i.e., adjusted gross income computed without regard to net operating loss carryback). These limits depend upon whether the gift is to a public charity or a private foundation (see page 497); and whether the gift is one of either cash or ordinary income property, or a gift of long-term capital gain property. The deduction cannot usually exceed the following percentages of the taxpayer's contribution base:

	Cash or Ordinary Income Property	Long-Term Capital Gain Property
Public Charities	50%	30%
Private Foundations	30%	20%

If the gift is made to a public charity there is a five-year carryover of any unused deduction.

A charitable remainder trust (CRT) that has unrelated business income (UBI) is subject to income taxation on all of its income. Generally, UBI is the net income from the conduct of a trade or business that is not substantially related to the exempt purpose of the CRT. Income from property that is debt-financed and not related to the exempt function of the CRT is generally considered UBI. However, debt-financed income is excluded from UBI for the first ten years following transfer to the CRT if the debt had been placed on the property more than five years prior to the transfer.

[5] The "wealth replacement trust" is another name for an irrevocable life insurance trust (see chart on page 55). For an expanded discussion of the gift and estate tax ramifications of an irrevocable life insurance trust, see the discussion on page 54. Funding with survivorship life insurance can be particularly attractive (see page 561).

GRANTOR RETAINED ANNUITY TRUST (GRAT)

The Grantor Retained Annuity Trust (GRAT) is an estate planning technique that can be used to transfer *future* appreciation to family members, or others, free of gift and estate taxes provided the grantor survives the trust term.[1]

TRUST ESTABLISHED. In order to implement a GRAT, the grantor creates an irrevocable trust for a specified number of years, names his or her children as trust beneficiaries, and transfers to the trust property that has a potential for substantial appreciation.[2] The grantor retains the right to receive, for the term of the GRAT, a "qualified annuity interest" based on either a specified sum or fixed percentage of the initial value of the property transferred to the trust. This annuity is mandatory and must be paid at least annually. The annual payment may be increased, provided the increase is not greater than 120 percent of the prior year's payment. Additional contributions to the GRAT are not permitted.

Only the value of the remainder interest payable to the trust beneficiaries is subject to the gift tax. This value is determined by subtracting from the fair market value of the property transferred to the trust the present value of the annuity retained by the grantor.[3] The value of this annuity is increased by a longer-term trust, larger annuity payments, and lower assumed interest rate used to make the present value calculation. To summarize, gift tax exposure is *reduced* if the present value of the retained annuity is increased and the value of the remainder interest is decreased:[4]

Exposure to Gift Tax ↓	↑ Value of Retained Annuity	Value of Remainder Interest ↓

DURING TRUST TERM. Tax-free annuity payments are made to the grantor. Trust assets may be used to make these payments. For federal tax purposes the GRAT is considered a grantor trust, meaning that the grantor pays taxes on all trust income.[5] Should the grantor die before the end of the trust term, the annuity payments continue to be made to the Grantor's Estate and the property is subject to estate taxes.[6]

AT END OF TRUST TERM. Any property remaining in the trust, including appreciation and earnings, is paid to the trust beneficiaries (i.e., the remainder interest). Provided the grantor lives to the end of the trust term (and does not die within 3 years of the transfer), this property is not subject to estate taxes.[7]

Footnotes on page 65

TRUST ESTABLISHED

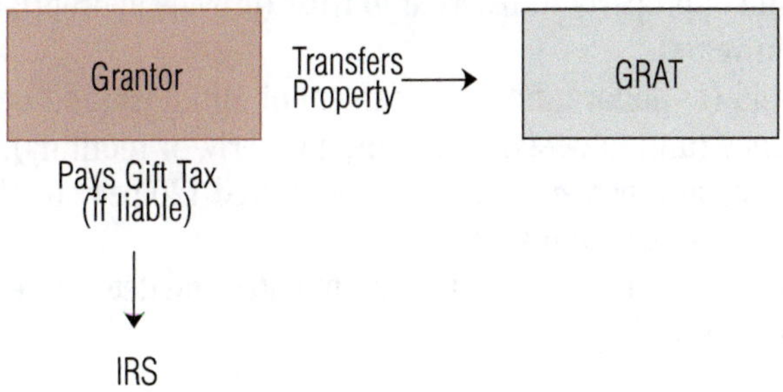

DURING TRUST TERM

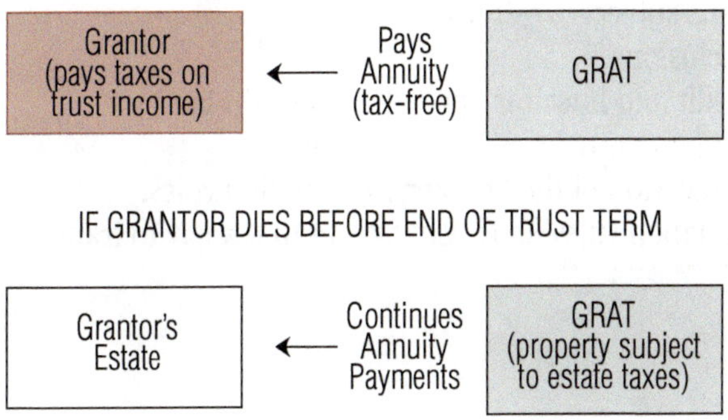

AT END OF TRUST TERM

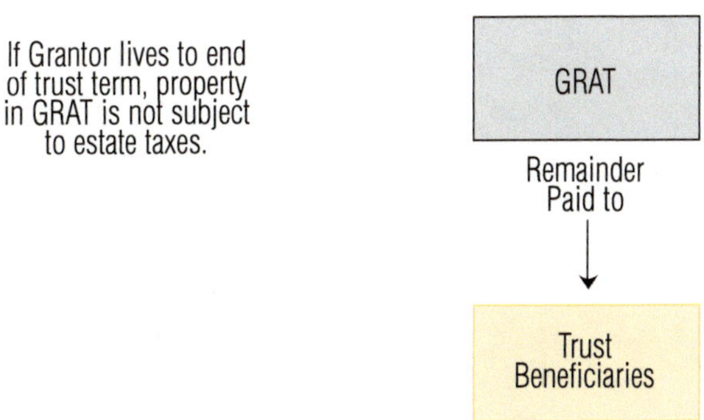

INFORMATION REQUIRED FOR ANALYSIS & PROPOSAL

1. Fair market value of property transferred to trust (provide appropriate appraisals).
2. Term of trust (in years).
3. Annuity to be paid (as dollar amount or percent of initial trust value).
4. Payment frequency (annually, semiannually, quarterly, or monthly).
5. Increase in annuity as a percent, if any (not to exceed 120 percent of prior year).
6. Age of grantor (if grantor retains reversion).
7. Date of transfer to trust (needed to set payment dates and determine Section 7520 interest rate as published monthly by IRS).

CROSS REFERENCES TO TAX FACTS ON INSURANCE & EMPLOYEE BENEFITS, VOL. 1 (2019)

Q 786. Grantor trust and how it is taxed.
Q 903. Types of gifts subject to gift tax.
Q 915. Gift tax exclusions.
Q 924. Unified credit and how it is applied against gift tax.
Q 926. Valuation of property for gift tax purposes.
Q 944. General discussion of the Chapter 14 valuation rules.
Q 948. Special valuation rules under Chapter 14 that apply to transfer of an interest in trust.

Footnotes

1 Section 2702 of the Internal Revenue Code provides the basic rule that if a transferor makes a gift in trust for the benefit of the *transferor's family*, for purposes of gift taxation any interest retained by the transferor (grantor) will be valued at zero (the so-called "zero-value rule"). If the retained interest has no value, then the gift tax value of the remainder interest is equal to the full fair market value of the property transferred to the trust (not a good gift-tax result for the transferor). But this zero-value rule does not apply when the retained interest is a "qualified annuity interest" meeting requirements set forth under Treasury Regulations (e.g., trust must be irrevocable, mandatory payments must be made at least annually, no payments may be made to anyone other than the grantor, and increases in annuity payments may not be greater than 120 percent of the prior year's payment). A "qualified annuity interest" is valued using the valuation tables provided by Code Section 7520 and a "Section 7520" interest rate in effect for the month in which the valuation date occurs (i.e., when the property is transferred to the GRAT). This chart describes a GRAT meeting the requirements for a qualified annuity interest (i.e., grantor's children are trust beneficiaries).

2 The effectiveness of the GRAT can be further enhanced by selecting assets that offer discounts for lack of control and marketability (e.g., a family limited partnership, page 211).

3 A "zeroed out" GRAT occurs when the value of the grantor-retained annuity is essentially equal to the value of the asset transferred to the trust, resulting in a nominal gift or no gift because the remainder interest has virtually no value for gift tax purposes. A zeroed out GRAT is sometimes referred to as a "Walton GRAT," for the well-known family in a court case addressing this type of planning.

4 Conversely, exposure to the gift tax is increased when the value of the retained annuity is decreased and the value of the remainder interest is increased. It is important to keep the value of the gift low, as the transfer to the trust is considered a gift of a future interest and the $15,000 gift tax annual exclusion is not available (see chart on page 51). To the extent there is available unified credit, it is allocated to the gift; otherwise, the grantor pays a gift tax on the transfer.

5 The grantor trust rules are discussed on page 393.

6 The effectiveness of the GRAT as a wealth transferring device is dependent upon: (1) the grantor surviving the trust term (i.e., not dying until the remainder interest passes to the trust beneficiaries); and (2) the property held in the trust appreciating at a rate that is higher than the Section 7520 interest rate used to determine the present value of the annuity paid to the grantor (i.e., the more the appreciation, the more that will pass to the trust beneficiaries free of both gift and estate taxes). Should the grantor die before the end of the trust term, any unified credit utilized when making the gift would be restored to the estate (i.e., the tax effect is the same as if the GRAT had never existed).

7 Lower Section 7520 interest rates make GRATs particularly attractive, since the effect is to allow more assets to be placed in trust with less exposure to the gift tax (see footnote 1 above). For example, assume that a grantor transfers an asset with a fair market value of $100,000 into either: (1) a 5-year GRAT paying the grantor a fixed annuity of $20,000 per year; or (2) a 10-year GRAT paying the grantor a fixed annuity of $10,000 per year; with the remainder interest passing to the grantor's children. The following table compares the results of varying Section 7520 interest rates and GRAT durations.

		GRAT Funded with $100,000			
		$20,000/year for 5 years		$10,000/year for 10 years	
Date	Section 7520 Interest Rate	Retained Annuity	Gift of Remainder	Retained Annuity	Gift of Remainder
Dec - 2009	3.2%	$91,074	$8,926	$84,438	$15,562
Dec - 2006	5.8%	$84,708	$15,292	$74,303	$25,697
Dec - 2000	7.0%	$82,004	$17,996	$70,236	$29,764

PRIVATE SPLIT-DOLLAR

Whereas a traditional split-dollar plan involves an employer and an employee, a private split-dollar plan is an agreement between individuals, or between an individual and a trust.[1] A private split-dollar plan enables an insured to *both* have the policy cash values available for emergency and retirement purposes and exclude life insurance proceeds from his or her estate. For example, assume that a married couple wishes to establish a private split-dollar plan.[2]

DURING LIFETIME. The individual who will become the insured (the "grantor") establishes an irrevocable life insurance trust with the grantor's spouse and children as trust beneficiaries.[3] The trustee then applies for life insurance on the grantor and enters into a collateral assignment split-dollar agreement with the spouse that provides for the sharing of premiums and death benefits between the spouse and the trust. Under the agreement the spouse owns all cash values (although the policy is trust owned) and retains the sole right to borrow against or withdraw policy cash values.[4]

The trust's share of the premium is equal to the "economic benefit" of the death benefit payable to the trust.[5] To fund the trust's portion of the premium, the insured makes annual gifts to the trust. These will qualify as "present interest" gifts provided the trust beneficiaries have Crummey withdrawal powers.[6]

The spouse pays the balance of the premium. These funds either come from the spouse's separate property or are given by the grantor (insured) to his spouse free of any gift tax liability (i.e., the marital deduction enables married persons to pass unlimited amounts of property to each other during lifetime or upon death free of gift or estate taxes).[7]

Prior to or during retirement the spouse can access policy cash values free of income taxes through withdrawals or loans against the policy. By this means the insured has indirect access to the cash values.[8]

UPON DEATH. The death benefit payable to the spouse is the greater of the total premiums paid by the spouse or the policy cash values (less any outstanding loans). The trust receives the balance of the death benefit. Since the insured had no incidents of ownership in the policy, none of the death benefit is included in the insured's estate.[9] Guided by the specific provisions of the trust, these estate tax-free proceeds are used to pay trust income and principal to the trust beneficiaries.

Footnotes on page 69

DURING LIFETIME

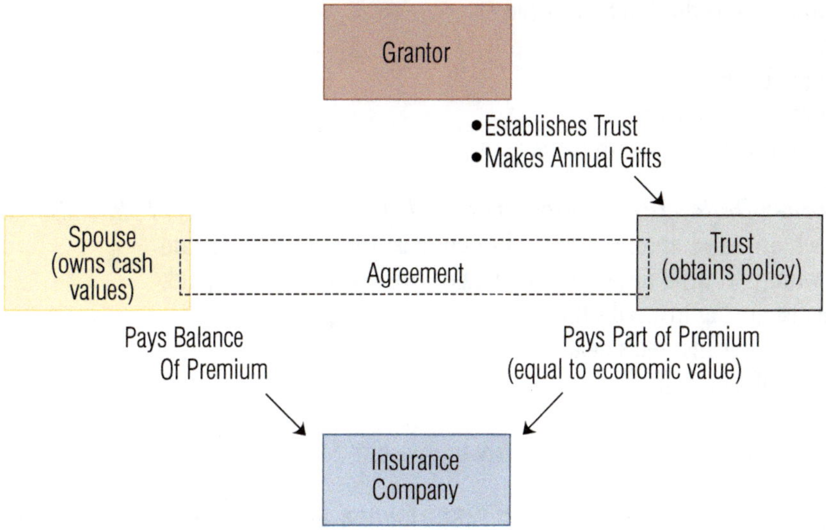

UPON DEATH

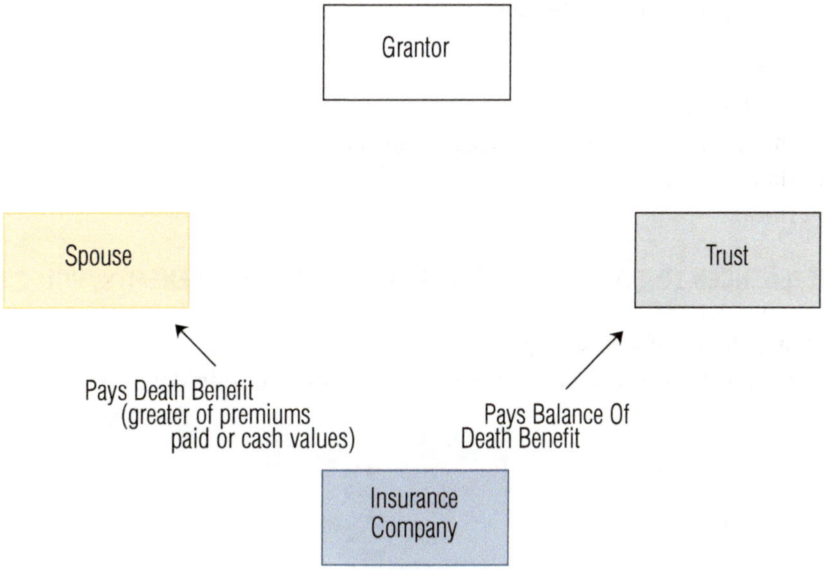

INFORMATION REQUIRED FOR ANALYSIS & PROPOSAL

1. Name of individual to be insured.
2. Sex.
3. Date of birth.
4. Smoker/nonsmoker.
5. Amount of desired death benefit.

Attorney Drafting Trust Instrument And Split-Dollar Agreement Must Also Know

6. To whom, in what amounts, and when trust *income* is to be paid.
7. To whom, in what amounts, and when trust *corpus* is to be paid.
8. Trustee during insured's lifetime.
9. Trustee after insured's death.
10. Names of beneficiaries.
11. Ages of minor beneficiaries.
12. Name of spouse who will be a party to the split-dollar agreement.

CROSS REFERENCES TO TAX FACTS ON INSURANCE & EMPLOYEE BENEFITS, VOL. 1 (2019)

Split-Dollar

Q 153. Death proceeds received by trust free of income taxes.

Estate Tax

Q 325. Estate taxation of split-dollar.

Gift Tax

Q 116. Gift taxation of split-dollar.
Q 159. Qualification for annual gift tax exclusion.
Q 161. Qualification for annual exclusion of gifts to trust to pay premiums (Crummey rules).

CROSS REFERENCES TO TAX FACTS ON INSURANCE & EMPLOYEE BENEFITS, VOL. 2 (2019)

Q 4009. Description of split-dollar.
Q 4015. Income tax consequences of transfer or "rollout" of split-dollar policy.

Footnotes

[1] Prior to 2002 there was little authority for private split-dollar plans. In Notice 2002-8 the IRS acknowledged the existence of private split-dollar plans without actually sanctioning them. The final split-dollar regulations issued in 2003 specifically state that they apply "for gift tax purposes, including private split-dollar life insurance arrangements." Such affirmative guidance on how to structure private split-dollar plans may encourage more of these plans to be established for wealth transfer purposes.

[2] When involving family members, such an arrangement is also referred to as "family split-dollar."

[3] This trust would be similar to that shown in the Life Insurance Trust chart on page 55. Private split-dollar involving both an irrevocable life insurance trust and a split-dollar plan requires a great deal of planning, implementation, and ongoing administration. If estate tax-free death benefits are important, but access to cash values is unimportant, then third party ownership or an irrevocable life insurance trust should be considered. On the other hand, if access to cash values is important, but estate tax-free death benefits are unimportant, then the insured might better own the policy (see the discussion of life insurance as property on page 98).

[4] This is a "nonequity collateral assignment plan" intended to be taxed under the economic benefit regime set forth in the split-dollar regulations (compare with other designs discussed on page 118). As the insured ages, a plan subject to gift taxation under the economic benefit regime can become difficult to maintain. This is due to the substantial gifts that must be made to the trust to cover the increasing value of the insurance coverage (see footnote 3, page 121). When there is a need for permanent life insurance, such as to pay estate taxes, it is important to establish an "exit strategy" for maintaining the policy (see Split-Dollar Rollout, page 553).

[5] Under the regulations, this "economic benefit" is measured by "life insurance premium factors" to be published by the IRS. Until these factors become available, the Table 2001 rates on page 596 should be permissible.

[6] For an expanded discussion of Crummey withdrawal powers, see page 332 and footnote 4 on page 57. As the insured gets older the trust's portion of the premium will increase substantially, particularly if the insured lives past age 80 (see footnote 3, page 121). If the spouse is also a trust beneficiary, failure of the trust to pay its portion of the premium could be considered a gift by the spouse to the trust with a retained life interest. This would cause a portion of death proceeds to be included in the *spouse's* estate (see discussion of retained life estate on page 375). To avoid imputed gifts from the spouse to the trust, the trust must continue paying for any death benefits it receives (even if premiums are not currently being paid). If the trust's portion of the premium exceeds the amount that can be qualified as a present interest gift to the trust, then a portion of the gift becomes taxable and the insured must either use some of his unified credit or pay gift taxes. Attempts to avoid these problems have involved: (1) establishing a trust-owned premium prepayment account; and (2) reducing in later years the death benefit paid to the trust.

[7] The marital deduction is more fully discussed on page 459.

[8] A stable marriage and confidence in the noninsured spouse is essential. To avoid income taxation, withdrawals are made up to the spouse's income tax basis in the policy. Thereafter, loans could be taken against the policy (see page 467). Other less attractive alternatives involve having the cash values owned by a QTIP trust, adult child, S corporation, or limited partnership.

[9] However, if the spouse dies *before* the insured, and the spouse's interests in the policy cash values pass in any way that cause the insured to have an incident of ownership in the policy, upon the insured's subsequent death the death proceeds will be included in his or her estate. This means that the insured cannot be a trustee of a trust holding the policy, nor can he act as executor of the deceased spouse's estate if the policy is part of the estate. See discussion of incidents of ownership on page 374.

MULTI-GENERATIONAL SPLIT DOLLAR

Multi-generational split dollar or inter-generational split dollar, sometimes called "discount split dollar," is merely a type of private split dollar involving multiple generations.[1] In the usual format, funding from the senior generation, matriarch or patriarch, is used to purchase life insurance on the funder's children for the benefit of grandchildren or more remote heirs.[2]

Despite the popularity of private split dollar arrangements since being sanctioned by IRS Notice 2002-8, some professionals remained reluctant to utilize split dollar in arrangements involving multiple generations because the final split dollar regulations did not specifically discuss multi-generational settings. However, the popularity of this planning technique for affluent families exploded as a result of two 2016 court cases specifically recognizing the ability to use split dollar in multi-generational situations.

The first court case involving this concept, *Estate of Clara Morrissette*, involved a split dollar arrangement created by the 93 year-old Mrs. Morrissette's conservator.[3] The purpose of the arrangement was to fund life insurance used to fund a buy-sell agreement for the family business.[4] What *Morrissette* confirmed is that split dollar can be used in a multi-generational situation if you have a legitimate business need for life insurance.[5]

But, despite this important confirmation, much remained unknown about this planning technique.[6] Maybe most importantly, the *Morrissette* decision did NOT address the issue of valuation. As already mentioned, multi-generational split dollar is sometimes marketed as "discount split dollar." This is because one of the primary reasons it is utilized is to move wealth from the patriarch and/or matriarch to trusts for remote beneficiaries without taxation.[7] In addition to the important discounting issue, many additional issues associated with multi-generational split dollar remain unresolved.[8]

In 2018, the Tax Court again looked at multi-generational split dollar in *Estate of Cahill*. In this case, which was merely a refusal of taxpayer's request for summary judgement, the court examined the application of 2036(a)(1), 2038(a)(2), and 2703 to pull the previously gifted (and heavily discounted) collateral assignments back into the taxable estate. Although merely a refusal to grant summary judgement, the court went into detail about possible ways in which the collateral assignments could be taxed in decedent's estate. So, while the 2016 decisions created considerable interest in this exciting strategy – the 2018 decisions remind us of the importance of caution. Although *Cahill* and *Morrissette* were both structured as collateral assignment economic benefit regime split dollar, professionals are divided on the viability of loan regime arrangements.

In summary, "discount multi-generational split dollar" remains a complex and risky planning strategy. When contemplated – it is extremely important that experienced tax counsel be retained. The issues associated here are among the most complex imaginable in tax planning and a small error could result in a very significant problem if the arrangement is looked at on audit.

Footnotes on page 73

MULTI-GENERATIONAL SPLIT DOLLAR

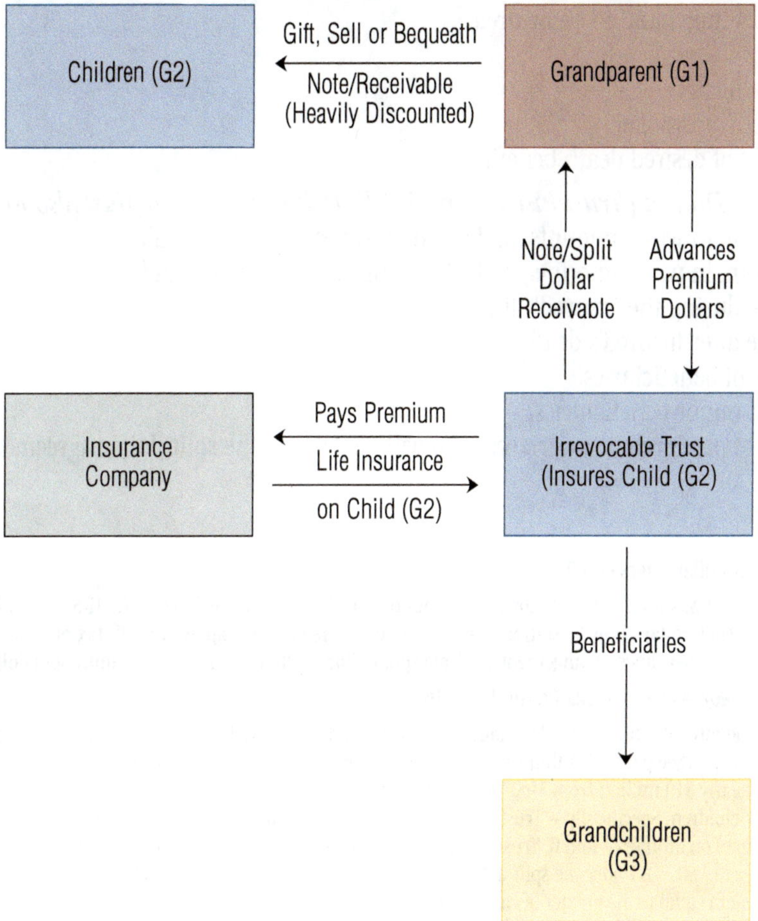

INFORMATION REQUIRED FOR ANALYSIS & PROPOSAL

1. Name of individual to be insured.
2. Sex
3. Date of birth
4. Smoker/Nonsmoker
5. Amount of desired death benefit

Attorney Drafting Trust Instrument & Split Dollar Agreement Must Also Know

6. To whom, in what amounts, and when trust income is to be paid.
7. To whom, in what amounts, and when trust corpus is to be paid.
8. Trustee during the insured's lifetime.
9. Trustee after insured's death.
10. Names of beneficiaries.
11. Ages of minor beneficiaries.
12. Name of patriarch or matriarch who will be party to the split-dollar agreement.

Footnotes

[1] See Private Split Dollar, pages 66-69.

[2] Prior to 2002 there was little authority for private split dollar plans. In Notice 2002-8, the IRS acknowledged the existence of private split-dollar plans by stating that the split dollar regulations apply "for gift tax purposes, including private split-dollar life insurance arrangements. Private split dollar is often referred to as "family split dollar."

[3] *Estate of Clara Morrissette*, 146 Tax Ct. No. 11 (2016).

[4] To help fund the buy-sell obligations, Mrs. Morrissette's conservator entered into a split dollar agreement with each of three Dynasty Trusts (See page 356) that were created for the benefit of each of her three children and their heirs. Each trust received nearly $10 million from Mrs. Morrissette which was used to pay lump sum premiums on the life insurance policies on her children. Specifically – Trust A purchased two policies (one on Brother B and one on Brother C). Trust B purchased policies on brothers A and C. Trust C purchased policies on brothers A and B. (See discussion of Cross-Purchase Buy Sell at pages 174-177). Under the split dollar agreement – Mrs. Morrissette's revocable trust would receive a portion of the death benefit equal to the greater of cash surrender value or total premiums paid. Each Dynasty Trust would receive that portion of the death benefit in excess of the amount paid to Mrs. Morrissette's revocable trust. The surviving children's Dynasty Trusts could then use the death benefit to purchase the shares of family stock owned by the deceased shareholder. If the split dollar agreement was terminated during life – Mrs. Morrissette's revocable trust would also receive the greater of premiums paid or cash surrender value (meaning that the Dynasty Trusts would receive nothing). The Dynasty Trusts provided the revocable trust with collateral assignments which secured payment of the amounts owed under the agreements. (See discussion of Split Dollar Funding Cross Purchase at pages 244-247). Mrs. Morrissette reported gifts to the Dynasty Trusts on her gift tax returns. The value of the gifts reported were the economic benefit of current death benefit protection determined using IRS Table 2001-10. After Mrs. Morrissette passed away, her estate engaged a valuation firm that determined the value of the amount due her revocable trust (i.e., the collateral assignments) totaled approximately $7.5 million (or about 25 percent of the amount advanced). That valuation was used in the estate tax filing.

[5] See also Estate of Marion Levine (Tax Ct. #9345-15) (summary judgment granted on basis of the *Morrissette* opinion).

[6] The Tax Court decision in *Morrissette* involved a very limited issue. That was if the arrangement could be taxed under the economic benefit split dollar regime set forth in Treasury Regulation 1.61-22. On this very limited issue – the court found that no economic benefit other than the cost of current life insurance protection was provided to the Dynasty Trust. Hence, the arrangement was properly taxed under the economic benefit split dollar regulations. Generally – the final split dollar regulations require use of loan regime split dollar in an arrangement between the owner and non-owner of the policy when

the non-owner advances the funds. In this case – the funds were advanced by Mrs. Morrissette's revocable trust to the Dynasty Trusts (owners of the policies). But, the final regulations contain an exception to this general rule that requires the economic benefit regime to be used when the donee receives no benefit other than current life insurance protection. In this instance – the Tax Court found that the donee (*i.e.*, the Dynasty Trusts) received NO benefit other than current life insurance protection.

[7] Although in *Morrissette*, the need for the life insurance was clear and independent of any discounting strategy – multi-generational split dollar is often promoted primarily for the discounting benefits with life insurance need as an ancillary benefit or as only a necessity to use the split dollar guidelines. Based on conversations with private practice attorneys and valuation firms who are active in this form of planning – it isn't uncommon for the reported discounts to be 80 or 90 percent. In *Morrissette*, the discount was 75 percent. It is important to remember that the court specifically did NOT address the discount issue in this court case.

[8] Among the important issues NOT addressed by the Morressette or Levine cases include the following:

- What is the proper value of the collateral assignment receivables?
- Would you receive a greater valuation if the policy cash value is significantly less than premiums paid?
- Is the value of the receivable more if the policy has long-term guarantees?
- What effect does the insured's age and health have on the value of the policy and hence the receivable?
- Morressette and Levine involved economic benefit split dollar. The court did not discuss the taxation of this arrangement had it been structured as loan regime split dollar rather than economic benefit split dollar. (See discussion of loan regime v. economic benefit regime on page 240). It is common for multi-generational split dollar to be intentionally structured as loan regime. The senior generation lends money to an irrevocable trust and takes back a note. The note is generally long-term in duration (30 years being most common) paying interest at the long-term Applicable Federal Rate (AFR) (see discussion of AFR at page 295).
- Mrs. Morrissette held the collateral assignment receivables until her death. What if she had transferred them to the Dynasty Trust or the kids shortly after entering into the arrangement? What if the IRS could have shown non-privileged discussions around this transfer and the discounts available?
- In *Morressette* – it was clear that insurance protection was desired and needed. The opinion went into detail about the need for the insurance to fund the buy-sell arrangement. What if there was no documented or obvious need for the life insurance? What if the insurance had been surrendered, perhaps while Generation 1 was still alive, or three or four years after issued when policy cash values equaled premiums paid and then the cash was invested in unrelated assets? Might the IRS have argued and the court agreed that the real benefit was not life insurance protection – but the transfer of cash?
- A number of factors sometimes seen in economic benefit split dollar arrangements were seemingly not found in this arrangement. But, would any of these facts have taken the case out of the economic benefit regime by being considered benefits in addition to current death benefit protection? What if the split dollar agreement provided that Mrs. Morrissette would have gotten not the greater of premiums paid and cash surrender value – but instead premiums paid and NET cash surrender value? What if the policy had included a living benefits rider – such as a chronic illness or long term care rider? (See discussion of Long-Term Care Hybrid Products at pages 454-457). What if the policy had a long-term guaranty or a "shadow account" structure? What if the arrangement had measured economic benefit based on the carrier's cost of term insurance (instead of Table 2001-10) and the carrier product had not met the technical (and vague) standards for use in split dollar?
- The premiums paid were from Mrs. Morrissette's liquid assets. What if premium dollars from a commercial lender had been attained and then used to enter into the split dollar arrangement? (See discussion of Premium Financing at page 494). Might the IRS have argued and the court re-classified the arrangement as a loan between the trust and the commercial lender (possibly with a guaranty by Mrs. Morrissette)? It is very common for the funds in multi-generation split dollar to be attained from a commercial lender. For illiquid older donors – it allows them to avoid capital gains taxes on appreciated assets. By using funding from a lender – appreciated assets can be held until death where the basis would be stepped up and capital gains avoided on sale by the heirs. (See discussion of Basis Planning at pages 106-109).

INTENTIONALLY DEFECTIVE TRUST

The intentionally defective trust is a wealth-transferring device used by larger estates. It is an irrevocable trust that has been carefully drafted to cause the grantor to be taxed on trust income, yet have trust assets excluded from the grantor's estate.[1] Once established, it can offer multiple planning opportunities and benefits, particularly when combined with both gifts and installment sales.[2]

TRUST ESTABLISHED. When establishing the trust, the grantor will typically retain a right to substitute assets of equivalent value. Retention of this right in a nonfiduciary capacity violates one of the grantor trust rules.[3] The grantor is then considered the "owner" of the trust for income tax purposes, but not for estate, gift, and generation-skipping tax purposes. As to income taxes, the grantor and the trust are considered one and the same; trust income, deductions, and credits are passed through to the grantor.

Once established, the grantor then makes a gift of cash or other liquid assets to the trust, equal in value to 10 percent or more of the value of the property that will be sold to the trust in the subsequent installment sale.[4]

INSTALLMENT SALE. Thereafter, the grantor and the trustee enter into a sales agreement providing for the purchase of additional assets from the grantor at fair market value. Under this agreement the trustee gives the grantor an installment note providing for payment of interest only for a number of years, followed by a balloon payment of principal at the end of the term.[5] The assets sold will typically consist of property subject to a valuation discount (e.g., a non-controlling interest in a limited partnership, a limited liability company, or an S corporation).[6] The amount of this valuation discount is immediately removed from the grantor's estate.[7]

SUBSEQUENT ADVANTAGES. Payment of taxes by the grantor upon the trust income enables the trust to grow income tax-free, and is a tax-free gift from the grantor to the trust beneficiaries. The interest and principal payments by the trust are "tax neutral," meaning that they have no income tax consequences for either the grantor or the trust. Any growth of invested trust assets is excluded from the grantor's estate.[8]

If appropriate, the trustee could also use cash flow in excess of required interest payments to purchase life insurance on the grantor. Since the grantor/insured is not the "owner" of the trust for estate tax purposes, the death proceeds would be excluded from the grantor's estate.

Footnotes on page 77

TRUST ESTABLISHED

INSTALLMENT SALE

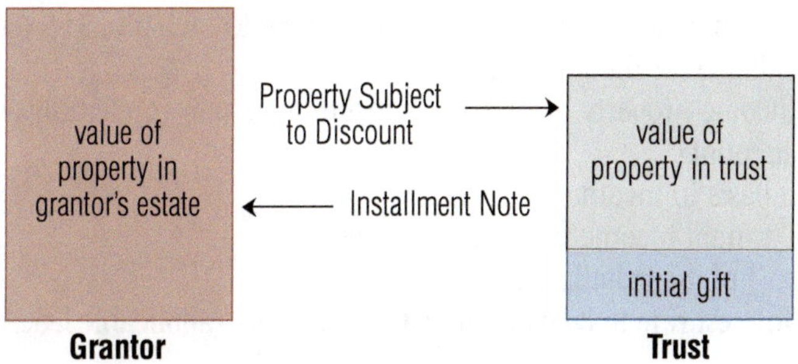

SUBSEQUENT ADVANTAGES

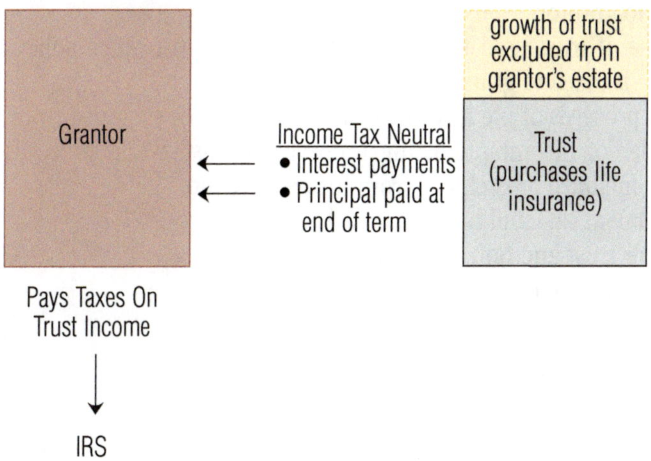

INFORMATION REQUIRED FOR ANALYSIS & PROPOSAL

1. Names and ages of trust beneficiaries.
2. To whom, in what amounts, and when trust income is to be paid?
3. To whom, in what amounts, and when trust corpus is to be paid?
4. Trustee(s) of trust (both before and after grantor's death).
5. Client's: (a) Date of birth; (b) Sex; (c) Smoker/nonsmoker.
6. Client's annual taxable income (to determine marginal tax bracket).
7. Approximate size of estates of both client and spouse (generally, gross estates less outstanding debts and liabilities).
8. Extent to which client and spouse have used their annual gift exclusion ($15,000 each in 2019 (projected)).
9. Extent to which client and spouse have each used their available gift tax unified credit ($4,417,700 each in 2019 (projected), allowing them to each give $11,400,000 of property).
10. Property available for the initial gift.
11. Nature of income-property available for installment sale (preferably, an asset subject to valuation discount).
12. Client's cost basis in income-property.
13. Anticipated annual income from income-property.
14. Length (term) of the installment note.
15. Minimum interest rate to be paid on installment note (applicable federal rate).

CROSS REFERENCES TO TAX FACTS ON INSURANCE & EMPLOYEE BENEFITS, VOL. 1 (2019)

Q 146. When life insurance trust will provide income tax savings for grantor.
Q 147. Income of trust used to pay premiums on life insurance policy insuring grantor is taxed to grantor.
Q 148. Income of trust used to pay premiums on life insurance policy insuring grantor's spouse is taxed to grantor.
Q 179. When proceeds of life insurance either included or excluded from insured's estate.
Q 183. Transfer of income-producing property to trust. When proceeds of life insurance either included or excluded from insured's estate.
Q 670. Installment sale and how it is taxed.
Q 786. Grantor trust and how it is taxed.
Q 924. Gift tax unified credit.

Footnotes

[1] This trust is also referred to as a "grantor trust," or an "intentionally defective irrevocable trust (IDIT)." Historically, the inadvertent inclusion of these powers in a trust resulted in the grantor being taxed on the trust income. Since the grantor was usually in a *higher* tax bracket than the trust, the results were undesirable, and the trust was considered defective. Today, the grantor will likely be in a *lower* tax bracket than the trust (compare the federal income tax tables on page 581).

[2] The intentionally defective trust is most often merely funded with a large gift of income-producing property. The additional installment sale funding is typically used when the grantor has no available gift tax exemption, or when the needs of the trust are very large (e.g., to pay premiums on a very large life insurance policy).

[3] See page 393 for a more complete explanation of the grantor trust rules, and other applications of the defective trust.

[4] In order to keep the trust free of any generation-skipping transfer taxes (GSTT), the grantor should file a gift tax return allocating GST exemption to the trust in the amount of the gift. However, provided it falls within the grantor's available annual exclusion and/or gift tax exemption, the gift can be made without paying gift taxes (see chart, Gifts & Split-Gifts on page 51). The primary reason for making this initial gift is to establish that the trust has a degree of independence from the grantor. The primary concern here is that the IRS might challenge the installment sale as a sham, by arguing that it is unlikely a valuable asset would be sold to someone who has no ability to pay. Sometimes this concern is alleviated by having trust beneficiaries (assuming they have significant independent wealth) guaranty the trust's payment of the note.

[5] Unlike the assets sold, the note will not appreciate in the grantor's estate. However, upon the grantor's death the assets will not receive a stepped-up basis. With the amount (temporarily) exempt from estate tax at $11,400,000 per person in 2019 (projected) – the basis issue is a bigger issue for most taxpayers than estate tax avoidance. Although the term of the note could be 20 years or more, some tax advisors recommend that the term should be less than the grantor's life expectancy. The federal mid-term rate is used for installment notes of more than three years, and not more than nine years; whereas, the higher federal long-term rate is used for notes of more than nine years. Choice of a shorter deferral period takes advantage of lower interest rates, reduces the amount paid to the grantor, and improves the chances that the loan will be paid off prior to the grantor's death. See footnote 7, below.

[6] Such discounts can range from 35 percent to as much as 65 percent. Rather than selling assets directly to the trust, the grantor will often place the assets in a family limited partnership, which is then sold at a discount to the trust.

[7] If the grantor dies prior to final payment, the estate includes the promissory note. There is disagreement among commentators, as to whether gain on the outstanding note must be recognized upon the grantor's death (i.e., at death the defective trust becomes non-defective, and the estate becomes a separate tax-paying entity).

[8] The installment sale to a defective grantor trust resembles a grantor retained annuity trust (GRAT). See page 394. Both are intended to remove an asset from the grantor's estate and affect a tax-free transfer of assets to heirs. Although many features of the defective grantor trust are superior to a GRAT, unlike the GRAT there is no specific statutory authority for a defective trust (the IRS will not issue a ruling on them). The defective trust is a sophisticated estate planning technique that should only be undertaken with the advice of competent tax counsel.

PLANNING FOR A DIGITAL AFTERLIFE

The age of digital assets is here. A client's digital life includes hard-drive data, electronic statements, online account balances, e-mail accounts, websites, blogs and stored media, including photographs. For many clients this will extent to digital works of art, copyrighted work and, increasingly, access to a client's financial accounts. As on-line and cashless payment platforms expand this issue will increase.

However, access to these accounts can be highly involved and difficult. This was brought into focus a few years ago when the family of a marine killed on duty was denied access to his Yahoo account, containing some of his final emails from the front, and eventually led to a long legal battle.[1] On one extreme, clients might hold substantial assets in the form of Bitcoins, or even substantial frequent flyer miles and even access to assets acquired through on-line gaming.[2]

Comprehensive estate and succession planning should involve a defined strategy for the property those lives create, both financial and digital. As valuable as it may be, digital property may be difficult or impossible to access upon the passing of the account holder.

Access to on-line accounts and assets is generally governed by what each site and account establishes between its users under the general name of Terms of Service Agreement (TOSA). These are intended to control not only content and use of sites and accounts, but also privacy and unauthorized access to accounts. In the case of the deceased Marine, the Yahoo TOSA limited access solely to the account owner and Yahoo was initially able to deny the family access to deeply personal assets. If the Marine was like most of us – do you suppose he even read the TOSA before establishing his account?

As quickly as the digital world has evolved, planning for these assets has also evolved. The genesis of the issue stems from laws governing digital assets fating back to the Stored Communications Act (SCA) of 1986. Although this greatly pre-dates the use of personal computers and the internet, that timeframe saw the earliest uses and pilots of data storage and email. The SCA established internet privacy and strictly prohibited certain internet providers from disclosing the content of electronic communications.

To address modern asset planning, on July 16, 2014 the Uniform Law Commission established the Uniform Fiduciary Access to Digital Assets Act (UFADDA). Within a year, this uniform law was substantially revised effective July 15, 2015. In part, the change was to address changes in the digital environment. It was also to address and mollify internet providers and other on-line platform concerns over access to accounts which they saw as subject to the privacy provisions in their TOSAs and viewed the UFADDA as operating in contravention to the SC.

Under the revised UFADAA, clients must specifically authorize access to others if the directions and access are different than the service provider's TOSA. The authorization must define the scope of access regarding what can be disclosed or not-disclosed. It also extends beyond estate and trust fiduciaries. In contrast to the original, 2014, UFADAA the current uniform act does not attempt to presume a fiduciary's access to an account without express authorization by the account holder. Moreover, the current UFADAA allows access by personal representatives, conservators, guardians and even agents acting under a power of attorney. However, without the express consent it is possible that access can be denied.

All this makes for certain planning that must be increasingly addressed while clients are healthy and of sound mind.

Footnotes on page 81

DIGITAL ASSETS CHECKLISTS

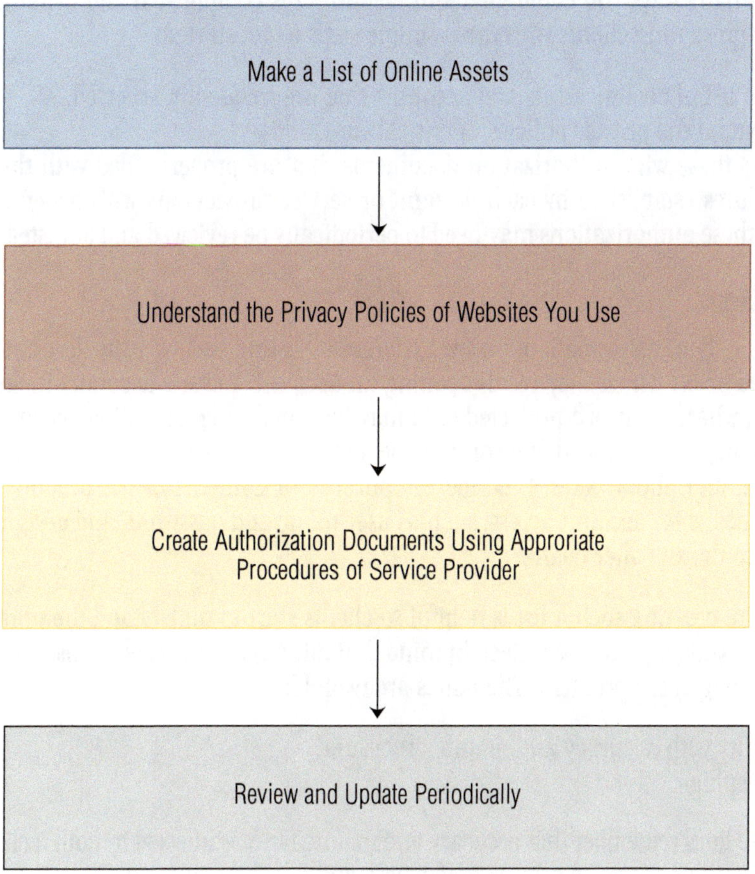

A Step-by-Step Approach

There are many ways you could go about tackling this complicated and dynamic landscape, but consider presenting clients with three simple steps to get started:

1. Make a list of on-line assets and accounts that are frequently accessed,
2. Understand the privacy policies of critical sites, and
3. Address these with authorization documents that are properly filed with the appropriate procedures established by each account or service provider. As with beneficiary designations, these authorizations may need to periodically be reviewed and adjusted as necessary.

1. Make a List

Start with a client assessment of online activities by listing each website account that is regularly accessed or on which they recall opening an account. Website accounts include any location, or URL, where password-protected data may be stored, such as online accounts for e-mail, financial management, social networking, personal or business websites, blogs, and media (music, video and photo) sites. Describe the purpose or contents of the account on that site, provide the means for account access, such as user name and password, and designate who may have access to the site after death.

The value of creating such a list is helpful so clients start to understand the number of issues related to accessing digital assets. Keep in mind that although these lists are useful, they can also become a management problem. The issues are twofold:

1. Difficulty with accuracy and maintenance, and
2. Safekeeping.

Along these lines remember that accuracy and maintenance is affected by both a client's personal habits, frequency of usage, by privacy preferences and advances in technology. The more security desired for digital assets, the more likely it is that passwords will change regularly and challenge the accuracy of any list soon after it is created. Certain websites actively require passwords to be changed on a periodic basis, while others only recommend it. Either way, it is certain that a list of passwords provided today will not be the same in a few years and lists will eventually be outdated.

2. Understand Service Provider Privacy Policies

On-line and e-mail accounts may be a source of significant information or intrinsic value that needs to be accessed or addressed after a client's passing. However, it is important to consider that many times they also include potentially sensitive information that a deceased person may not wish for family members to access. Private matters may be intended only for a select group or the deceased may desire to respect the privacy of communications received from others who are still living.

Primarily driven by the standards set in 1986 under the Stored Communications Act, provider TOSAs may be highly restrictive. Therefore, it is important for those with digital assets both to consider the types of information contained in each account and to understand each online account's privacy policies. Companies involved with digital asset accounts are subject to privacy laws, but application of those laws in forming procedures may result in widely different levels of privacy and they look different depending on what aspect of a digital asset is being addressed.

For example, e-mail service provider procedures for gaining access to a deceased family member's accounts are inconsistent and can be difficult to manage through. Prior to the UFADAA some e-mail providers only cooperated when a court order mandated access be provided. Others have established procedures for authorized individuals to access data in accounts after documentation is submitted and processed. Even post the revisions to the UFADAA these procedures may vary widely. Therefore, a critical portion of assembling digital assets is understanding the privacy and access policies of each online account

3. Build in Flexibility

The estate planning landscape has changed and will continue to change over time, making it necessary to build in flexibility. A planning strategy for access to digital assets must similarly have an element of flexibility built in. Not only do technological advances make the use of lists less than ideal, but privacy policies change and privacy laws related to digital assets will likely remain in flux.

Although broadly written authorization documents may be effective they may also need to vary based on the specifics of a service provider's TOSA, the nature of the asset and the nature of the authorization required.

In creating a plan to address these assets, contingency plans should be incorporated, such as password access alternatives and designated authorized representatives in the event that execution of the original plan fails. One option that can help to keep up with changes in life and the online world is to utilize available service-based websites that manage passwords and security questions, collecting and disseminating the data from disclosed online accounts to designated individuals in a designated manner. There are a number of these services available for a fee and each offers different features for managing digital assets. Another useful option to help manage financial information is the use of a site that focuses on consolidation of financial accounts. With a multitude of passwords and security clearances involved with each online account, having one service that manages around the hurdles can be useful.

Welcome to a new asset class.

Footnotes

[1] http://news.cnet.com/Yahoo-denies-family-access-to-dead-marines-e-mail/2100-1038_3-5500057.html.

[2] See http://tinyurl.com/kd6pg2z Forbes on-line cited in Trusts & Estates, November 2015 referencing an individual with over $500,000 of assets acquired via on-line gaming.

BLENDED FAMILIES

Many Americans live in a so-called "blended family." A blended family is generally considered one in which one or both spouses have children from a previous relationship.[1]

Although estate and retirement planning for blended families includes the same issues and concerns associated with "traditional families,"[2] blended families also present familiar and financial issues that are either unique to blended families or are more pronounced.

Like most people, couples in a blended family typically want to provide for the surviving spouse's needs while ensuring that children are also taken care of. However, common planning strategies like the qualified terminal interest property (QTIP) trust[3] may not be appropriate for a blended family. In a QTIP trust, assets pass to a trust for the surviving spouse at the first death and no one else can receive distributions from the trust during the spouse's lifetime. At the second death, any assets left in the QTIP trust typically pass to the children of the first spouse to die. But, in many second marriages, one spouse is considerably older than the other. It isn't uncommon for one spouse to have children who are close in age to the other spouse. In those situations, use of a QTIP trust can virtually disinherit the children of the older spouse. And, in situations where a QTIP isn't used, it is common for a will or revocable trust to simply leave all marital property to the surviving spouse – completely disinheriting the children of the pre-deceased spouse.

In addition to provisions in the will and revocable trust, upon remarriage it is especially important to look into things like qualified plan elections and life insurance policy beneficiary designations.[4] In many instances, the beneficiary designation may still reflect a divorced spouse or adult children. Even if that isn't the case – beneficiary designations leaving qualified plan assets and life insurance to the participant/insured's estate is often far from ideal planning.[5]

In blended families, it may be more appropriate to divide assets among the surviving spouse and children at the first death. Because it may not be practical to divide assets at the first death, life insurance is often used to create an inheritance for either the surviving spouse or the children of the older spouse.

It is not just finances that can get tricky in blended families. Although this is true of all families to some extent – the division of personal and sentimental items can often take center stage in a family dispute. A spouse's personal effects in the home may be meaningful to both the surviving spouse and the deceased spouse's children. In blended families, it is especially important to put together lists of personal items with the intended recipient. To insure that there are no disputes over personal effects – it may make sense to include this list in the will or revocable trust.

Because of the (temporary) increase in the amount of property that can pass free of estate tax to $11,400,000 under the 2017 Tax Act (projected value for 2019), fewer people are consulting estate planning professionals. Although federal estate taxes are now only a concern for the most wealthy, non-tax issues can be missed when a formal estate planning process is ignored. It is important that advisors remind clients that no estate tax exposure does not mean that there are not important issues to consider pertaining to their estates.

Footnotes on page 85.

Statistics on Blended Families

- 1 out of 3 Americans is either a step-parent, step-child, or has some form of blended family
- 1,300 new step families form every day in the U.S.
- The average marriage in the U.S. lasts 7 years.
- 66% of remarriages or couples living together break up when step-children are involved.
- 80% of remarried or recoupled adults with children are both employed.
- 75% of divorced people remarry.
- 35 Million step-parents in the U.S.

Source: U.S. Census Bureau

Common Examples of Blended Families

- Husband with children marries wife with no kids
- Wife with children marries husband with no kids
- Divorced mom with kids marries dad with kids
- Widow or widower with kids remarries
- Divorced or widowed parents with children have additional children in new marriage
- Divorced or widowed parents of adult children marry
- Divorced or widowed parent of adult children marry parent of minor children

Different types of blended families create different financial and interpersonal issues.

INFORMATION REQUIRED FOR ANALYSIS & PROPOSAL

Attorney Advising a Blended Family Must Know

1. Both spouse's name.
2. Both spouse's citizenship.
3. All children's names and legal relationship to spouses.
4. Name of executor/executrix.
5. Ages of minor children.
6. Copies of divorce decrees and custody agreements.
7. Pre-nuptual agreement.
8. Life insurance policies and beneficiary designations.
9. All qualified plans and beneficiary designations.

CROSS REFERENCES TO TAX FACTS ON INSURANCE & EMPLOYEE BENEFITS, VOL. 1 (2019)

Q 863. Description of the estate tax marital deduction (to include qualified terminable interest property).

Q 922. Description of the gift tax marital deduction (to include qualified terminable interest property).

CROSS REFERENCES TO TAX FACTS ON INSURANCE & EMPLOYEE BENEFITS, VOL. 2 (2019)

Q 3647. Description of the Transfer of Qualified Plan Funds Incident to a Divorce

CROSS REFERENCES TO TAX FACTS IN INDIVIDUALS AND SMALL BUSINESS (2019)

Q 9040-Q 9054. Discussion of tax planning considerations for estates with blended families

Footnotes

[1] According to the U.S. Census Bureau, as of 2010, there were 35 million step-parents and 18 million children living in step families. The number of households with step children is estimated to have doubled in the last decade. Each year nearly 500,000 adults become step parent.s

[2] Given today's demographics, it may be dangerous or confusing to use the term "traditional family." but for this discussion a "traditional family" is considered one where all children in the household were born into or adopted into the marriage.

[3] See discussion of QTIP Trust at pages 30-33.

[4] In some states, a life insurance beneficiary designation does not become void after divorce. It is possible that a former spouse could remain the beneficiary of a life insurance policy after divorce. And, it is usually not automatic that a new spouse becomes a beneficiary of an existing policy unless a new beneficiary designation is made.

[5] See Life Insurance as Property at pages 98-101 and IRA Distribution Planning at pages 411-413. Some states, including Michigan, Texas (in some situations), and Virginia provides that a divorced spouse can no longer receive life insurance proceeds even if named as beneficiary unless so provided in the divorce decree. However, in a many states, a divorced spouse named as beneficiary is still entitled to the death benefit. See also *Hillman v. Maretta*, 133 S. Ct. 1943 (2013) where Warren Hillman, a retired federal employee, divorced in 1998 and failed to change the beneficiary of his life insurance policy (provided to him as a retired federal employee). He remarried in 2002 and died in 2008. The U.S. Supreme held for the former spouse, despite a Virginia Statute that revoked a divorced spouse's right to receive life insurance proceeds. In Hillman, the U.S. Supreme Court ruled that federal law controlled (as the insurance was provided as a benefit of his employment) and under federal law the beneficiary designation dictated.

ASSET PROTECTION TRUST PLANNING

In today's litigious society, asset protection has become an integral part of estate and retirement planning. As the old saying goes – it isn't how much you make but how much you keep. This isn't only true of tax planning – it is equally true for asset protection planning.

State laws have traditionally provided limited protections against creditors. State law typically protects one's home, life insurance cash values and death benefits from creditors. States have a policy interest in protecting their citizens against economic ruin and dependency on the state. The federal government provides creditor protection against certain property as well such as certain qualified retirement assets.[1] Overall, the protections provided by state and federal law have been limited however.

Due to limited asset protection, for U.S. citizens and residents under state and federal law, a number of foreign jurisdictions have created what has become a cottage industry focused on asset protection for American citizens. Among the more popular foreign asset protection jurisdictions are the Bahamas, Belize, Bermuda, Cayman Islands, Channel Islands, Cook Islands, and Nevis. Switzerland and Liechtenstein have long been popular European tax and creditor protection havens.

On the other hand, there are also numerous examples where U.S. courts have not respected foreign asset protection trusts and have either gained access to foreign trust assets or at least made the life of the U.S. taxpayer miserable. A common approach taken by U.S. courts has been to claim jurisdiction over the taxpayer if the court doesn't have jurisdiction over the property itself. There are numerous examples of U.S. courts actually jailing debtors on contempt charges for failure to repatriate.[2] A number of these contempt cases have resulted in debtors spending years in jail.

In the 1990s, in response to the success of offshore asset protection trusts but also to a number of high profile instances where debtors were jailed for failure to repatriate offshore assets, Alaska introduced the first U.S. asset protection trust laws. Since that time, an increasing number of U.S. states have adopted various forms of "domestic asset protection trust" statutes (DAPTs).

DAPTs take a number of forms depending on state law, but what distinguishes DAPTs from typical irrevocable trusts is that it can be created by an individual who is also the beneficiary. When an individual (the settlor) creates an irrevocable trust for the settlor'sr own benefit, it is known as a "self-settled" trust. Traditionally, before Alaska introduced the DAPT, individuals were not able to create a trust for his or her own benefit to the detriment of creditors. A trust created by someone else (a parent or grandparent for example) could protect a beneficiary from creditors, but a trust created by the beneficiary for the beneficary was not valid. This ability to create a trust for one's own benefit that protects against creditors is what makes the DAPT both a controversial and popular planning tool.

Footnotes on page 89

9th Annual Domestic Asset Protection Trust State Rankings Chart

Rank	State	Statute (50% weight)	State Income Tax (5% weight)	Uniform Voidable Transactions Act (12.5% weight)	Statute of Limitations (Future/ Preexisting Creditor) (5% weight)	Spouse/ Child Support Exception Creditors (Spouse 3%, Alimony 1%, Child Support 1% weight)	Preexisting Torts Exception Creditors/Other Exception Creditors (5% weight)	Ease of Use – New Affidavit of Solvency required for every new transfer? (7.5% weight)	Fraudulent Transfer Standard (5% weight)	Decanting State Ranking (5% weight)	Total Score
1	NV	§§166.010 to 166.170	No	No	2 Yrs./2 Yrs. or 0.5 Yr. Discovery	No	No	No Affidavit Required	Clear and convincing	Ranked #2	99
2	SD	§§55-16-1 to 16	No	No	2 Yrs./2 Yrs. or 0.5 Yr. Discovery	Divorcing Spouse; Alimony; Child Support (only if indebted at time of transfer)	No	No Affidavit Required	Clear and convincing	Ranked #1	98
3	OH	Ch. 5816	No (except residents)	No	1.5 Yrs./1.5 Yrs. or 0.5 Yr. Discovery	Divorcing Spouse; Alimony; Child Support	No	Affidavit Required (with exceptions)	Clear and convincing	Ranked #6	85
4(tie)	MO	§456.5-505	No (except Missouri source income)	No	4 Yrs./4 Yrs. or 1 Yr. Discovery	Alimony; Child Support	State/U.S. to extent state/federal law provides	No Affidavit Required	Clear and convincing	Ranked #10 (tie)	84
4(tie)	TN	§§35-16-101 to 112	No (except dividends/ interest on residents)	No	2 Yrs./2 Yrs. or 0.5 Yr. Discovery	Divorcing Spouse; Alimony; Child Support	No	Affidavit Required	Clear and convincing	Ranked #3	84
6	DE	Tit. 12, §§3570-3576	No (except residents)	No	4 Yrs./4 Yrs. or 1 Yr. Discovery	Divorcing Spouse; Alimony; Child Support	Preexisting Torts	No Affidavit Required	Clear and convincing	Ranked #5	83
7	AK	§34.40.110; §13.36.310	No	No	4 Yrs./4 Yrs. or 1 Yr. Discovery	Divorcing Spouse	No	Affidavit Required	Clear and convincing	Ranked #7 (tie)	82.5
8	RI	§18-9.2	No	No	4 Yrs./4 Yrs. or 1 Yr. Discovery	Divorcing Spouse; Alimony; Child Support	Preexisting Torts	No Affidavit Required	Clear and convincing	Ranked #20	81
9	NH	§564-D:1-18	No (except dividends/ interest on residents)	No	4 Yrs./4 Yrs. or 1 Yr. Discovery	Divorcing Spouse; Alimony; Child Support	Preexisting Torts	No Affidavit Required	Limited clear and convincing standard	Ranked #4	79
10	WY	§§4-10-502, 504, 506(c), 510-523	No	No	4 Yrs./4 Yrs. or 1 Yr. Discovery	Child Support	Property listed on app. to obtain credit – but only as to that lender	Affidavit Required	Clear and convincing	Ranked #10 (tie)	78.5
11	HI	§554G	No (except residents)	No	2 Yrs./2 Yrs. Pers. Injury; 6 Yrs. Contract	Divorcing Spouse; Alimony; Child Support	Preexisting Torts/ Certain Lenders/ Hawaii Tax	No Affidavit Required	Limited clear and convincing standard	None	77
12	MI	§§700.1041 to 700.10502	No (except residents)	Yes	2 Yrs./2 Yrs. or 1 Yr. Discovery	Divorcing Spouse	No	Affidavit Required (with exceptions)	Clear and convincing	Ranked #21 (tie)	75.5
13	MS	§§91-9-701 to 91-9-723	Yes	No	2 Yrs./2 Yrs. or 0.5 Yr. Discovery	Divorcing Spouse; Alimony; Child Support	Preexisting Torts, State/ Criminal Restitution/ Up to $1.5MM if no $1MM Umbrella Policy	Affidavit Required	Clear and convincing	None	72.5
14	UT	§25-6-13	Yes	Yes	None/2 Yrs. or 1 Yr. Discovery (also 120-day mailing/ publication option)	No	No	Affidavit Required	Missing clear and convincing standard	None	65
NR	OK	Tit. 31, §§10 to 18	No (except residents)	No	4 Yrs./4 Yrs. or 1 Yr. Discovery	Child Support	Must be majority Oklahoma assets	No Affidavit Required	Clear and convincing	None	NR
NR	VA	§64.2-745.1; §64.2-745.2	Yes	No	None/5 Yrs.	Child Support	Creditor who has provided services to protect trust/ U.S./city, etc.	No Affidavit Required	Clear and convincing	Ranked #14 (tie)	NR
NR	WV	§44D-5-503A; §44D-5-503B	No (except residents)	No	None/4 Yrs.	No	No	Affidavit Required	Missing clear and convincing standard	None	NR

*9th Annual Domestic Asset Protection Trust State Rankings Chart created in April 2018. Original State Rankings Chart created in April 2010.

*The Decanting State Ranking column is based on the 5th Annual Trust Decanting State Rankings Chart (Jan. 2018) at http://www.oshins.com/state-rankings-charts.

Steve Oshins is a member of the Law Offices of Oshins & Associates, LLC in Las Vegas, Nevada. He is rated AV by the *Martindale-Hubbell Law Directory* and is listed in *The Best Lawyers in America®*. He was inducted into the NAEPC Estate Planning Hall of Fame® in 2011 and has been named one of the 24 "Elite Estate Planning Attorneys" by *The Trust Advisor* and one of the Top 100 Attorneys in *Worth*. He can be reached at 702-341-6000, ext. 2 or soshins@oshins.com. His law firm's website is www.oshins.com.

Asset Protection Trust Planning

Since Alaska introduced the first self-settled spendthrift DAPT in the late 1990s, Delaware, Hawaii, Mississippi, Missouri, Nevada, New Hampshire, Ohio, Oklahoma, Rhode Island, South Dakota, Tennessee, Utah, Virginia, and Wyoming have all adopted some version of DAPT legislation.

Not all DAPTs are the same, however, as states have adopted different approaches. Some DAPT statutes protect against pre-existing tort claims while other state laws specifically exclude these claims. The states have different statute of limitations as to pre-existing creditors that range from as few as two years to as many as five years. Based on public policy, some states do not protect one spouse against property division in divorce and alimony. Most states don't protect against child support awards.

In addition to asset protection, these trusts often offer income tax incentives. Many DAPTs are situated in states that have no state income tax and specifically exempt income earned on DAPT property from state income taxes. Some states, however, do not exempt DAPT property from taxation or only exempt income earned on DAPT assets by grantors who do NOT reside in that state. Whether self-settled spendthrift trusts, including DAPTs are subject to the estate tax is another issue that doesn't seem clear at this time.

Very little law addresses the validity of DAPTs. If the creditor and debtor are both situated in the state where the DAPT is created and the litigation occurs, then the DAPT would almost certainly be respected by the court. In many situations, however, debtors and creditors are from different jurisdictions. Given this, the creditor's attorney will ordinarily do everything possible to bring the action in a state other than the state where the DAPT is situated. These complications make for a difficult "conflicts of law" analysis to determine what law should apply and how that impacts the DAPT.

When contemplating a DAPT, it is important to carefully consider the various state options. A DAPT statute in the home state seemingly provides a strong protection against claims incurred in that state. If the client resides in a state that does not have a DAPT statute, the various out of state options be examined. Although Alaska had the first DAPT in the U.S., a number of other states have statutes that some advisors consider more comprehensive. In addition to Alaska, the more popular asset protection states include Nevada, South Dakota, and Delaware.

Although DAPTs have become relatively common, most states adhere to the long-standing rule that settlors cannot retain beneficiary rights in a trust while at the same time protecting the trust assets from creditors. Courts in these states will likely continue to issue judgments that provide creditors access to the assets in out-of-state trusts.While there is a fair number of states that allow for DAPTs, it is uncertain if these trusts will be upheld in all cases.

CROSS REFERENCES TO TAX FACTS ON INDIVIDUALS AND SMALL BUSINESS (2019)

Q 9001-Q 9018. Asset Protection Trusts.

Footnotes

[1] Please see a discussion of general asset protection provisions on page 299.

[2] *Reichers v. Reichers*, 679 NYS2d 333 (1998) (offshore trust assets included in marital estate for divorce purposes); *In re Brooks*, 217 B.R. 98 (D.Conn. Bkrpt. 1998)(offshore trust ignored and assets seized by U.S. court); *FTC v. Affordable Media LLC*, 179F.3d 1228 (9th Cir. 1999) (debtor jailed for refusing to repatriate assets); *SEC v. Bilzerian*, 131 F. Supp. 2d 10 (D.C. 2001) (debtor jailed for failure to repatriate assets); *In re Lawrence*, 279 F.3d 1294 (11 Cir. 2002) (debtor spent over six years in jail for refusing to repatriate assets to the U.S.); *Bank of American v. Weese*, 277 B.R. 241 (D. Md. 2002) (debtors paid settlement of $12 million to avoid jail for failure to repatriate assets); *U.S. v. Plath*, 2003-1 U.S.T.C. 50,729 (So. District Fla. 2003) (debtor held in contempt for failure to disclose offshore accounts despite no fraudulent transfer found); *Eulich v. U.S.* (N.D.Texas Aug. 2004) (debtor threatened with jail agreed to repatriate assets); *FTC v. AmeriDebt, Inc.*, 373 F. Supp. 2d 558 (D. Md. 2005) (debtor repatriated after threat of jail); *Morris v. Morris*, (11th Cir. 2006) (debtor jailed for contempt); *Chadwick v. Green*, (Del. County Ct. 2009) (Chadwick released after spending 14 years in jail on contempt charge for failure to produce hidden offshore assets); *SEC v. Solow*, 682 F. Supp. 2d 1312 (2010) (11th Circuit affirmed order jailing debtor for failure to repatriate offshore assets); *Advanced Telecommunication Network, Inc. v. Allen*, (11th Cir. 2011) (debtor jailed for failure to repatriate); *U.S.v. Rogan*, (N.D. Illinois 2012) (debtor and attorney who created trust indicted for perjury and obstruction): *U.S. v. Grant* (S.D.Fla. 2013) (widow and children of trust grantor enjoined from receiving benefits of offshore trust after death of grantor); *SEC v. Greenberg* (S.D. Fla. 2015) (debtor found in contempt for failure to pay judgment because he could have repatriated offshore assets).

RETIREMENT PLANNING AND SOCIAL SECURITY BENEFITS

For most Americans finances for retirement years is usually addressed by three assets groups:

- Qualified retirement funds
- Social Security Benefits
- Personal asset accumulations

Qualifying for Social Security Benefits?

American citizens and resident aliens who have contributed into the US Social security system during their working years can qualify for Social Security benefits. Workers who have "40 quarters" (10 years) of participating years can qualify for some benefit amount on their own. Spouses and divorced spouses may also be eligible for benefits.

Not all workers qualify to receive Social Security benefits. Those who have been employed by the federal government or state governments may be covered by other retirement funding arrangements. This group generally includes teachers in the public school systems.

Understanding the Basics

During a client's working years both they and their employers contribute to Social Security. An amount, currently 6.2 percent, is withdrawn from paychecks along with state and federal income taxes. There is a matching employer contribution for a combined contribution amount of 12.4 percent.

Compensation subject to the withdrawal is capped each year. In 2019 the compensation maximum is capped at $132,900. Once 40 quarters of contributions are credited, eligibility for benefits is sealed. However, the ultimate benefit amount is based on 35 years of compensation. For individuals who worked for 40 quarters or more, but less than 35 years total, values for the missing years will be filled in with zeroes for the final benefit calculations.

Understanding the Process

There are certain basic terms to know in understanding Social Security retirement benefits.

- Primary Insurance Amount: The "primary insurance amount" (PIA) is the benefit a person would receive if they elect to begin receiving retirement benefits at their "normal retirement age." At this age, the benefit is neither reduced for early retirement nor increased for delayed retirement.
- Normal Retirement Age: "Full or Normal Retirement Age" (NRA) refers to the age at which the participant will be eligible to receive 100 percent of their Social Security benefit.

The NRA varies based on the date of birth of the participant. For example, if born between 1943 and 1954 the NRA is age 66. If you were born after 1960 your NRA is age 67.

Applying for Social Security benefits before NRA will mean less than 100 percent benefits. If receipt of benefits is deferred to a future year, benefits will be greater than 100 percent.

Spousal Benefits

Special provisions exist for spouses. If eligible they are entitled to apply for their own Social Security benefits or if greater they can elect a spousal benefit. The spousal benefit is generally 50 percent of the other spouse's retirement benefit while they are alive. After the death of a spouse the survivor will be entitled to receive the deceased's benefit if greater than their own.

Divorced spouses may also have rights to a "spousal benefit" where they:

- are unmarried;
- are age 62 or older;
- their ex-spouse is entitled to Social Security retirement; and
- the benefit they are entitled to receive based on their own work is less than the benefit they would receive based on their ex-spouse's PIA.

Income Taxation of Benefits

Some clients may need to pay federal income taxes on their Social Security benefits. This usually happens only if there is other substantial income that must be reported on a tax return in addition to benefits.

For individual returns, the maximum Social Security benefits taxed is 85 percent of the Social Security benefit:

- For income between $25,000 and $34,000, they may have to pay income tax on up to 50 percent of their benefits.
- Income greater than $34,000, up to 85 percent of benefits may be taxable.

Joint Returns:

- For income between $32,000 and $44,000, they may have to pay income tax on up to 50 percent of benefits
- Income greater than $44,000, up to 85 percent of benefits may be taxable.

Some Planning for Social Security

Considerable planning can be done around the timing of benefits. This is especially true for married couples.

A spouse without 40 quarters of covered earnings can get up to 50 percent of the primary worker's income benefit. This is in addition to the benefit received by the primary worker himself or herself. In other cases, a spouse otherwise fully insured under Social Security, can elect to receive the larger of their own benefit or 50 percent of a spouse's benefit.

Another popular planning strategy was known "File and Suspend." Here spouses could accelerate the receipt of the lower earner's spousal benefits, while deferring the higher earner's benefits to age 70. But, under the Bipartisan Budget Act of November, 2015, the file and suspend technique was effectively eliminated. Under the terms of the new law, anyone who applies for an early retirement benefit or a spousal benefit is "deemed" to have APPLIED FOR ANY AND ALL AVAILABLE BENEFITS. Therefore anyone applying for reduced/early benefits would automatically get the benefit that was greater – the retirement OR the spousal, but not both. Under Section 831 (*Section 202(r)(1) of the Social Security Act*) changes, this "deemed filing" definition is changed to include ALL benefits rather than only EARLY benefits, essentially extending the "deemed filing" to age 70.

No other individual will be eligible for benefits based on the earnings of a person who has suspended benefits voluntarily.

INFORMATION REQUIRED FOR ANALYSIS AND PROPOSAL

1. Obtain all current copies of benefit statements from the Social Security Administration (www.socialsecurity.gov)
2. Determine current marital status
3. Determine birth date of client and birth dates of all potential beneficiaries
4. Discuss anticipated retirement dates with client and spouse

CROSS REFERENCES TO SOCIAL SECURITY AND MEDICARE FACTS (2019)

Q 1-Q 41. Understanding and Planning for Social Security
Q 191-Q 211. Social Security Coverage
Q 212-Q 229. Filing for Benefits
Q 230-Q284. Benefit Computation
Q 318-Q 342. Loss of Benefits because of "Excess" Earnings
Q 343-Q 351. Taxation of Social Security Benefits

EXCESS SOCIAL SECURITY AND LIFE INSURANCE AS PROPERTY

Affluent individuals who are nearing retirement or already retired may realize that they do not need their social security income.[1] They have brokerage accounts, pension plans, and other assets that they feel are sufficient for their own retirement needs. But, because social security is not a needs based program, these clients will still receive their benefits in retirement. However, these same clients may be concerned about leaving a legacy for their children or grandchildren. Although they are fortunate enough to receive a social security benefit, they may not be confident that social security will remain viable to assist their children's retirement.

These individuals who do not need their social security can either save it or use the social security income to purchase a life insurance policy. If they choose to save their social security income into a side fund, they would have to consider taxes affecting the side fund, a premature death which could mean less money to their heirs, and additional long-term care or chronic illness needs. Life insurance can provide tax benefits, an attractive rate of return at life expectancy, and can be structured to offer long-term care and chronic illness benefits.[2]

The first step in this type of strategy is to identify the social security income that is not needed. The client should factor in future needs — have they considered inflation? Have they factored in potential long-term care needs?

The second step is to create a plan for the excess Social Security Income (SSI). The client can either save the SSI in a side fund (and invest it into CDs, mutual funds, bonds, etc.) or they can use the SSI to fund a life insurance policy. By saving the money into a side fund, the money would always be accessible to the client. If the client were to pass away in the earlier years though, the benefit received by their heirs would be small. In addition, the side fund would most likely have income tax consequences.

The client can potentially increase the amount to heirs if they purchase a life insurance policy with the SSI instead. In addition, the death benefit is usually received on a tax-free basis. The cash surrender value of the life policy would also grow tax deferred. If needed, tax free distributions could be taken through withdrawals and loans.[3] In addition, for clients who are concerned with long-term care costs, a long-term care or chronic illness rider might be a solution.

If estate taxes are a concern, the client could create an Irrevocable Life Insurance Trust (ILIT). At death, the policy death benefit will pass to the ILIT, free of estate and income tax.[4]

Life insurance, of course, comes with its unique benefits and considerations.[5] It is important to understand the specifics of any life insurance policy that is purchased and to fully evaluate the risks associated with that product type, illustrated funding arrangement, and the issuing company ratings and stability.[6]

Footnotes on page 97

EXCESS SOCIAL SECURITY BENFITS AND LIFE INSURANCE PLANNING CASE STUDY

CLIENTS: Robert and Ann Schultz

STATUS: Ages 67 and 63, Preferred Non Smokers. Robert and Ann have an estimated monthly Social Security Benefit of $2,500 before taxes ($19,000 annually after taxes), and they have plenty of retirement income coming in from a pension and other retirement accounts.

PRODUCT: They purchase a Current Assumption Survivorship Universal Life policy, which buys approximately $1.7M of death benefit using a premium of approximately $19,000.

EFFECTS OF USING SOCIAL SECURITY BENEFITS TO FUND LIFE INSURANCE		
	CURRENT STRATEGY	**PROPOSED STRATEGY**
Social Security Benefit	$2,500	$2,500
Consumer Price Index (i.e. Benefit Inflation Rate)	1.00%	1.00%
Approximate Total Premiums Paid by Year 29	–	$551,000
Side Fund in Year 29 (A/T Growth rate of 2%)	$877,831	$126,037
Approximate Death Benefit in Year 29		$1,700,000
Net to Heirs in Year 29	**$877,831**	**$1,826,037**
Potential Gain Due from Planning	**–**	**$948,206**

The figures used in this case study are hypothetical, for discussion purposes only, are not guaranteed and may not be used to project or predict results. Actual results may be more or less favorable. Specific product and policy elements would be found in a policy illustration provided by an insurer. With any decision regarding the purchase of life insurance, a client would need to determine which type of life insurance product is most suitable for their specific needs.

INFORMATION REQUIRED FOR ANALYSIS & PROPOSAL

1. Name of individual to be insured.
2. Sex.
3. Date of birth.
4. Smoker/nonsmoker.

To Determine Type of Contract

5. Attitude toward risk – determine need for guarantees and suitability for variable life.
6. Possible need for lifetime distributions – determine need for long-term care or chronic illness rider.
7. Income – determine eligibility for insurance and suitability of product type.
8. New worth – determine eligibility for insurance and suitability of product type.

CROSS REFERENCES TO SOCIAL SECURITY & MEDICARE FACTS (2019)

Q 1-Q 41. Understanding and Planning for Social Security
Q 191-Q 211. Social Security Coverage
Q 212-Q 229. Filing for Benefits
Q 230-Q 284. Benefit Computation
Q 318-Q 342. Loss of Benefits Because of "Excess" Earnings
Q 343-Q 351. Taxation of Social Security Benefits

Footnotes

[1] See a discussion of considerations for determining when to begin taking Social Security benefits on page 637. Approximately 41.9 Million Americans are receiving Social Security benefits. The average benefit is $1,368 per month. Approximately 60% of those receiving Social Security benefits rely on it for at least half of their income. This strategy is obviously not for those in this 60%.

[2] See a discussion of Long-Term Care Hybrid Products at pages 454-457. Long term care riders and chronic illness riders are similar in many ways, but they are not identical. Moreover, there are significant differences even among long-term care or chronic illness riders. It is important to understand the differences between the various types of living benefit riders that have become very common in the market-place because of the continually increasing cost of stand-alone long-term care products and the high cost of long term care.

[3] Loans and withdrawals will reduce the death benefit, cash surrender value, and may cause the policy to lapse. Lapse or surrender of a policy with a loan may cause the recognition of taxable income.

[4] See a discussion of life insurance trust planning on pages 54-57.

[5] The potential benefits of using excess social security benefits to purchase life insurance for your heirs includes life insurance can increase the amount left to heirs, life insurance cash surrender values grow tax deferred and cash values can be accessed tax-free through loans and withdrawals, and the death benefit can be received tax free. Also, depending upon state law (see discussion of life insurance creditor protection by state on pages 431-446), life insurance policies may enjoy creditor protection.

[6] See a discussion of life insurance products at pages 102-105. See also a discussion of life insurance company ratings at pages 425-428.

LIFE INSURANCE AS PROPERTY

Life insurance differs from most other kinds of contracts because life insurance can potentially place specific rights in three types of persons: the ***insured***, the ***owner***, and the ***beneficiary***. These characteristics make life insurance unique when compared to other types of property. In fact, their arrangement will determine whether or not the death benefit will be subject to estate or gift taxes.[1]

A. Death proceeds *will* be included in the gross estate if the insured possesses any incidents of ownership in the contract at the time of his or her death, or within three years of his or her death, no matter who might be the beneficiary.[2]

B. Likewise, when the insured's estate is named beneficiary, the death proceeds will be included in the gross estate, even though the insured may have possessed no incidents of ownership.

C. Death proceeds *will not* be included in the gross estate of the insured if the insured possesses no incidents of ownership in the policy at death or within three years before death and proceeds are not payable to, or for the benefit of, the insured's estate. However, there may be gift tax problems where the insured, the owner, and the beneficiary are all different persons. This arises, for example, where one spouse is the insured, the other spouse the owner (with a right to change beneficiaries), and a child the beneficiary. When the insured dies, the surviving spouse will be considered as having made a gift of the death proceeds to the child. For purposes of the gift tax, property owned by one person (the surviving spouse) is transferred upon the insured's death to another (the child). This deemed transfer from owner to beneficiary is a gift and could result in the surviving spouse having to pay a ***gift tax***, or in having to use up some or all of the available unified credit.[3]

D. Where estate and gift tax issues are a concern, all incidents of ownership should be held by the beneficiary from the issuance of the policy.[4] For example, one individual would be the insured and the policy would be owned by and payable to either his spouse, a child, or an irrevocable life insurance trust.[5] This arrangement will assure that the proceeds from the life insurance contract are received untouched, untaxed, and on time: untouched in that they would be payable directly to the heirs; untaxed in that they would be free of income and estate taxes; and on time in that they would be paid when needed at death, whether death occurs immediately or at some indefinite time in the future.[6]

Footnotes on page 101

Death Proceeds WILL Be Included In Estate

A

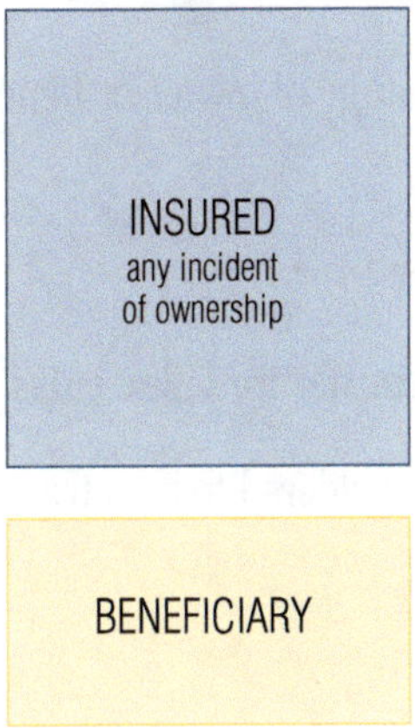

B

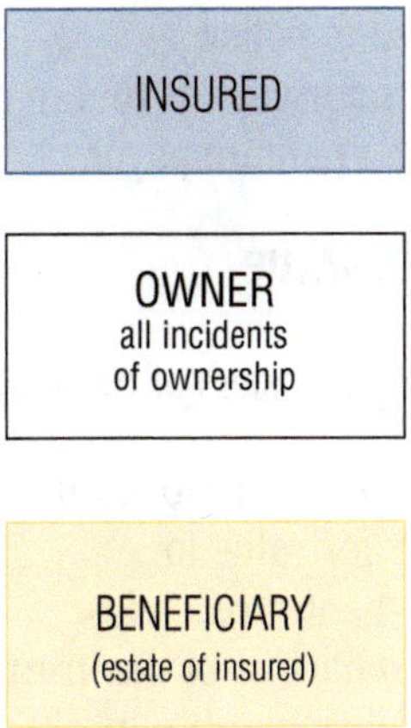

Death Proceeds WILL NOT Be Included In Estate

C

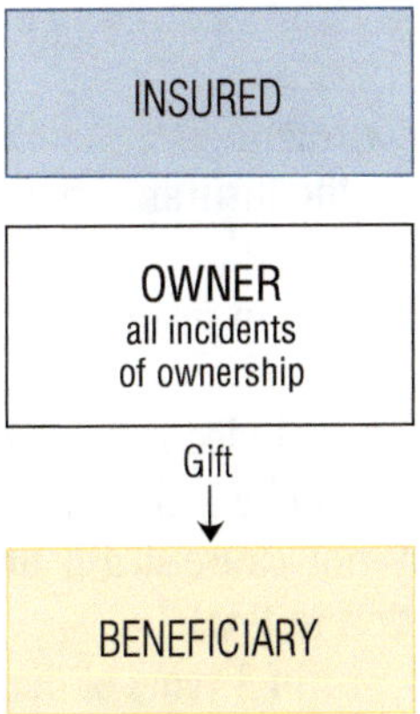

D

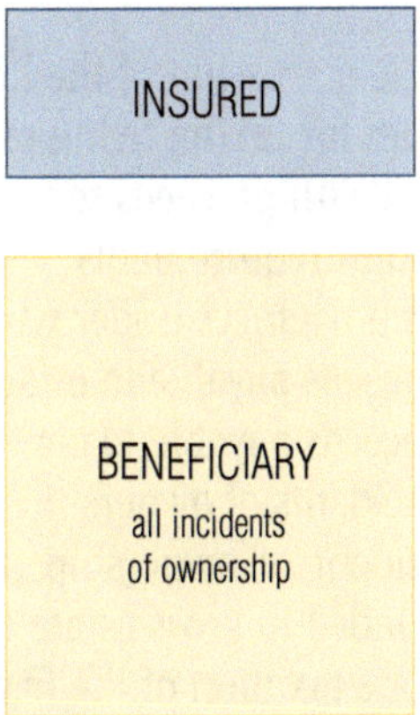

INFORMATION REQUIRED FOR ANALYSIS & PROPOSAL

1. Obtain copies of all insurance policies.
2. Determine original applicant, owner, and beneficiary from photostat copy of application contained in policy.
3. Review endorsements that may reveal a subsequent change of owner or beneficiary.
4. Ascertain premium payor.

TRANSFER FOR VALUE

The following transfers of ownership will not violate the transfer for value rules:

1. A bona fide gift (as to another family member)is not considered to be a transfer for value.
2. Transfers for value to:
    a. the insured.
    b. a partner of the insured.
    c. a partnership in which the insured is a partner.
    d. a corporation in which the insured is a stockholder or an officer.
    e. a corporation from another corporation in a tax-free reorganization.
    f. a spouse.

Note: An expanded discussion of these rules is contained on pages 568-569.

CROSS REFERENCES TO TAX FACTS ON INSURANCE & EMPLOYEE BENEFITS, VOL. 1 (2019)

Q 1. Basic discussion of the life insurance contract.
Q 10. Rules for taxing living proceeds of life insurance contracts.
Q 65. For death proceeds to be excludable from income, a life insurance policy must meet certain requirements.
Q 81. Circumstances under which death proceeds are included in insured's gross estate.
Q 82. Proceeds payable to estate are included in gross estate.
Q 85. Proceeds payable to beneficiary other than estate yet included in gross estate.
Q 86. "Incidents of ownership" which cause death proceeds to be included in estate.
Q 88. Incident of ownership as fiduciary will generally not cause death proceeds to be included in gross estate (but see Fifth Circuit position in text).
Q 96. Estate taxation of life insurance policy given away within 3 years of death.
Q 214. Policy owned by someone other than insured can result in gift if beneficiary is not also owner.
Q 279. Sale or other transfer for value will cause loss of income tax exemption for death proceeds.
Q 280. Transactions that constitute a "transfer for value."

Footnotes

[1] As property, the cash values of a life insurance policy are potentially subject to income taxes when there is a *withdrawal* from or *surrender* of the policy. However, when received, the cash values are taxed under the "cost recovery rules," meaning that such amounts are included in gross income only to the extent they exceed the investment in the policy (e.g., cash surrender values of $21,000 and total premiums of $15,000 would result in a $6,000 taxable gain, assuming no dividends and no prior distributions from the policy). A *loan* is not includable in income provided the policy is not a modified endowment contract. Distributions and loans from a modified endowment contract are taxed under different rules (see expanded discussion on pages 423-424).

[2] An incident of ownership includes the right to: (a) change the beneficiary; (b) surrender or cancel the policy; (c) assign the policy; (d) revoke an assignment; (e) pledge the policy for a loan; and (f) obtain a policy loan. Under Section 2035 if the insured owns a contract of insurance on his own life and then makes a *gift* of the policy to another, he would have to live *more than* 3 years before the proceeds would be excluded from his estate (see discussion on pages 374-375). However, if the policy were *sold* at fair market value to an irrevocable grantor trust, Section 2035 does not apply to a sale and the death proceeds payable to the trust would be excluded from his estate no matter when death occurred (this is often referred to as the "Swanson" Technique after a case holding that transfer to a grantor trust is a transfer to the insured). See also, the discussion of the grantor trust rules on page 393.

[3] As shown in Diagram "C" of the chart, *gift* tax consequences may result when owner and beneficiary are not the same (i.e., "non-parallel" owner and beneficiary and often referred to as the "Goodman Triangle"). However, when the deemed transfer of death proceeds occurs in a corporate setting, it can cause serious *income* tax problems when a contract owned by a corporation pays a death benefit to the widow of a stockholder. Payment of the death benefit will likely be non-deductible to the corporation and taxable as a *dividend* to the widow – despite the fact that under a different arrangement the payment could have qualified as a tax-free receipt of death proceeds. At best, the corporation could deduct the payment as a salary continuation expense, but the payment would be includable in the gross income of the estate or beneficiary as "income in respect of a decedent." See discussion on page 403.

[4] After numerous losses, including the *Leder*, *Headrick*, and *Perry* cases, the Internal Revenue Service issued an action on decision announcing it would no longer litigate the issue of whether life insurance proceeds are includable in the insured's estate, where the life insurance policy is procured by a third party at the instance of the insured, the insured pays the insurance premiums, and the insured dies within three years of procurement of the policy by the third person (i.e., the "beamed transfer" theory). For an expanded discussion, see Estate Taxation of Life Insurance, pages 374-375.

[5] With the unlimited marital deduction the decedent spouse's estate may well be free of federal estate taxes, but substantial taxes may be levied at the surviving spouse's death. For this reason, if it is desired to reduce exposure to estate taxes, the spouse of the insured should *not* be owner and beneficiary of the policy. Where the spouse is both owner and beneficiary, the arrangement is often referred to as a "cross-owned policy" and the death benefit received upon the insured's death will *increase* the surviving spouse's estate. In order to shift these death benefits from one generation to another free of estate taxes, it may be advisable to have the policy owned by an adult child, or placed in a Life Insurance Trust, as described in the chart on page 55. See also the discussion of minors and life insurance on page 469.

[6] The underlying principles discussed in this chart are as applicable to the analysis of existing policies as they are to proposed new insurance coverage. With many new clients, some of the easiest, yet most effective, estate planning recommendations will come from a policy audit involving an analysis and restructuring of the ownership and beneficiary provisions of existing insurance. As to new insurance, it is important to be familiar with the requirement that an applicant have an insurable interest in the life to be insured (see expanded discussion, page 408). Life insurance proceeds payable to a C corporation are not necessarily free of income taxes (see Corporate Alternative Minimum Tax, pages 327-329). Also, for the death benefits to be income tax-free, employer-owned life insurance must meet strict notice and consent requirements (see Company Owned Life Insurance (COLI), pages 319-321).

LIFE INSURANCE PRODUCTS

TERM INSURANCE. If an estate plan is to be built on a solid foundation, life insurance protection is essential. Term insurance provides protection for a *limited* period of time. However, the premium for this protection will usually increase, until it becomes prohibitively expensive for most people to maintain. While term insurance can provide a lot of protection for a lesser cost, it builds no cash values and has no permanent values. While some term insurance is "convertible" to permanent coverage and can preserve insurability, it is important to understand the policy details pertaining to conversion because sometimes the ability to convert is limited in time or to certain (undesirable) products in the carrier portfolio.

WHOLE LIFE INSURANCE, in contrast to term insurance, provides for a tax-deferred build-up of cash values over the life of the contract.[2] This cash value element, combined with level or limited premium increases, means that the death benefit will be available for an *unlimited* period. While the outlay for permanent insurance, including whole life, is greater than term insurance in the early years, most plans provide for payment of a level premium. Typically, both the cash values and the death benefits are guaranteed, unless they are dependent upon payment of projected dividends.[3]

UNIVERSAL LIFE INSURANCE offers flexible premium payments, an adjustable death benefit, and cash values that are sensitive to current interest rates.[4] Most contracts pay a *current interest rate* which can be higher than that available in the money market. However, these rates are subject to change and are not guaranteed over the life of the contract. The *guaranteed interest rate* is usually very modest and will likely result in a lapse of the policy if additional premiums are not paid. Likewise, most universal life policies offer lower *current (nonguaranteed) mortality* charges, but provided for higher *guaranteed mortality* charges. Taken together, the lower guaranteed interest rate and higher guaranteed mortality charges represent the "downside risk" of a universal life contract.

EQUITY INDEXED LIFE INSURANCE- is a product that ties the crediting rate to an index, such as the S&P 500. These products offer upside if the equity market increases (these products typically have a cap of 10 or 12 percent) but limit the exposure (usually to a floor of zero or 1 percent). See a detailed discussion of Equity-Indexed Products at pages 366-367. In recent years, sales of Equity Indexed products have been the fastest growing segment of the life insurance market.

VARIABLE LIFE INSURANCE is similar to universal life insurance, except that the underlying cash values can be invested in an equity portfolio, typically a mutual fund or bonds.[6] The policy owner is usually given the opportunity to redirect his or her investment to another portfolio although some limitations and restrictions may be imposed.[7]

Footnotes on page 105

TERM LIFE INSURANCE
(increasing premium)

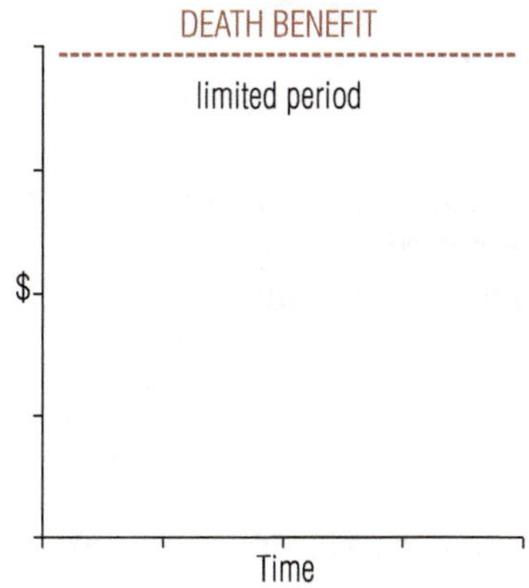

PERMANENT INSURANCE
(fixed premium)

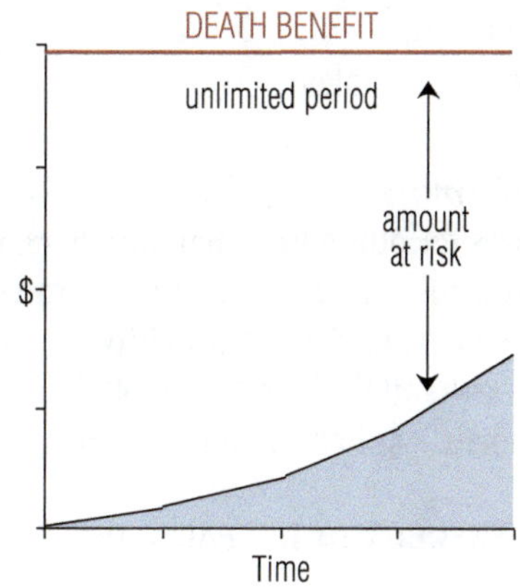

UNIVERSAL LIFE INSURANCE
(flexible premium)

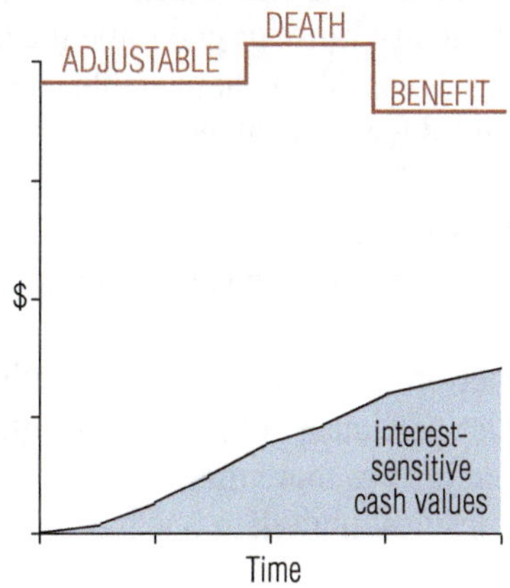

VARIABLE LIFE INSURANCE
(flexible premium)

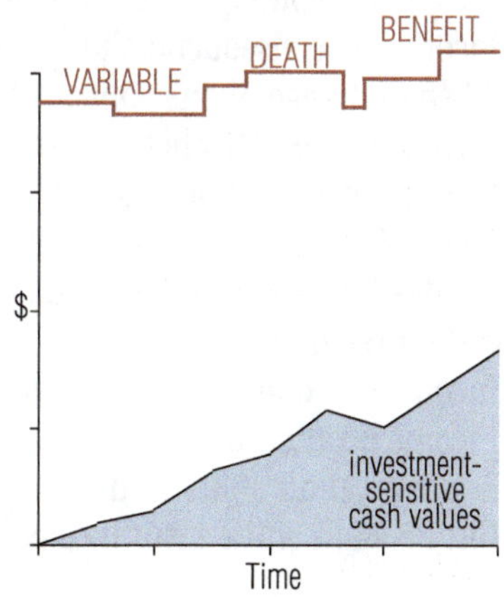

INFORMATION REQUIRED FOR ANALYSIS & PROPOSAL

1. Name of individual to be insured.
2. Sex.
3. Date of birth.
4. Smoker/nonsmoker.

To Determine Type of Contract

5. Reasons for purchase – temporary vs. permanent need.
6. Funds available for purchase – term vs. permanent (cash value).
7. Attitude toward risk – suitability for variable life.
8. Income – suitability for variable life.
9. Net worth – suitability for variable life.

CROSS REFERENCES TO TAX FACTS ON INSURANCE & EMPLOYEE BENEFITS, VOL. 1 (2019)

Q 1. Basic discussion of the life insurance contract.
Q 2. Premiums for personal life insurance not deductible.
Q 8. Annual cash value increases generally not taxable income to policyholder.
Q 13. Taxation of distributions from policies classified as modified endowment contracts.
Q 36. Income tax consequences to seller of life insurance or endowment contract.
Q 43. Income tax consequences to purchaser of life insurance or endowment contract.
Q 44. When exchange of one contract for another is considered nontaxable.
Q 51. Income tax results when contract surrendered for cash values.
Q 54. Income taxation of an "accelerated death benefit."
Q 63. Death proceeds generally received free of income taxes.
Q 65. For death proceeds to be excludable from income, a life insurance policy must meet certain requirements.
Q 77. Income taxation of death proceeds of policy previously transferred for value.
Q 78. Income taxation of death proceeds of policy previously transferred as a gift.
Q 199. Estate taxation of life insurance policy that insures more than one life.
Q 211. Gift taxation of life insurance policy that insures more than one life.

Footnotes

[1] Term insurance is available in many forms, the most common being annual renewable, five-year renewable (and/or convertible), 10-year renewable and convertible (R&C), 15-year R&C, 20-year R&C, and term to a specific age, such as age 65. A specialized form of term insurance, decreasing term, is also available, and usually purchased to cover a decreasing loan or mortgage obligation. Term insurance can be tailored to fit almost any temporary insurance need – level, decreasing, or even increasing.

[2] Permanent life insurance is often called "whole life." This is because, so long as the policy remains in force, it provides protection for the "whole of life." The whole of life is assumed to be to age 100 under many mortality tables, although in recent years lesser ages have been used (i.e., age 90 or 95). If the insured lives to age 100, the policy endows with the cash values equaling the face amount of the policy.

[3] Both term and permanent insurance are available as *participating* policies, which offer the opportunity for dividends that may be used to: reduce the premium outlay; purchase paid-up additions (which accrue their own cash values); enhance the amount of available death benefit through a combination of one-year term insurance and paid-up additions (the fifth dividend option); or augment the cash values by being left to accumulate at interest.

[4] Universal life insurance has many unique features not found in traditional whole life policies. Most importantly, your client *controls* many aspects of the contract because of the built-in flexibility of the universal life policy. Specific features of universal life include:

a. An adjustable death benefit that may be increased or decreased to suit the obligations and needs of the insured (often subject to insurability if the death benefit is increased).

b. Tax-deferred current interest earnings on cash values.

c. Flexible premiums that allow changes in payments to suit individual needs (but see the discussion regarding life insurance premium limitations, pages 423-424).

[5] Interest-sensitive whole life is a hybrid between permanent (whole life) insurance and universal life insurance. It is also known as excess-interest whole life, current assumption whole life, irreplaceable life, pseudo universal life, fixed premium universal life, and adjustable cash value whole life. The product typically requires a fixed premium, and in return provides a *guaranteed* death benefit and minimum interest rates, and current higher nonguaranteed interest rates. Premiums are usually fixed, although additional funds can be "dumped" into the policy in order to vanish, or short pay, premiums. As with universal life, a surrender charge is often assessed when the contract is surrendered in the early years, although some contracts allow withdrawals of "excess" earnings. A "bailout feature" may be offered, which enables the policyholder to withdraw funds without penalty if the credited interest rate drops below a certain level.

[6] While variable life insurance policies can provide a hedge against inflation, there is also the risk that investment performance will be poor and that the cash reserves will decrease or be lost. Since variable life insurance is a security, the agent must hold a valid federal securities license (and state license where required) in order to sell the product. In addition, *a prospectus must be delivered* with or preceding a specific proposal to a prospect or client.

[7] In recent years, joint life insurance policies insuring multiple-lives have become popular for funding a variety of insurance needs (see First-To-Die Insurance, page 380, and Survivorship Life Insurance, page 561). Company owned life insurance (COLI) is used to fund a number of nonqualified benefits (pages 319-321). A table of comparative Insurance Company Ratings is set forth on page 427. See also, Life Insurance Default Risk, page 418.

BASIS PLANNING AND CAPITAL GAINS

If property is classified as a "capital asset," then, upon its sale, any gain generally is considered a capital gain. Gain is the excess of the amount realized upon the sale over the basis (which might be adjusted downward for depreciation or upward for additions to the property). Gains and losses from the sale or exchange of capital assets are either short-term or long-term. Generally, in order for gain or loss to be long-term, the asset must have been held for more than one year.

Before assessing any taxes on capital gains, short-term gains and losses are netted against each other and long-term gains and losses are netted against each other. The excess of net long-term capital gain over net short-term capital loss (if any) is net capital gain.

Under the 2017 Tax Act, beginning on January 1, 2018 and scheduled to sunset at the end of 2025, a federal long term capital gain tax rate of 0 will apply to joint filers who earn less than $77,200 (half of that amount for married taxpayers filing separately), heads of households who earn less than $51,700, single filers who earn less than $38,600, and trusts and estates with less than $2,600 in income. A rate of 15 percent will apply to joint filers who earn more than $77,200 but less than $479,000 (half of these amounts for married taxpayers filing separately), healds of households who earn more than $51,700 but less than $452,400, single filers who earn more than $38,600 but less than $425,800, and trusts and estates with more than $2,600, but less than $12,700 in income. The 20 percent rate will apply to joint filers who earn more than $479,000 (half of that amount for married taxpayears filing separately), heads of hosueholds who earn more than $452,400, single filers who earn more than $425,800, and trusts and estates with more than $12,700 in income.

As had previously been the case, unrecaptured section 1250 gain will continue to be taxed at a maximum rate of 25 percent. Short-term capital gains continue to be taxed as ordinary income.

Added by the Affordable Care Act, for tax years after December 31, 2012, and unchanged by the 2017 Tax Act, there is an additional tax of 3.8 percent on passive income which includes most capital gains. The tax is levied on taxpayers with modified adjusted gross income over $250,000 (married filing jointly), $200,000 (single taxpayers), and $125,000 (married filing separately).

With an individual being able to pass (during life or at death) up to $11,200,000 from 2018 until 2025 (projected to increase to $11,400,000 for 2019, then returning to $5,000,000 in 2026 and indexed for inflation) – very few estates now face any federal estate taxes. In fact, even without the tempoary doubling of the exemption created by the 2017 Tax Act, only roughly two out of every one thousand estates face a federal estate tax according to the Joint Committee on Taxation. In addition to the federal estate tax, some states have state inheritance taxes which can apply to smaller estates. State taxes should be considered in the planning process.[1]

But, today, with the federal estate tax applying to only a small number of taxpayers, basis planning is the most important aspects of estate planning for many families. Assets gifted during life have a carry-over basis. In other words, if a parent (or grandparent) gifts highly appreciated assets to heirs duringlife – the heir takes the property with the donor's basis. Whereas assets that are held until death receive a basis step-up to the fair market value at the time of death – even if the decedent has no estate tax liability. Whereas estate planning has focused on reduction or elimination of estate taxes for decades – today the focus needs to shift to basis (capital gains) planning for the vast majority of taxpayers.

Footnotes on page 109

TAX BASIS PLANNING AND CAPITAL GAINS

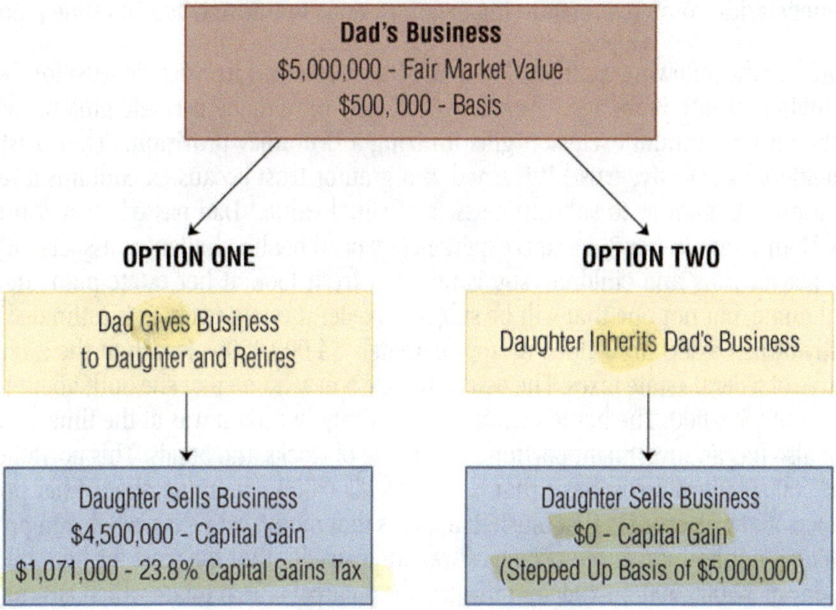

Basis Planning and Capital Gains

Despite the decreased number of individuals and married couples with estate tax exposure the use of irrevocable trusts in estate planning remains common. Trusts serve many important reasons other than avoidance of estate taxes. The ability to control the timing of distributions and protect beneficiaries from creditors are important reasons to utilize trusts in estate planning.

Let's consider the following example. Mom and Dad created an irrevocable trust for the benefit of their children twenty years ago. Over the years, they have made periodic gifts to the trust – often in the form of annual exclusion gifts utilizing a Crummey provision.[2] That trust is a so-called intentionally defective trust[3] It is taxed as a grantor trust because it contains a very common provision – the power to substitute assets of equal value.[4] Dad passed away a number of years ago. Mom is now in her 80s and is experiences typical health challenges associated with her age. With her advisors and children, she is taking a fresh look at her estate plan. Mom has a significant estate, but not one that will be subject to federal estate taxes. It is estimated that her individually owned assets are valued at approximately $4,000,000 – less than the amount that can pass free of federal estate taxes. The assets include a new home that she built about five years ago at a cost of $500,000. The home's value today is roughly what it was at the time of construction. Mom also has an investment portfolio consisting of stocks and bonds. This portfolio, values at about $3,000,000 has a cost basis that is about $3,000,000. The remainder of her property is cash and personal property. On first blush, it appears that mom's estate is probably in pretty good order. She does not have an estate tax exposure. But, consider that the trust for her children has a value today of $2,000,000. Included in this trust is a parcel of real estate which is situated near a popular new sub-division on the outskirts of the city. When the property was contributed to the trust nearly twenty years ago – the property was not near the current city limits and had nominal value. At the time, an appraisal placed the value of the property at $100,000. Recently, a developer has offered the family $1,000,000 for the property. The children suspect that the property will only continue to appreciate in value as the city expands in the vicinity of their parcel.

Assuming the family is comfortable holding onto the parcel – what can be done to minimize their tax exposure? Today, if the trust sold the property – mom would be taxed on the capital gain at her tax rate. If the property remains in the trust and isn't sold during mom's lifetime – the trust will cease being a grantor trust and will be taxed as a separate taxable entity. If the property is sold at that time – the capital gain (currently $900,000) would be taxed at then applicable capital gain rate. Because the property is owned in an irrevocable trust and is not included in mom's estate it will not receive a basis step up at the time of her death. Assuming a 15 percent tax rate – the "built in" capital gain is approximately $135,000 (ignoring possible state taxes). A third option is for mom to substitute other assets for the parcel of real estate and hold the parcel in her estate until death. Since the stock and bond portfolio has a basis roughly equal to cost basis; stocks and bonds valued at $1,000,000 could be exchanged for the real estate parcel with no tax consequences. At death, the parcel could pass under her will to the children or back to the irrevocable trust. If the family is correct and the parcel continues to appreciate in value – let's assume it has a value of $2,000,000 at the time of mom's death. Under the federal estate tax laws, even if mom owes no estate taxes because her estate does not exceed the amount that passes free of estate taxes, that parcel will receive a new basis equal to the value at the time of mom's death ($2,000,000). After mom's death – the family could sell the parcel for the then fair market value of $2,000,000 without any capital gains taxation.

Even if mom does not have an estate tax exposure – it doesn't mean that mom and the family are not in need of careful tax planning as they plan mom's estate. Depending on mom's tax bracket – maybe selling the property during mom's lifetime is the right answer. But, in this case, because the family believes the property is going to continue to grow in value, the best result is likely taking advantage of the basis step up at mom's death by utilizing the power of substitution contained in the irrevocable trust. What appears almost certainly to be the least desirable alternative is to stay the course – allowing the parcel to remain in the irrevocable trust without a basis step up at mom's death.

Today, planning to reduce capital gains taxes is a much more important issue than federal estate tax planning. Unfortunately, too many families and their advisors have not yet realized that just because they do not have an estate tax liability doesn't mean that they don't need to carefully consider the impact of capital gains taxation as part of the retirement and estate planning process.

CROSS REFERENCES TO TAX FACTS ON INSURANCE & EMPLOYEE BENEFITS, VOL. 1 (2019)

Q 694. Definition of tax basis.
Q 695. Tax basis of property acquired by purchase or exchange.
Q 696. Tax basis of property acquired from a decedent.
Q 700. Definition of capital asset.
Q 701. Short-term and long-term capital gain or loss.
Q 705. Individual taxation of capital gains or losses.

Footnotes

1 Nearly half of the states have some form of state inheritance or estate tax. In some states, including highly populated states such as New York, New Jersey, and Pennsylvania, the top state tax rate is 15 percent or more.

2 See discussion of Crummey Powers on page 332. Crummey powers are utilized to qualify gifts in trust as a present interest gift in order to qualify the gift for the gift tax annual exclusion. See a detailed discussion of annual exclusion gifts on page 297.

3 Intentionally defective trusts are discussed in detail in pages 74-77. An intentionally defective trust is generally one that is taxed as a grantor trust for income tax purposes (ie, it is ignored), but outside of the estate for estate, gift, and generation skipping transfer tax purposes.

4 IRC Section 675(4)(c) provides that a grantor's power to substitute assets of equal value for assets already in the trust makes the trust a grantor trust for income tax purposes. As a result, income and capital gains incurred at the trust level are taxed to the grantor. The trust, however, is outside of the estate for gift, estate, and generation skipping transfer tax purposes.

WITHDRAWAL SEQUENCING AND RETIREMENT SAVINGS

Money may be fungible, but not all retirement savings are the same. When planning for retirement, it is important to understand the tax consequences associated with various retirement assets. It's important to understand these basic rules while investing for retirement as well as when you begin taking distributions in retirement. Failure to consider taxation of various investment options, while saving for retirement and living in retirement, can needlessly reduce your retirement funds and/or the legacy you leave to your heirs.

It's important to have an understanding of the difference between ordinary income and capital gains. Today, the federal income tax is significantly biased toward capital gains. The tax rate on the gain from appreciated property is generally much higher than the tax rate on earned income. (See Basis Management on page 106). Whereas the highest federal marginal income tax rate is 39.6 percent, the highest capital gain tax rate is 20 percent. Essentially, the highest ordinary income tax rate is almost twice the highest capital gains rate. Different people have different views on the policy underlying this tax reality – but it's important to understand the difference between capital gains taxation and ordinary income taxation when investing. Obviously two investments both earning the same return (say 6 percent) are not identical if one is creating capital gains and the other ordinary income. The after-tax return could be very different. And, while most people are aware that municipal bond income is generally free of income tax – it is important to understand the taxation of specific bond purchases for both federal and state purposes. In short, not all municipal bonds are equal and state law varies as well.

When saving for retirement it is also important to consider the tax aspects of qualified retirement plan options. Many employers offer a 401(k) or other plan as an employee benefit. The ability to contribute to a 401(k) on a before tax basis is a major benefit. The advantage, of course, is more pronounced for taxpayers in higher marginal income tax brackets. But, what is often ignored by younger employees or those in lower income tax brackets is the potential employee match. It isn't uncommon for an employer to match a portion of an employee's contribution to a 401(k) or other retirement plan. Even if the employee is in a low marginal income tax bracket and the tax savings from the deferral is not great – an employee match can be a very significant benefit. Having an employer add 2 or 3 percent of salary to your qualified retirement can compound significantly over time.

Footnotes on page 113

It's equally important to understand which assets might be received income tax free. The decision between traditional IRA and 401(k) or "Roth IRA" and "Roth 401(k)" is another consideration that requires analysis on a case by case basis. (See Discussions of Roth IRA and Roth Conversions on pages 527-529).

Generally, most advisors would say that qualified retirement options should be exhausted before considering other retirement planning investments. However, this will vary from client to client. Various forms of savings and supplemental retirement investments come with various risks, tax liabilities and benefits. When considering saving for your own retirement – it's important to understand how various investment options are taxed. For example, deferred annuity contracts are purchased with after-tax dollars, but grow on a tax deferred basis. When withdrawals are taken from the deferred annuity, however, any gain in the contract is recognized first. That gain is recognized as ordinary income. As a result, a deferred annuity probably makes most sense for taxpayers who are currently in a high income tax bracket and want to avoid taxation on income and appreciation today. Generally, these are taxpayers who assume that their income will be lower in retirement making the deferral of taxation into the future most advantageous. An immediate annuity, however, is taxed much differently. An immediate annuity is taxed as a partial return of investment and partially as ordinary income.

Life insurance contracts enjoy their own rather unique taxation. The cash value of a life insurance policy that is not taxed as a modified endowment contract grows on a tax-deferred basis. Cash value in excess of premiums paid (i.e., the policy basis) is not taxed until/unless it is accessed during the insured's life. Even then, policy gain is only taxed after basis is recovered. In other words – the cash value of a life insurance policy is first treated as a return of basis (not taxed) and then as ordinary income when received. In most cases, to avoid taxation of the gain (after basis has been recovered), cash value is taken in the form of policy loans. Upon death, life insurance death benefits are ordinarily received free of income and capital gains tax. So, while it isn't completely accurate to say that life insurance is "tax-free," it is probably fair to say that life insurance is tax advanraged.

It's clearly important to understand how investment options are taxed while the taxpayer is in his or her working years and planning for retirement. But, understanding how investments are taxed and having a well-planned and systematic strategy for distributions is equally important. Advisors often refer to the systematic liquidation of retirement savings as "Savings Withdrawal Sequencing." There are numerous considerations that must be factored into savings withdrawal sequencing.

The tax bracket of the individual in retirement is an important consideration. The income tax (and capital gains) bracket will be important in understanding the "tax burn" rate of liquidating retirement assets. (See Discussion of Basis Management starting on page 106). See the table that accompanies this section on how using tax-free or lower tax assets, can help reduce a client's overall retirement taxation.[1]

Withdrawal Sequencing and Retirement Savings

Each taxpayer's situation will be unique and the savings withdrawal sequencing needs to be done in coordination with basis planning and qualified plan distribution planning to maximize what will be left to heirs when the family anticipates the individual will not use all of the assets during his or her lifetime. (See Basis Management at page 106).[2]

		Lower Tax Brackets		Higher Tax Bracket	
		Social Security, IRA, Pension Distributions and other Taxable Income		Taxable Income or Life Insurance Cash Values, Roth IRAs and Municipal Bond Interest	Total
		First $18,550	Next $56,850	Next $26,200	$100,000
Without Life	Tax Rate	10%	15%	25%	
Insurance Planning	Taxes Due	$1,855	$8,512	$6,550	$16,917
With Life Insurance	Tax Rate	10%	15%	0%	
Planning	Taxes Due	$1,825	$8,512	$0	$10,337

CROSS REFERENCES TO TAX FACTS ON INSURANCE & EMPLOYEE BENEFITS, VOL. 1 (2019)

Q 3644. Sequencing of Returns.

Footnotes

[1] As a general rule, qualified plans are the last assets that you want to tap for retirement income. That may sound counter-intuitive as they are the one asset specifically acquired for retirement purposes, but the tax deferred-advantages afforded qualified plans makes them generally the most desirable asset to retain. Although the qualified plan beneficiary designation rules are complex and deserving of a comprehensive section on their own merit – the rules are such that by utilizing a "spousal rollover" or by naming your children or grandchildren as the beneficiary you can "stretch" the distribution of qualified assets over an extended time period. Because qualified plan assets are generally not taxed until received (and Roth distributions are generally not taxed even upon receipt since the Roth is funded with after-tax dollars as opposed to other qualified plans) – being able to "stretch" the distributions over time creates maximum tax savings. To limit the ability to stretch qualified plan distributions and avoid taxation – there are "required minimum distribution" rules that generally require you to take distributions by April 1 of the year following the owner's attaining age 70½ years. (See IRA Distribution Planning on pages 411-413). Also keep in mind that while the policy behind this rule is less obvious than the RMD rules – you are generally (absent an unusual situation) not allowed to take distributions prior to age 59½ without also paying a 10 percent penalty tax.

So, generally, you will find that in retirement it is best to liquidate bank accounts first. Bank accounts have a low return and will not trigger capital gains taxation. Next are usually capital assets with a high basis. Qualified plan assets are ordinarily last. This general strategy should be combined with property qualified plan ownership and beneficiary designations (i.e., utilize "stretch" planning when appropriate). Other assets, such as capital assets with low basis, life insurance, and annuities need to be carefully considered as well. While life insurance has advantageous tax treatment that makes it an excellent retirement investment – because the death benefit is received completely income and capital gains tax free means that it may or may not be an asset that you want to access during life if you have other assets. And, because capital assets not used during life will receive a basis step up at death – whether to liquidate highly appreciated capital assets during life and before other assets probably depends mostly on the taxpayer's tax bracket and likelihood that the taxpayer will be leaving assets to his or her heirs at death

[2] A modified endowment contract (or "MEC") is a special type of life insurance policy that has a different tax regime. In summary, cash taken from a MEC is subject to taxation on gain first and return of basis after gain is recaptured. But, like a typical life insurance contract, gains are generally not taxed until cash is received and death benefits are ordinarily received free of income tax and capital gains tax. (See discussion of Modified Endowment Contracts on pages 423-424).

LONG-TERM CARE

Planning for long-term care is an integral part of retirement and financial planning. Long-term care consists of a continuum of services including nursing home care, assisted living, and home health and adult day care. The need can arise from an accident, illness, or advanced age.

THE RISK. Statistics make a very good case for long-term care planning. For example, a 65-year-old woman can expect to live another 20.1 years, and a 65-year-old man can expect to live another 16.8 years.[1] According to the U.S. Administration on Aging, 70 percent of people attaining age 65 will need some form of long term care during their lifetimes. During these years it is estimated that the risk of entering a nursing home is approximately 50 percent.

THE COST. Nursing care is expensive. Although there is a large variation from one region to another, the average nursing home cost was $85,775 per year in 2018.[2]

MANAGING THE RISK. For an individual with substantial retirement income and assets self-insurance may be a realistic option. However, for those who cannot self-insure reliance upon government programs may be ill advised. For example, after a minimum three-day hospital stay Medicare will only pay for the first 20 days of *skilled nursing* care. From days 21 through 100 the patient must pay in 2017 the first $164.50 per day, and all costs after 100 days. Medicare does not pay for *custodial* care.[3] Although Medicaid will pay for custodial care, the patient must first "spend down" assets in order to qualify.[4] Private insurance is often considered by those desiring independence and choice of care and benefits.[5] It also provides asset protection from the Medicaid spend down requirements.

PRIVATE INSURANCE provides flexibility by allowing individuals to obtain care in various settings and at different levels (skilled nursing, intermediate and custodial care). Contracts do not require prior hospitalization, are guaranteed renewable and offer level premiums.[6] Daily benefits run from $50 to $300 or more. The benefit periods are typically 2, 3, 4, or 5 years, or lifetime. Benefits are paid when the insured has a cognitive impairment or is unable to perform certain activities called "benefit triggers."[7] A deductible, in the form of an elimination period, will generally last from 0 to 180 days. Provisions for home health care and adult day care will allow the beneficiary to remain in the community. Of particular importance is waiver of premiums to limit premium costs and inflation protection to ensure an adequate daily benefit in the future.[8]

In addition to these basic components, other benefits are often available. These features include spousal discounts, respite care, hospice care, caregiver training, bed reservation, medical equipment, cognitive reinstatement, non-forfeiture benefits, case management and referral services.[9] Choosing from such a range of contract options requires a balancing of benefits and flexibility against premium costs.

Footnotes on page 117

THE RISK

The estimated risk of a 65-year-old person needing some form of long-term care during their life is 70 percent according to the U.S. Administration on Aging (see www.longtermcare.gov).

THE COST

The average cost of nursing home care in the United States is nearly $85,775 per year in 2018 for a semi-private room. There is, however, a large variation from one region to another around this national average. In many states the average cost exceeds $100,000 per year with the highest average state at over $200,000 per year.

MANAGING THE RISK

Government Programs

- Medicare
- Medicaid

Self-Insurance

- Income
- Assets

Private Insurance

- Independence & Choice
- Protection of Assets

PRIVATE INSURANCE

- Daily Benefit Amount
- Benefit Period
- When Benefits Paid
- Elimination Period
- Home Health Care
- Adult Day Care
- Waiver of Premium
- Inflation Protection

- Spousal Discounts
- Respite Care
- Hospice Care
- Caregiver Training
- Bed Reservation
- Medical Equipment
- Cognitive Reinstatement
- Non-Forfeiture Benefits
- Case Management
- Referral Services

LONG-TERM CARE/CHRONIC ILLNESS HYBRID PRODUCTS are becoming increasingly popular. In recent years, the cost of new and existing (inforce) private long term care insurance has increased at a rate far exceeding inflation. A number of companies previously selling stand alone long term care insurance have exited the market (see pages 454-457). As a result of price increases and few companies offering stand alone long term care insurance, there has a been a tremendous growth in "hybrid products." These products combine long term care or chronic illness riders with a life insurance or annuity contract. The cost of adding a long term care rider or chronic illness rider on a life insurance product will often increase the cost of the life product by ten percent or less making hybrid products an increasingly popular alternative to stand along long term care products.

INFORMATION REQUIRED FOR ANALYSIS & PROPOSAL

1. Name of individual to be insured.
2. Sex.
3. Date of birth (and spouse's date of birth).
4. Has individual or spouse been hospitalized in the last 5 years?
5. Has individual or spouse had any health problems?
6. What medications is the individual or spouse currently taking (include both dosage and frequency)?
7. What is the current monthly income and what monthly income is anticipated in retirement?
8. What is the net worth of the individual and spouse? (see page 12).

CROSS REFERENCES TO TAX FACTS ON INSURANCE & EMPLOYEE BENEFITS, VOL. 1 (2019)

Q 477. Description of a "qualified" long-term care insurance contract.
Q 481. Description of "qualified" long-term care services.
Q 482. Grandfathering of long-term care contracts issued prior to 1997.
Q 487. Within limitation premiums for a qualified long-term care insurance contract are deductible as medical expenses.
Q 488. Subject to a dollar limitation the self-employed may deduct premiums for a qualified long-term care insurance contract.
Q 489. Premiums paid by an employer for a qualified long-term care insurance contract should be excludable from the employee's gross income.
Q 490. Premiums paid by an employer for a qualified long-term care insurance contract for employees should be deductible by the employer.
Q 491. Description of limitations on the amount of benefits received under a qualified long-term care insurance contract that may be excluded from income.
Q 493. Taxation of a "nonqualified" long-term care insurance contract.
Q 494. Reporting requirements applicable to long-term care benefits.

Footnotes

[1] See Commissioners 2001 Standard Ordinary Mortality Table on pages 599-600.

[2] Source of 2017 nursing home costs for a semi-private room with skilled nursing care 24 hours a day: The median cost for a private room in the United States is $97,455 (growing an average of 4% a year for the past five years). Even assisted living has a $45,000 median average cost. Genworth Financial 2017 Cost of Care Survey (www.genworth.com/costofcare). Because of the wide range of charges a local cost survey of various levels of care is strongly recommended. The "cost of waiting" to buy long-term care insurance can be considerable. Not only are premiums substantially more at older ages but additional coverage must be purchased to cover inflation (see footnote 9, below).

[3] Medicare will pay for medically necessary home health visits that are restorative in nature (i.e., the patient must be improving). However, Medicare will not pay for intermediate care or custodial care (see page 463). It should also be noted that Medigap coverage only pays Medicare deductibles or coinsurance, it does not extend the basic coverage.

[4] Simply put, "spend down" means liquidating assets to pay for long-term care until a level of financial indigence is reached and it is possible to qualify for Medicaid. When does such a "financial meltdown" become significant? The answer depends upon marital status. In most states a single individual cannot have more than $2,000 in countable assets. But the "indigent spouse rules" provide better treatment to a married couple with an at-home spouse. In 2017, many states allowed them to retain up to $120,119, plus the home, automobile, household goods and personal belongings (and a minimum monthly income of $2,205.00 for the at-home spouse, as changed annually in July of each year). Amounts over these allowances are referred to as the "Medicaid deductibles."

[5] If an individual needs 24-hour-a-day custodial care, under Medicaid there is little or no provision for "community based care" (i.e., home care, assisted living or adult day care). It is understood that, on average, Medicaid pays about two-thirds as much as the private pay patient. Although a nursing home cannot, by law, treat patients differently depending on who is paying the bills, quality of care remains an issue. The Medicaid patients do not get private rooms. If the quality of care deteriorates, the family of a private pay patient can move him to a different facility.

[6] Premiums can be raised on a class basis. These features are offered either within the base contract or by contract rider. Long-term care insurance is also available on a group basis or as permanent life insurance that advances the death benefit.

[7] Typically, benefit payments are triggered by the loss of two or more activities of daily living (ADLs). These activities include eating, toileting, transferring, bathing, dressing and continence. There has been considerable debate over the quality of benefits under tax qualified versus nontax qualified products (e.g., the nontax qualified products will pay a benefit using the more liberal "medical necessity" standard). See the discussion of Qualified Long-Term Care Insurance on page 510.

[8] For younger insureds inflation protection is particularly important (e.g., a 50-year-old will not likely need coverage as soon as a 70-year-old, thus with inflation his care will cost more). Assuming 5 percent inflation per year, care that costs $3,750 a month today will cost $6,108 in 10 years and $9,948 in 20 years (see Future Value Table on page 617).

[9] It has been observed that eldercare may soon replace childcare as the number one dependent care issue. Good prospects for long-term care insurance are individuals in the so called "sandwich generation" (i.e., persons in their forties and fifties who still have children living at home, *and* are also providing for their own parents). In taking care of their parents these individuals have come to fully appreciate the problems of long-term care and generally do not want to be a burden on their own children.

SPLIT-DOLLAR FUNDING LIFE INSURANCE TRUST

Split-dollar offers a means of using employer-provided dollars to pay premiums for life insurance used for a variety of purposes, to include family income needs, estate taxes, and other estate settlement costs. When combined with an irrevocable life insurance trust, it is possible to take advantage of the gift tax laws while at the same time assuring that the proceeds will be received free of estate taxes.[1]

These plans will likely be structured as: (1) an "equity collateral assignment plan" using a trust-owned policy with employer-paid premiums treated as loans to the employee under the *loan regime* (cash values owned by the trust but assigned to the employer as security for the loans) or (2) a "nonequity collateral assignment" plan using a trust-owned policy with the employee taxed under the *economic benefit regime* (employer entitled to all cash values).[2] This last design offers the most flexibility and can be implemented as follows:[3]

DURING LIFETIME, the employee establishes a trust and the trustee applies for, or obtains, insurance on the employee's life.[4] Thereafter, at the employee's request, the employer and trustee enter into a split-dollar agreement providing for the allocation of premiums, cash values, and death benefits on the trust-owned insurance policy.[5] Under this agreement the employer pays all premiums and is entitled to all cash values (by virtue of a limited collateral assignment from the trust).[6]

Each year *income* is imputed to the employee in an amount equal to the "economic benefit" of the insurance protection received by the trust.[7] This same amount is then imputed as a *gift* by the employee to the trust. Provided the trust is properly funded, and the beneficiaries given appropriate withdrawal powers, these imputed gifts will qualify for the gift tax annual exclusion of $15,000 in 2019 (projected).[8] Of course, it is unlikely that they would exercise these powers, since to do so would defeat the purpose of the trust.

UPON DEATH of the employee, the policy proceeds are split between the employer and the trust. The employer is entitled to a death benefit equal to the *greater of* the cash values or the cumulative premiums paid. The balance of the proceeds are paid directly to the trust and are income and estate tax free.[9]

In recent years, split dollar has largely been used as a transfer tax tool. However, because of increases in the transfer tax exemption – fewer and fewer people are exposed to estate taxes. Therefore, split dollar arrangements were an infrequently used strategy limited to the very wealthy. However, the significant reductions in corporate tax rates established by the 2017 Tax Act have created new income tax strategies for business owners and executives using split dollar.

Footnotes on page 121

DURING LIFETIME

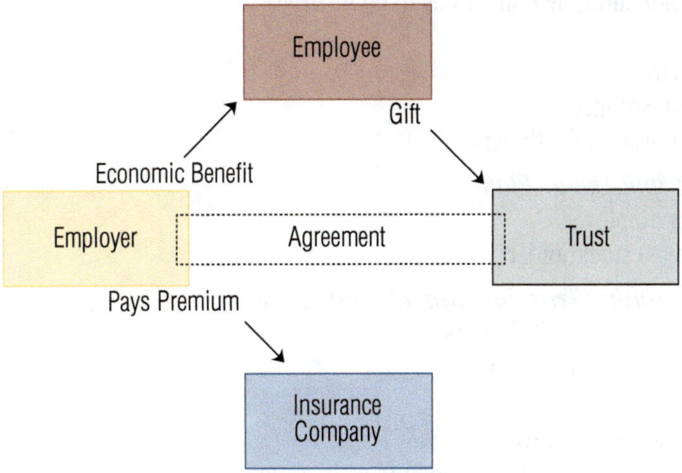

UPON DEATH

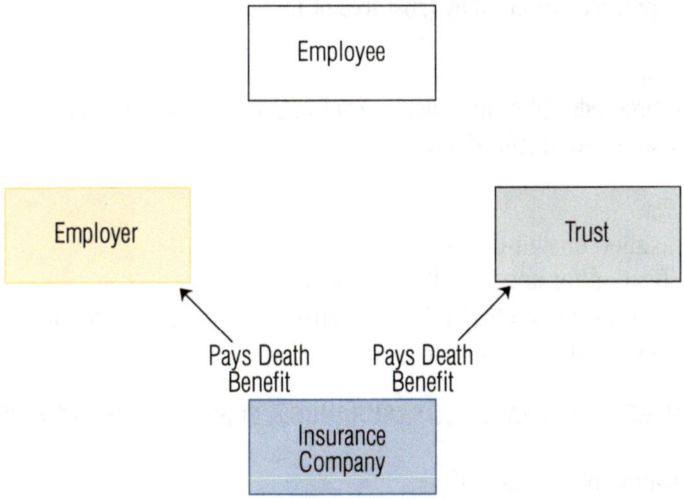

INFORMATION REQUIRED FOR ANALYSIS & PROPOSAL

1. Name of individual or individuals to be insured.
2. Sex.
3. Date of birth.
4. Smoker/nonsmoker.
5. Amount of desired death benefit.

To Design Split-Dollar Plan

6. Position of employee.
7. Is employee a stockholder?

Attorney Drafting Trust Instrument Must Also Know

8. Trustee during insured's lifetime.
9. Trustee after insured's death.
10. Names of beneficiaries.
11. Ages of minor beneficiaries.
12. To who, in what amount, and when trust income is to be paid.
13. To who, in what amount, and when trust corpus is to be paid.

CROSS REFERENCES TO TAX FACTS ON INSURANCE & EMPLOYEE BENEFITS, VOL. 1 (2019)

Income Tax

Q 153. Death proceeds received by trust free of income taxes.

Estate Tax

Q 179. When proceeds either included or excluded from insured's estate.
Q 325. Estate taxation of split-dollar.

Gift Tax

Q 116. Gift taxation of split-dollar.
Q 159. Qualification for annual gift tax exclusion.
Q 161. Qualification for annual gift tax exclusion when gifts made to trust for premium payments (Crummey rules).

CROSS REFERENCES TO TAX FACTS ON INSURANCE & EMPLOYEE BENEFITS, VOL. 2 (2019)

Q 4009. Description of split-dollar.
Q 4010. Income tax results of traditional split-dollar plan.
Q 4015. Income tax consequences of transfer or "rollout" of split-dollar policy.

See also cross references to life insurance trusts on page 56.

Footnotes

[1] If the insured is a majority stockholder the corporation can have no ownership interest in the policy if it is desired to remove the death benefits from his estate. It is important that the corporation not own the policy and have only a *limited* collateral assignment (see discussion, page 324).

[2] These regimes, or methods, are set forth in IRS regulations and are used to determine the tax treatment of *new* split-dollar plans (see Table C on page 276). Regarding the treatment of split-dollar plans established on or before September 17, 2003, see Tables A and B on pages 284-285.

[3] As an insured grows older the endorsement and nonequity collateral assignment plans taxed under the economic benefit regime become costly to maintain. This is due to the increasing "economic benefit" amount that is imputed as income to the employee and a gift to the trust. For example, using Table 2001 rates, $1,000,000 of insurance is valued at only $1,530/year for a male age 45, but this increases to $11,900/year for a male age 65, and to $88,760/year for a male age 85 (see table, page 596). When there is a permanent need for life insurance coverage, it is important to build flexibility into the split dollar plan to assure some means of maintaining the policy (often described as an "exit strategy"). For example, a *nonequity* collateral assignment plan, taxed under the economic benefit regime, might be converted to an *equity* collateral assignment plan, and taxed under the loan regime (i.e. at older ages reporting or paying loan interest costs less than paying income and gift taxes on imputed economic benefit.) See the discussion of Equity Split-Dollar on pages 362-365. However, if the conversion occurs after the accrual of policy cash values in excess of the trust's basis, this equity will be taxable income to the employee and a gift to the trust. Other exit strategies providing for a *termination* of the split-dollar plan should also be considered (see footnote 6, below).

[4] In a family-owned business it is possible that the reach of the attribution rules under new Code section 101(j) *might* treat this policy as "employer-owned." This could subject the death benefits to income taxation. To assure the proceeds are received free of income taxes, appropriate notice and consent should be obtained (see Company Owned Life Insurance (COLI) pages 319-321).

[5] When large amounts of insurance are required on older individuals, the premium requirements can often exceed the annual exclusion limits for present interest gifts (see footnote 4, page 57, and page 320). Split-dollar funding survivorship life insurance payable at the second death can substantially reduce the annual gifts to the trust, thereby allowing larger amounts of insurance to be purchased within these "present interest" limits (see Survivorship Life Insurance, page 561).

[6] If the split-dollar agreement is terminated and the employer releases the trust's assignment of cash values under a split-dollar "rollout," all cash values would then be owned by the trust. This release of employer-owned cash values would be treated as both taxable income to the employee and a gift by the employee to the trust (see Split-Dollar Rollout, page 553).

[7] Under the regulations this "economic benefit" is measured by "life insurance premium factors" to be published by the IRS. Until these factors become available the Table 2001 rates on page 596 should be permissible. The final regulations also continue to allow the economic benefit to be measured by the insurance company's cost of annual renewable term insurance (provided that the term policy is issued by the same company, is made available to all standard risks, and is "regularly sold" by that company). The requirements to utilize the (often considerably less expensive than Table 2001) carrier rates makes some tax advisors uncomfortable in utilizing this alternative method of valuation. In practice, however, the IRS has rarely challenged split dollar costs calculated by carrier term costs.

[8] Note that gifts to the trust are *imputed;* funds are not actually transferred to the trust. Also, unlike the typical life insurance trust, the trustee does not have any ownership interest in the policy cash values (see Life Insurance Trust chart, page 55). To qualify for the annual gift tax exclusion the trust beneficiaries must actually have an opportunity to withdraw funds from the trust. Partial funding of the trust with other liquid assets would allow the trustee to satisfy potential present interest demands of trust beneficiaries. See page 268 for a discussion of these withdrawal rights, which are often referred to as "Crummey" powers.

[9] Failure of the employee to report this economic benefit, or to contribute an equal amount of premiums, will result in the death benefits being taxed as ordinary income to his beneficiary (i.e., they will not qualify as income tax-free life insurance death benefits).

SURVIVOR INCOME

The sudden loss of income at the death of a breadwinner can be devastating to a surviving family.[1] A survivor income plan can assure that continuing income will be available and is based upon a written agreement between the employer and the employee.

Benefits under such a plan usually take the form of ongoing and periodic payments for a specified number of years following the employee's death. Typically, such benefits are set as a percentage of final pay for a period of years. For example, the plan may provide for 50 percent of final pay, per year, for 10 years.[2]

DURING LIFETIME, the employer and employee enter into an agreement providing for the employer to make periodic payments to the employee's beneficiary following the employee's death. In order to provide the funds to meet its obligation, the employer purchases a life insurance contract insuring the employee.[3] Neither the employee nor his family has any rights whatsoever in this policy. Because the employer is both owner and beneficiary of this contract, the premium payments are not tax-deductible to the employer. Nor will the premiums be taxable to the employee provided the policy is clearly not tied to the promise to pay the survivor benefit. In this sense, the policy is carried in the same manner as key person insurance, the difference being the *purpose* for which the death benefit will be used.

UPON DEATH, the insurance company pays a death benefit directly to the employer, as beneficiary of the policy insuring the employee.[4] Under the pre-existing agreement, the employer then provides a survivor income benefit to the family. While these payments are fully tax-deductible by the employer, they will be received as taxable income by the family.

Using life insurance to help meet the obligation under a survivor income plan offers tax-leverage to the employer, in that *receipt* of the death benefit by the employer should be tax-free, whereas *payments* made to the surviving family are fully tax-deductible. Before the 2017 Tax Act, for an employer in a 34 percent marginal tax bracket, payment of $1.00 in benefits would generate a tax savings of 34 cents.[5] Today, the deduction (at the federal level) is only 21 percent.

The *insured* survivor income plan provides the security of continuing income to the employee's family, while offering tax-leverage to the employer.[6]

Footnotes on page 125

DURING LIFETIME

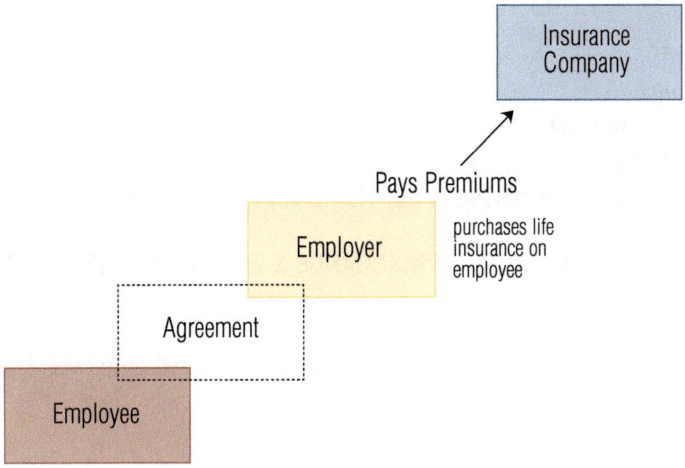

Agreement Provides For Periodic Payments Following Employee's Death

UPON DEATH

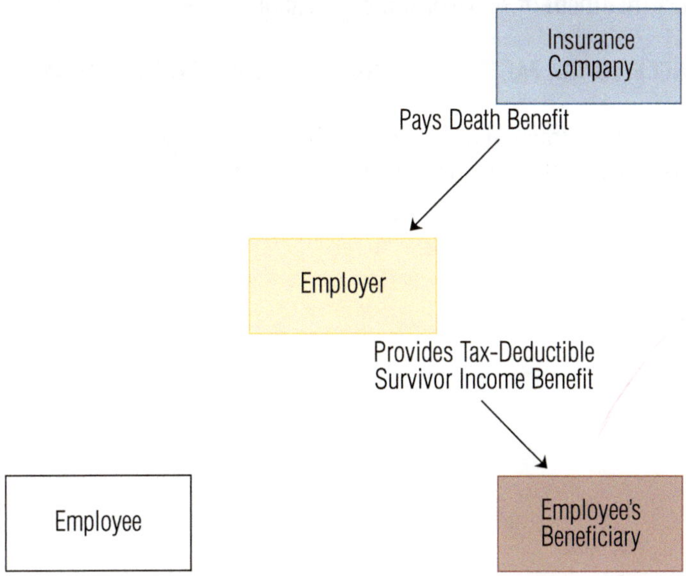

INFORMATION REQUIRED FOR ANALYSIS & PROPOSAL

1. Name of employee.
2. Sex.
3. Date of birth.
4. Smoker/nonsmoker.
5. Employer's tax bracket.
6. Amount of insurance coverage.
7. Method of payment to surviving family (lump-sum, period certain, annuity purchase, etc.).

CROSS REFERENCES TO TAX FACTS ON INSURANCE & EMPLOYEE BENEFITS, VOL. 1 (2019)

Income Tax

Q 267. Premiums paid by corporation not taxable to insured employee (provided corporation is owner and beneficiary).

Estate Tax

Q 100. Estate tax treatment when only benefit is survivor income.

Q 101. Estate tax treatment when employee has no rights to income (death benefit only plan).

Gift Tax

Q 118. Gift tax treatment of survivor income benefit.

CROSS REFERENCES TO TAX FACTS ON INSURANCE & EMPLOYEE BENEFITS, VOL. 2 (2019)

Q 3635. Taxation of contractual death benefits to surviving spouse.

Q 3636. Employer's deduction of survivor income payments.

Footnotes

1 To better appreciate the total amount of future income lost when a bread winner dies, refer to the table of Projected Earnings on page 638. Human Life Value is also dealt with in the table Life Insurance Needs As a Percentage Of Earnings on page 16. While many surviving families can expect to receive benefits from Social Security, it is probably not advisable for them to rely on the system for the greater part of their financial security. For example, in 2014 the *maximum* monthly survivor's benefits available under Social Security are:

Age of Worker	Surviving Spouse & 1 Child; or 2 Children	Surviving Spouse & 2 Children; or 3 Children	One Child (no parent)	Widow Age 60	or	Widower Age 66
25	4,112	4,797	2,056	1,960		2,741
30	4,103	4,787	2,051	1,956		2,735
35	4,052	4,727	2,026	1,931		2,701
40	4,040	4,713	2,020	1,925		2,693
45	4,022	4,692	2,011	1,917		2,681
50	4,077	4,675	2,003	1,910		2,671
55	3,990	4,655	1,995	1,902		2,660
60	3,939	4,596	1,970	1,878		2,626

The above table has been extracted from Social Security Table 11, *Social Security & Medicare Facts* (National Underwriter Company). Note that a surviving family is entitled to payments provided one or more children are under age 16. Once all children are 16 or over, no Social Security benefits are available until the surviving spouse is age 60. This period between the youngest child's age 16 and spouse's age 60 is often referred to as the Social Security "blackout period." In 2016, approximately 6.1 million people were receiving survivor benefits which averaged $1,115 per recipient.

2 Although a lump-sum payment could be made, it is usually preferable to provide the family with an income stream more suited to its needs. This will also allow for spreading out of the family's income tax liability and the employer's tax deductions.

3 Employer-owned life insurance must meet strict notice and consent requirements if the death benefits are to be received free of income taxes (see Company Owned Life Insurance (COLI), pages 319-321).

4 Under some circumstances the corporate alternative minimum tax could result in the indirect taxation of life insurance proceeds received by a corporation (see pages 327-329).

5 For each $1.00 received as a tax-free death benefit by the employer, this employer could afford to pay $1.52 in benefits. The calculations are as follows:

Desired After-Tax Cost	$ 1.00
Reciprocal Of Tax Bracket	÷ .66
Tax-Deductible Payment To Family	$ 1.52
Less Taxes Saved (34% tax bracket)	(.52)
After-Tax Cost	$ 1.00
Less Tax-Free Death Benefit	(1.00)
Cost To Make Payment	$ 0.00

Alternatively, the employer might prefer a return of all premiums, ***plus*** a tax-free gain to corporate surplus. For example, assume the tax-free death benefit from a $100,000 policy was invested in tax-free 6.6 percent municipal bonds. The employer could then afford to pay a survivor $10,000 per year for life, and eventually receive a return of all premiums and a tax-free gain. The yearly after-tax cost of the $10,000 payment would be covered by the $6,600 of tax-free income ($100,000 × .066). Of course, the above calculations would have to be adjusted downward if the death proceeds were subject to the corporate alternative minimum tax (see page 327-329).

6 "Death benefit only" plans allow payments from a survivor income plan to be excluded from the employee's federal taxable estate (see Death Benefit Only Plan on page 333).

DEFERRED COMPENSATION

In allowing *selected* management or highly compensated employees to defer income until after retirement, deferred compensation offers *multiple tax advantages* to both the employer and the participant.[1]

CORPORATE OBLIGATION. To illustrate, assume we have a key corporate manager who is currently age 45. Under its terms, the plan would provide for retirement payments, at age 65, of $10,000 per year for 10 years.[2] These payments would be *tax-deductible* to the corporation when made, and, although *taxable* to the retired employee, presumably he would pay less in taxes due to a reduced retirement income and resulting lower marginal tax bracket.

Typically, such plans also provide for survivor payments if the employee dies prior to retirement. For example, should the employee die at age 55, a typical plan might pay his surviving family $10,000 per year for 10 years. Since these payments would be tax-deductible to the corporation, each $10,000 payment would cost only $7,900 (assuming a 21 percent corporate marginal tax bracket). However, these payments would be taxable income to the family.[3] Life insurance cash values grow on an income tax deferred basis and death benefits are ordinarily received on an income tax free basis – making life insurance a common and tax-effective method of funding deferred compensation obligations.

The plan can also be structured to provide disability benefits to the employee. To assure itself of funds to meet its obligation, the employer could purchase a disability income contract, or it could *partially* protect itself by adding a waiver of premium rider to any life insurance contract on the employee's life.[4] Although standards for disability, long-term care, chronic illness, and critical illness differ – today it is common to see plans created with pre-retirement payouts based on a standard that is consistent with the payout language on a hybrid life insurance policy offering a lifetime benefits rider. See Long-Term Care Hybrid Products at pages 454-457.

LIFE INSURANCE on the employee can assure the employer that it will have the funds to meet its obligation.[5] For illustrative purposes, using life insurance for this purpose could require a corporate commitment to spend $4,000 per year during the first 20 years, and $6,600 per year during the 10 years following the employee's retirement (all after taxes).[6] The *cumulative* outlay by the corporation would be $80,000 during the 20 years prior to retirement at age 65, and $146,000 by time the employee reaches age 75.[7]

If life insurance with an increasing death benefit is purchased, it will likely produce a *gain* to corporate surplus when the employee dies, which amount can then be used to make the survivor payments. This gain is the amount by which the death benefit *exceeds* the cumulative outlay by the corporation (i.e., the sum of the premium payments prior to retirement and the after-tax cost of the retirement payments). For example, if the employee died at age 55, payment of a $120,000 death benefit would produce a gain to corporate surplus of $80,000 ($120,000 – $40,000 = $80,000).

Footnotes on page 129

CORPORATE OBLIGATION

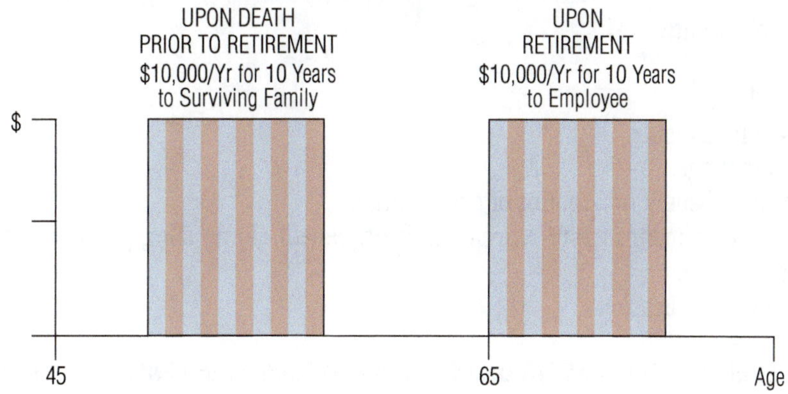

LIFE INSURANCE FUNDING

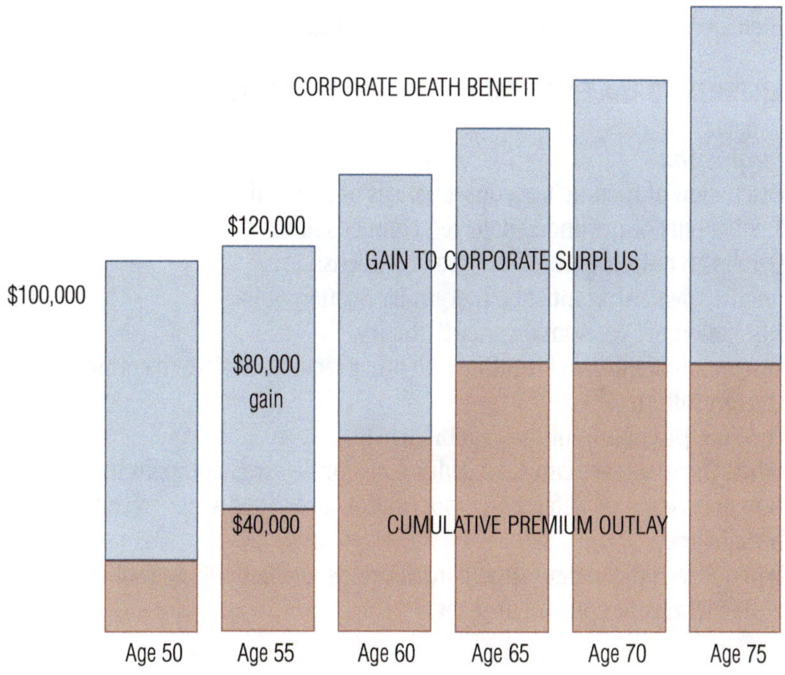

ASSUMPTIONS

Current Age 45 - Premium Outlay $4,000/year for 20 Years
Insurance Contract Provides Increasing Death Benefit
Retirement Outlay $10,000/year for 10 Years Beginning at Age 65
After-Tax Cost of Retirement Outlay is $6,600/year
(34% Tax Bracket)

INFORMATION REQUIRED FOR ANALYSIS & PROPOSAL

1. Name of executive.
2. Sex.
3. Date of birth.
4. Smoker/nonsmoker.
5. Retirement age.
6. Retirement benefit *or* amount of contribution.
7. Method of payment for pre-retirement death benefit (lump-sum, period certain, annuity purchase, etc.).
8. Employer's tax bracket.

CROSS REFERENCES TO TAX FACTS ON INSURANCE & EMPLOYEE BENEFITS, VOL. 1 (2019)

Estate Tax

Q 101. Inclusion of survivor benefit in employee's gross estate.

CROSS REFERENCES TO TAX FACTS ON INSURANCE & EMPLOYEE BENEFITS, VOL. 2 (2019)

Income Tax

Q 3532. Discussion of income tax consequences of a "secular" trust.

Q 3538. Tax benefits of unfunded deferred compensation.

Q 3539. General requirements for deferred compensation.

Q 3541. Requirements that must be met under Section 409A.

Q 3561. Discussion of "economic benefit" theory.

Q 3562. Discussion of informal funding and other security devices in connection with deferred compensation.

Q 3565-Q 3568. Discussion of the "rabbi" trust.

Q 3571. When the employer can take deductions for deferred compensation.

Q 3572. How payments of deferred compensation are taxed when received by employee or beneficiary.

Q 3574. When deferred compensation contributions and benefits are subject to social security and federal unemployment taxes.

Footnotes

1 The corporate owner who is also an employee will find many planning opportunities with deferred compensation that are not subject to the rules of "qualified" retirement plans. For example: (1) deferred reasonable compensation payments to a retired employee-stockholder are deductible to the corporation, whereas inflated payments for stock are not deductible; (2) the cash values of a life insurance contract, carried on the books and intended for deferred compensation, are usually considered to be for the reasonable needs of the business and thus immune from the accumulated earnings tax; (3) the liability for deferred payments to a surviving widow can have the effect of depressing the value of a deceased's stock for estate tax purposes; and (4) corporate owned cash values under a split-dollar arrangement can be used to provide the employer with funds to make deferred compensation payments.

2 There are two types of deferred compensation plans: "pure" deferred compensation plans and salary continuation plans. Under a pure deferred compensation plan, the employee agrees to defer receipt of some portion of his present compensation. This deferral of compensation is not currently taxable to the employee, provided it is subject to a substantial risk of forfeiture (see the discussion of Section 409A on page 538 and Constructive Receipt on page 322). Under a salary continuation plan, the employer provides a benefit in addition to all other forms of compensation (i.e., there is no reduction in the employee's present compensation). When used with a vesting schedule or a non-competition agreement, a deferred compensation plan provides the "golden handcuffs" to retain a valued employee.

3 Benefits paid to survivors are generally not subject to FICA and FUTA taxes. However, these taxes can be currently imposed upon participants if the plan provides nonforfeitable benefits. This will not be too great a problem for the executive whose other wages exceed the OASDI wage base.

4 Backing up the plan with a life insurance contract containing the waiver of premium benefit would relieve the employer of having to make premium payments in case of the employee's disability. Assuming a premium of $4,000, a corporation in a 21 percent tax bracket could pay $5,063 per year to the disabled employee, since the after-tax cost of these payments is equal to the nondeductible premiums being waived ($4,000 divided by one minus the employer's tax bracket, or $4,000 ÷ .79 = $5,063).

5 Employer-owned life insurance must meet strict notice and consent requirements if the death benefits are to be received free of income taxes (see Company Owned Life Insurance (COLI), pages 319-321).

6 During the first 20 years, it is assumed that $4,000 purchases either a universal life insurance contract providing for a death benefit equal to the face plus the cash values (Option 2), or a paid-up at age 65 participating contract (with dividends typically being used to purchase paid-up additions). Once the employee reaches age 65, the chart assumes that the corporation will make retirement payments from *current* cash flow, as opposed to utilizing the contract's cash values. By maintaining the contract, the corporation will eventually receive the death benefit, which may more than offset its cumulative outlay. Assuming a 21 percent tax bracket and no alternative minimum tax, the after-tax cost of making a $10,000 payment is $7,900 (for sample calculations see footnote 5, page 125). Use of computer-prepared illustrations can provide a variety of funding options and schedules.

7 Because the corporation is both owner and beneficiary of the life insurance contract, the premium payments that it makes are *not* tax-deductible. In this sense, the contract is carried in the same manner as key person insurance, the difference being the *purpose* for which the death benefit will be used. To avoid any current tax liability to the employee, it is essential that the employee have no vested interest in a fund or any investments intended to secure the deferred compensation payments. The life insurance contract must remain the unrestricted asset of the employer, available to general creditors of the employer, and the employee can have no interest in the contract (see discussion on page 322). Despite this, it is generally recognized that the use of life insurance to back up a deferred compensation agreement provides some psychological security to the employee, in the sense that the employer is preparing to follow through on its commitment. Alternatives such as a Restrictive Bonus Plan, a Rabbi Trust or a Secular Trust might also be considered (see pages 236, 514, and 540).

ESTATE AND GIFT TAXATION OF RESIDENT AND NONRESIDENT ALIENS

The method used to determine whether an alien is a resident for U.S. estate taxation is more subjective than the method used for income tax purposes. For estate tax purposes, the U.S. includes only the 50 states and the District of Columbia. A non-U.S. citizen may be domiciled in one of the U.S. possessions, such as Puerto Rico, and escape U.S. federal transfer tax, except on transfers of property sitused within the U.S. In addition, the rules governing which assets to include in the gross estate are significantly different for resident and nonresident aliens.

Residency Determination for Estate Tax Purposes

When trying to establish residency for estate tax purposes, courts generally rely on multiple factors. Since an individual can only be domiciled in one place, the U.S. determines residency for estate tax purposes with any, or a combination, of the following factors:

- Testimony and statements of intent, like an immigrant visa, U.S. trust, will, etc.
- Green card application and/or U.S. Social Security number
- Driver's license and/or voter registration
- Marital status and residence of individual's family
- Time spent in the U.S. versus other countries
- Location and size of residence and business
- Participation in community affairs and social affiliations

No single factor determines domicile for a resident alien, and this is by no means a comprehensive list of what could determine domicile. Each case is considered individually by a court, and other evidence may be taken into account. However, if it can be shown that an alien illustrates an indefinite intent to stay in the U.S., then they'll generally be considered a resident alien for estate tax purposes.

Estate Taxation of Resident and Nonresident Aliens

While the rules of estate taxation differ for resident and nonresident aliens, applicable estate tax rates are the same for both groups.

Resident aliens and U.S. citizens are subject to estate taxes on worldwide assets regardless of the properties' location. The rules pertaining to joint property and the marital deduction are different for resident aliens and U.S. citizens. A federal estate tax credit is allowed, with limitations, for taxes paid to a foreign country on property located in that country.

Nonresident aliens are only taxed on U.S. situs assets. A foreign country may allow a credit against its death taxes for U.S. estate tax paid.

A nonresident alien is entitled to a credit against estate taxes of $13,000. Effectively, this credit permits the nonresident decedent to pass $60,000 of assets at death without incurring U.S. estate tax, unless provided otherwise in an applicable tax treaty. The estate tax exemption for nonresident aliens is much lower than that of U.S. citizens or resident aliens, which is currently $11,400,000 (projected for 2019, scheduled to return to $5,600,000 in 2026).

As previously mentioned, asset situs rules are different depending on the type of property being transferred. In general, the gross estate for estate tax purposes for a nonresident alien includes: tangible assets situated in the U.S., like land and buildings; stocks and options issued by a U.S. corporation; compensation paid by U.S. entities; and annuity contracts enforceable against U.S. obligators. Not included in the gross estate are U.S. bank deposits and insurance on the life of the nonresident alien. Similarly, tangible property not considered U.S. situs is omitted from the gross estate valuation for estate tax purposes. Estate tax situs rules for nonresident aliens by property type are summarized in the table below.

Type of Property	U.S. Situs Property Subject to U.S. Estate Tax	Non-U.S. Situs Property Exempt from U.S. Estate Tax
Real Property	Real property (e.g., land, buildings, fixtures and improvements, condos and time-shares, growing crops, timber cutting rights and mineral rights) situated in U.S.	Real property located outside the U.S.
Tangible Personal Property	Property (e.g., cash/foreign currency, jewelry, paintings and automobiles) physically located in the U.S., except for certain works of art on loan for exhibition. Cash/currency is considered tangible personal property (although most forms of monetary instruments aren't).	Tangible property in the possession of the foreign national if only temporarily visiting the U.S.
Bank, Brokerage and Fiduciary Accounts	Funds held by U.S. banks or other financial institutions, if used in conjunction with a U.S. trade or business and funds held in brokerage accounts. Deposits with domestic branches of foreign banks are also subject to trade or business requirement	Savings accounts, checking accounts or certificates of deposit issued by a U.S. bank if not used in conjunction with a U.S. trade or business; funds held in a U.S. bank custody account; funds deposited in a foreign branch of a U.S. bank.
Qualified Retirement Plans	Assets held by plan administrators representing service for a U.S. company.	Pensions payable by non-U.S. persons.
Stocks	Shares issued by a U.S. corporation, irrespective of the situs of the certificates.	Shares issued by a foreign corporation even if the certificates are located in the U.S.
Debt Obligations	Debts held from U.S. persons, or of the United States, any state, any state political subdivision or the District of Columbia.	Exempt from U.S. estate tax where exempt from U.S. income tax or the interest is treated as sourced from outside the U.S.
Life Insurance	The value of a policy on the life of another (i.e., the interpolated terminal reserve or PERC value), issued by a U.S.-licensed insurance company and owned by the decedent.	The proceeds from an insurance policy on the life of a nonresident alien, owned by the nonresident alien, regardless of the insurance company's country of origin.
Annuities	The value of any commercial annuity issued by a U.S. insurance company on the life of another.	Annuities issued by foreign insurance companies.

Estate and Gift Taxation of Resident and Nonresident Aliens

The U.S. Internal Revenue Code (IRC) determines the situs of asset types and, depending on whether or not there's an estate tax treaty between the U.S. and the country of residence, situs could be modified. See the table below for a list of countries for which the U.S. has an estate and gift tax treaty.

Australia	Canada	France	Ireland	Netherlands	Switzerland
Austria	Denmark	Germany	Italy	Norway	United Kingdom
	Finland	Greece	Japan	South Africa	

Availability of the Marital Deduction

The Technical and Miscellaneous Revenue Act (TAMRA) of 1988 eliminated the unlimited marital deduction to estates where the surviving spouse is not a U.S. citizen. This was intended to prevent surviving noncitizen spouses from returning to their home countries with assets that would then escape U.S. estate taxes.

The noncitizen spouse may gain the unlimited marital deduction by becoming a U.S. citizen before the date for filing the decedent's estate tax return. The surviving spouse must remain a resident of the U.S. between the date of the decedent's death and becoming a U.S. citizen. Alternatively, the estate tax liability may be deferred until the noncitizen spouse's death by having the estate pass to a qualified domestic trust (QDOT). A QDOT may also be set up by a surviving noncitizen spouse with property that passes to him/her outright and must be established before the date for filing the decedent's estate tax return.

Requirements for a QDOT include the following:

- At least one trustee must be a U.S. citizen or domestic corporation.
- Except for income, no distribution may be made from the trust, unless the U.S. trustee has the right to withhold estate tax on the distribution.
- Generally, all income must be paid to the noncitizen spouse annually.
- An election must be made on the decedent's estate tax return.
- The QDOT must comply with regulations to assure the collection of any tax imposed.
- If the trust assets exceed $2 million, the trust must do one of the following:
- Require at least one trustee that is a U.S. bank or trust company.
- Obtain a bond or letter of credit equal to 65 percent of the estate tax value of the trust corpus.
- If the trust corpus isn't more than $2 million, the trust document must prohibit investment of more than 35 percent of the trust's annual fair market value in offshore real estate.

There's an estate tax on the distribution of any principal from a QDOT prior to the death of the surviving noncitizen spouse, unless it's for a hardship situation. The estate tax due on the QDOT's assets, either at the time of a principal distribution or at the surviving spouse's death, is based on the amount of the estate tax that would have been paid if the QDOT's assets had been included in the deceased spouse's estate at his/her death.

Jointly Owned Property

Where one member of a married couple is a non-U.S. citizen, the couple's jointly owned property isn't treated as though each spouse contributed equally to its cost. Instead, the deceased spouse is presumed to have paid for the entire value of the property and it's included in his/her estate for federal estate tax purposes. An exclusion is allowed, however, for the portion of the property that the non-U.S. citizen spouse can demonstrate represents his/her contribution.

Gift Taxes

U.S. citizens and residents are subject to gift tax on the transfer of worldwide assets. Both citizens and residents have a gift tax annual exclusion ($15,000 per donee in 2019 (projected)) for present interest gifts. Each also has a lifetime gift tax exemption ($11.4 million under the temporary increase included in the 2017 Tax Act) for transfers to U.S. citizens, or up to a $153,000 annual exclusion gift in 2019 (projected) to a non-U.S. citizen spouse, who would have qualified for the marital deduction if they were a U.S. citizen or resident alien.

Nonresident aliens don't have the lifetime gift tax exemption, but they do have the gift tax annual exclusion ($15,000 in 2019 (projected)) for present interest gifts. Gift splitting is not available, even where the spouse is a U.S. citizen. Gifts to a U.S. citizen spouse qualify for the unlimited gift tax marital deduction, but gifts to a non-U.S. citizen spouse don't. The annual exclusion gift ($153,000 for 2019 projected) to a non-U.S. citizen spouse is available. See the table below for a comparison of the U.S. transfer taxes for resident and nonresident aliens.

	Resident Aliens	Non-resident Aliens
Assets Subject to U.S. Gift Tax	Worldwide Assets	Real and Tangible Personal Property Located in the U.S.
U.S. Gift Tax Annual Exclusion	$15,000	$15,000
U.S. Gift Tax Marital Deduction	Gift to U.S. Citizen Spouse: Unlimited Otherwise: $153,000 Annually	Gift to U.S. Citizen Spouse: Unlimited Otherwise: $153,000 Annually
U.S. Lifetime Gift Exemption	$11,400,000 (projected)	None
Gift Splitting	Yes (with U.S. Citizen/Resident Spouse)	No
Assets Subject to U.S. Estate Tax	Worldwide Assets	U.S. Situs Assets
U.S. Estate Tax Exemption	$11,400,000 (projected, less Lifetime Taxable Gifts)	$60,000 (Approximately)
U.S. Estate Tax Marital Deduction	Gift to U.S. Citizen Spouse: Unlimited Otherwise: Need a QDOT	Gift to U.S. Citizen Spouse: Unlimited Otherwise: Need a QDOT

Nonresident aliens are subject to gift tax only on gifts of real and tangible personal property that have U.S. situs for the purpose of gift taxes. This means that nonresident aliens may make unlimited gifts to U.S. citizens as long as the property in question has a situs outside the U.S. Intangible property, such as stocks and bonds of U.S. corporations, U.S. business interests (e.g., partnerships), life insurance policies and mutual funds, generally don't have situs and are exempt from U.S. gift tax. Because transfers of intangible personal property aren't subject to gift tax, but are subject to the estate tax (except for life insurance death benefits) if located in the U.S., a nonresident alien should take advantage of gifting opportunities during his/her lifetime to transfer intangible personal property.

Gift Versus Estate Tax Situs for Non-resident Aliens

Type of Property	Gift Tax	Estate Tax
Real Property in the U.S.	Yes	Yes
Tangible Personal Property in the U.S.	Yes	Yes*
Cash, Cash or Property in U.S. Safety Deposit Box	Yes	Yes
Custodial/Brokerage Accounts	Yes	Yes
Debt Obligations of U.S. Government	No	No
Debt Obligations of U.S. Persons	Yes	Yes
Deposits in U.S. or Foreign Banks	No	No
Life Insurance on the Life of the Nonresident Alien	No	No
Life Insurance on the Life of Another Person	No	Yes
Shares of a U.S. Mutual Fund	No	Yes
Stock in Foreign Corporations	No	No
Stock in U.S. Corporations	No	Yes
U.S. Business Interests (Including Partnerships)	No	Yes

Except for certain works of art on loan for exhibition and tangible property in the possession of the foreign national if only temporarily visiting the U.S.

Life Insurance

Life insurance is a unique asset in that it provides an income-tax-free death benefit when paid out to beneficiaries at the insured's death. Life insurance also offers tax advantages to the policy owner during the insured's lifetime. Any earnings or cash accumulation within the policy is accumulated on a tax-deferred basis, and in some cases these earnings can be accessed by the policy owner income-tax-free. The income tax benefits and rules are exactly the same for U.S. citizens, resident aliens and nonresident aliens.

Life Insurance for Foreign Nationals

In addition to purchasing supplemental retirement income, college funding, debt reduction, emergencies and unexpected events, foreign nationals may be interested in purchasing life insurance for reasons a U.S. citizen or resident alien may not. For example, foreign nationals may simply want a contract based in the U.S. because they believe that U.S. companies are more stable than those of their home country or because the policy type isn't available in their home country. A foreign national may wish to invest some of their wealth in U.S. corporations or mutual funds in a tax-favored manner through the use of a U.S. variable life insurance policy that utilizes a variety of separate accounts in order to meet investment objectives.

Life insurance issued by a U.S. carrier on the life on a nonresident alien can provide the liquidity to pay estate taxes on U.S. situs property. Due to its income-tax-free death benefit, life insurance can be an extremely useful tool in mitigating the costs of estate taxes and maximizing inheritance to heirs. Resident aliens may consider having an irrevocable life insurance trust own the life insurance policy in order to keep the death benefit value outside of their taxable estate while still maintaining the ability to use the death benefit to pay estate taxes, as well as for additional layers of asset protection.

For estate tax purposes, life insurance death benefits in the estate of a nonresident alien insured policy owner are deemed to have a foreign situs and are therefore exempt from U.S. estate taxes. Since a nonresident alien can own the life insurance policy without income, gift or estate tax consequences, outright ownership is a popular model for nonresident aliens. However, a nonresident alien may wish to use an irrevocable trust if: (a) he or she is considering relocating to the U.S., (b) he or she wishes to take advantage of the asset protection function an irrevocable trust offers or (c) he or she would like the policy proceeds to pass through more than one generation free of estate or generation skipping transfer (GST) tax. The GST tax applies only where the transfer was subject to either U.S. gift or estate tax and was made to a "skip person" (e.g., grandchild, or a person two or more generations younger than the transferor).

The value of a policy issued by a U.S. company owned by a nonresident alien on the life of another (including survivorship, where the policyowner was the first to die) has U.S. situs, making its fair market value includable in the taxable estate of the policyowner.

Life Insurance Sales to Nonresident Aliens

U.S. carriers generally have certain parameters surrounding the sale of life insurance on nonresident aliens. These parameters include, but are not limited to:

- Solicitation, application, negotiation and policy delivery must occur in the U.S.
- The owner (individual or entity) must have a U.S. domicile and billing address.
- The owner must have a U.S. tax identification number (TIN) or Social Security number.
- The medical examination and labs must be done in the U.S.
- Premium payments must be drawn on a U.S. bank account in U.S. dollars.

CROSS REFERENCES TO TAX FACTS ON INSURANCE & EMPLOYEE BENEFITS (2019)

Q 961-Q 976. Taxation Issues as applied to Foreign Nationals.

DOMICILE

One of the most important decisions we face in retirement is where should we live? Our jobs and our children's schools are often the primary factors impacting where to live before we retire. But, after we retire and the children have started their own lives – many people decide to relocate. Many people let climate dictate where they retire. Other people move closer to the grandkids. But, in addition to climate and family – financial considerations are also important when deciding where to reside in retirement. And, for the affluent, state inheritance and estate taxes can have a significant impact on the legacy that is left to heirs.

Historically, the decision on where to retire was almost exclusively limited to the United States. In recent years, however, it has become more and more common for Americans (both citizens and resident aliens) to retire outside of the U.S. This section is intentionally limited to domestic considerations. A decision to leave the U.S. in retirement needs to be made after considering many additional items – including stability of government, availability of health care, language, culture, and tax.

Domicile is the place that an individual has freely chosen as the center of his or her domestic and legal relations. It is the place where the individual intends to remain indefinitely. However, residence without this intention to remain indefinitely does not constitute domicile. A person can have a number of residences, but only one domicile. Once acquired, a domicile is presumed to continue until it is shown to have been changed.

The impact of establishing domicile is far reaching. It determines a person's liability for state and local income taxes; liability for state and local gift and estate taxes; potential limitations on the right to choose fiduciaries such as executors or trustees; rights of surviving spouses to take against a will; community property rights between spouses; divorce and child custody issues; availability of homestead exemptions or similar laws that reduce real estate taxes on a primary residence; where wills must be probated; how property is passed if there is no will; liability for intangible personal property tax on stocks, bonds, and savings accounts; and the ability to vote in state and local elections.

To demonstrate the intent to establish a new domicile, the following actions should be taken: (1) register to vote in state and local elections; (2) obtain a new driver's license; (3) change automobile and boat registrations; (4) file for a homestead exemption on the new residence; (5) file a declaration of domicile, if the procedure is available in the new state; (6) remain physically present in the state for over one-half of the year; (7) file federal income tax with the Internal Revenue Service Center servicing the state and include new address on returns; (8) file state and local income tax returns for the new location; (9) file state and local intangible personal property tax returns, if imposed; (10) use the new address on all legal documents (e.g., contracts, wills, bills of sale, and deeds); (11) adopt new wills and trusts; (12) provide notice of the new address to banks, credit card companies, professional associations, insurance companies, publishers, friends, relatives, and others; (13) establish new relationships with doctors and dentists and have medical records transferred to them; (14) establish new relationships with professional advisers; (15) move stock brokerage accounts to local offices; (16) open checking and savings accounts at a local bank; (17) obtain a safe deposit box and place valuables and legal documents in it; (18) apply for a passport using the new address; and (19) become active in local social, civic, and religious organizations.

See also the discussion of noncitizen estate planning on page 473.

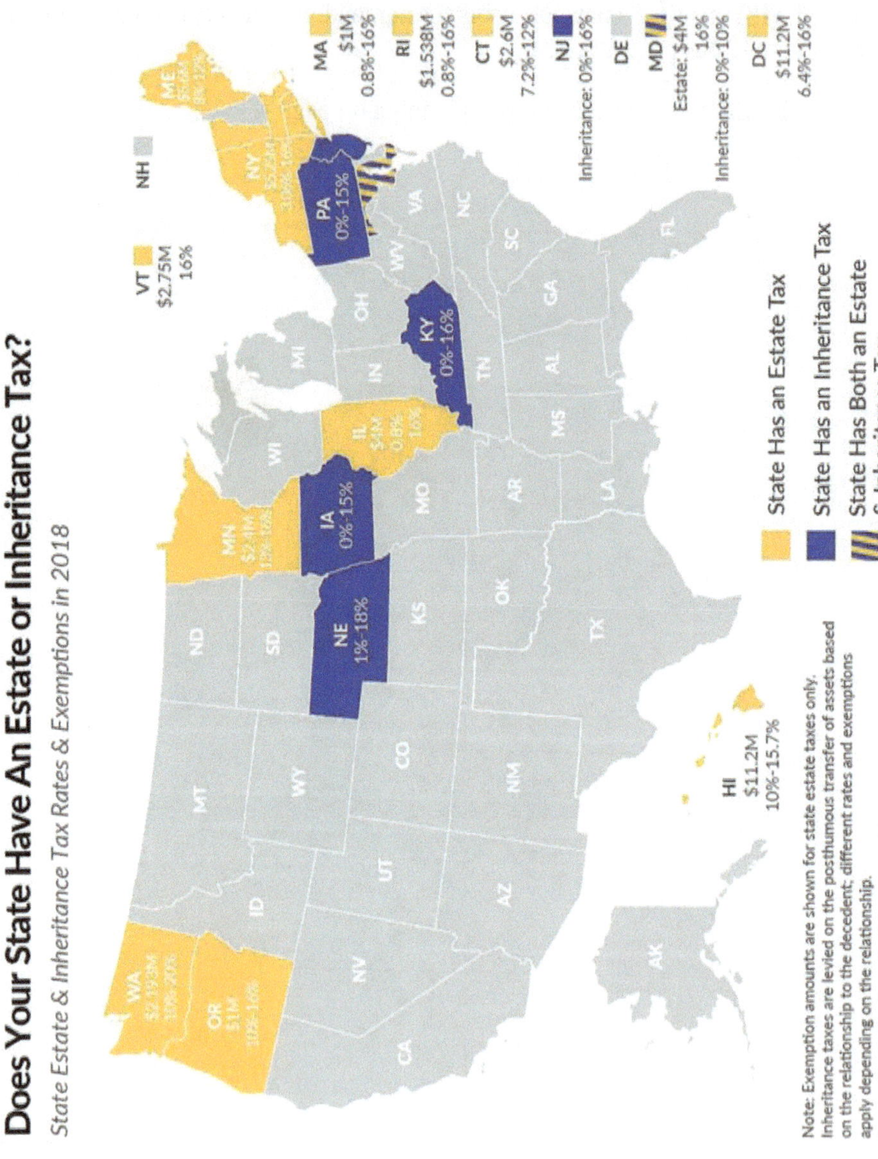
Does Your State Have An Estate or Inheritance Tax?
State Estate & Inheritance Tax Rates & Exemptions in 2018
WA $2.193M 10%-20%
OR $1M 10%-16%
MN $2.4M 13%-16%
IA 0%-15%
NE 1%-18%
IL $4M 0.8%-16%
KY 0%-16%
PA 0%-15%
NY $5.25M 3.06%-16%
ME $5.6M 8%-12%
VT $2.75M 16%
NH
MA $1M 0.8%-16%
RI $1.538M 0.8%-16%
CT $2.6M 7.2%-12%
NJ Inheritance: 0%-16%
DE
MD Estate: $4M 16% Inheritance: 0%-10%
DC $11.2M 6.4%-16%
HI $11.2M 10%-15.7%
AK
ND
SD
KS
OK
TX
MT
WY
CO
NM
ID
UT
AZ
NV
CA
WI
MI
MO
AR
LA
MS
AL
IN
OH
TN
GA
WV
VA
NC
SC
FL
State Has an Estate Tax
State Has an Inheritance Tax
State Has Both an Estate & Inheritance Tax
Note: Exemption amounts are shown for state estate taxes only. Inheritance taxes are levied on the posthumous transfer of assets based on the relationship to the decedent; different rates and exemptions apply depending on the relationship.
Source: Family Business Coalition; state statutes.

STATE TAX SUMMARIES

Planning for a client's needs requires attention to all factors with an influence on the client's life and assets, so having an awareness of the tax landscape in the client's jurisdiction of domicile is important. Also, as higher federal estate tax exemptions result in fewer clients being subject to federal estate tax, other taxes, including state and federal income taxes as well as state transfer taxes, become more important considerations by comparison. For example, reduced exposure to federal estate taxes brings new opportunities to plan for basis step-up at death, with the goal of reducing income and capital gain taxes of the recipient beneficiary. As clients' lives, families, and assets schedules grow more complicated, with assets and beneficiaries in multiple tax jurisdictions, this type of planning requires a consideration of the tax implications of proposed transfers in each such jurisdiction.

Of course, each of the laws and rates cited below is subject to change by the state legislature at any time. The reader should consult competent local counsel for current law.

Alabama

Income Tax: Top marginal rate, 5.00 percent; sales tax rate, 4.00 percent; capital gains taxed as ordinary income.

Estate/Inheritance Tax: (Ala Code § 40-15-2) Alabama imposes an estate tax in the amount "not to exceed the amount allowed to be credited against or deducted from such federal estate tax" ("sponge tax"). As it is not decoupled, the result is that the state estate tax amount is zero.

Generation-skipping transfer tax: (Ala Code § 40-15A-2) Alabama imposes generation-skipping transfer tax in the amount not to exceed the amount allowed to be credited against or deducted from such federal generation-skipping transfer tax.

Gift Tax: No state gift tax.

Alaska

Income Tax: No state income tax, or sales tax.

Estate/Inheritance Tax: (Alaska Stat. § 43.31.011) Alaska imposes an estate tax in the amount equal to the federal credit ("sponge tax"), minus amounts actually paid to other states. As it is not decoupled, the result is that the state estate tax amount is zero.

Generation-skipping transfer tax: No state generation-skipping transfer tax.

Gift Tax: No state gift tax.

Arizona

Income Tax: Top marginal rate, 4.54 percent; capital gains taxed as ordinary income.

Estate/Inheritance Tax: No state estate or inheritance tax.

Generation-skipping transfer tax: No state generation-skipping transfer tax.

Gift Tax: No state gift tax.

Arkansas

Income Tax: Top marginal rate, 6.90 percent; capital gains taxed as ordinary income, but only 70 percent of capital gains are taxed (equivalent to a rate of 4.9 percent on all capital gains).

Estate/Inheritance Tax: (A.C.A. § 26-59-103) State estate tax affirmatively repealed as of 2005.

Generation-skipping transfer tax: No state generation-skipping transfer tax.

Gift Tax: No state gift tax.

California

Income Tax: Top marginal rate, 13.30 percent; capital gains taxed as ordinary income.

Estate/Inheritance Tax: (Calif. Rev. Tax Code 2-8 § 13301 et seq.) State and political subdivisions prohibited from imposing any tax "on or by reason of any transfer

occurring by reason of a death" unless the federal tax code provides a credit for state taxes.

Generation-skipping transfer tax: (Calif. Rev. Tax Code 2-8 § 13301 et seq.) A tax is imposed equal to the federal credit under IRC §2604 for taxes paid.

Gift Tax: Prior law repealed in 1982, currently no state gift tax.

Colorado

Income Tax: Flat rate, 4.63 percent; capital gains taxed as ordinary income.

Estate/Inheritance Tax: (C.R.S. § 39-23.5-103 et seq.) Colorado imposes an estate tax in the amount equal to the federal credit for state death taxes allowable under §2011 of the Internal Revenue Code. As it is not decoupled, the result is that the state estate tax amount is zero.

Generation-skipping transfer tax: (C.R.S. § 39-23.5-106) Colorado imposes a tax on generation-skipping transfers equal to the federal credit under IRC §2604 for taxes paid.

Gift Tax: Prior law repealed in 1979, currently no state gift tax.

Connecticut

Income Tax: Top marginal rate, 6.99 percent; capital gains taxed as ordinary income.

Estate/Inheritance Tax: (Conn. Gen. Stat. §12-391 et seq.) Connecticut imposes a graduated estate tax on estates exceeding $2 million, nine brackets with rates ranging from 7.2 percent to 12 percent. The estate tax is unified with the gift tax below, and a credit is allowed against the estate tax for any gift taxes paid.

Generation-skipping transfer tax: No state generation-skipping transfer tax.

Gift Tax: (Conn. Gen. Stat. §12-640) Unified with the estate tax, same rates and tables.

Delaware

Income Tax: Top marginal rate, 6.60 percent; capital gains taxed as ordinary income; no sales tax.

Estate/Inheritance Tax: For decedents dying after 2018, Delaware imposes no estate tax or enheritance tax.

Generation-skipping transfer tax: No state generation-skipping transfer tax.

Gift Tax: No state gift tax.

District of Columbia

Income Tax: Top marginal rate, 8.95 percent; capital gains taxed as ordinary income.

Estate/Inheritance Tax: For decedents dying in 2015 and before, the District of Columbia imposes an estate tax is equal to the credit for state death taxes allowed for 2001, imposed on amounts exceeding the federal unified credit in 2001 ($1 million). For decedents dying in 2016 and after, the District will tax estates over $2 million in an amount determined by 11 brackets with rates ranging from 8 percent to 16 percent. The indexed federal exemption ($5.6 million indexed for inflation) will be phased in as revenue goals are met after 2016.

Generation-skipping transfer tax: No state generation-skipping transfer tax.

Gift Tax: No state gift tax.

Florida

Income Tax: No state income tax.

Estate/Inheritance Tax: (Fla. Stat. § 198.02) Florida imposes an estate tax in the amount equal to the federal credit ("sponge tax"). As it is not decoupled, the result is that the state estate tax amount is zero.

Generation-skipping transfer tax: (Fla. Stat. §198.021) Florida imposes a generation-skipping transfer tax in the amount equal to the credit against or deducted from such federal generation-skipping transfer tax for state taxes paid.

Gift Tax: No state gift tax.

Georgia

Income Tax: Top marginal rate, 6.0 percent; capital gains taxed as ordinary income.

Estate/Inheritance Tax: No state estate or inheritance tax.

Generation-skipping transfer tax: No state generation-skipping transfer tax.

Gift Tax: No state gift tax.

Hawaii

Income Tax: Top marginal rate, 11.00 percent; long-term capital gains rate, 7.25 percent.

Estate/Inheritance Tax: (HRS § 236E-1) For decedents dying after January 25, 2012, Hawaii imposes an estate tax on all estates that exceed the federal applicable exclusion amount ($5.49 million in 2017) in an amount determined by six brackets with rates ranging from 10 percent to 16 percent.

Generation-skipping transfer tax: (HRS § 236E-17) Hawaii imposes a flat 2.25 percent generation-skipping transfer tax on transfers (as defined under IRC §2611) in excess of the federal GSTT exemption under IRC §2631 ($5,49 million in 2017).

Gift Tax: No state gift tax.

Idaho

Income Tax: Top marginal rate, 7.40 percent; capital gains taxed as ordinary income.

Estate/Inheritance Tax: (Idaho Code § 14-403) Idaho imposes an estate tax in the amount equal to the federal credit ("sponge tax"). As it is not decoupled, the result is that the state estate tax amount is zero.

Generation-skipping transfer tax: (Idaho Code § 14-401 et seq.) Idaho imposes a generation-skipping transfer tax in the amount equal to the credit against or deducted from such federal generation-skipping transfer tax for state taxes paid.

Gift Tax: No state gift tax.

Illinois

Income Tax: 4.95 percent; capital gains taxed as ordinary income.

Estate/Inheritance Tax: (35 ILCS 405/3) Illinois imposes an estate tax equal to the state death tax credit allowed as of December 31, 2001, on estates exceeding $4 million. The top tax rate is 16 percent.

Generation-skipping transfer tax: (35 ILCS 405/4) Illinois imposes a tax on GST transfers (as defined by the IRC) equal to the federal credit under IRC §2604 for taxes paid allowed as of December 31, 2001.

Gift Tax: No state gift tax.

Indiana

Income Tax: Flat rate, 3.23 percent; capital gains taxed as ordinary income.

Estate/Inheritance Tax: No state estate or inheritance tax. (State inheritance tax repealed for decedents dying after 2012.)

Generation-skipping transfer tax: No state generation-skipping transfer tax.

Gift Tax: No state gift tax.

Iowa

Income Tax: Top marginal rate, 8.98 percent; capital gains taxed as ordinary income.

Estate/Inheritance Tax: No state estate tax; tax repealed for transfers made after July 1, 2014. (Iowa Code § 450.10) Iowa imposes a graduated inheritance tax on property received from a decedent in an amount determined by three brackets with rates of 10 percent, 12 percent, and 15 percent. Transfers received by surviving spouses or lineal ancestors or descendants are exempted. Transfers received by siblings and in-laws are taxed at more favorable rates.

Generation-skipping transfer tax: No state generation-skipping transfer tax. (Tax repealed for transfers made after July 1, 2014.)

Gift Tax: No state gift tax.

Kansas

Income Tax: Top marginal rate, 5.70 percent; capital gains taxed as ordinary income.

Estate/Inheritance Tax: No state estate or inheritance tax. (State estate tax repealed for decedents dying after 2009.)

Generation-skipping transfer tax: No state generation-skipping transfer tax.

Gift Tax: No state gift tax.

Kentucky

Income Tax: Top marginal rate, 6.00 percent; capital gains taxed as ordinary income.

Estate/Inheritance Tax: (KRS §140.010) Kentucky imposes an estate tax in the amount equal to the federal credit ("sponge tax"). As it is not decoupled, the result is that the state estate tax amount is zero. Kentucky also imposes an inheritance tax on the value of property received from a decedent, graduated by the class of beneficiary. Close lineal ancestors and descendants are generally exempted, and other recipients are taxed according to graduated tables with rates ranging from 4 percent to 16 percent. The exemption amount is $500.

Generation-skipping transfer tax: No state generation-skipping transfer tax.

Gift Tax: No state gift tax.

Louisiana

Income Tax: Top marginal rate, 6.0 percent; capital gains taxed as ordinary income.

Estate/Inheritance Tax: (La. Rev. Stat. Ann. §47:2431) Louisiana imposes an estate tax in the amount equal to the federal credit ("sponge tax"). As it is not decoupled, the result is that the state estate tax amount is zero.

Generation-skipping transfer tax: No state generation-skipping transfer tax.

Gift Tax: No state gift tax. (Gift tax law repealed for gifts made after June 30, 2008.)

Maine

Income Tax: Top marginal rate, 7.15 percent; capital gains taxed as ordinary income.

Estate/Inheritance Tax: (36 M.R.S. § 4101 et seq.) For decedents dying after 2012, Maine imposes an estate tax on estates over $5.6 million in an amount determined by the application of three brackets with rates of 8 percent, 10 percent, and 12 percent.

Generation-skipping transfer tax: No state generation-skipping transfer tax.

Gift Tax: No state gift tax.

Maryland

Income Tax: Top marginal rate, 5.75 percent; capital gains taxed as ordinary income.

Estate/Inheritance Tax: Maryland imposes both an estate tax and an inheritance tax. (Md. TAX-GENERAL Code Ann. § 7-301 et seq.) The estate tax is imposed on estate exceeding the state exemption (equal to $4 million, or $5 million in 2019 and after (Md. TAX-GENERAL Code Ann. § 7-301 et seq.) Maryland also imposes an inheritance tax on the value of property received from a decedent with a top rate of 16%. Transfers received by lineal ancestors and descendants are generally exempted.

Generation-skipping transfer tax: Maryland imposes a generation-skipping transfer tax in the amount equal to the credit against or deducted from such federal generation-skipping transfer tax for state taxes paid.

Gift Tax: No state gift tax.

Massachusetts

Income Tax: Flat rate of 5.10 percent; capital gains taxed as ordinary income.

Estate/Inheritance Tax: (M.G.L. Ch. 65C, §1 et seq.) Massachusetts imposes an estate tax of 16% on amounts in excess of $1,000,000 in an amount equal to the federal the credit for state death taxes that would have been allowable against a decedent's federal estate tax liability under IRC §2011, as in effect on Dec. 31, 2000, adjusted.

Generation-skipping transfer tax: (M.G.L. Ch. 65C, §14A) Massachusetts imposes a GST tax on taxable transfers equal to the amount allowable as a credit for state death taxes under IRC §2064 in effect on December 31, 1981.

Gift Tax: No state gift tax.

Michigan

Income Tax: Flat rate of 4.25 percent; capital gains taxed as ordinary income.

Estate/Inheritance Tax: (MCLS § 205.201 et seq.) Michigan imposes an estate tax in the amount equal to the federal credit ("sponge tax"). As it is not decoupled, the result is that the state estate tax amount is zero.

Generation-skipping transfer tax: Michigan imposes a generation-skipping transfer tax in the amount equal to the credit against or deducted from such federal generation-skipping transfer tax for state taxes paid.

Gift Tax: No state gift tax.

Minnesota

Income Tax: Top marginal rate, 9.85 percent; capital gains taxed as ordinary income.

Estate/Inheritance Tax: (Minn. Stat. §291.016 et seq.) Minnesota imposes an estate tax on estates exceeding the state exemption in an amount determined by the application of (presently) seven brackets with rates of ranging from 10 percent to 16 percent. The state exemption is $2.4 million in 2018, $2.7 million in 2019, and $3 million in 2020 and thereafter.

Generation-skipping transfer tax: No state generation-skipping transfer tax.

Gift Tax: No state gift tax. (Gift tax law repealed for gifts made after March 22, 2014.)

Mississippi

Income Tax: Top marginal rate, 5.00 percent; capital gains taxed as ordinary income.

Estate/Inheritance Tax: (Mississippi Code § 27-9-1 et seq.) Mississippi imposes an estate tax in the amount equal to the federal credit ("sponge tax"). As it is not decoupled, the result is that the state estate tax amount is zero.

Generation-skipping transfer tax: No state generation-skipping transfer tax.

Gift Tax: No state gift tax.

Missouri

Income Tax: Top marginal rate, 5.90 percent; capital gains taxed as ordinary income.

Estate/Inheritance Tax: (Missouri Revised Statutes § 145.011 et seq.) Missouri imposes an estate tax in the amount equal to the federal credit ("sponge tax"). As it is not decoupled, the result is that the state estate tax amount is zero.

Generation-skipping transfer tax: (Missouri Revised Statutes § 145.995) Missouri imposes a generation-skipping transfer tax in the amount equal to the credit against or deducted from such federal generation-skipping transfer tax for state taxes paid.

Gift Tax: No state gift tax.

Montana

Income Tax: Top marginal rate, 6.90 percent; capital gains taxed as ordinary income.

Estate/Inheritance Tax: (Rev. Code Mont. § 72-16-901 et seq.) Montana imposes an estate tax in the amount equal to the federal credit ("sponge tax"). As it is not decoupled, the result is that the state estate tax amount is zero.

Generation-skipping transfer tax: (Rev. Code Mont. § 72-16-1002) Montana imposes a generation-skipping transfer tax in the amount equal to the credit against or deducted from such federal generation-skipping transfer tax for state taxes paid.

Gift Tax: No state gift tax.

Nebraska

Income Tax: Top marginal rate, 6.84 percent; capital gains taxed as ordinary income.

Estate/Inheritance Tax:. (Rev. Stat. Neb. § 77-2001 et seq.) Nebraska imposes an inheritance tax in an amount, and subject to an exemption, that each depend upon the relation of the recipient to the decedent: "immediate relatives" taxed at 1 percent of value in excess of $40,000; "remote relatives" taxed at 13 percent of value in excess of $15,000; all others taxed at 18 percent of value in excess of $10,000.

Generation-skipping transfer tax: No state generation-skipping transfer tax.

Gift Tax: No state gift tax.

Nevada

Income Tax: No state income tax; sales tax rate, 6.85 percent.

Estate/Inheritance Tax: (NRS 375A.010 et seq.) Nevada imposes an estate tax in the amount equal to the federal credit ("sponge tax"). As it is not decoupled, the result is that the state estate tax amount is zero.

Generation-skipping transfer tax: (NRS 375B.010 et seq.) Nevada imposes a generation-skipping transfer tax on generation-skipping transfers other than a "direct skip" that occur as a result death in the amount equal to the credit against or deducted from such federal generation-skipping transfer tax for state taxes paid.

Gift Tax: No state gift tax.

New Hampshire

Income Tax: Flat tax of 5.00 percent; capital gains taxed as ordinary income.

Estate/Inheritance Tax: (New Hampshire Revised Statutes Annotated § 87:1 et seq.) New Hampshire imposes an estate tax in the amount equal to the federal credit ("sponge tax"). As it is not decoupled, the result is that the state estate tax amount is zero.

Generation-skipping transfer tax: No state generation-skipping transfer tax.

Gift Tax: No state gift tax.

New Jersey

Income Tax: Top marginal rate, 8.97 percent; capital gains taxed as ordinary income.

Estate/Inheritance Tax: (New Jersey Revised Statutes Annotated § 54:33-1 et seq.) New Jersey imposes an inheritance tax that exempts many types of property (and receipt by a spouse or lineal ancestor or descendant), and otherwise taxes the receipt of property from a decedent according to the relation to the decedent, with a maximum rate of 16 percent. (New Jersey Revised Statutes Annotated § 54:38-1 et seq.)

Generation-skipping transfer tax: No state generation-skipping transfer tax.

Gift Tax: No state gift tax.

New Mexico

Income Tax: Top marginal rate, 4.90 percent; capital gains taxed as ordinary income.

Estate/Inheritance Tax: (New Mexico Statutes Annotated § 7-7-1 et seq.) New Mexico imposes an estate tax in the amount equal to the federal credit ("sponge tax"). As it is not decoupled, the result is that the state estate tax amount is zero.

Generation-skipping transfer tax: No state generation-skipping transfer tax.

Gift Tax: No state gift tax.

New York

Income Tax: Top marginal rate, 8.82 percent; capital gains taxed as ordinary income.

Estate/Inheritance Tax: (New York Tax Code §951 et seq.) New York imposes an estate tax on estates exceeding the state exemption in an amount determined by the application of 15 brackets with rates of ranging from 3.06 percent to 16 percent. The state exemption is $5.25 million in 2018, and was set to be tied to the $5 million federal exemption under IRC §2010(c) in 2019 and thereafter, although it is uncertain whether the state will continue with this course in light of the 2017 tax reform changes. If the taxable estate is greater than 105 percent of the exemption amount, no exemption is available and the entire estate is taxable.

Generation-skipping transfer tax: No state generation-skipping transfer tax.

Gift Tax: No state gift tax.

North Carolina

Income Tax: Flat tax of 5.499 percent; capital gains taxed as ordinary income.

Estate/Inheritance Tax: No state estate or inheritance tax. (State estate tax repealed for decedents dying after 2012.)

Generation-skipping transfer tax: (General Statutes of North Carolina § 105-32.7) North Carolina imposes a tax on generation-skipping transfers equal to the federal credit under IRC §2604 for taxes paid.

Gift Tax: No state gift tax.

North Dakota

Income Tax: Top marginal rate, 2.0 percent; capital gains taxed as ordinary income.

Estate/Inheritance Tax: (North Dakota Century Code § 57-37.1-01 et seq.) North Dakota imposes an estate tax in the amount equal to the federal credit ("sponge tax"). As it is not decoupled, the result is that the state estate tax amount is zero.

Generation-skipping transfer tax: No state generation-skipping transfer tax.

Gift Tax: No state gift tax.

Ohio

Income Tax: Top marginal rate, 4.997 percent; capital gains taxed as ordinary income.

Estate/Inheritance Tax: No state estate or inheritance tax. (State estate tax repealed for decedents dying after 2012.)

Generation-skipping transfer tax: (Ohio Revised Code Annotated § 5731.181) Ohio imposes a tax on generation-skipping transfers equal to the federal credit under IRC §2604 for taxes paid.

Gift Tax: No state gift tax.

Oklahoma

Income Tax: Top marginal rate, 5.00 percent; capital gains taxed as ordinary income.

Estate/Inheritance Tax: No state estate or inheritance tax. (State estate tax repealed for decedents dying after 2009.)

Generation-skipping transfer tax: No state generation-skipping transfer tax.

Gift Tax: No state gift tax.

Oregon

Income Tax: Top marginal rate, 9.90 percent; capital gains taxed as ordinary income.

Estate/Inheritance Tax: (Or. Rev. Stat. §118.005 et seq.) Oregon imposes an estate tax on estates exceeding $1 million in an amount determined by the application of ten brackets with rates of ranging from 10 percent to 16 percent.

Generation-skipping transfer tax: No state generation-skipping transfer tax.

Gift Tax: No state gift tax.

Pennsylvania

Income Tax: Flat tax of 3.07 percent; capital gains taxed as ordinary income.

Estate/Inheritance Tax: (20 Pa. Code §37.1 et seq.) Pennsylvania imposes an inheritance tax on the receipt of property from a decedent. Transfers received by spouses are generally exempt. Transfers received by lineal ancestors and descendants are taxed at 4.5 percent of the value of the property; by siblings at 12 percent of the value; and by all others at 15 percent of the value. Pennsylvania also imposes an estate tax in the amount equal to the federal credit ("sponge tax"). As it is not decoupled, the result is that the state estate tax amount is zero.

Generation-skipping transfer tax: No state generation-skipping transfer tax.

Gift Tax: No state gift tax.

Rhode Island

Income Tax: Top marginal rate, 5.99 percent; capital gains taxed as ordinary income.

Estate/Inheritance Tax: (R.I.G.L. §44-22-1 et seq.) Rhode Island imposes an estate tax in an amount equal to the federal state death tax credit allowed as of December 31, 2001, on estates in excess of $1,537,656 million (indexed for inflation annually).

Generation-skipping transfer tax: (R.I.G.L. §44-40-1 et seq.) Rhode Island imposes a tax on generation-skipping transfers equal to the federal credit under IRC §2604 for taxes paid.

Gift Tax: No state gift tax.

South Carolina

Income Tax: Top marginal rate, 7.00 percent; capital gains taxed at 3.92 percent.

Estate/Inheritance Tax: (S.C. Code §12-16-10 et seq.) South Carolina imposes an estate tax in the amount equal to the federal credit ("sponge tax"). As it is not decoupled, the result is that the state estate tax amount is zero.

Generation-skipping transfer tax: (S.C. Code §12-16-720 et seq.) South Carolina imposes a tax on generation-skipping transfers equal to the federal credit under IRC §2604 for taxes paid.

Gift Tax: No state gift tax.

South Dakota

Income Tax: No state income tax.

Estate/Inheritance Tax: (S.D. Compiled Laws § 10-40A-1 et seq.) South Dakota imposes an estate tax in the amount equal to the federal credit ("sponge tax"). As it is not decoupled, the result is that the state estate tax amount is zero.

Generation-skipping transfer tax: No state generation-skipping transfer tax.

Gift Tax: No state gift tax.

Tennessee

Income Tax: No income tax, 3.00 percent tax on capital gains.

Estate/Inheritance Tax: (Tenn. Code Ann. § 67-8-301 et seq.) For property received from a decedent before 2016, Tennessee imposes an inheritance tax of property received in excess of $5 million per class of beneficiary in an amount determined by four brackets with a top rate of 9.5 percent. The tax is repealed as of 2016. (Tenn. Code Ann. § 67-8-301 et seq.) Tennessee also imposes an estate tax in the amount equal to the federal credit ("sponge tax"). As it is not decoupled, the result is that the state estate tax amount is zero.

Generation-skipping transfer tax: (Tenn. Code Ann. § 67-8-601 et seq.) Tennessee imposes a tax on generation-skipping transfers equal to the federal credit under IRC §2604 for taxes paid.

Gift Tax: No state gift tax.

Texas

Income Tax: No state income tax.

Estate/Inheritance Tax: (Vernon's Texas Codes Ann., Tax Code § 211.001 et seq.) Texas imposes an estate tax (although denominated an "inheritance tax") in the amount equal to the federal credit ("sponge tax"). As it is not decoupled, the result is that the state estate tax amount is zero.

Generation-skipping transfer tax: (Vernon's Texas Codes Ann., Tax Code § 211.054) Texas imposes a tax on generation-skipping transfers equal to the federal credit under IRC §2604 for taxes paid.

Gift Tax: No state gift tax.

Utah

Income Tax: Flat tax of 5.00 percent; capital gains taxed as ordinary income.

Estate/Inheritance Tax: (Utah Code §101 et seq.) Utah imposes an estate tax in the amount equal to the federal credit ("sponge tax"). As it is not decoupled, the result is that the state estate tax amount is zero.

Generation-skipping transfer tax: No state generation-skipping transfer tax.

Gift Tax: No state gift tax.

Vermont

Income Tax: Top marginal rate, 8.95 percent; capital gains taxed as ordinary income.

Estate/Inheritance Tax: (Vermont Stat. Ann. § 7441 et seq.) Vermont imposes an estate tax equal to the state death tax credit allowed (up to 16%) as of December 31, 2001, on estates exceeding $2.75 million.

Generation-skipping transfer tax: (Vermont Stat. Ann. § 7460) Vermont imposes a tax on GST transfers (as defined by the IRC) equal to the federal credit under IRC §2604 for taxes paid allowed as of December 31, 2001.

Gift Tax: No state gift tax.

Virginia

Income Tax: Top marginal rate, 5.75 percent; capital gains taxed as ordinary income.

Estate/Inheritance Tax: No state estate or inheritance tax.

Generation-skipping transfer tax: No state generation-skipping transfer tax.

Gift Tax: No state gift tax.

Washington

Income Tax: No state income tax.

Estate/Inheritance Tax: (Rev. Code Wash. § 83.100.010 et seq.) Washington imposes an estate tax determined by eight brackets with rates ranging from 10 percent to 20 percent on estates exceeding an exemption amount of $2,193,000.

Generation-skipping transfer tax: No state generation-skipping transfer tax.

Gift Tax: No state gift tax.

West Virginia

Income Tax: Top marginal rate, 6.50 percent; capital gains taxed as ordinary income.

Estate/Inheritance Tax: (W.V. Code §11-11-2 et seq.) West Virginia imposes an estate tax in the amount equal to the federal credit ("sponge tax"). As it is not decoupled, the result is that the state estate tax amount is zero.

Generation-skipping transfer tax: No state generation-skipping transfer tax.

Gift Tax: No state gift tax.

Wisconsin

Income Tax: Flat tax of 7.65 percent; capital gains taxed at 5.36 percent.

Estate/Inheritance Tax: (Wisconsin Stat. §72.01 et seq.) Wisconsin imposes an estate tax in the amount equal to the federal credit ("sponge tax"). As it is not decoupled, the result is that the state estate tax amount is zero.

Generation-skipping transfer tax: No state generation-skipping transfer tax.

Gift Tax: No state gift tax.

Wyoming

Income Tax: No state income tax; sales tax rate, 4.00 percent.

Estate/Inheritance Tax: (2015 Wyoming Stat. 39-19-103 et seq.) Wyoming imposes an estate tax (denominated as an "inheritance tax") in the amount equal to the federal credit ("sponge tax"). As it is not decoupled, the result is that the state estate tax amount is zero.

Generation-skipping transfer tax: No state generation-skipping transfer tax.

Gift Tax: No state gift tax.

TABLE OF CONTENTS

Page

POINTERS

Value And Control.

It is essential for any successful business continuation or disposition plan to consider the factors of value and control. Complete control of a business with no value is worthless; and value in a business you do not control is tenuous. With most successful operating businesses, value and control are typically fixed and determined. In the small closely-held business it is generally accepted that the same individual, or group of individuals, both controls the business and owns the value. But what happens to control and value upon the death of the business owner? This is the essential question you must address in developing an effective business succession plan. By charting the interrelationship of these two factors you can better appreciate how control dictates value. Greater control means greater value – less control means less value. But the relationship is not linear! Having a controlling interest (i.e., more than 50 percent) in a closely-held corporation produces a "control premium," as can be seen from the sharp increase in value in the chart. The flip side of the control premium is the discount allowed for a minority interest (page 376).

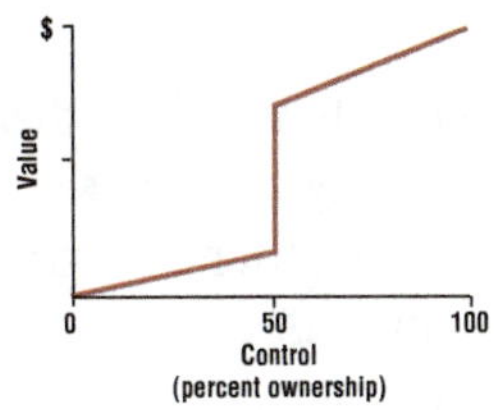

Continued – Sold – Liquidated.

There is no better place to begin a discussion of business succession planning than by asking the questions set forth on page 163. But before you begin the discussion, visit the chart on page 161. Where would you place your client on this chart? Just as importantly, where would your client place himself or herself on this chart? This insight should enable you to more effectively work with your client in developing and implementing a business disposition plan.

Know The Entity.

Before proceeding, it is essential to identify the type, or format, of the business: C corporation, S corporation, partnership, limited liability company, or sole proprietorship. The form of organization is an important consideration in selecting an agreement to be used if it is intended that the business will be sold. In this regard, you may wish to consult the materials on pages 449, 481-483, 501, 531-533, 622-624, and 625-626. Knowing the type of business is also important when considering employee benefits.

Pointers

Retain Control ... Shift Value.

If your client's business is to be continued by a family member, there are many techniques that can be used to reduce estate taxes – while at the same time maintaining control (e.g., family limited partnerships or recapitalizations, see pages 210-217). Implementation of a specific arrangement will often depend not only upon your client's willingness to proceed, but also upon the ability of your client's professional advisors to work as a team.

Compare The Charts.

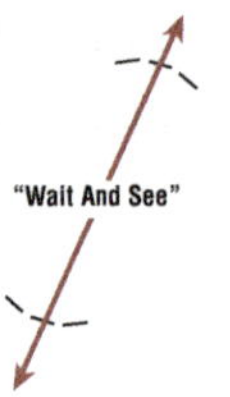

The cross purchase agreement involves an agreement between the owners to buy and sell their respective interests. You might think of it as a horizontal obligation running from business owner to business owner. On the other hand, the entity purchase agreement, also referred to as a stock redemption agreement if used with a corporation, involves an agreement by the owners to sell their respective interests to the business. You might think of it as a vertical obligation running between the business owners and the business. However, because of changing individual and business circumstances, choosing between a cross purchase agreement and an entity purchase agreement can be difficult. To keep their options open, your clients may prefer to use the highly flexible "wait and see" or "cross endorsement" buy/sell arrangements All of these agreements provide for the complete sale of a business interest, and can be used with either a corporation or a partnership, but not with a sole proprietorship. To gain a better understanding of these plans, compare the charts on pages 171, 175, 183, and 187.

Business Valuation Is Art ... Not Science.

With the business owner the subject of business valuation is a wonderful "ice breaker." However, do not promise more than you can deliver. Business valuation is art, it is not science. The chart on page 167 provides a good place to begin, but a capitalization of earnings approach is not relevant in valuing many businesses (e.g., a medical practice or professional corporation). Do not hesitate to advise your client to retain an accredited expert to perform a comprehensive business valuation.

Company Owned Life Insurance (COLI)

Employer-owned life insurance contracts must meet certain notice and consent requirements in order for the death proceeds to be excluded from taxable income. Application of a "related persons" provision, together with complicated attribution rules, will likely cast a very wide net (see discussion, pages 319-321). The general rule is that death proceeds from these contracts are taxed as ordinary income. Exceptions to this general rule are based upon the insured's status, or how death proceeds are paid or used. However, to qualify for any exception, it is essential to first meet strict notice and consent requirements. For each tax year the contract(s) is owned a reporting requirement mandates that all employers owning one or more employer-owned life insurance contracts must file Form 8529 (Report of Employer-Owned Life Insurance Contracts). *It is strongly recommended that notice be given, and consent be obtained, at the time an application is taken for virtually any life insurance contract that might conceivably fall within the scope of this law.*

Understand The Attribution Rules.

These rules have been aptly described as "infamous and insidious." While at first they may appear esoteric and difficult, they are important to understand. In family held corporations, if stock owned by one family member is to be sold to the corporation it is extremely important to consider the effect of the attribution rules (pages 218-223). Violation of these rules means that the sale will be treated and taxed as a stock dividend.

Reality Checks ... They Are Important!

Often your business owner client will want to retain the business for the benefit of a son or daughter. Good planning will usually help this happen, but not if the child is a 2-year-old. Then there is the sole proprietor, who is convinced that his key person will take over the business and run it for the benefit of his survivors. This sounds just fine, until you discover that the "keyman" is a stock clerk hired just a year ago – but he is a "bright" young man. And then there is the physician, who is practicing as a sole proprietor, and who is convinced that his practice is easily worth five or six times annual billings, plus the book value of all the equipment purchased a few years back. These clients will be well served if you help them perform a "reality check-up."

With recent changes in estate and gift tax rules, most small business owners will not have an estate tax exposure. Planning techniques previously used to avoid estate and gift taxes may no longer be necessary. Although it was always important to not let the "tax tail" wag the dog – today planning for business owners should start with non-tax issues. Start with identifying a viable successor. One will often not exist. In those cases – the plan should center on monetizing the business for the family. Often, the value is greater while the primary owner is living.

DEVELOPMENT CYCLE OF A BUSINESS

This chart will help us to better understand the typical life cycle of the owner-managed business. Such businesses are usually owned by rugged individualists who were drafted into business in a variety of ways. Although the growth curve is different for each business, it can generally be separated into four distinct phases, with the first two involving a lot of hard work.

The first stage is best described as the **Wonder Stage**, because sooner or later the business owner will wonder, "How in the world did I get into this mess?" A seven-day workweek is the norm, for which the business owner gets *freedom*, *power*, and the *last word* on how the job is to be done. Undercapitalized and overextended, the business owner expends maximum energy just to keep creditors at bay and end up with a profit to finance future growth. The large majority of new businesses don't survive this stage.

It is during the **Blunder Stage** that the last of the failures quit, while the survivors experience substantial growth, work 18-hour days, learn to trust no one, and become *highly secretive*. This leads to a reluctance to teach the business to others.

By the time the **Thunder Stage** is reached, the business owner has often become a respected and substantial member of the community. The business owner enjoys his or her success! Secrecy and a *total lack of review* of decisions have often become his or her management style. The creation of myths at this stage is commonplace. These include the notion that the business is too unusual for anyone else to run; his or her experience is all that counts; business practices should stay the same; the business is the owner's to do with as he or she pleases; that HE or SHE is *truly immortal*. It is now that the successful business owner draws the collective attention of the community's life underwriters and financial advisers. He or she desperately needs their services, but proves to be distrustful of advice. This dilemma could have been avoided had a relationship of trust and service been established *before* the thunder stage.

During the **Plunder Stage** the owner may tend to lose his or her appetite for risk, preferring instead just to keep what he or she has. The owner must learn to teach and share, not destroy on the way down what the owner built on the way up. Such teaching and sharing will allow for a renaissance of wonder, the opportunity for a successor's hard work and continued business growth. All too often the alternative is liquidation!

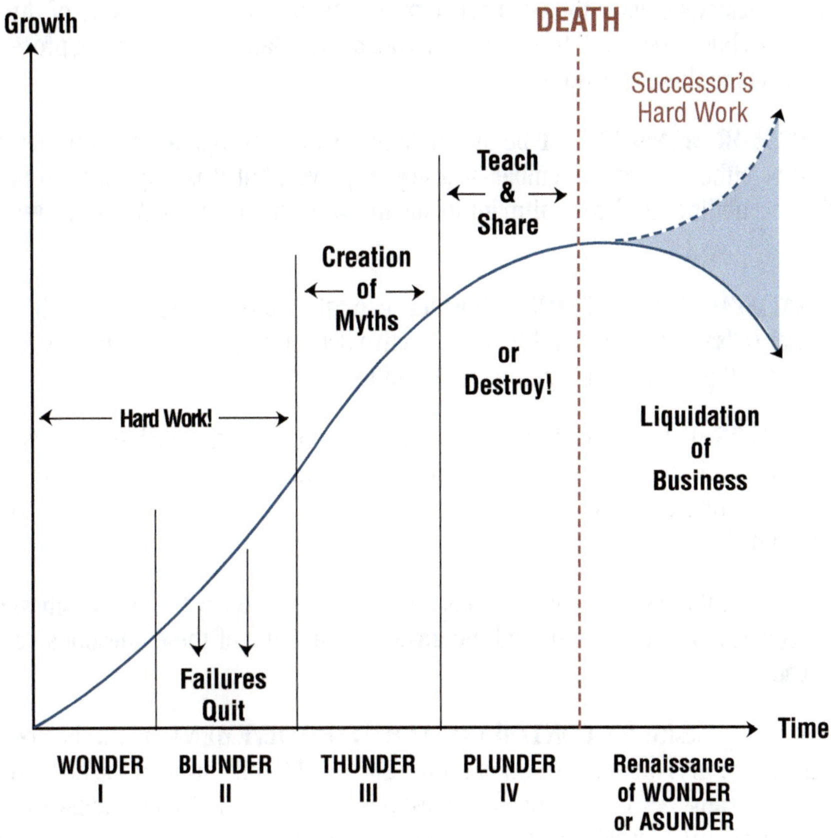

This chart and the accompanying text have been taken from Chapter Three of *Beyond Survival*, by the late Léon A. Danco, Ph.D., and are reprinted by permission of the publisher. This book has proven to be an invaluable guide to the advisor who desires to understand and effectively communicate with the owner of the closely held business. In addition, Dr. Danco has written *Inside The Family Business*, and *Outside Directors In The Family Owned Business*. Dr. Danco was a pioneer in the field of family businesses and spent over 50 years mentoring family businesses and advisors on the nuances of family business.

DISPOSITION OF A BUSINESS INTEREST

For our purposes, there are three primary risks facing the business owner: death, disability, and retirement. Likewise, upon the occurrence of one of these events, only one of three things can happen to his business: it will be continued, sold, or liquidated. The planning process should reveal the answers to these questions:

Will **SUCCESSOR MANAGEMENT** be available and willing to operate the business? Such a person could be either a family member or a key employee, but it is important to be realistic about both their abilities and commitment to staying with the business. A *yes* answer will lead to ...

Would a **SATISFACTORY RETURN** on business capital be provided for the family? The decision as to what is "satisfactory" is a highly subjective determination, but it usually falls within the range of 6 to 20 percent.[1] A *yes* answer will lead to ...

Could **TAX-FAVORED PROFITS** be withdrawn for the family? If the business is a corporation, then payment of a salary to the stockholder-employee is "tax-favored" as a deductible business expense. However, the same payments to a surviving spouse might be characterized as nondeductible dividends.[2]

If the answers to all three of these questions are *yes*, then it is likely that the business could be successfully **continued**. However, should the answer to any one of these questions be *no*, then this would lead to ...

Is there a *strong* desire for **CONTINUING FAMILY INVOLVEMENT** in the business? A *yes* answer to this question is often the result of a strong sense of family pride in the business, despite one or more "no" answers to the previous questions. Under such circumstances the business might well be **continued**, provided steps are now taken to assure that continuation is possible.[3] A *no* answer to this question will lead to ...

Would a **BUYER** be readily available? If the answer is *yes*, then the business should be **sold**, with a binding agreement and adequate funding in order to assure that the sale takes place. A *no* answer to this question means that the business is likely to be **liquidated** and its assets sold for pennies on the dollar.

But, even if all of the above questions can be answered "yes," it's prudent to ask if family wealth and happiness could be maximized by a sale. Just because a family business can be continued doesn't always mean that it should be. Sometimes family wealth, harmony, and happiness is maximized by monetizing the business while the founder is still living and the business is prospering.

Footnotes on page 165

UPON DEATH, DISABILITY OR RETIREMENT

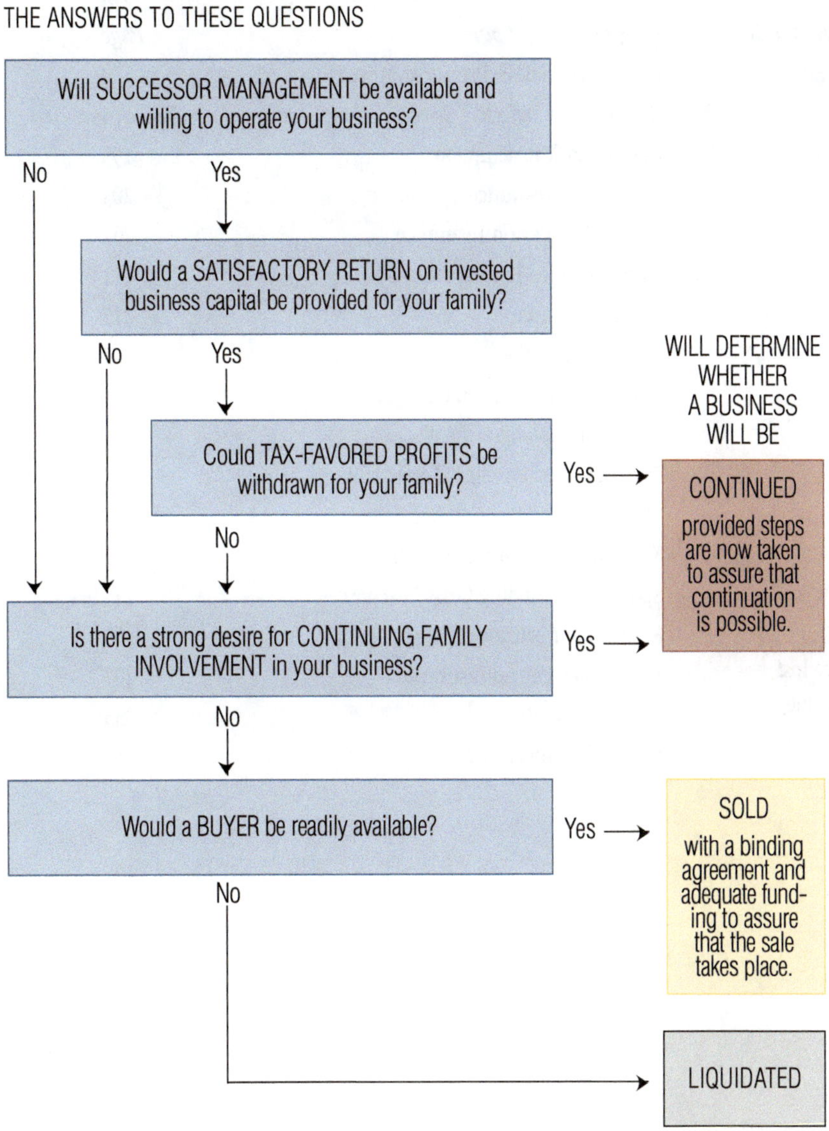

PLANNING MATRIX

Footnotes

1 A determination of business value would be a starting point for deciding what would be a "satisfactory" return on business capital. For example, $10,000 of annual income from a business worth $500,000 would probably not be satisfactory. If the business could be sold for $400,000, and the funds invested at 8 percent, the resulting before-tax income would be $32,000 per year, more than three times that provided if the business were retained.

2 There are numerous cases that have held that payments to stockholder-heirs are not deductible to the corporation. In the case of *The Barbourville Brick Company v. Commissioner*, 37 T.C. 7 (1961), the United States Tax Court held that payments to the surviving widow were dividends. Judge Brown, concurring in the denial of any income tax deduction to the corporation, considered the payments nondeductible as not a "reasonable business expense." In his written opinion, Judge Brown observed that:

> "[A]pparently there were no employees, stockholders, or members of [the decedent's] family, qualified to take over the management of petitioner's business. There is neither claim nor evidence that the widow performed any services for [the business]. Finally there is neither claim nor showing that the payments in question were in the nature of extra compensation for past services rendered by petitioner's deceased president ... income tax deductions are a matter of legislative grace ... and are to be justified as ordinary and necessary expenses of carrying on a trade or business."

3 The "steps" relate to preparing for the eventual transfer of a healthy business to other family members or key employees. In this regard, the business planning charts on the following pages demonstrate techniques that will assist in providing the plans and funds for such a smooth transfer of the business.

BUSINESS VALUATION

There are many reasons why the owner of a closely held business must have some idea of the value of his business:

- When *obtaining loans* a higher, yet realistic, value could result in increased credit.
- If the *reasonableness of compensation* to an employee-stockholder is challenged by the IRS, knowing the value of the business will be helpful.[1]
- In *determining a price* for the business when it is sold upon death, disability, or retirement.[2]
- For *estate planning* purposes, the higher the value, the greater the potential estate tax.[3]
- For *estate planning* and *business continuation* purposes, it is important to know the value when selling or gifting interests.

Valuation is an art; it is not a science.[4] With the closely held business, the concept of valuation is often elusive. Pat answers rarely exist. However, with many businesses, "capitalizing" expected earnings can be a useful starting point for determining fair market value.

For example, we know that assets, plus the talents of good management, are expected to produce earnings. Assume that a business had assets of $1,400,000 and liabilities of $400,000. By subtracting liabilities from assets, we can determine that book value is $1,000,000.[5] This is the net worth of the business, which is often referred to as stockholder's equity. Also assume that the business has earnings of $220,000.

The first step in capitalizing expected earnings is to determine what rate of return an outside purchaser would expect on his investment. Assume that, after a careful consideration of the risks inherent in this particular business, the *expected* rate of return is determined to be 12 percent.[6] If the sales price were set at book value, or only $1,000,000, expected earnings would then be $120,000. This means that there are *excess* earnings of $100,000, which should be reflected in the sales price as goodwill.

Goodwill is determined by deciding how much a purchaser should pay for these excess earnings, which are the product of such intangibles as reputation and market position. A careful consideration of both the age of the business and the likelihood of continuing excess earnings might reveal that the purchaser should pay for five years of excess earnings, or $500,000. By adding this $500,000 of goodwill to the $1,000,000 of book value, we get a fair market value for the business of $1,500,000.[7]

Footnotes on page 169

CAPITALIZING EXPECTED EARNINGS

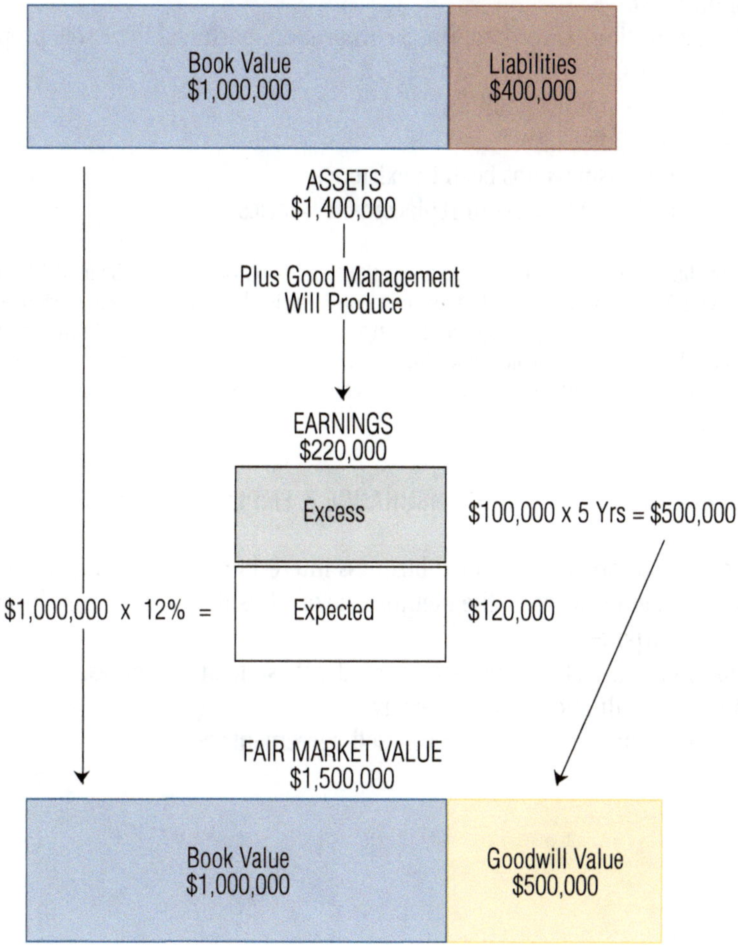

INFORMATION REQUIRED FOR ANALYSIS & PROPOSAL

1. Name of business.
2. Form of organization (C corporation, S corporation, partnership *or* sole proprietorship).
3. Nature of business.
4. Book value (assets minus liabilities).
5. Average earnings (after-tax).
6. Number of years business has been in existence.
7. Salaries of principals in excess of replacement salaries.

Note: Whenever possible, at least a 3-year average of earnings and book value should be used. The salaries of principals in excess of salaries that would be paid to replacements is typically added to average earnings. The nature of the business is relevant to determining the appropriate *expected rate of return* ("12%" in the chart). The number of years the business has been in existence, and thus its stability, reputation and market position, is relevant to determining the appropriate *capitalization of earnings* factor ("5" in the chart). For a further discussion of these rates, see footnote 6, page 169.

CROSS REFERENCES TO TAX FACTS ON INSURANCE & EMPLOYEE BENEFITS, VOL. 1 (2019)

Q 322-Q 323. Valuation of closely held business interest for federal estate tax purposes.
Q 329. An agreement restricting the lifetime sale of a business interest may be considered for gift tax purposes.
Q 937. Valuation of investment property for federal estate tax purposes.
Q 944. Chapter 14 valuation rules generally.
Q 953. Impact of Chapter 14 rules on buy/sell agreements.

Footnotes

[1] Knowing the value of the business will help defend the reasonableness of salary and other fringe benefits. In this regard, see the expanded discussion of Unreasonable Compensation on page 576.

[2] Common means of selling businesses are set forth in the Entity Purchase Agreement chart on page 171 and the Cross Purchase Agreement chart on page 175.

[3] Under the Chapter 14 special valuation provisions, the value of property for gift and estate tax purposes is determined without regard to any agreement to acquire the property at less than fair market value. However, this rule does not apply if the agreement is: (1) a *bona fide* business arrangement; (2) not a *device* to transfer the property to members of the decedent's family for less than full and adequate consideration; and (3) in its terms, *comparable* to similar arrangements entered into by persons in an arm's length transaction. All three of these tests are presumed to be met if the agreement is between unrelated individuals (i.e., an agreement exclusively among persons who are not the natural objects of each other's bounty).

In agreements between related individuals maintenance of family ownership and control could be a *bona fide* reason for using a particular business value, thereby satisfying the first test. But the stipulated value will not be controlling for estate tax purposes unless the agreement also meets the *device* and *comparable* tests. In order to satisfy all three of these requirements in family held businesses there is likely to be an increased utilization of both *appraisal* and generally accepted *formula* methods of business valuation.

For estate tax purposes, the executor of an estate may elect special methods for valuing *real property* used in a farm, trade, or business. A discussion of the strict qualifications and restrictions imposed appears on pages 518-519.

[4] When valuation is left to chance, it opens the door to litigation with the Internal Revenue Service. The state of the art is at best uncertain for those who fail to "peg" properly the value of their business interests. It is also important to recognize that valuation may mean different things to different people, depending upon the purpose of the valuation. However, as far as the Internal Revenue Service is concerned, it is based upon a consideration of *all relevant facts*, and in particular those eight factors set forth in the expanded discussion of Fair Market Value on page 376. Financial ratio analysis provides another means of determining business value.

[5] In using this approach to business valuation, care must be taken to assure that Book Value accurately reflects the true value of business assets (see page 301).

[6] Selection of appropriate expected *rate of return* and *capitalization of earning* factors is very subjective. Nevertheless, the following may provide some idea of the ranges used:

Expected rate of return		Capitalization of earnings	
8-11%	safe business	1-3	volatile earnings
12-17%	average business	4-6	average, variable earnings
18-22%	speculative business	7-9	stable earnings

[7] This chart demonstrates an application of what has come to be known as the "ARM 34" formula. It is most appropriately used with manufacturing firms involving substantial investments of both plant and equipment. The letters "ARM" stand for "Committee on Appeals and Review Memorandum." This committee no longer exists under the present judicial system. Another, more direct, method of capitalizing earnings is sometimes referred to as the "straight capitalization method" and is best demonstrated by the following question: "If a buyer expects to make 12 percent on his investment, and the business is producing earnings of $220,000 per year, what would the buyer be willing to pay for the business?" The calculation required to answer this question produces a substantially higher valuation than the ARM 34 formula shown in the chart:

$$\text{Value} \times .12 = \$220{,}000 \quad \textit{or} \quad \text{Value} = \$220{,}000 \div .12 = \$1{,}833{,}333$$

ENTITY PURCHASE AGREEMENT

The entity purchase agreement is another means of providing for the complete disposition of a business interest. Under such an arrangement the contract is with the business rather than with the other owners.[1]

DURING LIFETIME. To illustrate how it works, assume that we have a corporation that is owned equally by A and B.[2] They would each enter into an agreement with the business for the purchase and sale of their respective interests. Typically, this agreement is *binding*, in that it obligates both A and B, and their estates, to sell, and the business to buy, upon the death, disability, or retirement of either one of them.[3]

Rather than relying on its ability to accumulate or borrow sufficient funds to meet its obligations to purchase these interests, the business obtains separate life insurance contracts insuring A and B.[4] The business pays the premiums and is owner and beneficiary of the contracts. In this manner, the business pre-funds its obligations with life insurance. With the use of life insurance to fund an entity purchase agreement the business is in effect *amortizing* the cost of the purchase over the lifetime of the insured.[5]

UPON DEATH. Should A die first, his stock interest passes to his family or estate. At the same time, the insurance company pays a potentially tax-free death benefit to the business as beneficiary of the contract insuring A's life.[6]

Pursuant to the agreement, in return for cash, A's family, or estate, will then transfer A's *entire interest* to the business.[7] In this way a fully funded agreement *guarantees* that the surviving family will receive a fair price for A's interest.[8] If A's estate is subject to estate taxes, the agreement can also serve to help "peg," or establish, the value of the stock for estate tax purposes, thereby avoiding the extensive negotiations and potential litigation with the Internal Revenue Service that may occur when valuation is left to chance.[9]

The biggest draw-back of an entity purchase agreement is that the cost basis in B's interest is not increased by the purchase price paid by the business. Given the importance of income tax planning; the cross-purchase arrangement discussed in the following sections is usually more tax efficient.

Footnotes on page 173

DURING LIFETIME

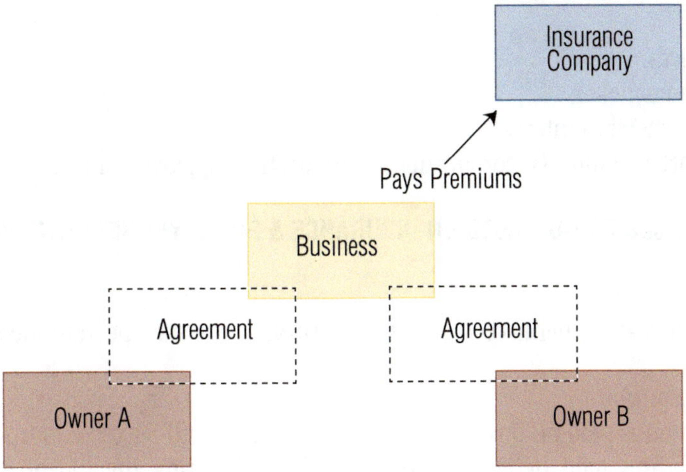

The Business Obtains Life Insurance On Each Owner

UPON DEATH

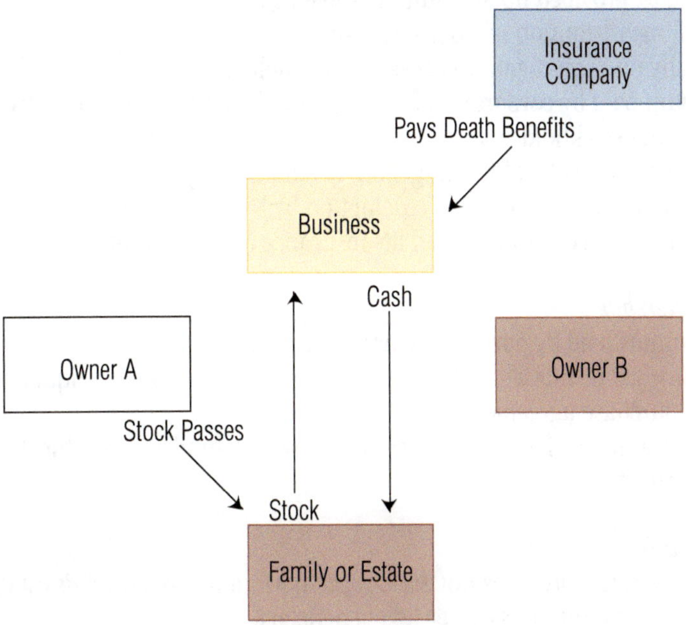

INFORMATION REQUIRED FOR ANALYSIS & PROPOSAL

1. Name of owner to be insured.
2. Sex.
3. Date of birth.
4. Smoker/nonsmoker.
5. Value of ownership interest.
6. Form of organization (C corporation, S corporation *or* partnership).

CROSS REFERENCES TO TAX FACTS ON INSURANCE & EMPLOYEE BENEFITS, VOL. 1 (2019)

Income Tax

Q 276. When death benefits of business life insurance are exempt from income tax.

Corporation

Q 263. Premiums paid on business life insurance not usually taxable to insured employee.

Q 264. Premiums paid by corporation on policies insuring the life of a stockholder or employee usually not deductible.

Q 268. Premiums paid by corporation to fund stock redemption not taxable to insured stockholder.

Q 300. Amount paid by corporation for decedent's entire stock interest generally not dividend to estate, provided no attribution problems.

Q 301. Avoiding attribution of stock ownership.

Q 305. Usually no capital gain to deceased stockholder's estate.

Q 306. Amount paid by corporation for stock usually not taxable as constructive dividend to surviving stockholder(s).

Q 307. Income tax results of funding stock redemption agreement with life insurance.

Q 310. Taxation of payments when redemption by S corporation.

Q 316. Treatment of corporate owned life insurance for purpose of alternative minimum tax.

Partnership

Q 274. Premiums paid by partnership are not deductible.

Q 311. Income tax results when deceased partner's interest is sold or liquidated under a business purchase agreement.

Q 315. Tax treatment of life insurance purchased to fund partnership business purchase agreement.

Estate Tax

Q 321. Life insurance proceeds not directly included in insured owner's estate when partnership or corporation is owner and beneficiary.

Footnotes

[1] Note that in contrast to the cross purchase agreement, the entity agreement requires that the *business* purchase the interest, not the other owners (compare entity purchase agreement with cross purchase agreement using the materials on page 625). The entity agreement can be used by either a partnership or a corporation with more than one stockholder. It is often the preferred method with *multiple* stockholders or partners, since only one policy on the life of each owner is required (but see, Trusteed Cross-Purchase, pages 178-181, and Cross-Endorsement Buy-Sell, pages 182-185 to fund multiple-owner cross purchase agreements). An entity purchase agreement cannot be used by a corporation with only one stockholder or a sole proprietorship, since the corporation cannot own itself and the sole proprietorship is not a separate entity that can make the purchase. When used to fund the purchase of corporate stock, it is usually referred to as a "stock redemption" or "section 302(b)(3) stock redemption" agreement (see footnote 8, page 197). In this sense, the terms "entity purchase" and "stock redemption" are interchangeable.

[2] It is also assumed that A and B are *not* related to each other. If they were, and the business was a corporation, then the attribution rules would have to be considered (attribution is more fully explained on pages 218-223).

[3] If the agreement is binding upon disability as well as death, consideration should also be given to funding the agreement with disability buy-out insurance (see expanded discussion on page 342-343). The tax treatment of various disability income arrangements is set forth on page 646. Although a life insurance policy with a long-term care or critical illness rider is not a substitute for a disability policy – these types of "hybrids" are sometimes used to help fund lifetime buyouts. If this strategy is used – it is important that the conditions for buy-out match the conditions for making benefit claims under the contract.

[4] Employer-owned life insurance must meet strict notice and consent requirements if the death benefits are to be received free of income taxes (see Company Owned Life Insurance (COLI), pages 319-321).

[5] By having the corporation purchase and pay the insurance premiums, it is often possible to utilize after-tax "enhanced dollars." Corporate borrowing as an alternative to life insurance funding is usually unattractive.

[6] Under some circumstances a portion of annual cash value increases and death proceeds could be subject to the Corporate Alternative Minimum Tax, as discussed on pages 327-329.

[7] Note that B is now the sole owner of the business. However, B's cost basis for purposes of income taxes has not been increased, because the business, not B, purchased A's interest. If the business were subsequently sold by B, he would have substantially more gain than would have been the case had B previously purchased A's interest under a cross purchase agreement at A's death. With regard to a corporation, once an entity purchase agreement has been funded with life insurance, it *is generally not* possible to use the same policies when changing to a cross purchase agreement. This is because of the Transfer For Value rule, as more fully explained on pages 568-569. See also Cross Endorsement Buy-Sell at pages 182-185.

[8] Various means can be used in the agreement to determine the purchase price. A *fixed price* could be established, with a further provision providing for periodic review and redetermination between the business and the owners. Alternatively, a *formula method* could be used, under which specific factors would be employed to calculate a value. For an example of a *capitalization formula*, see the Business Valuation chart on page 167. Another approach to determining a price is to provide for an *appraisal* at the time of sale (i.e., after the first owner's death, or earlier if a lifetime sale is contemplated). Determination of the purchase price is a key aspect of the buy-sell agreement and is too infrequently considered only when there is a triggering event.

[9] To help "peg" the value of the business for estate tax purposes, the parties must be required to sell during lifetime for the same price as provided for a sale at death. Also, the agreement must specifically *bind* A's estate or family and further comply with the Chapter 14 requirements (see footnote 3, page 169).

CROSS PURCHASE AGREEMENT

The cross purchase agreement is one means of providing for the complete disposition of a business interest.[1] Under this arrangement the owners agree, among themselves, to buy and sell their respective interests.[2]

DURING LIFETIME. To illustrate how this works, assume that we have a corporation equally owned by two individuals, A and B. They enter into an agreement providing for the purchase and sale of their respective interests. Typically, this agreement is *binding* and obligates both parties, or their representatives, to either buy or sell upon the death, disability, or retirement of either A or B.[3]

Rather than trying to accumulate or borrow sufficient funds to buy B's interest, A obtains a life insurance contract insuring B. A applies for this coverage, pays the premiums, and is both owner and beneficiary of the contract. Likewise, B applies for a life insurance contract insuring A, pays the premiums, and is both owner and beneficiary.[4] By this means, A and B can use life insurance to *fully* fund their mutual obligations to each other.[5]

UPON DEATH. Assuming that A dies first, his stock interest would then pass to his family or estate. At the same time, the insurance company pays a death benefit to B, as beneficiary of the contract insuring A's life. B receives these funds free of all income taxes, since they are received as the death benefit of a life insurance contract.[6]

Pursuant to the agreement, A's family, or estate, transfers A's entire stock interest in the corporation to B, in return for which B pays the cash received from the insurance company.

The fully funded agreement can *assure* that A's surviving family receives a fair price for his or her interest in the business. But such an agreement can also serve another very important function. If the estate had been subject to estate taxes, it is possible that extensive negotiations and even litigation could result if the estate tax value of the business had been left to chance. These problems of delay and litigation can be avoided by having a cross purchase agreement which helps establish, or "peg," the value of the stock.[7]

Given the importance of income and capital gains tax planning, a cross-purchase arrangement increases the remaining owners' cost-basis by the purchase price. This is the primary advantage over an entity buy-sell arrangement.

Although term insurance alone can provide funding for a buy-out at death, the reality is that disability, retirement, and disagreement among owners is a far more common reason for an owner to leave a business. It is important that planning and funding for those eventualities also be considered.

Footnotes on page 177

DURING LIFETIME

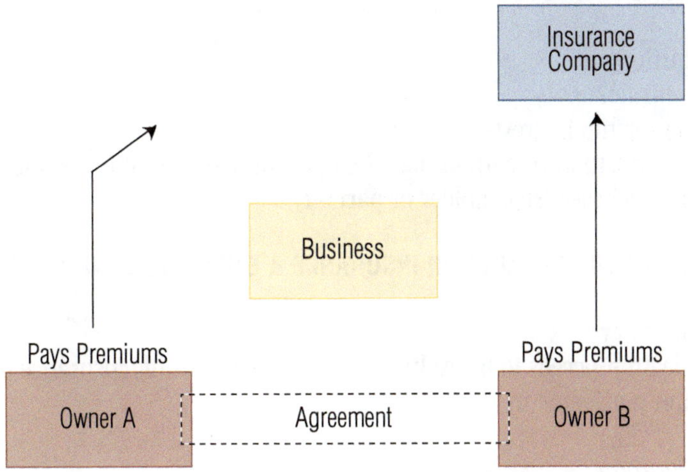

Each Owner Obtains Life Insurance On The Other

UPON DEATH

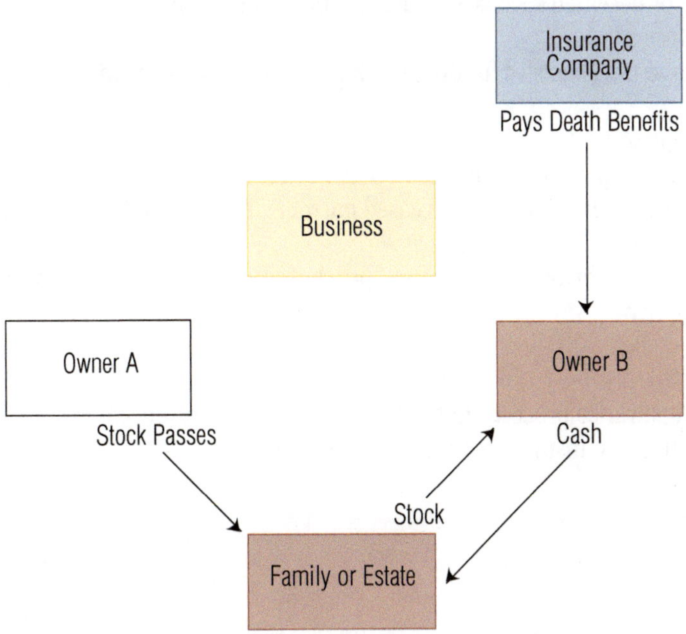

INFORMATION REQUIRED FOR ANALYSIS & PROPOSAL

1. Names of owners to be insured.
2. Sex.
3. Dates of birth.
4. Smoker/nonsmoker.
5. Value of ownership interests.
6. Form of organization (C corporation, S corporation, partnership, or sole proprietorship).
7. Identity of purchaser (stockholder or partner).

CROSS REFERENCES TO TAX FACTS ON INSURANCE & EMPLOYEE BENEFITS, VOL. 1 (2019)

Income Tax

Q 65. For death proceeds to be excludable from income, a life insurance policy must meet certain requirements.

Corporation

Q 266. Stockholder cannot deduct premiums paid on policy purchased on life of another stockholder.

Q 271. Premiums paid by corporation on policies owned by stockholders are taxable income to stockholders.

Q 298. Sale of deceased's stock will usually not result in income tax liability to deceased's estate.

Q 299. Income tax effects of funding stock purchase agreement with life insurance.

Partnership

Q 274. Premiums paid by partner for insurance on life of copartner are not deductible.

Q 311. Income tax results when deceased partner's interest sold or liquidated under a business purchase agreement.

Q 315. Tax treatment of life insurance purchased to fund partnership business purchase agreement.

Estate Tax

Q 320. Life insurance proceeds not included in insured's estate when partners or stockholders purchase insurance on lives of each other.

Footnotes

1 Compare the cross purchase agreement with the entity purchase agreement using the materials on page 625. The cross purchase agreement can be used with either a corporation or a partnership. With a sole proprietorship, a similar arrangement could be established between the sole proprietor and a key employee (chart, page 191. The sole proprietor would merely be obligated to sell and the key employee obligated to buy. Life insurance funding involves the key employee purchasing a contract on the life of the sole proprietor in order to fund the obligation to purchase.

2 Various means can be used in the agreement to determine a purchase price. A *fixed price* could be established, with a further provision providing for periodic review and redetermination by mutual agreement among the owners. Alternatively, a *formula method* could be employed, under which specific factors would be used to calculate a value. For an example of a *capitalization* formula, refer to the valuation chart on page 167. Another approach to determining a price is to provide for an *appraisal* at the time of sale (i.e., after the first owner's death, or earlier if a lifetime sale is contemplated).

3 A cross purchase agreement will avoid the attribution problems that can occur in a family held corporation (attribution is more fully explained on pages 218-223). However, a cross purchase agreement with *multiple* stockholders can be cumbersome when the agreement is to be funded with life insurance. For example, with three stockholders, six policies would be required because each stockholder would have to be the owner and beneficiary of a policy on each of the other stockholders. If there were four stockholders, twelve policies would be required. To avoid the problem of multiple policies, preference is often given to using an entity purchase agreement (chart, page 171) or a trusteed cross purchase agreement (chart, page 179 and comparison page 598). However, the death of one owner could create a transfer for value problem with respect to remaining policies insuring the surviving owners (pages 568-569). See also the discussion of Cross-Endorsement Buy-Sell at pages 182-185.

4 In a family-owned business the attribution rules under Code section 101(j) *may* treat these policies as "employer-owned." This would subject the death benefits to income taxation. To assure the proceeds are received free of income taxes, appropriate notice and consents should be obtained (see Company Owned Life Insurance (COLI) pages 319-321).

5 When the obligation is not fully funded, borrowing as an alternative to life insurance is usually unattractive. The real risk of a death among multiple owners of a business can be estimated by using the Odds Of Death figures on pages 611-612. Executive equity or split-dollar could be used to assist A and B in purchasing the life insurance (see charts, pages 233 and 245).

6 Receipt of the death proceeds allows B to purchase A's business interest *and* obtain an income tax cost basis equal to the purchase price. To illustrate, assume that both A and B originally paid $100,000 for each of their 50 percent stock interests which are now each worth $750,000 (for a total corporate value of $1,500,000). If A dies and the corporation buys A's stock for $750,000, B is then left as the sole stockholder of a corporation valued at $1,500,000. If B then subsequently sells the corporation, his gain on the sale would be $1,400,000 (the $1,500,000 sales price less the $100,000 he originally paid for his stock). However, if upon A's death B had purchased A's stock under a cross purchase agreement, B's basis in his corporate stock would be increased by $750,000. Under these circumstances, B's gain on a later sale of the corporation would be only $650,000 (the $1,500,000 sales price less his basis of $850,000, which includes the $100,000 he paid for his original stock plus the $750,000 he paid for A's shares).

7 To help "peg" the value, the parties must be required to sell during lifetime for the same price as provided for a sale at death. In addition, the agreement must specifically *bind* A's estate or family and further comply with the Chapter 14 requirements (see footnote 3, page 169 and pages 371-372).

TRUSTEED CROSS PURCHASE AGREEMENT

The trusteed cross purchase agreement is one means of providing for the complete disposition of a business interest.[1] Under this arrangement the owners use a third party to carry out their cross purchase agreement.[2] Although sometimes referred to as a "trustee," this individual is not acting as a trustee in a formal trust sense. Rather, the trusteed cross purchase agreement more closely resembles an escrow arrangement, under which an escrow agent acts as agent for the owners in carrying out their mutual obligations to each other.

DURING LIFETIME. To illustrate how this works, assume that we have a corporation owned by four stockholders, A, B, C, and D. They enter into an agreement providing for the purchase and sale of their respective interests.[3] Typically, this agreement is *binding* and obligates all stockholders, or their representatives, to either buy or sell upon their death, disability, or retirement.

To implement the agreement the stockholders transfer their stock certificates to the escrow agent, and further have the escrow agent purchase life insurance on each stockholder.[4] The escrow agent is both owner and beneficiary of these contracts and pays any required premiums.[5] By this means the stockholders can use life insurance to *fully* fund their agreement, while having the assurance that their mutual obligations to each other will be carried out by the escrow agent.[6] Use of an escrow agent can substantially reduce the number of policies required to fund the agreement.[7]

UPON DEATH. Assuming that A dies first, the insurance company pays a death benefit to the escrow agent, as beneficiary of the contract insuring A's life. The escrow agent receives these funds free of all income taxes, since they are received as the death benefit of a life insurance contract. Pursuant to the agreement, the escrow agent then transfers A's entire stock interest in the corporation to the surviving stockholders, in return for which the escrow agent pays the cash received from the insurance company to A's family.[8]

The fully funded agreement will *assure* that A's surviving family receives a fair price for his interest in the business. But such an agreement can also serve another very important function. If the estate had been subject to estate taxes, it is possible that extensive negotiations and even litigation could result if the estate tax value of the business had been left to chance. These problems of delay and litigation can be avoided by having a trusteed cross purchase agreement which helps establish, or "peg," the value of the stock.[9]

Footnotes on page 181

DURING LIFETIME

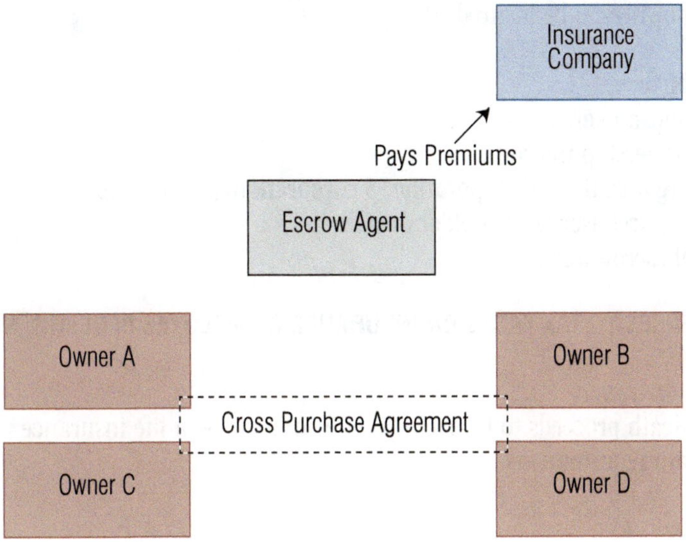

The Escrow Agent Obtains Life Insurance On Each Owner

UPON DEATH

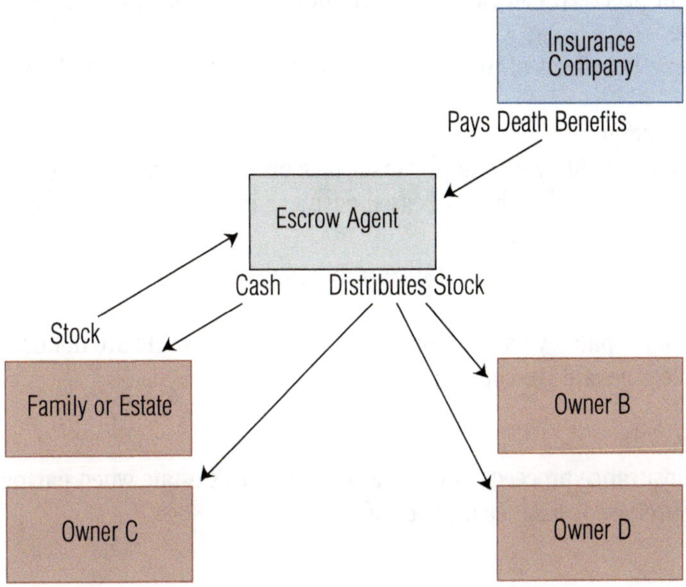

INFORMATION REQUIRED FOR ANALYSIS & PROPOSAL

1. Names of owners to be insured.
2. Sex.
3. Dates of birth.
4. Smoker/nonsmoker.
5. Value of ownership interests.
6. Form of organization (C corporation, S corporation, partnership, or sole proprietorship).
7. Identity of purchaser (stockholder or partner).
8. Identity of escrow agent.

CROSS REFERENCES TO TAX FACTS ON INSURANCE & EMPLOYEE BENEFITS, VOL. 1 (2019)

Income Tax

Q 65. For death proceeds to be excludable from income, a life insurance policy must meet certain requirements.

Corporation

Q 266. Stockholder cannot deduct premiums paid on policy purchased on life of another stockholder.

Q 271. Premiums paid by corporation on policies owned by stockholders are taxable income to stockholders.

Q 298. Sale of deceased's stock will usually not result in income tax liability to deceased's estate.

Q 299. Income tax effects of funding stock purchase agreement with life insurance.

Partnership

Q 274. Premiums paid by partner for insurance on life of copartner are not deductible.

Q 311. Income tax results when deceased partner's interest sold or liquidated under a business purchase agreement.

Q 315. Tax treatment of life insurance purchased to fund partnership business purchase agreement.

Q 437. Premiums paid by partner for insurance on his own life are not deductible by him if proceeds payable to copartner.

Estate Tax

Q 320. Life insurance proceeds not included in insured's estate when partners or stockholders purchase insurance on lives of each other.

Footnotes

[1] Trusteed cross purchase agreements are also known as "custodian" or "escrowed" agreements. The provisions for an escrow agent can be part of the cross purchase agreement, or provided for in a separate agreement. The trusteed cross purchase agreement can be used with either a corporation or a partnership. With a sole proprietorship, a similar escrowed arrangement could be established between the sole proprietor and a key employee (chart, page 181). However, since the key employee has no ownership interest, there are no reciprocal obligations to buy and sell. The sole proprietor would merely be obligated to sell and the key employee obligated to buy.

[2] In recent years there has been a substantial increase in the use of cross purchase agreements (as opposed to entity purchase agreements). The factors contributing to this include: (1) the avoidance of the attribution rules with a family-held corporation (see pages 218-223); (2) the increase of cost basis for the surviving stockholders, (see footnote 6, page 177); and (3) the ability to convert to a entity purchase agreement using the same policies without running afoul of the transfer for value rules (see page 568-569).

[3] See footnote 2, page 177, for an explanation of the various means that can be used in the agreement to determine a purchase price.

[4] In a family-owned business the attribution rules under Code section 101(j) *may* treat these policies as "employer-owned." This would subject the death benefits to income taxation. To assure the proceeds are received free of income taxes, appropriate notice and consents should be obtained (see Company Owned Life Insurance (COLI) pages 319-321).

[5] Since the escrow agent pays the premiums on behalf of the owners he or she obtains the funds from the owners (e.g., B, C and D benefit from and therefore must pay the premiums for the policy insuring A). Although the premiums are not tax-deductible, split-dollar plans could be used to assist the owners in paying for the life insurance (chart, page 245).

[6] When the obligation is not fully funded, borrowing as an alternative to life insurance is usually unattractive. The real risk of a death among multiple owners of a business can be estimated by using the Odds Of Death figures on pages 611-612.

[7] With multiple stockholders the typical cross purchase agreement has the disadvantage of requiring that each stockholder be the owner and beneficiary of a policy on each of the other stockholders. Example 1, below, requires twelve policies to fund a cross purchase agreement involving just four stockholders (i.e., A must own policies insuring B, C, and D, etc.). Example 2 uses an escrow agent under a *trusteed* cross purchase agreement to reduce the number of policies to the number of insured stockholders.

EXAMPLE 1	**Owner →**	**A**	**B**	**C**	**D**
	12 policies insuring	B C D	A C D	A B D	A B C
EXAMPLE 2	**Owner →**	**ESCROW AGENT**			
	4 policies insuring	A	B	C	D

[8] After the first death there is a potential transfer for value problem upon the transfer of the deceased stockholder's ownership interests in the remaining policies insuring the surviving stockholders (pages 568-569). Sometimes a similar partnership structure is used to avoid this concern.

[9] To help "peg" the value, the parties must be required to sell during lifetime for the same price as provided for a sale at death. In addition, the agreement must specifically *bind* A's estate or family and further comply with the Chapter 14 requirements (see footnote 3, page 169 and pages 371-372).

CROSS ENDORSEMENT BUY-SELL AGREEMENT

The trusteed cross purchase agreement is one flexible means of providing for the complete disposition of a business interest.[1] However, the cross endorsement buy-sell agreement is an alternative which can provide the benefit of basis-step up typically found in a cross purchase agreement with the simplicity and flexibility of individual policy ownership by the insured shareholders. Unlike the trusteed cross purchase agreement and the escrow and partnership versions of that structure, each shareholder simply purchases a permanent policy on his or her own life.[2] No third party is required to own or facilitate the arrangement. This type of arrangement is sometimes referred to as the Retirement Buy-Sell because of the flexibility to utilize cash value policies for dual use.

DURING LIFETIME. To illustrate how this works, assume that we have a corporation owned by four stockholders, A, B, C, and D. They enter into a buy-sell agreement providing for the purchase and sale of their respective interests.[3] Typically, this agreement is *binding* and obligates all stockholders, or their representatives, to either buy or sell upon their death, disability, or retirement.

To fund the agreement the stockholders simply endorse some or all of the death benefit on a policy (or policies) insuring their own life to the other shareholders. For example, A would endorse a portion of the death benefit on his or her life insurance policy (equal to the purchase obligation of that shareholder) to each of B, C, and D.[4] Likewise, B would endorse his or her death benefit to A, C, and D. C and D would do the same with the result that each of A, B, C, and D could own a single permanent policy on his or her life that would be partially endorsed to each of the other three shareholders. A, B, C, and D can continue to own their own life insurance policy and their own shares of stock without the need to make a transfer. Like a trusteed cross purchase agreement, a cross-endorsement arrangement can substantially reduce the number of policies required to fund a cross-purchase buy-sell agreement.[5]

UPON DEATH. Assuming that A dies first, the insurance company pays the death benefit to the shareholders as provided for under the split dollar endorsement agreements. Assuming A, B, C, and D were equal shareholders – the death benefit would be paid (tax-free) one-third to each of B, C, and D.[6] Pursuant to the buy-sell agreement, A's estate would transfer A's entire stock interest (one-third each) to B, C, and D in exchange for the cash received from the insurance company.[7] The fully funded agreement can *assure* that A's surviving family receives a fair price for his or her interest in the business. But such an agreement can also serve to establish, or "peg," the value of the stock.[8] The remaining shareholders would have their cost basis in the business increased by the amount paid to A's heirs. Most importantly, under this structure, if the business is sold or otherwise terminated during the insureds' lifetimes, the life insurance policies are owned by the individual insured. All that is required is that the parties cease the annual rental of the death benefit under the endorsement split dollar arrangement.[9]

Footnotes on page 185

CROSS-ENDORSEMENT BUY/SELL FUNDING

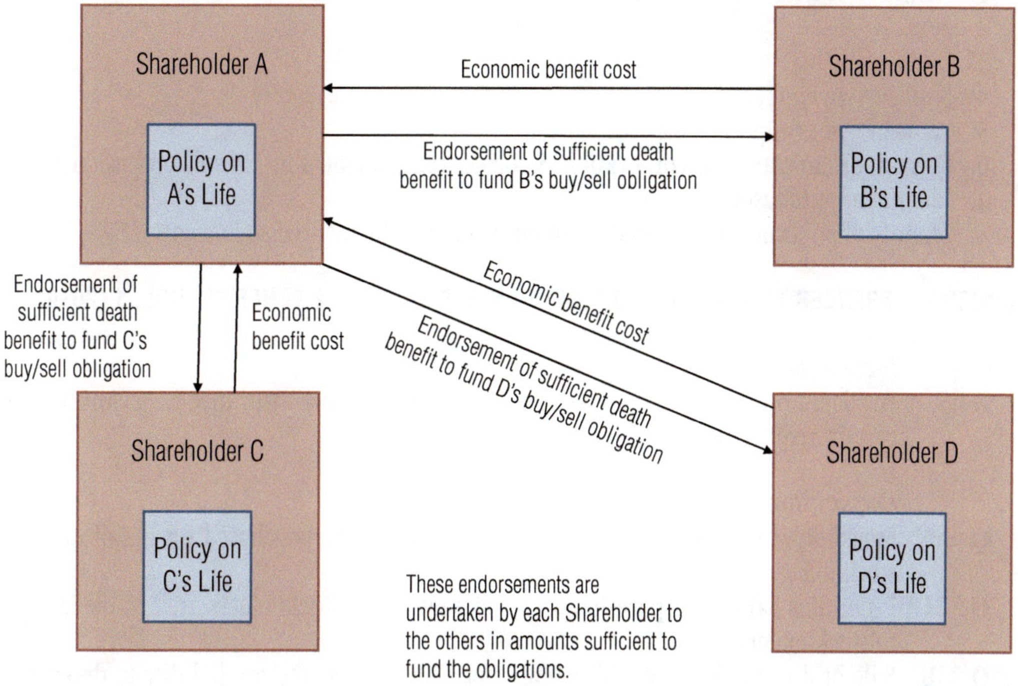

INFORMATION REQUIRED FOR ANALYSIS & PROPOSAL

1. Names of owners to be insured.
2. Sex.
3. Dates of birth.
4. Smoker/nonsmoker.
5. Value of ownership interests.
6. Form of organization (C corporation, S corporation, partnership, or sole proprietorship).
7. Identity of purchaser.
8. Identity of policyowner (insured or an entity created by insured such as an ILIT).

CROSS REFERENCES TO TAX FACTS ON INSURANCE & EMPLOYEE BENEFITS, VOL. 1 (2019)

Income Tax

Q 65. For death proceeds to be excludable from income, a life insurance policy must meet certain requirements.

Corporation

Q 266. Stockholder cannot deduct premiums paid on policy purchased on life of another stockholder.

Q 271. Premiums paid by corporation on policies owned by stockholders are taxable income to stockholders.

Q 298. Sale of deceased's stock will usually not result in income tax liability to deceased's estate.

Q 299. Income tax effects of funding stock purchase agreement with life insurance.

Partnership

Q 311. Income tax results when deceased partner's interest sold or liquidated under a business purchase agreement.

Q 315. Tax treatment of life insurance purchased to fund partnership business purchase agreement.

Q 437. Premiums paid by partner for insurance on his own life are not deductible by him if proceeds payable to copartner.

Footnotes

1 See discussion of the Trusteed Cross Purchase Agreement on pages 178-181. A common alternative to the Trusteed Cross Purchase Agreement is the Partnership Cross Purchase Agreement in which a partnership is used rather than a trust or escrow arrangement. The partnership arrangement is used to void what some tax professionals consider a possible transfer for value issue created when beneficial ownership of the policies is transferred in the Trusteed Cross Purchase Agreement structure. See a discussion of Transfer for Value on pages 568-569.

2 Sometimes the policy is owned by a trust created by the insured rather than by the insured individually. Use of a trust brings with it the advantages and disadvantages of trust ownership discussed in various places throughout the text including pages 54-57.

3 See footnote 2, page 177, for an explanation of the various means that can be used in the agreement to determine a purchase price.

4 The arrangement between the shareholders is a simple endorsement split dollar agreement whereby the policy owner simply "rents" the death benefit to the other shareholders using the IRS 2001-10 rates or the carrier cost of term insurance. See a discussion of endorsement split dollar at pages 240-243.

5 With multiple stockholders the typical cross purchase agreement has the disadvantage of requiring that each stockholder be the owner and beneficiary of a policy on each of the other stockholders. Example 1, below, requires twelve policies to fund a cross purchase agreement involving just four stockholders (i.e., A must own policies insuring B, C, and D, etc.). Example 2 uses a cross-endorsement arrangement to reduce the number of policies to the number of insured stockholders.

EXAMPLE 1	**Owner** ⟶	**A**	**B**	**C**	**D**
	12 policies insuring	B C D	A C D	A B D	A B C
EXAMPLE 2	**Owner** ⟶	**INDIVIDUAL INSURED**			
	4 policies insuring	A	B	C	D

6 Each of B, C, and D would receive the death benefit free of all income taxes since they are received as the death benefit of a life insurance contract.

7 With a trusteed buy-sell agreement there is a potential transfer for value problem after the first death upon the transfer of the deceased stockholder's ownership interests in the remaining policies insuring the surviving stockholders (pages 568-569). With the cross-endorsement arrangement no such problem exists at that time since no policy is transferred. Rather, the endorsement split dollar agreement in future years is merely modified to accommodate the new ownership percentages. However, some tax advisors have expressed concern that the cross-endorsement itself is a transfer for value. To avoid this concern, a common strategy is to create a separate partnership between the shareholder to hold a piece of business property such as land, building, or vehicles.

8 To help "peg" the value, the parties must be required to sell during lifetime for the same price as provided for a sale at death. In addition, the agreement must specifically *bind* A's estate or family and further comply with the Chapter 14 requirements (see footnote 3, page 169 and pages 371-372).

9 This avoids potential conflict among shareholders upon sale or liquidation of the business. In most instances, once the business is sold or terminated, the parties to the buy-sell arrangement want to acquire the policies on their own life. Traditional entity purchase, cross purchase, and trusteed cross purchase arrangements require complicated planning to insure that this can be done and that a fair price for the policy is set. With the cross-endorsement buy sell arrangement no transfer is required. Each surviving shareholder simply stops endorsing his or her policy to the other shareholders when the buy-sell agreement ceases to exist.

"WAIT AND SEE" BUY/SELL AGREEMENT

Choosing between a cross purchase and entity purchase agreement is often made difficult because of changing individual and business circumstances, as well as the inevitable "reforms" to our tax laws. One solution to this dilemma is the highly flexible "wait and see" buy/sell agreement, under which the owners agree among themselves, and with the business, to buy and sell their respective interests.[1]

DURING LIFETIME. To illustrate how this works, assume that we have a corporation which is owned equally by A and B.[2] As with both cross purchase and entity purchase agreements, the "wait and see" agreement provides for valuation of their interests, sale upon death, disability, or retirement, and the specific terms of payment.[3] However, unlike cross purchase and entity purchase agreements, the "wait and see" buy/sell agreement does not specifically identify the purchaser. The purchaser and amounts of purchase are not determined until after the death of either A or B.

Life insurance funding of the agreement can be accomplished in a number of ways.[4] A and B ordinarily purchase life insurance contracts on each other (as with cross purchase agreements). Alternatively, the business could purchase life insurance contracts on both A and B (as with entity purchase agreements). A third alternative involves a combination of the first two methods.[5] Our example assumes that A and B purchase life insurance contracts on each other, are the policy owners, premium payors, and beneficiaries.[6] Under current tax law, having A and B own the insurance and buy the deceased shareholder's interest at death creates the best tax result by providing for an increase in the survivor's cost basis equal to the purchase price.

UPON DEATH. For example, should A die first, his stock passes to his family or estate. At the same time, the insurance company pays a tax-free death benefit to B, as beneficiary of the contract insuring A's life. Pursuant to the agreement the following steps are implemented:

1st – The business has a *first option to purchase* A's stock.[7]

2nd – If the business does not exercise its option, or purchases less than all of A's stock, B has a *second option to purchase* A's stock.[8]

3rd – The business *is required to purchase* any of A's stock not previously purchased by either the business or B.[9]

Under the first and third steps the business could obtain funds for purchasing A's stock by borrowing the death proceeds received by B.[10] As with cross purchase and entity purchase agreements, the "wait and see" buy/sell agreement can also serve to help "peg," or establish, the value of the stock for estate tax purposes.[11]

Footnotes on page 189

DURING LIFETIME

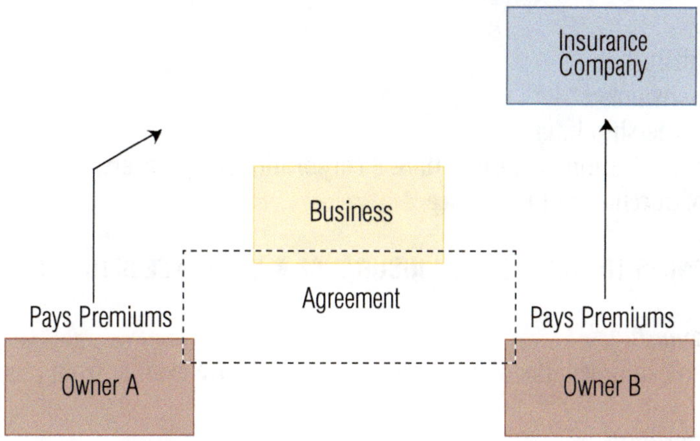

Each Owner Obtains Life Insurance On The Other

UPON DEATH

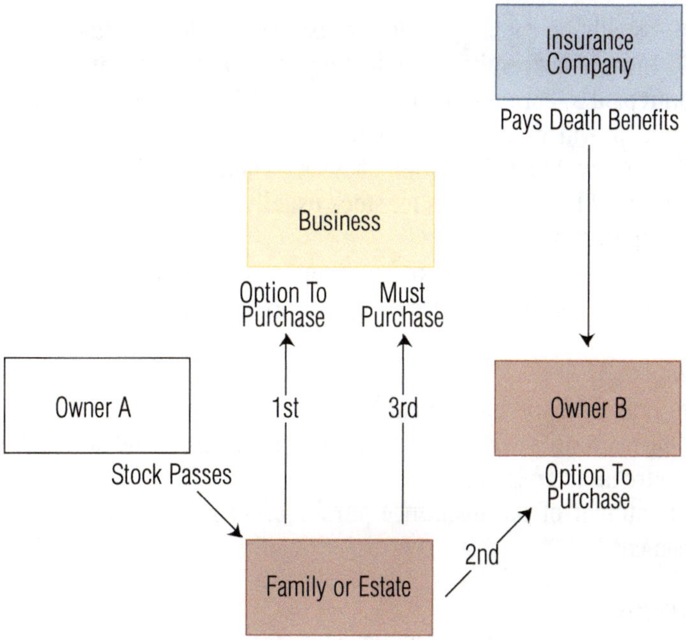

INFORMATION REQUIRED FOR ANALYSIS & PROPOSAL

1. Names of owners to be insured.
2. Sex.
3. Dates of birth.
4. Smoker/nonsmoker.
5. Value of ownership interests.
6. Form of organization (C corporation, S corporation, or partnership).
7. Identity of purchaser of insurance.

CROSS REFERENCES TO TAX FACTS ON INSURANCE & EMPLOYEE BENEFITS, VOL. 1 (2019)

Income Tax

Q 276. When death benefits of business life insurance are exempt from income tax.

Corporation

Q 263. Premiums paid on business life insurance not usually taxable to insured employee.

Q 264. Premiums paid by corporation on policies insuring the life of a stockholder or employee usually not deductible.

Q 268. Premiums paid by corporation to fund stock redemption not taxable to insured stockholder.

Q 298-Q 305. Usually no capital gain to deceased stockholder's estate.

Q 299-Q 307. Income tax results of funding agreement with life insurance.

Q 300. Amount paid by corporation for decedent's entire stock interest generally not dividend to estate, provided no attribution problems.

Q 301 and Q 302. Avoiding attribution of stock ownership.

Q 306. Amount paid by corporation for stock usually not taxable as constructive dividend to surviving stockholder(s).

Q 310. Taxation of payments when redemption by S corporation.

Q 316. Treatment of corporate owned life insurance for purpose of alternative minimum tax.

Partnership

Q 274. Premiums paid are not deductible.

Q 311. Income tax results when deceased partner's interest is sold or liquidated under a business purchase agreement.

Q 315. Tax treatment of life insurance purchased to fund partnership business purchase agreement.

Estate Tax

Q 321. Life insurance proceeds not directly included in insured owner's estate when partnership or corporation is owner and beneficiary.

Footnotes

[1] The "wait and see" buy/sell agreement is also referred to as the "option" or "flexible" buy/sell. The agreement is not appropriate when a corporation has only one stockholder, or with a sole proprietorship, since the corporation cannot own itself and the sole proprietorship is not a separate entity that can make the purchase.

[2] It is also assumed that A and B are *not* related to each other. If they were, and the business were a corporation, then the attribution rules would have to be considered if there is a purchase of stock by the business under either the 1st or 3rd step (attribution is more fully explained on pages 218-223).

[3] Various means can be used in the agreement to determine the purchase price. A *fixed price* could be established, with a further provision providing for periodic review and redetermination between the business and the owners. Alternatively, a *formula method* could be used, under which specific factors would be employed to calculate a value. For an example of a *capitalization formula*, see the Business Valuation chart on page 167. Another approach to determining a price is to provide for an *appraisal* at the time of sale (i.e., after the first owner's death, or earlier if a lifetime sale is contemplated).

[4] If the agreement is binding upon disability as well as death, consideration should also be given to funding the agreement with disability buy-out insurance. Such coverage will generally provide a lump-sum payment after a stated period of total and permanent disability. The premiums are nondeductible and the benefits are received free of income taxes. An expanded discussion of disability buy-out insurance is on page 342-343.

[5] No matter which method is chosen, to assure the death proceeds are received free of income taxes, appropriate notice and consents should be obtained (see Company Owned Life Insurance (COLI), pages 319-321).

[6] Funding of the life insurance owned by A and B could be accomplished with split-dollar (chart, page 245) or executive equity (chart, page 233). Having the stockholders as owners and beneficiaries of the policies avoids any potential corporate alternative minimum tax problem, as discussed on pages 327-329. This also allows the survivor to obtain a stepped-up basis by purchasing some or all of the deceased's stock at the 2nd step (i.e., a cross purchase agreement). The survivor would not have received an increased cost basis if the corporation purchases all of the deceased's stock at the 1st step (i.e., an entity purchase agreement).

[7] Typically the corporation would have from 30 to 90 days to exercise its option at the 1st step. If the corporation purchases all of A's stock the result would be an entity purchase agreement (chart, page 171).

[8] If the corporation does not purchase all of the stock at the 1st step, and B purchases all of A's stock at the 2nd step, the result is a cross purchase agreement (see chart, page 175). Typically B would have from 30 to 90 days to exercise his option. Note that it is important for the surviving stockholder to have an *option*, but not an *obligation*, to purchase stock at the 2nd step. If B had a legal obligation to purchase A's stock, and failed to do so, then the corporation's purchase of stock at the 3rd step would be treated as a dividend to B (i.e., the corporation would be considered as having discharged B's legal obligation).

[9] Note that despite the options involved in the 1st and 2nd steps, the mandatory purchase by the corporation in the 3rd step provides the *binding* agreement that assures A's stock will be sold for the benefit of his family (see footnote 11, below).

[10] Alternatively, the corporation could borrow funds from other sources, or B could make a capital contribution to the corporation, thereby increasing his cost basis in his stock. This also has the advantage of avoiding any problems with the corporate alternative minimum tax, which could occur if the corporation received the death proceeds (see pages 327-329).

[11] To help "peg" the value of the business for estate tax purposes, the parties must be required to sell during lifetime for the same price as provided for a sale at death. In addition, the agreement must specifically *bind* A's estate or family and further comply with the Chapter 14 requirements (see footnote 3, page 169).

KEY PERSON BUY-OUT AGREEMENT

The key person buy-out agreement is one means of providing for the complete disposition of a business interest.[1] Under this arrangement the owner agrees to sell all of his or her business interest to a key person.[2]

DURING LIFETIME. To illustrate how this works, assume that we have a corporation owned by A. A would enter into an agreement providing for the sale to B, a key person in the business. Typically, this agreement is *binding* and obligates both parties, or their representatives, upon the death, disability, or retirement of A.

Rather than trying to accumulate or borrow sufficient funds to buy A's interest, B obtains a life insurance contract insuring A. B applies for this coverage, pays the premiums, and is both owner and beneficiary of the contract.[3] By this means, B can use life insurance to *fully* fund his obligation to A.[4]

UPON DEATH. Assuming that A dies first, his or her stock would then pass to his or her family or estate. At the same time, the insurance company pays a death benefit to B, as beneficiary of the contract insuring A's life. B receives these funds free of all income taxes, since they are received as the death benefit of a life insurance contract.[5]

Pursuant to the agreement, A's family, or estate, transfers A's stock interest in the business to B, in return for which B pays the cash received from the insurance company.

The fully funded agreement will *assure* that A's surviving family receives a fair price for his interest in the business. But such an agreement can also serve another very important function. If the estate had been subject to estate taxes, it is possible that extensive negotiations and even litigation could result if the estate tax value of the business had been left to chance. These problems of delay and litigation can be avoided by having an agreement that helps establish, or "peg," the value of the stock.[6]

Footnotes on page 193

DURING LIFETIME

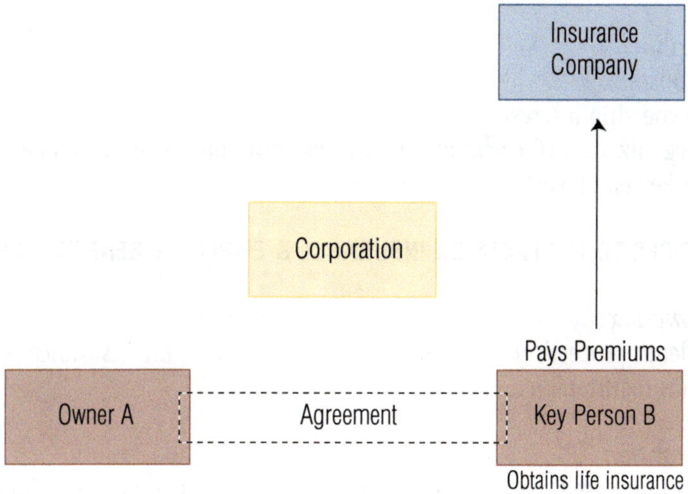

UPON DEATH

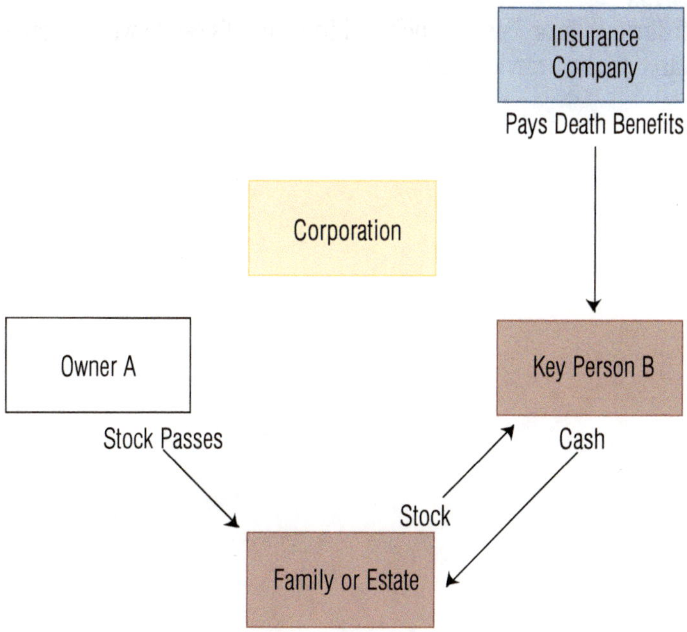

INFORMATION REQUIRED FOR ANALYSIS & PROPOSAL

1. Name of owner to be insured.
2. Sex.
3. Date of birth.
4. Smoker/nonsmoker.
5. Value of ownership interest.
6. Form of organization (C corporation, S corporation, partnership, or sole proprietorship).
7. Identity of key employee.

CROSS REFERENCES TO TAX FACTS ON INSURANCE & EMPLOYEE BENEFITS, VOL. 1 (2019)

Income Tax

Q 65. For death proceeds to be excludable from income, a life insurance policy must meet certain requirements.

Corporation

Q 298. Sale of deceased's stock will usually not result in income tax liability to deceased's estate.

Q 299. Income tax effects of funding stock purchase agreement with life insurance.

Estate Tax

Q 320. Life insurance proceeds not included in insured's estate when partners or stockholders purchase insurance on lives of each other.

Footnotes

1 Such an agreement can be used with a corporation, a partnership, or a sole proprietorship. Since the key employee has no ownership interest, unlike the cross purchase agreement on page 175, there are no reciprocal obligations to buy and sell. The owner is merely obligated to sell and the key employee obligated to buy.

2 Various means can be used in the agreement to determine a purchase price. A *fixed price* could be established, with a further provision providing for periodic review and redetermination by mutual agreement among the owners. Alternatively, a *formula method* could be employed, under which specific factors would be used to calculate a value. For an example of a *capitalization* formula, refer to the valuation chart on page 167. Another approach to determining a price is to provide for an *appraisal* at the time of sale (i.e., after the owner's death, or earlier if a lifetime sale is contemplated).

3 In a family-owned business it is possible that the reach of the attribution rules under Code section 101(j) *might* treat this policy as "employer-owned." This would subject the death benefit to income taxation. To assure the proceeds are received free of income taxes, appropriate notice and consent should be obtained (see Company Owned Life Insurance (COLI) pages 319-321).

4 When the obligation is not fully funded, borrowing as an alternative to life insurance is usually unattractive, as can be appreciated. Although the premiums paid for this coverage are not tax-deductible, a split-dollar plan could be used to assist B in purchasing the life insurance (chart, page 245). As an alternative, consider Executive Equity (chart, page 233).

5 Receipt of the death proceeds allows B to purchase A's business interest *and* obtain an income tax cost basis equal to the purchase price. Assume that A originally paid $100,000 for the stock interest that is now worth $750,000. If A dies and B purchases A's stock under a key person buy-out agreement, B's basis in the stock would be equal to the $750,000 purchase price. B's gain on a later sale of the stock would be equal to the amount by which the sales price exceeds $750,000.

6 To help "peg" the value, A must be required to sell during lifetime for the same price as provided for a sale at death. In addition, the agreement must specifically *bind* A's estate or family and further comply with the Chapter 14 requirements (see footnote 3, page 169 and pages 371-372). The table of Contested Business Valuations on pages 193-198 provides specific examples of what happens when there is a failure to properly "peg" the value of stock in a closely held corporation.

PARTIAL STOCK REDEMPTION

A partial stock redemption under Section 303 offers a very attractive way of paying estate settlement costs, particularly for a corporation that will be continued by the surviving family.[1]

Under most circumstances, a stockholder who has the corporation redeem less than his entire stock interest will be fully taxed on the proceeds as ordinary income. However, under the special provisions of Section 303, his surviving family can do after death what the stockholder generally cannot do during his lifetime . . . namely, sell only a *portion* of his stock interest to the corporation, and have the sale treated as a capital transaction rather than as a dividend.

DURING LIFETIME. If the stock interest will be *more than* 35 percent of the stockholder's adjusted gross estate, then his stock will qualify under Section 303 for a partial redemption at his death.[2] The *amount* of stock which can be purchased is limited to the sum of all federal and state death taxes, funeral, and administrative expenses. The purchase must also be made from whoever has the obligation to pay these costs, usually the family or estate.[3]

Since few corporations can be expected to accumulate sufficient cash for such a purchase, typically the corporation obtains a life insurance contract insuring the stockholder in his capacity as an employee. The corporation pays the premiums and is both owner and beneficiary of the contract.[4] This is generally a much better solution to the funding problem than attempting to accumulate large cash reserves over a period of time, borrowing at high interest rates, or selling corporate assets.[5]

UPON DEATH, the stock passes to the family or estate. At the same time, the insurance company pays a death benefit to the corporation.[6] This money is usually received free of all income taxes.[7] The corporation can then use the cash to purchase *some* of the stock from the family or estate.

The tax-favored treatment under Section 303 has been made available to the family-owned corporation in order to protect it from being sold or liquidated to pay death taxes and other estate settlement costs. When a corporate interest is the bulk of an estate, it only makes sense to use corporate dollars to provide the necessary cash to pay these costs.[8]

Footnotes on page 197

DURING LIFETIME

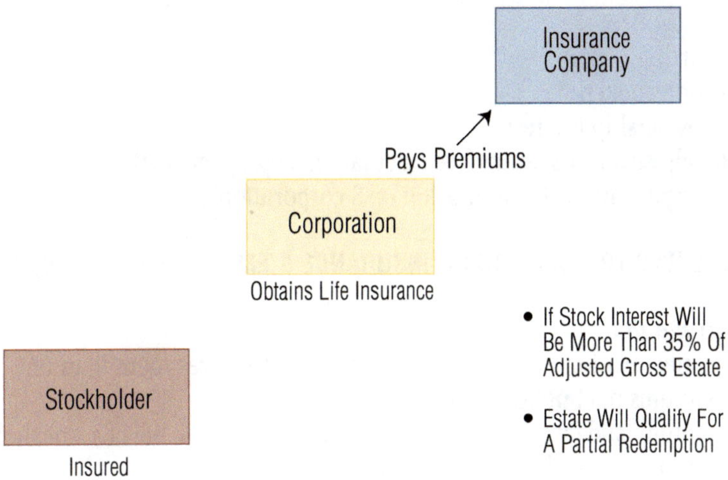

UPON DEATH

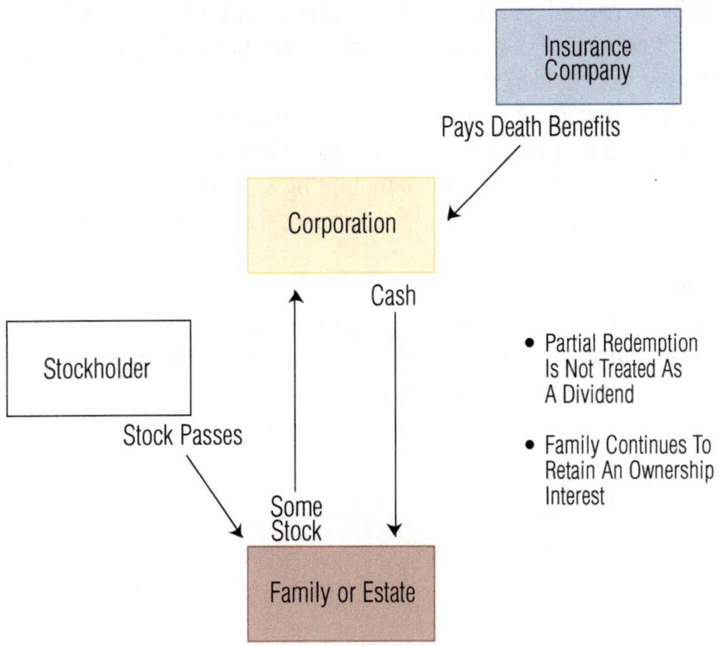

INFORMATION REQUIRED FOR ANALYSIS & PROPOSAL

1. Name of owner to be insured.
2. Sex.
3. Date of birth.
4. Smoker/nonsmoker.
5. Value of ownership interest.
6. Value of adjusted gross estate (see calculation steps, page 584).
7. Form of organization (C corporation *or* S corporation).

CROSS REFERENCES TO TAX FACTS ON INSURANCE & EMPLOYEE BENEFITS, VOL. 1 (2019)

Income Tax

Q 143. Income taxation of life insurance policy that insures more than one life.
Q 262. Premiums paid not deductible.
Q 264. Premium paid by corporation on policies insuring the life of a stockholder or employee usually not deductible as business expense.
Q 268. Premium paid by corporation to fund stock redemption not taxable to insured stockholder.
Q 276. When death benefits of business life insurance are exempt from income tax.
Q 303. Requirements for a Section 303 stock redemption.
Q 305. Usually no capital gain to deceased stockholder's estate caused by a redemption.
Q 306. Amount paid by corporation for stock usually not taxable as constructive dividend to surviving stockholder(s).
Q 307. Income tax results of funding stock redemption agreement with life insurance.
Q 308. Accumulated earnings tax and purchase of business life insurance.
Q 310. Taxation of payments when redemption by S corporation.
Q 316. Treatment of corporate owned life insurance for purposes of alternative minimum tax.

Estate Tax

Q 199. Estate taxation of life insurance policy that insures more than one life.
Q 321. Life insurance proceeds not directly included in insured stockholder's estate when corporation is owner and beneficiary.

Footnotes

[1] Partial stock redemptions are also referred to as "Section 303 Redemptions." Code section 303 authorizes a redemption of less than the entire stock interest of the decedent to be treated as a *sale* of stock, as opposed to a *dividend*. Because of the step-up in basis at death, a sale of stock will generally result in little, if any, taxable gain, since under a capital transaction the seller is not taxed on the basis of the property sold. In contrast, a dividend would be fully taxable as ordinary income (see Stepped-Up Basis, on page 556).

[2] The adjusted gross estate is determined by subtracting debts, funeral, and administrative expenses from the gross estate. This requirement provides you with the opportunity to conduct an estate analysis involving a full review of a client's assets. Without this information, it is not possible to determine whether an estate would qualify for a partial stock redemption (see page 12). If a client has more than one corporation, the stock of two or more corporations may be combined to meet the 35 percent test, provided the stockholder owns 20 percent or more of the value of each corporation, and the stock of the corporation is included in his gross estate. Even though an estate may *presently* be expected to qualify for a partial stock redemption, it is important to monitor estate assets to assure that there is not a subsequent disqualification. For example, the corporate stock could become 35 percent or less of the adjusted gross estate if: (1) other estate assets appreciate more than the stock interests; (2) the stock interests decline in value; (3) stock is either sold or given away.

[3] The redemption can be made only by that party having liability for the federal and state death taxes, funeral, and administrative expenses. It must usually be made within 3 years and 90 days after the estate tax return is filed (the estate tax return must be filed within 9 months after death). The effectiveness of a Section 303 redemption is limited when the unlimited marital deduction is used. See discussion on page 536.

[4] Employer-owned life insurance must meet strict notice and consent requirements if the death benefits are to be received free of income taxes (see Company Owned Life Insurance (COLI), pages 319-321).

[5] It is questionable whether many corporations could accumulate sufficiently large cash reserves for effective partial stock redemptions without running afoul of the prohibition against the unreasonable accumulation of earnings (see Accumulated Earnings Tax on page 294). With the purchase of life insurance to fund a partial stock redemption, the corporation is in effect amortizing the cost of the redemption over the lifetime of the insured stockholder. The insurance carried is similar to key person insurance as shown in the chart on page 203. If the corporation is in a relatively low tax bracket, the required premium payments can be made with enhanced dollars. Another variation of insurance ownership and beneficiary designation is shown in the Reverse Section 303 stock redemption chart, on page 199. Funding a partial stock redemption with survivorship life insurance can be particularly attractive when the unlimited marital deduction is used at the first death, since it provides death proceeds at the second death, when the estate taxes can no longer be deferred.

[6] This death benefit will *increase* the value of the decedent's stock in his gross estate in proportion to the decedent's interest in the corporation. For example, if the decedent owned 100 percent of the stock, a $100,000 death benefit might increase the value of the stock in the estate by $100,000. However, if the decedent owned only 40 percent of the stock, a $100,000 death benefit might increase the value of the stock in the estate by only $40,000. It could always be argued that there was a loss of corporate value caused by the death of a key employee that offsets some or all of the increase in stock value.

[7] Under some circumstances a portion of annual cash value increases and death proceeds could be subject to the Corporate Alternative Minimum Tax, as discussed on pages 327-329.

[8] In this chart, only *some* stock is redeemed, whereas a redemption of *all* stock is referred to as a "Section 302(b)(3) redemption." Section 302(b)(3) is that section of the Code that enables the redemption, or sale to the corporation, of the *entire* stock interest of a stockholder to be treated as a *sale* of stock, as opposed to a *dividend*. The Entity Purchase Agreement chart, on page 171, explains the Section 302(b)(3) redemption. Unlike the entity purchase agreement, in a family held corporation a partial stock redemption does not cause potential attribution problems (see pages 218-223).

REVERSE SECTION 303

A reverse stock redemption under Section 303 offers a very attractive way of paying estate settlement costs by having an entity other than the corporation purchase insurance to fund the redemption.[1]

DURING LIFETIME. If the stock interest will be *more than* 35 percent of the stockholder's adjusted gross estate, then his stock will qualify under Section 303 for a partial redemption at his death.[2] The *amount* of stock that can be purchased is limited to the sum of all federal and state death taxes, funeral, and administrative expenses.[3] However, the purchase must be made from whoever has the obligation to pay these costs, usually the family or estate.

One way to implement a reverse Section 303 is for the stockholder to establish a life insurance trust.[4] A life insurance contract insuring the stockholder is then obtained by the trust.[5] The trust pays the premiums and is both owner and beneficiary of the contract.[6]

UPON DEATH. The stock passes to the family or estate. At the same time, the insurance company pays a death benefit to the trust, which is received free of all income taxes.[7] The trust then loans the money to the corporation, which uses it to purchase *some*, but not all, of the stock from the family or estate.

In repaying this loan the corporation can make tax-deductible interest payments to the trust. Although these interest payments would be taxable income to the trust, repayments of the loan principal would be received by the trust free of income taxes. By this means the family can continue to retain ownership and control of the corporation, while at the same time receiving, as trust beneficiaries, the benefits of the untaxed repayment of loan principal.

Of course, it is not necessary for a trust to be established. Anyone who has substantial funds can loan them to the corporation for the purpose of a partial stock redemption. For example, a son or daughter of the stockholder could be owner and beneficiary of life insurance contracts insuring the parent. After receipt of the death benefit, the proceeds could be loaned by the children to the corporation, which would then repay the loan together with interest.[8]

Footnotes on page 201

DURING LIFETIME

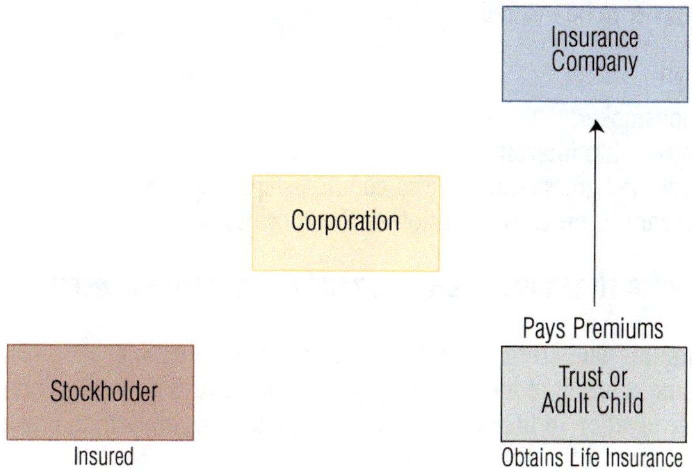

UPON DEATH

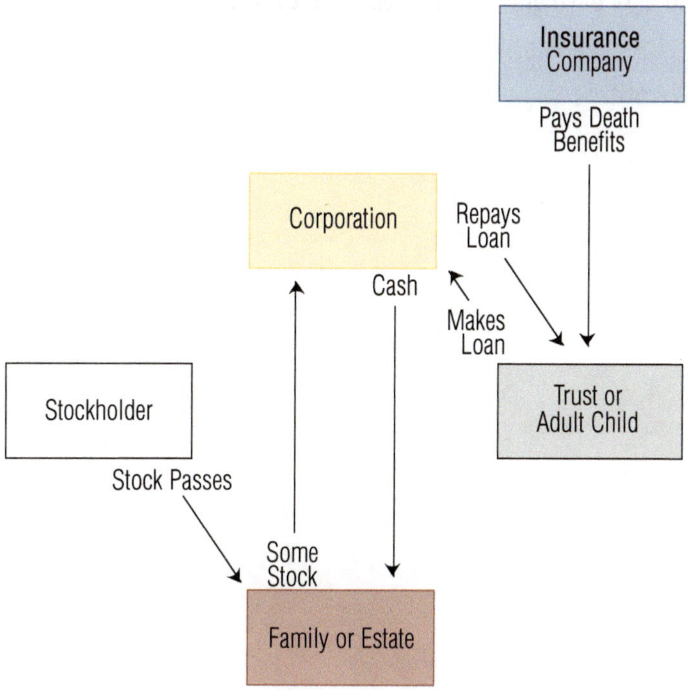

INFORMATION REQUIRED FOR ANALYSIS & PROPOSAL

1. Name of owner to be insured.
2. Sex.
3. Date of birth.
4. Smoker/nonsmoker.
5. Value of ownership interest.
6. Value of adjusted gross estate (see calculation steps, page 584).
7. Form of organization (C corporation *or* S corporation).

CROSS REFERENCES TO TAX FACTS ON INSURANCE & EMPLOYEE BENEFITS, VOL. 1 (2019)

Q 2. Premiums paid on life insurance generally not deductible.
Q 143. Income taxation of life insurance policy that insures more than one life.
Q 199. Estate taxation of life insurance policy that insures more than one life.
Q 303. Requirements for a Section 303 stock redemption.
Q 305. Usually no capital gain to deceased stockholder's estate.
Q 306. Amount paid by corporation for stock usually not taxable as constructive dividend to surviving stockholder(s).
Q 310. Taxation of payments when redemption by S corporation.

Footnotes

[1] Section 303 is that section of the Code that authorizes a redemption of less than the entire stock interest of the decedent to be treated as a *sale* of stock, as opposed to a *dividend*. Because of the step-up in basis at death, a sale of stock will generally result in little, if any, taxable gain, since under a capital transaction the seller is not taxed on the basis of the property sold. In contrast, a dividend would be fully taxable as ordinary income (see Stepped-Up Basis, on page 556).

[2] The adjusted gross estate is determined by subtracting debts, funeral, and administrative expenses from the gross estate. This requirement provides you with an opportunity for an estate analysis involving a full review of a client's assets (see page 12). Without this information, it is not possible to determine whether an estate will qualify for a partial stock redemption. If a client has more than one corporation, the stock of two or more corporations may be combined to meet the 35 percent test, provided the stockholder owns 20 percent or more of the value of each corporation, and the stock of the corporation is included in his gross estate. Even though an estate may *presently* be expected to qualify for a Section 303 redemption, it is important to monitor estate assets in order to assure that the estate continues to qualify. For example, the corporate stock could become 35 percent or less of the adjusted gross estate if: (1) other estate assets appreciate more than the stock interests; (2) the stock interests decline in value; (3) some of the stock is either sold or given away.

[3] The permanent reduction of the federal estate tax under the American Taxpayer Relief Act of 2012 (combined with the temporary doubling of the exemption under the 2017 Tax Act) reduced the utility of a Reverse Section 303.

[4] The details of establishing a life insurance trust are set forth in the chart on page 59.

[5] In a family-owned business it is possible that the reach of the attribution rules under Code section 101(j) *might* treat this policy as "employer-owned." This would subject the death benefit to income taxation. To assure the proceeds are received free of income taxes, appropriate notice and consent should be obtained (see Company Owned Life Insurance (COLI) pages 319-321). Funding a reverse Section 303 stock redemption with survivorship life insurance can be particularly attractive when the unlimited marital deduction is used at the first death, since it provides death proceeds at the second death, when the estate taxes can no longer be deferred. If survivorship life insurance is used, then appropriate notice and consents should be obtained from *both* insureds.

[6] Since premiums must come from after-tax dollars, having someone other than the corporation own the insurance contract and pay the premiums could take advantage of a lower tax bracket.

[7] Use of a reverse Section 303 may be advisable when there is a concern regarding the Corporate Alternative Minimum Tax (see pages 327-329). With the usual Section 303 redemption, as shown in the chart on page 195, the payment of the death benefit to the corporation exposes the corporation to the alternative minimum tax. With a reverse Section 303 redemption the death benefit is paid outside the corporation, meaning that there is no increase in adjusted current earnings, and thus no exposure to the alternative minimum tax.

[8] When the insurance is owned by and payable to either children or a trust, the reverse 303 technique avoids the problem of increasing the value of the deceased's taxable estate, as occurs when death proceeds are paid to a corporation under the usual Section 303 arrangement (see the chart on page 195, and footnote 6 on page 197).

KEY PERSON INSURANCE

Multipurpose key person insurance protects a business from the financial losses that can occur when a key employee dies. Such a key employee could be the owner of the business, or a non-owner employee whose very specialized abilities are critical to the operation of the business and difficult or costly to replace.[1] Adequate amounts of key person insurance are essential in any risk management program. A discussion of key-person valuation formulas can be found on page 203.

Since the existence of business debt "signals a need for insurance," key person insurance can function as a form of commercial loan protection, as well as provide needed funds when a business is to be continued, sold, or liquidated.[2]

DURING LIFETIME. This protection is provided by having the business obtain insurance on the life of the key employee.[3] As both owner and beneficiary of the contract, the business pays the premiums directly to the insurance company.[4] The contract's cash values are carried as a business asset, and are available as collateral for securing commercial loans, or for direct borrowing from the insurance company at generally favorable interest rates.[5]

Many guidelines are used in estimating the *dollar value* of a particular key employee. However, the value can be most easily estimated by using a factor of three to ten times the employee's salary. Other guidelines that have been employed involve either a determination of the employee's replacement cost, or an estimation of lost profits or credit.[6]

UPON DEATH of the key employee the insurance company pays the death benefit directly to the business. The funds are treated as an addition to surplus and are received free of any direct income taxes.[7]

The proceeds can then be used for various purposes. Should it be determined that the business will be *continued*, these can be used to obtain a qualified replacement, replace lost profits, protect its credit position, provide a financial cushion, fund a partial stock redemption or make survivor income payments. If the business is to be *sold*, then there is money available to fund a full stock redemption. In case of *liquidation*, the cash will benefit the surviving family by offsetting lost business value.[8]

Footnotes on page 205

KEY PERSON VALUATION FORMULAS

No single formula is accepted for valuing a key person or employee. In fact, valuing a key person is much like valuing a business, it is more art than science. Much depends upon the characteristics of the key person (e.g., a sales manager who has a substantial impact upon sales or a financial officer who has access to credit). However, there is little doubt that key persons can have considerable value; and their death or disability can cause substantial financial losses, or even failure of a business. One or more of the following formulas should provide a useful starting point for determining value.

Contribution To Profits. This method evaluates the key person's contributions to profits and then capitalizes this amount to determine value. For example, assume the business has a book value of $500,000, an expected rate of return on book value for this particular type of business is 8 percent and average profits are $120,000. The excess earnings are $80,000 ($500,000 × .08 = $40,000; $120,000 – $40,000 = $80,000). Assuming the key person's contribution to excess earnings is 50 percent, capitalization of the key person's contribution at 12 percent yields a value of $333,200 (.50 × $80,000 = $40,000; 100 ÷ 12 = 8.33 × $40,000 = $333,200). Note that a similar capitalization approach to valuing a business is discussed on page 166. A variation on the contributions to profits method does not capitalize the contribution, but rather reduces the key person's annual contribution as a replacement is recruited, trained, and becomes fully effective. Using this variation, the key person's value would be $120,000, assuming annual contributions to profits of $40,000 and 5 years to complete the replacement. The basic method and the variation are calculated as follows:

		Variation	
Average Profits	$120,000		
Book Value At 8%	40,000	Year 1	$40,000
Excess Earnings	$80,000	Year 2	32,000
Percent Of Contribution	.50	Year 3	24,000
Key Person's Contribution	$40,000	Year 4	16,000
Capitalization Factor	8.33	Year 5	8,000
Key Person Value	$333,200	Key Person Value	$120,000

Business Life Value. This is a variation of the method commonly used to determine human life value. The business estimates its annual loss of earnings if the key person were to die, multiplies that amount by the number of working years to retirement, and then discounts the results by an appropriate interest rate. Assuming annual loss of earnings of $40,000, 15 years to retirement, and 12 percent interest, the value would be calculated as follows:

Loss Of Earnings	$40,000	
Present Value Factor	6.811	(from table on page 620)
Key Person Value	$272,440	

Multiple Of Salary. This method recognizes that the salaries paid to key persons are an indication of their value. Typically a factor of from 3 to 10 times annual salary is used. Assuming an annual salary of $75,000 and a factor of 5, the value would be calculated as follows:

Annual Salary	$75,000
Factor	5
Key Person Value	$375,000

Discount Of Business. This method simply discounts the value of the business to reflect the loss of the key person. Assuming a business value of $900,000 and a discount of 20 percent, the value would be calculated as follows:

Value Of Business	$900,000
Discount	.20
Key Person Value	$180,000

INFORMATION REQUIRED FOR ANALYSIS & PROPOSAL

1. Name of employee.
2. Sex.
3. Date of birth.
4. Smoker/nonsmoker.

To Determine Amount of Coverage

5. Salary of employee.
6. Position of employee in business.

CROSS REFERENCES TO TAX FACTS ON INSURANCE & EMPLOYEE BENEFITS, VOL. 1 (2019)

General Rules

Q 3. Deduction of interest on indebtedness incurred to purchase or carry life insurance contract.
Q 13. Taxation of distributions from policies classified as modified endowment contracts.
Q 29. Taxability of policy loans.
Q 30. Deduction of interest on policy loans.
Q 262. Premiums paid usually not deductible as business expense.
Q 263. Premiums paid usually not taxable to insured employee.

Corporation

Q 228. Tax consequences of attaching disability income rider to key person life insurance policy.
Q 264. Premiums paid by corporation on policies insuring the life of a stockholder or employee usually not deductible as business expense.
Q 267. Premiums paid by corporation not taxable to insured employee.
Q 316. Treatment of corporate owned life insurance for purposes of alternative minimum tax.

Partnership

Q 274. Premiums paid by partnership are not deductible.

Estate Tax

Q 304. Life insurance payable to partnership generally not includible in insured partner's estate (but included as part of partnership interest).
Q 305. Life insurance payable to corporation generally not includible in insured's estate, provided insured had no "incidents of ownership" in policy (but included in valuing corporate stock).

Footnotes

[1] The classic statement regarding the need for key person insurance was made by the U.S. Court of Appeals, 3rd Circuit (1951), in the case of *The Emeloid Co., Inc. v. Commissioner*:

> "What corporate purpose could be more essential then key [person] insurance? The business that insures its buildings and machinery and automobiles from every possible hazard can hardly be expected to exercise less care in protecting itself against the loss of two of its most vital assets – managerial skill and experience."

[2] Key person insurance can also be thought of as a "line of credit." As such, it will assure that money is available when needed, without any repayment of the debt, i.e., a forgiveness of the "loan." Relying on borrowed funds may be ill advised.

[3] Employer-owned life insurance must meet strict notice and consent requirements if the death benefits are to be received free of income taxes (see Company Owned Life Insurance (COLI), pages 319-321).

[4] The "cost" of key person insurance is sometimes measured as the difference between the premium paid and the cash value increase. This view tends to argue in favor of permanent insurance with cash values, as opposed to term insurance with no cash values (but such an approach ignores the time value of money, as discussed in Interest Adjusted Net Cost on page 408). It should also be recognized that the cash values of permanent insurance, carried for a bona fide business purpose, are not subject to the unreasonable accumulation of earnings tax. An expanded discussion of this subject is contained on page 294. If cash values are borrowed, it would be to the business's advantage to be sure it could deduct interest paid on the borrowed funds (see Minimum Deposit Insurance, on page 467). If borrowing of cash values is contemplated, then it is important to avoid having the policy classified as a Modified Endowment Contract (see expanded discussion on pages 423-424).

[5] Under some circumstances a portion of annual cash value increases and death proceeds could be subject to the Corporate Alternative Minimum Tax, as discussed on pages 327-329. However, this problem is not present in an S corporation, since it is not subject to the alternative minimum tax adjusted current earnings adjustment. In fact, key person insurance in an S corporation may be particularly attractive in view of the opportunity to make tax-free withdrawals of the death proceeds where the S corporation has no accumulated earnings and profits (see S Corporation, pages 531-533). With a C corporation the alternative minimum tax problem can be avoided by using the Reverse Key Person Insurance technique (see chart, page 207).

[6] See the discussion on page 203 for various formulas used to value a key person. No matter which approach is used, valuation of a key person is much like valuation of a business, the process may be more art than science.

[7] An explanation and illustration of proper accounting entries for policy premiums and values is set forth in Accounting For Business Life Insurance on pages 292-293.

[8] Whether a business is likely to be continued, sold, or liquidated upon the death of a key employee, will depend upon answers to the questions set forth in the Disposition Of A Business Interest chart on page 163.

REVERSE KEY PERSON INSURANCE

Reverse key person insurance offers an alternative means of providing key employee insurance by having someone other than the business purchase insurance on the life of the key employee. It was considered particularly useful with C corporations, where the corporate alternative minimum tax ("AMT") could previously reduce by up to 15 percent the death benefit received by the corporation.[1] However, the 2017 Tax Act eliminated the corporate AMT, reduced the top marginal income tax rate to 21 percent, and significantly reduced the federal estate tax.[2]

DURING LIFETIME. Such a program can be established by having the trustee of an irrevocable life insurance trust purchase insurance on the key employee.[3] As both owner and beneficiary of the contract, the trustee pays the premiums directly to the insurance company.[4]

Many guidelines are used in estimating the dollar value of a particular key employee. However, the value can be most easily estimated by using a factor of three to ten times the employee's salary. Other guidelines that have been employed involve either a determination of the employee's replacement cost, or an estimation of lost profits or credit.

UPON DEATH of the key employee the insurance company pays the death benefit directly to the trustee of the trust.[5] The proceeds are received free of income taxes as the death benefit of a life insurance contract.

The funds can then be loaned by the trustee to the corporation.[6] In repaying this loan the corporation makes tax-deductible interest payments to the trust.[7] Although these interest payments are taxable income to the trust, repayments of the loan principal are received by the trust free of income taxes.

Of course, it is not necessary for a trust to be established. Anyone who has the funds can loan them to the corporation for the purpose of key person insurance. For example, an adult child could be the owner and beneficiary of a life insurance contract insuring his parent. After receipt of the death benefit, the child could loan the proceeds to the corporation, which would then repay the loan together with interest.[8]

Footnotes on page 209

DURING LIFETIME

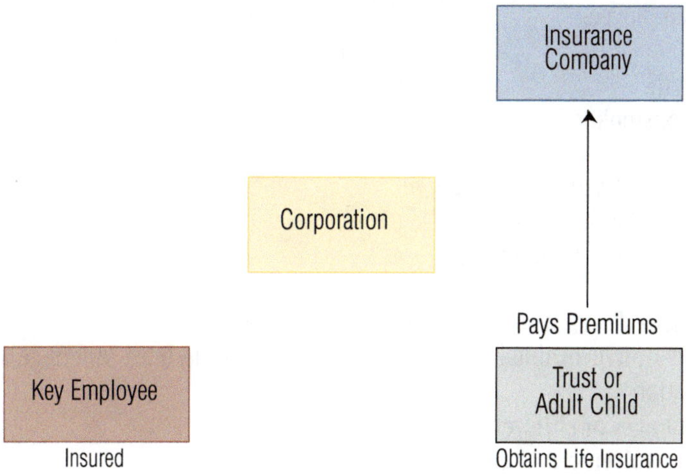

UPON DEATH

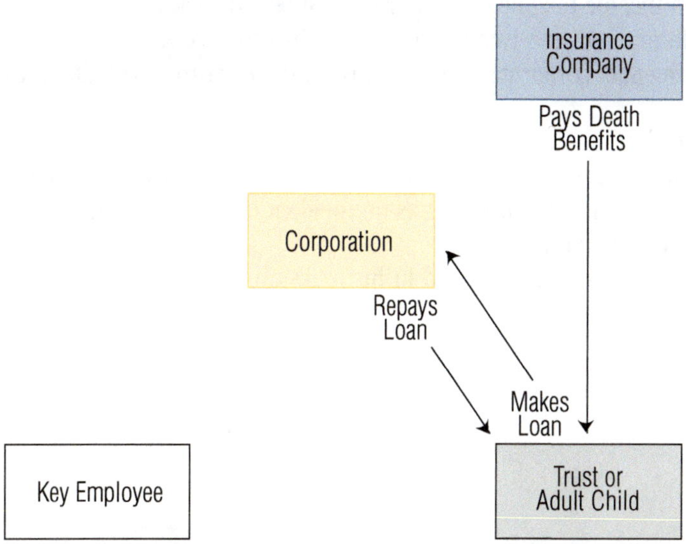

INFORMATION REQUIRED FOR ANALYSIS & PROPOSAL

1. Name of employee.
2. Sex.
3. Date of birth.
4. Smoker/nonsmoker.

To Determine Amount of Coverage

5. Salary of employee.
6. Position of employee in business.

To Determine Party Who Will Own Insurance Contract

7. Availability of irrevocable life insurance trust (including trust language authorizing loan to corporation).
8. Names and ages of children.
9. Degree of involvement of children in business.

CROSS REFERENCES TO TAX FACTS ON INSURANCE & EMPLOYEE BENEFITS, VOL. 1 (2019)

Income Tax

Q 150. When income taxable to trust or to trust beneficiaries.
Q 153. Death proceeds received by trust free of income taxes.
Q 316. Treatment of corporate owned life insurance for purposes of alternative minimum tax.

Estate Tax

Q 80. Circumstances under which life insurance proceeds are includable in insured's gross estate even though insured has no incident of ownership in policy and proceeds are not payable to estate.
Q 182. Insurance proceeds included in insured's estate when trustee *required* to pay estate debts and taxes.

Footnotes

[1] This reduction is only likely with a C corporation; there is no exposure with an S corporation or a partnership. With Key Person Insurance, as shown in the chart on page 203, the death benefit paid to a C corporation is included in adjusted current earnings as part of the alternative minimum tax calculations. The larger the death benefit relative to anticipated corporate earnings, the greater the likelihood that the corporate alternative minimum tax will reduce the death benefit. Alternatively, the smaller the death benefit relative to anticipated corporate earnings, the lesser the likelihood of a reduction in death benefits on account of the alternative minimum tax. A more detailed explanation of the Corporate Alternative Minimum Tax is contained on pages 327-329. The table on page 329 provides examples of the relationship between the amount of the death benefit and anticipated corporate earnings.

[2] When the insurance is owned by and payable to either a trust or an adult child, the Reverse Key Person Insurance technique also avoids the problem of increasing the value of the deceased's estate, as can occur when death proceeds are paid to a corporation under the typical Key Person Insurance arrangement (see the chart on page 203, and footnote 6 on page 197). In this regard, note the similarity between Reverse Key Person Insurance and Reverse Section 303 (see chart, page 199). Although the estate tax is much less a problem today as a result of recent tax changes, the estate tax is still a concern for the most affluent taxpayers.

[3] In a family-owned business it is possible that the reach of the attribution rules under Code section 101(j) *might* treat this policy as "employer-owned." This would subject the death benefit to income taxation. To assure the proceeds are received free of income taxes, appropriate notice and consent should be obtained (see Company Owned Life Insurance (COLI) pages 319-321).

[4] The details of establishing and administering an irrevocable life insurance trust are set forth on pages 54-57.

[5] When considering Reverse Key Person Insurance it is important to determine how the premiums will be paid. With Key Person Insurance the premium is an obligation of the corporation as owner of the insurance contract. In contrast, with *Reverse* Key Person Insurance the contract is owned by a trustee, or an adult child, who has the obligation to make the premium payments. Corporate funds could be used to assist in paying the premiums using either Executive Equity, chart page 233, or Split-Dollar Insurance, chart page 241.

[6] The trustee must have authority (preferably in the trust agreement – or otherwise under applicable state law) to make a loan to the corporation. Although many irrevocable life insurance trusts will give the trustee broad authority to purchase assets and make loans to the estate and others, it would be prudent to give the trustee specific authority to make loans at prevailing interest rates to the corporation. However, the trust language *should not* require the trustee to make such loans, as this would likely cause the death proceeds to be included in the insured's estate. Although the trustee cannot be required to make the loan, preserving the family business for the trust beneficiaries would likely motivate the trustee to make the loan, particularly if the trustee was also responsible for maintaining and preserving the business (see footnote 6, page 57).

[7] Interest payments are deductible by the corporation but taxable to the trust unless the trust is taxed as a grantor trust or payments are distributed and taxed to the trust beneficiaries. On the other hand, creation of a debt from the corporation to the trustee, or an adult child, offers the advantage of being able to subsequently withdraw the loan principal from the corporation free of income taxes. This is similar to the same advantage offered by the Reverse Section 303 (see chart, page 199).

[8] Because it is not possible to obligate the adult child to loan the death proceeds to the corporation, it is extremely important to be sure the child will be highly motivated to make such a loan (e.g., the child is the "heir apparent" to the business and would suffer financially should the corporation fail to continue operations).

FAMILY LIMITED PARTNERSHIP

The family limited partnership (FLP) is a valuable planning technique offering numerous advantages to the owners of a closely held business.[1] With this technique, business interests and other assets can be transferred to family members at reduced values while maintaining indirect yet effective control.[2]

ESTABLISHING PARTNERSHIP. The FLP is established by an agreement setting forth the partnership's operating rules and the filing of a certificate of limited partnership with state authorities.[3] The typical FLP agreement places restrictions and limitations on ownership of partnership interests, and cannot be changed or terminated for a specified number of years without the concurrence of all partners.[4]

Once the agreement is drawn, the parents then contribute assets to the FLP, which in turn issues both *general* and *limited* partnership interests.[5] Thereafter, the parents make gifts of the limited partnership interests to their children. These gifts can be structured to fall within the gift tax annual exclusion, or the $5,000,000 ($5,600,000 as indexed in 2018 and temporarily doubled to $11,200,000 by the 2017 Tax Act) estate tax exclusion amount and used to immediately transfer large amounts of limited partnership interests.[6]

ADVANTAGES OF PARTNERSHIP. The principal advantages of the FLP are both *control* and *flexibility*.[7] As general partners, the parents have complete power and authority to manage the partnership.[8] As limited partners, the children have no say in the management of the partnership, no liability for partnership debts, and a priority over the general partners in the event of a liquidation.

Income can be shifted to children in lower income tax brackets.[9] Periodic gifts of limited partnership interests can reduce the parent's taxable estate.[10] Gifts of limited partnership interests are subject to valuation discounts for both minority interests and lack of marketability. Such valuation discounts, which can often range up to 30 percent and more, offer the opportunity to "leverage" these tax-free gifts.[11] Even for those families without federal or state transfer tax concerns, an FLP allows gifts to be made of assets that are otherwise not easily divisible (e.g., the family farm). Transferring real estate located in another state to the partnership can avoid ancillary probate.

Because the children cannot transfer their limited partnership interests without the consent of all other partners, partnership assets are protected from claims against the individual partners (including those arising out of a divorce). Although creditors might succeed in obtaining a right to partnership distributions, the general partners have the power to withhold distributions by retaining income within the partnership.[12]

Footnotes on page 213

ESTABLISHING PARTNERSHIP

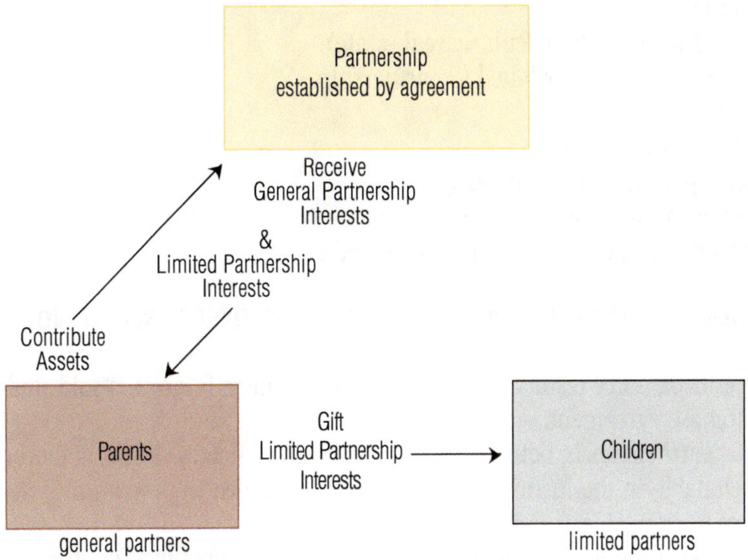

ADVANTAGES OF PARTNERSHIP

Control and Flexibility

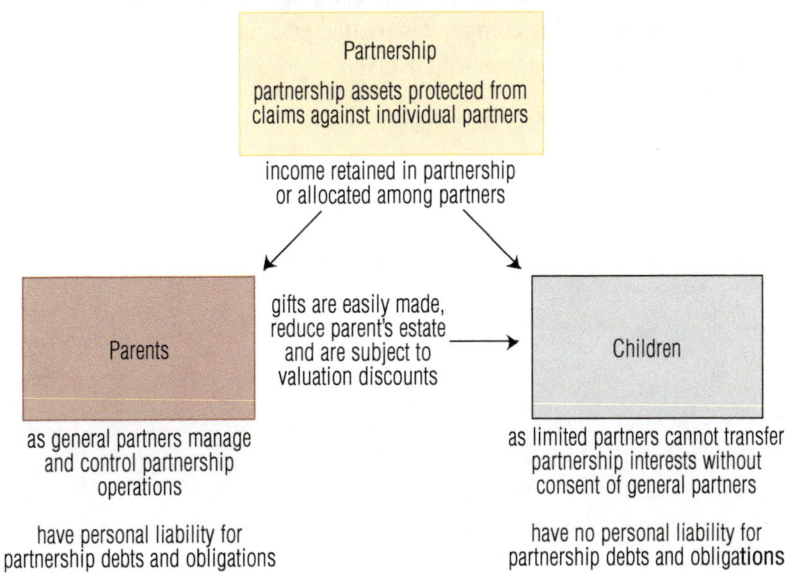

INFORMATION REQUIRED FOR ANALYSIS & PROPOSAL

1. Nature of family business.
2. Other assets in estate (particularly real estate).
3. Value of assets to be contributed to partnership.
4. Marital status.
5. Names and ages of donee(s).
6. Relationship of donee(s) to donor(s).
7. Attitude toward making gifts to family members.
8. Prior gifts made and prior use of unified credit.

CROSS REFERENCE TO TAX FACTS ON INSURANCE & EMPLOYEE BENEFITS, VOL. 1 (2019)

Q 311. The income tax results when a deceased partner's interest is sold under a business purchase agreement.

Q 318. If a partnership is both policy owner and beneficiary, insurance proceeds are not includable in the insured's estate (but are included in determining the value of the deceased's partnership interest).

Q 320. Proceeds from a policy purchased by a partner on the life of another partner to fund a cross purchase agreement are not included in the insured partner's gross estate.

Q 321. Proceeds from a policy purchased by a partnership on the life of a partner to fund the purchase of the insured partner's interest are not included in the insured's gross estate.

Q 322-Q 323. How a closely held business interest is valued for federal estate tax purposes.

Q 802. When a limited liability company is treated as a partnership.

Q 803. How the income of a partnership is taxed.

Footnotes

[1] Partnerships are also used as an alternative to the irrevocable life insurance trust and to avoid transfer for value rules, but the latter use is sometimes considered aggressive (see page 483).

[2] Although the family limited partnership is an innovative use of existing laws regarding limited partnerships, it should always be established for legitimate business and non-tax estate planning purposes.

[3] The principal requirements for a family limited partnership are: (1) capital must be a material income-producing factor, meaning that a personal service business where income consists primarily of fees or commissions would not qualify for operation as a family limited partnership (i.e., lawyer, doctor, photographer, plumber, etc.); (2) if the partnership has been created by gift, the donor (parent) must be given a reasonable salary for services rendered to the partnership before profits can be allocated among the partners (the concept of "gift" also includes intra-family sales); (3) profits of the partnership must be allocated, or divided, in proportion to each partner's capital investment; and (4) all partners must actually own a "capital interest" (i.e., an interest in partnership assets which is distributable to the partner upon his withdrawal from the partnership or upon partnership liquidation).

[4] Generally, the partnership agreement will limit ownership of partnership interests to family members. The agreement is also likely to contain provisions for settling disputes.

[5] Transfer of assets to the partnership is generally done without recognition of either gain or loss. Alternatively, the parents could make a gift of assets to the children who will then contribute these assets to the family limited partnership in return for limited partnership interests.

[6] Often the ultimate goal is for the parents to eventually own only modest partnership interests, with the bulk of the family limited partnership being held by other family members. Although this example assumes that both parents will be general partners, family limited partnerships are often established with only one spouse as the general partner and the other spouse as a limited partner.

[7] Some disadvantages of the family limited partnership include: (1) the traditional partnership freeze is subject to the impact of the Chapter 14 valuation rules, see pages 371-372 (however, most of the techniques used to reduce the effect of, or to avoid, these rules with respect to recapitalizations will also work with partnerships); (2) much of the ability to reduce taxes by shifting income from parent to younger children has been curtailed by the "kiddie tax" (see discussion on page 575); (3) there are additional expenses associated with establishing and accounting for a FLP (e.g., an information tax return must be filed); (4) gifts do not receive a step-up in income tax basis; and (5) retained partnership interests continue to appreciate in the parent's estate until they are transferred during lifetime or at death.

[8] The general partners also have liability for all partnership debts and obligations.

[9] Effective income shifting requires that the partnership be one in which capital is a material income-producing factor (see also item (2) in footnote 7, above).

[10] These gifts could be made in trust for minor children (see page 571).

[11] Lack of marketability can be established by prohibitions in the partnership agreement against terminating the partnership without the concurrence of all partners (usually limited to 40 years or less). Although valuation discounts of up to 70 percent have been claimed, such overly aggressive discounts are likely to be challenged by the IRS.

[12] The right to partnership distributions is secured by obtaining a charging order. However, because the general partners have the ability to retain profits, the flow-through nature of partnership income taxation gives them the ability to create a tax liability without making cash distributions for tax payments (i.e., an "ugly" asset).

RECAPITALIZATION

A recapitalization through a preferred stock recapitalization can offer an effective and versatile estate planning technique for corporate stockholders. For example, when combined with a subsequent gifting program, it can:

- Shift substantial future appreciation to children.
- Retain control of the corporation.
- Freeze the value of stock for estate tax purposes.
- Provide an ongoing income stream for retirement.
- Transfer corporate control when, and if, appropriate.
- Motivate younger employees.
- Facilitate distribution of stock at death.

PREFERRED STOCK RECAPITALIZATION. The design of stock to be received in a recapitalization can take many forms. For example, a parent might make a tax-free exchange of *all* his original common stock for a combination of voting cumulative preferred stock and nonvoting common stock.[1] Income would be provided by requiring annual dividends from the preferred stock at a fixed rate. The common stock will often receive appreciation while the preferred stock remains fixed in value.

The parent retains the voting preferred stock in order to maintain control of the corporation, and the nonvoting common stock is given to the children, or other donees. As long as the retained preferred stock is entitled to dividends, it will be considered to have a value generally equal to the present value of the right to future payments. Because the value of the common stock is determined by subtracting the value of the preferred stock from the total corporate value, the preferred stock's value has the effect of *decreasing* the value of the common stock, thereby lessening exposure to gift taxes when the common stock is given to the children.[2] However, in order to obtain this increase in value of the retained preferred stock it may be necessary to obligate the corporation to pay substantial cumulative preferred stock dividends.[3]

EFFECT OF SUBSEQUENT APPRECIATION. The prior "freezing" of the value of the preferred stock means that most, if not all, future appreciation is shifted to the common stock owned by the children.[4]

Recapitalizations can be an effective estate planning technique for corporate stockholders who desire to make gifts of stock to children or other heirs.[5] However, they should be undertaken only with the assistance of competent tax counsel.[6]

Footnotes on page 217

PREFERRED STOCK REDEMPTION

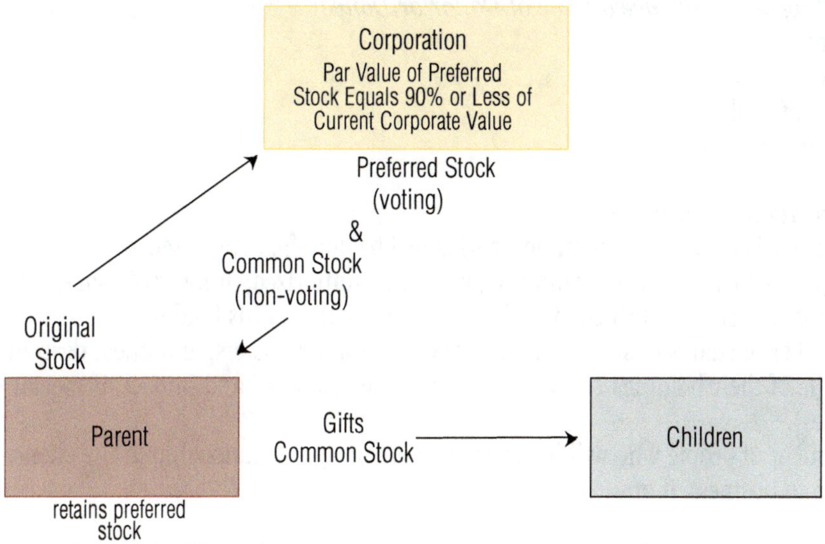

EFFECT OF SUBSEQUENT APPRECIATION

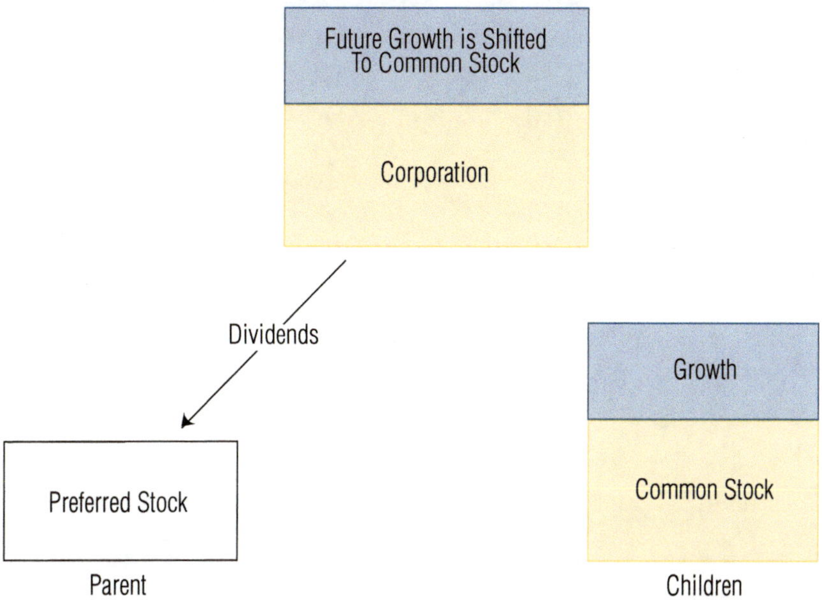

INFORMATION REQUIRED FOR ANALYSIS & PROPOSAL

To Propose Insurance on Life of Donor or Donee

1. Name.
2. Sex.
3. Date of birth.
4. Smoker/nonsmoker.

Attorney Must Also Know

5. Fair market value of corporation performed by qualified appraiser.
6. Capital structure of corporation (type of stock authorized, number of shares outstanding).
7. Number of shares of stock owned by client and value of his holdings.
8. Number of shares of stock owned by client's brothers, sisters, and lineal descendants, and value of their holdings (in order to determine "control" and impact of special valuation rules).
9. Number of people who will be given stock, their ages, relationship to the client, and position in business, if any.

CROSS REFERENCES TO TAX FACTS ON INSURANCE & EMPLOYEE BENEFITS, VOL. 1 (2019)

Q 945. Effect of Chapter 14 valuation rules on recapitalization.

Footnotes

[1] This chart does not demonstrate a "true" recapitalization in which there is an exchange of *all* of a stockholder's stock (usually common) for a different class of stock (usually preferred). What is demonstrated is essentially a "preferred stock" distribution, under which the stockholder receives another class of stock (the voting preferred) without actually giving up his common stock that represents the future equity growth of the corporation. Although this receipt of preferred stock is non-taxable, it is essentially equivalent to a stock dividend and will likely be considered "Section 306 stock" (see discussion, page 537). If it were then subsequently sold, the proceeds would be treated as ordinary income, not capital gain.

[2] Because of the special valuation provisions of Chapter 14 all common stock must be given a value of at least 10 percent of the total value of the corporation (e.g., if the corporation had a value of $1,000,000, the common stock value must be at least $100,000, meaning that the retained preferred stock could, at most, be valued at $900,000). For this purpose the total value of the corporation includes the amount of all corporate indebtedness to the transferor and family members (see discussion on pages 371-372). Obtaining an accurate fair market value of the corporation at the time of recapitalization can also avoid unexpected tax problems. For example, if the value placed on the new preferred stock is *greater than* the original common stock, the stockholder may be considered as having received a dividend from the corporation. On the other hand, when a second stockholder exists at the time of the recapitalization, undervaluing the new preferred can lead to either income or gift tax liabilities. If the value placed on the new preferred is *less than* the original common stock the amount of the undervaluation might be treated as taxable income to the co-stockholder (either salary, or worse yet, a nondeductible corporate dividend). It could be treated as a gift if the co-stockholder were a family member.

[3] Under Chapter 14 these cumulative dividends *must actually be paid*, or there will be exposure to *future* gift or estate taxes. If the retained preferred stock is to have a value greater than zero the stock dividend rights must constitute "qualified payments" (i.e., dividends payable on a periodic basis and at a fixed rate or at a variable rate with a fixed relationship to market value). See the expanded discussion of qualified payments on pages 371-372. In the desire to have the retained preferred stock highly valued in order to reduce the exposure to gift taxes when the common is given to children, care must be taken not to obligate the corporation to unrealistic and onerous preferred stock dividends, which are not deductible to the corporation.

[4] Because *future* appreciation is being shifted out of the estate, a recapitalization will generally not reduce *present* estate settlement costs. The value of the stock retained by the donor will still be included in his gross estate. A partial stock redemption under Section 303 can provide an effective means of paying these costs, particularly when funded with life insurance. Dividends paid on the stock transferred by gift can be used by the donee to pay for insurance on the life of the donor using the reverse section 303 technique described in the chart on page 199. However, because of the grantor trust rules, the donee should be an individual, not a trust. Since there is some possibility that the donee will predecease the donor, the donor may wish to insure the donee in order to purchase stock from the donee's estate.

[5] A recapitalization can also be an effective way to accomplish the non-tax objectives of transferring growth and control to one child while providing income for another child. For example, assume that both nonvoting preferred and voting common were issued pursuant to a recapitalization. If Child A were not involved in the business he could be given the *nonvoting* preferred stock (with an income stream provided by dividends). Child B, who is working in the business, might then be given the voting common stock (with both its control and potential for future appreciation).

[6] These less restrictive anti-freeze provisions in the form of special valuation rules are contained in Chapter 14 of the Code.

ATTRIBUTION

When it is intended that continued ownership would be held within a family, it is extremely important to consider the effect of the attribution rules when planning for the sale of stock to a corporation. Unfortunately, all too often the operation of these rules is poorly understood, and the adverse tax consequences can be disastrous (they have been aptly described as "infamous and insidious").

The basic problem arises under Section 302(b)(3) of the Code, that requires that to qualify as a "capital transaction" the sale of stock to a corporation must result in a *complete* disposition of the stockholder's interest (both actually owned and constructively owned). If there is a redemption of *less* than the stockholder's entire interest, then the transaction is likely to be treated and taxed as a stock dividend. However, merely selling all directly owned stock to the corporation, may not satisfy this requirement if stock owned by others is attributed to the selling stockholder or his estate. There are two types of attribution, family attribution and entity attribution. Whereas family attribution can be waived (charts, pages 222-223), entity attribution cannot be waived (charts, page 221). To summarize the rules of family attribution:

1. An individual is deemed (i.e., considered) to own any stock owned directly or *indirectly* by his:
   a. parents
   b. spouse
   c. children
   d. grandchildren

2. There is *no* family attribution with respect to one's grandparent, brother, sister, uncle, aunt, nephew, cousin, or in-law.

3. There is no "secondary" attribution under the family attribution rules (e.g., stock attributed from daughter-in-law to son cannot then be again attributed from the son to his parents).

Depending upon the particular family relationship, an individual may, or may not, be considered to own the stock of other members of his family. For example, assume we have an extended family composed of a husband, his wife, his grandfather, grandmother, father, mother, and brother; as well as his son, daughter-in-law, and grandson. In this family the **husband** is considered as owning the stock of *his* father, mother, wife, son and grandson. On the other hand, his **wife** will be considered as owning the stock of only *her* father, mother, husband, son, and grandson.

FAMILY ATTRIBUTION

Husband is considered to own the stock of *his* Father, Mother, Wife, Son and Grandson.

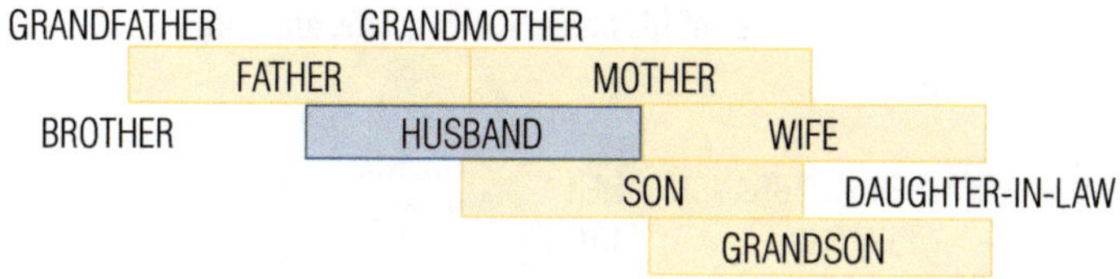

Wife is considered to own the stock of *her* Father, Mother, Husband, Son and Grandson.

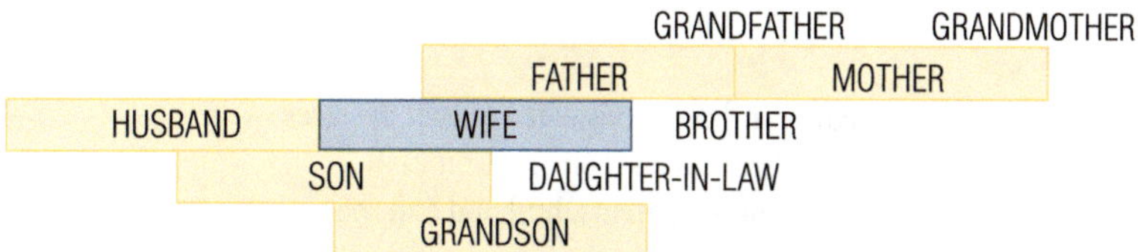

Moving Up One Generation

Father is considered to own the stock of Grandfather, Grandmother, Mother, Brother, Husband, and Son (i.e., of *his* father, mother, wife, sons, and grandson).

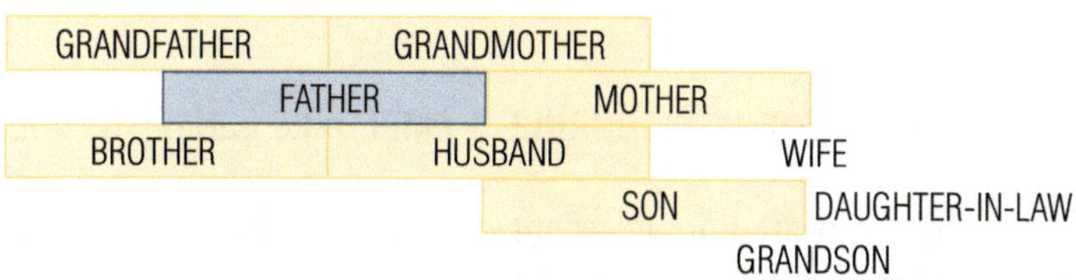

FAMILY ATTRIBUTION

Moving Down One Generation

Son is considered to own the stock of
Husband, Wife, Daughter-in-law, and Grandson
(i.e., of his father, mother, wife, and son).

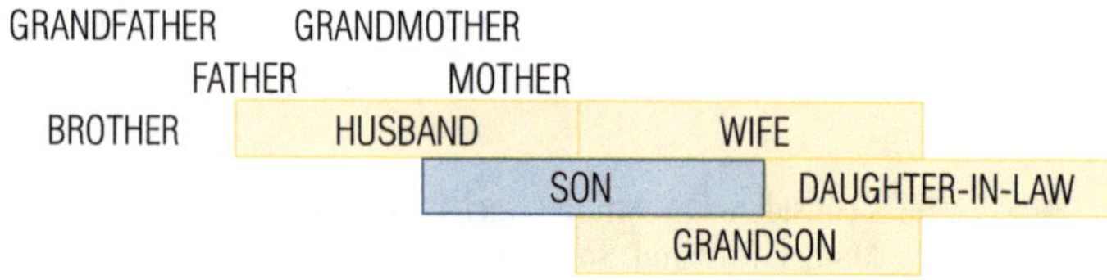

Daughter-in-law is considered to own the stock of
her Parents, Son and Grandson
(i.e., of her parents, husband and son).

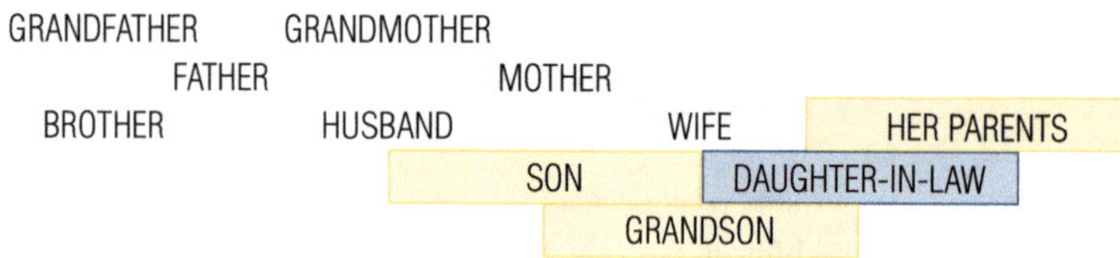

CROSS REFERENCES TO TAX FACTS ON INSURANCE & EMPLOYEE BENEFITS, VOL. 1 (2019)

Q 300. Amount paid by corporation for decedent's entire stock interest generally not dividend to estate, provided no attribution problems.
Q 301. Avoiding attribution of stock ownership among family members.
Q 302. Avoiding attribution of stock ownership from estate beneficiary to estate.

ENTITY ATTRIBUTION

Attribution From An Estate

Stock owned by an Estate is attributed to the Beneficiaries in proportion to their interests in the estate.

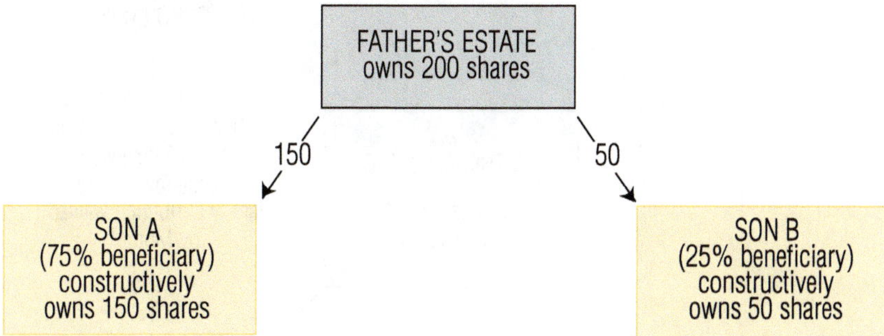

Attribution To An Estate

Stock actually or constructively owned by a beneficiary is attributed in full to the estate, without regard for the beneficiaries' percentage of interest in the estate (the attribution of Son A's 100 shares to the estate cannot be waived).

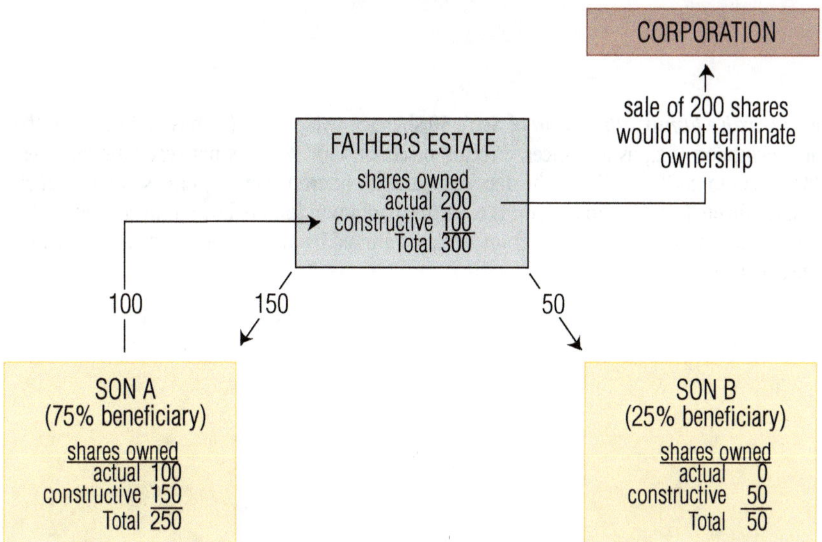

FAMILY & ENTITY ATTRIBUTION

Waiver Of Family Attribution
Sale by Mother

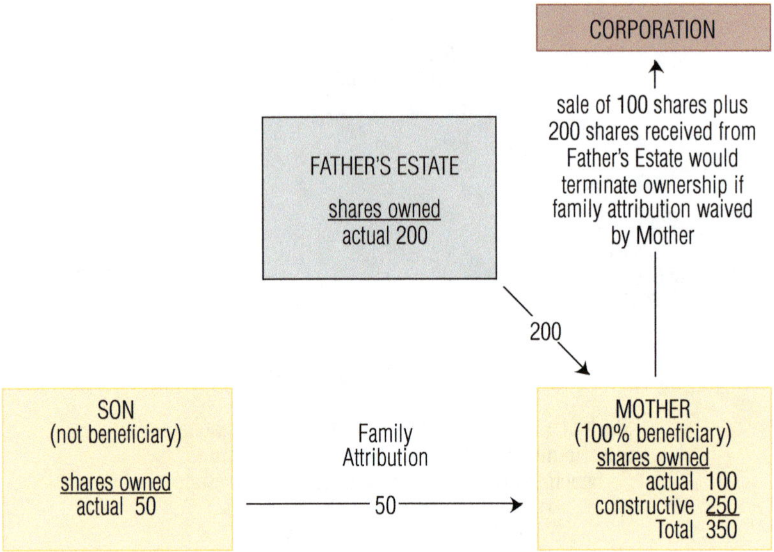

Note: Mother can *waive family attribution* of Son's 50 shares provided she: (1) has no interest in the corporation following the redemption (i.e., as an officer, director, or employee); (2) does not reacquire an interest within 10 years; and (3) agrees to notify the IRS if she does reacquire an interest. Note also the secondary attribution of the estate's 200 shares through Mother to the Son (i.e., entity attribution followed by family attribution). However, you cannot have entity attribution to the estate from Mother followed by another entity attribution from the estate to another estate beneficiary.

FAMILY & ENTITY ATTRIBUTION

Waiver Of Family Attribution
Sale by Estate

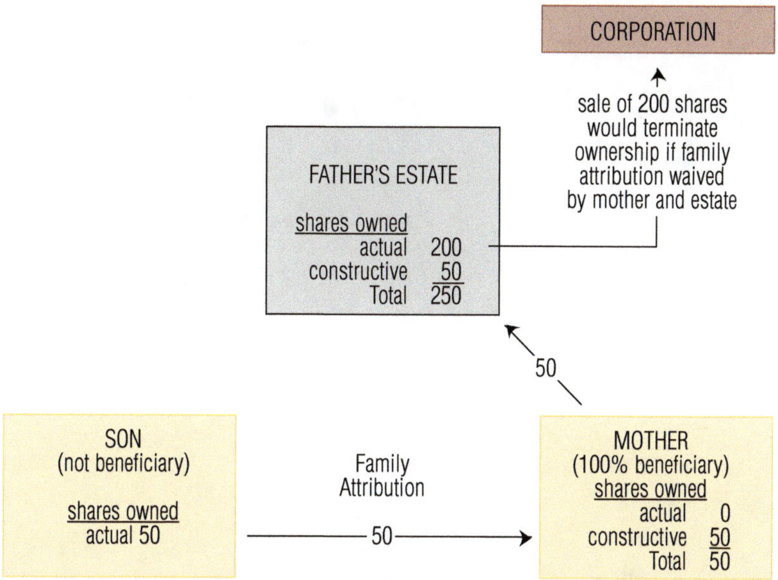

Note: Even though an entity, Father's estate can *waive* family attribution of Son's 50 shares to Mother. This breaks the chain of secondary attribution from Son to Mother to Father's estate (i.e., family attribution followed by entity attribution). The waiver by the estate is dependent upon both the entity (i.e., the estate) and those through whom ownership is attributed (i.e., the mother) agreeing to join in the waiver. Both the entity and the beneficiary must hold no interest in the corporation, cannot acquire an interest within 10 years of the redemption, and must agree to notify the Internal Revenue Service should an interest be acquired. If Son predeceased Mother, as an estate beneficiary Son's 50 shares would be attributed in full to the estate (see bottom chart, page 221). There can be no waiver of entity attribution.

TABLE OF CONTENTS

POINTERS

Will The Plan Fit?

Employers and employees come in many shapes and forms. Before proceeding with recommendations as to a specific benefit plan, it is essential to ascertain whether your client is doing business as a C corporation, S corporation, partnership, limited liability company, or sole proprietor (see pages 377, 449, 481-483, 487, 500, and 531-533). In general, the S corporation, partnership, and sole proprietorship provide limited opportunities for creative employee benefit plans for the owner/employee (pages 622-624).

In contrast, C corporations are taxable entities, separate and apart from their stockholders. They offer attractive opportunities for using tax-advantaged employee benefits for employee/stockholders. For example, a deferred compensation plan can be used in the medium to large sized corporation to reward key executives who are stockholders in the corporation (page 127). However, deferred compensation is not appropriate if your client is a sole proprietor or the only owner of a "Pass-through entity" such as an S-corporation or limited liability company. The threshold question is simple: are your client and his or her business separate taxable entities? If they are, then your client is able to use a "business check" for funding employee benefits, and can take advantage of any tax leverage provided by the difference between employer and employee income tax brackets (see pages 230-231).

Because of recent tax changes, consideration should be given to the tax status of the business. In recent years, individual tax rates were generally lower than corporate tax rates – helping to drive many businesses to select subchapter S status. However, today, top individual tax rates are higher than corporate tax rates. As a result, it is becoming more common to see businesses convert to C status. This has become especially true as a result of the 2017 Tax Act that lowered the top marginal income tax rate for C-corporations to 21%. With the top individual marginal income tax rate temporarily lowed from 39.6% to 35% – there is now potentially a 14% difference between the corporate and individual marginal income tax rate which has again made deferral of business-owner income within their c-corporations a popular strategy. Cash value life insurance can play a signficant role in this type of planning.

You should refer to the following footnotes for guidance regarding the appropriateness of specific employee benefits: executive equity (footnote 2, page 235); split-dollar insurance (footnote 2, page 243); deferred compensation (footnotes 1 and 7, page 129); disability income plan (footnote 1, page 255); and health reimbursement arrangements (footnote 1, page 259). See also the discussion of Top-Hat Plans on page 565.

With Whom Are You Working?

It is also important to consider whom you are working with and what their objectives are. Is your client the owner of a small closely held business who wants to fund his or her corporate buy/sell agreement with split-dollar life insurance, or is your client the chief financial officer of a larger corporation charged with the responsibility of assembling a selective supplemental retirement plan for a group of key executives? Is the benefit for a "pure" employee (i.e., a non-owner)? Is the nonowner/employee related to your client? Is it expected that the nonowner/employee will eventually become an owner? Answers to these questions will help you design an employee benefit plan that is responsive to your client's objectives. A relevant and responsive plan improves your credibility with your client, and is far more likely to be accepted and implemented.

Time Can Work For You ... And Against You.

Dollars can grow, but they need time. Some people have more time, and some people have less time. If you are just starting out, time is your friend; the stock market will go up, maybe not today,

tomorrow, next week, next month, or even next year, but it will go up. If you are about to retire, time is not your friend, particularly if you did not take advantage of time when it was your friend. By allowing before-tax dollars to grow tax-deferred, tax-favored retirement plans offer a very effective way of using time to secure your retirement years. The materials on pages 264-267, 615, 616, 638, and 643, will help you better understand and explain concepts involving the time value of money.

Education Funding And Taxation.

Many educational tax benefits that were scheduled to expire at the end of 2012 have been either extended or made permanent by the American Taxpayer Relief Act of 2012. These include the $2,500 American Opportunity Credit (as of date of publication set to expire after 2017); the $5,250 exmployer education assistance exclusion (made permanent); and the $2,000 maximum contribution to Coverdell Education Savings Accounts ("ESA") including elementary school expenses as qualified expenses (made permanent).To help sort out the multiplicity of these education tax incentives and their interrelationships, see pages 313-315, 330, 539, and a handy summary comparison at page 634.

Life Insurance In Qualified Plans.

Qualified plans can offer an attractive way of using pretax dollars to purchase life insurance for the benefit of plan participants. In pension plans the plan trustee determines to purchase life insurance as a plan asset. In defined contribution plans, such as profit sharing and 401(k) plans, participants have the ability to elect to purchase life insurance with part of their accounts (e.g., from self-directed accounts). See generally, pages 419-420.

Providing For Retirement.

Minimum distribution rules. With qualified retirement plans there are strict rules regarding when, how much, and for how long money can be put away (pages 268-283, 547-549, and 627-633). The minimum distribution rules allow your clients to significantly defer income taxes with post-retirement and post-death distribution planning, particularly with regard to IRAs (pages 411-413, and 595). Under rollover rules your clients have a great deal of flexibility to transfer, or consolidate, their retirement funds between IRAs, 403(b) plans, 457 plans, and qualified plans including 401(k) plans.

Retirement income planning. Retirees are living longer, healthier, and more active lives (see table, Healthy Life Expectancy, page 601). No longer is it adequate to merely help clients save for retirement. Your soon-to-retire clients must have a plan that will provide an inflation-adjusted stream of income that will not be outlived (see pages 522-523). In this regard, see the Longevity In Retirement table on pages 613-614. This table can be used to estimate the odds of living to a specific retirement age. For example, a 65-year-old male has a 55.6 percent chance of living to age 80, and a 34.6 percent chance of living to age 85; but only a 15.5 percent chance of living to age 90. Given those odds, a healthy 65-year-old male should be very concerned about having sufficient retirement funds for at least the next 20 years (age 85), if not the next 25 years (age 90).

Contribution limits. Many contribution limits for employee retirement plans changed in 2019, including the Section 415 defined contribution limit of $56,000 and the defined benefit limit of $225,000. Elective deferrals for traditional and safe harbor 401(k) plans, 403(b) plans, TDAs, SEPs, and Section 457 plans are $19,000 in 2019. See table on page 630.

Self-employed individuals. A variety of retirement plans are available for the self-employed. The discussion on page 543 generally lists them in the order of amount of maximum annual contribution, costs to set up, complexity, and difficulty of administration.

Disability, Long-Term Care, And IRAs.

As with retirement planning concepts, disability income, long-term care, and IRAs are included in this employee benefits section. However, these important needs may well be provided for outside the context of an employer-employee relationship. For example, some of your clients will establish IRAs that have nothing to do with their employer, while other clients may participate in SIMPLE IRAs established by their employer (pages 405 and 548). Likewise, many clients acquire individual disability income contracts outside of a formal disability income plan; while other clients are covered by plans with varying degrees of employer participation (pages 248-251, 252-255, 344, and 646).

Long-term care. Long-term care planning is an important part of financial and retirement planning. Therefore, long-term care has been included in this employee benefits section together with the subjects of retirement and disability planning. In 2018 average nursing home costs were over $95,000 per year (see chart, page 115). The average stay is over 800 days with about 10 percent staying for 5 years or more.

Minors and IRAs. IRA accounts are the major asset many of your clients rely upon for their retirement. Given the size of these accumulations, IRA owners often desire to control the timing and nature of distributions to IRA beneficiaries while fully maximizing the benefits of tax deferral for their beneficiaries. In this regard, see the discussions of Minors And IRAs on page 468 and See-Through Trust on page 541.

TAXATION OF EMPLOYEE BENEFITS

Employee benefits, once considered an "addition" to wages, have now become an integral part of virtually all compensation packages. This overview evaluates the tax attributes of various employee benefit plans.

Characterization of a benefit as either bad, better, or best, can be made according to its effect upon the income taxes of the employer and the employee. Because of reductions in the top C corporate marginal tax rate from 34 percent to 21 percent and a much smaller reduction (actually an increase for some taxpayers) in the individual tax rates – the analysis of various employee benefits has changed since the 2017 Tax Act. In 2017, this book assumed an example where we had an employer in a 34 percent marginal tax bracket and an employee in a 25 percent tax bracket.[1] Today, the analyis will be done with a 21 percent employer rate and a 25 percent employee rate.

BAD. A bad employee benefit is one that is *nondeductible* to the employer yet *taxable* to the employee, such as one that results in unreasonable compensation or is treated as a dividend. Because it is nondeductible, on each $1.00 of income the employer must pay 21 cents in taxes (34 percent in 2017). Since the remaining 79 cents is taxable to the employee, 20 cents of employee taxes will further reduce the original $1.00 to only 59 cents (49 cents in 2017). So while reductions in corporate tax rates make nondeductible benefits less inefficient – it is still prudent to avoid this tax treatment in most instances.

BETTER. A better employee benefit is one that is *deductible* to the employer, although still *taxable* to the employee. Since there are no employer taxes, the full $1.00 is taxable income to the employee. Now 25 cents goes to pay employee taxes, and the remaining 75 cents actually benefits the employee. With little change to the individual income tax rates as a result of the 2017 Tax Act, this analysis remains mostly unchanged from 2017.

Better benefits include salary allotment plans, executive equity plans, split-dollar insurance, survivor income plans, disability income plans, and deferred compensation.

BEST. The best employee benefit is one that is *deductible* to the employer and either *nontaxable* or *tax deferred* to the employee. Now the entire $1.00 benefits the employee, without any current reduction for either employer or employee taxes.

"Best" benefits include group term insurance, medical expense reimbursement plans, SIMPLE IRAs, and qualified retirement plans, including 401(k) plans.[2]

---

[1] However, for the first time in recent memory, it is possible (if not likely) for the corporate income tax rate to be less than the individual income tax rate. For this reason, it is very important to consider relative tax brackets when considering employee benefit planning.

[2] Specific benefits may not be available to all employees and employers. Although SIMPLE IRAs and qualified retirement plans, including 401(k) plans, are listed among the "best," it must be recognized that the employee pays taxes when retirement income is actually received. Tax-free group term insurance is limited to $50,000 of coverage. The term "leveraged benefit" can be used to describe some of the best employee benefits, as discussed further on page 415.

BAD

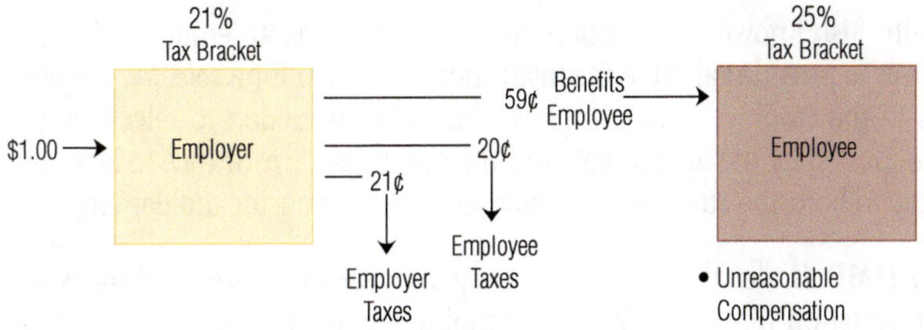

- Unreasonable Compensation
- Dividends

BETTER

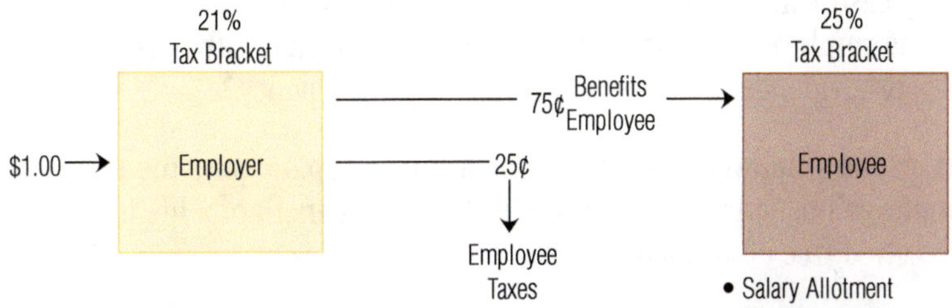

- Salary Allotment
- Executive Equity
- Bonused Split-Dollar Insurance
- Survivor Income Plans
- Disability Income Plans
- Deferred Compensation

BEST

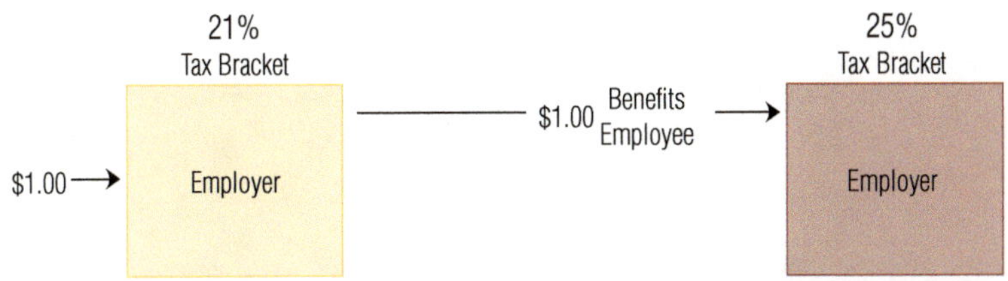

- Group Term Insurance
- Medical Expense Reimbursement Plans
- SIMPLE IRAs
- Qualified Retirement Plans
- 401(k) Plans

EXECUTIVE EQUITY

Executive equity, also known as a Section 162 Bonus Plan, is an employee benefit plan that allows an employer to provide valuable life insurance protection for a *selected* employee on a tax deductible basis to the employer.[1] The employer has total discretion to select the employee, or employees, to be covered by the agreement, and the amounts of insurance to be provided. It can be made available to both the stockholder-employee and the nonstockholder-employee.[2]

DURING LIFETIME. Under the agreement, the employee purchases and owns a permanent life insurance contract on his or her life.[3] The employer pays premiums to the insurance company, which are fully tax-deductible by the employer as compensation to the employee.

These premiums are considered taxable income to the employee, upon which the employee is responsible for paying taxes to the IRS.[4] However, the *employee owns* the life insurance contract, including all policy cash values, and the annual increase in these values may more than offset any taxes paid by the employee. If desired, these taxes could be paid with borrowed or withdrawn policy cash values, or dividends, if funded with a participating policy.[5]

UPON DEATH. At the employee's death, the insurance company pays the total death benefit directly to the employee's beneficiary. Because it is the death benefit of a life insurance contract, this payment is received free of all income taxes.

Executive equity offers something for everyone – tax deductibility to the employer, cash value accumulations for the employee, ease of installation, and premium payments with a business check.[6] If the employee-stockholder's marginal tax bracket is less than his corporation's marginal tax bracket, then executive equity should be attractive to the employee-stockholder who wishes to withdraw profits from the corporation. However, because of the 2017 Tax Act, employee-stockholders will less frequently have a lower marginal tax bracket than the business making this planning technique less used for employee-stockholders and mostly focused on non-owner key-employees.

Footnotes on page 235

DURING LIFETIME

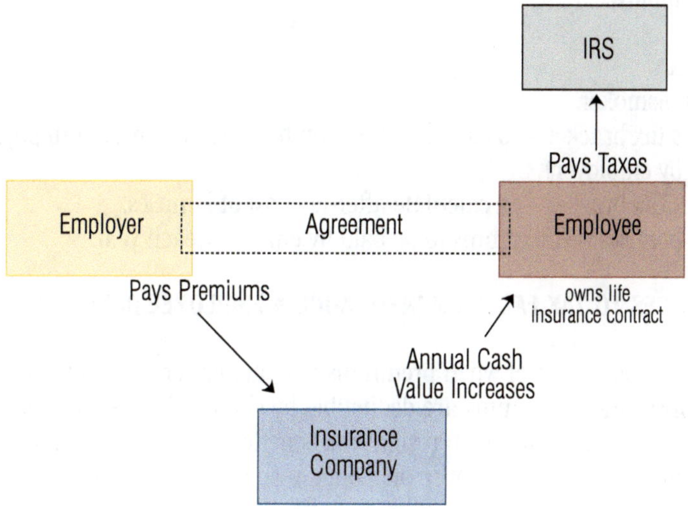

UPON DEATH

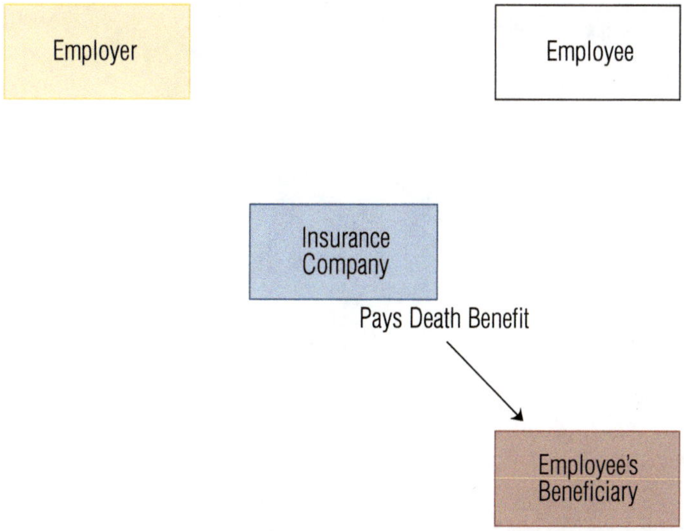

INFORMATION REQUIRED FOR ANALYSIS & PROPOSAL

1. Name of employee.
2. Sex.
3. Date of birth.
4. Smoker/nonsmoker.
5. Employee's tax bracket – to calculate taxes on bonuses (i.e., premium payments made for employee by employer).
6. Employer's tax bracket – to calculate after-tax cost of bonuses.
7. Projected bonuses or premiums to be paid by employer each year.

CROSS REFERENCES TO TAX FACTS ON INSURANCE & EMPLOYEE BENEFITS, VOL. 1 (2019)

Q 262. General discussion of when premiums paid are either deductible or nondeductible.

Q 264. Life insurance premiums are deductible by corporation as additional compensation provided it has no ownership rights or beneficial interest in policy.

Q 269. Premiums paid by employer on policy owned by employee are taxable income to employee.

Q 272. Income tax consequences of Section 162 Bonus Plan.

Footnotes

[1] Executive Equity plans are also referred to as "Executive Bonus Plans," "Executive Retirement Bonus Plans," and "Section 162 Bonus Plans" (after Section 162(a)(1) of the Internal Revenue Code, which authorizes a business to deduct a "reasonable allowance" for salaries or other compensation for personal services actually rendered).

[2] If executive equity is to be effective with owner-employees, it must usually be used in a regular C corporation (not an S corporation). Neither the sole proprietorship nor the partnership provides the separate taxable entity that is essential for the concept to be an attractive benefit for owner-employees.

[3] Because the contract is entirely owned by the employee, it is not essential that the agreement be in writing. However, it is good practice to have the terms of any important agreement in writing; and the agreement could help defend against an IRS attempt to characterize the bonuses as nondeductible dividends.

[4] The premiums paid by the employer are reported as "other compensation" on the employee's W-2 form. Likewise, this compensation is subject to both the Social Security Tax (FICA) and the Federal Unemployment Tax (FUTA). Underlying any discussion of employee benefits is the assumption that, if challenged by the Internal Revenue Service, the increased compensation would be considered "reasonable." For an expanded discussion of Unreasonable Compensation, see page 576.

[5] In designing the column arrangements of executive equity illustrations, it is particularly important to emphasize the direct comparison between the yearly *income taxes* paid by the employee and the annual *cash value increases*, all of which are owned by the employee. For example, if the employer pays a premium of $2,500 for $100,000 of insurance protection, this $2,500 will constitute taxable income to the employee. Assuming the employee is in a 25 percent tax bracket, the employee will have to pay $625 of additional income taxes (.25 × $2,500). However, if the cash values *owned* by the employee increased by $1,300 in that year, this more than offsets the taxes paid. The increase in cash surrender value is not taxable.

[6] Note that with executive equity, the employer has no interest in either the cash values or the death benefits. This contrasts with a split-dollar arrangement, under which the employer usually owns most, if not all, of the cash values, and receives a portion of the death benefits. To better appreciate these differences, see the Split-Dollar Insurance chart on page 241 and the comparison of Executive Equity. The Restrictive Bonus Plan discussed in the chart on page 237 provides an interesting alternative to both Executive Equity and Split-Dollar plans.

RESTRICTIVE BONUS PLAN

The restrictive bonus plan is an employee benefit that allows an employer to provide valuable life insurance protection for a *selected* employee on a tax deductible basis to the employer.[1] The employer has total discretion to select the employee, or employees, to be covered by the agreement, and the amounts of insurance to be provided. It is typically made available to a minority stockholder or a nonstockholder-employee since there is no reason for a majority owner to restrict his or her access to the bonus.

DURING LIFETIME. Under the agreement, the employee purchases and owns a permanent life insurance contract on his or her life. Added to the policy is a restrictive endorsement that requires the employer's consent for the employee to: (1) surrender the policy; (2) assign or pledge the policy for a loan; (3) change ownership of the policy; or (4) withdraw or borrow the cash values of the policy.[2] The endorsement will typically provide for these restrictions to expire upon the earliest to occur of: (1) the retirement of the employee; (2) disability of the employee, (3) attainment of a specific age; (4) a period of years; (5) release by the employer; or (6) the bankruptcy or dissolution of the employer.

By *separate* written agreement, the employer agrees to provide a bonus to the employee by paying all premiums to the insurance company, which is fully tax-deductible by the employer as reasonable compensation to the employee.[3] These premiums are considered taxable income to the employee, upon which the employee is responsible for paying taxes to the IRS.[4]

UPON DEATH. At the employee's death, the insurance company pays the total death benefit directly to the employee's beneficiary. Because it is the death benefit of a life insurance contract, this payment is received free of all income taxes.[5]

The restrictive bonus plan offers something for everyone – tax deductibility to the employer, a simple yet attractive "golden handcuff" for attracting and retaining a key employee, life insurance protection together with cash value accumulations available to the employee upon retirement, ease of installation, and premium payments with a business check.[6]

Footnotes on page 239

DURING LIFETIME

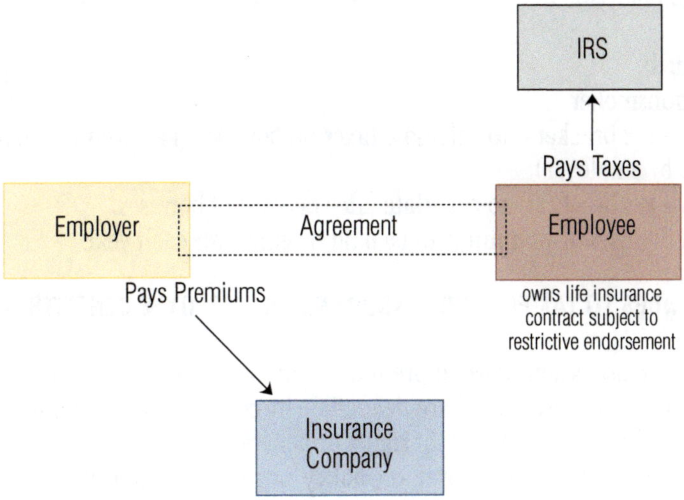

UPON DEATH

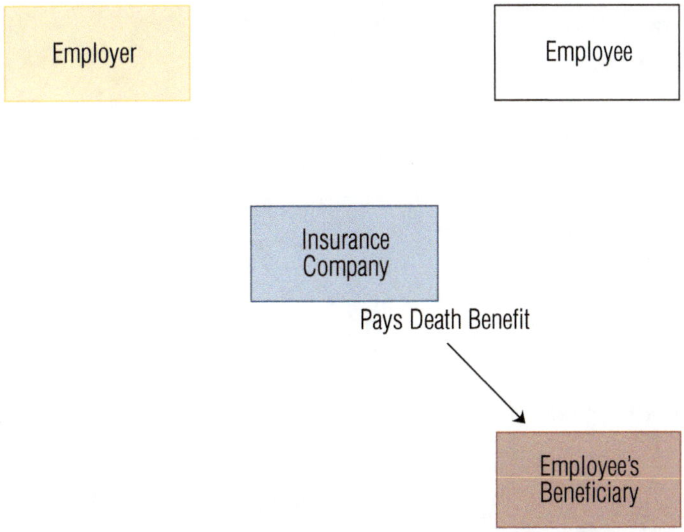

INFORMATION REQUIRED FOR ANALYSIS & PROPOSAL

1. Name of employee.
2. Sex.
3. Date of birth.
4. Smoker/nonsmoker.
5. Employee's tax bracket – to calculate taxes on bonuses (i.e., premium payments made for employee by employer).
6. Employer's tax bracket – to calculate after-tax cost of bonuses.
7. Projected bonuses or premiums to be paid by employer each year.

CROSS REFERENCES TO TAX FACTS ON INSURANCE & EMPLOYEE BENEFITS, VOL. 1 (2019)

Q 262. General discussion of when premiums paid are either deductible or nondeductible.

Q 264. Life insurance premiums are deductible by corporation as additional compensation, provided it has no ownership rights or beneficial interest in policy.

Q 269. Premiums paid by employer on policy owned by employee are taxable income to employee.

Footnotes

[1] The restrictive bonus plan is also referred to as a "Restrictive Endorsement Bonus Arrangement (REBA)," a "Golden Executive Bonus Arrangement (GEBA)" and a "Controlled Executive Bonus Plan."

[2] One objection to executive equity plans is that the employee can terminate employment at any time, yet have full access to the cash values of the life insurance contract (see chart, page 233). The restrictive bonus plan is an extension of the executive equity concept that in part answers this objection by giving the employer some measure of control over the employee's use and enjoyment of the policy (i.e., a "golden handcuff").

[3] If desired, a "double bonus" could be given (i.e., the bonus is large enough to pay not only the premium, but also the tax on the bonus). The premiums paid by the employer are reported as "other compensation" on the employee's W-2 form. Likewise, this compensation is subject to both the Social Security Tax (FICA) and the Federal Unemployment Tax (FUTA). Underlying any discussion of employee benefits is the assumption that, if challenged by the Internal Revenue Service, the increased compensation would be considered as "reasonable." For an expanded discussion of Unreasonable Compensation, see page 576.

[4] A more aggressive plan design requires the employee to reimburse the employer for some or all of the premiums paid, should the employee terminate employment prior to normal retirement date (or within a certain period of time). While the tax results of this reimbursement are not entirely clear, it seems likely the employee would not be allowed to deduct the repayment and the employer would be required to include the repayment in income. Also, see footnote 6 below regarding the need for the employee's interest to fully vest in order for the employer to get a current deduction for the premiums paid (i.e., not subject to a substantial risk of forfeiture, thus taxed on bonus).

[5] Note that with both the restrictive bonus plan and executive equity, the employer has no interest in either the cash values or the death benefits. This contrasts with a split-dollar arrangement, under which the employer usually owns most, if not all, of the cash values, and receives a portion of the death benefits.

[6] It is important that the employer have no interest in the life insurance contract, because Code section 264 would seem to disallow the employer's tax deductions for the bonuses if the employer is directly or indirectly a beneficiary under the policy. It is also important to keep the written agreement entirely separate from the policy endorsement, particularly if the employer has a right to be reimbursed for bonuses given the employee. Code section 83 provides, in effect, that the employee is not taxed on property "transferred in connection with the performance of services," if the property: (1) is not transferable by the employee; *and* (2) is subject to a substantial risk of forfeiture. It is clear that the first condition is met since the endorsement prohibits the employee from transferring the policy. Therefore, if the second condition is met, the employee is not taxed and the employer cannot take a current tax deduction.

SPLIT-DOLLAR INSURANCE

Split-dollar insurance is an agreement between two parties to *allocate* between them the costs and benefits of a life insurance policy.[1] It is *not* a particular type of life insurance policy. When adopted by an employer split-dollar insurance allows the employer to provide valuable life insurance protection for *selected* employees.[2]

Under regulations issued by the IRS there are two ways for an employer to establish a new split-dollar plan.[3]

(1) **Loan regime**. Under this method the *employee* purchases and is the owner of a life insurance contract. The employee-purchased policy is then collaterally assigned to the employer to secure employer premium payments. Each employer premium payment is treated as a loan from the employer to the employee. The employee will either: (a) pay to the employer a market rate of interest on these loans; or (b) receive additional compensation equal to the foregone interest.[4] Under this regime, policy cash values will inure to the benefit of the employee. Upon death, the employer will receive an amount equal to premiums paid plus any accrued interest. The named beneficiary will receive the balance.

(2) **Economic benefit regime**. This method offers a straightforward means of providing to the employee a supplemental executive life insurance death benefit during the years prior to retirement. It is often (although it can be structured as a collateral assignment arrangement owned by the employee) implemented as follows:

DURING LIFETIME. The *employer* purchases and owns a permanent life insurance policy insuring the employee's life.[5] Pursuant to the split-dollar agreement the employer typically pays the entire premium (an "employer pay all" plan) and owns all cash values.[6] Each year income is imputed to the employee in an amount equal to the "economic benefit" of the insurance protection received by the employee.[7] The employee is responsible for paying taxes to the IRS on this imputed income. Provided it is reasonable compensation, the employer could consider paying a bonus to assist the employee in paying taxes on the imputed income.

UPON DEATH. The death benefit payable to the employer can vary according to the provisions of the split-dollar agreement. Unlike with collateral assignment split dollar, the employer need not be entitled to a death benefit equal to the *greater* of the cash values or the cumulative premiums paid. By endorsement to the policy the employee's personal beneficiary is entitled to the death benefits in excess of the amount paid to the employer.[8]

Footnotes on page 243

DURING LIFETIME

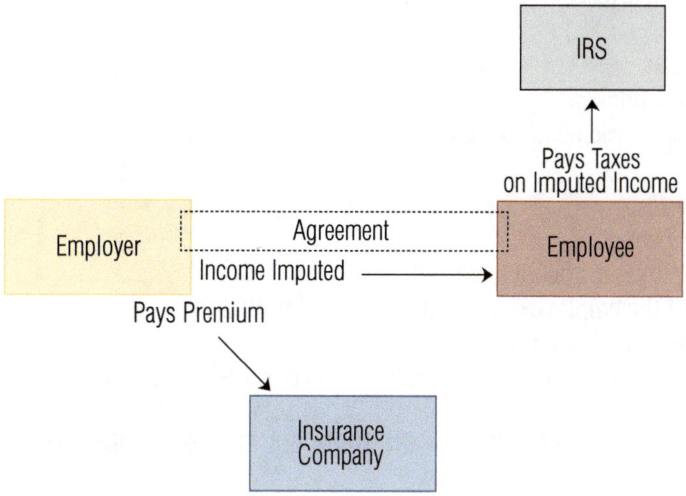

UPON DEATH

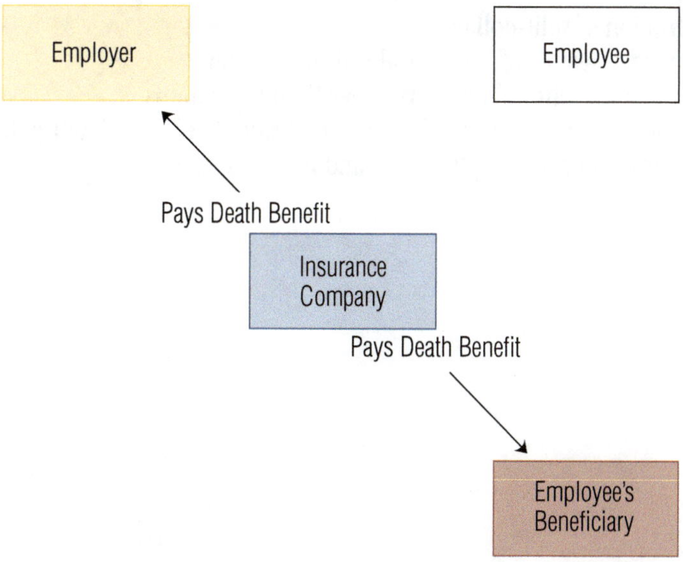

INFORMATION REQUIRED FOR ANALYSIS & PROPOSAL

1. Name of employee.
2. Sex.
3. Date of birth.
4. Smoker/nonsmoker.
5. Amount of desired death benefit.

To Design Plan

6. Position of employee.
7. Is the employee a stockholder?
8. Purpose of the employee's insurance need – family income, estate liquidity, etc. (i.e., how long is the death benefit needed?).
9. Employee's tax bracket – to calculate employee's after-tax cost of imputed income.

CROSS REFERENCES TO TAX FACTS ON INSURANCE & EMPLOYEE BENEFITS, VOL. 1 (2019)

Q 116. Gift taxation of split-dollar.
Q 325. Estate taxation of split-dollar.

CROSS REFERENCES TO TAX FACTS ON INSURANCE & EMPLOYEE BENEFITS, VOL. 2 (2019)

Q 4009. Description of split-dollar.
Q 4010. Income tax results of traditional split-dollar plan.
Q 4014. Treatment of split-dollar plans under final regulations.
Q 4015. Income tax consequences of transfer or "rollout" of split-dollar policy.
Q 4018. Description of private split-dollar and how it is taxed.

Footnotes

[1] The split-dollar plan described in this chart is intended to comply with the requirements of the final split-dollar regulations (effective for plans established after September 17, 2003). Given that the employer pays *all* life insurance premiums and is entitled to *all* cash values, it is better to use the word "allocate" rather than the word "share" (i.e., the premiums and the cash values are allocated to the employer, they are not shared with the employee). See tables A and B on pages 284-285 concerning the treatment of Employer/Employee Split-Dollar Plans established on and before September 17, 2003.

[2] Split-dollar insurance can be provided for the employees of a corporation, a partnership, or a sole proprietorship.. Split-dollar is generally not appropriate for partners or employee-stockholders of S corporations because of the pass-through nature of taxation (except to reallocate premiums among owners and when used with a life insurance trust to reduce the value of gifts to the trust, see footnote 5, page 121, and pages 531-533). In contrast, Private Split-Dollar involves an agreement between individuals, or between an individual and a trust (see chart on page 67).

[3] Based upon policy ownership the split-dollar regulations use a formalistic, yet straight forward, approach in providing two "mutually exclusive regimes" (or methods) for the taxation of split-dollar plans. The economic benefit regime which is illustrated in this chart (as in the typical endorsement arrangement) applies where the employer owns the contract. The loan regime (as in the typical collateral assignment arrangement) applies where the employee owns the contract. However, as an exception to the general rule, even if the employee owns the contract the split-dollar plan is subject to the economic benefit regime if all cash values belong to the employer. This is useful in majority stockholder situations when it is desired to remove all employer death benefits from the insured's estate (see the discussion of Controlling Stockholder on page 324).

[4] In contrast to the chart on page 241 illustrating a split-dollar plan under the economic benefit regime, see the chart on page 363 illustrating a split-dollar plan under the loan regime (the "during lifetime" portion of the chart looks quite different). See also the discussion of Equity Split-Dollar on pages 362-365 for an explanation of the complicated tax treatment of imputed loans.

[5] It is essential to meet strict notice and consent requirements to preserve the employer's income tax-free death benefit (see Company Owned Life Insurance (COLI), pages 319-321).

[6] These employer-owned cash values can be used to informally fund a nonqualified deferred compensation plan (see chart, page 127). Under the economic benefit regime any direct or indirect access to the cash values is immediately taxable to the employee-nonowner, who cannot obtain any income tax basis in a policy owned by the employer. Also, the employee does not share in the premium payments, since under the split-dollar regulations any premiums paid by the *employee* under the economic benefit regime are considered taxable income to the *employer* (under the theory that the employee is paying premiums on a contract owned by the employer).

[7] Under the regulations this "economic benefit" is measured by "life insurance premium factors" to be published by the IRS. Until these factors become available, the Table 2001 rates on page 596 are permissible. Failure of the employee to report this economic benefit, or to contribute an equal amount of premiums, will result in the death benefits being taxed as ordinary income to his beneficiary (i.e., they will not qualify as tax-free life insurance death benefits). Assuming the employee will live to normal retirement age or beyond the taxable economic benefit will get very expensive. This means that an "exit strategy" must be in place if the employee's death benefit is to be maintained after retirement (see Split-Dollar Rollout, page 553).

[8] Provided the employer is willing to have no interest in either the cash values or the death benefit, Executive Equity offers a simpler approach to obtaining needed life insurance protection. It is easier to install, in that there is no required formal agreement between the employer and the employee (see chart, page 233). The Restrictive Bonus Plan in the chart on page 237 provides an interesting alternative.

SPLIT-DOLLAR FUNDING CROSS PURCHASE

Split-dollar insurance is not limited to merely funding the personal insurance needs of an employee. For example, the employee could choose to enter into a split-dollar agreement insuring someone other than himself, such as a spouse or a child. Alternatively, the employee could choose to enter into a split-dollar agreement insuring another stockholder whose stock he is obligated to purchase.[1]

DURING LIFETIME. Assume that we have a corporation owned by two individuals, Employee A and Employee B. They enter into a cross-purchase agreement providing for the purchase and sale of their respective interests.[2] This business funded strategy should not be confused with the Cross-Endorsement Buy-Sell Agreement discussed at pages 182-185.

The *corporation* purchases and owns a permanent life insurance policy insuring the life of each employee.[3] In order to fund their mutual obligations to each other, A and B enter into split-dollar agreements with the corporation providing for the allocation of premiums, cash values and death benefits. In contrast to the typical employer/employee split-dollar plan that provides death benefits for the insured's personal beneficiary, these agreements provide for A to receive the death proceeds from the policy insuring B, and for B to receive the death proceeds from the policy insuring A.[4]

The corporation typically pays the entire premium for each policy ("employer pay all" plans) and owns all cash values.[5] Each year income is imputed to the employee in an amount equal to the "economic benefit" of the insurance protection received by the employee on the life of the other employee.[6] Rather than having to come up with expensive after-tax dollars to pay premiums, A and B pay taxes to the IRS on only this imputed income.[7]

UPON DEATH. Assuming that A dies first, his stock interest would then pass to his family or estate. At the same time, the insurance company pays a portion of the death benefit to the corporation to reimburse it under the terms of the split-dollar agreement. The remainder of the death benefit is paid income tax-free to B, which is then used by B to purchase A's entire stock interest from A's family or estate.[8] As with a traditional cross-purchase buy-sell arrangement, this structure allows B to increase his or her basis by the amount to purchase A's interest in the business.

Because of the 2017 Tax Act that reduced the top C corporation marginal tax rate to 21 percent, use of corporate dollars rather than individual dollars to fund a business buy-sell arrangement is especially appealing to many business owners. This arrangement provides the benefit of a traditional cross-purchase agreement (basis step-in and reduction in capital gains taxes) while allowing business owners to use corporate dollars for funding purposes.

Footnotes on page 247

DURING LIFETIME

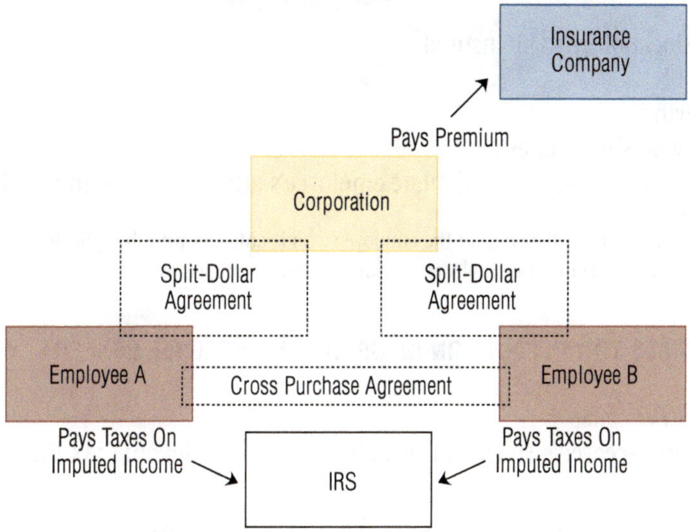

Corporation Obtains Life Insurance On Each Employee

UPON DEATH

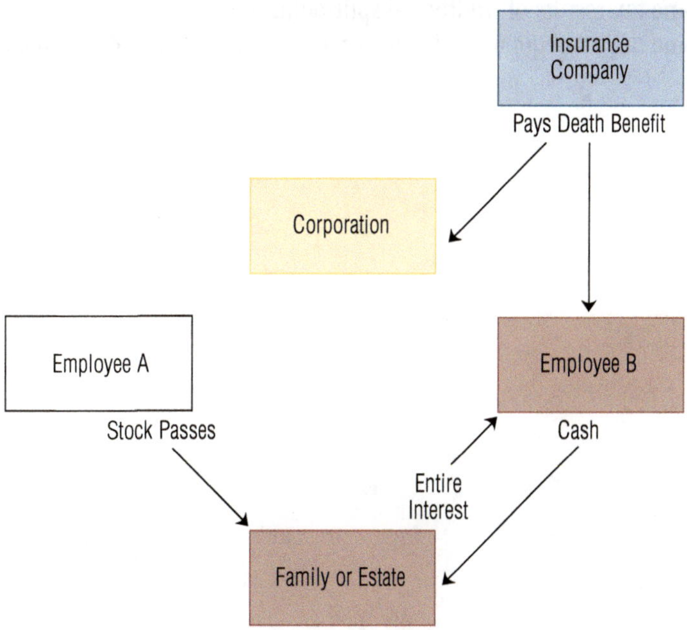

INFORMATION REQUIRED FOR ANALYSIS & PROPOSAL

1. Name of stockholder to be insured.
2. Sex.
3. Date of birth.
4. Value of ownership interest.
5. Employee's tax bracket – to calculate employee's after-tax cost of imputed income.

Note: The "employee's tax bracket" is that of the employee who is entering into the split-dollar agreement with the corporation, *not* the tax bracket of the employee-stockholder who is the insured.

CROSS REFERENCES TO TAX FACTS ON INSURANCE & EMPLOYEE BENEFITS, VOL. 1 (2019)

Cross Purchase

Q 298. Sale of deceased's stock will usually not result in income tax liability to deceased's estate.

Q 299. Income tax effects of funding stock purchase agreement with life insurance.

CROSS REFERENCES TO TAX FACTS ON INSURANCE & EMPLOYEE BENEFITS, VOL. 2 (2019)

Split-Dollar

Q 4009. Description of split-dollar.

Q 4010. Income tax results of traditional split-dollar plan.

Q 4015. Income tax consequences of transfer or "rollout" of split-dollar policy.

Footnotes

[1] In working with a business client it is important to remember that it is usually far easier to obtain payment of premiums with the *corporate* check than the *personal* check. Split-dollar enables employee-stockholders to use a corporate check to pay for life insurance to fund their cross purchase agreement. (Where there is a disparity in ages between the insureds, split-dollar can also help to de-emphasize the difference because substantial portions of the premiums are paid with corporate dollars.) To fund a cross purchase agreement between employee-stockholders, in some situations executive equity may offer a simpler solution, provided there is no requirement that the corporation have any interest in either the cash values or the death benefits (see the Executive Equity chart, page 233).

[2] See the Cross Purchase Agreement chart, page 175. To be viable, split-dollar usually requires that the employer and employee each be a separate taxable entity. Therefore, other than situations where split-dollar is being used primarily for estate and gift tax leverage, funding a cross purchase agreement between two owners of a business is generally limited to a regular C corporation, and would *not* be applicable to an S corporation or a partnership. However, it would be feasible to use split-dollar to fund a ***key employee*** purchase of a stockholder's interest in a corporation, a partnership, or even a sole proprietorship, since in each of these situations the key employee represents a separate taxpayer from his employer (see the Key Person Buy-Out Agreement chart, page 191).

[3] The corporation's ownership of the policy under an endorsement split-dollar plan (see footnote 5, below) could result in a prohibited "transfer for value" if the policy is subsequently transferred to a co-stockholder (e.g., the split-dollar arrangement is terminated and the policy is transferred to a co-stockholder to fund an ongoing cross purchase obligation). This problem only occurs if the transfer does not fit within any of the transfer for value exceptions (see the expanded discussion on page 568). If it is considered important to avoid this *latent* transfer for value problem, the split-dollar agreement could be implemented using the loan regime (i.e., the policy is *owned by the co-stockholder* who collaterally assigns the cash values to the corporation, see the expanded discussion on pages 362-365).

[4] It is essential to meet strict notice and consent requirements to preserve the employer's income tax-free death benefit (see Company Owned Life Insurance (COLI), pages 319-321).

[5] Under the split-dollar regulations this is a "nonequity endorsement plan" intended to be taxed under the economic benefit regime (see the Split-Dollar Insurance chart, page 241). Under the economic benefit regime any direct or indirect access to the cash values is immediately taxable to the employee-nonowner (see also footnote 6, page 243). However, these employer-owned cash values could be used to informally fund a nonqualified deferred compensation plan (see the Deferred Compensation chart, page 127).

[6] Note that the life used to measure the "economic benefit" is that of the insured co-stockholder, not the employee-stockholder who enters into the split-dollar agreement with the corporation. Under the regulations this "economic benefit" is measured by "life insurance premium factors" to be published by the IRS. Until these factors become available, the insurance company cost of annual renewable term insurance or the Table 2001-10 rates on page 596 are permissible. Use of the insurance company term rates is subject to a number of IRS requirements – some of which are not well defined.

[7] The typical corporate split-dollar agreement involving an employee/stockholder is intended to provide an employee ***benefit***, not a stockholder benefit. However, lowered maximum tax rates on qualified corporate dividends (permanently reduced by the American Taxpayer Relief Act of 2012) to 0 percent, 15 percent, and 20 percent after 2012 may cause some split-dollar agreements to be established as stockholder plans, with the stockholder's imputed income taxed at these lower dividend tax rates. Of course, any imputed dividends would not be deductible by the corporation.

[8] Failure of the employee to report this economic benefit, or to contribute an equal amount of premiums, will result in the death benefits being taxed as ordinary income (i.e., they will not qualify as tax-free life insurance death benefits).

DISABILITY PLANNING

No estate or financial plan can be considered complete unless there has been an evaluation of the risks of disability. *Planning to live* is as important as *planning to die*, and the risk is greater.

Before disability, most people are able to acquire savings to the extent income exceeds expenses. However, **after disability** caused by a sickness or injury, income will *fall* and expenses will *rise*.[1]

WITHOUT PLANNING, the expenses of a disability can quickly exhaust the family's savings and create substantial debt. This is true despite the availability of Social Security after six months of continuous and total disability. For most people these payments will rarely fill the gap created between falling income and increasing expenses. When available, Social Security disability payments to a disabled wage earner with children will be substantially more than those to a disabled wage earner without children. The fact that a disabled wage earner is married – and often responsible for the financial needs of a spouse – does not result in an increase in Social Security payments.

Attempting to reduce expenses by selling personal possessions, a car, or even the family home, is unlikely to eliminate the substantial debt which is created by a long-term disability, which is often referred to as "the living death."

WITH PLANNING, the cornerstone of any disability plan is **disability insurance**. Just as life insurance protects a family in case of the insured's death, disability income insurance protects *both* the insured and his family in case of the insured's disability. In addition, before disability strikes, the purchase of a comprehensive **major medical expense plan** offers one of the most effective ways of paying the major expenses of many disabilities. A **waiver of premium rider** on existing or new life insurance policies will provide for payment of premiums after a stated period of disability.[2]

Disability, although a common reason for a business owner to leave a business, is often ignored or not addressed when funding a buy-sell agreement.. Planning for disability can be as important as planning for death when advising a client on business succession and buy-sell matters.

Today, many life insurance contracts can be purchased with riders that also protect against long-term care events or chronic illness. See pages 454-457. While these hybrid life products are not disability insurance they can provide a lower cost alternative that can protect against some of the same risks.

Footnotes on page 251

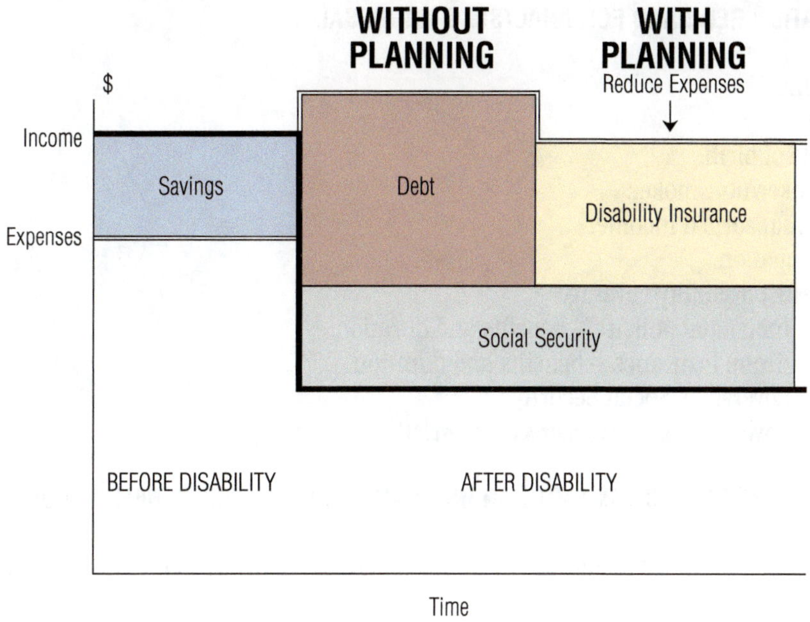

RISK OF LONG-TERM DISABILITY - RISK OF DEATH

	Male	Female
Age 30 –	4.0 times more likely	7.6 times more likely
Age 40 –	2.9 times more likely	5.9 times more likely
Age 50 –	2.3 times more likely	3.8 times more likely

INFORMATION REQUIRED FOR ANALYSIS & PROPOSAL

1. Name.
2. Sex.
3. Date of birth.
4. Smoker/nonsmoker.
5. Annual earned income.
6. Occupation.
7. Present disability coverage:
   a. Individual policies – benefits and duration.
   b. Group insurance – benefits and duration.
   c. Covered by Social Security?
   d. Covered by state worker's compensation?

CROSS REFERENCES TO TAX FACTS ON INSURANCE & EMPLOYEE BENEFITS, VOL. 1 (2019)

Q 330. Employer can deduct as a business expense amounts paid for disability income policy for employee.

Q 343. Disability income benefits received from personally paid policies are tax free.

Q 346. Taxation of benefits when provided for stockholder-employees only.

Q 759. Tax credit for the permanently and totally disabled.

Footnotes

1 The expenses associated with a long-term disability can be devastating. With death, the funds required are those needed to support a surviving family. With disability, the living death, not only is there a need to provide for the family, but the living and medical expenses of the disabled person must also be provided. The advances of modern medicine and equipment, which have enabled many more people to survive crippling accidents and illnesses, have further added to the expenses of long-term care. See the chart on page 115 regarding the risk and costs of long-term care.

2 In addition to disability income insurance, the owners of a business should consider funding their buy/sell agreements with disability buy-out insurance (see page 342). Also, business overhead expense insurance can provide for payment of specific business expenses during a period of disability (see discussion, page 302).

DISABILITY INCOME PLAN

When a disabled employee is faced with increasing expenses and decreasing income, some employers will informally continue the disabled employee's salary for an extended period of time. Such an approach can be unwise when the disabled employee is a stockholder. To illustrate, assume that a corporation's income is $150,000 before paying a $50,000 salary to its employee-stockholder.[1]

NO PLAN. If this employee-stockholder becomes disabled without a pre-existing plan, continued salary payments of $50,000 could be treated by the IRS as *nondeductible dividends*, which must come from after-tax profits. Assuming the taxable income of the business does not suffer because of the key employee's disability, taxable income would then be $150,000, upon which $31,500 (assuming a flat 21 percent tax rate) of taxes must be paid, with $68,500 remaining after-tax and after payment to the disabled stockholder-employee.

PLAN. A pre-existing disability income plan would enable the corporation to preserve the tax-deductibility of these continued salary payments to the disabled employee-stockholder. This would place the corporation in the same position as existed prior to the employee-stockholder's disability.

To establish a plan, three things are required: (1) a corporate resolution must be adopted; (2) a plan document must be prepared; and (3) notification of the plan's existence must be given to the covered employees.[2] By doing this, the corporation could deduct continued salary payments and retain $79,000 after paying taxes of $21,000. Compared to "no plan," this represents a saving of $10,500 per year. Such plans may be *highly selective*, and a class may consist of just one employee, provided it is a "reasonable" classification. If stockholders are covered, it must be in their capacity as employees.

REDUCED RISK PLAN. Under the reduced risk plan, the corporation shifts a part of its liability to an insurance company.[3] With an individual disability income contract, an insured benefit of $25,000 per year could be paid directly to the disabled employee-stockholder.[4] The corporation would deduct a continued salary payment of $25,000, with $125,000 of taxable income remaining with the corporation. After paying taxes of $26,250, the corporation then retains $98,750. When compared to "no plan," this represents a saving of $30,250 per year.

With a reduced risk plan the premium is deductible by the corporation, yet not taxable to the employee, who is *assured* of receiving disability payments if the corporation should fail.[5]

Footnotes on page 255

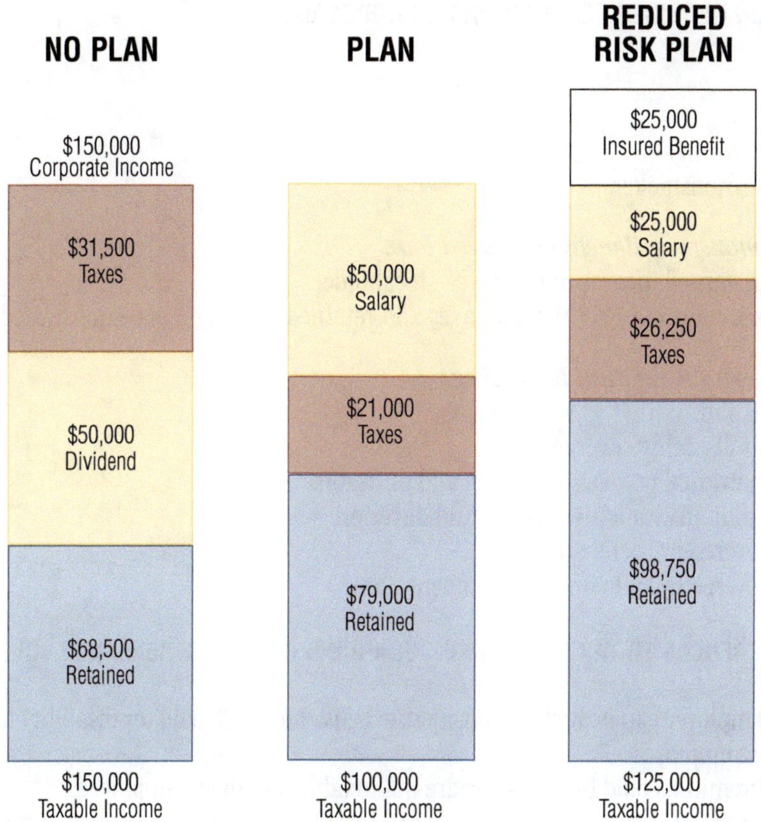

REQUIREMENTS FOR A "PLAN"

- Corporate Resolution
- Plan Document
- Notification to Employee

KEY FEATURES OF THE "REDUCED RISK PLAN"

- Premiums Deductible by Corporation
- Premiums Not Taxable to Employee
- Employee is Assured of Payments

INFORMATION REQUIRED FOR ANALYSIS & PROPOSAL

1. Name.
2. Sex.
3. Date of birth.
4. Smoker/nonsmoker.

To Demonstrate Benefit of Insured Plan

5. Annual earned income of employee-stockholder.
6. Corporate income (to calculate taxes and retained earnings, as demonstrated in chart).

To Determine Amount of Coverage

7. Occupation.
8. Present disability coverage:
   a. Individual policies – benefits and duration.
   b. Group insurance – benefits and duration.
   c. Covered by social security?
   d. Covered by state worker's compensation?

CROSS REFERENCES TO TAX FACTS ON INSURANCE & EMPLOYEE BENEFITS, VOL. 1 (2019)

Q 330. Employer can deduct as a business expense amounts paid for disability income policy on employee.
Q 332. Premiums paid by employer are not taxable income to employee.
Q 334. Disability income payments are fully taxable to employee (except portion of income attributable to employee's contributions, if any).
Q 343. Disability income benefits received from personally paid policy are tax-free.
Q 346. Taxation of benefits when provided for employee-stockholders only.
Q 759. Tax credit for the permanently and totally disabled.

Footnotes

1 Although a corporation has been selected to demonstrate the tax problems that can occur when an employee-stockholder becomes disabled, a disability income plan can be established for the *employees* of a partnership or a sole proprietorship. However, the partners and the sole proprietor are not "employees" and cannot exclude from their incomes premiums paid for disability income insurance. On the positive side, benefits received by a partner or sole proprietor are totally free of income taxes, because premiums are paid with after-tax dollars. For this purpose, the stockholder who owns more than two percent of an S corporation will be treated the same as a partner in a partnership (see pages 531-533).

2 Notification given by himself as an officer, to himself as an employee, that the board of directors, on which he serves, has established a disability income plan for him, may appear unnecessary, but that is what is required. For appearance's sake, it would be preferable to have another officer sign the letter of authorization. Theoretically, it may be possible to include only the owner-employee; however, it may help avoid IRS scrutiny if other key employees are covered.

3 Despite the tax advantages of having a pre-existing plan, it alone *will not guarantee* that salary continuation payments will be made to a disabled employee. This is particularly true if the corporation is liquidated because of the extended absence of the owner during a long-term disability.

4 The maximum coverage that most insurers will issue for long-term disability is generally limited to 60 percent of pre-disability earned income, reduced to account for other disability insurance and anticipated Social Security or state lump-sum benefits. However, reliance upon Social Security to provide the needed disability benefits may be ill-advised in view of the strict qualification requirements (see Disability Under Social Security, page 345).

5 Provided they are *reasonable*, corporate premium payments are deductible as a business expense. Although the *premium* is not taxable to the employee, if and when disability *payments* are received by the employee, they will be taxed as salary. In order for the employee to receive tax-free payments, the employee must have paid the premiums. By including the premiums paid by the employer in his or her taxable income, the employee will be considered as having paid the premiums with his or her own after-tax dollars. The employee can then receive the disability payments tax-free. This is a decision to be made by the employee, and it will not affect the deductibility of the amount equal to the premium paid by the employer. To determine the various tax ramifications of premium and benefit payments under different arrangements, see the table on page 646.

HEALTH REIMBURSEMENT ARRANGEMENTS

Under a health reimbursement arrangement, it is possible to pay for the medical expenses of an employee and the employee's dependents.[1]

MEDICAL EXPENSES include items such as doctor bills, dentist bills, hospital bills, transportation, prescription drugs, dentures, nursing services, eyeglasses, and hearing aids. The ideal plan has the cost of the benefit tax deductible to the employer and not includable in the employee's income.

SELF-INSURED ARRANGEMENTS will cause highly compensated individuals to be taxed on part or all of any reimbursements, unless the arrangement is nondiscriminatory as to benefits provided and meets one of three eligibility requirements:[2]

1. The IRS has found specific eligibility classifications within the arrangement to be nondiscriminatory;
2. 70 percent or more of employees benefit from the arrangement; or
3. 70 percent or more of all employees are eligible, and at least 80 percent of the 70 percent actually benefit from the arrangement.

If a self-insured arrangement does not meet one of these three requirements, then the highly compensated individuals who will be taxed include:

- Any stockholder who owns more than 10 percent of the stock.
- The five highest paid officers.
- Any employee who is among the 25 percent highest paid of all employees.

These arrangements must also comply with many of the requirements of the Patient Protection and Affordable Care Act (the Health Care Act). Some of the more significant include: (1) prohibition of preexisting condition exclusions; (2) prohibition on excessive waiting periods; (3) no lifetime or annual limits; (4) prohibition on rescissions; (5) coverage of preventive health services; and (6) extension of dependent coverage.

INSURED ARRANGEMENTS cannot be used to provide tax benefits to stockholder-employees or officers by segregating them from other employees.[3] Under the Health Care Act, policies purchased on or after September 23, 2010, will be subject to nondiscrimination requirements (i.e., these arrangements can no longer be used to benefit a select class of employees).

Footnotes on page 259

MEDICAL EXPENSES

Doctor Bills - Dentist Bills - Hospital Bills
Transportation - Prescription Drugs - Dentures
Nursing Services - Eyeglasses - Hearing Aids

SELF-INSURED ARRANGEMENTS

will cause highly compensated
individuals to be taxed, unless
plan is nondiscriminatory as to benefits
and

Classifications Found By IRS As Nondiscriminatory

OR

70% Of Employees Benefit

OR

70% Of Employees Eligible And 80% Of The 70% Actually Benefit

HIGHLY COMPENSATED INDIVIDUALS INCLUDE

Stockholder Who Owns More Than 10% Of Stock

5 Highest Paid Officers

25% Highest Paid Employees

INSURED ARRANGEMENTS

Cannot Benefit A Select Class of Employees

INFORMATION REQUIRED FOR ANALYSIS & PROPOSAL

1. Name of employee.
2. Date of birth.
3. Smoker/nonsmoker.
4. Salary.
5. Status of employee (full time or part time).
6. Employment date.
7. Employer's tax bracket.

CROSS REFERENCES TO TAX FACTS ON INSURANCE & EMPLOYEE BENEFITS, VOL. 1 (2019)

Q 332. Value of health coverage not generally taxable to employee.
Q 334. Employee taxation of payments received under employer provided health insurance.
Q 335. Employee taxation of benefits provided under employer's noninsured plan.
Q 336. Nondiscrimination requirements that apply to employer provided health benefits.
Q 337. Nondiscrimination requirements that apply to self-insured health plans.
Q 341. Taxation of amounts paid to highly compensated employees under a discriminatory self-insured medical reimbursement plan.
Q 345. Taxation of "domestic partnership" benefits.
Q 346. Taxation of benefits when provided by C corporations for stockholder-employees only.
Q 347. Taxation of health insurance coverage for partners and sole proprietors.
Q 348. Taxation of health insurance coverage for S corporation stockholders.
Q 356. Coverage continuation requirements under "COBRA."
Q 441. New health insurance nondiscrimination rules affect on insured plans.
Q 442. How to determine if a health plan is discriminatory.
Q 443. The consequences of violating the nondiscrimination rules.
Q 445. Application of health reform to self-insured plans.

Footnotes

[1] A health reimbursement arrangement can be provided for the *employees* of a C corporation, a partnership, or a sole proprietorship. However, the partners of a partnership and the sole proprietor cannot be covered and receive the same tax benefits, as they are not considered "employees." Only the stockholders of a corporation who are also employees of the corporation can be covered and receive the tax benefits. For this purpose, the stockholder-employees of an S corporation who own more than 2 percent of the outstanding stock or voting power are treated the same as partners (see pages 531-533). Sole proprietors and partners can deduct 100 percent of amounts paid during the taxable year for medical insurance for themselves and their dependents. To take the deduction, the individual must not be eligible to participate in any subsidized health plan maintained by his employer or his spouse's employer. The deduction is allowable in determining adjusted gross income (but is limited to the amount of the individual's income from the business for which the plan was established).

[2] Routine physical examinations, blood tests, and X-rays (that are not for a known illness or symptom) are not subject to the nondiscrimination requirements (i.e., the "medical diagnostic procedures" exception). In addition, despite having to include in income reimbursements under a discriminatory self-insured plan, a "highly compensated individual" may be able to claim a portion of his or her reimbursements as an itemized deduction. Medical and dental expenses, prescription drugs, and medical insurance premiums, which in total exceed 10 percent of adjusted gross income, may be deducted if the taxpayer itemizes deductions. This amount is limited to 7.5 percent of AGI for 2017 and 2018 after which it returns to 10%. However, because of the elimination of other itemized deductions under the 2017 Tax Act, far fewer taxpayers will itemize deductions and be able to use this deduction.

[3] The Patient Protection and Affordable Care Act generally extended the *nondiscrimination rules* applicable to non-insured plans to insured plans. However, employer-provided health insurance policies in existence on March 23, 2010, were grandfathered and may continue to discriminate in favor of highly compensated employees. Policies purchased after March 23, 2010, and before September 23, 2010, are subject to the nondiscrimination requirements beginning with the first plan year beginning after September 23, 2010. Failure to satisfy the nondiscrimination requirements will subject the employer to a $100 per day/per affected participant excise tax.

HEALTH SAVINGS ACCOUNTS

Offering an attractive means of funding future health care costs, a health savings account (HSA) can be established by eligible individuals covered by a high deductible health plan (HDHP), provided they are not claimed as a dependent on another person's income tax return and are not entitled to benefits under Medicare (i.e., have not reached age 65).[1] The required HDHP must provide for a *minimum* annual deductible of at least $1,350 for individual coverage and $2,700 for family coverage; and *maximum* annual out-of-pocket expenses must be limited to $6,750 for individual coverage and $13,500 for family coverage (as adjusted in 2018 for inflation). As an exception to these deductibles, preventive care services may be covered on a first-dollar basis.[2]

Annual contributions to the HSA are limited to a maximum of $3,500 for an individual, or $7,000 for a family (as adjusted in 2019 for inflation). Account holders and covered spouses, aged 55 and over, may each make additional contributions of $1,000 in 2019.[3] Both the account holders and their employers can make contributions, but total contributions cannot exceed these annual limits.[4] Employer contributions for all similarly situated employees must be "comparable" (i.e., the same dollar amount or percentage of the annual deductible limit). The account is entirely owned by the employee. Because unused funds may be carried over from year-to-year, for many individuals it may be possible to accumulate substantial amounts prior to retirement.[5]

HSAs offer substantial tax advantages.[6] Contributions made by an individual are fully deductible from income as an "above the line" deduction (i.e., without regard to whether deductions are itemized). Employer contributions are deductible by the employer, are not taxable to the employee, and are not subject to Social Security and federal unemployment taxes. Earnings within the account are tax-deferred. Distributions are tax-free, provided they are for "qualified medical expenses," a term that is broadly construed to include items such as braces and nursing home costs (but not over-the-counter medications or cosmetic surgery). Distributions other than for qualified medical expenses are taxable and subject to a 20-percent-penalty tax.[7]

Although payments of health insurance premiums are not considered qualified medical expenses, exceptions allow tax-free reimbursements for premiums paid for a qualified long-term care insurance contract, premiums for COBRA continuation coverage, and premiums for healthcare while receiving unemployment compensation. For those who are eligible for Medicare, tax-free distributions can be made for post-age 65 health insurance such as Medicare Parts A, B, C, and D, and employer-sponsored retiree health insurance (but not for a Medicare supplement policy).[8]

Footnotes on page 263

Individual

Covered By

HDHP
High Deductible Health Plan

Minimum Deductible
- Individual $1,350
- Family $2,700

Maximum Out-Of-Pocket
- Individual $6,750
- Family $13,500

May Establish

HSA
Health Savings Account

Contribute Maximum of
- Individual $3,500
- Family $7,000

Plus Catch-Up Contribution If Age 55+
- Individual $1,000
- Spouse $1,000

TAX ADVANTAGES OF HSA

CONTRIBUTIONS
Tax-Deductible

EARNING
Tax-Deferred

DISTRIBUTIONS
Tax-Free

TAX-FREE DISTRIBUTION MUST BE FOR "QUALIFIED MEDICAL EXPENSES"

- Medical Care For Individual, Spouse & Dependent
- Premiums For Qualified Long-Term Care Insurance
- Premiums For Health Insurance During Period:
    - COBRA Continuation Coverage
    - Unemployment Compensation
- Premiums For Post-Age 65 Health Insurance Such As:
    - Medicare Part A, Part B, Part C, or Part D Coverage
    - Employer-Sponsored Retiree Health Insurance

INFORMATION REQUIRED FOR ANALYSIS & PROPOSAL

1. Name of individual.
2. Date of birth.
3. Annual income.
4. Names and ages of dependents.
5. Details regarding current health insurance (to include coverage, deductibles, and maximum out-of-pocket expense).
6. Employment status (i.e., employee of another or self-employed).

CROSS REFERENCES TO TAX FACTS ON INSURANCE & EMPLOYEE BENEFITS, VOL. 1 (2019)

Q 397. Description of a Health Savings Account (HSA) and how it can be established.
Q 400. Definition of an "eligible individual" for purposes of a HSA.
Q 401. Definition of a "high deductible health plan" for purposes of a HSA.
Q 404. Limits on contributions to a HSA.
Q 406. An employer offering a HSA to its employees must make "comparable" contributions for comparable employees.
Q 412. Penalty for making excess contributions to a HSA. Treatment of excess contributions.
Q 417. Taxation of funds accumulated in a HSA prior to distribution.
Q 418. Taxation of amounts distributed from a HSA.
Q 420. Transfer of funds into a HSA.
Q 422. Transfer of an individual's interest in a HSA as part of a divorce or separation.
Q 424. Disposition of a HSA upon the death of the account holder. Treatment of a surviving spouse as account owner.
Q 425. Amounts contributed to a HSA are not subject to social security taxes.
Q 426. Employer contributions to a HSA on behalf of an employee are not subject to withholding.
Q 427. Tax reporting requirements that apply to a HSA.
Q 457. Distributions from a HSA that do not qualify as medical expenses under the Patient Protection and Affordable Care Act (i.e., nonprescription drugs).

Footnotes

1 HDHPs can also include self-insured medical reimbursement plans that are sponsored by an employer. See chart on page 257.

2 The "preventive care" safe harbor allows HDHP coverage for items such as periodic physical exams, routine pre-natal and well-child care, immunizations, tobacco cessation programs, obesity weight-loss programs, and a long list of health screening services that includes, among others, mammograms and PSA tests (i.e., these services can be provided without regard to the $1,350 and $2,700 deductibles). If prescription drug coverage provides a benefit before satisfying the required deductible it would prevent tax-deductible contributions to a HSA. Permitted is insurance for a specific disease or illness, accident and disability insurance, and coverage for dental care and vision care. In sum, only preventive care services, permitted insurance, and permitted coverages are allowed in conjunction with a HDHP.

3 Calendar year taxpayers have until April 15 of the following year to make contributions for the previous year (filing extensions do not extend the time). No contributions are allowed once an individual has reached age 65.

4 A participant in a health reimbursement arrangement (HRA), or a health flexible spending account (FSA), may, one time per arrangement, make an employer-to-trustee transfer to an HSA (see overview of Medical Expense Programs, on page 644). This transfer will be treated as a rollover contribution to the HSA (i.e., it will not count toward the annual HSA contribution limit). In addition, individuals who own either a traditional or a Roth IRA may make a one-time trustee-to-trustee transfer from their IRA to a HSA (referred to as an "IRA-HSA rollover"). This transfer will not be included in the individual's income, nor will it be subject to the 10-percent penalty tax for premature withdrawals. However, the amount cannot exceed the individual's maximum HSA contribution limit for the year (in 2019, $3,500 for individuals and $7,000 for families). There is also an additional $1,000 per year contribution allowable for individuals who attain age 55 before the close of the taxable year.

5 Tax-deferred accumulation of earnings and no requirement to withdraw funds at any particular time makes the HSA particularly advantageous as a savings vehicle for future health care expenses (e.g., expenses incurred after age 65). For example, assume a family is covered by a HDHP. In 2019 this allows a maximum annual deposit into the HSA of $7,000 (indexed by the 2017 Tax Act and increasing as per the so-called "chained CPI"). Contributions to a HSA may be invested in the same manner as contributions to an IRA (e.g., in stocks and bonds). Of course, the HSA is also available for spending on current medical costs or to reimburse the account holder for incurred health care costs.

6 Lower-paid employees in the lowest tax brackets are less likely to benefit from these tax-deductions. Critics of HSAs maintain that for lower-paid employees with substantial health care costs these tax benefits may prove largely illusory. The perceived cost-shifting of the cost of health care to workers is also of concern when an employer switches from a comprehensive coverage program to a high-deductible health plan in order to reduce premium costs. In response, proponents of HSAs maintain that increases in health care costs have excluded many people (particularly the self-employed) from having any health care insurance; and HSAs, together with HDHPs, will make insurance more affordable. It is also argued that savings will come from engaging the health care consumer in health care choices.

7 Under the Patient Protection and Affordable Care Act of 2010 the penalty-tax was increased from 10 percent to 20 percent for distributions made on and after January 1, 2011. The penalty tax does not apply if the distribution is on account of the beneficiary's death, disability, or after reaching age 65 (i.e., has become eligible for Medicare).

8 Prior to age 65, HSAs cannot be used to make tax-free reimbursements of an employee's share of health insurance premiums.

TAX-FAVORED RETIREMENT PLANS

Tax-favored retirement plans can be established in a variety of ways.

- Qualified retirement plans such as defined benefit pension plans, money-purchase pension plans, and 401(k) plans, can be installed in a corporation, a partnership, or a sole proprietorship.[1]

- Individual retirement arrangements (IRAs), including both individual retirement accounts and individual retirement annuities, can be established by many taxpayers. With a simplified employee pension plan (SEP) or a SIMPLE IRA, employer contributions can also be made to individual retirement accounts.

- Section 403(b) plans are available to employees of public schools and colleges, and certain non-profit hospitals, and charitable, religious, scientific, and educational organizations.

- Section 457 plans are available to employees of state and local governments and tax-exempt organizations.

To better appreciate the advantages of tax-favored retirement plans, we can compare the growth of a tax-favored account to the results obtained when after-tax funds are invested outside a tax-favored plan … for example, in certificates of deposit, savings accounts, or treasury bills. Assume that there are $1,000 of before-tax funds available for investment per year over the next 20 years.[2]

Taxable Growth. If after-tax dollars were invested outside of a tax-favored plan, assuming a 25 percent tax bracket, of the original $1,000 only $750 per year would remain after-taxes for investment.[3] The earnings will also be taxed, which means that although the investment might pay 8 percent interest, it would yield only 6 percent after-taxes. The reduced after-tax funds available for investment, combined with the reduced after-tax yield, means that in 10 years $10,478 will have accumulated, and in 20 years $29,245.

Tax-Deferred Growth. The tax leverage provided by a tax-favored plan offers the opportunity for substantially increased accumulations, because there are no current taxes on contributions, and no current taxes on investment earnings. This means that each year $1,000 will actually be invested, and a full 8 percent rate of return will actually be credited, neither being subject to current income taxation. A tax-deferred growth of 8 percent will accumulate $15,645 in 10 years, and $49,423 in 20 years. Although payments received during retirement will be taxable, after-tax income will usually far exceed that available with investments that are not tax-favored.

Footnotes on page 267

TAX LEVERAGE

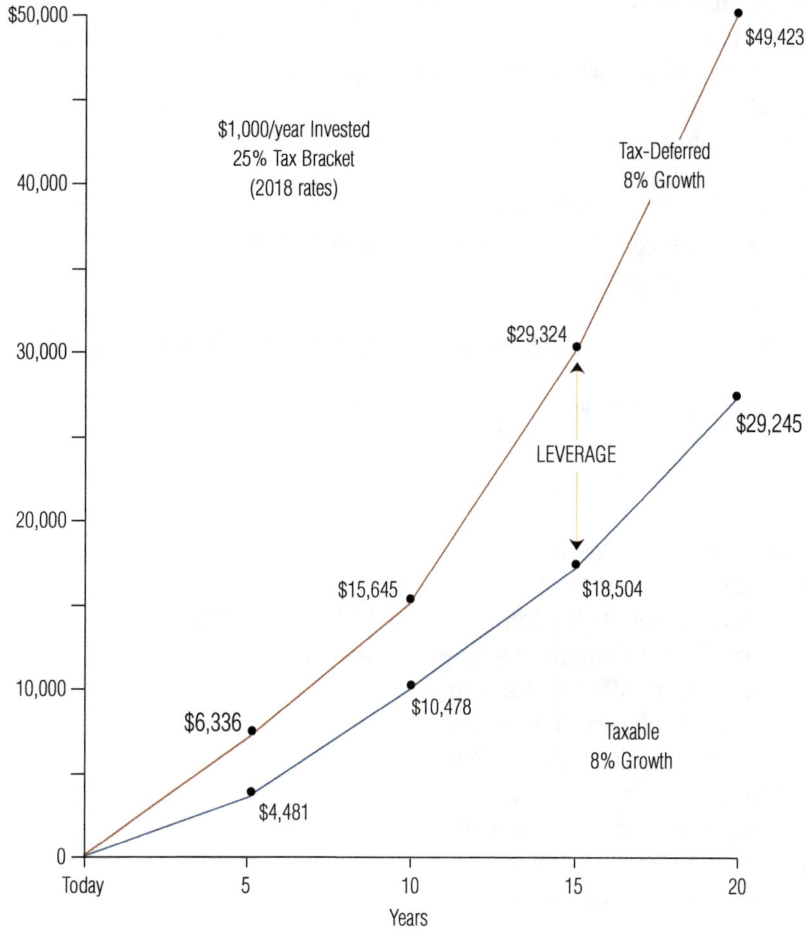

NO CURRENT TAXATION ON CONTRIBUTIONS & INVESTMENT EARNINGS

- Money Purchase Pension Plans
- Target Benefit Plans
- Profit Sharing Plans
- 401(k) Plans
- ESOPs
- Stock Bonus Plans
- Age-Weighted Profit Sharing Plans
- Thrift Plans
- Defined Benefit Plans
- Cash Balance Plans
- Keogh Plans For Self Employed (HR-10)
- Individual Retirement Arrangements (IRAs)
- SIMPLE IRAs
- Simplified Employee Pension Plans (SEPs)
- 403(b) Plans
- 412(i) Plans
- 457 Plans

INFORMATION REQUIRED FOR ANALYSIS & PROPOSAL

1. Names of employees.
2. Dates of birth.
3. Smoker/nonsmoker – when life insurance is to be used.
4. Salary schedule.
5. Status of employees – full time *or* part time.
6. Employment dates.
7. Retirement benefit – if defined benefit; *or*
   Dollar or percent contribution – if defined contribution.
8. Employer's tax bracket.

CROSS REFERENCES TO TAX FACTS ON INSURANCE & EMPLOYEE BENEFITS, VOL. 2 (2019)

Q 3579. Nonqualified deferred compensation tax benefits that are available to employees of state or local governments and other tax-exempt employers.
Q 3582. Requirements that a Section 457 plan must satisfy.
Q 3638. Description of individual retirement plan (IRA).
Q 3642. Description of a "deemed IRA."
Q 3656. Description of Roth IRA.
Q 3659. Rollover or conversion from traditional IRA to Roth IRA.
Q 3698. Description of simplified employee pension plan (SEP).
Q 3703. Description of SIMPLE IRA plan.
Q 3716. Description of defined benefit plan.
Q 3725. Description of defined contribution plan.
Q 3733. Description of pension plan.
Q 3734. Description of profit sharing plan.
Q 3752. Description of 401(k) plan.
Q 3762. Description of solo 401(k) plan.
Q 3770. Description of SIMPLE 401(k) plan.
Q 3802. Description of a 412(i) plan.
Q 3817. Description of Keogh (HR-10) plan.
Q 3827. Tax advantages of qualified pension and profit sharing plans.
Q 3828. Requirements for a plan to be "qualified."
Q 4014. Tax benefits of 403(b) tax sheltered annuities.
Q 4015. Organizations that can make 403(b) tax sheltered annuities available to their employees.
Q 4018. Requirements that must be met by 403(b) tax sheltered annuities.

Footnotes

[1] The Qualified Plans Checklist on pages 627-628 provides a brief overview of some of the characteristics of qualified plans. Although some plans allow contributions of after-tax dollars, the chart on page 265 assumes all contributions are made from pre-tax dollars.

[2] To estimate the total before-tax dollars that a wage earner can expect to receive assuming annual increases in earnings of either 5 percent or 8 percent, refer to the tables of Projected Earnings on page 638. To demonstrate the importance of starting early to save for retirement, refer to the Penalty Of Waiting table on page 639. The table entitled Early Saver vs. Late Saver on page 640 also illustrates the advantage of saving early for retirement. The table entitled How Money Grows on page 642 provides the accumulations for given amounts of monthly savings. How long these savings will last during retirement can be demonstrated using the table How Money Goes on page 643.

[3] In return for *nondeductible contributions*, the Roth 401(k) feature permits *tax-free distributions* (see discussion on page 495). In contrast to the traditional IRA, the Roth IRA also permits tax-free distributions in return for nondeductible contributions (see discussions and analysis on pages 405, 411, 527, and 631-633).

401(k) PLAN

These plans allow eligible employees to defer compensation or bonuses and contribute the funds to an employer-sponsored profit sharing plan.[1] They are funded entirely or in part through salary reductions elected by the employees.[2] Because employee participation in 401(k) plans is entirely voluntary, employers will often encourage participation by matching employee contributions. These matching contributions are typically limited to a maximum percentage and/or maximum dollar amount.[3]

One of the better ways of explaining the advantages of participating in a 401(k) plan is to contrast current nonparticipation with the benefits of participation (i.e., a "before and after" presentation).

WITHOUT PARTICIPATION. Assume that in 2019 a thirty-five-year-old married employee with an annual salary of $52,000 currently pays $2,979 in federal income taxes, $840 in state income taxes and $3,978 in Social Security taxes. This leaves $44,203 of "take-home pay," with nothing set aside for retirement. (Calculation assumes: joint filing, standard deduction, and 3 percent of federal AGI state income tax.)

WITH PARTICIPATION. Now assume that this same employee has the opportunity to participate in a plan with a 50 percent employer match, (i.e., the employer will contribute one dollar for every two dollars of employee elective deferral).[4] If the employee elects to defer 6 percent of salary ($3,120 per year), the employer would then make a matching contribution of $1,560.[5] The total annual deposits to the employee's account are $4,680, consisting of the employee's elective deferral of $3,120 and his employer's matching contribution of $1,560. Because his contributions are before tax, the employee's federal income taxes are reduced to $2,605 and his state income taxes are reduced to $746. Social Security taxes are not affected by employee elective deferrals.[6] Take home pay will be reduced to $41,551.

Note that a reduction in take-home pay of only $2,652 has produced a deposit of $4,680 into the employee's retirement account. The efficiency of this is even greater for taxpayers in a higher tax bracket (the top marginal federal rate is 37 percent in 2019) than this example where the taxpayer's top marginal rate is (temporarily because of the 2017 Tax Act) only 12 percent.

A thirty-five-year-old employee can accumulate $393,720 by age sixty-five; assuming level plan contributions of $390 at the beginning of each month and 6 percent interest on plan assets. Over the same 30-year period, total employee contributions amount to only $93,600. Waiting just five years to begin participation would reduce age sixty-five projected accumulations to $271,619, which is $122,101 less than would accumulate assuming immediate participation (393,720 – 271,619 = 122,101).[7]

Footnotes on page 271

WITHOUT PARTICIPATION

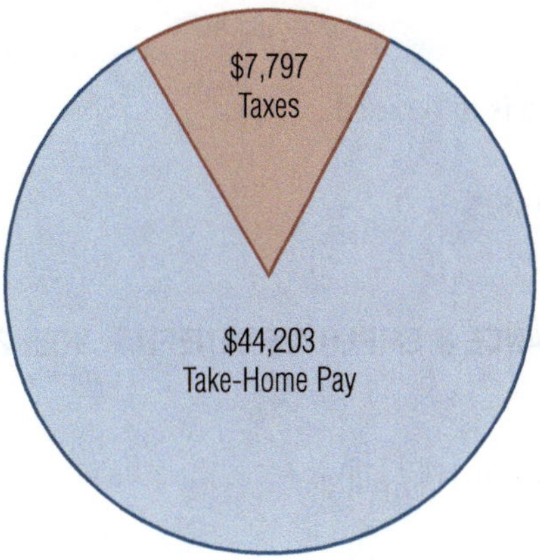

Annual Salary	$52,000
Less: Federal Income Tax	2,979
State Income Tax	840
Social Security	3,978
Take-Home Pay	$44,203

WITH PARTICIPATION

Assuming 6% Deferral and 50% Employer Match

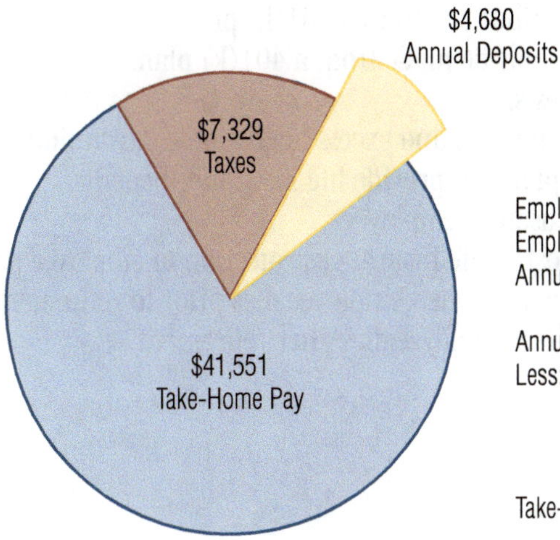

Employee Deferral	$3,120
Employer Match	1,560
Annual Deposits	$4,680

Annual Salary	$52,000
Less: Employee Deferral	3,120
Federal Income Tax	2,605
State Income Tax	746
Social Security	3,978
Take-Home Pay	$41,551

An annual reduction in Take-Home Pay of $2,558 produces Annual Deposits of $4,680.

Assuming 6.00% interest and level contribution levels, an employee age 35 would accumulate $393,720 by age 65. Total employee contributions would be $93,600.

Waiting 5 years to begin participation would reduce age 65 projected accumulations to $271,619.

INFORMATION REQUIRED FOR ANALYSIS & PROPOSAL

1. Names of employees.
2. Dates of birth.
3. Smoker/nonsmoker – when life insurance is to be used.
4. Salary schedule.
5. Status of employees – full time *or* part time.
6. Employment dates.

CROSS REFERENCES TO TAX FACTS ON INSURANCE & EMPLOYEE BENEFITS, VOL. 2 (2019)

Q 3752. General description of 401(k) plan.
Q 3753. Special qualification requirements for 401(k) plans.
Q 3760. Limits on elective deferrals.
Q 3761. Description of catch-up contributions.
Q 3762. Description of a solo 401(k) plan.
Q 3763. Description of an automatic enrollment safe harbor 401(k) plan.
Q 3765. Requirements for a 401(k) safe harbor plan.
Q 3770. Requirements for a SIMPLE 401(k) plan.
Q 3771. Requirements for Roth 401(k) feature.
Q 3789. Restrictions that apply to distributions from a 401(k) plan.
Q 3790. When hardship withdrawals may be made from a 401(k) plan.
Q 3792-Q 3795. The ADP and ACP tests.
Q 3798. Distributions of excess contributions and excess aggregate contributions.
Q 3820. Extent to which a qualified plan can provide life insurance benefits.
Q 3919. Definition of "highly compensated" employees.
Q 3937. Method used to determine cost of life insurance protection to employee participant.
Q 3962-Q 3963. Taxation of death benefit when employee dies prior to retirement.
Q 3964. Taxation of death benefit when employee dies after retirement.

Footnotes

[1] In addition to meeting the requirements necessary to qualify as a profit sharing or stock bonus plan, traditional 401(k) plans must: (1) limit the forfeitability and distribution of employee elective deferrals; (2) permit participation by the later of age twenty-one or one year of service; (3) limit elective deferrals to $19,000 in 2019; and (4) meet an annual nondiscrimination requirement (the ADP test), by comparing ratios of elective deferrals for highly compensated and nonhighly compensated employees. In contrast, employers can avoid the nondiscrimination testing required of traditional 401(k) plans if they are willing to make required contributions and meet other design requirements. See 401(k) Plan Designs, page 629.

[2] These amounts are referred to as "elective deferrals." It is helpful to remember that 401(k) plans can contain the following:

a. **Employee elective deferrals** – amounts the employee elects to have the employer contribute instead of receiving cash (the source might be existing salary, salary increases, or bonuses).

b. **Employer matching contributions** – made by the employer in some ratio to employee elective deferrals (if immediately 100 percent vested and subject to certain withdrawal restrictions, they are known as "qualified matching contributions").

c. **Employer nonelective contributions** – made by the employer on behalf of employees and not conditioned upon employee elective deferrals (if immediately 100 percent vested and subject to certain withdrawal restrictions, they are known as "qualified nonelective contributions").

d. **Catch-up contributions** – made by employees age fifty or over (see page 630).

[3] The typical plan design provides for the employer to match from 25 to 100 percent of employee *contributions* to a maximum of 5 to 10 percent of employee compensation.

[4] The employee elective deferral is limited to $19,000 in 2019 for traditional and safe harbor plans. Amounts deferred in excess of this limit (other than catch-up contributions) are not excludable from income, and, if not timely corrected by distribution, will be taxed a second time when distributed from the plan.

[5] Unless the plan is a safe harbor design (see page 629), the amount of elective deferrals must satisfy the ADP test. Matching contributions are often used to improve ADP results. The Actual Deferral Percentage (ADP) test is applied by dividing employees into two groups … the *highly* compensated, and the *nonhighly* compensated. The ADP test is met if either: (1) the deferral percentage for eligible highly compensated employees during the year does not exceed the deferral percentage of all other eligible employees in the *preceding* year multiplied by 1.25; *or* (2) the deferral percentage for eligible highly compensated employees during the year is not more than 2 percent higher than, nor more than 2 times, the deferral percentage for all other eligible employees in the *preceding* year (in either case, an election is available to compare current instead of preceding year results). An employee is potentially within the group of "highly compensated employees" if he:

a. Was a 5 percent owner at any time during the current or preceding year, or

b. Earned from his employer more than $125,000 for the preceding year (in 2019, as indexed for inflation) and, if the employer elects to apply this clause, was in the top 20 percent in relation to compensation for that year.

[6] Although most states allow an employee to exclude 401(k) contributions from taxable income, it would be advisable to check with individual state authorities.

[7] Provided it is an "incidental benefit," life insurance can be purchased within a 401(k) plan. Up to 49.9 percent of annual contributions can be used to purchase whole life insurance (24.9 percent if used to purchase universal life). The participant must include in gross income the "cost" of the insurance coverage (measured by multiplying the difference between the face amount and the cash surrender value by either the Table 2001 rates or the insurance companies' rates for individual 1-year term life insurance). If the employee dies prior to retirement, death proceeds in excess of cash surrender values are received free of income taxes.

403(b) PLANS

403(b) plans are available to employees of public schools and colleges, and certain non-profit hospitals, charitable, religious, scientific, and educational organizations.[1] The employee may supply the funds by agreeing to a salary reduction, or by foregoing a salary increase, or the employer may make contributions as additional compensation to the employee.[2] Contributions are *before taxes*, meaning that a participant is able to exclude the contributions from his current taxable income.[3]

Generally, with a salary reduction plan the lowest of these two limits may be excluded from income each year:

- A limit of $19,000 in 2019, which also includes total salary reduction contributions to Section 401(k) Plans, Simplified Employee Pension Plans and SIMPLE IRAs. "Catch up" provisions allow: (1) certain employees with 15 years of service to increase this amount by an additional $3,000; and (2) employees who have attained age 50 to increase this amount by an additional $6,000 in 2019.
- The lesser of $56,000 in 2019, or 100 percent of compensation, made to all defined contribution plans by the same employer.

The compounding effect of before tax contributions and tax-deferred growth may result in substantially increased accumulations.[4] Because the annuity is generally portable to another qualified employer, contributions may be continued when changing employment.

Distributions from tax deferred annuities are subject to ordinary income taxes, unless rolled over into a traditional Individual Retirement Arrangement (IRA), another 403(b) plan, a 401(k) plan, a 457 government plan, or a 401(a) qualified retirement plan.[5] In addition, withdrawals may be subject to a 10-percent penalty tax. However, penalty-free withdrawals are allowed once the participant has attained age 59½, separated from service after attaining age 55, or under other specific circumstances.[6] With some restrictions, tax-free loans are also available.[7]

Required distributions of amounts accruing after 1986 generally must begin by April 1st of the year following the year in which the employee retires or attains age 70½, whichever is later.[8] Payments made under an annuity contract may be for the life of the employee (or lives of the employee and his beneficiary), or a period certain not longer than the life expectancy of the employee (or joint and last survivor life expectancy of the employee and his beneficiary).

Footnotes on page 275

SALARY REDUCTION PLAN

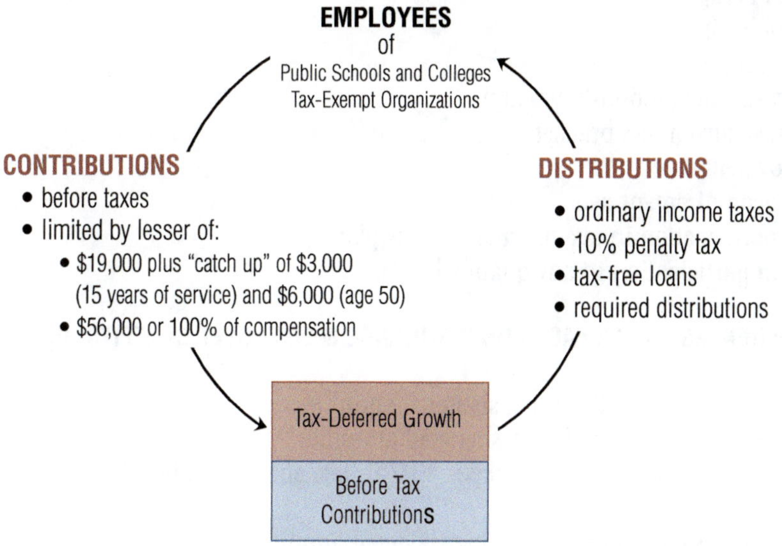

INFORMATION REQUIRED FOR ANALYSIS & PROPOSAL

1. Name of employee.
2. Date of birth.
3. Marital status.
4. Salary (annual, monthly, weekly).
5. Assumed current tax bracket.
6. Employment date.
7. Projected retirement age.
8. Prior participation in tax deferred annuity plan.
9. Current participation in any qualified plan.

CROSS REFERENCES TO TAX FACTS ON INSURANCE & EMPLOYEE BENEFITS, VOL. 2 (2019)

Q 3994. Rollovers from 403(b) tax sheltered annuities.
Q 4019. Tax benefits of 403(b) tax sheltered annuities.
Q 4020. Organizations that can make 403(b) tax sheltered annuities available to their employees.
Q 4021. Methods of funding 403(b) tax sheltered annuities.
Q 4022. Requirements that must be met.
Q 4023. Nine requirements of a tax sheltered annuity contract.
Q 4025. Minimum nondiscrimination requirements.
Q 4029. Limits on excludable contributions.
Q 4030. Section 415 overall limits.
Q 4034. Salary reduction limits.
Q 4048. Taxation of incidental life insurance protection.
Q 4050. Loans under a 403(b) tax sheltered annuity.
Q 4061. Distributions subject to penalties.
Q 4062-Q 4074. Required distributions.
Q 4075. Taxation of payments received by employee.
Q 4077. Taxation of death benefits received by employee's beneficiary.
Q 4079. Effect of salary reduction on social security tax and income tax withholding.

Footnotes

[1] A 403(b) plan is also referred to as a "tax sheltered annuity," or "TSA." Rather than "tax *sheltered* annuity," the Securities and Exchange Commission prefers the term "tax *deferred* annuity." Many companies now use the terms "tax deferred annuity" and "TDA," particularly when marketing variable annuities (see footnote 3, page 45, regarding licensing and prospectus requirements). 403(b) plans are also referred to as: (1) "qualified" annuity plans; and (2) "501(c)(3) plans" or "501(c)(3) pensions" (Section 501(c)(3) describes certain tax-exempt organizations).

[2] Nondiscrimination rules may apply to both salary reduction and employer contributions.

[3] Where a reduction in salary is taken to provide the premium payments for a 403(b) plan, Social Security taxes and benefits are based upon the *unreduced* salary (i.e., although income taxes are reduced, there is no reduction in Social Security taxes).

[4] The chart on page 265 demonstrates the leverage afforded by the typical tax-favored retirement plan. Investing in a *variable* 403(b) plan provides a particularly attractive opportunity for dollar cost averaging (see graph, page 641).

[5] However, if the employee has an investment in the contract, he or she is allowed a tax-free recovery of his or her investment. Examples of an employee's *investment in the contract* include: (1) any premiums that the employee has paid with nondeductible dollars; (2) any employer contributions that were taxable to the employee by virtue of having exceeded his or her exclusion allowance in years before 2002 or the overall limit; (3) the sum of the annual one-year term costs that were taxable to the employee (where the contract provided life insurance protection); and (4) the amount of any loans included in income as a taxable distribution. When benefits are received in installments, or as a life income, the employee's investment in the contract requires the calculation of an exclusion ratio. The method used to determine the exclusion ratio depends upon the annuity starting date. Distributions are generally subject to mandatory withholding of 20 percent unless the employee elects a direct rollover.

[6] These additional specific circumstances include: (1) death; (2) disability; (3) as a part of substantially equal periodic payments beginning after separation from service; (4) when used for medical expenses exceeding 7.5 percent of adjusted gross income; (5) distribution of excess contributions within the same calendar year; (6) payments to an alternate payee under a qualified domestic relations order; and (7) penalty-free withdrawals for military reservists.

[7] The maximum tax-free loan is generally one-half the contract value, or $50,000, whichever is less. However, an exception is available for the first $10,000 of cash value, all of which may be borrowed. Loan repayments must be made at least quarterly and in amounts that allow for amortization over five years, except for loans to purchase a primary residence, which may be repaid over a longer "reasonable" period.

[8] These rules apply whether the distribution is calculated under the 1987, 2001, or 2002 regulations. However, different rules apply when distributions are not made as an annuity. See pages 411-413.

412(e)(3) PLANS

A 412(e)(3) plan is a defined benefit plan that is funded by life insurance and annuities.[1] Prior to the Pension Protection Act of 2006, these plans were governed by IRC Section 412(i) and are, therefore, sometimes promoted as 412(i) plans. These plans provide high-earning business owners who have stable cash flow an opportunity to make maximum deductible retirement contributions while offering a high degree of security to plan participants.

PLAN REQUIREMENTS. 412(e)(3) plans are subject to all the requirements that apply to other defined benefit plans, including nondiscrimination, vesting and benefit limitations.[2] In addition, they must generally meet the following six additional requirements: (1) the plan must be funded exclusively by life insurance policies and/or annuities guaranteed by a state licensed insurance company; (2) contracts must have level premiums; (3) benefits must be provided entirely by these contracts; (4) premiums must be paid without lapse; (5) contract rights cannot be subject to a security interest; and (6) no policy loans are allowed.[3]

FUNDING. Known as "fully insured" plans, 412(e)(3) plans are typically funded with a combination of life insurance and annuities.[4] The primary purpose of the plan must be to provide retirement income. Therefore, when life insurance is used it must provide participants with no more than an "incidental" death benefit. To satisfy this requirement defined benefit plans often limit the insured death benefit to not more than 100 times the expected monthly benefit.[5] Excessive funding may result in nondeductible contributions and "listed transaction" status. Each plan participant has the right to name the beneficiary of this death benefit and must include in income an amount equal to the "economic benefit" of the life insurance benefit.[6]

THE TRADEOFFS. Because 412(e)(3)plans are exempt from the full funding limit that otherwise applies to defined benefit plans, they offer (within limits) the opportunity to make accelerated contributions resulting in large upfront tax deductions. Simplicity is achieved with conservative low-risk life insurance and annuity contracts that shift investment risks from the employer to the insurance company. The IRS has scrutinized these plans in recent years because of questionable actuarial assumptions being used to increase the level of funding. These plans offer pre-retirement death benefits that are easy to calculate and plan benefits that are easier to understand.[7]

In contrast, other defined benefit **plans** provide more flexibility in both plan design and investment options. This offers the potential for high investment returns, but this entails fewer guarantees and increased risk (i.e., risk and return go hand in hand). Initial costs tend to be lower, but ongoing administrative and actuarial costs tend to be higher in comparison to 412(e)(3) plans.[8]

Footnotes on page 279

PLAN REQUIREMENTS

Subject to the same qualification requrements as any other defined benefit plan, including:

- Nondiscrimination
- Vesting
- Benefit Limits

Must also meet the following additional requirements:

- Funded exclusively by life insurance contracts and/or annuities
- Level annual premiums
- Benefits guaranteed by insurance company
- Premiums paid without lapse
- Not subject to security interests
- No policy loans

FUNDING

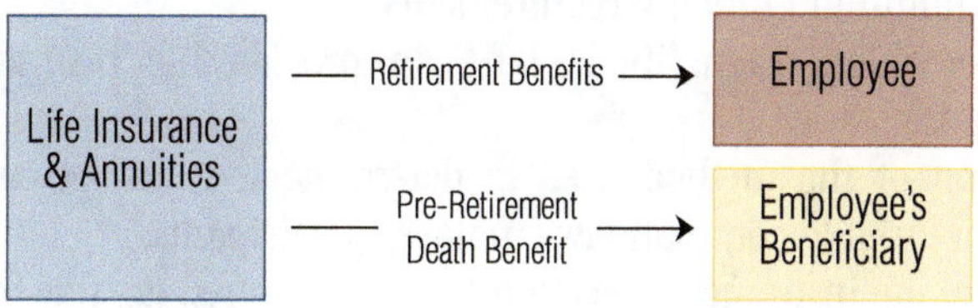

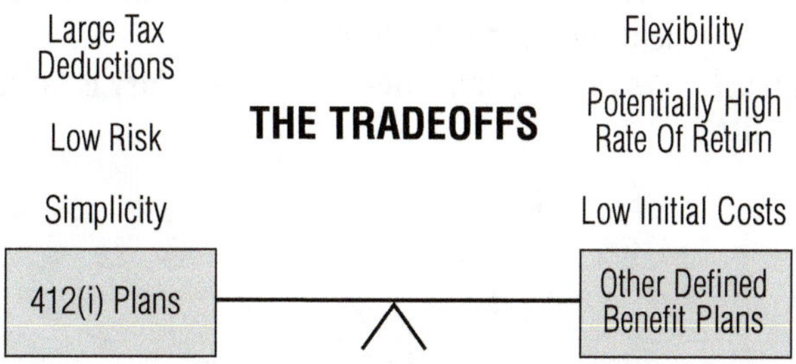

INFORMATION REQUIRED FOR ANALYSIS & PROPOSAL

1. Names of employees.
2. Sex.
3. Dates of birth.
4. Dates of employment.
5. W-2 salary.
6. Hours worked per year.
7. Tax status of business (sole proprietor, C corporation, S corporation, professional corporation, partnership, limited liability company).
8. Ownership percentage.
9. Projected retirement age.
10. Other pension plans in force.

CROSS REFERENCES TO TAX FACTS ON INSURANCE & EMPLOYEE BENEFITS, VOL. 2 (2019)

Q 3717. Special qualification requirements that apply to defined benefit pension plans.
Q 3742. Minimum funding standard for pension plans.
Q 3802. Basic description of 412(i) plans.
Q 3803. Requirements a Section 412(i) fully insured plan must meet in order to be exempt from the minimum funding requirements.
Q 3820. Extent to which a qualified plan can provide life insurance benefits for its participants.
Q 3937. Description of the method used to determine the cost of current life insurance protection taxed to common law employee participants.
Q 3941. The cost of life insurance protection can be recovered tax free from plan benefits.
Q 3962. When employee dies *before* retirement – how beneficiary is taxed on a single sum cash payment of the death benefit.
Q 3963. When employee dies *before* retirement – how beneficiary is taxed on life income or installment payments of the death benefit.
Q 3964. When employee dies *after* retirement – how beneficiary is taxed on payments of the death benefit.

Footnotes

[1] In consolidating the funding rules of Section 412, the Pension Protection Act of 2006 eliminated Section 412(i) and moved its provisions without substantive changes to Section 412(e)(3). Although Section 412(i) no longer exists, the fully insured plans described in this chart are often still referred to as"412(i) plans."

[2] For example, the plan must generally include all full-time non-union employees, except for employees younger than 21 and those with less than one year of service. See the Qualified Plan Checklist, page 627 (but 412(e)(3) plans are exempt from the stated "maximum limits").

[3] It is important to recognize that a defined benefit plan entails an obligation on the part of the employer to fund the plan each and every year. Failure to make regular premium payments could cause it to fail the IRS requirement that the plan be "permanent."

[4] Most 412(e)(3) plans provide a death benefit, but it is not required. Guidance released by the IRS in 2004 announced a crackdown on 412(i) plans in three major areas: (1) valuation of life contracts – regulations require that a contract's fair market value be included in the distributee's income, not merely the cash value (a safe harbor definition of fair market value is provided); (2) discrimination in the types of contracts provided to highly compensated employees – discrimination against nonhighly compensated employees with respect to purchase or surrender rights, cash value growth terms, exchange features, or other benefits rights and features, will be considered to violate the nondiscrimination requirement; and (3) deduction of premiums for "excessive" amounts of life insurance – premiums attributable to excessive coverage will not be deductible, a 10 percent excise tax on nondeductible contributions may be applied, and the plan may be classified as a "listed transaction."

[5] This "incidental" death benefit requirement is also satisfied if: (1) the cost of the benefit is less than 25 percent of the cost of all benefits provided under the plan (the 25 percent rule); or (2) less than 50 percent of the employer contribution credited to each participant's account is used to purchase "ordinary life insurance" (if either *term* insurance or *universal life* insurance is purchased the 50 percent is reduced to 25 percent).

[6] This value is taxed at the lower of the Table 2001 rates (page 596) or the life insurance company's actual term rates for standard risks (beginning in 2004 the use of the insurance company's term rates was more restricted). When life insurance protection under a plan is provided by a cash value policy the aggregate costs taxed to the employee are considered to be a part of the employee's basis and may be recovered tax free from the *retirement benefits* received under the policy. Income taxation of this *death benefit* is as follows: (1) the pure insurance element (death benefit less cash values) is received free of taxes; (2) the total of "economic benefit" costs paid by participant are also received free of taxes; and (3) any remaining death benefit is taxed as a qualified plan distribution (generally as ordinary income). Qualified plan death benefits are included in the decedent's estate for estate tax purposes unless the participant avoids having any "incidents of ownership" in the policy (see page 374).

[7] If there are excess earnings they must be used to reduce future contributions that fund plan benefits. 412(i) plans also avoid both excise and income taxes on reversions to the employer, since they are fully funded by the annuity values and life insurance cash vales that determine the retirement benefit.

[8] When compared to other funding vehicles, such as variable annuities or equity investments, the question of whether the large and accelerated tax deductions produced by 412(e)(3) plans adequately compensate for their comparatively low guaranteed rates of return is controversial. Ultimately the decision may be more influenced by a desire to: (1) fund life insurance on a tax deductible basis; and (2) avoid the risks associated with equity investments.

457 PLANS

Section 457 plans are nonqualified deferred compensation plans available to employees of state and local governments and tax-exempt organizations.[1] By deferring income, employees are able to reduce current income taxes while saving more for retirement than they would with the typical after-tax savings plan.[2]

ELIGIBLE PLANS. Under "eligible" plans, in 2019 deferrals are limited to the lesser of $19,000, or 100 percent of includable compensation.[3] Benefits usually are not subject to forfeiture. Eligible plans are most often used for the "rank and file" employees of state and local governments, who desire to defer *limited* amounts of compensation on an attractive tax deferred basis.[4] Employees of *state and local governments* are not taxed until benefits are actually paid. In contrast, employees of *tax-exempt organizations* are not taxed until the benefits are actually paid *or* otherwise made available to them. Tax-exempt organizations can only make eligible plans available to a select group of management or highly compensated employees.[5] (These higher paid employees of tax-exempt organizations often prefer "ineligible plans" providing for greater deferrals.) The *earliest* plan distributions can be made is at severance of employment, death, an "unforeseeable emergency," or in the calendar year in which the participant reaches age 70½. Plan distributions must generally begin by April 1 of the year following the year in which the employee retires or attains age 70½, whichever is later. Distributions from Section 457 plans are subject to ordinary income taxes. Rollovers are permitted to and from an eligible Section 457 plan of a state or local government, a qualified plan, a Section 403(b) tax sheltered annuity, or an IRA.

INELIGIBLE PLANS. Under "ineligible" plans, employees may make *unlimited* deferrals of compensation, provided the benefits are subject to a "substantial risk of forfeiture."[6] These plans are most often used by tax-exempt organizations to provide substantial deferrals for a *select* group of management or highly compensated employees (the "top hat" group). Use of ineligible plans by state and local governments is generally limited to highly paid employees who can accept a risk of forfeiture, since such a risk is often unacceptable to the "rank and file" employee. Because employees are taxed when there is no longer a substantial risk of forfeiture, vesting provisions must be carefully drafted.[7] Ineligible plans are not required to comply with any specific distribution requirements. Non-qualified or ineligble plans for tax-exempt organizations differ primarily from those used in for-profit businesses because of the fact that deferral of taxation cannot be pushed beyond retirement.

Both eligible and ineligible plans may *not* be formally funded, except for eligible governmental plans. However, it is customary and desirable for employers to "informally" fund their obligations through the purchase of life insurance, annuities, or investment products.[8] Any deferrals, and assets purchased with the deferrals, must remain the property of the employer and are subject to the employer's general creditors.

Footnotes on page 283

EMPLOYEES
of
State and Local Governments
Tax-Exempt Organizations

ELIGIBLE PLANS

- Deferrals limited to lesser of:
  $19,000
  or 100% of compensation
- Benefits not subject to forfeiture
- Coverage - State and Local Governments have no specific coverage requirements (Tax-Exempt Organizations must limit coverage to "top hat" group)
- Employee taxed when benefits actually paid or otherwise made available
- Distribution requirements:
  - seperation from service
  - unforeseeable emergency
  - age 70½

INELIGIBLE PLANS

- Deferrals unlimited
- Benefits subject to a "substantial risk of forfeiture"
- Coverage - Tax-Exempt Organizations must limit coverage to "top hat" group (State and Local Governments have no specific coverage requirements)
- Employee taxed when there is no substantial risk or forfeiture
- No distribution requirements

Both

- May not be formally funded except for eligible governmental plans
- Deferrals subject to employer's creditors except for eligible governmental plans

INFORMATION REQUIRED FOR ANALYSIS & PROPOSAL

1. Name of employee.
2. Date of birth.
3. Marital status.
4. Salary (annual, monthly, weekly).
5. Assumed current tax bracket.
6. Projected retirement age.
7. Prior and current participation in any qualified plans (including state teacher's retirement plans), 403(b) plans, and Section 457 plans.
8. Smoker/nonsmoker – when life insurance is to be used.

CROSS REFERENCES TO TAX FACTS ON INSURANCE & EMPLOYEE BENEFITS, VOL. 2 (2019)

Q 3579. Nonqualified deferred compensation tax benefits that are available to employees of state or local governments and other tax-exempt employers.

Q 3582. Requirements that a Section 457 plan must satisfy.

Q 3598. Taxation of cost of life insurance protection and death benefits provided under Section 457 plans.

Q 3599. Income taxation of death benefits provided under Section 457 plans.

Q 3600. Taxation of participants in eligible Section 457 plans, and "ineligible" plans.

Q 3601. Taxation of participants in "ineligible" Section 457(f) plans.

Footnotes

[1] "State and local governments" include a state, a political subdivision of a state, or any agency or instrumentality of either of them (e.g., a school district or sewage authority). Tax-exempt organizations include those types of nongovernmental organizations exempt from tax under Code Section 501 (i.e., most nonprofit organizations that serve their members or some public or charitable purpose, but not a church or synagogue). Under "eligible" plans, only individuals may participate, not partnerships or corporations. Partnerships and corporations may participate in "ineligible" plans (see footnote 5, below). Section 457 plans can also be made available to independent contractors, but under somewhat different rules.

[2] The chart on page 265 can be used to demonstrate the leverage afforded by the typical tax-favored retirement plan. Investing in a ***variable*** tax deferred annuity provides a particularly attractive opportunity for dollar cost averaging (see graph, page 641).

[3] The dollar limit on deferrals to a Section 457 plan is $19,000 for 2019. When appropriate, cost-of-living adjustments are made in $500 increments. This conforms to the elective deferral limits for 401(k) plans and Section 403(b) plans. "Catch-up" provisions may permit larger deferrals. See the table of Employee Benefit Limits on page 630.

[4] The term "eligible plans" is used to describe the deferred compensation plans of state and local governments and tax-exempt organizations that comply with the provisions of Section 457. When a plan provides for deferrals in *excess* of the lesser of $19,000 or 100 percent of compensation, Section 457(f) states, "compensation shall be included in the gross income of the participant or beneficiary for the 1st taxable year in which there is no substantial risk of forfeiture." Plans falling under Section 457(f) are variously referred to as "ineligible" plans and "Section 457(f)" plans.

[5] Unlike plans of state and local governments, plans of tax-exempt organizations can be subject to the participation, vesting, and funding requirements of ERISA (see page 368). These ERISA requirements are in conflict with the "no funding" requirements of Section 457 for tax-exempt organizations. This prevents most tax-exempt organizations from having a Section 457 plan unless the plan fits within the ERISA "top hat" exemption (i.e., an unfunded plan for a select group of management or highly compensated employees). This also means that "rank and file" employees of tax-exempt organizations cannot participate in Section 457 plans.

[6] A "substantial risk of forfeiture" is said to exist if a participant's right to the compensation is conditioned upon the future performance of substantial services. The risk of forfeiture must be both real and substantial.

[7] For example, payment of compensation might be conditioned upon the continued employment of the participant for a specified period, measured by a pre-established service completion date. At the end of the service completion date, when there are no longer any future service requirements, and therefore no risk of forfeiture, the deferred amount (including earnings accumulated prior to the lapse of the risk) is included in the participant's taxable income. However, the *earnings* credited to the participant's account after the substantial risk of forfeiture ends generally will not be taxable as compensation until actually paid or otherwise made available. It may be desirable to release compensation over a specific period of years in order to reduce the tax burden as the contract conditions are met.

[8] If life insurance is purchased with amounts deferred, the premiums are not taxed to the participant as long as the employer remains the owner and beneficiary of the contract. However, upon the employee's death, payment of the proceeds to the employee's beneficiary would be taxed under the normal annuity rules and would not be treated as tax-free death proceeds.

EMPLOYER/EMPLOYEE SPLIT-DOLLAR PLANS

In light of Notice 2002-8 & Final Regulations

<table>
<tr><th colspan="3">Table A - Plans Entered Into Before January 28, 2002</th></tr>
<tr><th></th><th>Taxation of Cash Values</th><th>Economic Benefit</th></tr>
<tr><td>Plan Terminated
Before January 1, 2004</td><td>SH1: Employee not taxed on cash value in excess of employer's interest (referred to as the rollout safe harbor). See Planning Point 1, bottom page 285.</td><td>n/a</td></tr>
<tr><td rowspan="3">Plan Terminated
On Or After January 1, 2004</td><td>SH2: Employee not taxed on equity if plan converted to a loan from employer to employee for all periods beginning January 1, 2004 (pre-2004 employer outlays considered beginning loan balance, and subsequent employer premiums added to loan balance). After conversion to a loan there is no reportable economic benefit.</td><td rowspan="3">1. Use insurer's published term premium rates, or

2. Until further IRS guidance use Table 2001 rates as first set forth in Notice 2001-10, or

3. If specified by split-dollar agreement, may use P.S. 58 rates.</td></tr>
<tr><td>SH3: Employee taxed on existing employee equity if plan converted to a loan on or after January 1, 2004. However, employee not taxed on equity accruing after conversion.</td></tr>
<tr><td>Upon termination employee subject to being taxed on all equity if plan not previously converted to a loan from employer to employee. Would have to rely on interpretation of prior split-dollar rulings (i.e., Revenue Rulings, Technical Advice Memorandums, Private Letter Rulings, etc.). Under no inference language of Notice 2002-8 would ignore Notice 2001-10 and Notice 2002-8.</td></tr>
<tr><td rowspan="2">Plan Not Terminated
(and not materially modified)</td><td>SH4: Employee not taxed on equity provided the employee continues to report the receipt of the economic benefit and the employer retains some economic interest.</td><td></td></tr>
<tr><td>SH5: Employee not currently taxed on equity merely because cash surrender value exceeds the amount payable to employer.</td><td></td></tr>
<tr><td colspan="3">SH1: This safe harbor (SH) provides that, as long as the employer is entitled to receive full repayment of premiums, if plans entered into before January 28, 2002, are terminated before January 1, 2004, (i.e., are rolled out) the IRS will not assert that there is a taxable transfer (under Section 83). Interestingly, this appears to apply to endorsement plans as well as collateral assignment plans.</td></tr>
<tr><td colspan="3">SH2-SH5: See bottom of page 285.</td></tr>
</table>

EMPLOYER/EMPLOYEE SPLIT-DOLLAR PLANS (cont'd)

<table>
<tr><td colspan="3">Table B – Plans Entered Into After January 28, 2002 & Before September 18, 2003</td></tr>
<tr><td></td><td>Taxation Of Cash Values</td><td>Economic Benefit</td></tr>
<tr><td rowspan="2">Plan Terminated</td><td>SH3: If plan converted to a loan employee not taxed on equity accruing after conversion. However, any existing employee equity at time of conversion would be taxable. See Planning Point 2, bottom page 286.</td><td>n/a</td></tr>
<tr><td>Employee subject to being taxed on all equity if plan not converted to a loan. Would have to rely on interpretation of prior split-dollar rulings (i.e., Revenue Rulings, Technical Advice Memorandums, Private Letter Rulings, etc.). According to the no inference language of Notice 2002-8 would not consider Notices 2001-10 and 2002-8.</td><td rowspan="3">1. Use insurer's published premiums rates, but for periods after December 31, 2003, insurer must actually make known and sell term insurance at these rates, or
2. Until further IRS guidance use Table 2001 rates as first set forth in Notice 2001-10.</td></tr>
<tr><td rowspan="2">Plan Not Terminated
(and not materially modified)</td><td>SH4: Employee not taxed on equity provided the employee continues to report the receipt of the economic benefit and the employer retains some economic interest.</td></tr>
<tr><td>SH5: Employee not currently taxed on equity merely because cash surrender value exceeds the amount payable to employer.</td></tr>
<tr><td colspan="3">SH2: This safe harbor provides that, as long as the employer is entitled to receive full repayment of premiums, if the plan is converted to loan treatment the IRS will not assert that there is a taxable transfer (under Section 83) upon eventual termination.</td></tr>
<tr><td colspan="3">SH3: This safe harbor allows taxation under the Loan Regime (see Table C, page 286).</td></tr>
<tr><td colspan="3">SH4: This safe harbor provides that, as long as the plan is maintained by having the employee continue to report the economic benefit, the IRS will not challenge the arrangement as terminated (with resulting transfer of equity to employee).</td></tr>
<tr><td colspan="3">SH5: This safe harbor provides that there will be no deemed transfer under Section 83 of a portion of the cash surrender value that exceeds the amount payable to the employer.</td></tr>
</table>

EMPLOYER/EMPLOYEE SPLIT-DOLLAR PLANS (cont'd)

Table C - Plans Entered Into *After* September 17, 2003		
Plan Structured As	Taxation Of Cash Values	Economic Benefit
Economic Benefit Regime: *employer* owns policy (endorsement method).	Employee *taxed* on annual increase in value (not just at rollout). This is likely to present a difficult problem of valuation, particularly regarding variable life. Employee *taxed* on equity upon transfer of policy from employer to employee (i.e., when there is a "rollout"). But "taxable equity" is reduced by amounts paid at time of transfer and amounts of equity previously included in employee's income.	According to final regulations the IRS will issue new "life insurance premium factors." Until then, use Table 2001 rates as first set forth in Notice 2001-10.
Loan Regime: *employee* owns policy (collateral assignment method).	Employee *not taxed* on equity (i.e., employee owns the policy, is obligated to repay the employer, and the policy is subject to the employer's security interest for loans made to employee). Note: If employee owns policy, but employer is entitled to all cash values (a non-equity collateral assignment arrangement), the IRS will treat it as employer-owned under the economic benefit regime. See Planning Point 3.	n/a (all employer outlays are treated as loans to employee)
Planning Point 2: In order to secure potentially lower economic benefit reporting (as opposed to assumed higher cost of loan interest) a plan might be established under SH4 and SH5 as collateral assignment split-dollar until such time as the employee is about to acquire an equity interest (employee equity = cash value - employer interest - employee basis, if any). At that time the plan could be switched to SH3 (referred to as "switch dollar"). This would avoid taxation of any employee interest at time of switch (i.e., none exists) and avoid taxation of future employee equity interests (unless cash value withdrawals exceed employee's basis). Also, might consider switching to SH3 if cost of economic benefit exceeds cost of nondeductible loan interest (i.e., the crossover point).		
Planning Point 3: This could be useful in *controlling stockholder* situations when using a limited collateral assignment to keep corporate employer from having prohibited incidents of ownership (see Controlling Stockholder, page 324).		

ANNUITY MATRIX

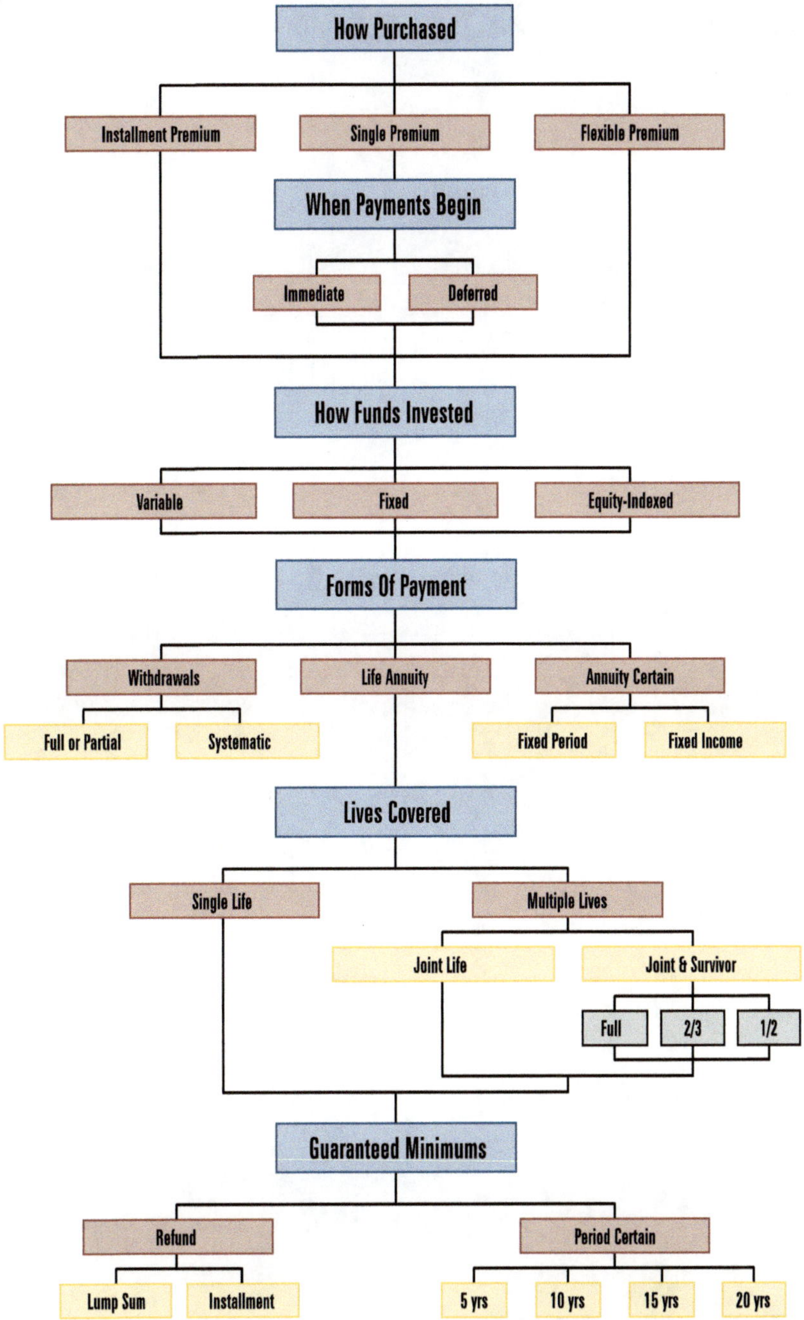

TABLE OF CONTENTS

Page

ACCELERATED DEATH BENEFIT

An accelerated death benefit (ADB) is a type of living benefit. Most accelerated death benefit riders are included with a life insurance policy at no additional cost. These riders pay a portion of the death benefit, usually no more than either 50 percent or 75 percent of the face amount, if the insured has been certified by a physican to have an illness or physical condition that is reasonably expected to result in death within twelve months. Payments received because of terminal illness under an accelerated death benefit rider are ordinarily excluded from federal taxable income as the death benefit would be.

An accelerated death benefit rider limited to terminal illness should not be confused with today's more flexible living benefit riders which may cover chronic illness, critical illness, or long-term care events. These more flexible riders (often referred to as "Hybrid Products" are discussed on page 454). These Hybrid products are usually provided at an additional premium cost or for a cost at the time of claim. Whereas, a person is considered *terminally* ill if certified by a physician to have an illness or physical condition that is reasonably expected to result in death within twelve months, a person is considered *chronically* ill if certified by a health care professional as unable to perform for a period of at least ninety days, without substantial assistance, at least two activities of daily living (i.e., eating, toileting, transferring, bathing, dressing, and continence) or requires substantial supervision to protect himself from threats to health and safety due to severe cognitive impairment (i.e., a deterioration or loss of intellectual capacity that places the individual in jeopardy of harming self or others). These standards for the chronically ill also apply to long-term care benefits (see chart, page 115).

There is no limitation on the amount or use of payments made to a *terminally* ill person outside of the life insurance contract language.. However, payments made to a *chronically* ill individual generally must be for the actual costs incurred that have not been compensated for by insurance or otherwise. The tax treatment will depend on the Tax Code section the policy was filed under. Amounts received from a qualified long-term care contract in 2018 are generally not includable in income up to the greater of $420 per day or actual costs incurred (see discussion on page 510). The terms of the contract must comply with certain provisions of the Internal Revenue Code, standards adopted by the National Association of Insurance Commissioners (NAIC) and standards adopted by the state in which the policyowner resides. These are the same limits and requirements that apply to payments for long-term care (see chart, page 115).

In contrast to an accelerated death benefit *received* under a life insurance policy, when a chronically or terminally ill insured *sells* a death benefit at a discount to a third party it is known as a life settlement or viatical settlement (see discussion, pages 447-448).

ACCOUNTING FOR BUSINESS LIFE INSURANCE

Premium Payments. With cash value insurance the excess of net premiums paid (i.e., the premiums paid less dividends declared, if any) over the increase in cash surrender values is considered an insurance expense. Because premium payments are generally *not* deductible as a business expense, they are usually considered an "Extraordinary Item" and placed on the profit and loss statement before "Net Income Before Taxes," as at **B** on page 293. Alternatively, the insurance expense could be shown on the balance sheet as a direct charge to capital, with no entry being made on the profit and loss statement (note that this method highlights the non-tax-deductible nature of the expense).

Cash Values. The general rule is that net cash surrender values are carried on the balance sheet under "Noncurrent Assets," as at **A** on page 293 ("noncurrent assets" are also referred to as "other assets"). It has been suggested that with universal life containing surrender charges the full cash values should be carried as an asset. However, this is not consistent with the position taken by the Financial Accounting Standards Board in FASB Technical Bulletin No. 85-4, entitled "Accounting for Purchases of Life Insurance." When responding to the question of how to account for an investment in life insurance, the bulletin states: "*The amount that could be realized* under the insurance contract *as of the date of the statement* of financial position should be reported as an asset.... the current capacity to realize contract benefits is limited to settlement amounts specified in the contract" [emphasis added]. When it is intended to surrender a universal life policy value during the normal operating cycle, the *surrender* values might be carried on the balance sheet as a "Current Asset," as opposed to a "Noncurrent Asset."

Policy Loans. Usually there is no intention of repaying the policy loan within the current year, in which case the loan should be reflected on the balance sheet as a deduction from the cash surrender value (i.e., net cash surrender values should be shown). If there is an intention to repay within the current year, the loan should be carried as a current liability and the full cash surrender value shown as an asset.

Death Benefits. The amount of the death benefit in excess of the cash surrender values is considered a gain to corporate surplus. The entry can be made as a negative expense under Extraordinary Items on the profit and loss statement (**B** on page 293). Assuming cash surrender values of $36,000 and a death benefit of $250,000, the actual entry would read, "Plus: proceeds of officers life insurance in excess of cash surrender value ... 214,000."

(continued on next page)

ACCOUNTING FOR BUSINESS LIFE INSURANCE (continued)

BALANCE SHEET

ASSETS			
CURRENT ASSETS:			
Cash	$450,000		
Notes and accounts receivable	850,000		
FIXED ASSETS:			
Land	300,000		
Buildings	550,000		
Machinery and equipment	220,000		
NONCURRENT ASSETS:			
Prepaid insurance, taxes, etc.	18,500		
Life insurance cash surrender values	36,000 **A**		
Total Assets			$2,424,500
LIABILITIES AND STOCKHOLDER EQUITY			
CURRENT LIABILITIES:			
Notes and loans payable banks	$145,000		
Accounts payable	85,000		
Liability for income taxes	42,500		
LONG-TERM LIABILITIES:			
Mortgages	735,000		
Total Liabilities		$1,007,500	
STOCKHOLDER EQUITY:			
Common stock authorized and issued	$900,000		
Retained earnings	517,000		
Total Stockholder Equity		1,417,000	
Total Liabilities and Stockholder Equity			$2,424,500
PROFIT AND LOSS STATEMENT			
Net Sales		$ 869,000	
Less: Cost of Sales and Operating Expenses			
Cost of goods sold	$260,000		
Depreciation	95,000		
Selling and administrating expenses	184,000		
		(539,000)	
Operating Profit			$ 330,000
Other Income			
Interest and dividends			5,000
Total Income			$ 335,000
Extraordinary Item			
Less: life insurance expense			(7,000) **B**
Net Income before Taxes			$ 328,000
Provision for Income Tax			(113,900)
Net Profit for Year			$ 214,100

ACCUMULATED EARNINGS TAX

Accumulating corporate earnings and profits in excess of the reasonable needs of the business and for the purpose of avoiding income tax can in 2018 result in a surtax of 20 percent of accumulated taxable income. This surtax is imposed on the current year's earnings, and once taxed, accumulated earnings are not again taxed in subsequent years during which the accumulation is retained.

However, a corporation is allowed to accumulate at least $250,000 without being subject to this surtax. This figure is reduced to $150,000 for personal service corporations, whose principal business consists of the performance of services in the fields of health, law, engineering, architecture, accounting, actuarial science, performing arts, or consulting.

Reasonable needs of the business can include: (1) providing for plant expansion; (2) acquiring another business through purchase of either stock or assets; (3) retiring indebtedness; and (4) making loans to suppliers or customers in order to maintain the business of the corporation. Insurance carried as *key person insurance*, or to help meet an employer's obligation under a *deferred compensation plan* or *entity purchase agreement (§302)*, is generally considered as carried for reasonable business needs. However, under Section 303 (partial stock redemption) only accruals in the year of death or thereafter are considered as carried for reasonable needs of the business.

For example, if a corporation in its first year of existence in 2018 has $425,000 of retained earnings for which no reasonable need exists, it would be subject to a penalty tax of $35,000. It is calculated as follows:

First $250,000 is exempt from tax
Excess $175,000 is subject in 2018 to a tax of 20 percent, or $35,000

The penalty tax is imposed *in addition to* the regular corporate income tax. It is important for the corporation to document the reasons for retaining earnings in excess of the $250,000 limit. Purchasing cash value key person insurance can reduce accumulated earnings while avoiding a distribution and retaining liquidity inside of the business.

In recent years, accumulated earnings tax was generally not a problem because corporate tax rates were roughly equal to those of the business owner. However, with C corporation tax at 21 percent and the top marginal individual tax rate at 35 percent – business owners have a greater incentive to retain earnings in the business. Permanent cash value life insurance on the business owners and key people can be a valuable planning strategy to reduce tax exposure and avoid accumulated earnings taxes. However, it is important that the business document the insurance need.

APPLICABLE FEDERAL RATE ("AFR")

While interest-free loans are generally not allowable, today's low interest rate environment lends itself to the use of loans as a planning tool. One of the more common estate planning transactions is the sale of assets to an "intentionally defective trust" using loans at the "applicable federal rate" or "AFR." See discussion of Intentionally Defective Trust planning on page 74.

The AFR is determined by the Secretary of the Treasury on a monthly basis as outlined in IRC Section 1274(d). The publication takes the form of a revenue ruling and is available to the public on the IRS website.

One of the main uses of the AFR is to compare them with the interest on loans or installment sales between related parties, such as family members and closely-held businesses. If the interest on a loan is lower than the AFR – it may result in a taxable event for the parties involved.

There are three distinct AFRs, short-term, mid-term, and long-term. Short-term AFR rates are determined from the one-month average of the market yields from marketable obligations, such as U.S. government T-bills with maturities of three years or less. Mid-term AFR rates, are from obligations of maturities of more than three and up to nine years. Long-term AFR rates are from bonds with maturities of more than nine years. The AFRs include various compounding periods – including annually, semi-annually, quarterly, and monthly.

When making a loan to a related party, taxpayers should consider two factors to select the correct AFR. The length of the loan should correspond to the AFRs: short-term (demand and less than three years), mid-term (three years and less than nine years), and long-term (nine years or more). The parties must use the AFR that is published by the IRS at the time when the lender initially makes the loan.

In September of 2018, the AFRs were as follows: short-term (2.51 percent), mid-term (2.86 percent), and long-term (3.02 percent). These rates are higher than the past few years, but are still very low by historical comparison. For example, in August of 2017, the rates were 1.29 percent (short-term), 1.94 percent (mid-term), and 2.60 percent (long-term). However, by comparison, in March of 2000 the rates were 6.45 percent (short-term), 6.8 percent (mid-term), and 6.75 percent (long-term).

The most common use of the AFR is probably in estate planning where the AFR is used as the safe-harbor interest rate in "sales to intentionally defective grantor trusts," "private financing," and "loan regime split dollar." For example, if Bob owns real estate growing at an average of 6 percent a year and he sells it to an intentionally defective grantor trust on a long-term AFR note – an average of 2.98 percent (6 percent less the 3.02 percent long-term AFR) will appreciate outside of his taxable estate (in the grantor trust). In this example, nearly half of the appreciation will avoid transfer (gift, estate, and generation-skipping) taxes. In today's relatively low interest rate environment – the AFR is used as means to freeze the estate by replacing appreciating assets with a low interest rate loan. By selling assets or lending money on a low interest rate AFR loan – you may be able to actually reduce your estate by replacing the taxpayer's current asset (property or cash) with a note which may be discounted for valuation purposes.

AGE-WEIGHTED PROFIT SHARING PLAN

Pension plans, both defined contribution (money purchase and target benefit) and defined benefit, require that the employer make recurring annual contributions. These annual obligations can be avoided with profit sharing plans. Under a traditional profit sharing plan employer contributions are generally allocated each year to employees in proportion to relative compensation, either with or without Social Security integration. However, with an age-weighted profit sharing plan the participant's age is taken into account when making these allocations. The results are similar to those produced in target plans, with significantly larger allocations (as a percentage of compensation) to older employees, but with the added flexibility of a profit sharing plan (e.g., fixed annual contributions are required under a target plan, but there is no such requirement under an age-weighted profit sharing plan).

One of the most common types of age-weighted profit sharing plans is the "cross tested" or "new comparability" plan. The name is derived from the cross testing that is used in order to satisfy the nondiscrimination regulations. An age-weighted plan that discriminates as to contributions may be permissible, provided it does not discriminate when compared to benefits that could be provided using the benefits testing. With respect to defined contribution plans, cross testing is an "end justifies the means" or "benefit justifies the contribution" test. It is permissible for a profit sharing plan to fail the nondiscrimination tests for defined contribution plans, provided it actually produces nondiscriminatory benefits using the nondiscrimination tests applicable to defined benefit plans. Final regulations define three methods under which a cross tested defined contribution plan can satisfy the nondiscrimination in amount requirement.

To summarize, compared to defined benefit plans and other pension plans (both money purchase and target benefit), profit sharing plans offer the flexibility of not having to make annual contributions, but age-weighted profit sharing plans offer the additional advantage of providing significantly larger allocations to older employees.

See also, the discussion of qualified retirement plans on page 512.

ANNUAL EXCLUSION GIFTS

Individuals have the ability to make annual gifts, each year, up to certain indexed amounts without these gifts eroding into one's other gift options, such as one's lifetime exemption. For 2018 and projected for 2019 the annual exclusion gift amount is $15,000. These annual gifts can be made from an individual (the donor) to any number of individuals (the donee). For example, a parent with 2 children can make annual exclusion gifts to each of the children totaling $30,000, or $15,000 each year. Gift limits are indexed annually.

To qualify for the annual exemption, a gift must be of a current rather than a future interest. This means the gifts must be unrestricted and not contingent on the occurrence of an event or the performance of certain duties or tasks.

Additionally, spouses may be able to expand on this dollar amount. Where a spouse consents, they can gift their annual exclusion amount through a concept known as gift-splitting. Using the example in the first paragraph a married couple is able to gift up to $60,000 to their two children. So long as the spouse consents to use their own annual exclusion amount the larger gift is allowed even if the transferred funds all come from one spouse's assets.

An annual exclusion gift does not need to be reported on a gift tax form (Form 706), but reporting on such a form has the advantage of beginning the statute of limitations in the event the IRS might question the valuation of a gift. For split gifts, spouses should file a Form 706 so as to document the consent of the spouse allowing the split gift. The gift splitting election covers all gifts made that tax year.

When gifting to a trust, care must be taken in drafting to ensure trust assets are not included in the estate, and certain withdrawal powers generally have to be provided to qualify the gifts for the annual exclusion. These withdrawal powers are often referred to as Crummey Powers or Crummey Notices. See page 332.

The complexity of gifts to trusts aside, annual exclusion gifts offer a tremendous opportunity to use life insurance to provide for a client's beneficiaries. In the example at the start of this section, a couple was able to currently gift up to $60,000 per year into a trust. That amount could be used to purchase life insurance and, effectively, leverage the gift through the death benefit. For many clients, however, with the estate and gift tax lifetime exemption (temporarily at least) increased to $11.2 million – simply making gifts against the exemption is often thought to be an easier alternative. However, it is wise to use annual exclusion gifts when possible – especially with younger taxpayers or those with property and/or businesses that could increase in value.

Finally, in the case of gifts related to medical and education donors are allowed larger amounts than the $15,000 annual exclusion. Gifts can be made by donors directly to health care providers and educational institutions on behalf of individuals without triggering gift tax consequences.

ANNUITIES NON-NATURAL OWNER TAXATION

A qualified annuity is taxed like other qualified accounts, such as an IRA, 401(k), and profit sharing plans. However, deferred nonqualified annuities are taxed differently from most investments. Although variable annuities remain popular, equity index annuities have become more popular in recent years. See Variable Annuities at page 578 and Equity-Indexed Products at page 366-367. Because of recent low interest rates and changes to rules pertaining to insurance company reserves, fixed annuities have become less common – as well as less popular with both insurance companies and consumers.

Deferred nonqualified annuities generally grow on a tax-deferred basis until withdrawals begin or the policy is annuitized. Gains are taxed when distributed as ordinary income. Gains are deemed to be distributed before principal is returned (i.e., amounts distributed are ordinary income until the annuity value is reduced to the amount of the investment in the contract after which withdrawals are a return of cost basis). As a general rule, if the annuitant is less than age 59 ½ years old, there is also a 10 percent penalty in addition to ordinary income tax imposed on withdrawals.

If the annuity is annuitized – only a portion of the amount received will be subject to income tax. The remaining portion will be deemed a return of basis. The amount treated as taxable ordinary income is determined based on an "exclusion ration" which is determined based on age at the time of electing annuitization. An older annuitant will have a shorter life expectancy and, hence, a larger portion of the amount received is treated as a return of basis and excluded from taxable income. For example, a 65 year old has a life expectancy of approximately 240 months (IRS Table V). If an annuity is purchased with $100,000 then $416.67 of each annuity payment ($100,000/240) is non-taxable as a return of basis. In other words, if the monthly distribution was $700 - the "exclusion ratio" would be 59.5 percent ($416.67/$700.00).

Unlike many assets, the basis is not stepped-up at death and the deferred earnings will be taxable as ordinary income to a non-spousal beneficiary. The annuity is generally included in the owner's estate for estate tax purposes.

However, under IRC Section 72(u) annuity payments made to a "non-natural person" are subject to different taxation than payments made to a natural person unless that "non-natural person" is "acting as an agent for a natural person." This non-natural person issue comes up most often when an annuity is owned by a corporation or a trust. There are a number of letter rulings where the IRS has found a trust to be an agent for a natural person. One example is PLR 1999905015 where the terms of the trust provided that the trustee would terminate the trust and distribute an annuity to each trust beneficiary after a certain period of time. The most common trust example is a trust that is taxed as a grantor trust (see Intentionally Defective Grantor Trust at pages 74-77) being deemed an agent for the grantor.

If a non-natural person owns an annuity and is not treated as an agent for a natural person – distributions from the annuity contract are treated as ordinary income to the extent there is gain. Instead of an exclusion ratio – all income is deemed received first and basis is only returned after income is received.

ASSET PROTECTION

The term "asset protection" refers to techniques that offer protection from the claims of personal and business creditors.

These techniques can range from the simple to the complex. For example, in some states, much, if not all, of a personal residence is protected from creditors. Many states exempt annuity values, substantial life insurance cash values, and all death benefits. The assets of most retirement plans covered by ERISA are also protected (but not from tax deficiency claims or divorce disputes). The Supreme Court has strengthened IRA protection, and the Bankruptcy Abuse Prevention and Consumer Protection Act of 2005 provides increased protection for most retirement plan assets. However, in light of the Supreme Court decision in *Clark, et ux v. Rameker*, 134 S. Ct. 2242 (2014), IRAs inherited by non-spouses may not necessarily have the same protection. That decision disallowed retirement plan status of inherited IRAs. Prior to the *Clark* decision spouses could receive special protection; however, in light of the *Clark* decision that protection may not continue. It is important to also look to state law as a number of states have either passed laws or had favorable court decisions that specifically protect inherited IRAs under state bankruptcy exemptions for federal bankruptcy purposes.

Gifts can be made to family members or charitable organizations; provided they are not made with intent to defraud creditors (see charts on page 51). Gifts may also be made to an irrevocable trust or custodial account.

More complex techniques include limited liability companies and family limited partnerships (see chart on page 211 and discussion on pages 481-482). Trusts can be established with "spendthrift" provisions to prevent the creditors of trust beneficiaries from reaching trust assets. But this technique does not provide protection from existing creditors.

The most sophisticated of all asset protection techniques is probably the offshore or asset protection trust (APT). It is thought that using an APT to remove assets to a foreign jurisdiction will lead to more favorable terms in disputes with creditors. Just as some states have laws that are more favorable to asset protection; certain countries have gained similar reputations. Jurisdictions considered most favorable as a situs for APTs do not recognize foreign judgments (thereby forcing a retrial of claims), have weakened or no fraudulent conveyance laws, and permit a trust settlor to retain trust powers and benefits without subjecting the trust to the claims of creditors. APTs are not intended to avoid income taxes.

In our litigious society, it is understandable why monied individuals and high-risk professionals have long been interested in adopting asset protection techniques. However, a few words of caution: not only will the concealment of assets from a known creditor be set aside by the courts, but assisting a debtor will likely subject both the debtor and his advisor to ethical, civil, and criminal liability (e.g., Code section 7206, see page 484). Therefore, asset protection planning must begin long before there is a need. Also, state laws vary widely in the protection they offer and should be specifically consulted. See Domestic Asset Protection Trust Comparison grid on page 87.

BANK OWNED LIFE INSURANCE (BOLI)

In many respects, Bank Owned Life Insurance (BOLI) is similar to Company Owned Life Insurance (COLI), in that BOLI enables banks to recover, or to informally fund, the costs of nonqualified benefit plans (see page 319). However, there are important differences.

Banks are considered highly "balance sheet sensitive." From a bank investment perspective, the life insurance contract has been described as "a perpetual municipal with a yield that resets to the market." From a bank accounting perspective, the purchase of life insurance has been described as a "repositioning" of assets on the balance sheet, "from the securities portfolio to the BOLI portfolio," that generates "incremental income." Unlike traditional taxable investments, the cash value increases of BOLI are reflected on the balance sheet as "other non-interest income," without any reduction for income taxes (accounting for BOLI policies is subject to FASB Technical Bulletin 85-5, see page 293). When compared to currently taxed investments, BOLI can produce improved after-tax yields and a positive impact on earnings per share.

Unlike COLI, the purchase of BOLI by national banks is very tightly regulated by the Office of Comptroller of the Currency (OCC) (FDIC regulated state-chartered banks are typically subject to similar regulation). When purchasing BOLI, OCC Bulletin 2000-23 requires an informed decision "consistent with safe and sound banking practices." To that end, the bank must perform a *pre-purchase analysis* that includes determination of need, quantification of amount, vendor and carrier selection, review of insurance product characteristics, determination of reasonableness of compensation, analysis of benefits and risks, and alternatives. The purchase of BOLI, "... must address a legitimate need of the bank for life insurance. Life insurance may not be purchased to generate funds for the bank's normal operating expenses [or for] speculation ..." However, the purchase of "key-person insurance, insurance on borrowers, insurance purchased in connection with employee compensation and benefit plans, and insurance taken as security for loans," are all found to fall within the "incidental powers [that are] necessary to carry on the business of banking."

If purchased with a single premium, a BOLI policy is classified as a modified endowment contract (MEC), with the resulting LIFO taxation of policy withdrawals, loans and surrenders; and application of a 10-percent-penalty tax on amounts includable in gross income (see Life Insurance Premium Limitations, pages 423-424). However, if the contract is held until the insured's death, the policy proceeds are received income tax-free (provided strict notice and consent requirements are met, see pages 319-321 and there is no prior "transfer-for-value," see pages 568-569). Because of a bank's low cost of capital, it is ordinarily easy for a bank to achieve cash value growth that exceeds the bank's cost of capital. This arbitrage makes BOLI a popular investment for banks. In selecting the employees to be insured, a bank must be mindful of the state "insurable interest" requirements (see discussion, page 407).

BOOK VALUE

Many approaches to valuation require a consideration of book value. Simply stated, book value is assets less liabilities, or the net worth of the business. However, because assets are often carried at substantially *below* their fair market value, care must be taken to assure that book value is adjusted upward to reflect accurately the value of these underlying assets. This adjustment in book value results in an ***adjusted book value.***

For example, land purchased many years ago is likely to have appreciated in value, yet it is often carried on the books at the original purchase price. Machinery and equipment may be depreciated for income tax purposes, yet be worth substantially more than is shown on the books (when carried at its depreciated value). If the LIFO (last in, first out) method of inventory valuation is used, the value of inventory will likely be carried at below market value. Because of this, book value produces a valuation that is often below fair market value for most types of businesses. Generally, this is not recommended as a method for buy-sell valuation (See Business Valuation at pages 166-169).

This can be seen in the following example:

1000 units purchased at $1.00 on June 1	$1,000
1000 units purchased at $1.50 on July 1	1,500
1000 units purchased at $2.00 on August 1	2,000
Total cost of inventory	$4,500
Less 1000 units sold on August 2 (charged to inventory at $2.00 per unit)	(2,000)
Remaining 2,000 units carried at	$2,500
But to replace these units it would cost	$4,000
Inventory is undervalued by	$1,500

BUSINESS OVERHEAD EXPENSE INSURANCE

Business overhead expense insurance is designed to provide funds to cover overhead expenses during a business owner's disability. Business overhead expense insurance is intended to help maintain the business; it is not intended to replace disability income insurance (see chart, page 253) or disability buy-out insurance (see discussion, page 342-343).

Covered expenses include those that are tax deductible to the business. Typically these expenses include employee salaries, utilities, professional fees, rent, mortgage payments, lease payments for furniture and equipment, premiums for health, property and liability insurance, laundry services, janitorial services, and maintenance services. Not included are the insured's salary, salaries of co-workers who perform the same duties as the insured, salaries of family members, and depreciation.

Monthly benefits are paid upon the insured's total and continuous disability, and are limited to a maximum amount. Partial disability benefits are also available. During disability a "carry-forward" provision allows unused benefits to be carried forward from month to month. Extension of the benefit period allows unused benefits to be received beyond the original benefit period.

Waiting periods are typically either 30, 60, or 90 days. The cash flow requirements of the business are considered when selecting an appropriate waiting period.

Benefit periods are typically limited to 12, 18, or 24 months. Limited benefit periods assume that the insured will dispose of the business interest if disability lasts longer then the benefit period.

Optional coverages are often similar to individual disability income policies (e.g., partial disability riders, guaranteed insurability riders, and lump-sum survivor benefits). Other optional coverages are unique to business overhead expense insurance (e.g., a professional replacement rider covering the cost of hiring someone to perform the insured's duties).

Eligible businesses include regular C corporations, S corporations, limited liability companies, partnerships, and sole proprietorships. The business must have been in operation for a minimum period of time (e.g., 3 years). The business cannot have more than a specific number of owners (e.g., 5 professionals working in the business). This requirement recognizes that a substantial loss of revenue is less likely if the business has a large number of owner-employees. There are specific issue ages and medical underwriting requirements; and the insured must be actively at work full time (e.g., a minimum of 30 hours per week).

Premiums are deductible as a business expense. Although the *proceeds* are taxable, they are used for tax-deductible business expenses (i.e., taxable proceeds are offset by deductible business expenses).

CAFETERIA PLANS

Cafeteria plans, also described as "flexible benefit" plans or Section 125 plans, allow participating employees to choose between a number of non-taxable qualified benefits or taxable cash. Plans typically offer participants a "cafeteria menu" of items, including group term life insurance, medical expense insurance, dependent group term life insurance, child care, and dental expense coverage.

Among the advantages to an *employer* that establishes such a plan are reductions in FICA (Federal Insurance Contributions Act) and FUTA (Federal Unemployment Tax Act) taxes, expansion of employee benefits, and enhanced employee appreciation of the benefit package.

Employee advantages include the opportunity: (1) to select benefits most suited to individual needs; (2) to pay for these benefits with before-tax rather than after-tax dollars; (3) to obtain benefits that may not be available for individual purchase; and (4) to pay less FICA taxes by reducing taxable income.

The design of cafeteria plans can range from simple "premium only" plans to full-blown flexible benefit plans including flexible spending accounts. **Premium-only plans**, which are also referred to as "premium-conversion" plans, merely allow employees to use their before-tax, rather than after-tax, dollars for plan contributions. In contrast, **flexible spending accounts** allow employees to defer before-tax dollars to pay for dependent care expenses and unreimbursed medical expenses (such as deductibles and coinsurance payments, glasses, and eye exams).

The election to defer dollars must be made in advance of the plan year and can be changed only under limited circumstances. With flexible spending accounts, employees forfeit fund balances that are not used up by the end of the plan year, except for a 2½ month grace period if permitted by the plan. An additional period is allowed after the close of the plan year for submission of claims incurred during the plan year. Forfeitures may be used to offset the employer's cost of administering the plan, reallocated proportionately to other employees, or given to charity.

Former employees may participate, but self-employed individuals may not. All plans are subject to special nondiscrimination rules. Proper administration of cafeteria plans requires preparing plan documents, conducting annual enrollments, tracking claims and benefit payments, and filing yearly 5500 reports.

See also, SIMPLE Cafeteria Plans, page 547.

CAPTIVE INSURANCE ARRANGEMENTS

Captive insurance (sometimes referred to as a Section 831(b) Plan) is a name given to a corporation created for the purpose of insuring against risk, usually some type of property and casualty insurance to a relatively small group of insureds, usually including the party or parties that created the Captive. These are set up when an entity believes it may be more cost effective to carve out the risk from their standard coverage. Like all insurance companies, the Captive is regulated as an insurance carrier by either a state or an offshore jurisdiction. The Captive collects premiums, sets aside reserves, and pays claims.

Captives are often used as an alternative to self-insuring certain risks. A business cannot deduct the cost of setting aside reserves to self-insure against risk. The business can only deduct the cost of self-insuring a risk when the loss is incurred, whereas premiums paid to a Captive to insure the same risk, if reasonable and meeting other certain requirements, are currently deductible. For this reason, Captives have become popular with businesses having substantial risk – like real estate developers and trucking companies.

Premium contributions made by the parent company to the Captive are deductible pursuant to Section 162 if ordinary and reasonable. If certain conditions are met, pursuant to Section 831(b), a Captive receiving less than $2.2 million (increased from $1.2 million and indexed for inflation by the PATH Act for tax years beginning in 2017) of annual premium is taxed only on investment income. Thus, it is possible that the parent can currently deduct the premium under Section 162 and the Captive not take the premium into income pursuant to Section 831(b).

To obtain the tax treatment outlined above, the Captive must qualify as an insurance company. As previously mentioned, the Captive must be formed under the law of a U.S. state or a foreign jurisdiction. The Captive must operate within the guidelines of that local jurisdiction. The IRS also requires that there be both risk shifting and risk distribution. The IRS has provided safe harbor rulings defining risk distribution. In effect, the risk distribution requirement should be met if at least 50 percent of the premium received by the Captive relates to unrelated third-party risk or there are at least twelve entities insured by the Captive. The "twelve-insured" requirement can be satisfied by related, but separate legal, entities. The risks insured must be real and not illusory and the rates must be appropriate for the risk insured.

Although Captives are an attractive alternative for some businesses to self-insurance and commercial insurance coverage, they are not for every business owner. A Captive is a separate legal entity that is regulated by a state or offshore insurance commissioner. It has significant reporting requirements as an insurance carrier plus a complicated federal tax regime. A Captive must be adequately reserved – creating a significant initial capitalization. In summary, the cost to create and maintain a Captive can be significant. A Captive must have risk shifting and risk distribution – meaning that the premium paid by a business owner could be used to pay a claim by another business owner.

(continued on next page)

CAPTIVE INSURANCE ARRANGEMENTS (continued)

There is also a "diversification" requirement under IRC Section 831(b) that was added by PATH. Under the diversification reqirement the insurance company can qualify for Section 831(b) treatment if (1) it receives no more than 20 percent of its written premium from a single policyholder or (2) if no spouse nor lineal descendant of an owner of the policyholder has a percentage interest in the insurance copany that exceeds his or her intrest in the policyholder by more than 2 percent (the so-called "Relatedness Test"). The Relatedness Test was added to limit the ability of excess premiums (premiums over claims) to be moved tax-free from a business owner to lineal descendants. By overcharging for insurance coverage – Captives are sometimes promoted as a "wealth transfer" strategy.

Like all insurance companies, a Captive must hold reserves that are deemed sufficient under the local law (jurisdiction of domicile) to pay future claims. Different jurisdictions have different reserve requirements as to the amount of the reserve and the type of allowable investments.

Recently, life insurance has become a popular investment for funding a Captive's reserve. The argument in favor of life insurance goes something like this: (1) the premiums are deducted by the business under Section 162; (2) the first $2.2 million of premiums received by the Captive are not taxed pursuant to Section 831(b); (3) dollars then paid into permanent life insurance products can grow income tax deferred under the rules governing cash value life insurance; and (4) life insurance cash values can be used by the business owner in retirement. In short, it is sometimes argued that Captives are a means of tax deductible non-qualified deferred compensation.

Caution should be taken when Captives are being promoted with focus on the tax deductions. Remember, the risk must be real and the amount of the premium fair to get the deduction. Captives are a means of spreading risk – not taking deductions for an imaginary risk. A recent case, *Avrahami v. Commissioner*, 149 T.C. 7 (2017), provides an example of a so-called "Captive" that the court found was not opperating as an insurance company. Because it wasn't acting as an insurance company – it could not take advantage of the tax benefits provided by IRC Section 831(b).

Life insurance may have a place in Captives, just like life insurance has a place with other businesses, but one should become suspicious when life insurance becomes the focus of the Captive. Remember that a Captive needs to be a real insurance company which complies with local law – including those governing reserves. Also, it shouldn't be forgotten that premiums paid to purchase life insurance are generally not deductible. Past attempts at creating tax-deductible life insurance arrangements have usually not been successful (see, for example, Retired Lives Reserve, page 521; Welfare Benefit Fund, page 579). Some commentators have even wondered if some of the Captive arrangements marketed today as tax-deductible non-qualified deferred compensation are governed by the IRS tax-shelter (i.e., listed transaction) rules.

In short, caution should be taken when a promoter is suggesting a Captive. That caution should be even greater when life insurance is a significant aspect of the Captive arrangement. Captives can be an effective tool in the right situation and life insurance may be an appropriate investment, but be sure that the primary purpose of the arrangement is for insuring property and casualty risk and not for retirement planning. Consultation with independent tax and legal advisors, not affiliated with the Captive arrangement, is highly recommended.

CASH BALANCE PENSION PLAN

A cash balance plan is a defined benefit plan that calculates benefits in a manner similar to defined contribution plans. Each employee has a hypothetical account or "cash balance" to which contributions and interest payments are credited. Under the typical plan a fixed percentage of each employee's salary is contributed each year, and both the level of contribution and a minimum rate of return are *guaranteed* by the employer (i.e., the employer bears the investment risk). Contributions may be weighted for age or years of service. Unlike a true defined contribution plan, individual accounts are not maintained and participants may not direct the investments in their accounts. As with the defined benefit pension plan the plan benefits are guaranteed up to specific limits by the Pension Benefit Guaranty Corporation (PBGC). See page 485.

Compared with traditional defined benefit plans, cash balance plans generally provide greater benefits to younger employees and those with shorter service (but at a higher cost), and lower benefits to older, longer service employees (at lower cost).

In an effort to reduce the costs of employee retirement plans, and offer more attractive plans to younger workers with few years of service, employers can convert their traditional defined benefit plans into cash balance plans. This conversion benefits younger workers, who not only can accrue benefits more rapidly, but will also enjoy the added advantages of portability (i.e., if the employee leaves prior to normal retirement age vested account values can be taken in a lump sum, rolled over into an IRA, or otherwise invested). However, these conversions are generally detrimental to older employees, since they occur just as these workers are reaching the age where the defined benefit formulas began to sharply raise the value of their future pension payouts. The effect is that some cash balance conversions have arguably lowered the rate of future benefit accruals. In response to this concern, the Pension Protection Act of 2006 required that future conversions of defined benefit plans to cash balance plans preclude the possibility of "wear-away" (i.e., a time after conversion during which additional benefits do not accrue).

See also, the discussion of qualified retirement plans on page 512.

CHARITABLE GIFT ANNUITY

A charitable gift annuity is received pursuant to a contractual obligation by a charity to make annuity payments to a donor in exchange for the transfer of property to the charity. In comparison to charitable trusts they are less costly and relatively simple to adopt, typically requiring only an application and a one or two page agreement. The donor's tax-deductible gift is measured by the difference between the market value of the gift and the value of the retained life annuity. The annuity can be immediate or deferred and for a single life or the joint lives of two annuitants.

The actual rates used to calculate the annuity payout are typically based upon those published by the American Council of Gift Annuities. The council meets periodically in order to review interest rates and mortality assumptions and update the annuity rates. Although these rates are published in an attempt to avoid "rate bidding wars" between charities, the council has no enforcement authority. However, charities using the rates need not retain their own actuaries and have the assurance that the underlying actuarial assumptions will likely produce an ultimate charitable benefit.

The annuity receives favorable tax treatment. A portion of each payment is received tax-free as a return of principal (but excludable only until the investment has been recovered, thereafter taxed as ordinary income). The remaining portion is taxed as ordinary income. However, if the donor has transferred appreciated property to the charity, the donor has a gain (either capital gain or ordinary income depending on the property) to the extent the fair market value exceeds the donor's adjusted basis. The basis in the property must then be allocated between the charitable gift and the donor's investment in the annuity contract. As a result the return of principal element of each annuity payment is divided into two parts, one representing a return of gain (taxed as capital or ordinary gain) and the other representing a return of basis (excluded from income).

The contractual obligation to the annuitant is solely the charity's and the annuity payments are dependent upon the continuing financial stability of the charity. If desired, the charity can reinsure its obligation to the donor by purchasing a commercial annuity. This relieves the charity of the burden of investing the proceeds to assure that all payments will be made to the annuitant. To the extent that the cost of a commercial annuity is less than the amount realized from the gift the excess funds become immediately available to the charity.

CHARITABLE GIFTS OF LIFE INSURANCE

Gifts of life insurance policies and premiums have become a popular way of providing substantial gifts to a donor's favored charity. Generally, the charitable deduction for the gift of an existing life insurance policy is limited to the lesser of the policy current fair market value or cost basis (See Valuation of Life Insurance on page 577). When properly implemented, the donor should receive charitable deductions for the value of the insurance contract and for all future premium payments.

In order to obtain the anticipated income, gift, and estate tax deductions, the donor must make a gift of his *entire* interest in the policy. The donor will not qualify for these deductions if he retains the right to name or change the beneficiary, or gives less than his entire interest (e.g., assignment of death benefit but retention of cash values).

However, even when the donor appears to have given his entire interest in the policy to a charity, or where the charity originally applies for the insurance, a 1991 private letter ruling (withdrawn when state law changed) provided that the charity's lack of an insurable interest under state law would be a basis for denying the income, gift and estate tax deductions.

Following this ruling virtually all states have passed legislation that specifically provides that charities have an insurable interest in the lives of their donors.

The variety of state laws and likely changes to these laws make it imperative that specific state statutes be consulted prior to making gifts of life insurance and premiums, or having a charitable organization apply for life insurance (for an expanded discussion of insurable interest, see page 407).

CHARITABLE TRUSTS

Charitable trusts can benefit both individual and charitable beneficiaries. The requirements for charitable remainder trusts are specific and detailed in order to assure that an accurate determination can be made of the benefit the charity will eventually receive. Such trusts can offer both income and estate tax benefits, and include:

1. **Charitable Remainder Annuity Trusts (CRATs)** are trusts under which a *fixed amount* of at least 5 percent and no more than 50 percent of the initial fair market value of trust assets is paid annually to a noncharitable beneficiary. Payments to the noncharitable beneficiary may be for a set term not exceeding 20 years or for the life of the beneficiary. The amount of the grantor's tax deduction is measured by the present value of the charity's remainder interest at the time property is given to the trust. The value of the remainder interest must be at least 10 percent of the initial fair market value of all property placed in the trust. If the trust income is insufficient to make the required payments to the noncharitable beneficiary, then capital gains or trust principal must be used. If the trust income is more than required to make the payments, the excess is reinvested in the trust. See chart on page 59.

2. **Charitable Remainder UniTrusts (CRUTs)** are trusts under which a *fixed percentage* of the net fair market value of the trust (valued annually) is paid at least annually to a noncharitable beneficiary. This percentage cannot be less than 5 percent and no more than 50 percent. Payments to the noncharitable beneficiary may be for a term not exceeding twenty years or for life. The amount of the grantor's tax deduction is the present value of the charity's remainder interest. The value of the remainder interest must be at least 10 percent of the net fair market value of each contribution as of the date the property is contributed to the trust. See chart on page 59 and discussion of NIMCRUT on page 472.

3. **Pooled income funds** are trusts created by public charities rather than private donors. The donors, or other income beneficiaries, receive from the commingled funds in the trust an income for life that is based upon the earnings of the trust. The amount of the grantor's tax deduction is the present value of the charity's remainder interest.

4. **Charitable lead trusts** allow a grantor to place funds in trust with an annuity or unitrust interest going to a charitable beneficiary and the remainder interest returning to the grantor or some other noncharitable beneficiaries. Although the grantor continues to be taxed on trust income under the grantor trust rules, the grantor is entitled to an income tax deduction at the time of the gift equal to the present value of the charity's annuity or unitrust interest.

CHARITY AS DESIGNATED BENEFICIARY OF RETIREMENT PLAN

Naming a charity as beneficiary of some or all of a retirement plan can be a simple and tax-efficient way to make a charitable bequest. The many benefits include the following:

1. Payments made from a tax-deferred retirement account to individual beneficiaries are considered "income in respect of a decedent" and taxed as ordinary income (see page 403). However, charities are exempt from state and federal income taxes and can receive retirement funds without any reduction for taxes paid.
2. Payments made to a charity are deductible from the gross estate and not subject to estate taxes. With larger estates this can save substantial amounts of estate taxes. (But an income tax credit is available to the beneficiaries for any estate tax paid.)
3. By satisfying charitable objectives with retirement account assets the decedent can then pass appreciated property to non-charitable beneficiaries. Since this property is entitled to a stepped-up basis at death, it can then be sold at fair market value without paying income taxes (see page 556).

Before making a charity a beneficiary, it should be determined if: (1) the plan contains any restrictions against naming a charity as beneficiary; and (2) the account holder is married (retirement plans other than IRAs require that the spouse waive his or her rights under the retirement plan). The mere naming of a charity as beneficiary will not adversely impact the calculations of the owner's required minimum distributions (RMDs) during his or her lifetime (prior rules would have prevented using the joint life expectancy of the owner and another person if a charity was a named beneficiary).

A "designated beneficiary" must be determined for the purpose of calculating the required post-death distributions from a retirement account. Designated beneficiaries are living persons for whom a life expectancy can be calculated. (An exception to this rule allows some trusts to qualify as designated beneficiaries provided they meet specific requirements.) A charity is considered to be a "non-designated beneficiary" since it has no life expectancy.

When the **charity is the only beneficiary**, the RMD is determined as if there were no designated beneficiary and there is limited flexibility as to when distributions may be taken (see page 413). However, this is rarely a concern as most charities have no tax incentive to delay distribution and want to receive the funds as soon as they are available.

When there are **multiple individual beneficiaries** (i.e., multiple "designated beneficiaries") the RMD calculation is based upon the oldest beneficiary, unless separate accounts are established before September 30th of the year following the owner's death, in which case each individual beneficiary should be able to calculate RMD (based upon their individual life expectancies).

(continued on next page)

CHARITY AS DESIGNATED BENEFICIARY OF RETIREMENT PLAN (continued)

When a **charity is among the beneficiaries**, the individual beneficiaries will be unable to use their life expectancies to calculate RMDs if the charity is included among the beneficiaries on September 30th of the calendar year following the year of the account owner's death (the deadline for determining the identity of account beneficiaries for the purpose of determining RMDs). The reason for this is that an account that has both designated and non-designated beneficiaries is treated as if it has no designated beneficiaries. However, the problem can be avoided and the individual beneficiaries can preserve their ability to stretch out annual withdrawals over the course of their lifetime by either:

1. Establishing separate accounts for the charitable and the non-charitable beneficiaries after the death of the account owner, but not later than the September 30th deadline.
2. Paying out the charity's share prior to the September 30th deadline. Unlike individual beneficiaries, a charity has no incentive to stretch out distributions from the retirement account. The individual beneficiaries may then take minimum distributions over the life expectancy of the oldest remaining beneficiary or over their individual life expectancies if the account is divided into separate accounts for each remaining individual beneficiary.

A retired married couple might wish to make a charity a partial beneficiary of their retirement assets, but be reluctant to do so because of a need to provide for the surviving spouse and a desire to leave the bulk of the account to adult children. The following beneficiary designation addresses that concern and passes a ten percent interest in the retirement account to a charity, with the remaining ninety percent to any surviving children, but only upon the death of the surviving spouse: "In the event of my death, transfer ownership of my account to my spouse if he/she survives me. If my spouse predeceases me, transfer ownership of my account to the following beneficiaries who survive me and make payment in the following proportions: Son A – 30%; Son B – 30%; Daughter C – 30%; XYZ Charity – 10%. If any of my individual beneficiaries predeceases me, his or her share shall be divided among the other individual beneficiary(ies) who survive me in the relative proportions assigned to each such surviving Individual Beneficiary. If there is no surviving individual beneficiary(ies) at the time of my death, transfer ownership of my Account to my estate (unless otherwise required by the laws of my state of residence)."

Should the **account owner's spouse die first**, then the charity would receive a ten percent interest and the adult children would receive their ninety percent interest in the retirement account. Should the **account owner die first**, the spouse would either remain a beneficiary of the account or transfer the funds to the spouse's IRA. In this event, the spouse should consider using the same beneficiary designation as above, but with the underlined text deleted. In either case, if the individual beneficiaries desire to delay receipt of their distributions over the longest possible time, it is important to take the actions set forth in paragraphs 1 or 2 above.

CHILDREN'S LIFE INSURANCE

Children's insurance, also referred to as "juvenile insurance," offers many advantages. The death proceeds can be used to pay medical bills and funeral expenses, provide a financial cushion for a grieving family or establish a lasting memorial (e.g., a scholarship fund in the child's name). Loans or withdrawals from policy cash values can be used for educational expenses, as a down payment on the purchase of a home, to start a business, or for emergency expenses. Adding a guaranteed purchase option will assure that in future years the child can purchase additional death benefits without evidence of insurability (see discussion on page 397).

Despite these advantages, placing insurance on a child's life is not without controversy. Opponents maintain that the lack of an underlying economic risk makes the purchase inappropriate and, further, that the wrong person is being insured. Clearly, if family resources are limited they should first be used to obtain adequate amounts of insurance on a child's parents (upon whom the child is economically dependent). Opponents also contend (ignoring the tax-free growth of policy cash values) that if cash accumulations are desired it is better to save outside of a life insurance contract, thereby avoiding charges for the death benefit. Obviously, insuring a child can raise different issues than those encountered when insuring a spouse, parent, estate owner, employee, or stockholder.

Since a minor cannot directly own a policy on his or her own life, it is important that the individual applying for the insurance have an insurable interest in the child's life (see discussion on page 407). Initially the contract will typically be owned by a parent, grandparent, trust, or obtained as a custodial gift under the Uniform Transfers to Minors Act or Uniform Gifts to Minors Act (see discussions on pages 469 and 575).

A grandparent's purchase of insurance on the life of a grandchild can provide a meaningful gift to the grandchild while taking advantage of the gift tax laws (see chart on page 51). Virtually any form of permanent life insurance policy can be used. Single premium or limited payment plans are often used, or additional funds can be placed in a prepaid premium account (also referred to as a "premium deposit fund").

The amount of death benefit that can be purchased may be limited by state law and will be limited by insurance company underwriting standards. Purchase of a low death benefit with higher premiums will produce larger cash values. However, in making premium payments it is important to avoid classification as a modified endowment contract, since loans or surrenders of cash values could be subject to less favorable income taxation (see discussion on pages 423-424). It should also be recognized that a lower initial death benefit means that smaller amounts of additional insurance can be purchased under the guaranteed purchase option.

COLLEGE EDUCATION FUNDING

1. **Financial Aid**. In order to determine who qualifies for financial aid, a formula provided by the federal government subtracts the expected family contribution from the cost of attendance. Among other factors, this formula takes into consideration the assets and income of the parents and child. Because the formula gives substantially greater weight to the child's income and assets, large gifts should not be made to a child if financial aid is likely to be sought.

2. **Life Insurance And Annuities**. One advantage of life insurance cash values and annuities is that they are not included in the formula used by the government in determining eligibility for financial aid. Tax-deferred cash value accumulations, favorable loan provisions and a preferred status under the financial aid laws make permanent life insurance attractive for funding a college education. But there should be a real need for the insurance; otherwise, funds might better be invested where there would be no charges for a death benefit. And since a parent is most likely to be paying for college, it makes sense that a parent be the insured (with parent or trust the owner). Provided the parents are adequately insured, life insurance on the child might also be considered. However, a minor child should not be the owner of an annuity or life insurance contract (see page 469). Note also, that when the owner of an annuity is under age 59½, there is a 10-percent-penalty tax upon surrender.

3. **Gifts**. Gifts can be made to a minor under either the Uniform Transfers to Minors Act or in trust (see page 575). However, most authorities agree that the actual payment of college costs falls within a parent's obligation to support a child; therefore, such payments are not subject to gift taxation. Grandparents can take advantage of the annual exclusion to make gifts to the parents or grandchildren (see chart, page 51). Tuition costs paid directly to a university are free of gift and estate taxes.

4. **Section 529 Plans**. Also known as Qualified Tuition Programs, initial contributions to these plans must come from after-tax income. Contributions must be in cash, are not tax deductible, and are treated as completed gifts eligible for the gift tax annual exclusion ($15,000 in 2018). Under the 2017 Tax Act, Section 529 Plans were expanded to cover qualifying expenses for private, public, and religious kindergarten through twelfth grade. However, under the new guidelines applying to kindergarten through twelfth grade, only $10,000 per year per child can be withdrawn from the plan. Amounts in excess of this limit are subject to a 10 percent penalty tax. See the table of Educational Tax Incentives on page 634, and the discussion of Section 529 Plans on page 539.

5. **American Opportunity Credit**. This credit replaced what was previously known as the Hope Scholarship tax credit. It provides an income tax credit of up to $2,500 per year for each of the first *four* years of college, calculated as 100 percent of the first $2,000 of qualifying expenses and 25 percent of the next $2,000. Up to 40 percent of the credit is refundable (i.e., low income students without a federal income tax liability can receive up to $1,000 a year). Books and course materials are included among eligible expenses. The credit is against amounts actually paid during the calendar year – not those billed.

(continued on next page)

COLLEGE EDUCATION FUNDING (continued)

The student must be enrolled at least half-time in a qualifying educational institution and may be the taxpayer, his spouse or any dependent. However, the credit may not be taken by an individual who is eligible to be claimed as a dependent on another taxpayer's return. The credit may not be taken if the student has ever been convicted of a state or federal charge of felony drug possession or distribution. There is no limit in any given year as to the number of American Opportunity Credits a taxpayer may claim as to his dependents (i.e., the limit is on a per-student basis). The credit is phased out ratably between modified adjusted gross income of $80,000 to $90,000 for unmarried taxpayers and $160,000 to $180,000 for married taxpayers filing joint returns.

6. **Lifetime Learning Credit**. The Lifetime Learning Credit is 20 percent of the first $10,000 of qualifying education expenses (i.e., a maximum of $2,000 per year). The Lifetime Learning Credit limit is on a per-return basis, meaning that only $10,000 of educational expenses covering all students in the household qualifies each year. In 2018 the credit is phased out ratably between modified adjusted gross income of $55,000 to $65,000 for unmarried taxpayers and $110,000 to $130,000 for married taxpayers filing joint returns. Unlike the American Opportunity Credit, it is not limited to the first four years of post secondary education and the student need not be full-time to qualify.

7. **Deducting Interest On Education Loans**. This deduction allows the taxpayer to deduct up to $2,500 of interest paid on any qualified education loan (the debt must be incurred solely to pay qualified higher education expenses). In 2018, the deduction is phased out ratably between modified adjusted gross income of $65,000 to $80,000 for unmarried taxpayers, and $135,000 to $165,000 for married taxpayers filing joint returns (as indexed for inflation). It is an "above the line" deduction, meaning that the taxpayer does not have to itemize in order to claim the deduction.

8. **Coverdell Education Savings Account**. An annual non-deductible contribution of $2,000 per beneficiary can be made to these accounts. This contribution limit is phased out ratably for individual taxpayers with modified AGI between $95,000 and $110,000, and for married taxpayers filing jointly with modified AGI between $190,000 and $220,000. Amounts are contributed on an after-tax basis, but funds grow free of taxation and amounts distributed to pay qualified education expenses are income tax-free (see page 330). These accounts had previously been known as "Education IRAs."

9. **Penalty-Free Withdrawals From Traditional IRAs**. Withdrawals from an IRA for qualified higher education expenses of the taxpayer are not subject to the 10-percent-penalty tax for premature distributions (but are subject to regular income taxes).

(continued on next page)

COLLEGE EDUCATION FUNDING (continued)

10. **Series EE Bonds and Series I Bonds**. Interest on Series EE and I bonds is ordinarily taxable on your federal return, but not at the state or local level. However, bonds purchased on or after January 1, 1990, can provide tax-free interest if the proceeds are used for the tuition and fees of a dependent. However, there is a phase-out of this exclusion once modified adjusted gross income exceeds a designated amount (in 2018 for single taxpayers the phase-out is between $79,700 and $94,700; for joint tax return filers the phase-out is between $119,550 and $149,550).

11. **Education Expense Deduction**. This provides an above-the-line $4,000 deduction for qualified educational expenses for taxpayers in certain income ranges. The expenses must be for tuition and fees at an eligible post-secondary educational institution. A maximum deduction of $4,000 is available for employees who file a single return with adjusted gross income of $65,000 or less and for those who file jointly with adjusted gross income of $135,000 or less. The deduction decreases to $2,000 for employees who file a single return with adjusted gross income that is greater than $65,000 but less than or equal to $80,000, and for those who file jointly with adjusted gross income that is greater than $130,000 but less than or equal to $160,000.

12. **Employer Tuition Reimbursement**. Also known as "educational assistance plans," or "Section 127 plans," under these nondiscriminatory programs an employee may exclude up to $5,250 of employer-provided educational assistance each calendar year. Amounts over $5,250 are included in income and subject to employment and income tax withholding (but expenses related to the employee's current job may be deductible, see paragraph 13 below). The education expenses need not be job related or lead to a degree. Covered expenses include tuition, fees, books, and supplies. Expenses for both undergraduate and graduate-level courses are covered. The American Tax Relief Act of 2012 made permanent this exclusion from income.

13. **Trade Or Business Expense**. Reimbursements to an employee outside of an educational assistance plan are included in the employee's income. These reimbursements were previously *deductible* as miscellaneous itemized deductions if the education expense was incurred for maintaining or improving skills required in employment – but this below-the-line deduction, subject to a "2-percent-floor," was suspended by the 2017 Tax Act. These reimbursements are *not deductible* if the education expense was incurred for meeting minimum requirements for employment or qualifying for a new trade or business.

COMMON DISASTER CLAUSE

The term "common disaster clause," also known as a "simultaneous death provision," has been loosely used to describe a variety of clauses dealing with presumptions as to the order of death of the insured and the beneficiary. The basic intent of these clauses is to prevent the death benefit from passing to a named beneficiary if that person dies at the same time or shortly after the insured. Thus, it is an attempt by the deceased to better control the disposition of property after death. Although this discussion refers to an insured and the death benefit paid from a life insurance contract, the same concepts apply to a testator and the transfer of property under a will.

Under a "true" common disaster clause, when the beneficiary and the insured die as a result of a common disaster there is a *conclusive* presumption that the insured was the last to die, despite the fact that the beneficiary might survive the insured by days, or even months. Under the Uniform Simultaneous Death Act, enacted in almost all states, there is a *nonconclusive* presumption that the insured survived the beneficiary. However, if it can be shown that the beneficiary survived the insured, even for a moment, then the beneficiary receives the death proceeds. A "reverse common disaster clause" is used to assure that the marital deduction will be available. This clause assumes that a beneficiary-spouse survives the insured and therefore the death benefit passes to the estate of the beneficiary-spouse.

A "time clause" (or "short term survivorship clause"), on the other hand, refers not to the cause of death, but to the length of time the beneficiary must survive the insured. The time period is typically thirty days, but may be as long as six months. Periods longer than six months should be avoided if a surviving spouse is the beneficiary and the insured desires to take advantage of the marital deduction (see page 459). This is because property that does not vest in the surviving spouse within six months does not qualify for the marital deduction. For example, assume a time clause requires the spouse to survive for nine months after the insured's death. Once the spouse has survived the required nine months the death benefit is paid, but since it did not vest within six months, it does not qualify for the marital deduction, and could be subject to estate taxes.

Because of the difficulty of determining what time period to specify, it is often better to name contingent beneficiaries and have the insurance proceeds paid under a settlement option (other than a life income option that would terminate upon the beneficiary's death). Under such an arrangement, the primary beneficiary might receive a few payments, but the bulk of the death benefits would pass to the contingent beneficiaries upon the death of the primary beneficiary (which occurs after the death of the insured). Providing the primary beneficiary with an unlimited right of withdrawal under the settlement option would qualify the death proceeds for the marital deduction.

COMMUNITY PROPERTY

Community property is a specialized form of property ownership that exists only between a husband and wife who are considered to have an undivided one-half interest in such property during marriage. In most community property states, both spouses have an equal right and duty to manage community property, but neither spouse has the right to convert to his or her separate use or give away any substantial amount of community property without the other's consent (the gift can be voided by the nondonor spouse). In case of divorce, each spouse becomes a tenant in common of his or her share of the former community property (see footnote 1, page 13). Upon death, each may dispose of his own share of community property however he wishes. Without a will, community property passes by state law (generallyto the surviving spouse), with the deceased spouse's separate property passing according to the state's intestacy statute.

The nine states that have adopted community property are: Arizona, California, Idaho, Louisiana, Nevada, New Mexico, Texas, Washington, and Wisconsin. Wisconsin uses the term "marital property". In addition, Alaska allows for the affirmative election of community property and Tennessee allows for the creation of a Tennessee Community Property Trust.

In the nine states with community property, the community property laws are not exactly the same in each of these states. A married couple living in a community property state does not have the option of being governed by the state's community property law (except Alaska, where they may opt into the community property system). However, all community property states have provisions allowing for the partition of existing community property into separate property by gift from one spouse to the other, but this must be evidenced by a clear intention (retitling of assets will not suffice). During marriage, merely placing newly acquired property in the name of either spouse is not enough to assure that it will be treated as separate property. Prenuptial and postnuptial agreements can be used to fix the property rights of existing or after-acquired property. Community property generally consists of: (1) property purchased during the marriage; (2) earned income during marriage; (3) fringe benefits derived from employment; (4) dividends, interest, and capital gains earned on community property; and (5) dividends and interest earned on separate property during the marriage (Texas, Louisiana, and Idaho). In addition, property that is otherwise separate property can become community property if it becomes so commingled with community property that it cannot be identified.

Separate property consists of: (1) property owned by either spouse before marriage; (2) earned income from work before marriage; (3) gifts and inheritances received before or during marriage; (4) capital gains on separate property; and (5) dividends and interest earned on separate property during the marriage (Arizona, California, Nevada, New Mexico, and Washington).

(continued on next page)

COMMUNITY PROPERTY (continued)

A particular asset can be a mixture of both community property and separate property (e.g., purchase of home using funds earned before marriage and subsequent mortgage payments with community funds). Many community property states provide for other forms of co-ownership, such as joint tenancy and tenancy in common. For example, owning a home in joint tenancy rather than as community property avoids probate (but must be titled using explicit language). On the other hand, community property enjoys the specific advantage of getting a full step-up in income tax basis upon the death of one of the spouses (not available in common law states). There are also advantages to maintaining separate property, since it is generally not subject to pre-marriage debt or debt connected with the other spouse's separate property (but separate property could be subject to claims arising from "community debt").

Problems can occur when married couples move between community property and common law states. Common law property rights have been addressed by California's "quasi-community property" laws, whereas community property interests in common law states have been addressed by the Uniform Disposition of Community Property Rights at Death Act (adopted in a number of common law states).

When a life insurance policy is considered community property, generally one-half of the proceeds will be included in the insured's estate. But unique problems can arise when life insurance is community property. If the insured spouse dies first and the beneficiary is someone other than the surviving spouse, then one-half of the proceeds received by the beneficiary will be deemed a gift by the surviving spouse to the beneficiary, and subject to gift taxes on the surviving spouse's community share of the proceeds. If the noninsured spouse dies first, the deceased's one-half interest in the policy is included in his probate estate.

Merely naming the noninsured spouse owner of a newly issued policy will likely not avoid the policy becoming community property. The ownership designation should read: "John Doe as his sole and separate property and for his sole use and benefit," or words to that effect. With an existing policy, a transfer can be made to the noninsured spouse using a formal release of the community property interest. Thereafter, all premiums should be paid from the noninsured spouse's separate funds. If premiums are paid with both separate and community funds, one of two approaches will be used to determine the amount included in the insured's estate, either the "premium tracing" rule or the "inception of title" doctrine (see **Q 167**, *Tax Facts on Insurance & Employee Benefits (2018)*).

Buy-sell agreements involving community property business interests should contain the written consent of both spouses to be bound by the agreement. They should also include provisions limiting the disposition of stock or partnership interests upon death or divorce.

COMPANY OWNED LIFE INSURANCE (COLI)

The term "company owned life insurance" (COLI), also referred to as corporate owned life insurance, or employer-owned life insurance, is used to describe a wide variety of life insurance products that are purchased to fund both employee benefit plans and business insurance needs. These products include virtually all forms of permanent life insurance, including participating whole life, interest sensitive whole life, indexed universal life, universal life, and variable life.

Employee benefit plans. COLI products are purchased on the lives of key employees to fund survivor income plans (chart, page 123), deferred compensation plans (chart, page 127), post-retirement medical benefits, and supplemental executive retirement plans (SERPs) (discussion, page 560). When used for funding employee benefit plans, key features of COLI products include: (1) high early cash values ordinarily exceeding 90 percent of first-year premiums (and sometimes equal to or higher than first-year premiums); (2) underwriting considerations providing either guaranteed issue or simplified issue; (3) flexibility in funding variable benefits from both cash values and death proceeds; (4) change of insured provisions; (5) levelized commissions; (6) limited pay features; and (7) contract guarantees relating to mortality charges, expense charges, credited interest rates, and interest rates charged on borrowed funds. Tax and investment considerations often weigh heavily in the design and implementation of these plans. You will sometimes find products with lower cash value to premiums that focus more on returns at death, but the underwriting concessions on those products are often not as significant as the simplied issue and guaranteed issue programs offered on high cash value products.

Business insurance needs. COLI products are also purchased on the lives of business owners and key employees to fund a wide variety of needs related to risk planning, business continuation, and succession planning. These include entity purchase agreements (chart, page 171), "wait and see" buy/sell agreements (chart, page 187), partial stock redemptions (chart, pages 195), and key person insurance (chart, page 203).

Income Taxation of COLI Death Benefits

In response to the regrettable practice of insuring rank-and-file workers without their knowledge and consent, Congress included in the Pension Protection Act of 2006 major provisions affecting the income tax treatment of business owned life insurance policy death benefits. Employer-owned life insurance contracts, entered into after August 17, 2006, must meet certain requirements in order for the death proceeds to be excluded from taxable income. The general rule is that death proceeds from these contracts are taxed as ordinary income, except to the extent of any premiums paid for the policy. Exceptions to this general rule are based upon the insured's status, or how death proceeds are paid or used. The requirements and meeting the exceptions to the general rule are now generally referred to as Employer Owned Life Insurance (EOLI). See pages 357-359 for a more detailed discussion of these rules.

(continued on next page)

COMPANY OWNED LIFE INSURANCE (COLI) (continued)

The above concepts are obvious examples of "employer-owned" life insurance. Not so obvious is the application of the "related persons" provision, which treats individuals as "related" if they own more than 50 percent of a corporation (i.e., life insurance contracts owned by a majority stockholder are treated as "employer-owned"). For example, in the cross purchase agreement on page 175, assume that Owner A is a 60 percent stockholder, and Owner B is both a stockholder and an employee of the business. Insurance purchased by Owner A on Owner B's life to fund their cross purchase agreement is treated as employer-owned, and the death benefit is subject to income taxation. Payment of the proceeds to B's heirs would provide relief from taxation, but only if there had been the required notice and consent (see below).

The "related persons" provision is further complicated by application of the attribution rules. For example, assume Owner A is a 40 percent owner, Owner B (A's brother) is a 35 percent owner, and Owner C is a 25 percent owner. By family attribution B's stock is attributed to A, making A a majority stockholder (A's 40 percent + B's 35 percent = 75 percent). Insurance A owns on C is treated as employer-owned, and the death benefit is subject to income taxation. These attribution rules may even cause life insurance contracts owned by individuals, who themselves are not business owners, to be treated as employer-owned (e.g., insurance on A owned by A's spouse treated as employer-owned). Hopefully, the IRS will clarify and limit the scope of these rules. Until then, it is essential to fall within the exceptions by first meeting the following notice and consent requirements. As a practical matter, because the rules governing what is and what isn't covered by the notice and consent requirements are not as clear as they could be, it is prudent to give notice and consent before the policy is issued in any situation that could conceivably be covered. The requirements are not onerous and the consequences for non-compliance are draconian.

Notice and consent requirements. To qualify for an exception, it is essential to first meet strict notice and consent requirements. Under these requirements, the employee must: (1) be notified in writing that the employer intends to insure the employee's life and the maximum face amount to be issued; (2) be informed that the employer will be the policy beneficiary; and (3) give written consent, before the policy is issued, to being insured and consent to the coverage continuing after the insured employee terminates employment. *It is strongly recommended that notice be given, and consent be obtained, at the time an application is taken for virtually any life insurance contract that might conceivably fall within the scope of this law.* The statute provides no means of obtaining relief from these requirements. The potential cost of non-compliance is income taxation of the death proceeds in excess of premiums paid.

(continued on next page)

COMPANY OWNED LIFE INSURANCE (COLI) (continued)

Reporting requirements. Every employer (technically referred to as the "applicable policy-holder"), owning one or more employer-owned life insurance contracts issued after August 17, 2006, must file a return showing for each year: (1) the number of employees at the end of the year; (2) the number of employees insured under such contracts at the end of the year; (3) the total amount of insurance in force at the end of the year under such contracts; (4) the employer's name, address, and taxpayer identification number, and the employer's type of business; and (5) that the employer has a valid consent for each insured employee (if any consents were not obtained, the number of insured employees for whom such consent was not obtained).

CONSTRUCTIVE RECEIPT

A general rule of taxation is that income becomes taxable when it is "made available" to the taxpayer. The constructive receipt doctrine is used to currently tax cash basis taxpayers on income that is available to them, but which they have not actually received. The purpose of the rule is to prevent taxpayers from turning their backs on available income and thereby avoiding current taxation on that income. However, even though the taxpayer could, under some circumstances, currently receive the money, he will not be taxed provided his control of its receipt is subject to substantial limitations or restrictions. For example, a substantial limitation or restriction might be a forfeiture of the right to continued participation in the plan, a suspension of plan participation for a period of time, or a reduction in plan benefits.

If an employee's rights to deferred compensation are *forfeitable*, there is no constructive receipt. Even where the employee's rights are *nonforfeitable*, there will be no constructive receipt, provided (1) the agreement to defer compensation is entered into before the services are performed, and (2) the employer's promise to pay is not secured in any way.

Employers will often informally fund a deferred compensation plan through the purchase of a life insurance contract. This can be done without adverse tax consequences to the employee provided the employee has no interest in the contract and it remains the unrestricted asset of the employer and, as such, subject to the employer's general creditors. The employer should be the applicant, owner, and beneficiary of the contract. However, it is common for an employer owned policy to have the death benefit endorsed to the insured under an endorsement split dollar plan where the employee rents the death benefit annually for the economic benefit value of the net amount at risk. See pages 240 and 595.

Code section 409A has tightened up the deferral and distribution rules that apply to nonqualified deferred compensation plans. Under prior law the constructive receipt doctrine was the only restriction on the time and manner of deferred compensation *distributions* (e.g., provided a significant penalty was imposed, an employee could be given the right to withdraw funds at any time). Now a participant must make the *deferral* election before the start of the year in which the compensation is earned (prior law required that the election be made before the compensation was payable). See the expanded discussion of Section 409A on page 538.

See also, the discussion of Rabbi Trusts on page 514.

CONTINGENT OWNERSHIP OF SECOND TO DIE LIFE POLICY

In planning their estates, clients are sometimes reluctant to give up control of policy values and death benefits. In these situations, "contingent" ownership of a survivorship life policy can be used to provide some measure of flexibility. However, with this technique there is ongoing estate tax exposure that could be avoided by using a third party as the original policy owner (see Life Insurance Trust chart, page 55). Flexibility is achieved by maintaining individual ownership of the life insurance policy and designating an irrevocable trust as contingent owner of the policy (which could subsequently be changed to a new irrevocable trust with different provisions and beneficiaries).

Assume that husband and wife need life insurance to cover estate taxes and/or other estate settlement costs. They apply for a survivorship life policy paying a death benefit at the death of the second spouse to die. The policy owner should be that person who is most likely to die first. For example, since the husband is older than his wife, he is named policy owner. An irrevocable life insurance trust is designated as both beneficiary and "contingent" owner.. One of three scenarios is likely to occur:

1. **Husband dies first**. The trust becomes policy owner and the value of the policy at the time of death is its fair market value (often measured as its interpolated terminal reserve). See discussion of Life Insurance Policy Valuation at page 577. This is the value of the policy to be included in the husband's gross estate (because many survivorship policies provide for a large cash value increase upon the first death this amount could be substantial). Since the wife never owned the policy, upon her subsequent death the policy proceeds paid to the trust are not included in her estate.
2. **Wife dies first**. If the husband continues to own the policy, the death proceeds will be included in his estate upon his subsequent death. However, the husband could give the policy to the irrevocable trust (or to any third party), in which case the proceeds will be excluded from his estate *provided* he lives for more than three years after the gift (see pages 374-375). Although this exposure to estate taxation is aptly described as "estate planning roulette," with some clients it may be an acceptable risk if they are unwilling to give up control from the inception of the policy. It may be possible to sell the policy to an intentionally defective grantor trust and avoid the "three year rule." See Intentionally Defective Trust at pages 74-77.
3. **Husband and wife die in a common disaster**. A "reverse common disaster" clause might be used to establish a conclusive presumption that the wife survives her husband (i.e., husband dies first). See discussion on page 316.

It is strongly recommended that this technique only be resorted to when a client is unwilling to have the insurance policy owned by an irrevocable life insurance trust. Such a trust can *assure* that both cash values and death proceeds are not subject to estate taxation (see chart, page 55). But, because of increases in the estate tax exemption (currently increased to \$11.2 million (\$11.4 million projected for 2019) on a temporary basis per person by the 2017 Tax Act), many people are uncertain as to the application of the estate tax at their death. Because of constantly changing politics and increasing budget deficits, many people anticipate a future Democratic Congress once again decreasing the exemption. However, despite the possibility of this happening, it is impossible to be sure when and if it will happen. As a result, advisors are more frequently recommending purchasing insurance for the non-tax benefits (and to lock in insurability) – but recommending ownership in the most flexible structure. As a result, where it was once unusual, it has become more common for second-to-die insurance not to be trust owned.

CONTROLLING STOCKHOLDER SPLIT DOLLAR

The concept of a controlling stockholder, also referred to as a "majority stockholder," is important with respect to split-dollar plans in which the death benefit is shared between the corporation and the insured's personal beneficiary. As with any key person insurance, that part of the *death benefit received by the corporation* on a policy insuring a controlling stockholder is included with other assets in valuing the corporation, and thus in determining the value of stock in the controlling stockholder's estate. But that part of the *death benefit received outside of the corporation* by a personal beneficiary or a trust will also be included in the insured's estate where the insured was a controlling stockholder, since any incidents of ownership held by the corporation are attributed to the insured through his stock ownership as a controlling stockholder. A person is considered a controlling stockholder when, at the time of his death, he owns more than 50 percent of the voting stock of a corporation. A "bare bones" collateral assignment strategy where the trust retains all rights other than the lone right for the employer to be reimbursed at death is generally believed to avoid inclusion.

Assume a split-dollar plan is funded by a $5,000,000 policy paying $1.000,000 to the corporation and $4,000,000 to the employee's beneficiary. Because corporate ownership is attributed to the controlling stockholder, the $4,000,000 death benefit paid to the personal beneficiary is also included in the estate. Despite stockholders often using split dollar today for income tax reasons (using corporate dollars because they are taxed at a lower rate than individual dollars), many business owners still have estate tax concerns when factoring in the death benefit of their life insurance. And, even for those without a current estate tax concern, the ever changing political environment and the increasing federal budget deficit create a very real possibility that the estate tax exemption will be reduced by a future Congress.

Controlling stockholder split dollar can be illustrated as follows:

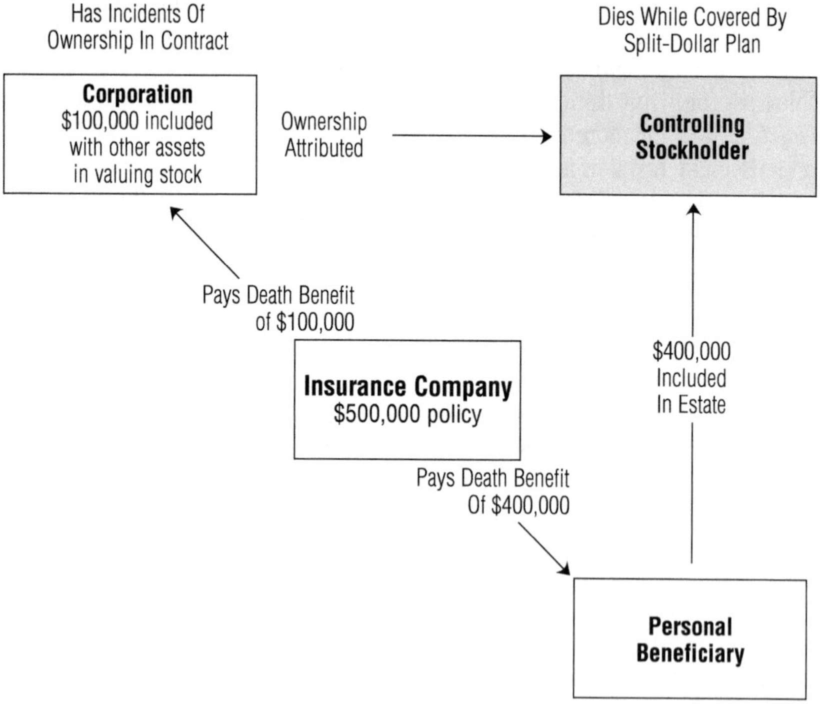

Note: See the Life Insurance as Property chart on page 96, discussion in footnote 3 on page 243, and **Q 325**, *Tax Facts on Insurance & Employee Benefits (2019)*.

CONVERSION FROM S CORPORATION TO C CORPORATION

The most significant change made by the 2017 Tax Act was the permanent reduction of the C Corporate tax rate to a flat 21 percent. As the focus of the Republican Tax Reform strategy – it was widely argued by the GOP that U.S. corporate tax rates were unreasonably high compared to other countries – discouraging U.S. business and hurting American workers. Much of the $1.5 trillion cost (estimated over ten years) is a result of this aspect of the 2017 Tax Act. While it is probably fair and safe to say that lower U.S. Corporate tax rates have further spurred the economy – what is not clear is the impact that the increased deficit and tax-stimulus will have on the economy and workers over a longer time-horizon.

However, regardless of your personal view on this aspect of tax policy – business owners need to consider whether it makes sense for them to convert their businesses to C corporation status if not currently operating as a C corporation. After many years of seeing businesses change from C-status to S-corporation status – taxpayers and their tax and legal advisors are now focusing on the desirability of moving to C-status (rather than away from it).

Although, while on first glance the "permanent" 21 percent flat rate seems to make C corporate status very desirable – there is much more to the analysis. Here are some of the items that should be considered.

1. C corporations are taxed at a flat 21 percent rate whereas partnerships (including S corporations electing partnership status) are taxed at individual rates. Individual tax rates are graduated – meaning that even though the top marginal rate is 37 percent for federal purposes an individual's effective rate can be significantly lower. In fact, the 22 percent marginal rate does not apply until a married filing joint taxpayer reaches over $77,000 of taxable income. The 24 percent rate doesn't begin until taxable income is over $165,000. For many small business owners the individual tax rates will be lower than the C corporation rate.
2. Pass-through income (such as S corporations or partnerships) may be eligible for a 20 percent deduction for "qualified business income" or "QBI." While this is a meaningful deduction for owners of such businesses – it should be remembered that even with a 20 percent deduction the top marginal rate for income from these businesses would still be taxed at 29.6 percent (80% of 37%). The 29.6 percent is considerably higher than the 21 percent C corporate rate for high-income business owners.
3. Not all pass-through income is eligible for the 20 percent deduction. Service business owners have the 20 percent deduction capped starting at $315,000 and totally phased out at $415,000 for married filing joint returns. There are also limitations tied to the number of employees and the amount of depreciable tangible property. In other words, it is necessary to do a full analysis to determine how much, if any, the 20 percent deduction will benefit. See discussion of Qualified Business Income at pages 504-506).

(continued on next page)

CONVERSION FROM S CORPORATION TO C CORPORATION (continued)

4. Corporations are subject to TWO levels of tax – or as commonly known as "Double Taxation." A C corporation is taxed at 21 percent on earnings and dividends distributed to shareholders would be taxed a second time at 20 percent. Such dividends could also be subject to the 3.8 percent excise tax on investment income. The C corporation does not receive a deduction for dividends paid. In other words, a key consideration is how much will be distributed in the form of dividends. If the business owner is only compensated in the form of reasonable compensation and if excess profits are going to be permanently retained in the business – potential double taxation is a much lesser consideration.
5. The Personal Holding Company Tax can apply to certain closely-held C corporations if 60 percent or more of the income is passive. See discussion of Personal Holding Company at page 487.
6. The Accumulated Earnings Tax can apply to C corporations. Many business owners considering a switch to C corporation status assume that they can simply pay themselves as much compensation as they desire (avoiding the need for dividends) and retain the balance of earnings in the company without consequence. While Accumulated Earnings Taxes have not been a major IRS focus in recent years – it is very likely that the reduction in C corporate tax rates will increase the focus on this tax.
7. Taxpayers assuming that they can simply pay themselves unlimited compensation when needed to avoid paying dividends need to consider the doctrine of unreasonable compensation. The IRS has the ability to re-classify compensation as a dividend when it exceeds what is "reasonable." Reasonable compensation has not been an IRS focus in recent years, but it too is likely to see increased attention because of the tax law changes.
8. If a business owner is contemplating the sale of his or her business, it is important to consider the impact that this will have on taxation. A sale structured as an asset sale, the most common type of business sale, will result in two levels of tax for a C corporation. The business will have potential gain when it sells assets and the shareholders have potential tax when they exchange low-basis stock for sales proceeds.
9. On a positive note, owners holding C corporation stock will get a basis step-up on the value of the stock at death. This would allow heirs to avoid one level of tax on the liquidation of the business – although it would not avoid the business gain on an asset sales as discussed above.
10. Unlike a partnership, corporate losses do not flow through to the shareholders. For businesses that may operate at a loss, this can be an important consideration.

These are only some of the primary issues that should be considered when analyzing the relative merits of converting to C corporation status. For many business owners, the conversion will make sense because of the lower corporate tax rates. However, this won't be universally true for business owners. It is important for each closely-held business and its owner(s) to consider specific facts.

CORPORATE ALTERNATIVE MINIMUM TAX

The corporate alternative minimum tax (AMT) is designed to assure that the taxpayer with substantial economic income will not be able to avoid taxes merely by using available tax exclusions, deductions, and credits.

A corporation qualifying as a "small corporation" is not subject to the alternative minimum tax. A small corporation is a corporation that for its first tax year beginning after 1996 has average annual gross receipts not exceeding $5,000,000 for the preceding three-year period (if the corporation was in existence less than three years, then the test will be applied to whatever period it was in existence). Annualization of receipts is required for any short taxable year. Once a corporation qualifies as a small corporation, it will continue to be treated as a small corporation as long as its average gross receipts for the three-year period preceding the taxable year do not exceed $7,500,000.

Gross receipts include total sales (net of returns and allowances) and all amounts received for services. In addition, gross receipts include any income from investments, and from incidental or outside sources. For example, gross receipts include interest, dividends, rents, royalties, and annuities, regardless of whether such amounts are derived in the ordinary course of the taxpayer's trade or business. Gross receipts are generally not reduced by the cost of goods or property sold.

The following discussion applies only to those corporations that do not qualify as a "small corporation" and therefore are subject to the alternative minimum tax.

As it applies to corporations, the AMT requires that the corporate tax base be determined with certain adjustments and increased by specific tax preferences. Two of the more common tax preference items are accelerated depreciation and certain tax-exempt interest. In the process of determining the alternative minimum taxable income (AMTI) of a C corporation, 75 percent of the amount by which adjusted current earnings (ACE) exceed the tentative AMTI is added to the tentative AMTI (or 75 percent of the amount by which the tentative AMTI exceeds ACE is subtracted from the tentative AMTI). The resulting amount is then reduced by an exemption of $40,000 less 25 percent of the excess of AMTI over $150,000. The resulting tax base is multiplied by 20 percent to determine the tentative minimum tax. The corporation then pays a tax equal, in effect, to the greater of this amount or its regular tax.

Although ACE is not equivalent to current earnings and profits (E&P), some of the adjustments used in computing ACE rely on E&P concepts. For example, life insurance will increase ACE, since

(continued on next page)

CORPORATE ALTERNATIVE MINIMUM TAX (continued)

under generally accepted accounting principles E&P increased by: (1) yearly cash value increases in excess of annual premiums; and (2) death proceeds (including outstanding loans) in excess of basis increased for cash value increases previously included in AMTI. Proceeds from disability income and buy-out policies payable to the corporation are also included in ACE.

Conversely, if premiums are paid for term insurance, or the cash value increase is less than the annual premium, there is a *decrease* of ACE that reduces exposure to the AMT. However, redemption of the deceased or disabled owner's stock in the same year as the proceeds are received will not avoid an increase in ACE.

The existence of the AMT does not mean that all, or even most, life insurance cash values or death proceeds will be subject to the tax. Much depends upon the corporation's taxable income, tax preference items, and other factors (e.g., S corporations are not subject to the ACE adjustment). Only a portion of cash value increases and death proceeds will be potentially exposed to this tax, since cash value increases will be partially offset by premiums; and death proceeds will be offset by cash values. Even when there is exposure, generally **the maximum rate is 15 percent** (i.e., a 20 percent tax on 75 percent of ACE). With many corporations payment of the tax will be an *acceleration of* rather than an *increase of* tax liability, since it then becomes a credit available to offset a portion of the corporation's tax liability in future years (unlimited carry forward). However, this credit may be useless to the closely held or professional corporation that will have little, if any, taxable income.

(continued on next page)

CORPORATE ALTERNATIVE MINIMUM TAX (continued)

Impact of Alternative Minimum Tax On Life Insurance Death Benefits Payable to C Corporation

Taxable Income	Death Benefit				
	100,000	250,000	1,000,000	2,500,000	5,000,000
0	**7,000**	**31,375**	**150,000**	**375,000**	**750,000**
	7,000	31,375	150,000	375,000	750,000
25,000	**12,000**	**37,625**	**155,000**	**380,000**	**755,000**
	8,250	33,875	151,250	376,250	751,250
50,000	**17,000**	**43,875**	**160,000**	**385,000**	**760,000**
	9,500	36,375	152,500	377,500	752,500
100,000	**28,250**	**56,375**	**170,000**	**395,000**	**770,000**
	6,000	34,125	147,750	372,750	747,750
250,000	80,750	**87,500**	**200,000**	**425,000**	**800,000**
		6,750	119,250	344,250	719,250
500,000	170,000	170,000	**250,000**	**475,000**	**850,000**
			80,000	305,000	680,000
1,000,000	340,000	340,000	**350,000**	**575,000**	**950,000**
			10,000	235,000	610,000
2,000,000	680,000	680,000	680,000	**775,000**	**1,150,000**
				95,000	470,000

Note: This chart assumes the C corporation is not exempt from the alternative minimum tax (AMT) as a "small corporation." Small figure represents that portion of the income tax that is attributable to the death benefit (i.e., additional tax imposed under the AMT calculations). The corporation is assumed to have no tax preference items. No adjustments are made for cumulative premiums paid and for possible annual cash value increases in excess of premiums paid (i.e., "basis for ACE"). As an example of how to use this chart, assume a corporation has $500,000 of taxable income in a given year and also receives a death benefit payment of $1,000,000. The corporation will owe federal income taxes of $250,000 of which $80,000 is attributable to the effect of the AMT and the receipt of the life insurance death benefit. If this corporation received the same $1,000,000 death benefit but had $2,000,000 of taxable income, the corporation would owe $680,000 in taxes, none of which would be attributable to the death benefit and the AMT. This chart also indicates that a corporation with taxable income of $1,000,000 could consider increasing its key person life insurance on a key employee from $100,000 to $250,000 without additional exposure to the AMT (i.e., the income taxes remain at $340,000).

COVERDELL EDUCATION SAVINGS ACCOUNT

A Coverdell Education Savings Account, originally called an "Education IRA," may be created for the purpose of paying the qualified education expenses of a designated beneficiary. The American Tax Relief Act of 2012 made permanent the annual non-deductible contributions of $2,000 per beneficiary that can be made to these accounts (it had been scheduled to be reduced to $500). The beneficiary must be under age eighteen (except in the case of a special needs beneficiary). This $2,000 annual contribution limit is phased out ratably for individual taxpayers with modified AGI between $95,000 and $190,000, and for married taxpayers filing jointly with modified AGI between $190,000 and $220,000. Contributors with modified AGI above this phase-out range are not allowed to make contributions to an Education Savings Account. This contribution limit is per beneficiary, meaning that multiple contributors cannot exceed the $2,000 per beneficiary per year limit (e.g., if grandfather contributes $1,800 for grandson then grandmother is limited to contributing an additional $200 for grandson).

Contributions to an Education Savings Account are not tax deductible, but will be treated as completed present interest gifts from the contributor to the beneficiary at the time of the contribution. A taxpayer may claim a American Opportunity Credit or Lifetime Learning Credit for the same taxable year there are distributions from an Education Savings Account, provided the distributions are used to pay for different education costs.

When the funds are distributed to pay the beneficiary's qualified education expenses, *neither the* principal *nor the earnings will be included in the beneficiary's income*. Qualified education expenses include elementary and secondary school tuition, expenses of special needs beneficiaries, post-secondary tuition, fees, books, supplies, uniforms, equipment, and certain room and board expenses. The earnings portion of distributions that are not used to pay for qualified education expenses is not only taxed to the beneficiary, but is also subject to an additional 10-percent-penalty tax. For this purpose, the "earnings portion" means any growth in the funds in excess of the nondeductible contributions.

Any balance remaining in an Education Savings Account at the time a beneficiary becomes thirty years old (except in the case of a special needs beneficiary) or dies, if earlier, must be distributed. The earnings portion of such a distribution will be includable in gross income of the beneficiary and will be subject to the additional 10-percent-penalty tax because the distribution was not for educational purposes. However, it is possible to avoid taxation by rolling the account balance over to another Education Savings Account benefiting a different beneficiary, who is a member of the family of the original beneficiary and who has not attained age thirty as of such date (except in the case of a special needs beneficiary).

CRITICAL ILLNESS INSURANCE

Major advances in medical sciences in recent years have resulted in substantial increases in the number of people surviving a critical illness. For example advancements in treatment have caused more forms of cancer to be viewed as chronic illnesses rather than terminal diseases. Critical illness insurance is designed to provide for those suffering from, and surviving, such illnesses.

Critical illness insurance typically pays a benefit upon the *diagnosis* of the first occurrence of a named critical illness or condition. Some products provide for payments for a limited number of conditions, such as heart attack, stroke, or cancer. Other products pay upon such wide ranging conditions as Alzheimer's Disease, multiple sclerosis, major organ transplant, kidney failure, loss of sight, loss of use of two or more limbs, any terminal illness, or death.

Although often resembling the more common "dreaded disease" products, critical illness insurance typically offers substantially greater coverages and benefits. For example, proceeds might be used to provide for home health care needs, replace lost wages of the insured or a caregiver, provide for housekeeping or child care services, pay for "experimental" treatment or drugs, pay medical copayments and deductibles, or make modifications to automobiles and homes for a disabled survivor. Benefits can vary widely. The amount can be either a fixed sum or a percentage of a life insurance death benefit. Payments can be made as a lump sum or over a number of years. Some policies offer coverage that terminates at specified age such as sixty-five or seventy.

While critical illness insurance has apparently gained wide acceptance in the United Kingdom, Australia, and Japan, within the United States it is not as popular. The product is likely to have wide application, not just to the married couple or business owner but also to the single person, who, after suffering a critical illness becomes his or her own dependent (traditionally a difficult market for life insurance). The proliferating consumer-directed health plans, larger medical deductibles, and lower reimbursement caps are all likely to increase interest in the product.

It is currently offered in the form of a stand-alone product, as a rider to a life insurance policy, as group insurance, or as part of a health, term life, or universal life policy. However, payment of critical illness benefits from a life insurance policy could reduce death benefits and reduce or eliminate accumulated cash values. See Long Term Care Hybrid Products on pages 454-457.

CRUMMEY POWERS

By using the gift tax annual exclusion, in 2018 and 2019 (projected) up to $15,000, as adjusted for inflation, can be given tax free each year to as many people (donees) as desired. However, this exclusion is available only when the donee has a right to the immediate use, possession, or enjoyment of the property that is the subject of the gift (i.e., a "present interest" in the property as opposed to a "future interest").

Although outright gifts present no difficulty with this requirement, gifts made to trusts are often subject to substantial restrictions on the beneficiaries' (donees') rights to the trust property. Under these circumstances, in order to assure the availability of the annual exclusion it is important for the beneficiaries to be given powers to withdraw gifts placed in a trust. These powers are often referred to as "Crummey powers." The term is derived from the case of *D. Clifford Crummey v. Commissioner*, 397 F.2d 82 (9th Cir. 1968). A trust containing such powers is often referred to as a Crummey Trust.

Typically these withdrawal rights, or "Crummey powers," are exercisable only during a specific period of time (e.g., for 30 days after receiving notice of the gift to the trust). For the power to be effective, the beneficiary must receive timely notice of the gifts, but the withdrawal rights are noncumulative and will lapse after the designated period of time.

For example, an irrevocable life insurance trust might provide for each beneficiary to have "the right to demand up to $5,000, not to exceed the amount placed in the trust during the calendar year." Note that the power is usually limited to $5,000, rather than the full $15,000 allowed as the annual exclusion or the $30,000 allowed as a split-gift (the $15,000 annual exclusion is subject to indexing for inflation). Such a limitation avoids creating adverse gift and estate tax consequences for the beneficiaries of the trust (for a further explanation, see page 50). A "hanging" Crummey power used to avoid a lapse of a power of withdrawal in excess of the greater of $5,000 or 5 percent of the trust corpus should be drafted by reference to such "5-or-5" limitation and not as a tax savings clause (see footnote 4, page 57).

An alternative to the Crummey power is the cumulative power, which is a vested withdrawal right that does not lapse. Use of a cumulative power enables the trust grantor to make annual gifts of $15,000 (subject to indexing) per beneficiary without causing problems with lapsing powers of withdrawal. However, these nonlapsing withdrawal powers are always subject to being exercised in case of bankruptcy or divorce, and would be included in the beneficiary's estate.

DEATH BENEFIT ONLY PLAN

Under the usual survivor income plan, the present value of the survivor income payments is considered to be a part of the employee's taxable estate. With a larger estate, the "death benefit only plan" (DBO plan) offers a particular type of survivor income plan that can be designed to keep these benefits out of the employee's taxable estate and thereby avoid federal estate taxes. However, because of the unlimited marital deduction, there is no exposure to federal estate taxes unless benefits are payable to someone other than the surviving spouse (e.g., children or other heirs). In addition, because of increases to the federal estate tax exemption (increased by the 2017 Tax Act to \$11.2 million for 2018 and \$11.4 million projected for 2019 per taxpayer through 2025) far fewer employees have estate tax concerns making a survivor income plan more tax efficient for employees.

Typically, the employer and employee enter into a legally binding agreement under which the employer agrees to provide a specified payment, or payments, to a named beneficiary of the employee. The actual payments are usually either a fixed amount or based upon some multiple of salary.

If life insurance is used to provide the employer with funds to meet the obligation under the agreement, the policy should be carried as key person insurance and the agreement itself should contain no specific mention of the insurance funding. As with all key person insurance, since the premiums paid by the employer come from after-tax dollars, none of the premiums are included in the employee's income. With the corporate tax rate now at 21 percent and corporate taxpayers able to immediately deduct many expenditures previously subject to capitalization, loss of a corporate tax deduction may be less important than in past years to the employer. Should the employee die, the employer's payments to the employee's beneficiary under the DBO plan are received as ordinary income and are deductible by the employer, provided they are considered as "reasonable compensation" for the employee's services (see page 576).

There is some question as to whether a DBO plan would be successful in removing the death benefit from the estate of a controlling stockholder, since his or her voting control of the corporation gives the controlling stockholder the right to alter, amend, or terminate the agreement. See discussion of Controlling Shareholder on page 324.

DECANTING

Decanting refers to the revision or updating of an otherwise irrevocable trust. Decanting statutes have introduced new flexibility into rules governing the modification of an irrevocable trust.

The states of Alabama, Alaska, Arizona, Colorado, Delaware, Florida, Illinois, Indiana, Kentucky, Michigan, Minnesota, Missouri, Nevada, New Hampshire, New Mexico, New York, North Carolina, Ohio, Rhode Island, South Carolina, South Dakota, Tennessee, Texas, Virginia, Washington, Wisconsin, and Wyoming have adopted decanting statutes. Because additional states continue to add and amend their trust law frequently, it is important to consult a local trust and estate lawyer. Procedural requirements for decanting differ from state to state. Where allowed, typically all that is required is for the trustee to sign a document carrying out the decanting, provide a copy to all interested persons and file the document with the appropriate court. While court approval or beneficiary consent is generally *not* required to decant a trust, state laws can restrict the elimination of beneficiary rights (e.g., provision of fixed income for beneficiaries). Although decanting generally will not create income tax issues, there are gift, estate, and generation-skipping tax issues that require careful consideration by qualified tax counsel (e.g., the trustee should not be a beneficiary under the trust). As a result of decanting the original trust may be merely amended, or replaced by one or more new trusts.

The potential reasons for decanting trusts are many and varied. Decanting can be used to correct drafting errors, provide for more flexible trust administration, change governing law, assist in paying life insurance premiums, remove or add spendthrift provisions, expand trustee powers, appoint investment advisors, consolidate similar trusts, extend the trust termination date, authorize the use of investment advisors, and change from nongrantor to grantor trust or vice versa (see chart on page 75 and discussion on page 393).

In addition to decanting statutes, either specific trust language or a state's version of the Uniform Trust Code (UTC) can provide trustees with substantial flexibility to change the original provisions of an irrevocable trust. The UTC provides for the reformation or modification of trusts that are subject to the laws of states that have adopted the UTC. With *reformation*, amendments to the trust do not change the grantor's original intent. In contrast, with *modification* amendments to the trust change the grantor's original intent. Unlike the decanting statutes, changes to a trust under the UTC require a court proceeding. Generally the UTC aims to adhere to the grantor's original objectives and the trust may only be modified or terminated upon either: (1) the consent of the grantor and all of the beneficiaries; (2) the consent of all of the beneficiaries – if the trust's material purposes have been accomplished; or (3) the consent of less than all of the beneficiaries – provided the trust could have been modified or terminated if all the beneficiaries had consented and the interests of the nonconsenting beneficiaries are protected.

DECOUPLING OF STATE DEATH TAXES

Prior to the Economic and Tax Relief Act of 2001 (EGTRRA), the majority of states imposed a state death tax that was equal in amount to the allowable state death tax credit under federal law (known as a pick-up or sponge tax). Other states, that maintained an independent state death tax system, imposed a tax at least equal to the state death tax credit (i.e., the tax imposed was the greater of the state death tax credit or the separately computed state tax). Under this system of revenue-sharing, all states imposed a tax at least equal to the federal credit. For example, in 2001 the maximum federal estate tax of 55 percent was effectively split into two parts, with 39 percent paid to the federal government and 16 percent paid to the state government (lesser percentages were provided in a table for taxable estates under $11,200,000).

Under EGTRRA, the state death tax credit was eliminated and replaced with a deduction from 2005 to 2009 (for the taxpayer a deduction provides less than half the benefit of a credit). This elimination of the state death tax credit effectively repealed the state inheritance tax in those states that levied a tax exactly equal to the state death tax credit. Threatened with the loss of significant revenue, many states responded by "decoupling" from the federal estate tax. The laws designed to recoup lost revenues have taken a number of different forms, to include:

(1) **Decoupling as to the tax rate but not the exempt amount.** For example, in the chart on page 21, no state tax would be imposed on up to $11,200,000 going to the family trust (state exemption is equal to federal exemption), but upon the second death the amount in excess of $11,200,000 would be subject to a maximum tax of 16 percent.

(2) **Decoupling as to both the tax rate and the exempt amount.** For example, assume a pick-up state decouples by imposing a tax based on the law immediately prior to EGTRRA 2001 (i.e., $675,000 is exempt and the top rate is 16 percent). In the chart on page 31, placing $11,200,000 in the family trust to take full advantage of the federal unified credit would expose $10,525,000 to *state* death taxes (11,200,000 – 675,000 = 10,525,000).

Although sunset provisions provided for return of the state death tax credit, the deduction was temporarily extended through the end of 2012. However, The American Tax Relief Act of 2012 permanently replaced the credit with a deduction, effectively denying a return to revenue-sharing with the states.

To cope with the lack of uniformity from state to state, additional flexibility should be added to estate plans (e.g., post mortem planning with disclaimers, see page 346). See also the planning pointers on pages 5-7 and the discussion of post mortem planning on page 492.

DEFERRAL OF ESTATE TAX

The federal estate tax is normally due and payable in cash within nine months after death. However, special deferral provisions are available for a "closely held" business, provided: (1) the business interest exceeds thirty-five percent of the adjusted gross estate; and (2) the decedent was a sole proprietor, a partner in a partnership with forty-five or fewer partners (or owning 20 percent or more of the partnership capital interest), or a stockholder in a corporation with forty-five or fewer stockholders (or owning 20 percent or more of the voting stock in a corporation).

If an estate meets these requirements, then the estate taxes attributable to the business interest may be deferred for four years during which interest only is payable. Thereafter, there is a maximum period of ten years during which annual installments of principal and interest must be paid (Code section 6166).

The interest rate was only 2 percent on the tax attributable to the first $1,550,000 in business value (as indexed in 2019 for inflation) in excess of the "applicable exclusion amount." Under prior law the applicable exclusion amount was known as the "exemption equivalent." As a result of temporary changes sunsetting in 2026, in 2018 the applicable exclusion amount was increased from $5,600,000 to $11,200,000. Because of the uncertainty of planning for a temporary tax bill, planning for Section 6166 is ordinarily based on the 2017 exemption of $5,600,000 and unified credit of $2,185,800.

For example, using 2017 estate tax exemptions, the tax on $6,900,000 of assumed business value would be $2,717,800 and the tax on the first $5,600,000 of business value would be $2,185,800 (i.e., the unified credit). Therefore, the maximum amount of tax deferrable at the 2 percent rate would be $532,000 ($2,717,800 – $2,185,800 = $532,000). Any estate tax that is attributable to the business interest in excess of $532,000 would be deferrable at 45 percent of the rate applicable to underpayment of tax.

Before relying on the Section 6166 deferral provisions as an alternative to life insurance, a business owner should give serious consideration to **the following qualifications and restrictions**:

1. **The business** interest **must meet strict qualification standards and percentage**s in order for the deferred payment provision to be available.
2. **Not all settlement costs can be deferred**. For example, federal estate taxes on non-business assets, state death taxes, income taxes, debts, and administrative expenses must normally be paid in cash when due.
3. The interest payments are not deductible.
4. **Only a limited** amount **of tax** can qualify for the 2 percent interest rate (in 2018 the amount is limited to $532,000).
5. **All remaining** payments **may be accelerated** if either installment or interest payments are not made within six months of the due date, in addition to the payment of a 5 percent per month penalty.
6. **The executor is** personally **liable** for payment of the tax and must post a bond of up to twice the amount of the deferred tax unless a special IRS tax lien is placed on the estate.
7. **Extensive delays** in the final disposition of the estate will often occur when there is a deferral of the estate tax.
8. **The** tax must be paid. The deferral provisions only allow the business to continue with another creditor (the IRS) making demands on cash flow.

DEFERRAL OF GAINS ON CERTAIN STOCK OPTIONS & RSU

The 2017 Tax Act created IRC Section 83(i) that significantly changes the taxation of stoock options and restrictive stock units ("RSU") by allowing for tax deferral on certain stock options and RSUs. Ordinarily, under Section 83(a), property (including options and RSU) received in exchange for services becomes taxable at the earlier of when it becomes transferrable or when it becomes vested (or is no longer subject to a substantial risk of forfeiture). As a result, appreciation on such stock or RSUs from the time of grant to the time of vesting becomes taxable and subject to taxation as ordinary income.

Under Section 83(b), taxpayers may make an irrevocable election to pay income taxes on the unvested stock at its fair market value on the date of receipt – rather than date of vesting. This allows future appreciation (between date of grant and vesting) to be taxed at capital gain rates. However, in many instances, taxpayers may not have the resources to pay taxes on stock that is not readily tradeable.

New Section 83(i) allows employees who receive certain equity grants to elect to defer taxation for up to five years AFTER the stock vests. This will be very helpful to employees when the equity grant received is not readily tradeable. It is also beneficial for recipients of start-up companies that anticipate significant growth in the stock received and would rather not liquidate portions of the stock to pay the tax bill. Specifically, the income must be recognized at the earlier of: (1) the date the qualified stock becomes transferable, (2) the date the employee becomes an "excluded employee," (3) the date on which the stock becomes readily tradeable on an established equities market, (4) five years after the stock becomes substantially vested, or (5) the date upon which the employee revokes the deferral election.

An "excluded employee" includes (1) a 1 percent or greater owner or former owner (1 percent within the past ten years), (2) the current or a former CEO or CFO, (3) a family member of someone described in (1) or (2), or (4) one of the four most highly compensated officers in any of the past ten years.

Eligible employers must be a private company that has a written plan in place whereunder at least 80 percent of U.S.-based full-time employees will be granted stock options or RSUs on substantially the same terms. The number of shares need not be the same – but no grant can be de minimis. Presumably, this would allow for a grant formula tied to salary. The 80 percent test is based upon all employees within a controlled group (as defined under IRC Section 414(b)). Only corporations (specifically excluding LLCs making a partnership tax election) are eligible employers.

(continued on next page)

DEFERRAL OF GAINS ON CERTAIN STOCK OPTIONS & RSU (continued)

Employers are REQUIRED to provide notice of the potential to defer income to the employee receiving the grantor. The election must be made within 30 days after the date upon which the employee's rights in the stock are transferrable or are no longer subject to a substantial risk of forfeiture (whichever is earlier). The election must be filed with the IRS and the employee must also provide a copy to the employer.

At the end of the deferral period, the employee recognizes income based upon the value of the stock on the vesting date (regardless of weather the value has increased or decreased during the deferral period). However, it is important to note that long-term capital gains treatment begins to run during the deferral period. As a result, if the property's value increases during the deferral period, ordinaruy income tax rates will only apply to the value at the start of the deferral period. The remainder will be taxed at the lower long-term capital gains rates if the stock is not sold for at least one year.

A Section 83(b) election is not available for property on which an 83(i) election to defer has been made. Equity grants qualifying under this new section will not be treated as non-qualified deferred compensation for purposes of Section 409A.

See also, the discussion of Incentive Stock Options on page 401.

DEFINED BENEFIT PENSION PLAN

Under the defined benefit pension plan the employer guarantees a specified benefit at "normal retirement age." Based upon actuarial calculations the employer is required to maintain a level of "minimum funding" such as will assure that funds will be available to pay this guaranteed retirement benefit. In contrast to defined contribution pensions, such as the money purchase pension plan, there are no individual accounts.

The maximum amount of the projected annual benefit at age sixty-five (paid as a life annuity or as a joint and survivor benefit) is limited to the lesser of $225,000 (projected for 2019) or 100 percent of compensation averaged over the three highest-earning consecutive years (if normal retirement age is earlier than age sixty-two these maximum limits are reduced). In contrast to the money purchase pension plan, a defined benefit pension plan has maximum benefit limits but not maximum contribution limits (i.e., the regulatory concern is directed toward assuring that minimum funding standards are met). However, plan contributions must be suspended if the plan is found to be overfunded. In determining the specified benefit integration with Social Security is allowed.

Under a defined benefit pension plan the employer bears the investment risk of the plan (i.e., the employer is obligated to pay a specified benefit upon the employee's retirement). Up to specific limits the benefits of a defined benefit pension plan are guaranteed by the Pension Benefit Guaranty Corporation. See page 485.)

Various formulas are used to determine the employee's benefit: (1) **Flat amount formula** – all employees receive the same stated dollar monthly benefit without regard to the employee's level of compensation (e.g., $600 per month for life beginning at age sixty-five). However, some minimum years of employment might be required for the maximum monthly benefit, with reduced benefits for lesser years of employment. (2) **Flat percentage formula** – each employee receives a benefit that is based upon a percentage of his average earnings (e.g., 50 percent of average earnings for life beginning at age sixty-five). However, some minimum years of employment might be required for the maximum monthly benefit, with reduced percentages for lesser years of employment. (3) **Unit credit formula** – each employee receives a benefit that is based upon his years of employment (e.g., assuming 1¼ percent credit for each year of service an employee with 20 years of service and $100,000 of average earnings would receive a benefit of $25,000, calculated as $1.25 \times 20 = 25 \times .01 = .25 \times 100{,}000 = 25{,}000$).

See also, the discussion of qualified retirement plans on page 512, and the discussion of life insurance in qualified plans on pages 419-420.

DEPARTMENT OF LABOR ("DOL") FIDUCIARY RULES

In 2016 the Department of Labor (DOL) announced regulations that would have affected producers receiving compensation when working with qualified retirement accounts and funds coming out of retirement accounts including various forms of Individual Retirement Accounts (IRAs). The regulations would have affected IRAs, even though these are not normally within the scope of the DOL's reach. These regulations were scheduled to become effective in phases over 2017 with final implementation pushed back to July of 2019. However, on June 21, 2018, the Fifth Circuit Court of Appeals ruled that the guidelines were an "arbitrary and capricious exercise of administrative power". This ruling by the Court of Appeals effectively killed implementation of the Fiduciary Rules – leaving the future of these regulations very much in doubt. As of the time this edition went to press, this project was on hold and the DOL and SEC were reconsidering their next steps. Despite this setback, it is likely that some changes will eventually be implemented in how fiduciaries are governed. As a result, and because the reality is that courts are increasingly holding producers to a higher standard of care, it is important to consider what these guidelines would have required. For purposes of this edition – the remaining section of this text has been left in due to the possibility that the Fifth Circuit decision is reversed by the U.S. Supreme Court.

Under the DOL's guidelines, or so-called fiduciary rule, certain commission-paying accounts would become problematic. This is because the rule is perceived as making it difficult, or - risky, for some professionals to sell commission-based business when planning advice is also being provided. Opponents of the rule believe it could be detrimental, rather than protective, to small investors as advisors and firms will likely make commission accounts unattractive with higher minimums or less product options. As a result, smaller investors may find themselves being pushed into self-directed arrangements.

The rule, initially promulgated on April 10, 2016 became applicable for some arrangements in April of 2017 with a transition period for some aspects of the rule stretching out to July 1, 2019.

The rule expands the definition of "fiduciary" and significantly expands the definition of fiduciary investment advice applicable to ERISA plans, IRAs, and recommendations regarding plan rollovers and distributions. The new rule applies with respect to advice given regarding plans subject to Title I of ERISA and to entities (such as IRAs and Health Savings Accounts) subject to the Prohibited Transaction Rule in IRC Section 4975.

Advice is defined broadly so that not only is it believed to cover what would traditionally be viewed as investment advice – but will likely cover recommendations regarding the timing of qualified plan distributions. Commentators suggest that something as common as suggesting that a client use qualified plan distributions to purchase a fixed life insurance policy could be viewed as fiduciary advice under this rule – even though the purchase of a life insurance policy itself would not be covered.

An exception to the definition of fiduciary advice includes "investment education" – which has been the subject of much discussion because of the inherent difficultly in determining where "education" ends and "advice" begins. Also exempted are the activities of a "wholesaler" who can provide "advice" to a fiduciary (as opposed to advice to the client or plan fiduciary). The reason for this exception is to allow manufacturers of financial products to educate advisors without the encumbrance of the rule (since the advisor is the one with fiduciary responsibility to the client).

Where commissioned sales do take place financial professionals must operate under certain guidelines set by their Broker Dealers, or other financial institutions, as described below. There are three general approaches that advisors can take to limit or avoid problems under the new fiduciary rules.

(continued on next page)

DEPARTMENT OF LABOR ("DOL") FIDUCIARY RULES (continued)

First, DOL Prohibited Transaction Exception ("PTE") 84-24 remains available for the sale of certain products to employee benefit plans and IRAs. As recently modified, it continues to exempt life insurance products and fixed annuities from the new DOL Fiduciary rule. However, PTE 84-24 will no longer protect variable and equity indexed annuities which will make it more difficult to sell these products to qualified plans. The DOL specifically explained this change by citing perceived aggressive sales practices in the sale of variable and indexed annuities. Furthermore, PTE 84-24 was modified to include an "impartial conduct" standard that requires the fiduciary to act in the "best interest" of the plan or IRA without regard to his or her own financial interests and those of the insurer. So although life insurance and fixed annuities remain protected by PTE 84-24 – the standard of the professional working in this space is heightened. Moreover, PTE 84-24 has been modified to include disclosure of insurance commissions to plans and IRAs. Specifically, the disclosure must be "to the extent feasible as an absolute dollar figure, or otherwise, as a percentage of gross annual premium payments, asset accumulation, or contract value..."

Second, the rule introduces what is generally referred to as the "Best Interest Contract" ("BIC") or "Best Interest Contract Exemption" ("BICE"). Under the BIC Exemption, an advisor is allowed to sell commission-based products with unlevel compensation under certain circumstances. To some, the explanation and examples provided by the DOL as to how advisor compensation may permissibly vary under the BIC Exemption appears subjective – creating a perceived risk of litigation for advisors or firms utilizing the BIC approach. If a BIC Exemption approach is used the client must sign a document setting forth the fiduciary relationship and the inherent conflict of interest. This appears to be the approach that is being considered by most large Broker Dealers, although given the explanation and examples institutions might vary widely as to how they apply the BIC Exemption approach.

Third, the BIC Exemption also has a provision allowing protection for advisors generally utilizing a level fee arrangement for their services. In the event of a transaction such as an IRA rollover or change in account type from brokerage to fee-based, the BIC Exemption can be used to protect the additional fee collected on the isolated transaction so long as the advisor has (1) provided a written acknowledgment that they are a fiduciary, (2) abides by the "impartial conduct" requirement, and (3) documents why the transaction is in the client's best interest.

A shift away from commission-based accounts to fixed fee arrangements could be tricky and costly for retirement investors who prefer to buy and hold investments for long periods. Some major investment advisors have already stated that they will begin limiting commission-based accounts and move customers to fee-based arrangements.

While the DOL rule does not ban commissions, the BIC Exemption makes it much harder for people who prefer a variable compensation structure. Smaller investors may find themselves forced to move their account from a full-service brokerage firm into a self-directed option.

The new fiduciary rule described above was invalidated by the Fifth Circuit Court of Appeals in *Chamber of Commerce of the U.S. v. U.S. Dep't. of Labor*, No. 17-10238, 2018 U.S. App. LEXIS 6472 (5th Cir. Mar. 15, 2018).

DISABILITY BUY-OUT INSURANCE

Disability buy-out insurance is designed to provide funds for the purchase of a disabled owner's interest in a corporation or partnership after an extended period of *permanent and total* disability. The benefits of such insurance include: (1) providing funds for the purchase, which funds are not tied to the continued success of the business; and (2) assuring that the disabled owner will no longer be a drain on business income and assets. In contrast, see the discussion of business overhead expense insurance on page 302.

A business is usually not eligible for coverage until it has been in existence for two years, although exceptions can be found (e.g., professional corporations). Maximum amounts of coverage typically range from $300,000 to $1,000,000, with specific amounts limited to a percentage of the owner's interest (e.g., 80 percent of fair market value). As with disability income insurance, definitions of disability vary widely, from inability to engage in one's "own occupation," to inability to perform the duties of "any other occupation" for which one is reasonably suited. It is ***absolutely essential*** that the provisions of the purchase agreement be consistent with the definitions and terms of the disability buy-out policy.

Because a disabled individual's chances of recovery are highest in the early months of his disability, the waiting period is extended and typically lasts from twelve months to three years (see disability statistics, page 645). This attempts to avoid the forced sale of a business interest while the disabled owner might reasonably expect to return to work. Benefits are paid to the "loss payee," who is that individual or business entity having the contractual obligation to purchase the disabled owner's interest (i.e., entity purchase or cross purchase, see charts on pages 171 and 175). Payment of proceeds can vary from lump sum to installment, with lump sum having the advantage of simplicity, but losing the tax advantage of spreading gain over a number of years.

Successive disabilities can cause a problem when the insured returns to work after being disabled for less than the waiting period, and thereafter suffers a second period of disability. Some policies require satisfaction of a new waiting period, while others consider both disabilities to be "continuous," provided the gap between them does not exceed a certain period. If the insured recovers after the end of the waiting period, but prior to the last indemnity payment, some policies will stop all future payments, while others disregard the recovery and make payments as originally scheduled (i.e., a form of "presumptive" disability).

Although the premiums are not tax deductible, the benefits are received tax-free by the loss payee. As with any other lifetime sale of a business interest, the disabled owner is subject to capital gains taxation of any gain on the sale of his business interest.

(continued on next page)

DISABILITY BUY-OUT INSURANCE (continued)

An alternative to traditional disability buy-out insurance is the use of a hybrid long-term care product combined with life insurance. These are usually attached to life insurance contracts in the form of a rider that carries an additional cost. Although these riders do not address the full range of disabilities, they can allow the acceleration of a life insurance death benefit when an insured has a long-term care triggering event. These are usually the inability to perform one of the traditional activities of daily living or a mental impairment. These riders may be a cost efficient alternative to true disability buy-out coverage. However, care needs to be exercised in the type of long term care rider that is selected. These riders may vary widely in terms of the ability to have a payment made to the business entity to tax efficiently fulfill the buy-out and receive funds, the circumstances under which a rider might be triggered. These are often driven by the underlying insurance carrier, the underlying filing and the state requirements. By its contract language, at least one major life insurance carrier requires that reimbursement for long-term care benefits be made to the insured. Such a reimbursement rider, as opposed to an indemnity type rider payable to the policy owner, creates tax, as well as fiduciary, issues if owned by a third-party (such as a trust, business, or co-shareholder).

Increasingly a number of life insurance carriers are offering long term care (or chronic or critical illness) riders or combination products associated with their life insurance policies. For an additional premium (often a reasonably modest amount – such as 10 percent to 15 percent) a policy owner can accelerate some or all of the death benefit covering the insured upon the triggering of a long term care event. Some combination (or Hybrid) products can be purchased for no additional premium – instead the product may only have a cost if/when the rider is activated by the policyholder.

These Hybrid products do not always cover every disabling contingency but can cover many events. These can be low cost alternatives to traditional disability policies, but can also be complex. The state filing, policy structure and ownership of these products are critical. However, in the right conditions they can be effective in a business continuation setting. See Long Term Care Hybrid Products, pages 454-457.

DISABILITY INCOME TAXATION

The general rule is that disability income payments under an employer's plan are included in gross income and fully taxable to the disabled employee, including both pre-retirement and post-retirement payments. However, if the payments have been received under a plan to which the employee has contributed part of the premium, that portion of the benefit attributable to the employee's contributions will be received free of income taxes. The tax treatment is the same, whether such payments are characterized as disability payments, salary continuation, wage continuation, or sick pay. See page 550 for an explanation of the taxation of Social Security disability payments.

Under some circumstances, there is a tax *credit* available to individuals who are: (1) age sixty-five or older; or (2) under age sixty-five and retired on permanent and total disability. The credit is equal to 15 percent of the taxpayer's "Section 22" amount of income for the year: $5,000 for single taxpayers or married taxpayers filing jointly when only one spouse qualifies for the credit (i.e., $750 credit), and $7,500 for married taxpayers when both qualify for the credit (i.e., $1,125 credit). If the taxpayer is under age sixty-five, the base amount is limited to the amount of taxable disability income.

The base amount used to figure the credit must also be reduced: (1) for nontaxable pension or disability benefits received under social security, railroad retirement and certain other nontax laws; and (2) by one-half of the amount by which adjusted gross income exceeds $7,500 for single taxpayers, and $10,000 for married taxpayers filing jointly. The calculation of the credit is done on Schedule R to the IRS Form 1040. The impact of these rules means that *no credit is available* if a taxpayer receives more than the following amounts of income:

	Nontaxable Social Security, pension, or disability benefits	*or*	Adjusted gross income
Single	$ 5,000		$ 17,500
Married filing jointly with one spouse qualified*	5,000		20,000
Married filing jointly with both spouses qualified*	7,500		25,000

* A qualified individual is one who is either age sixty-five or older, or under age sixty-five and retired on permanent and total disability.

DISABILITY UNDER SOCIAL SECURITY

In order to qualify for Social Security disability benefits an applicant must meet *all* nine of the following tests:

1. He or she is fully insured by: (1) accumulating forty quarters of coverage (a total of ten years of covered work); or (2) accumulating at least six quarters of coverage provided he has acquired at least as many quarters of coverage as there are years elapsing after 1950 (or, if later, after the year in which he reaches age twenty-one) and before the year in which he becomes disabled.
2. He or she has worked under Social Security for at least five of the ten years (twenty out of forty quarters) just before becoming disabled, or if disability begins before age thirty-one but after age twenty-three, for at least one-half of the quarters after reaching age thirty-one and before becoming disabled (but not less than six).
3. He or she is unable to engage in "any substantial gainful work that exists in the national economy," whether or not such work exists in the area, a specific vacancy exists, or the applicant would be hired if he or she applied for the work (however, consideration is given to age, education, and work experience).
4. Such inability results from "a medically determinable physical or mental impairment" which is expected to result in death, or which has lasted (or can be expected to last) for a continuous period of not less than twelve months. A special definition of the term "disability" is provided for individuals age fifty-five or over who are blind.
5. He or she is under sixty-five years of age.
6. He or she has filed an application.
7. He or she has furnished the required proof of disability.
8. He or she has fulfilled a five-month waiting period.
9. He or she accepts state vocational rehabilitation services or has good cause for refusal.

DISCLAIMER

The use of disclaimers in estate planning can often result in obtaining greater flexibility by providing the opportunity for post mortem decisions when more facts are likely to be available regarding assets, taxes, and beneficiaries. Disclaimers can be used for both tax and nontax purposes. For example, an individual might disclaim an inheritance in order to avoid losing eligibility for public benefits. Under limited circumstances disclaimers are sometimes used to benefit a charity and produce an estate tax charitable deduction. Disclaimers can also be employed outside an estate with respect to gifts, employee benefits, or life insurance proceeds.

To be effective, disclaimers must comply with state as well as federal tax law, must be made in writing prior to acceptance of the property or any of its benefits, contain an irrevocable and unqualified refusal to accept an interest in the property, and must be given to the holder of legal title to the property within nine months after the date that the transfer was made which created the interest (i.e., after death or date of gift). Because of their inherent flexibility, disclaimers have been increasingly used to deal with uncertainty (e.g., to allow a surviving spouse the opportunity to make post death adjustments to the amount placed in the family or non-marital trust under a Trust Will, see chart on page 21).

For example, the chart on page 21 shows an example of a trust will under which the testator directs that an amount equal to or less than the applicable exclusion amount be placed in the family trust ("B" Trust). Similar results could be obtained by passing all property to the surviving spouse, but with provision for a "disclaimer trust." The disclaimer trust would come into being only if the surviving spouse disclaimed, or refused to accept, a portion of the estate under the will. When funded as a result of such a disclaimer, the trust would function in exactly the same way as the family trust illustrated in the chart, except that the surviving spouse would decide exactly how much property, if any, was to go into the trust.

DIVORCE AND LIFE INSURANCE

Transfer of an existing policy incident to a divorce can generally be made without recognition of gain to the transferor spouse. Because the transferor spouse is treated as having acquired the property by gift, the transferor's cost basis is carried over to the transferee, and since the transfer is within an exception to the transfer for value rule, the death proceeds can be received by the wife free of income taxes. A transfer is "incident to a divorce" if it is made within one year after the marriage is terminated or is made within six years after the divorce and pursuant to a divorce or separation instrument.

Payment of premiums pursuant to a divorce or separation agreement that qualify as alimony payments are deductible by the payor and taxable to the recipient, provided the wife is owner of the policy. To qualify as "alimony": (1) the payment must be made in cash; (2) the divorce or separation instrument must not stipulate that the payments are not alimony; (3) there must be no liability to make payments after the death of the payee (wife); and (4) the parties must not be members of the same household. Beginning in 2019 (as a revenue offset in the 2017 Tax Act), alimony payments made pursuant to a new agreement (existing arrangements are grandfathered) cease being deductible to the payor spouse and are no longer taxable to recipient spouse. Presumably, this would impact the payment of premiums pursuant to a divorce or separation agreement as well.

Payment of death benefits to the former divorced spouse would be taxable as income if the policy had been owned and maintained by the insured spouse pursuant to a divorce decree or agreement as security for post-death payments. However, if the policy had been owned by and payable to the divorced wife, the death benefits would be received free of income taxes.

DOMESTIC PARTNERS

Also referred to as nontraditional couples and unmarried partners, the term "domestic partners" includes both opposite-sex and same-sex couples that are not married. There currently exists a legal patchwork across the states on this topic. Rights and benefits afforded to domestic partners in some jurisdictions may not be available or recognized elsewhere. On June 26, 2015, the U.S. Supreme Court held, in *Obergefell v. Hodges*, that state laws prohibiting marriage between two individuals of the same sex (or prohibiting the recognition of a same-sex marriage lawfully licensed and performed elsewhere) violated the Fourteenth Amendment to the U.S. Constitution. In all U.S. jurisdictions, all couples may exercise the fundamental right to marry in all U.S. jurisdictions and can enjoy recognition of their lawful marriage performed in any other jurisdiction. While a few legal challenges continue, this is the law of the land. While this development would appear to uncomplicate the national marital landscape and simplify planning for all couples, married or contemplating marriage, there are some remaining transitional complexities. For example, many states carry laws that provide protections for non-marital relationships between same- or different-sex couples, often denominated "domestic partnership" or "civil union." While there may be many reasons for entering into any such relationship, some states provided these legal protections primarily as an alternative for same-sex couples who could not legally marry. Now that any two individuals can choose to marry, some state have introduced measures that will alter or phase out the alternatives that are seen as less necessary. For example, after the *Obergefell* decision, the State of Washington passed laws that automatically "convert" a domestic partnership to a marriage if the couple was same-sex and both individuals were under age sixty-two.

(continued on next page)

DOMESTIC PARTNERS (continued)

Despite this complex and evolving legal environment and the unique issues facing domestic partners, both same sex and opposite sex, there are effective techniques that domestic partners can use in planning their financial affairs and estate plans. As with a marriage, every domestic partnership or other non-marital relationship will sooner or later end with either separation or death.

Domestic partnership agreement. It is generally acknowledged that individuals can contract for most anything, provided it is legal and not against public policy. Domestic partnership agreements, also called cohabitation agreements, are similar to premarital (antenuptial) agreements in that they provide for a division of income, expenses, and assets, as well as provisions relating to termination of the relationship. See Prenuptial Agreements at page 495.

Wills. Domestic partners generally have no right to take under state intestacy laws. A will, or will substitute, assuring that property passes to a domestic partner should cover issues relating to qualification of a survivor to take under the will (e.g., defining the beneficiary as "that person living with me at my death," and disqualify a survivor from taking in case of "separation due to domestic disharmony"). It is also important to define exactly those children or other heirs that are to take under the will (e.g., children born or adopted prior to or after the domestic partnership agreement).

Revocable living trusts. As a will substitute, the living trust is particularly attractive to domestic partners, as it avoids probate and reduces the chances of a successful will challenge by the decedent's relatives (see page 24). However, unlike the exemption trust will on page 20, a "marital trust" will not shield assets from the estate tax (i.e., the federal unlimited marital deduction is not available).

Gifts. Present interest gifts of $15,000 (in 2018 and projected for 2019) and gifts that use the $11.2 million (projected for 2019) gift tax applicable exclusion amount are both effective with domestic partners (see page 52). However, under federal law, split-gifts are available only to a married couple (see page 50).

(continued on next page)

DOMESTIC PARTNERS (continued)

Life insurance. It is generally required that an individual who is issued a life insurance contract on another person's life has an insurable interest (see page 407). Although an insurable interest may exist because of a financial dependence in the relationship, this isn't always the case when both individuals are economically independent. However, in such instances, domestic partners should be able to avoid insurable interest problems by having the policy initially issued to the insured, and then later transferring the policy by gift to the other partner. An individual has an unlimited insurable interest in his or her own life and insurable interest need only exist at the time a policy is issued. An irrevocable life insurance trust offers many advantages to domestic partners (see page 54).

Joint tenancy. Although the simplicity of joint ownership is attractive, the following should be considered: (1) federal law includes the entire value in the first decedent's estate, unless the survivor can prove contributions; (2) the account is subject to the creditors of both partners; and (3) to pass the asset at death, the title must include the words "rights of survivorship.

DURABLE POWER OF ATTORNEY

A power of attorney is a written document executed by one individual, the "principal," authorizing another person, the "attorney-in-fact," to act on his or her behalf. Under a *general* power of attorney, the powers are very broad and authorize the attorney-in-fact to enter into and discharge virtually all legal obligations on behalf of the principal. Under a *special* power of attorney, the powers are very limited and authorize the attorney-in-fact to perform only specific functions on behalf of the principal. Typically, either power of attorney is limited to acts being performed at a time when the principal himself has legal capacity (e.g., is not deceased, disabled, mentally incompetent, or under some other incapacity).

A *durable* power of attorney authorizes the attorney-in-fact to act even if the principal is incapacitated. The durable power of attorney has been recognized in some form in all states. Such powers of attorney may be either *immediate*, giving the attorney-in-fact power to act prior to an incapacity, or *contingent*, giving the attorney-in-fact power to act only when the principal has become incapacitated. This is particularly useful in estate planning situations where it may be desired to make gifts, file tax returns, or provide for the lifetime management of assets.

See also, Health Care Power Of Attorney, page 400, and Living Will, page 453.

DUAL LOAN

Combining Commercial Premium Financing with a Private Financing Arrangement

The Dual Loan approach funds large life insurance needs with outside liquidity. Through a combination of an institutional loan to an individual (See discussion of Premium Financing on page 494) followed by a Private Financing loan (also known as "Private Split Dollar") to a grantor trust created by that individual – a large life insurance premium can be efficiently funded to provide for the purchase of a large life insurance policy without placing personal wealth or assets in the trust. (See discussion of Private Split Dollar on pages 66-69).

Because personally-owned assets are not transferred to the trust, this option is excellent for clients with significant net worth but limited liquidity. It is also a valuable planning tool for individuals who have appreciated property and do not want to incur a capital gain on the liquidation of those assets. Like both commercial premium financing and private financing – Dual Loan works well for anyone interested in funding their trust without making taxable gifts.

Commercial Premium Financing may be a viable option in many scenarios for funding a large life insurance premium, but Dual Loan is a more efficient alternative in many instances. Dual Loan allows the client to use outside liquidity to create estate liquidity and minimizes gift taxes while taking advantage of the generally more favorable "applicable federal rate" or "AFR" loan interest rates. (See discussion of AFR at page 295). It allows the client to utilize an existing line of credit or banking relationship rather than utilizing a premium financing lender.

How it Works

STEP 1. CREATE AN IRREVOCABLE GRANTOR TRUST

Avoidance of Estate Taxes. Property owned by an irrevocable trust, assuming it is properly structured and administered, is outside of the taxable estate of the person creating the trust. To avoid estate taxation on the proceeds of large life insurance policies – it is common for large policies to be owned by irrevocable trusts for the benefit of the insured's heirs.

Income Tax Considerations. Because the Dual Loan approach involves the lending of cash from the grantor of the trust to the trust – the irrevocable trust utilized in the Dual Loan approach is typically what is known as a "Grantor Trust" or "Intentionally Defective Grantor Trust." (See discussion of Intentionally Defective Trust at pages 74 to 77). Simply put – this means that the trust is one that is respected for estate and gift tax purposes (i.e., property in the trust is out of the grantor's estate for estate tax purposes) but is ignored for income tax purposes. Because the trust is ignored for income tax purposes transactions between the grantor and the trust are not taxable. Hence – even though the trust will make interest payments to the grantor on money loaned to the trust there will be no requirement that the loan income be reported for tax purposes. Likewise, property sold by the grantor to the trust would not be considered sold for income tax reporting purposes (you can't sell something to yourself).

(continued on next page)

DUAL LOAN (continued)

What Makes an Irrevocable Trust an "Intentionally Defective Grantor Trust"? While the Internal Revenue Code contains a number of trust provisions that cause a trust to be ignored for income tax purposes, an Intentionally Defective Grantor Trust for insurance and/or estate planning purposes is typically made a grantor trust by including a "power of substitution" in the trust. All this means is that the grantor of the trust is allowed to substitute assets of equal value for trust assets. Not only does this make the trust a grantor trust for income tax purposes and allows for a loan or sale of property without tax consequences – this is a generally important trust feature in that it creates flexibility for future planning. Under current tax law – assets in a trust retain their cost basis (carry-over basis) whereby assets in an individual's estate at death receive a basis step up at death to their then fair market value. So, sound estate planning including a constant monitoring of assets by individuals with taxable estates to see that their low basis assets are in their estate at death (basis stepped up and capital gains avoided on future sale) and high basis assets are in their trust (since there will be no basis step-up at death). See Basis Planning and Capital Gains at pages 106-109.

STEP 2. APPLY FOR THE LIFE INSURANCE POLICY

Avoid Estate Tax Inclusion. Ordinarily, the life insurance policy will be the applicant and initial owner of the life insurance policy. By making the trust the applicant and owner of the policy – the policy should avoid estate tax inclusion. A policy purchased outside of the trust and then gifted to the trust will ordinarily be included in the insured's estate for period of three years (known as the "three year rule").

STEP 3. ATTAIN AN INSTITUTIONAL LOAN

Source of Funds. The grantor will utilize existing banking relationships to attain a loan. The terms of the loan are negotiated between the grantor and their institution of choice. Frequently, the grantor will use an existing credit line. Most business owners and investors have existing lending arrangements where they can get access to cash at interest rates which are often below those made available by traditional premium financing specialty lenders. This is especially true of some businesses – such as farmers, ranchers, real estate investors, and hedge fund managers.

Interest. Interest is paid by the grantor to the institutional lender based on the terms negotiated by the grantor. If the grantor has an existing relationship with the institution, the grantor may be able to negotiate favorable loan terms. The loan may require regular interest payments or may allow for the accrual of interest. The terms of the loan are between the grantor and the lender.

(continued on next page)

DUAL LOAN (continued)

Collateral. The collateral used to secure the loan from the institutional lender generally will be in the form of real estate, business interests, or an investment portfolio. The life insurance policy should not be the collateral for the loan because the loan is between the grantor and the lending institution. The loan is not between the lending institution and the trust.

Loan Repayment. The institutional loan will be repaid by the grantor from either the funds received when the ILIT repays the Private Financing Loan or from the grantor's personal assets.

STEP 4. The Private Financing Transaction

Source of Funds. The grantor will utilize the cash attained from the institutional loan and enter into a separate Private Financing loan with the intentionally defective grantor trust.

Interest. Generally, it is believed that a Private Financing loan must be at a rate at least equal to the Applicable Federal Rate (See AFR at page 295) to avoid possible treatment as a gift.

Collateral. Most times, the Private Financing loan is not collateralized. It is merely repayable from general trust assets. However, some tax advisors use the policy as collateral to give the loan arrangement more of a commercial feel. Some advisors like to "seed" that trust with assets before entering into the Private Financing loan. These tax advisors feel that if the trust has assets other than the life insurance policy that the arrangement looks more commercially reasonable and less like a possible gift. In these instances, assets equal to at least 10 percent of the Private Financing loan amount are often gifted into the trust. Sometimes, instead of gifting seed money, the trust beneficiaries will guaranty the loan. There are no regulations or case law that clearly make collateral or seed money a necessity.

Loan Repayment. Generally, but not always, the loan is repaid at death from life insurance death benefits. In some instances, for example if the trust has property in addition to the life insurance policy, the Private Financing loan is repaid during life. Generally, however, it makes sense to renew the AFR loan as long as the trust return on assets is higher than the AFR rate.

(continued on next page)

DUAL LOAN (continued)

Benefits.

- Minimizes the need to liquidate assets to fund large life insurance premiums
- Minimizes loan interest costs by taking advantage of low interest rates often available to business owners and investors
- Facilitates the use of low fixed interest rates on the Private Financing arrangement
- Can protect against loan interest rate duration exposure by completing the transaction in less than nine years with a short-term or mid-term AFR loan
- Minimizes the institutional loan financing costs and shifts them from the ILIT to the grantor
- Puts the risk of higher commercial loan rates outside of the estate tax-free trust assets
- Loan interest rate payments made under the Private Financing note are generally not subject to income tax if the ILIT is designed as a grantor trust
- Gift taxes may be eliminated when premiums are funded through Private Financing
- The overall net to heirs may be increased with the Dual Loan approach
- Since the policy is not collateral for the loan – the arrangement is more flexible in that it can be utilized to fund all types of life insurance policies (including VUL)

DYNASTY TRUST

The term "dynasty" trust is often used to describe a trust created for the benefit of multiple generations. Such trusts are also referred to as "generation-skipping," "legacy," "mega," "dynastic," or "super" trusts. They are often similar to the typical irrevocable life insurance trust, but adapted to take advantage of the generation-skipping transfer tax (GSTT) exemption. A dynasty trust can be very flexible and clients often ignore the benefits because they mistakenly believe that "generation-skipping" means that their children cannot benefit from the trust. In reality, a Dynasty Trust can be very flexible and provide significant discretion to benefit children. In reality, the "generation-skipping" refers to the payment of taxes and not the enjoyment of the inheritance.

The federal transfer tax system is designed to tax property each time it is passed from one generation to the next. To assist in accomplishing this objective, the GSTT applies an additional tax to the normal gift or estate tax whenever property is transferred to persons two or more generations younger than the transferor, or whenever there are taxable distributions or terminations from a trust (see chart, page 35). However, a GSTT exemption is available which allows aggregate transfers of $11.2 million projected in 2019, to be exempt from this tax ($22.8 million projected for 2019 total for both husband and wife). The increased exemption passed as part of the 2017 Tax Act is scheduled to sunset after 2026. It remains unclear how sunsetting will work for transfers made during the temporarily increased transfer tax exemptions. Some professionals have suggested that a "claw-back" process could exist – whereby lifetime transfers are added back at death and the then existing exemption (scheduled to revert to $5 million indexed for inflation) will reduce the date of death estate value (increased by lifetime gifts). Most professionals believe, despite little or no guidance on this subject, that transfers made during this temporary period will not be subject to a claw-back at death.

A dynasty trust can be created during lifetime or upon death. In order to avoid the GSTT, the donor will typically allocate a portion of his or her GSTT exemption to each transfer to the trust. Purchase of life insurance upon the life of the grantor, or upon the lives of trust beneficiaries, can result in a leveraging of trust assets through life insurance. Once assets are placed in the trust, and shielded from the GSTT, a properly drafted trust document would avoid subjecting the trust corpus to estate and gift taxes applicable to the trust beneficiaries (e.g., the trust beneficiaries would have no powers over trust assets such as would cause inclusion in their estates). However, a disinterested trustee could be given authority to make discretionary distributions of both trust income and corpus. Trust assets could be made available for use by trust beneficiaries and spendthrift provisions could protect trust assets from a beneficiary's estranged spouse and creditors. Special powers of appointments held by trust beneficiaries could also provide added flexibility (see page 495). In its purest form, a dynasty trust would forever avoid application of the federal estate tax by providing that trust beneficiaries in each generation never have anything more than an income interest in trust property. However, this is generally prevented by the rule against perpetuities, which requires that trust assets must vest in the trust beneficiaries after a certain period of time (see page 530). However, this limitation can be avoided by establishing a trust in those states where the rule has been eliminated by statute.

The complexity of both the GSTT and state property laws make it extremely important to seek the advice of knowledgeable legal counsel when considering a dynasty trust.

EMPLOYER OWNED LIFE INSURANCE (EOLI)

Life insurance can serve many business purposes. Life insurance death benefits can be used to offset the loss of a key employee. The death benefit and/or tax-advantaged cash value can provide a source for the indirect funding of employee benefits – such as a salary continuation or salary deferral plan. Life insurance is an important means of funding a buy-sell arrangement. And, with C corporation tax rates reduced to 21 percent by the 2017 Tax Act, the purchase of life insurance by businesses has become even more common. However, to avoid taxation on the death benefit, one of the key advantages to life insurance over other financial assets, it is important that the purchase be done in accordance with rules set forth in the Pension Protection Act of 2006.

Ordinarily, life insurance death benefits are received income tax-free. However, because of the Pension Protection Act of 2006, death benefits paid to employers are generally taxable to the extent they exceed the employer's premium payments unless certain requirements and exceptions are met for policies that were bought (or substantially changed) after August 17, 2006.

To qualify for an exception that will allow the death proceeds to be received income tax free (under IRC Section 101(a)), all employers must meet certain notice and consent requirements. Moreover, for all but a limited number of employees the life insurance cannot continue beyond twelve months following a separation of service, and still hope to receive the income tax free death benefit even if the notice and consent requirements are met. However, for certain employees, an employer may continue to own the life insurance policy and can receive the death proceeds income tax free, again, provided specific notice and consent requirements are met. See Sections 2 and 3 in the Notice and Consent Requirements Section. Note that there are certain state specific requirements for Massachusetts, New York, and Washington State.

Notice and Consent Requirements. To qualify for an exception, it is essential to first meet strict notice and consent requirements. Under these requirements, the employee must: (1) be notified in writing that the employer intends to insure the employee's life and the maximum face amount to be issued; (2) be informed that the employer will be the policy beneficiary; and (3) give written consent, before the policy is issued, to being insured and consent to the coverage continuing after the insured employee terminates employment. This must be obtained before the life insurance policy is issued. *It is strongly recommended that notice be given, and consent be obtained, at the time an application is taken for virtually any life insurance contract that might conceivably fall within the scope of this law.* The statute provides no means of obtaining relief from these requirements. The potential cost of noncompliance is income taxation of the death proceeds in excess of premiums paid.

(continued on next page)

EMPLOYER OWNED LIFE INSURANCE (EOLI) (continued)

If the Notice and Consent requirements are met then death benefits received are income tax free when:

1. Proceeds are from a life insurance contract insuring the life of an employee who was employed at time of death, or was employed within twelve months of death (this includes rank-and-file employees).
2. Proceeds from a life insurance contract insuring the life of an individual who was (at the time the contract was issued):
   a. Among the highest-paid 35-percent of all employees, or
   b. One of the five highest-paid officers, or
   c. Received in the preceding year compensation in excess of $120,000 (as adjusted for inflation in 2018), or
   d. A 5-percent or greater owner of the business at any time during the preceding year, or
   e. A director.
3. Proceeds paid to the insured's heirs, to include:
   a. A member of the insured's family (i.e., spouse, brother, sister, ancestor, or lineal descendant).
   b. An individual who is the insured's designated beneficiary (other than the employer).
   c. A trust established for a member of the insured's family or such designated beneficiary.
   d. The estate of the insured.
   e. Proceeds used to purchase an interest (including partnership capital, or profits) in the employer from any of the above individuals or entities.

The chart that follows shows where the EOLI rules may or may not apply in certain common business owned life insurance situations.

Reporting requirements. Every employer (technically referred to as the "applicable policy-holder"), owning one or more employer-owned life insurance contracts issued after August 17, 2006, must file a return showing for each year: (1) the number of employees at the end of the year; (2) the number of employees insured under such contracts at the end of the year; (3) the total amount of insurance in force at the end of the year under such contracts; (4) the employer's name, address, and taxpayer identification number, and the employer's type of business; and (5) that the employer has a valid consent for each insured employee (if any consents were not obtained, the number of insured employees for whom such consent was not obtained).

(continued on next page)

EMPLOYER OWNED LIFE INSURANCE (EOLI) (continued)

EOLI Rules in Common Business Situations			
	Probably Subject to EOLI Rules	**Probably Not Subject to the EOLI Rules**	**Unclear, Best to Require Notice and Consent**
Sole Proprietors			
Owner		X	
Employee	X		
Employer Benefit Plans			
Employer Owned – Economic Benefit Regime	X		
Employee Owned – Split Dollar Loan		X	
Employee Owned – Non Equity Collateral Assignment			X
Section 162 Bonus		X	
VEBA		X	
Qualified Plan Trust		X	
Nonqualified Deferred Compensation or SERP	X		
Death Benefit Only (DBO) Plan	X		
Rabbi Trust	X		
Business Planning			
Key Person	X		
Redemption	X		
Cross Purchase – majority owner	X		
Corporate Cross Purchase – policy owned by a minority owner		X	
Cross Purchase – policy owned by a partnership, LLC or LLP			X
Charitable Owned Coverage – otherwise tax exempt			
Employee			X
Donor		X	

EMPLOYEE STOCK OWNERSHIP PLAN (ESOP)

An employee stock ownership plan, or ESOP, is a stock bonus plan, or a stock bonus plan combined with a money purchase plan, that is designed to invest primarily in the common stock of the employer (see pages 470 and 534). However, unlike a pure stock bonus plan, the ESOP is typically used as a device for implementing the business continuation and estate planning objectives of its stockholders. The benefits provided by an ESOP are similar to those provided by a profit sharing plan, but they are distributable in stock of the employer, and contributions are not dependent upon employer profits. The National Center for Employee Ownership (NCEO) estimates that as of 2018 there are almost 7,000 employee ESOPs covering more than 14 million employees.

An ESOP must meet specific requirements pertaining to coverage, nondiscrimination in contributions, limits on contributions, diversification of investments, and nonforfeiture of rights upon termination of employment. If these requirements are met, then the plan can be useful in:

1. Motivating employees toward increased productivity (the value of corporate stock held by the trust is dependent upon the corporate profitability).
2. Providing retirement income as a supplement to Social Security and other retirement benefits.
3. Generating liquidity for principal stockholders through the sale of stock to the ESOP during lifetime or after death.
4. Securing funds for corporate growth and expansion with untaxed dollars.
5. Avoiding taxation of accumulated earnings.
6. Securing income tax deductions for an employer with little or no cash outlay.
7. Paying for life insurance on key employees with before-tax dollars.

Leveraged ESOP. A "leveraged" ESOP can be used to borrow money from a financial institution based on the credit (and guarantee) of the employer. (Normally, loans or extensions of credit between an employer and its plans are "prohibited transactions," but the ESOP is exempt from these restrictions.) The borrowed funds are then used by the ESOP trustee to purchase stock from the employer. In turn, the employer typically uses these funds to finance expansion and capital purchases.

(continued on next page)

EMPLOYEE STOCK OWNERSHIP PLAN (ESOP) (continued)

Subsequent employer *contributions* to the ESOP are used by the ESOP trustee to repay the debt. In effect, provided employer contributions to the ESOP are within the annual additions limitations, this technique has enabled an employer to: (1) obtain funds for expansion by selling shares to the ESOP; and (2) repay the ESOP's bank loan with fully tax deductible dollars (i.e., in the form of deductible contributions to the ESOP). Had the employer borrowed the funds directly the interest payments would have been deductible, but repayment of principal would not have been deductible.

Distributions to employees may be made entirely in cash or partly in cash and partly in employer securities. Participants must be given the right to demand the entire distribution in the form of employer stock. If the stock is not readily tradable on an established market the participants must also be given the right to require the *employer* to purchase any distributions of employer stock made to them (a "put option").

It has been suggested that the complexity of establishing a leveraged ESOP is usually not necessary since the same tax benefit can be accomplished if the employer borrows funds directly from a financial institution and contributes an amount of its stock to a stock bonus plan each year equal in value to the amount of its loan repayment.

Non-Leveraged ESOP. ESOPs are also used to purchase an owner's stock interest upon death (sometimes referred to as a "non-leveraged ESOP"). These arrangements entail giving the ESOP an *option* to purchase stock upon the stockholder's death. To fund the purchase the trustee of the ESOP acquires life insurance on the life of the stockholder. However, requiring the ESOP to purchase the stock under a formal stock purchase plan should be avoided, since it is likely that this purchase would be treated as a fully taxable stock dividend paid by the corporation to the estate. In contrast, if treated as a sale the transaction would likely produce little or no taxable gain due to the estate's stepped-up basis in the stock (see page 556).

EQUITY SPLIT-DOLLAR

Under a split-dollar plan the term "equity split-dollar" is derived from the employee's interest in policy cash values (i.e., the employee has an "equity" interest). By sharing the ownership of cash values and limiting the employer's interest in the policy to its cumulative premium payments it was often possible for the employee to accrue substantial interests in the remaining cash values, with little or no adverse income taxation.

Until the final split-dollar regulations issued in 2003 there had been a great deal of uncertainty surrounding the tax treatment of equity split-dollar. However, Notice 2002-8 (issued in January of 2002) and proposed regulations (REG-164754-01 released in July of 2002) appeared to provide workable transition rules, safe harbors, and limited grandfathering of existing plans. The final split-dollar regulations (Treasury Decision 9092 issued in September of 2003) generally adopted the proposed regulations and dramatically altered the tax treatment of split-dollar plans. The tax treatment of new split-dollar plans is now governed by policy ownership.

Plans Established Prior To September 18, 2003

To better understand the transition rules for existing split-dollar plans and the application of the regulations to new split-dollar plans, it is helpful to break plans out according to the date they were entered into:

1. In split-dollar plans *entered into before January 28, 2002, and terminated before January 1, 2004*, the employee's equity will not be taxed. In split-dollar plans entered into before January 28, 2002, and terminated on or after January 1, 2004, the employee's equity will not be taxed, provided the plan was converted to a loan from the employer to the employee for all periods beginning on or after January 1, 2004 (if the plan was not converted to a loan, the employee will be taxed on all equity if the plan is eventually terminated). See the treatment of Employer/Employee Split-Dollar Plans (Table A) on page 284.

2. In split-dollar plans *entered into on or after January 28, 2002 and before September 18, 2003*, if the plan was not converted to a loan the employee is subject to taxation on all equity in excess of the employee's basis when the plan is terminated (employee basis does not include amounts reported or paid for life insurance protection). But if the plan was not terminated the employee will not be currently taxed on equity as it builds up, provided the employee continues to report the receipt of the economic benefit and the employer retains some economic interest in the policy. See the treatment of Employer/Employee Split-Dollar Plans (Table B) on page 285.

(continued on next page)

EQUITY SPLIT-DOLLAR (continued)

Plans Established After September 17, 2003

In split-dollar plans entered into after September 17, 2003 (or prior plans that are "materially modified") taxation of employee equity depends upon how the plan is structured. Based upon policy ownership the split-dollar regulations use a formalistic, yet straight forward, approach in providing two "mutually exclusive regimes" (or methods) for the taxation of split-dollar plans (see also Table C on page 286).

Economic Benefit Regime. This regime applies when the *employer* owns the contract and the employee's death benefit is accomplished by a policy endorsement (known as endorsement split-dollar). By exception this regime also applies when the employee owns the contract but the employer owns all cash values. (See Split-Dollar Insurance chart, page 241.) In addition to being taxed for the value of the life insurance protection (i.e., the "economic benefit" as imputed income), the employee is also taxed on any increased interest in policy cash values (not just at rollout). Also, if the policy is subsequently transferred from the employer to the employee the employee is taxed on any employer equity (see Split-Dollar Rollout, page 553). The employee's basis in the policy is equal to the amount paid at the time of transfer, but *does not* include amounts that had been taxed to the employee on account of prior increases in policy cash values and amounts reported or paid for life insurance protection. Any premium amounts contributed by the employee are taxable income to the employer. Given these harsh rules it is doubtful whether the employee should be given an equity interest in plans established and taxed under the economic benefit regime. However, nonequity endorsement plans taxed under the economic benefit regime avoid many of these adverse tax consequences (see Split-Dollar Insurance chart, page 241).

Loan Regime. This regime applies when the *employee* owns the contract and collaterally assigns the policy cash values to the employer in order to secure repayment of the employer's premium advances (known as collateral assignment split-dollar). Because the employee already owns the policy and is obligated to repay any employer loans the employee is not taxed on the equity interest in policy cash values.

Each premium payment by the employer is treated as a separate loan to the employee ("deemed loan" in the chart below). If the employee fails to pay an adequate rate of interest they are classified as below-market split-dollar loans and the employee is considered to have received compensation equal to the foregone interest (taxable to the employee and deductible by the employer). This foregone interest is then imputed back to the employer (taxable to the employer but not deductible to the employee since it is considered personal in nature). The complexity of *loan regime* taxation, as illustrated in the following chart, should be compared with the simplicity of *economic benefit regime* taxation, as illustrated in the chart on page 241.

(continued on next page)

EQUITY SPLIT-DOLLAR (continued)

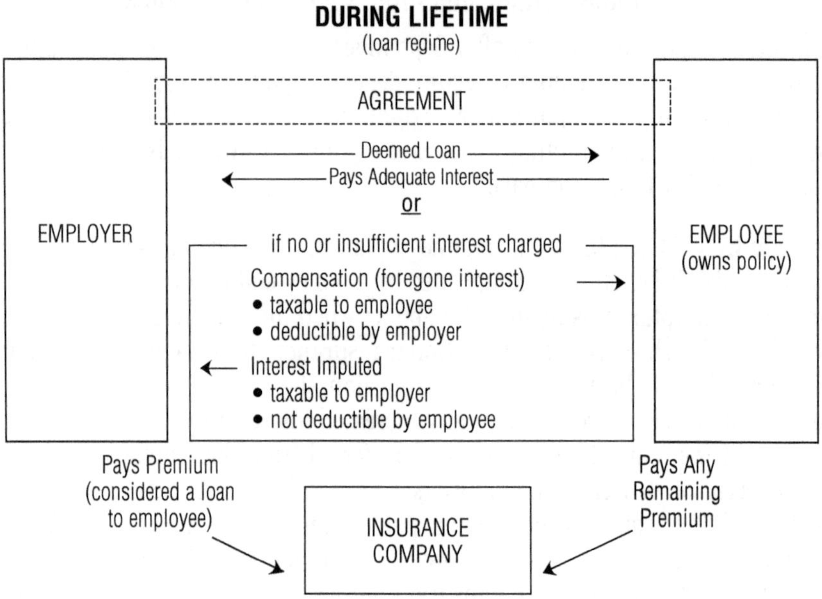

For the purpose of determining whether the employee has paid an adequate rate of interest, loans are generally classified as either demand loans or term loans.

1. **Demand loan**. A split-dollar demand loan is due in full upon demand of the employer. If the employer reserves the right to terminate the split-dollar plan it is a demand loan (e.g., upon the employee's terminating his or her employment). These loans are tested each year for adequate interest by comparing the interest rate to the *blended* applicable federal rate (AFR) published in July of each year. The 2018 blended rate was 2.03 percent - up from the 2017 rate of 1.09 percent. This is still relatively low, but the highest rate since 2008). The foregone interest for that particular year is taxed as shown in the chart above. Classification as loan offers the advantages of being relatively easy to calculate with taxation spread over the term of the agreement, but has the disadvantage of being subject to yearly changes in the blended AFR.

   For example, assume the employer advances a $10,000 premium payment without interest in a year in which the blended AFR is 2 percent. The employee includes $200 in income ($10,000 × .02). Each employer premium payment is considered a separate loan and each loan must be tested every year for adequate interest rates.

(continued on next page)

EQUITY SPLIT-DOLLAR (continued)

2. **Term loan**. A split-dollar term loan is any loan that is not a demand loan (e.g., a loan payable in full in fifteen years). Loans payable upon the death of the insured are also treated as term loans. The amount of the interest over the period of the loan is discounted to present value and then all of the interest is taxed in the very first year (i.e., all up-front). Classification as a term loan offers the advantage of knowing the interest rate for the loan's duration (it is not redetermined annually), but has the distinct disadvantage of being accelerated to the first tax year in which the loan is created (i.e., borrower must include all of foregone interest in the very first year, but lender reports interest income ratably over the term of the loan). The appropriate applicable federal rate (AFR) is based upon the original term of the loan (short-term for loans of three years or less, mid-term for loans between three and nine years, and long-term for loans nine years or greater). These AFR rates change monthly (in October of 2018 the AFR was 2.55 for short-term loans, 2.83 percent for mid-term loans, and 2.99 percent for long-term loans). Because the interest rates are condensed, most planners are currently using the long-term rate for planning strategies. These rates remain low by historical standards, but are considerably higher than in recent years.

   For example, assume the employer advances a $10,000 premium payment repayable in fifteen years without interest. Also assume that the AFR for a long-term loan is 3 percent. Discounted at 3 percent the present value of $10,000 payable in fifteen years is approximately $7,430 ($10,000 times the factor of .7430 as obtained from the table on page 619). The employee is taxed on $2,570 (the difference between the $10,000 loan and the present value of the $7,430 repayment amount). For comparitive purposes, if the long-term AFR were 5 percent the employee would be taxed on $5,190.

Sarbanes-Oxley Act. This law generally makes it a *crime* for any publicly traded company to make loans to officers or directors (the law does not apply to closely held companies). Enforcement of the Act falls within the jurisdiction of the Securities and Exchange Commission (SEC) and the SEC has yet to provide any guidance regarding its impact on split-dollar plans.

It is likely that new split-dollar plans taxed under the loan regime (employer premium payments considered employee loans) are prohibited, whereas new split-dollar plans taxed under the economic benefit regime are not prohibited (i.e., plans providing only death benefit protection for the employee). As to existing split-dollar plans, it is not clear whether the "grandfathering" provisions of this Act will apply (e.g., employer-paid premiums secured by employee-owned cash values considered as extensions of outstanding credit). Pending clarification, it may be prudent to consider: (1) using existing cash values to pay premiums; (2) reducing coverage to obtain a paid-up policy; or (3) paying premiums with employee bonuses.

EQUITY-INDEXED PRODUCTS

These are life insurance and annuity products where the crediting rate is tied to the performance of an index (most commonly the S&P 500, but it can involve other indices). These products have been available for some time, but they have become much more popular since late 2010 when the Securities and Exchange Commission withdrew a proposal that might have treated equity indexed annuities as regulated products. That proposal, Rule 151A, was withdrawn after the rule was vacated by the U.S. Court of Appeals for the District of Columbia in July 2010. Under proposed Rule 151A the SEC could have considered an equity indexed annuity a security that would have required selling agents to be equity licensed.

The workings of an EIA can be quite complicated and it is important to fully understand the product. Because they can have so many "moving parts," the following discussion provides, at best, only a general outline of Equity indexed products. Individual contracts can vary greatly from company to company. Second and third generation products are being introduced with new features and new complexities.

Equity indexed products are particularly attractive to individuals who are concerned about the safety of principal but who want the opportunity to experience market related gains. Typically a premium payment is allocated to one or more indices offered by a carrier. Although the premiums are credited to the carrier's general account (as opposed to a variable product with separate accounts).

Insurance companies typically fund indexed products by investing in high grade bonds in order to cover the end-of-term guarantee of principal, pay commissions and make a profit. However, a portion of the remaining funds are used to purchase options (i.e., the right to purchase stock at a fixed price at some future time). If the market goes up selling the call options provides funds for meeting the contract obligations.

The most common index is the S&P 500 for a one-year period. Other indices and time periods (two, three, and five years) are also common. Based on the performance of that index more or less might be credited to the policy owner.

Generally the policy owner will receive credit to their policy based on the performance of the selected index up to a certain cap. For example in a year where the S&P index increased 20 percent, a policy with a 12 percent cap will credit 12 percent to the policy owner's contract. There are wide variations in how the crediting works with certain contracts offering percentages of the underlying index and other contracts offering no cap, or limit, to the crediting.

(continued on next page)

EQUITY-INDEXED PRODUCTS (continued)

The attraction of most indexed products is that there is a floor below which the credit rate cannot fall. This is the most meaningful difference between an equity indexed product and a variable life insurance contract. Typically the floor is zero, although some carriers may offer a slightly higher floor. The attraction is that in a period of time where the selected indices have negative performance (there is a loss below zero) the policy will not be reduced in value. In effect, prior year's crediting is locked in.

In reality there are multiple moving parts to an equity indexed product. For example, carriers may offer high cap rates and, therefore, high illustrated rates. However, there may also be high internal charges within the contract, effectively negating the benefit of a credit received by a high cap rate. A credit to a policy is often not received until the end of the index period (again, often one year). Carriers may charge policy expenses in a variety of ways even before a policy credit is received; this can have an effect on long-term policy performance. Additionally, in years where there is little or no crediting to the policy, internal charges will continue to be assessed on the policy.

Unlike the other methods, this has the effect of locking in gains and annually resetting the starting point of the index. Earnings are typically not credited until the end of the term, thus there is no compounding of interest earned. Averaging can be done daily, monthly, or annually. The usual effect of averaging is to increase the rate in a decreasing market and reduce the rate in a rising market.

A cap (maximum rate) may be set on annual gains in the contract. The participation rate is the percentage of the index movement that will be credited (this can vary widely from 60 to over 100 percent). Some contracts guarantee the participation rate for the term of the contract, while other contracts reserve the right to change the participation rate or even lower the cap.

In effect, equity indexed products offer upside potential with downside protection. However, the long-term performance of these policies remains to be determined. Although numerous carriers show how their indices might have performed based on historic averages, many of these indices did not offer options for much of these periods. As a result true back-testing may not be available. Moreover, future performance is impossible to predict.

ERISA

The purpose of the Employee Retirement Income Security Act of 1974 (ERISA) is to protect the interests of workers and their beneficiaries who depend on benefits from employee pension and welfare plans. Among other things, the law requires disclosure of plan provisions and financial information, establishes standards of conduct for trustees and administrators, and sets up funding, participation, and vesting requirements for pension plans.

ERISA covers employee pension and welfare plans that are established or maintained: (1) by any employer engaged in commerce or in any industry or activity affecting commerce; or (2) by an employee organization or organizations representing employees of such employers.

A **pension plan** includes any plan that provides *retirement income* to employees or results in a *deferral of income* by employees to the termination of employment or beyond.

A **welfare plan** includes any plan that provides medical, surgical, or hospital care, or benefits in the event of sickness, accident, *disability*, *death*, or unemployment (other miscellaneous benefits are also covered).

Title I, Subtitle B, of ERISA contains requirements relating to the following:

Part 1 - Reporting and Disclosure
Part 2 - Participation and Vesting
Part 3 - Funding
Part 4 - Fiduciary Responsibility
Part 5 - Administration and Enforcement

Deferred Compensation Plans

Unfunded deferred compensation plans for a select group of management or highly compensated employees are generally considered pension plans and are subject to the following requirements:

Part 1 - Reporting and Disclosure. Can comply with by: (1) providing a letter to the Secretary of Labor giving the employer's name and address, IRS identification number, a statement that the employer maintains a plan or plans primarily for the purpose of providing deferred benefits for a select group of management or highly compensated employees, and the number of plans and number of employees in each plan; and (2) providing plan documents to the Secretary of Labor upon request.

Part 2 - Participation and Vesting. Not applicable.

Part 3 - Funding. Not applicable.

(continued on next page)

ERISA (continued)

Part 4 - Fiduciary Responsibility. Not applicable, unless considered a welfare benefit plan because death or disability benefits are provided. Can then comply by naming the employer, through one of its officers, as the plan's fiduciary. These requirements may be met in a properly drafted deferred compensation agreement.

Part 5 - Administration and Enforcement. Can comply by providing a definite procedure for handling claims, including providing a written explanation of any denial of benefits. These requirements may be met in a properly drafted deferred compensation agreement.

Split-Dollar Plans

Plans providing split-dollar insurance are generally considered welfare benefit plans under ERISA and are subject to the following requirements:

Part 1 - Reporting and Disclosure. Compliance is generally dependent upon the type of split-dollar plan, for example:

1. A noncontributory split-dollar plan (e.g., an endorsement employer-pay-all plan) for a select group of management or highly compensated employees is exempt from these requirements, except for the requirement that plan documents be provided to the Secretary of Labor upon request.
2. A contributory split-dollar plan (e.g., a collateral assignment plan) having less than 100 participants is also exempt from these requirements, except for the requirement that plan documents be provided to the Secretary of Labor upon request and the need to provide the employee with a summary plan description. Generally, the summary plan description requirement can be satisfied by providing the employee with a copy of the split-dollar agreement and any policy ledgers prepared as part of the proposal.

Part 2 - Participation and Vesting. Not applicable.

Part 3 - Funding. Not applicable.

Part 4 - Fiduciary Responsibility. Can comply by naming the employer, through one of its officers, as the plan's fiduciary. Additionally, the plan documents must set forth procedures for funding the plan, allocating operational responsibilities, amending the plan, and making payments from the plan. These requirements may be met in a properly drafted split-dollar agreement.

Part 5 - Administration and Enforcement. Can comply by providing a definite procedure for handling claims, including providing a written explanation of any denial of benefits. These requirements may be met in a properly drafted split-dollar agreement.

ESTATE EQUALIZATION

For many people, dividing property among heirs is among the most difficult aspects of estate planning. The family home, a vacation property, antiques, and art are sometimes very difficult to divide because of the personal nature of the property.

However, for a business owner, estate equalization can be an even greater hurdle to effective estate planning. Take for example, David, a business owner with three children. He has an estate valued at $4.5 million – primarily stock in a family business. One of the children (Kevin) is active in the business and appears to be the natural successor. A second child (Mark) has an office, but he is rarely seen at the business. The third child (Randy) lives out of the state and has shown no interest in the family business. How does David divide his estate?

Should he leave one-third of the stock to each of the three children? If he does that, will the three children each have a one-third vote? That arrangement nearly guarantees that the business will not succeed after David's death. He could reconfigure the stock into voting shares and non-voting shares and leave one-third to each child – leaving the voting stock to Kevin. That arrangement provides a better chance of long-term success, but is it fair to Kevin? He is now being asked to run the family business for the benefit of his siblings. Will Mark and Randy allow Kevin to run the business without interference?

David could simply disinherit Mark and Randy and leave the business to Kevin. But, of course, that result probably insures that Mark and Randy will have nothing to do with Kevin after their father's death. Maybe the most important aspect of estate planning is preservation of family harmony. This strategy almost insures that the family will be torn apart after their father's death.

Life insurance is often the solution to difficult situations like this. Assuming he could qualify medically and financially, David could purchase $9 million of life insurance. The entire $4.5 million business could be given to Kevin so he could run the business without interference from his siblings. Mark and Randy could each be given $4.5 million of insurance to equalize the estate. This approach is sometimes known as the "equal amount" approach to estate equalization.

On the other hand, even if David could afford and qualify for $9 million of life insurance, is it fair to leave the same amount of property to all three kids when only one of the three is active in the family business? Another common approach is to purchase $3 million of insurance to divide between Mark and Randy. Kevin would get the entire family business and Mark and Randy would get $1.5 million of insurance proceeds. This leaves them with the amount that they would have received if the original $4.5 million estate had been divided equally among the three children. This approach is sometimes referred to as the "equal share" or "equitable division" approach.

ESTATE FREEZES

Intra-family transfers of property, particularly closely held businesses, have always garnered the attention of the Internal Revenue Service and Treasury. They have long questioned the valuation of certain business interests and whether gifts of interests made to family members were made at their true value.

Estate freeze techniques, such as splitting a corporate business interest into preferred stock, with priority rights in income distributions, and common stock, with appreciation potential have long caught the eye of the IRS. These bifurcations of business interests and value typically froze the current value in the preferred stock, which retained distributions of the business as evidence of their preferred status and the current business value. This devalued the common stock, which could be gifted with little or no transfer tax consequences, but these shares were designed to capture future appreciation. The IRS's belief was that the preferred interests were designed to minimize gifts of the business interest to the younger generation(s), but that the freeze may not have been properly valued for gift tax purposes. They often believed the older generation had little or no interest in retaining a preferred income stream, as that might continue to build their asset base.

As a result of these concerns, Code sections 2701-2704, together referred to as "Chapter 14," contain special valuation rules that govern the gift tax value of many intra-family transfers. These sections do so by assigning a zero value to specific retained interests unless the retained interest is entitled to defined "qualified payments."

With Chapter 14 it is still possible for a stockholder to freeze the value of a retained corporate interest (the preferred stock) and have a minimal gift tax value assigned to the common stock given to family members (see chart on page 215). However, careful detail and compliance with the guidelines established in Chapter 14 is critical. To enforce the values represented by the older generation when making reduced gifts to younger generation(s) this section of the Tax Code has established recapture rules. These recapture rules insure that the stockholder actually receives the anticipated dividends that are claimed to increase the value of the retained preferred stock (similar rules apply to partnership interests).

These valuation rules affect three categories of retained rights:

1. A cumulative distribution right with a preference upon liquidation is generally valued as the present right to future "qualified payments."
2. A noncumulative distribution right, or one that lacks preference upon liquidation, is valued at zero unless a "qualified payment" election is made.
3. A retained liquidation, put, call, or conversion right is valued at zero, unless the right must be exercised at a specific time and amount, or the right contains certain provisions which insure that its holder can share in appreciation.

(continued on next page)

ESTATE FREEZES (continued)

For example, assume that pursuant to a recapitalization a stockholder transfers common stock to a family member and retains *noncumulative* preferred stock (item 2 above). Since the preferred stock (the retained interest) does not encompass a "qualified payment" (cumulative rights), the retained right is valued at zero. This has the result of no premium being assigned to the preferred shares, meaning that the common stock represents the entire value of the corporation and is subject to gift taxes on that amount. To avoid this result, the transferor could elect into "qualified payment" treatment, with dividends to be paid in the amounts and at the times specified in the election.

Alternatively, assume that after the transfer of common stock to a family member the transferor retains *cumulative* preferred stock with a liquidation preference (item 1 above). In this instance, the transferor has retained a right to a "qualified payment" (i.e., to a dividend payable on a periodic basis and at a fixed rate or at a variable rate with a fixed relationship to the declared market value at the time the interests were created). The value of the gift of common stock is then determined by subtracting the value of the present value of these qualified payment/preferred stock interests from the total value of the corporation. The effect is that the common stock will have substantially less gift tax value. However, this reduction in the value of the common stock is limited by a provision requiring that all common stock (termed the "junior equity" interest) be given a value of at least 10 percent of the total value of the corporation (which, for this purpose, includes a gross-up equal to the total amount of corporate indebtedness to the transferor and family members).

It is important to note that the Tax Code sections that make up Chapter 14 only apply to specified family relationships. For the statute to apply: (1) the transfer must be to the transferor's spouse, lineal descendants of the transferor or the transferor's spouse, and the spouses of such descendants; and (2) the transferor and applicable family members immediately before the transfer must "control" the entity by owning, by vote or value, 50 percent of the stock. For purposes of this 50 percent "control" a person is treated as holding (aggregating) any interest(s) held by his ancestor or his spouse's ancestor, or a spouse of such ancestor, or a lineal descendant of his parent or his spouse's parent.

The valuation rules assume that payments on the cumulative preferred will be made as scheduled. If payments are not made in accordance with a statutorily provided grace period, the rules provide for additional gift tax to be paid at the time of a subsequent lifetime transfer, or for additional estate tax at the death of the transferor (i.e., recapture). The increase in the taxable gift or taxable estate is the compounded value of the unpaid dividends using the same discount rate employed in determining the preferred stock's value.

Excluded from the scope of these valuation rules are interests in publicly traded stock, interests of the same class as the transferred interest, and interests that are proportionately the same (without regard to differences relating to nonlapsing voting power). Chapter 14 encompasses a wide range of planning techniques where discounted interests might be transferred, which are discussed elsewhere in this book.

ESTATE PLANNING STRATEGY: LEGACY FLOOR

When the federal estate tax exemption was $1 million, many life insurance agents didn't look past funding for the estate tax liability as a strategy with their clients. The life insurance "need" on nearly all large permanent life insurance sales was sold as "estate tax liability" or "estate planning." But, in many cases, was that really the case?

Let's look at an example. James is sixty years old. He is reaching retirement age and has accumulated $5 million in assets. After looking at his retirement needs, he has ear-marked $2.5 million of his current assets for his heirs. Given solid investment, he hopes that he can grow his projected legacy from $2.5 million to $4.5 million. Given his approximate twenty year life expectancy (see page 613), this should be a very realistic goal for James. But, reality is that nearly 20 percent of sixty year old males will not survive to age seventy. And, by definition, life expectancy means that point where half a population is deceased. So, even though James' life expectancy is approximately age eighty – that is a 50/50 proposition.

So, James' agent has discussed the idea of creating a "Legacy Floor" with him. Legacy Floor is a simple idea. While the terminology may be relatively new and the way it is presented may be new to some insurance professionals – Legacy Floor simply protects against early death. In our example, James anticipates growing his "savings" during the remainder of his lifetime to leave as a legacy to his heirs. What could derail his plan? James could not achieve his desired or expected growth rates on his assets. This could be a result of investment mistakes or simply an inopportune economic collapse. However, the biggest risk to James reaching his legacy goal is early death.

Using a modest portion of his current legacy portfolio (ie., the $2.5 million that James doesn't anticipate needing during lifetime and his considers his legacy portfolio), James can protect his heirs against James' early death. At age sixty, a healthy male can purchase $2 million of permanent life insurance for approximately 1 percent of the $2.5 million legacy portfolio.

In addition to providing an immediate bump in James' legacy of $2 million, by purchasing insurance James has created a floor that could protect his heirs against untimely market downturns.

ESTATE TAXATION OF LIFE INSURANCE

Section 2042 Proceeds of Life Insurance.

Incidents of ownership – Any incidents of ownership in a policy held by a decedent at the time of death will cause the proceeds to be included in his or her estate. The regulations under Section 2042 state that the term "incidents of ownership" is not limited in its meaning to ownership of the policy in the technical legal sense. These rights include the power to: (1) change the economic benefit of the policy, including the power to change the beneficiary; (2) surrender or cancel the policy; (3) assign the policy; (4) revoke an assignment; (5) pledge the policy for a loan; or (6) obtain a policy loan. However, direct or indirect payment of premiums is not an incident of ownership. See also, Life Insurance in Qualified Plans, pages 419-420.

Proceeds payable to estate – When proceeds are payable to or for the benefit of the deceased's estate they are subject to taxation in the insured's estate (e.g., when a trustee or third party is required to use the proceeds to pay estate taxes or other estate obligations).

Controlling stockholder – If the insured is a controlling stockholder and the corporation has any incidents of ownership in the policy, then proceeds paid to someone other than the corporation will be included in the estate of the insured. Under a split-dollar plan, an incident of ownership includes the right to borrow cash values.

Fiduciary capacity – Under the regulations, an individual is considered to have an "incident of ownership" in an insurance policy on his life which is held in trust if he (either alone or in conjunction with another person or persons) has the power (as trustee or otherwise) to change the beneficial ownership of the policy or its proceeds, or the time or manner of enjoyment of the policy or its proceeds, even if he has no beneficial interest in the trust. It has been held that a co-trustee who has the right to elect a settlement option has a power to effect the time and manner of enjoyment of the policy proceeds insuring himself (i.e., he has an economic benefit). The courts are not consistent in their interpretation of the regulations (see **Q 84** *Tax Facts on Insurance & Employee Benefits (2018)*).

Section 2035 Transfers of Life Insurance.

Transfer of a policy by an insured within three years of his death will cause the proceeds to be included in his or her gross estate. It is not necessary that the insured have outright ownership of the policy, since transfer within three years of death of any of the above "incidents of ownership" is sufficient to cause the policy proceeds to be included in his or her estate.

(continued on next page)

ESTATE TAXATION OF LIFE INSURANCE (continued)

Under the pre-1982 versions of Section 2035, using a "beamed transfer" theory the courts found constructive transfers of life insurance policies by insureds within three years of death where: (1) the policy was purchased on the initiative of the insured; (2) the insured supplied the funds used to purchase the insurance; and (3) the insured died within three years of the purchase. However, after the change to Section 2035 in 1981, the courts have refused to extend this beamed transfer theory to insureds dying after 1981 (*Estate of Leder*, 10th Cir. 1989, *Estate of Headrick*, 6th Cir. 1990, and *Estate of Perry*, 5th Cir. 1991).

In July of 1991, the IRS issued an action on decision in which the Service announced that it would no longer litigate the issue of whether life insurance proceeds are includable in the insured's estate where the life insurance policy is procured by a third party at the instance of the insured, the insured pays the premiums, and the insured dies within three years of procurement of the policy by the third person (i.e., the "beamed transfer" theory). This means that the incidents of ownership in a policy on the decedent's life that is issued to a trustee of an irrevocable life insurance trust will not be imputed to the decedent by reason of the fact that the decedent initiated the procurement of the policy, paid the premiums, or filled out the application for the policy in his or her capacity as the prospective *insured* (as distinguished from the prospective *owner* of the policy).

Recommended method of purchase and ownership. Despite the Service's favorable decision, it is recommended that whenever possible: (1) a third party be the original applicant, owner, and premium payer; (2) premiums come from an account held in the name of someone other than the insured, i.e., a trustee or adult child; (3) gifts should not be in the same amount as the premiums; (4) the gifts should be made at times other than premium due dates; (5) the insured not be named trustee of an irrevocable trust which owns a policy on his life; and (6) split-dollar plans involving controlling stockholders should avoid giving the corporation any incidents of policy ownership (see page 324).

Section 2036 Retained Life Estate.

Section 2037 Reversionary Interests.

Section 2038 Revocable Transfers.

Property given away is still included in the decedent's estate if the decedent: (1) retained the income from, use or enjoyment of, or the right to designate who will ultimately receive the property or its income; or (2) had a reversionary interest worth more than 5 percent of the value of the property at death, and the person to whom the gift was made could obtain possession or enjoyment only by surviving the decedent; or (3) reserved the power to alter, amend, revoke, or terminate the gift.

FAIR MARKET VALUE

Property included in a decedent's gross estate is valued at its fair market value on the date of the decedent's death or, if the executor elects, its fair market value six months after death (i.e., the "alternate valuation date"). Fair market value is defined in Treasury Regulations as the price at which an item of property, or a business interest, would change hands between a willing buyer and a willing seller, neither of whom is under any compulsion to buy or sell, and both of whom have a reasonable knowledge of all the relevant facts.

When it comes to valuing an interest in a closely held business, the above definition of fair market value is often of little practical assistance. In Revenue Ruling 59-60, the Internal Revenue Service set forth the following eight factors that are considered essential in valuing a closely held corporation:

1. The nature of the business and the history of the enterprise from its inception.
2. The economic outlook in general and the condition and outlook of the specific industry in particular.
3. The book value of the stock and the financial condition of the business.
4. The earning capacity of the company.
5. The dividend-paying capacity.
6. Whether the enterprise has goodwill or other intangible value.
7. Sales of stock and the size of the block to be valued.
8. The market price of stocks of corporations engaged in the same or a similar line of business having their stocks actively traded in a free and open market, either on an exchange or over the counter.

It is interesting to note that factor number 6 is goodwill, and that four of the other factors play a part in the capitalization of earnings formula demonstrated in the chart on page 167.

In determining fair market value, discounts are allowed for minority interests and lack of marketability. For publicly traded stock, it is also possible to obtain discounts using the "blockage" theory, which recognizes that placing a large block of stock on the market would likely have a depressing effect on its price. However, a "control premium" might increase the stock value of a person owning more than 50 percent of the business.

FAMILY HOLDING COMPANY

The family holding company, or asset holding company, which is a method of recapitalization, should not be confused with the personal holding company. When a new family holding company is formed, it is authorized to issue both voting preferred stock and non-voting common stock. The business owner then transfers his common stock in the original operating corporation to the family holding company in exchange for the voting preferred stock and the non-voting common stock.

Traditionally, the intention is to "freeze" the interest of the business owner in the operating corporation by subsequent gifts of the non-voting common stock of the family holding company. Although gifts of family holding company stock would be subject to the impact of Chapter 14, the techniques used to reduce or avoid the effect of these valuation rules will also work with a family holding company (see pages 371-372, and **Q 944-Q 945**, *Tax Facts on Insurance & Employee Benefits (2019)*).

The problems with Section 306 stock do not exist with respect to the formation of the family holding company. A family holding company could become a personal holding company if it generates personal holding company income (i.e., passive income such as dividends, rents, and royalties). If there were personal holding company income, a distribution could avoid the personal holding company tax of 20 percent (as increased from 15 percent by the American Taxpayer Relief Act of 2012).

As with a recapitalization, there is a definite need to establish an accurate fair market value of the operating corporation prior to a transfer of its common stock to the family holding company.

FIDUCIARY

A fiduciary is an individual or organization who stands in a relationship of trust with another. The law imposes the highest standard of care upon fiduciaries, who must have complete loyalty to their principals in exercising their fiduciary duty. Attorneys, accountants, trust officers, physicians, registered investment advisers, trustees who manage money, and company directors and officers are all fiduciaries.

Under ERISA, a person who exercises discretionary control over plan management or plan assets, or regularly provides investment advice for a fee, is considered to be a fiduciary. When found to have exercised "functional control" over the plan's insurance decisions, life insurance salespersons have been held to be "inadvertent fiduciaries" under ERISA (e.g., when an unsophisticated purchaser trustee relies on the salesperson's advice as the primary basis for insurance decisions).

In contrast, as suggested by their state licenses, stock brokers and insurance sales agents who act only in a traditional sales capacity by limiting their advice to recommended purchases are typically considered salespersons, not fiduciaries. In declining to offer an opinion regarding an agent's alleged "fiduciary duty for recommending one policy over another," the State of New York Insurance Department has stated that: "the suitability of an insurance policy is a business decision for the insured to make based upon the insured's unique situation." However, under New York law, insurance agents and brokers are responsible in a fiduciary capacity for all funds received or collected from their customers.

Even if not a fiduciary, the agent or broker who undertakes to obtain insurance for a client owes a duty to exercise reasonable skill, care, and diligence in obtaining the coverage. Insurance agents and brokers can be held liable to their clients if they: (1) commit a fraud by either making a fraudulent statement or by withholding material information; (2) violate a state insurance code or other state statute; or (3) breach an express or implied contract; among other actions.

The line between *sales* activities and *fiduciary* activities is not always clear. Insurance producers who hold themselves out as professionals, with numerous credentials and high levels of expertise, may well be taking the first steps toward creating fiduciary relationships. It has been argued that fiduciary relationships are created when unsophisticated clients rely on these professionals for advice regarding complex insurance products and tax planning. If the facts and circumstances establish that fiduciary relationships exist, then these professionals will be held to fiduciary standards. Insurance professionals, particularly those holding themselves out as "financial planners," are well advised to maintain a high level of expertise through continuing study and education, and to further protect themselves with appropriate levels of errors and omissions insurance.

The line would have been further blurred by the Department of Labor Fiduciary Rules discussed at pages 340-341. These rules would have created a heightened standard of care when working with qualifed retirement funds. Despite implementation of these rules being struck down by the 5th Circuit Court of Appeals, many producers (and attorneys) speculate that these standards will be considered by future courts.

FINANCIAL UNDERWRITING

Underwriting is the process of risk selection. In addition to *medical* underwriting it is also important to consider *financial* underwriting, where the objective is to issue an amount of insurance that indemnifies but does not enrich the beneficiary.

The key to good financial underwriting is good communication and information. The more information that can be supplied the more likely that a case will be fairly and efficiently underwritten. Typically, the following kinds of information will be required: (1) sales proposals establishing reasons for the life insurance; (2) W-2 forms or latest income tax returns; (3) certified personal financial statements; (4) reports of assets, liabilities and operating income of the business; (5) business purchase agreements; and (6) letters of transmittal setting forth reasons for the insurance, details of the agent's knowledge of the applicant, and other pertinent information about the case.

When applying for life insurance it is important to be familiar with the insurance company's specific financial underwriting guidelines. Although different carriers may have similar guidelines, carriers will often differ in their published standards and the application of these standards.

Personal life insurance is intended to provide ongoing income to a surviving family by replacing human life value. The maximum amount is typically based upon the insured's age and annual *earned* income (but not including *unearned* income such as interest, dividends, rents and royalties). For example, between ages fifty and fifty-four the amount might be ten times income, whereas between ages twenty and thirty the amount might be increased to fifteen times income. These guidelines are sometimes exceeded when the proposed insured has a potential for substantially increased future income (e.g., the young medical intern).

Key person life insurance is intended to protect a business from the loss of technical and business talent and the resulting loss of profits (see chart, page 203). The amount of insurance is typically limited to some multiple of the insured's compensation (e.g., from three to ten times annual compensation).

Estate liquidity life insurance provides for final expenses, debts and estate taxes (see charts, pages 15, 19, and 21). Projections of liquidity needs at reasonable rates of estate growth for five to ten years are often allowed (e.g., 8 percent growth over ten years).

Buy/sell life insurance is issued to fund the purchase of a business interest. Determining the amount of insurance requires a consideration of the reasonableness of the value placed upon the business under the agreement (see Business Valuation pages 166-169). Insurance will likely be required on all owners, but not necessarily with the same carrier (see charts, pages 171, 175, 179, 183, and 187).

FIRST-TO-DIE LIFE INSURANCE

First-to-die life insurance, also known as "joint life insurance," insures two or more lives, and pays a benefit upon the *first* death. Generally, the premium required for a permanent product is substantially less than those for individual policies on each insured.

Uses for first-to-die life insurance include: (1) income replacement in two wage-earner families (e.g., to pay off mortgage); (2) social security replacement for retirees; (3) estate tax payment to facilitate early transfer of appreciating assets to heirs; (4) key person insurance (chart, page 203); (5) funding split-dollar rollout of survivorship life insurance (page 553); and (6) funding both entity purchase and cross purchase agreements (charts, pages 171 and 175).

When funding a cross purchase agreement it is appropriate to have joint *ownership* of the contract. With equal ownership interests an appropriate *beneficiary* designation would be: "surviving insureds, equally." With unequal interests an appropriate designation would be: "surviving insureds as their interests may appear in the cross purchase agreement dated _____."

First-to-die life insurance is very effective in reducing the number of policies required to fund multiple-owner cross purchase agreements. For example, funding of a four stockholder cross purchase agreement requires twelve individual policies, but only four first-to-die policies (Options 1 and 2 below). A trusteed cross purchase agreement using an escrow agent requires four individual policies, but only one first-to-die policy (Option 3 that follows). If available, a survivor purchase option provides an effective means of acquiring ongoing insurance for surviving stockholders. Exercising this option appears to resolve the "transfer for value" problem caused by a transfer of policy interests following the death of a stockholder under a trusteed cross purchase agreement funded with individual policies (see footnote 8 on page 181, and pages 568-569).

However, first-to-die insurance has not proven to be commercially successful for insurance companies. Because the cost of a first-to-die policy is not always materially less expensive than two individual policies (assuming a two life application), the use of first-to-die product is not as common as might be expected. For this reason, it is increasingly difficult to find life insurance companies that issue this product.

OPTION 1	Owner ⟶	**A**	**B**	**C**	**D**
	12 individual policies insuring	[B] [C] [D]	[A] [C] [D]	[A] [B] [D]	[A] [B] [C]
OPTION 2	Owner ⟶	**A**	**B**	**C**	**D**
	4 first-to-die policies insuring	[B C D]	[A C D]	[A B D]	[A B C]
OPTION 3	Owner ⟶	**ESCROW AGENT**			
	1 first-to-die policy insuring	[A B C D]			

FOREIGN TRUSTS[1]

The topic of foreign trusts is often not a topic that United States (U.S.) estate planning lawyers or financial advisors have familiarity with. The purpose of this section is to provide a basic understanding of the topic so that the lawyer or advisor can spot the key issues and provide informed advice to the client.

U.S. lawyers must recognize that the concept of a trust exists in the U.S. (and in other countries that have adopted the common law) but does not exist in many parts of the world. In particular, Europe, Latin America and even China have adopted civil law, which does not recognize trusts. Arab countries which adopt Sharia law likewise do not recognize trusts. In those countries that have not adopted the common law, other types of entities – but not trusts – are used to hold passive investments for the benefit of family members.

You probably have a trust in the U.S. if you have an "arrangement by which title to property is held by a person or entity with a fiduciary responsibility to conserve or protect the property for the benefit of another person." Under Treasury Regulation Section 301.7701-4(a). The beneficiaries merely accept the benefit of the trust property. An arrangement will be classified as a trust, at least for U.S. tax purposes, if it can be shown that the purpose of the arrangement is to vest in a trustee the responsibility for the protection and conservation of property and the beneficiaries cannot share in the discharge of this responsibility. The beneficiaries are not associates in a joint venture for the conduct of a business for an activity for profit. An entity that conducts an active trade or business will likely be classified for tax purposes as either an association taxable as a corporation or a partnership under Treasury Regulation Section 301.7701-4(b).

Why is this Important?

Once an entity has been classified for U.S. tax purposes as a trust, the next question is whether the trust is a (U S) domestic or foreign trust? The answer to this question determines what U.S. (federal) taxes apply at the trust level and at the beneficiary level, and what informational reporting to the IRS, if any, will be required. As discussed below in greater detail, if the trust is considered to be a U.S. domestic trust, the trust's worldwide income will be subject to U.S. income tax. A foreign trust, in contrast, is generally subject to U.S. income tax only on its U.S. source income. If the trust is a foreign trust with either a U.S. grantor or U.S. beneficiary, there likely will be considerable U.S. tax information reporting that is required.

(continued on next page)

[1] The author of wishes to thank Michelle Graham, Esq. of Withersworldwide based in its Rancho Santa Fe, California office who is the original author of this material. Michelle is a Partner on the Withersworldwide Private Client and Tax Team. She leads a team of international estate planning lawyers based in California, who focus on estate planning and tax planning strategies for both domestic and international clients. This outline prepared for the Field Guide is a condensed version inspired by a longer presentation prepared by Michelle Graham, Esq. and co-delivered by Michelle and Elizabeth Bawden, a Partner in the Los Angeles office of Withersworldwide, which they presented at the STEP Wyoming Conference on September 15, 2017 in Jackson Hole, Wyoming.

FOREIGN TRUSTS (continued)

Foreign or U.S. Domestic Trust

Post-1996 Objective Rules

The Small Business Job Protection Act of 1996 established a two part objective test for determining the situs (location) of a trust for U.S. tax purposes. That Act added a new code section which provides that a trust will be treated as a U.S. domestic trust only if a) a court within the U.S. is able to exercise primary supervision over the administration of the trust (known as the "Court Test"), and b) one or more U.S. persons have the authority to control all substantial decisions of the trust (known as the "Control Test").

The Court Test

The Treasury Regulations provide that a trust will meet the Court Test if a) the trust instrument does not direct that the trust be administered outside of the U.S.[1] the trust in fact is administered exclusively in the U.S.[2] the trust is not subject to an automatic migration provision (a provision that causes the situs/location of the trust to change if a court attempts to exercise jurisdiction over the trust).[3]

Are there any bright-line rules of when a trust satisfies the Court Test? The Regulations contain four bright-line rules for satisfying the Court Test. A trust will satisfy the Court Test under the following circumstances:

A) When a trust is registered by an authorized fiduciary of the trust in a court in the U.S. pursuant to a state statute that has provisions that are substantially similar to the provisions found in the Uniform Probate Code.[4] Registering trusts is rare in the U.S. (although in Wyoming private trust companies may register a trust pursuant to state statute).

B) In the case of a trust created under the terms of a will probated within the U.S. (excluding ancillary probate) if all fiduciaries of the trust have been qualified as trustees of the trust by a court within the U S.[5] Many testamentary trusts do not require that a local probate court qualify a trustee of a trust created under a will. Such prior court approval qualifying the trustees is often explicitly waived in most wills or trusts created under wills.

C) In the case of a trust other than a testamentary trust (i.e. an inter vivos trust), if the fiduciaries take steps with a court within the U.S. that cause the administration of the trust to be subject to the primary jurisdiction of the court, the trust will meet the Court Test.[6] A U.S. court and a foreign court are able to exercise primary supervision over the administration of the trust. If both a U.S. court and a foreign court are able to able to exercise primary supervision over the administration of the trust, the trust meets the Court Test.[7]

(continued on next page)

1 Treas. Reg. §301.7701-7(c)(1)(i); (b).
2 Treas. Reg. §301.7701-7(c)(1)(ii); and c.
3 Treas. Reg. §301.7701-7(c)(1)(iii).
4 Treas. Reg. §301.7701-7(c)(4)(i)(A).
5 Treas. Reg. §301.7701-7(c)(4)(i)(B).
6 Treas. Reg. §301.7701-7(c)(4)(i)(C).
7 Treas. Reg. §301.7701-7(c)(4)(i)(D).

FOREIGN TRUSTS (continued)

The Control Test

A trust will meet the Control Test if one or more U.S. persons have the authority to control all "substantial decisions" of the trust. A U.S. person includes a U.S. citizen or a resident of the U.S. (for income tax purposes; not for immigration or transfer tax purposes).[1] Substantial decisions mean those decisions that persons are authorized or required to make under the terms of the trust instrument and applicable law and which are not ministerial.[2] Decisions that are ministerial include decisions regarding details such as maintaining books and records, collecting rent and executing investment decisions.[3]

Substantial decisions include whether and when to distribute income or principal to beneficiaries; the amount of any distribution; the selection of a beneficiary; whether to terminate the trust; whether to settle or abandon claims of the trust; whether to sue on behalf of the trust or to defend lawsuits against the trust; whether to remove, add or replace a trustee; whether to appoint a successor trustee who has died, resigned or otherwise ceased to act as a trustee. If a U.S. person hires an investment advisor for the trust, investment decision made by the investment advisor will be considered substantial decisions controlled by the U.S. person if the U.S. person can terminate the investment advisor's power to make investment decisions at will.[4]

If the trust contains certain powers, such as the power to remove and replace the trustee, this power could be exercised in such a way as to cause the trust to become a foreign trust (e.g., appointing a foreign person as sole successor trustee). If this happens the trust will be treated as having made, immediately before becoming a foreign trust, a gratuitous transfer of all of its assets to the foreign trust. As a result such a transfer will be treated as a sale or exchange of the assets of the formerly U.S. domestic trust to the foreign trust for an amount equal to the fair market value of the trust property transferred in excess of the adjusted basis of the property in the hands of the formerly U.S. domestic trust.

Some practical considerations in applying the Control Test:

- If a U.S. NRA (non-resident alien) is the grantor of the trust and has the power to revoke the trust and revest the assets in himself but selects a U.S. person as trustee, the trustee does not control all substantial decisions. The foreign grantor's power to have all the trust assets revert to the grantor is a substantial decision exercisable solely by a foreign person, and the trust will be a foreign (grantor) trust in the U S.
- If the U.S. trustee hires a foreign person as investment manager but can terminate such investment manager at will, the Control Test is satisfied and the trust is a U.S. trust.

(continued on next page)

1 Treas. Reg. §301.7701-7(d).
2 Treas. Reg. 301.7701-7(d)(1)(ii).
3 *Id.*
4 Treas. Reg. §301.7701-7(d)(1)(ii)(A)-(J).

FOREIGN TRUSTS (continued)

- If a U.S. person creates a trust for the benefit of two beneficiaries one of whom is a U.S. citizen and the other is a NRA, and the NRA beneficiary has the power to replace the trustee, the Control Test is not satisfied and the trust is a foreign trust.
- If a trust requires three trustees, and one of the trustees is a NRA, is the trust a foreign or U.S. domestic trust? If the trust instrument, or in default local law, requires that all three trustees must act unanimously in making all substantial decisions, the trust is a foreign trust. On the other hand, if the trust instrument, or in default local law, provides that a majority (two out of three) of the trustees can make all substantial decisions for the trust, then the trust is a U.S. domestic trust.

In the event of an inadvertent change in status of any person that has the power to make a substantial decision of the trust that would cause the domestic or foreign residency of the trust to change, the trust is allowed twelve months from the date of the change of status to make necessary changes either as to the persons who control substantial decisions or as to the residency of such person to avoid a change in the residency of the trust. An inadvertent change means the death, incapacity, resignation or change in residency or other change as to a person who has a power to make a substantial decision of the trust that would cause a change in the residency of the trust but that was not intended to change the residency of the trust. If the necessary change is made within twelve months, the trust is treated as retaining the pre-change residency during the twelve month period.[1]

Income Taxation of Foreign Trusts

Once a determination has been made that the entity is a foreign trust, it will be classified as either a foreign grantor trust or a foreign non-grantor trust.

Foreign Grantor Trust

If Established by a U.S. Person. For U.S. income tax purposes, a trust is a grantor trust when the grantor is treated as the owner of the trust assets because the grantor or another non-adverse party retained certain powers over the trust income and principal.[2] A foreign trust established by a U.S. person that has, or may have, U.S. beneficiaries will be considered a grantor trust, even if the grantor has retained no interest in or powers over the trust.[3] Also, a foreign trust established by a non-U.S. person who becomes a U.S. person within five years of transferring property to the trust will be a grantor trust if, at the grantor's residency starting date, the trust has a U.S. beneficiary[4] established by a non-U.S. person. It is more difficult for a trust to be classified as a foreign grantor trust. A trust will be treated as a (foreign) grantor trust only if a) it is revocable by the grantor (either alone or with the consent of a related or subordinate party), or b) distributions of income or principal may be made only to the grantor or the grantor's spouse during the grantor's lifetime.[5]

(continued on next page)

[1] Treas. Reg. §301.7701-7(d)(2).
[2] IRC Sec. 671.
[3] IRC Sec. 679.
[4] IRC Sec. 679(a)(4).
[5] IRC Sec. 672(f).

FOREIGN TRUSTS (continued)

Foreign Non-Grantor Trust (FNGT)

If a foreign trust is not a grantor trust, then it is considered a (foreign) non-grantor trust ("FGNT"). In a FNGT the grantor is not considered the owner of the trust assets for federal income tax purposes. A FNGT is treated as a separate taxpayer for federal income tax purposes and is treated the same, for incomes tax purposes, as an NRA individual.

In computing its taxable income, a trust (either a U.S. domestic non-grantor trust or a FGNT) will receive a deduction for distributions made to its beneficiaries to the extent such distributions carry out the trust's "distributable net income" ("DNI") for the tax year.[1] The term DNI is generally defined to mean the taxable income of the trust with certain modifications, such as adding back certain deductions (e.g., distribution deduction, personal exemption, capital losses, extraordinary dividends and tax exempt income).[2]

However, FGNTs are subject to three special tax rules which when combined cause the U.S. tax on FGNT income to become draconian.

First, one major difference in the taxation of FNGTs and domestic non-grantor trusts is that FGNTs remain subject to the "throwback" tax rules. The throwback tax rules effectively result in tax being imposed at the U.S. recipient's (beneficiary's) highest marginal income tax rate for the year in which the income or gain was earned by the trust.

Second, in addition to the throwback tax itself, an interest charge accrues for the period beginning with the year in which the income or gain is recognized and ending with the year that the undistributed net income amount is distributed. This interest charge is assessed at the same rate applicable to underpayments of tax, compounded daily.[3]

Third, any capital gain accumulated by the FGNT for distribution in a later tax year will lose its favorable tax status as capital gain property. Instead such accumulated (formerly) capital gain property will be converted to ordinary income and taxed at the currently higher ordinary income tax rates when distributed to a U.S. beneficiary.

Transfers to Foreign Trusts by U.S. Persons

The tax code provides that any transfer of property by a U.S. person to a foreign trust will be treated as a taxable exchange of the property subject to tax.[4] There is a major exception to this gain recognition rule for transfers to foreign trusts if any person is treated as the owner of the foreign trust under the grantor trust rules. See Treasury Regulation Section 1.684-3(a)-(f) for other exceptions. This tax code provision also provides that any outbound trust migration, by

(continued on next page)

[1] IRC Sec. 661(a).
[2] IRC Sec. 667.
[3] IRC Sec. 668.
[4] IRC Sec. 684.

FOREIGN TRUSTS (continued)

which a U.S. domestic trust becomes a foreign trust, is treated as a taxable transfer by the domestic trust of all its property (including all appreciated property) to a foreign trust immediately before the trust's change of residence status, unless one of the exceptions to this rule applies.[1]

Immigration to the U.S.

If a non-U.S. citizen/NRA transfers property to a trust and then becomes a U.S. resident within five years of transferring property to this trust, the trust will become a grantor trust if it has "or may have" U.S. beneficiaries.[2]

Death of Grantor

On the death of a U.S. citizen-grantor of a foreign trust, the appreciation in value of the trust assets from date of contribution until date of death will be subject to U.S. income tax. If the trust property, however, is included in the U.S. grantor's estate for estate tax purposes, the basis in the trust property will be "stepped up" to fair market value on the U.S. grantor's date of death.[3] If the grantor is a non-U.S. citizen/resident, the grantor will be subject to U.S. estate tax on the assets owned by the trust. To avoid this result, it is important that a transfer into trust be a completed gift, and that the grantor not retain sufficient actual or implied powers over the trust to cause the trust assets to be taxable on the grantor's death. Potential U.S. estate tax can be eliminated if the situs of the trust assets is moved to a non-U.S. entity (i.e., foreign portfolio investment company) and the transfer is respected for U.S. estate tax purposes.

Loans or Rent-Free Use of Trust Property Treated as Trust Distributions

If a foreign trust makes a loan of cash or marketable securities to or permits the use of other trust property (e.g., rent-free use of real estate owned by trust) by a U.S. beneficiary of the trust or the U. S. grantor of the trust, the amount of such loan or the fair market value of the use of such trust property shall be treated as a distribution by such trust to such grantor or beneficiary. This means that for FNGTs U.S. individuals who are trust beneficiaries may no longer be able to use such trust property free from rent without tax consequences.

U.S. Information Reporting Requirements

Transactions of U.S. Beneficiaries with Foreign Trusts

For over twenty years the tax code has included provisions imposing reporting U.S. tax reporting requirements on U.S. beneficiaries of foreign trusts. There are now new more extensive reporting requirements for U.S. beneficiaries of foreign trusts who fail to file information as to foreign trusts. Further, the tax code was expanded to add new reporting requirements for U.S. persons who receive large gifts or bequests from foreign persons.

(continued on next page)

1 IRC Sec. 684(c).
2 IRC Sec. 679(a)(4).
3 Treas. Reg. §1.684-3(c).

FOREIGN TRUSTS (continued)

At the same time, additional provisions were added to the tax code requiring reporting by U.S. persons who directly or indirectly transfer money or other property to a foreign trust. A primary purpose of this reporting requirement is to ensure that U.S. transferors comply with IRC Section 679, which treats a U.S. person as the owner of a foreign trust if the U.S. person transfers property to the foreign trust and the trust could have as permissible beneficiaries a U.S. person.

U.S. Persons Responsibility to Ensure Reporting if Considered the "Owner" of the Foreign Trust

Each U.S. person who is treated as the "owner" of a foreign trust under the U.S. grantor trust rules is required to ensure that the foreign trust files an annual return setting forth a full and complete accounting of all trust activities, trust operations and other relevant information on Form 3520-A (Annual Return of Foreign Trust with a U.S. Owner).[1] The burden is on the U.S. owner to ensure the foreign trust annually furnishes all such information because the trustee will be a non-U.S. person.[2] If the U.S. person fails to furnish this information, a penalty equal to 5 percent of the gross value of the foreign trust assets treated as owned by such U.S. owner will be assessed by the IRS.[3]

Appointment of U.S. Agent

If a foreign trust with a U.S. owner does not have a U.S. agent, the Treasury Department or IRS can determine the amounts required to be taken into account with respect to a U.S. owner of the foreign trust.[4] To avoid this result, it is highly recommended that a U.S. owner of a foreign trust appoint a U.S. person to act as the foreign trust's limited agent for purposes of any request by Treasury or the IRS to inspect the records or produce testimony.

U.S. Beneficiaries of Foreign Trusts

A U.S. beneficiary who receives a direct or indirect distribution from a foreign trust is required to report on Form 3520 the name of the trust, the total amount of the distributions received from the trust during the tax year, and any other information required by the Treasury Department.[5] Reporting is required only if the U.S. beneficiary knows or has reason to know the trust is a foreign trust. A U.S. beneficiary who fails to report a distribution is subject to a 35 percent penalty on the gross amount of the distribution.[6]

Sample Transactions that are Reportable to IRS

A distribution generally includes any gratuitous transfer of money or property from a foreign trust, regardless of whether the trust is owned by another person (i.e., the grantor as trust creator).

(continued on next page)

---

1 IRC Sec. 6048(b)(1).
2 IRC Sec. 6048(b)(1)(B).
3 IRC Sec. 6677(b) and (c)(2).
4 IRC Sec. 6048(c).
5 IRC Sec. 6048(c).
6 IRC Sec. 6677(a).

FOREIGN TRUSTS (continued)

This means that the distribution from a foreign trust includes the receipt of trust principal and the receipt of a gift or bequest described in the tax code. A distribution is reportable if it is either actually or constructively received.

What are some examples of transactions that are reportable by a U.S. person?

If a U.S. beneficiary uses a credit card and charges on that credit card are paid or otherwise satisfied by a foreign trust or guaranteed or secured by the assets of a foreign trust, the amount charged on that credit card will be treated as a distribution to the U.S. beneficiary that must be reported to the IRS for the year charged.

If a U.S. beneficiary writes a check on the foreign trust's bank or brokerage account or incurs a debt charged to the foreign trust, the amount incurred will be treated as a distribution to the U.S. beneficiary that must be reported to the IRS.

If a U.S. beneficiary receives a payment from a foreign trust in exchange for property transferred to the trust or for services rendered to the trust, and the fair market value of the payment received by the U.S. beneficiary exceeds the fair market value of the property transferred or services rendered to the trust, the excess will be treated as a distribution from the foreign trust that must be reported to the IRS.

No Reporting for Services Rendered to the Foreign Trust That Are Taxable as Compensation

If the recipient of a distribution from a foreign trust is treated and reported as taxable compensation income by the recipient, reporting to the IRS is not required. (If the services are rendered in the U.S. by the recipient then he or she must report the compensation income to the IRS regardless of the tax status of the recipient as a U.S. citizen/resident or NRA).

U.S. Beneficiary Statements

If adequate records are not provided to the IRS to determine the proper U.S. tax treatment of a distribution, then any such distribution from a foreign trust, whether from income or principal, will be treated as an accumulation distribution includable in the gross income of the U.S. beneficiary (and subject to the throwback tax, interest rate deferral charge and recharacterization as ordinary income).

Form 3520, Annual Return to Report Transactions with Foreign Trusts and Receipt of Certain Foreign Gifts

IRS Form 3520 is used to report certain (larger) transactions with foreign trust receipt by U.S. persons who receive in a tax year (large) gifts or bequests from certain foreign persons. The responsible person required to file the Form 3520 is a U.S. person who has any connection with a foreign trust, such as a U.S. beneficiary. For U.S. persons who during the year receive either more than a) US $100,000 from a NRA individual or a foreign estate, or b) more than US $15,797

(continued on next page)

FOREIGN TRUSTS (continued)

(for 2017) from a foreign corporation or foreign partnership must also report such transactions to IRS on Form 3520.

Form 3520-A, Annual Information Return of Foreign Trust with a U.S. Owner

IRS Form 3520-A provides information to the IRS about a foreign trust, its U.S. beneficiaries and any U.S. person who is treated as the owner of any portion of the foreign trust. The trustee of a foreign trust is required to a) file a return with the IRS for each tax year setting forth a full and complete accounting of all trust activities, and b) furnish specified income and other information to each U.S. grantor and U.S. trust beneficiary who directly or indirectly receives a trust distribution for that year.[1]

Foreign Bank Accounts; Report of Foreign Bank and Financial Accounts (FBAR)

Fin CEN Report 144 (Report of Foreign Bank and Financial Account or "FBAR") is required to be filed annually by any U.S. citizen or resident who has a "financial interest" in or "signatory authority" over or any "other authority" over a financial account (foreign bank, brokerage or financial account such as a foreign life insurance policy) located outside the U.S. and the aggregate value of these financial accounts exceed $10,000 at any point in the tax year. In addition, any U.S. citizen or resident who has such a foreign account must complete Schedule B, Part III to report information about such "foreign accounts on his or her annual IRS Form 1040.

Disclosure of this information is mandatory. FBAR is required under the Bank Secrecy Act. Currently, the FBAR form is due April 15 of the subsequent year with a maximum extension of six months ending Oct 15.

IRS Form 8938, Statement of Specified Foreign Financial Assets

In addition to FBAR reporting, an individual with an interest in a "specified foreign financial asset" during the year must attach a disclosure statement (i.e., Form 8938) to their U.S. income tax return for any year in which the total value of all such assets exceeds the reporting threshold. The reporting threshold varies depending on whether the individual lives in the U.S. or files a joint income tax return with a spouse. Moreover, IRC Section 6038D applies to any U.S. domestic entity formed or availed of for purposes of holding specified foreign financial assets.

"Specified foreign financial assets" are depository or custodial accounts at foreign financial institutions and to the extent not held at a financial institution, stocks or securities issued by foreign person or any other financial instrument or contract held for investment that is issued by or has as a counterpart a non-U.S. person and any interest in a foreign entity (including a foreign trust).

(continued on next page)

[1] IRC Sec. 6048(B)(1)(B).

FOREIGN TRUSTS (continued)

Perhaps the most crucial takeaway here is that under IRC 6038D compliance with the filing requirements of IRS Form 8938 does not relieve a person of the responsibility to file Form TD F 90-22.1 to comply with the FBAR rules. The FBAR form must be filed in addition to filing the IRS Form 8938. The bottom line is that if, for example, IRS Form 3520 has been filed identifying a specific foreign financial asset, the taxpayer is not required to fully identify the same asset again on IRS Form 8938 but must still file Form 8938 identifying the IRS form (i.e., IRS Form 3520) on which the specific asset was fully identified.

FUNERAL TRUSTS

A funeral trust is an arrangement under which an individual, during his lifetime, purchases funeral services or merchandise from the provider of funeral and burial services. Pursuant to a contract between the individual and the provider, the individual selects the services and merchandise to be provided at death and agrees to make payments during lifetime into a trust.

A "qualified funeral trust" is a trust arising out of a contract with a person in the business of providing funeral or burial services, the sole purpose of which is to hold, invest, and reinvest funds in the trust and to use such funds to make payments for the funeral or burial services of beneficiaries under the trust. Contributions to the trust can only be made for the benefit of beneficiaries. There are no dollar limit on contributions to funeral trusts. Contributions to the trust are not deductible for income tax purposes. However, the trustee of the trust can elect to have the trust earnings taxed to the trust and payable by the trustee (i.e., elect exemption from the grantor trust rules that would cause trust income to be taxed to the grantor). Each beneficiary's interest is treated as a separate trust for this purpose. However, a qualified funeral trust is not allowed a personal exemption.

An alternative to a funeral trust is a "pre-need" life insurance contract which provides a guaranteed death benefit typically tied to the average funeral cost for the insured's county of residence. These policies are usually available on a guaranteed issue or simplified issue basis even to insureds with health issues. The cost of these policies, because they are guaranteed issue, are typically more expensive than traditional life insurance policies.

GOLDEN PARACHUTE RULES

Under these rules, a corporation is barred from taking an income tax deduction for an "excess parachute payment" made to an officer, shareholder, or highly compensated individual when the payment is contingent upon a change in ownership or control of the corporation. In addition, a nondeductible 20 percent excise tax is imposed on the employee's excess payment.

Parachute payments are generally defined as any payments in the nature of compensation, which are contingent upon a change of ownership or effective control of the corporation when the present value of such payments equals or exceeds three times the individual's average annual compensation in the five taxable years ending before the date of the change. If the individual has been employed by the corporation for fewer than five years, then average annual compensation is determined by using the years actually employed.

These rules can adversely impact a *supplemental* deferred compensation plan if the plan calls for an acceleration of vesting or payment of benefits due to a change in control. However, these rules do not impact a pure *deferral* plan under which the executive has made an election to actually defer income previously earned. There are also limited exceptions for payments made by closely held corporations.

The golden parachute rules should not be confused with the $1,000,000 compensation deduction limitation placed upon publicly held corporations (i.e., those that issue stock required to be registered under the Securities Exchange Act of 1934). Under this limitation, such corporations may not deduct compensation in excess of $1,000,000 paid to the chief executive officer and the four highest paid officers of the corporation. In effect, this limitation declares such excess compensation to be unreasonable per se, and therefore not deductible. Both split-dollar and executive bonus plans for this group of executives could be impacted. However, excluded from the limitation are: (1) amounts paid by reason of worker's compensation, medical or hospitalization expenses, or payments made to any qualified plan or SEP; (2) commission payments; (3) performance-based compensation meeting strict qualifications and standards; and (4) stock options and stock appreciation rights.

GRANTOR TRUST RULES

Under the grantor trust rules, a grantor who retains interests in a trust created by the grantor may be treated for income tax purposes as the owner of all or part of the trust and thus taxed on all or a portion of the trust income. Retention of the following powers or interests, among other powers, can cause a trust to be considered a grantor trust: (1) reversionary interests in the income or principal of any portion of a trust that exceed five percent of the value of the trust; (2) the power to control the beneficial enjoyment of any portion of the trust that can be exercised without the approval of an adverse party (excepted is the power to limit distributions of principal to a beneficiary using a "reasonable definite standard"); (3) administrative powers, including the power to deal with trust funds for less than full and adequate consideration and to borrow without adequate interest or security; (4) power to revoke the trust; (5) power to substitute assets of equal value: and (6) income of the trust is *or may be* distributed to or held for the future use of the grantor or the grantor's spouse, used to discharge a legal obligation of the grantor, or used to purchase life insurance on the life of the grantor or the grantor's spouse.

Thus, transfer of income-producing property to a trust and the subsequent use of that income to pay life insurance premiums will result in the income being taxed to the grantor. The results are less clear when a trust merely authorizes the payment of premiums from trust income but does not use trust income for this purpose. In order to avoid grantor trust status, most authorities recommend that the trust language specifically prohibit the use of trust income to pay life insurance premiums on the life of the grantor or the grantor's spouse. To insure grantor trust status when considered beneficial for planning purposes, most attorneys favor use of the power to substitute assets of equal value as a grantor trust power.

A "defective" trust is an *irrevocable* trust that intentionally violates one or more or the grantor trust rules (see chart, page 75). With a defective trust, application of the grantor trust rules can work to the taxpayer's advantage: (1) *To transfer additional amounts to trust beneficiaries without gift tax consequences*. Income taxes paid by the grantor on trust income distributed to beneficiaries will not be included in the value of gifts made by the grantor. (2) *To avoid the transfer for value rules*. A grantor trust that is taxed as if owned by the grantor/insured can purchase or obtain existing policies on the grantor's life without adverse tax consequences (i.e., the transaction falls within the "transfer to the insured" exception, see page 568). (3) *To avoid disqualification of the S corporation election*. An irrevocable grantor trust can be a stockholder, but limited to two years after the grantor's death.

Some, but not all, grantor trust powers also cause estate tax inclusion. Hence, when doing estate planning for taxable estates it is important that any powers or interests retained by the grantor not cause the trust to be included in the grantor's taxable estate. Clearly, application of the grantor trust rules can be very complicated and the advice of competent tax counsel should always be sought.

GRITs, GRUTs, AND GRATs

GRITs. Prior to the changes brought about by the special valuation rules of Chapter 14, a grantor retained *income* trust (GRIT) was an effective technique for transferring property between generations. For example, a GRIT was created by having a grantor establish an irrevocable trust from which he retained the right to trust income for a specified period. At the end of this period, the succeeding trust beneficiaries (or remainderpersons) received the trust principal. Because of the reserved income interest, the gift tax value of the transferred remainder interest was usually substantially less than the current value of the property. However, except for a personal residence, for most taxpayers, Chapter 14 effectively eliminated the GRIT as a viable estate planning tool, since the grantor's right to trust income is deemed to have no value, meaning that the gift tax value of the remainder interest is equal to the *entire* value of the trust property (see pages 371-372). The gift tax cost is exactly the same as if the grantor had made a direct gift of the property to the remainderpersons. In place of a GRIT, the grantor retained unitrust (GRUT) and the grantor retained *annuity* trust (GRAT) are available to leverage gifts between generations.

GRUTs. The GRUT is an irrevocable trust in which the grantor retains the right to receive a *fixed percentage* of the trust's assets payable at least annually for life or for a term of years (and which must be revalued annually). However, in contrast to the GRAT, the GRUT will provide increasing payments to the grantor if the value of the trust increases (or decreasing payments if the value of the trust decreases). The GRUT is actuarially similar to the charitable remainder unitrust (see page 58).

GRATs. The GRAT is an irrevocable trust in which the grantor retains the right to receive *fixed payments* payable at least annually for life or for a term of years (see chart, page 63). In contrast to the GRIT, the GRAT *must pay* a fixed annual payment to the grantor, regardless of the income earned (whereas the GRIT often experienced substantial appreciation while yielding only a modest income). The GRAT is actuarially similar to the charitable remainder annuity trust (see page 58).

With both the GRAT and the GRUT, the value of the transferred remainder interest is equal to the present value of the entire property reduced by the present value of the retained interest. If the grantor is seeking to reduce his estate, additional smaller gifts that qualify for the annual exclusion can be made with the funds provided by trust payments. See the discussion of recessionary estate planning on pages 515-516.

GROUP CARVE OUT

The term "group carve out" is often used to describe the *replacement* of group term insurance for a selected class of executives with individual permanent insurance policies. Increased popularity of this concept has been due to the prohibition against individual selection in providing amounts of coverage to key employees.

Although a variety of plans are used to fund a group carve out, the more popular include Executive Equity (see chart, page 233) and Split-Dollar Insurance (see chart, page 241). The advantages of group carve outs include: (1) the provision of permanent post retirement insurance for the executive; (2) lower long term cost for the employer; (3) elimination of the increasing term cost after retirement to both the executive and the employer; (4) flexible structure with little or no ERISA or nondiscrimination requirements; (5) cost recovery options for the employer; and (6) portability of the policy for the executive.

The design of individual illustrations will differ widely depending upon the circumstances of the existing group program and the proposed method of funding the group carve out. However, it is essential to compare annual costs to both the employer and executive, both before and after the carve out. This includes estimates of the current and projected group premiums for the executive's coverage under the group plan, together with the after-tax costs of bonuses, if any, given the executive to cover his tax cost of amounts of coverage in excess of $50,000. These same employer after-tax dollars are then placed in an executive equity or split-dollar program. Should the group carve out plan require additional executive costs (i.e., either direct premium payments or increased tax costs), then it is important to make a direct year-by-year comparison of this cost to the executive's ownership of policy cash values.

GUARANTEED MINIMUM WITHDRAWAL BENEFIT

When an annuity is annuitized, the owner loses all control over the underlying funds, has no right to make investment decisions, and gives up any rights to accelerated payments. The owner's only right is to receive the periodic payments as stipulated in the contract. The guaranteed minimum withdrawal benefit (GMWB) is a variable annuity living benefit that allows the contract owner to retain control.

The GMWB guarantees the contract owner can withdraw each year a fixed percentage of the premiums, *until all premiums have been completely recovered*, regardless of the actual account value. The amount against which this percentage is applied is variously referred to as the total premiums, the principal, the protected value, or the benefit base. Although annual withdrawals can be stopped and started at any time, failure to make a withdrawal does not entitle the contract owner to subsequently recover the amount not withdrawn. If a withdrawal in any one year exceeds the guaranteed percentage, the benefit base can be reset, which in a declining market could result in a lower guaranteed payment (i.e., same percentage applied to a lower benefit base). The contract can be surrendered at any time, provided the underlying funds are positive (i.e., a form of liquidity guarantee). The GMWB addresses the fear of losing control, but it does nothing to protect the contract owner from running out of money.

The GMWB "for life," or guaranteed lifetime withdrawal benefit (GLWB), addresses the fear of running out of money. Whereas the GMWB is essentially a money-back guarantee for the original premium, the GLWB guarantees a lifetime of income, regardless of the performance of the underlying funds (both single and joint spousal lifetime withdrawal options are available). In order to control risk, the owner is contractually limited as to the types of investments in the annuity subaccounts. A "step-up," or "ratchet-up," feature in many contracts allow the withdrawal amount to be increased on specified contract anniversaries, provided the actual account value is higher than the benefit base. Withdrawing more than the annual guaranteed percentage will generally void the lifetime guarantee.

Although the GLWB guarantees an income stream that may appear similar to annuitization, there are substantial differences between withdrawals and annuitization. For example, *withdrawals* from an annuity are first taxed at ordinary income tax rates on any growth within the annuity (first-in last-out), whereas when a contract is *annuitized*, use of an exclusion ratio allows a portion of each payment to escape taxation as a return of principal.

It is important to recognize that the "guarantees" offered by these living benefits (GMWB and GLWB) are subject to the claims-paying ability of the issuing life insurance company (i.e., guaranteed may not *really* mean guaranteed). See Life Insurance Default Risk, page 418 and Life Insurance Ratings Agencies, pages 425-428. The evolving nature and variety of contract provisions make these complex products. This makes it essential that the agent fully understand the product and the purchaser carefully read the prospectus.

GUARANTEED PURCHASE OPTION

At the time a life insurance policy is issued it is sometimes possible to purchase an option that provides the policy owner with the right to purchase, without evidence of insurability, additional amounts of permanent insurance at stated intervals or upon stated events. This option is usually issued as a rider to the basic policy and terminates at a specified policy anniversary. Most options provide an overall limit on the amount of additional insurance that may be purchased. Premiums for the option are based upon the insured's attained age and are payable until the rider terminates. Guaranteed purchase options are also referred to as "insurability options." Use of a guaranteed purchase option is particularly attractive when insurance is issued on the life of a child (see the discussion of children's life insurance on page 312).

When the option is exercised the insurance purchased does not have to be the same plan as the basic policy. Premiums for the additional insurance are often offered at the same underwriting class as the initial coverage (locking in today's health) and sometimes at standard rates (creating a hedge against future health deterioration). For example, a typical rider might provide for the option to purchase $20,000 of additional insurance every three years until the policy anniversary nearest the insured's age forty. Additional option dates might also include the insured's marriage and the birth of each of the insured's children.

Other forms of guaranteed purchase options offer guaranteed insurance under cost-of-living adjustments that are tied to increases in an economic inflation indicator, such as the Consumer Price Index. Another variation, known as a "beneficiary purchase option," allows the beneficiary, upon the death of the insured, to elect to use part or all of the proceeds to purchase insurance without evidence of insurability. However, at the time the underlying policy is issued the beneficiary must prove insurability. This option is sometimes used as a substitute for survivorship life insurance and may offer greater flexibility (i.e., the surviving spouse uses some of the proceeds to pay estate taxes at the first death and the remaining proceeds to exercise the "last to die" option). Still another variation, known as a "surviving spouse option," is used with survivorship insurance (see the discussion of survivorship life insurance on page 561). This option allows the policy owner to purchase an additional amount of insurance on the primary insured following the death of his or her spouse.

HARDSHIP DISTRIBUTIONS

A retirement plan may, but is not required to, provide for hardship distributions. Thus many, but not all, 401(k), 403(b), and 457(b) plans have provisions allowing hardship distributions. The 401(k) plan documents or 403(b) plan documents must have provisions specifically allowing for hardship distributions and must specify nondiscriminatory and objective standards as well as the criteria used to make a determination. A 457(b) plan must contain specific language defining what constitutes a distribution on account of an "unforeseeable emergency."

For a distribution from a 401(k) plan to be on account of hardship, the Treasury Regulations provide that it must be made on account of "an immediate and heavy financial need of the employee" and the amount "must be necessary to satisfy the financial need." Generally, the need must be that of the employee, spouse, or dependent.

Facts and circumstances determine if a need is "immediate and heavy" and not all needs must be allowed for in the plan documents. In fact, it isn't uncommon for a plan document to only allow for hardship distributions associated with medical exepenses and funeral expenses. The following expenses are delineated in the Treasury Regulations as being potentially "immediate and heavy:"

(1) medical expenses incurred by the employee, spouse, or dependents;

(2) costs relating to the purchase of the employee's principal residence;

(3) tuition and related educational fees and expenses of the employee, spouse, or dependents;

(4) payments necessary to prevent eviction or foreclosure on the employee's principal residence;

(5) burial or funeral expenses for the employee's parent, spouse, children or other dependents; and

(6) certain expenses for the repair of damage to the employee's principal residence that would qualify for the casualty deduction under IRC Section 165.

The amount of the distribution can also include an amount necessary to pay federal, state, and local taxes anticipated from the distribution.

(continued on next page)

HARDSHIP DISTRIBUTIONS (continued)

A distribution is NOT considered necessary to satisfy an immediate and heavy financial need of an employee if the employee has other resources available to satisfy the need, including assets of the spouse and minor children. The regulations provide an example of an employee with a vacation home who would be expected to first liquidate that property, if possible, before receiving hardship distributions.

When making a hardship distribution, the employer may reasonably rely on the employee's written representation that the need cannot be relieved through reimbursement or compensation by insurance, by reasonable liquidation of the employee's assets, by cessation of future elective contributions to the plan, by other distributions or nontaxable loans from another plan, or by a commercial loan. Hardship distributions are generally limited to the employee's total elective contributions as of the date of distribution reduced by the amount of previous hardship distributions.

In recent years, it seems that natural disasters have brought unprecedented loss of life and property. 2017 was especially notable for hurricanes Harvey and Irma that brought mass destruction to large portions of Texas and Florida.

Specifically, as to hurricanes Harvey and Irma, the IRS announced that special hardship provisions were available for employees and certain members of their families who lived or worked in disaster areas designated for individual assistance by the Federal Emergency Management Agency (FEMA). See IRS Announcement 2017-3. An employee living in such a designated area could take a hardship distribution up to the statutory limit. And, it also meant that an employee who was not in such an area could take a hardship withdrawal to assist a child, parent, grandparent or other dependent who did live or work in the disaster area. However, to qualify under these specific 2017 hurricane rules, hardship withdrawals had to be requested by January 21, 2018. No such rules have, as of the date of print, been implemented for hurricane Florence or other 2018 disasters.

HEALTH CARE POWER OF ATTORNEY

A health care power of attorney is a document that allows an individual to designate another person to make health care decisions when the individual is unconscious or mentally incompetent. The powers given include the power to consent to the giving, withholding, or stopping of medical treatment, service, or diagnostic procedures, including the withdrawal of life support. (The privacy rules of the Health Insurance Portability and Accountability Act of 1996, or HIPAA, make it important that the power-holder also be given the right to obtain and review medical records.) The power does not become effective until the individual has been declared by an attending physician to be incapacitated. In order to avoid conflicts between power-holders, it is best that only one power-holder be appointed at a time, but successor power-holders should be named. In general, a subsequent marriage automatically revokes a health care power of attorney held by someone other than the new spouse. Likewise, a subsequent divorce or separation usually revokes a health care power of attorney held by the divorced or estranged spouse. While there may be slight distinctions from state to state, the health care power of attorney is also referred to as a:

- Durable Power Of Attorney For Health Care
- Medical Power Of Attorney
- Health Care Proxy
- Health Care Surrogate Designation

In various ways, virtually all states recognize the right of a person to designate another person to make end-of-life choices for them in case of their mental incapacity. Other documents used for these purposes include:

1. **Living Wills** that merely express individuals' wishes with regard to life-sustaining procedures. They do not appoint another person to make specific health care decisions (see page 453).
2. **Advanced Health Care Directives** that provide instructions as to what should be done if grantors are unable to make future health care decisions. Health care power of attorneys and living wills are both considered to be advanced health care directives (AHCDs). In some states, documents referred to as AHCDs contain elements of both the health care power of attorney and the living will.
3. **Medical Directives** that contain elements of both the health care power of attorney and the living will, by allowing individuals to state their wishes regarding various types of specific medical treatments, appoint a proxy, and record wishes regarding organ donation (see www.caringinfo.org).

Because of potential differences between states, it is strongly recommended that individual state laws be consulted.

INCENTIVE STOCK OPTION

The incentive stock option (or "ISO"), also known as a qualified or statutory stock option, is an employee benefit used to attract and retain key corporate employees. Provided the required holding period is met, the employee is not taxed at the time the option is exercised and receives favorable capital gains treatment on the sale of the stock. In contrast to the incentive stock option, with the nonqualified stock option (also referred to as a non-statutory stock option) the employee is generally taxed at the time the option is exercised and does not receive favorable capital gains treatment. However, due to the required holding periods, the holder of the incentive stock option assumes more risk than the holder of the nonqualified stock option.

An incentive stock option must: (1) be granted under a plan that sets forth the number of shares to be issued and the employees or class or employees to receive the option; (2) be granted under a plan that is approved by the stockholders within twelve months before or after the plan is adopted; (3) be granted within ten years after the plan is adopted or approved by the stockholders, whichever comes first; (4) be exercisable within ten years after it is granted; (5) have an exercise price that is not less than the fair market value of the stock at the time it is granted; (6) be nontransferable and exercisable only by the transferee (except that it may be transferred by will or the laws of descent and distribution); and (7) be granted only to an employee who owns no more than 10 percent of the voting stock of the corporation (an exception applies when the option price is at least 110 percent of the fair market value of the stock).

Provided the employee does not sell the stock until at least a year and a day after the stock is purchased (option exercised) and at least two years after the option is granted, any profit on the sale is treated as long-term capital gain. For example, assume the employee is granted an option to purchase 100 shares at $75.00 per share on April 5, 2015 (stock has a fair market value of $74.00; thus exercise price is not less than the fair market value). The employee then uses part of his year-end bonus to exercise the option on February 15, 2016 and purchases 100 shares at $75.00 per share. Waiting until February 16, 2017 to sell the stock will comply with the *over one-year-after-purchase* holding period, but it would not comply with the *at least two-year-after-grant* holding period. The employee needs to wait until April 5, 2017 to sell the stock in order to received capital gains treatment. If the stock had a value of $86.00 on the day option was exercised (February 15, 2016) the difference between that value and the grant price of $75.00 is referred to as the bargain element. In this case the total bargain element would be $1,100 (86 – 75 = 11 × 100 = 1,100). In the year the option is exercised this bargain element must be reported as taxable compensation for alternative minimum tax (AMT) purposes (but Congress has provided some specific relief for taxpayers with incentive stock options).For additional information, see **Q 7545-Q 7552**, *Tax Facts on Investments (2018)*.

INCENTIVE TRUST

The dilemma faced by many wealthy individuals is how to pass down the family fortune without taking away their children's ambition, drive, and willingness to lead productive lives. The incentive trust is a response to these concerns.

In contrast to the traditional trust, with its set distribution times and amounts, the incentive trust goes beyond the age-linked distribution formulas by attaching conditions to distributions. For example, the incentive trust might contain provisions that tie the timing and size of distributions to the achievement of certain goals by the beneficiaries, such as receipt of good grades, graduation from college, obtaining a graduate degree, a first job, or the attainment of specific levels of income. More controlling provisions might reward certain conduct or community service, such as staying at home to take care of children, serving as a missionary, or remaining alcohol or drug free (i.e., "tough love" when there has been a prior history of abuse).

The potentially restrictive and controlling nature of such trusts is a matter of some debate. To some, incentive trusts might be seen as nothing more than an attempt to unduly "control from the grave." Yet it seems most laudable when parents desire to teach their children to be good stewards of family wealth. Establishing such a values-oriented trust will likely require a great deal more thought and effort then is required of the typical tax-savings and distribution trust.

When creating an incentive trust, a "one size fits all" approach is not appropriate. Ideally, the trust will accomplish the grantor's objectives without unduly restricting the trustee's ability to respond to changing circumstances, such as a beneficiary's marriage, medical emergency, or behavior. A good trust must be carefully drafted. While encouraging positive social goals and distributing income, the trust should also act as an economic safety net for children and other heirs.

Use of an institutional trustee together with an individual co-trustee who is either a family member or friend will avoid the undue pressure that can be placed on an individual trustee by beneficiaries demanding distributions that are inconsistent with trust objectives. It also seems quite reasonable to include provisions for the replacement of an unsatisfactory trustee by the beneficiaries.

In addition to the incentive trust, private foundations (see page 497) are also used as a means of involving children and other heirs in the responsible charitable distribution of a family's wealth.

INCOME IN RESPECT OF A DECEDENT

The term "income in respect of a decedent" (IRD) refers to those amounts which a decedent was entitled to as gross income, but which were not includable in the decedent's income for the year of his death. For example, the following are considered IRD: (1) payments to a surviving spouse under an individual deferred compensation agreement; (2) compensation for services rendered before death; (3) renewal commissions of a life insurance agent; (4) dividends declared but unpaid to a stockholder prior to death; (5) interest owed the decedent at the time of his death; (6) the decedent's distributive share of partnership income; (7) amounts paid for unrealized receivables upon the sale or liquidation of a partnership interest; (8) distributions from a 403(b) plan; (9) distributions from a decedent's individual retirement account; and (10) proceeds from sales on the installment method.

It is important to recognize that, unlike other property included in an estate, the recipient of IRD does not receive a stepped-up basis for the purpose of computing gain or loss (see the discussion of stepped-up basis on page 556). Thus, the estate or beneficiary who receives IRD will pay tax on that income in the same manner as the decedent. If the income would have been ordinary income to the decedent, then it is ordinary income to the estate or beneficiary. Likewise, if the income would have been treated as capital gains to the decedent, then it is treated as capital gains to the estate or beneficiary.

However, an income tax deduction is available which somewhat (albeit not entirely) alleviates this "double" taxation (i.e., subjecting the IRD to both estate taxation and income taxation). The recipient of IRD generally may take an income tax deduction for any estate taxes paid by the estate on the IRD. The amount of the deduction is determined by comparing the actual estate tax paid with the amount of estate tax that would have been paid had the IRD asset not been included in the estate (i.e., the deduction is determined at the highest estate tax rates to which the estate was subject). The deduction can also be taken for generation-skipping taxes paid on the IRD asset. This is a *deduction* to be used in determining the income taxes of the estate or beneficiary receiving the IRD, it is not a *credit* against the income tax due.

Income tax deduction to alleviate double taxation (for any estate taxes pd by the estate

INDIVIDUAL 401(k) PLAN

Also referred to as a "Solo 401(k) Plan," the Individual 401(k) Plan is a regular 401(k) plan combined with a single-participant profit sharing plan (the name itself has been created by the marketplace; it is not found in the Code). Individual 401(k) Plans are limited to self-employed individuals or small business owners who have no other full-time employees (an exception allows coverage of both the self-employed individual or business owner and his or her spouse who is employed full time). Like an IRA, an Individual 401(k) plan can be either a traditional or Roth version (see Roth IRA on page 527.)

Individual 401(k) Plans can provide for increased retirement contributions without many of the complex administrative rules and nondiscrimination testing required of 401(k) plans and profit sharing plans covering multiple employees. Should the sponsoring employer add additional employees to the plan, it is subject to the same minimum participation, coverage, nondiscrimination, and other requirements that apply to any other qualified defined contribution plan. Other advantages include availability of loans, year-to-year contribution flexibility, availability of hardship withdrawals, rollovers from other retirement arrangements, and the ability to purchase permanent life insurance (see pages 419-420).

The Individual 401(k) Plan contribution limit is effectively the lesser of 100 percent of compensation or $56,000 ($62,000 if age fifty or over). Annual contributions to an Individual 401(k) Plan consist of two parts: a tax deductible salary deferral contribution plus an additional tax deductible profit sharing contribution:

1. **Salary Deferral Contribution**. In 2018, 100 percent of compensation up to a maximum of $19,000, or $25,000 if age fifty or older ($19,000 plus $6,000 catch-up), can be contributed in salary deferrals. For S and C corporations compensation is based on W-2 wages. For businesses taxed as sole proprietorships and partnerships compensation is based on net earnings (net profit less the deduction taken for one-half of the self-employment tax).

2. **Profit Sharing Contribution**. For S and C corporations profit sharing contributions can be made up to 25 percent of W-2 wages. For sole proprietorships and partnerships profit sharing contributions can be made up to 20 percent of net earnings.

The sum of the salary deferral and profit sharing contributions cannot exceed the 2019 Individual 401(k) Plan contribution limit. For example, a self-employed individual age forty-five (limit of $56,000) doing business as a sole proprietor and having $100,000 in net earnings can contribute $39,000 ($19,000 of salary deferrals plus 20 percent of $100,000 in net earnings). Likewise, a self-employed individual age fifty-two (limit of $61,000) doing business as an S corporation and having $100,000 in W-2 wages can contribute $49,000 ($24,000 of salary deferrals plus 25 percent of $100,000 in W-2 wages). Deferral contributions reduce taxable W-2 wages (or net earnings) and profit sharing contributions are generally tax deductible as a business expense. See also, simplified employee pension (SEP) on page 549.

INDIVIDUAL RETIREMENT ARRANGEMENTS (IRAs)

There are two types of regular individual retirement arrangements, individual retirement accounts and individual retirement annuities. Each is often referred to as an "IRA" (see also pages 527, 567, and 633). Generally an individual retirement *account* is set up as a trust or custodial account with a bank, a federally insured credit union, or a savings and loan association, whereas an individual retirement *annuity* is established by purchasing an annuity contract from a life insurance company. Life insurance may not be purchased by the IRA.

Contributions may be made up to the time when the individual's tax return is due (excluding extensions). In order to deduct contributions an individual must: (1) have compensation (including earned income as an employee or self-employed person, or alimony); and (2) not have attained age 70½ during the taxable year for which the contribution is made.

In 2018 a deduction may be taken for amounts contributed up to the lesser of $5,500 or 100 percent of compensation includable in gross income. An additional "catch-up" contribution of $1,000 is allowed in 2018 for individuals who attain age 50 before the close of the taxable year. Deductions may be reduced or eliminated if the individual is an "active participant" in a qualified plan. In 2018 the phase-out range for a *married couple filing jointly* is between $189,000 and $199,000 for a spouse who is not an active participant and between $101,000 and $121,000 for a spouse who is an active participant. The phase-out range for a *single individual* who is an active participant is between $63,000 and $73,000. Similar deductions may be taken for contributions to the IRA of a lesser-compensated spouse.

Generally, funds accumulated in a plan are not taxable until they are actually distributed. However, amounts distributed prior to age 59½ are considered early distributions and are subject to a 10-percent-penalty tax. Exceptions to the penalty tax include distributions: (1) made on or after death; (2) attributable to disability; (3) which are part of a series of substantially equal periodic payments made (at least annually) for the life or life expectancy of the individual or the joint lives or joint life expectancy of the individual and a designated beneficiary (e.g., an annuity payout); (4) for medical expenses in excess of 7.5 percent of adjusted gross income; (5) for health insurance premiums for those receiving unemployment compensation; (6) to pay for a first home; or (7) to pay for qualified higher education expenses. Distributions from a plan must usually begin by April 1 of the year after the year in which the individual reaches age 70½.

In order to prevent current taxation IRAs are frequently used for "rollovers" of distributions from qualified plans, 403(b) plans, or eligible 457 government plans. An IRA that meets certain requirements may accept an expanded rate of contribution as a simplified employee pension (SEP). SEPs are discussed on page 549.

INSTALLMENT SALE

An installment sale provides a method by which the gain on the sale of property, and the income tax on that gain, can be spread over a period of time. No payment is required in the year of sale; the only requirement is that at least one payment be made in a taxable year after the year of the sale. Payments can be tailored to fit both the seller's income and tax requirements, since gain and the payment of tax on that gain is prorated according to the amount received each year.

When there is a sale between related parties (spouses, children, etc.), any resale by the buyer within two years accelerates the gain to the seller unless such resale occurs after the death of either of the related parties. The seller's gain will also be accelerated if the seller cancels the buyer's obligation (this may also include a cancellation by bequest or by the seller's executor). However, it appears that this technique of making gifts is available with an installment sale, provided there is a forgiving of each installment payment as it comes due. See the expanded discussion of self-cancelling installment notes, page 542.

The installment method cannot be used to report a loss. Moreover, the sale of inventory, stock, or securities traded on an established exchange cannot be reported using the installment method.

INSURABLE INTEREST

The issuance of an insurance contract to someone who does not have an insurable interest in the life of the insured is, as a matter of public policy, depending upon the jurisdiction, either void or voidable by the carrier who issued the policy. Generally stated, an insurable interest arises from the relation of the party obtaining the insurance to the insured, provided there is a reasonable expectation of advantage or benefit from the continuance of the insured's life. An insurable interest is based upon relationships which involve: (1) pecuniary or economic advantage through the continued life of the insured or loss by reason of his death; or (2) love and affection in case of individuals closely related by blood or marriage.

The following are generally considered to have insurable interests: (1) a person on his own life; (2) a wife in her husband's life and a husband in his wife's life; (3) a fiancée in her fiancé's life and a fiancée in his fiancée's life; (4) a parent on a minor child's life (but not necessarily on an adult child's life); (5) a creditor in the life of his debtor; (6) an employer in the life of a key employee (but not a rank and file employee); (7) each of the partners, and the partnership itself, in the life of a partner whose death would result in a substantial loss; (8) each of the partners to a buy/sell agreement in the life of another partner, provided the beneficiaries do not stand to gain upon the death of the insured; and (9) among stockholders in a closely held corporation to the extent, and on the same basis, that an insurable interest exists among partners. See page 308 regarding charities having an insurable interest in the lives of donors.It is important to note that an insurance company cannot issue a life insurance policy when there is no insurable interest. However, an insurance company underwriting guidelines can limit issuance of policies where a legal insurable interest does exist. In other words- just because an insurance company can issue a policy doesn't mean it that it must.

Provided the insurable interest requirements are satisfied at the inception of the contract, a policy remains valid thereafter even if at the insured's death the policy owner-beneficiary no longer has an insurable interest. In recent years, there has been considerable litigation pertaining to insurable interest. In many states, it appears unlikely that insurable interest will be respected when the original legal owner had insurable interest but an arrangement was already in place to transfer the poliicy after issue to someone lacking insurable interest. The original insurable interest must be more than a mere formality or the court may look to the substance of the transaction rather than the mere form. See Stranger-Originated Life Insurance (STOLI), page 558, for a discussion of the controversy surrounding programs and arrangements intended to abuse or circumvent insurable interest statutes to facilitate acquisition of life policies by third-party investors without insurable interest

If the applicant has no insurable interest at the time a policy is taken out, the proceeds will be taxed as gain from a wagering contract. Since the existence of an insurable interest is governed by the case and statutory law of each state, it is essential to refer to these specific state laws for answers to questions regarding an insurable interest.

INTEREST ADJUSTED NET COST

Net Cost Method. Prior to introduction of the interest adjusted net cost method, the cost of life insurance was frequently determined by the "net cost" method, which consisted of simply adding up the net premiums (premiums less dividends), subtracting out any cash values, dividing by the number of years, and then dividing by the number of thousands of insurance. For example, assume a $150,000 nonparticipating contract with premiums of $900 per year yields $6,000 of cash values in the tenth year:

Premiums per year	900
Number of years	x 10
Total premiums paid	9,000
Less cash values	(6,000)
	3,000
Number of years	÷ 10
Cost per year	300
Number of thousands	÷ 150
Cost per year per thousand	2.00

Interest Adjusted Net Cost Method. But the above calculation fails to account for the time value of money. The *interest adjusted* net cost (IANC) method has been adopted by most states in order to provide some index for comparing one life insurance contract with another, and is particularly useful where there is a difference in amount and timing of premiums, availability of dividends, and amounts of cash values. The IANC method assumes that the purchaser would be helped by comparing the results of his purchase to those that he could obtain by investing his money in a 5 percent savings account, with interest compounded annually. The basic question involves determining what amount of annual deposit would be required to end up with the same cash accumulation. Assuming the same $150,000 nonparticipating contract:

Life Insurance Contract		
Premiums per year		900.00
Cash values in 10 years	6,000	
5% Savings Account		
Cash value objective	6,000	
Future Value factor (table, page 607)	÷ 13.207	
Annual deposit required		(454.30)
Cost per year for insurance		445.70
Number of thousands of coverage		÷ 150
Cost per year per thousand		2.97

INTEREST DEDUCTION

The deductibility of interest depends on its classification. For example, *investment interest* is generally deductible only to the extent of investment income, *qualified residence interest* is generally deductible in full, *trade or business interest* is generally deductible as a business expense, and *personal interest* is not deductible at all (except student loan interest; see page 314).

Personal interest includes interest on personal loans and interest on personal life insurance policy loans used to pay premiums on the policy. Investment interest may be deducted to the extent of net investment income. There are no limitations on deductibility of interest on amounts borrowed for ordinary and necessary business purposes.

Thus, loans used to purchase a personal life insurance policy or loans used to carry a personal life insurance policy are not deductible.

INTEREST-FREE LOANS

At one time the use of interest-free, or below market, loans between parent and child, or employer and employee, was generally considered an effective means of transferring income that offered many tax advantages. The Supreme Court decision in *Dickman*, the introduction of the concept of "forgone interest," and the phasing out of the deduction for personal interest limited these tax advantages. Nevertheless, there may still be circumstances in which such loans would be appropriate to accomplishing nontax objectives (parent loans to child to buy life insurance, or corporation loans to nonstockholder-employee as a form of "golden handcuffs").

Gift Loans. When a below market or term loan is treated as a "gift loan" the lender is deemed to have transferred (imputed gift) to the borrower, and the borrower is deemed to have retransferred (imputed payment) to the lender, an amount equal to the foregone interest. The effect of this retransfer is that the foregone interest is included in the gross income of the lender, and the borrower is considered as having paid the interest (for individuals, there is no deduction for personal interest, as discussed on page 409) and the lender will have interest income.

Compensation-Related Loans. The same transfer and retransfer of foregone interest is deemed to have occurred with loans between employers and employees, or corporations and stockholders, as with gift-loans. The employer will be deemed to have interest income in the amount of the foregone interest, which would be offset by a corresponding deduction for compensation paid (if reasonable). The employee will have taxable income and is considered as having paid the interest. However, with stockholder-employees, the foregone interest will be treated as a nondeductible dividend payment. The Sarbanes-Oxley Act of 2002 adopted new securities law provisions that prohibit below-market loans made by a *public* corporation to its executives. Note in this regard the split-dollar regulations that consider some split-dollar arrangements as employee-loans subject to deemed loan and imputed interest treatment (see pages 362-365).

Exceptions. There is a $10,000 de minimis exception for compensation-related or corporation-stockholder loans that do not have tax avoidance as a principal purpose. Another exception is available when the total loans between individuals (husband and wife are considered one individual) do not exceed $10,000 unless the gift loans are directly attributable to the purchase or carrying of income-producing assets. These exceptions may protect low interest loans used to purchase life insurance, unless the life insurance is considered an income-producing asset in the case of a gift loan, or there is a tax avoidance purpose in the case of a corporation-employee or corporation-stockholder loan.

Low Interest Rate Loans. However, while interest-free loans are generally not allowable, today's low interest rate environment lends itself to use of loans as a planning tool. One of the more common estate planning transactions today is the sale of assets to an "intentionally defective trust" using loans at the "applicable federal rate ('AFR')." See a discussion of Intentially Defective Trust planning on page 74. Loan regime split dollar to shareholder-employees or key non-shareholder employees is also a popular and effective employee benefit in a low interest rate environment.

IRA DISTRIBUTION PLANNING

Funds cannot be kept in an IRA indefinitely. Eventually they must be distributed. Effective distribution planning requires a careful consideration of both tax and nontax issues. The first and most important consideration should be the owner's need for income. If funds are required before age 59½, the early distribution penalty tax must be avoided. If funds are left to accumulate after age 70½, the 50 percent excise tax on undistributed minimum required distributions must be avoided. And finally, selection of beneficiaries not only determines those individuals who will inherit the IRA, but how and when the IRA will be subject to income taxation.

Early Distribution Penalty Tax

Distributions prior to the owner's age 59½ are subject to an additional 10 percent early distribution penalty tax, unless an exception applies (see pages 405 and 535). With a SIMPLE IRA, early distributions within two years of beginning participation are subject to a 25 percent penalty tax (see page 548). Beneficiaries of inherited IRAs are not subject to this tax.

Required Minimum Distributions

Distributions that are less than the required minimum are subject to a 50 percent excise tax (i.e., it is levied on any amount not distributed as required). The amount and timing of these distributions will vary, and is dependent upon a number of factors, including the attained age of the owner, when the owner dies, the existence of a surviving spouse or designated beneficiaries, and the ages of these individuals. Roth IRA owners are generally not subject to these distribution requirements during their lifetimes (and are treated as dying before their RBD, see below). (See page 527.)

Owner during lifetime. The owner of a traditional IRA must start receiving distributions by April 1 of the year following the owner's attaining age 70½. This date is referred to as the required beginning date (RBD). Although this first distribution can be delayed, distributions for the second and future years must be made by December 31 (e.g., two distributions would have to be made in a single year if the first distribution was not made until April 1). If the IRA owner dies after reaching age 70½, but before April 1 of the next year, no distribution is required (i.e., death occurred before the RBD).

The amount of the required minimum distribution (RMD) is calculated by dividing the IRA account balance at the end of the previous year by the life expectancy of the IRA owner and another person. This is also referred to as the applicable distribution period, or the RMD factor.

(continued on next page)

IRA DISTRIBUTION PLANNING (continued)

For example, assume that an IRA owner is age seventy-five and has an account balance of $100,000. The RMD uniform lifetime table on page 595 provides an RMD factor of 22.9. The required minimum distribution is $4,367 (100,000 ÷ 22.9 = 4,367). This table is used when the owner is alive, and there is no designated beneficiary or the designated beneficiary is either: (1) a spouse not more than ten years younger than the owner; or (2) a nonspouse beneficiary of any age. Under the incidental benefit rule, this table treats a nonspouse beneficiary as no more than ten years younger than the IRA owner, thereby assuring that distributions are primarily for the benefit of the IRA owner.

When the owner is alive, and a spouse more than ten years younger than the owner is the sole beneficiary, then the RMD joint and last survivor table can be used (see Appendix F of *Tax Facts on Insurance & Employee Benefits (2018)*). Use of this table is particularly helpful if the spouse is substantially younger than the IRA owner (i.e., a longer joint life expectancy reduces the amount of the annual required minimum distribution). For example, assume that an IRA owner age seventy-five is married to a spouse age forty-five, and the account balance is $100,000. The RMD factor from this table is 39.2, and the required minimum distribution is $2,551 (100,000 ÷ 39.2 = 2,551).

Surviving spouse as beneficiary. A surviving spouse who is the sole primary beneficiary of the deceased's IRA can either:

1. Elect to be *designated as the account owner* of the IRA (or use a "spousal rollover" to transfer assets to the spouse's traditional IRA). This allows for using the surviving spouse's age in determining required minimum distributions, and for the naming of new designated beneficiaries (i.e., the so-called "stretch IRA," see page 413). However, if withdrawn by a surviving spouse under age 59½, these funds may be subject to the 10 percent early distribution penalty tax (a spouse who remains a beneficiary is not subject to this tax), or
2. Remain a *beneficiary* of the IRA, with the following results:
    a. Distributions must generally be taken over the surviving spouse's lifetime (using the single life expectancy of the spouse). The first distribution must be made by the end of the year following the owner's death.
    b. If the IRA owner dies *on* or *after* the RBD, the life expectancy of the owner can be used for any year if it is greater than the spouse's life expectancy.

Non-spouse as beneficiary. Distributions to a designated beneficiary (see definition on page 413) are determined by whether the IRA owner dies before the required beginning date (RBD):

(continued on next page)

IRA DISTRIBUTION PLANNING (continued)

1. If the owner dies *before* the RBD, distributions must be made using the beneficiary's life expectancy under the RMD single life table (see Appendix F of *Tax Facts on Insurance & Employee Benefits (2018)*). This life expectancy is determined by using the beneficiary's age in the year following the owner's death, reduced by one for each year after the year of death. For example, assume the owner died in 2010 and the beneficiary was age fifty in 2011. Using the single life table, the factor is 34.2 in 2011, 33.2 in 2012, and 32.2 in 2013 (applying the subtract-one method).

2. If the owner dies *on* or *after* the RBD, distributions are generally based upon the longer of:

   a. The life expectancy of the *beneficiary* under the RMD single life table, or
   b. The life expectancy of the *owner* under the RMD single life table using the owner's age as of his or her birthday in the year of death, reduced by one for each year after the year of death.

No designated beneficiary. Distributions are again determined by whether the IRA owner dies before the required beginning date (RBD):

1. If the owner dies *before* the RBD, distributions must be made under the five-year rule. The entire account must be distributed by the end of the fifth year (sixth year, if 2009 is one of the five years) after the owner's death, but no distribution is required before then.

2. If the owner dies *on* or *after* the RBD, distributions continue to made based upon the life expectancy of the owner under the RMD single life table using the owner's age as of his or her birthday in the year of death, reduced by one for each year after the year of death.

Trust as beneficiary. A trust cannot technically be a designated beneficiary for RMD purposes, but the oldest beneficiary of a trust will be treated as the designated beneficiary if the trust meets certain specific requirements. (This is commonly known as a "see-through" trust, see page 541.) If the trust fails to meet these requirements, then distributions must be made under the five-year rule. Before making a trust the beneficiary of an IRA, the advice of qualified counsel should be sought.

Designated beneficiary. This is the individual (or certain trusts) who is designated to receive the IRA proceeds by the terms of the IRA document. Generally, the designated beneficiary will be determined as of September 30 of the calendar year following the year of the owner's death.

LEGAL EXPENSE BENEFIT

Given our litigious society, it is hardly surprising that the legal expense benefit has grown in popularity as an employee benefit. Intended to provide affordable access to legal services, these benefits are referred to as "legal service plans," "prepaid legal services," and "discount legal plans." Plans providing legal expense benefits are offered in a variety of forms, including legal referral networks, prepayment plans, and indemnity plans.

Prepayment plans are similar in concept to HMOs, and provide for services from specific groups of lawyers employed by or under contract to the plan, specific lists of attorneys, or attorneys of choice. Less common are indemnity plans that provide benefits by reimbursing employees for specific legal services, with reimbursements limited to flat amounts, hourly rates, and maximum annual benefits.

Benefits are provided on either a comprehensive or scheduled basis. Plans providing comprehensive benefits typically provide full legal services, with specific services excluded. More common are plans providing only scheduled services. Typical of all plans is their emphasis on preventative law.

A variety of services are available. Most plans offer telephone consultations, document review, phone calls on the client's behalf, letter writing, and contract review. While many services are available without limit, limits are likely to be placed on some services (e.g., contract review limited to ten pages; trial preparation and representation limited to seventy-five hours of attorney time). Excess time is typically charged at reduced rates.

Covered are family law matters such as divorce, adoption, child custody, will services, and estate planning; property rights such as real estate and probate matters; IRS audit representation; and trial defense on civil matters. Criminal defense work is excluded, except for moving vehicle violations and work-related criminal charges. Generally no coverage is provided for plaintiff actions, and virtually all nonunion plans specifically exclude actions against the sponsoring employer.

In evaluating a plan, it is important to determine the availability of attorneys, as well as the specific services offered (e.g., attorneys may not be available for face-to-face consultations, or appointments may be difficult to get).

Most plans are enrolled by payroll deduction, with the individual employee paying for his or her share of plan costs. These costs are not deductible, but the benefits are tax-free. If the plan is paid for by the employer, the costs are deductible by the employer, provided the employee's total compensation is reasonable. Although the employee must include in income his or her prorata share of these costs, any benefits received are tax-free.

LEVERAGED BENEFIT

The "best" type of fringe benefit is one that is not taxable to the employee, or at least not currently taxable, yet currently deductible by the employer. Because of this favorable tax treatment, it can be considered a leveraged benefit.

For example, assume that in 2018 an *employee* in a 25 percent marginal tax bracket is in need of $30,000 of additional life insurance protection and is presently receiving only $20,000 of group term coverage. If insurance were individually purchased by the employee for $200, the employer could pay for the benefit by giving the employee a salary of $267 ($200 ÷ .75 = $267). The tax cost of the additional salary of $267 is $67, leaving the employee with $200 to pay the insurance premium. Assuming an *employer* in a 21 percent marginal tax bracket, the after-tax cost to the employer of the salary increase is $211 ($267 × .79 = $211).

To provide a leveraged benefit, the employer could increase the group term coverage by $30,000, which would be tax-free to the employee. Assuming this would cost the employer $200, the after-tax cost of providing the same benefit to the employee is now only $158 ($200 × .79 = $158). The employee gets the needed $30,000 of additional life insurance protection, but the employer has saved $53 by using a leveraged benefit.

Other leveraged benefits include physical examinations, increased mileage allowances, medical expense reimbursement, and employer paid premiums for disability income insurance.

LIFE INSURANCE COST BASIS

Life insurance is being looked upon more and more as a tax-efficient investment for supplemental retirement income. LIRP (see pages 429-430), or sometimes referred to as Life Insurance in Retirement Planning, has become a standard retirement planning strategy. In addition to the purchase of life insurance as a supplement retirement strategy – the life settlement industry (see pages 447-448) has become an accepted industry with thousands of inforce life insurance policies being sold each year.

Most agents and tax advisors recognize that life insurance cash values grow on an income tax deferred basis and that death benefits are ordinarily received income and estate tax free. Most advisors also understand that withdrawals from a policy during life are tax-free up to the policy's tax-basis. Likewise, most advisors recognize that an ordinarily gain is generally recognized on the disposition of a life insurance policy on an amount equal to the excess of the amount received (in cash or boot – such as extinguishment of debt) over cost basis (see pages 421-422). However, how to calculate policy cost basis is not universally understood. And, in fact, basis calculation seems to be subject to different interpretations by different carriers. Moreover, based on the limited tax authority available – basis seems to be calculated differently when a policy is sold to a buyer lacking insurable interest (i.e., a settlement company).

Ordinarily, the starting point for determining cost basis is premiums paid. However, that is only a starting point. Premium payments attributed to "supplemental benefits" such as waiver of premium on disability, double indemnity, accidental death protection, and disability income are probably not included in cost basis. Also subtracted from premiums paid to arrive at cost basis are cash dividends and dividends used to purchase riders. But, dividends used to purchase paid-up additional insurance ("paid up ads") or reduce premiums do not reduce cost basis.

Compounding the difficulty in determining the cost basis of a life insurance policy are deficiencies in life insurance carrier administration systems. For starters, a large number of life insurance policies are issued as a Section 1035 like-kind exchange (see page 563). Ordinarily, when a policy is issued as a 1035 Exchange, the carrier will simply start with the transferred policy's cash value as the beginning basis of the new policy or they will actually ask the policyholder what the basis was in the old policy. Obviously, neither of these approaches is likely to create an accurate cost-basis in the new policy. And, even for policies not purchased as part of a 1035 Exchange, carrier administration systems often make assumptions and interpretations of law that are sometimes not accurate.

Further complicating a discussion of life insurance cost basis is Revenue Ruling 2009-13 and the IRS position on policies sold as life settlements. In this Ruling, the IRS held that the cost basis in the life insurance policy must be reduced by the portion of the premium allocable to the cost of insurance ("COI"). In this Ruling, taxpayer had paid premiums totaling $64,000 and had not received any distributions or loans from the policy. The policy cash surrender value was $78,000.

(continued on next page)

LIFE INSURANCE COST BASIS (continued)

Taxpayer received $80,000 from the settlement company. Most would have assumed that the gain would be $16,000 (the amount received less the amount of the premiums paid). If the policy had been surrendered, it is a near certainty that the life insurance carrier would have reported the gain as $14,000 (cash surrender value less premiums paid). However, the IRS ruled in this case that the gain was $26,000. It found that the "cost of insurance" charges had been $10,000 so it reduced cumulative premiums by this amount in arriving at a cost-basis of $54,000 ($80,000 received less adjusted basis of $54,000 was $26,000 gain). Further complicating the result was that the IRS held that the first $14,000 was ordinary income (the amount that would have been recognized on surrender) and the balance was a capital gain.

The 2017 Tax Act modified the taxation of life insrance policies sold. Retroactively to transactions entered into after August 25, 2009, no adjustment is made for mortality, expense, or other reasonable charges (presumably including "cost of insurance" or "mortality"). This would negate (retroactively) Rev. Rul 2009-13. Taxpayers who reported taxation based on this ruling should consider amending their returns for open policy years.

Policy loans can also confuse the determination of cost basis. A loan from a life insurance policy not classified as a modified endorsement contract, or MEC (See pages 423-424), is not included in income because it is not treated as a distribution under IRC Section 72. Hence, if the loan is still outstanding when the policy is surrendered or allowed to lapse, the borrowed amount becomes taxable at that time to the extent the cash value exceeds the owner's basis in the contract as if the borrowed amount was actually received at the time of surrender or lapse and used to pay off the loan. An internal policy loan is treated as a reduction in cost-basis for purposes of determining future gain when a withdrawal, surrender, or lapse takes place. A loan received from a MEC is treated as a withdrawal from the policy.

Determination of cost basis is a complicated matter. It's important to know what the insurance company will report before surrendering a policy or taking a withdrawal. The gain on the policy may also be different if it is sold than if it is allowed to lapse or surrender. It's important to consult a qualified tax advisor.

LIFE INSURANCE DEFAULT RISK

Life insurance default risk refers to the possibility that an insurance company might default on its obligations to individual policyholders. The near financial meltdown of the banking industry of the first decade of the twenty-first century, and its subsequent potential spillover into the insurance industry, is likely to have made the life insurance purchaser far more aware of this risk (see Insurance Company Ratings, page 427).

Life insurance companies are subject to strict regulation by state regulatory agencies. This regulation includes conservative accounting rules, mandatory annual CPA audits, minimum capital/surplus requirements, and investment regulations/limitations. As a result, in down-market cycles life insurance companies are better positioned to handle greater losses than other companies in the financial sector, and thus better able to maintain adequate reserves to cover their financial obligations to policyholders. That said, life insurance and annuity products with lengthy guaranty provisions can put considerable financial stress on the companies that issue them in times of extended low interest rates which reduce returns on the general account.

If an insurance company does become financially unstable the insurance department in its home state takes control of the company in a "receivership process." The first step in this process involves an attempt to *rehabilitate* the company by improving its financial status. Sale of the distressed company is often brokered to a stronger company that assumes policyholder obligations. If rehabilitation is not successful, then the company is declared insolvent and the receivership process moves into the *liquidation* stage. Here the receiver attempts to maximize the company's assets in order to pay off as many creditors as possible, including individual policyholders who are given priority over other creditors.

Insolvent insurance companies frequently do not have enough funds to meet their obligations to policyholders. When this occurs state guarantee associations provide policyholders with benefits up to specified limits. The amount varies from state to state, but most states provide at least $100,000 in cash surrender or withdrawal values for life insurance and $300,000 in life insurance death benefits (a quick link to each individual state association website is available by going to www.nolhga.com/policyholderinfo/main.cfm/location/ga). Unfortunately, 100 percent of policyholder benefits are not covered in full, particularly as to high-dollar policies.

It is important to distinguish between separate account products and general account products. Assets backing variable products such as variable life insurance, are held in separate accounts that are insulated from the general creditors of the company. In contrast, assets backing fixed products, such as whole life and universal life insurance, are held in the company's *general* account, which is subject to the claims of all the creditors of the insurance company. (The general account also backs guaranteed death benefits and other available riders and endorsements.) Although this credit-risk exposure may be low, it nevertheless exists. Now, more than ever, it is important to consider the ratings of the issuing carrier as an essential part of the life insurance purchase process (see Insurance Company Ratings on page 427).

LIFE INSURANCE IN QUALIFIED PLANS

Qualified plans can offer an attractive way of using pretax dollars to purchase life insurance for the benefit of plan participants. In pension plans the plan trustee determines to purchase life insurance as a plan asset; plan participants do not have the power to direct plan investments. In defined contribution plans, such as profit sharing and 401(k) plans, each participant has the ability to elect to purchase life insurance with part of his or her account (e.g., from a self-directed account). Qualification rules do not require that all employees actually purchase life insurance. Discrimination against non-highly compensated employees is prohibited and if life insurance benefits are available to the highly compensated employees they must be available to all employees. Generally, the plan trustee is named owner and beneficiary of the life insurance policy.

Amount of insurance. Pension plans exist primarily to provide retirement benefits and profit sharing plans are primarily plans of deferred compensation. When these plans provide life insurance coverage for plan participants the life insurance must be an "incidental benefit" under the plan. This incidental benefit limitation is satisfied if the cost of providing a current life insurance benefit is less than 25 percent of the cost of providing all the benefits under the plan (both deferred and current). Staying within either of the following will satisfy this incidental benefit limitation:

1. The death benefit is no more than 100 times the expected monthly retirement benefit, or
2. At all times over the life of the plan total premiums paid for the insurance death benefit are less than the following percentages of total funds allocated to that participant:

   50 percent - for ordinary life insurance or variable life insurance

   25 percent - for term life insurance or universal life insurance

These limits may be used by any type of plan, although the "100 times" limit has typically been used by defined benefit plans and the "percentage limit" by defined contribution plans (e.g., profit sharing plans). See table, Types Of Qualified Retirement Plans, on page 512.

Profit sharing plans are an exception to these limits. There is no limit on the amount of life insurance that may be purchased with trust funds that have accumulated for two or more years, provided the plan requires that only such funds can be used to purchase life insurance (i.e., the "seasoned money" concept). Individual retirement accounts are prohibited from owning life insurance.

Premiums. With a defined benefit plan the additional cost associated with the purchase of life insurance increases the total amount deductible as a plan contribution (i.e., the cost of life insurance is on top of the maximum funding limits). In contrast, with a defined contribution

(continued on next page)

LIFE INSURANCE IN QUALIFIED PLANS (continued)

plan premiums are paid from the participant's account without increasing the annual additions limit (in 2018, the lesser of 100 percent of compensation, or $55,000).

Insured. Insurance is generally provided on the life of the plan participant for family protection or estate needs. However, in profit sharing plans where life insurance is purchased in self-directed accounts, insurance may be purchased on the lives of third parties (e.g., a spouse for family protection, a business partner to fund a buy/sell agreement, or a survivorship life policy on both the participant and spouse for estate liquidity needs).

Taxation. Each year the plan participant must include in income the economic value of the current life insurance protection (i.e., death benefit less cash values, if any). This includable cost is calculated using the lower of (a) the Table 2001 rates on page 596, or (b) the insurer's published rates for initial issue one-year term for standard risks. Except for owner-employees of unincorporated businesses, the cumulative value of these taxable amounts constitutes the participant's "basis" in the contract. (This can be a substantial benefit for the highly rated individual who reports an economic benefit based upon standard rates.) If the insured dies while the policy is held within the plan, the death benefit in excess of the policy's cash value (the amount "at risk") is received by the beneficiary free of income taxes. The remaining distribution, reduced by the participant's basis in the contract, is taxed as a qualified plan distribution. Death benefits from a qualified plan are generally includable in a decedent's estate for federal estate tax purposes, under the theory that the participant has an "incidents of ownership" in the policy (see page 374). Account values payable at death to a named beneficiary are classified as income in respect of a decedent and are subject to both income and estate taxes (see page 403).

Disposition of policy. If the insured does not die prior to retirement, the life insurance policy must be either surrendered, distributed, or sold. In making transfers from the plan to third parties, it is important to fall within the parameters set forth in Prohibited Transaction Exemption 92-6 (e.g., sold for "fair market value"). To avoid current income taxation, a policy with cash values may be sold to the insured and then passed by gift from the insured to a third party. If estate taxation is a concern, the policy may be sold directly to an irrevocable life insurance trust established by the insured (see chart, page 55). Provided this trust is considered a grantor trust, this sale would not violate the transfer for value rules (see discussions on pages 393 and 568-569).

See also, the fully insured 412(e)(3) plan, pages 276-279.

LIFE INSURANCE POLICY LOANS

The cash value of a life insurance contact generally grows free of income taxation. If paid at death as part of the death benefit, it avoids taxation at death. Not only can cash be taken out of the policy in an amount equal to cost-basis without taxation, but a policy loan in excess of basis is not included in income provided the policy is not a modified endowment contract (MEC).[1]

However, cash values of a life insurance policy are potentially subject to income taxes when there is a withdrawal from the policy, surrender of the policy, or transfer of the policy. When received, the cash values are taxed under the "cost recovery rules" meaning that such amounts are included in gross income only to the extent they exceed the investment in the policy (e.g., cash surrender values of $1,000 and total premiums of $600 would result in a $400 taxable gain, assuming no dividends and no prior distributions from the policy). Despite the very powerful tax advantages offered by life insurance, it is important to remember the events that can trigger taxation.

Section 1035 Exchanges

Generally, a "1035 exchange" is a tax-free exchange. A life insurance policy can be exchanged for another life insurance policy, an endowment contract or an annuity. An endowment contract can be exchanged for another endowment contract or an annuity. Whereas, an annuity contract can only be exchanged for another annuity contract.[2] But, when a life insurance policy has a policy loan on it – caution must be taken when entering into a 1035 exchange.

In many instances, the easiest approach is to pay off the policy loan with outside funds prior to the exchange. Repayment of the loan will not result in a taxable event. If it isn't practical to repay the loan, often times the safest approach is to simply carry the loan over to the new policy. Today, life insurance policy loan provisions are generally more consumer friendly than they were years ago. It isn't uncommon to be able to considerably reduce the interest rate by exchanging policies. If the insured is in good health, doing a 1035 exchange into a new policy with a reduction in loan interest rate by even a couple of percentage points can make a big difference.

If an existing loan is carried over to the new policy on a 1035 exchange, the owner will not recognize any income on the exchange. The cost basis on the new policy will equal the basis in the old policy plus any additional premiums paid with respect to the new policy.[3] But, if the policy loan had been repaid shortly before or shortly after the exchange, the loan amount will be considered "boot" received in the exchange and thus will not be deferred under IRC Section 1035.[4] Thus, in the example above, the taxpayer would recognize gain of $200 and have a basis of $700 on the new policy.[5]

If there is a sufficient time gap between the repayment of the loan and the 1035 exchange, the payoff value of the loan will not be deemed boot and will have no effect on the tax-free nature of the 1035 exchange.[6] The basis of the new contract would be $500 in this example if the repayment from policy cash surrender value was made after a sufficient period of time.[7]

(continued on next page)

---

1 See Life Insurance Premium Limitations at page 423-424.

2 See Tax Free Exchanges at page 563.

3 See IRS regulation Sect. 1.1031.(d)(2). Assume that a policy has a gross cash surrender value of $1,000, an outstanding loan balance of $200, and a basis of $700. Assume that the policy is exchanged for a new policy (with no additional premiums). The basis of the new policy will be $700 and the new policy will have a carry-over loan of $200. No taxation results from this exchange.

4 There is no clear law on what constitutes repayment of a loan "shortly" before or after an exchange. Some life insurance companies treat repayment from policy cash values within six months after the 1035 Exchange as boot. Other companies use a year as a benchmark. Six months and twelve months are also generally regarded as the benchmark for repayment from cash values prior to the exchange.

5 The calculation is as follows: (a) $800 value of new policy + (b) $200 boot (loan payoff value) = (c) $1,000 total consideration received. $1,000 consideration received less $700 cost basis = $300 gain realized. Therefore, the gain is recognized to the extent of the boot received or $200. The new policy would have a $700 basis.

6 If the policy loan is repaid through a partial surrender of the policy within the first fifteen years, there may be a recapture tax under IRC Section 7702.

7 The calculation is as follows: (a) $800 value of the new policy – (b) $500 basis ($700 less $200 cash value used to repay loan) = (c) $300 gain realized AND deferred. The basis of the new contract would be $500.

LIFE INSURANCE POLICY LOANS (continued)

Gift of Policy with Outstanding Loan

Ordinarily, the recipient of a gifted life insurance contract takes the basis of the policy at the time of the transfer (ie., carry-over basis). But, if a policy is given away with a loan – it is deemed to be a part sale/part gift transaction. The value of the loan is treated as consideration received (ie., the sale portion). The fair market value of the policy[1] is deemed to be the gift portion.

For example, if the policy has a value of $1,000 with an outstanding loan of $400 and a basis of $600 the transaction would not result in realized or recognized gain. $400 is the amount received (boot) – which is less than the $600 basis. The policy would have a carry-over $600 basis in the hands of the donee. On the other hand, if the loan was $800 – the gift would result in a $200 gain recognized by the donor ($800 boot less $600 basis). The $800 deemed paid by the donee would be the donee's new basis.[2]

Although a gift of a policy to an irrevocable trust could trigger taxation under these rules, most irrevocable trusts are taxed as grantor trusts. If the trust is a grantor trust – the transfer is ignored for income tax purposes and the gain is avoided.[3]

It is also common for policyholders with large loans to make gifts of policies to charity. When the policy is on the verge of lapsing because of the loans – rather than repaying the loan the policyholder believes that they can get out from under the loan by giving the policy to a charity. To the surprise of taxpayers – this strategy can result in unexpected taxation. And, also in many instances – the taxpayer is surprised to learn that the value of the policy for charitable income tax deduction purposes is limited to the lesser of cost basis or fair market value.[4]

In summary, it is rather uncommon to have taxation of cash value in a life insurance contract. But, when considering disposition of a policy with an outstanding loan – it is important to understand the rules governing loan encumbered policies.

---

1 See Valuation of Life Insurance at page 577. The method for determining the fair market value of a life insurance policy is not as clear as one would expect. Although cash surrender value is often assumed to be the fair market value of a life insurance policy – it is probably more likely that the IRS would look to the policy's reserve value (Interpolated terminal reserve on a whole life product and tax reserve value on other policies).

2 Not only can the gift of the policy cause taxation – but the gift of the policy can create a situation where the policy death benefit becomes taxable under the transfer for value rule. Under Treas. Reg. Sect. 1.1014-4, in the case of a part gift/part sale, such as the gift of a life insurance policy with an outstanding loan, the basis in the hands of the donee would be determined by reference to how much the donee is deemed to have paid for the policy (ie., the amount of the loan) and not with reference to the donor's basis. Because the basis is NOT determined by reference to the donor's basis, the carry-over basis exception of IRC Sect. 101(a) does not apply to this gift of the policy. See also PLR 891056. As a result – if the loan exceeds the basis you have a transfer for value that will cause the amount of the death benefit in excess of cost basis to be taxable unless there is an exception to the transfer for value rule. See Transfer for Value at pages 568-569.

3 See Rev. Rul. 85-13 (a transfer from a grantor to a grantor trust is ignored for income tax purposes as a transfer to oneself). See also 2017-13 (a transfer to a grantor trust is deemed to be a direct transfer to the grantor – which is an exception to the transfer for value). See Taxation of Grantor Trusts at pages 74-77.

4 For example, assume that the policy's fair market value is $1,000, the loan is $800 and the basis is $600. In a gift to charity (treated as a part sale/part gift) the basis is allocated between the sale portion and gift portion. The sale portion (ie., the boot – loan) is 80 percent of the allocation and, hence, $480 of the basis is allocated to the sale and $120 allocated to the gift portion. The contribution will result in $320 of taxable gain to the donor ($800 boot in form of loan forgiveness reduced by $480 basis). The charitable deduction will be limited to $120 (the lesser of basis or fair market value). By making a charitable gift of the policy – the donor may end up with a net tax liability.

LIFE INSURANCE PREMIUM LIMITATIONS

TAMRA limitations. Under TAMRA (Technical and Miscellaneous Revenue Act) a life insurance contract issued on or after June 21, 1988, is subject to being classified as a modified endowment contract (MEC) if cumulative premiums paid during the first seven contract years exceed the sum of "net level premiums" (the seven-pay test). Net level premiums are determined by each carrier and reflect the premiums required to pay up the contract during the first seven years using guaranteed mortality costs and interest rates. Distributions from a MEC are subject to "gain first" taxation to the extent there is gain in the contract (i.e., cash values exceed investment in the contract). Such distributions include withdrawals, loans, and use of the policy as collateral for a loan. Generally, the investment in the contract is the sum of premiums paid, less dividends received, plus prior taxable loans (but not prior taxable withdrawals).

Additionally, a 10-percent-penalty tax is imposed on amounts includable in gross income if the distribution is made prior to the contract owner's attaining age 59½, unless the owner is disabled or receives the cash values under a life annuity settlement option. However, the penalty tax is always applicable if the contract owner is a "non-natural person" (e.g., a corporation)

For example, assume that the "net level premium" for a particular contract is $2,500 and the following payment plans are being considered:

	Cumulative Net	Plan A		Plan B	
Year	Level Premium	Annual	Cumulative	Annual	Cumulative
1	2,500	2,000	2,000	2,500	2,500
2	5,000	1,000	3,000	2,500	5,000
3	**7,500**	1,500	4,500	3,000	**8,000**
4	10,000	5,500	10,000	2,000	10,000

Plan A is not a MEC, since at no time did the cumulative amount paid exceed the cumulative net level premiums. However, Plan B became a MEC in year 3, since the cumulative amount paid ($8,000) exceeded the allowable cumulative net level premium ($7,500). In summary, a policy owner can "catch up" after falling behind, but he cannot "get ahead" by paying premiums in advance.

Now assume premiums are paid according to Plan B, and at the end of year 4 the cash values are $11,000. A withdrawal of $2,500 would result in a taxable gain of $1,000, since there is gain of $1,000 in the contract (cash values of $11,000 less cumulative premiums of $10,000).

(continued on next page)

LIFE INSURANCE PREMIUM LIMITATIONS (continued)

Once a contract becomes a MEC, it forever stays a MEC (except for limited opportunities given insurance companies to correct procedural errors). In addition, even though a contract is "grandfathered" because it was issued prior to June 21, 1988, it can become a MEC if a "material change" occurs with respect to its benefits or terms. Since it is very broadly defined, virtually any alteration in benefits is likely to be treated as a material change, except for death benefit increases of up to $150,000 (or cost of living increases tied to a broad-based index). Potential material changes can occur when: (1) exchanging an old contract for a new contract; (2) converting term insurance to permanent cash value insurance; (3) adding a new insured to the contract; and (4) increasing the death benefit voluntarily. Contracts issued after June 21, 1988, are also subject to the material change rules.

While it is important to be aware of the potential adverse tax implications of TAMRA, there will be no adverse effect if: (1) the contract was issued prior to June 21, 1988; (2) the death proceeds are the only payments received under the contract; (3) the premium payments do not exceed the seven-pay limits; or (4) the only payment received is pursuant to a complete surrender of the contract after age 59½.

DEFRA limitations. In contrast to TAMRA, it is ***absolutely essential*** to comply with the guideline premium and corridor test or meet the cash value accumulation test of DEFRA (Deficit Reduction Act). A failure to abide by these limitations will produce disastrous tax results since the contract will immediately lose its status as life insurance, all cash value increases will be subject to current income taxation, and the death benefit will be taxed as ordinary income (to the extent it exceeds cumulative net premiums paid).

For example, assume Plan A is being tested for DEFRA compliance:

	TAMRA	DEFRA		Plan A	
	Cumulative	Guideline	Cumulative		
Year	Net Level	Single	Annual	Annual	Cumulative
1	2,500	9,000	1,000	2,000	2,000
2	5,000		2,000	1,000	3,000
3	7,500		3,000	1,500	4,500
4	10,000		4,000	5,500	10,000

In year 4, Plan A violates both DEFRA guideline premium tests. Under this test the cumulative annual premiums cannot exceed either the greater of: (1) the guideline single premium ($9,000); or (2) the guideline cumulative annual premiums ($1,000 per year). Although the cumulative annual premiums were exceeded beginning year 1, Plan A cumulative premiums fell within the guideline single premium ($9,000) until year 4.

LIFE INSURANCE RATINGS AGENCIES

The life insurance industry has been remarkably solid over the years. Insurance companies are heavily regulated by state insurance commissioners and are required to hold considerable reserves to protect their abilities to pay claims. In addition, many larger insurance companies are publicly traded so, in addition to regulation by state insurance commissioners, these companies are governed by federal agencies as a publicly traded corporation.

Historically, in the rare instances when life insurance carriers have experienced financial difficulties, other carriers have typically stepped in and acquired the struggling company or their in-force block of policies. As a result of heavy state and (sometimes) federal regulations, combined with insurance industry leaders protecting the industry by acquiring distressed companies and policies, the insurance industry has done a remarkably good job of paying insurance claims.

Despite the industry's strong record of solvency and honoring claims, it is important to note that state guaranty associations provide only limited protection to their residents. The maximum death benefits protected by these state guarantee funds often fall short of the coverage that a family should buy. In fact, death benefits are protected only up to $300,000 in many states, so consumers with larger policies could be left out in the cold. Moreover, many states provide only $100,000 coverage for cash surrender or withdrawal value of permanent policies and annuities.

As previously noted, before state guaranty fund payouts kick in, regulators will try to rehabilitate, sell, or liquidate the company. If that happens, you could see an acquiring company adjust your coverage by increasing the premium or otherwise making the terms less favorable. Moreover, if you die while your carrier is in state receivership or liquidation, the payment of benefits, up to state limits, could even be delayed.

Despite the insurance industry's strong track record of paying claims, there are real risks associated with a long-term obligation like life insurance. For this reason, it remains important to consider the size, ratings, and stability of the company issuing your policy. Not surprisingly, you sometimes see lower premium costs and aggressive policy features from carriers with lower ratings. In essence, the insured (and his or her beneficiary) is paying less in exchange for accepting a degree of solvency risk. When purchasing life insurance protection, it isn't enough to simply "spreadsheet" premium costs. Consideration of policy features and flexibility is important – as is consideration of the stability of the issuing company. Reviewing carrier financial statements can be an important means of determining carrier financial strength, but obtaining third party rating agency summaries is probably the easiest and most widely used method of evaluating claims paying ability.

(continued on next page)

LIFE INSURANCE RATINGS AGENCIES (continued)

The following page introduces you to A.M. Best, Standard & Poor's, Moody's, and Fitch. These ratings agencies are generally regarded as the leaders in evaluating claims paying ability. Although the various agencies generally look at similar information and seek to make similar assessments – it is generally wise to consider multiple ratings when making your evaluation of carrier strength. Page 428 shows you select ratings for a number of the larger life insurance companies. Ratings are not the only important consideration when selecting a life insurance company, but they can help you reach an informed decision regarding policy selection or retention. We also provide a chart below with many of the largest life insurers in the United States along with each companies' ratings by the various agencies.

(continued on next page)

LIFE INSURANCE RATINGS AGENCIES (continued)

INSURANCE COMPANY RATINGS

Rating Categories[1]	A.M. Best[2]	S&P[3]	Moody's[4]	Fitch[5]
Superior	A++ A+	AAA	Aaa	AAA
Excellent	A A–	AA[6]	Aa[7]	AA[6] A[6]
Good	B++ B+	A[6]	A[7]	
Fair (Adequate)	B B–	BBB[6]	Baa[7]	BBB[6]
Marginal	C++ C+	BB[6]	Ba[7]	BB[6]
Weak	C C–	B[6]	B[7]	B[6]
Poor (Below Standards)	D	CCC CC	Caa[7] Ca C	CCC[6] CC, C
Failed	E[8], F[9]	D[10]		

[1] The comparative distribution of rating categories is approximate. Therefore, the ratings definitions of each agency should be consulted. The basic mission of all of these independent agencies is to assess an insurer's financial strength in terms of its ability to meet policyholder and other contractual obligations, and to communicate those findings to the financial and investment communities. Due diligence requires not just a determination of the assigned rating, but an understanding of how each rating agency determines its published ratings.

[2] A.M. Best's Financial Strength Rating provides an independent opinion of an insurer's financial strength and ability to meet its ongoing insurance policy and contract obligations (has rated insurers since 1899).

[3] Standard & Poor's (S&P) publishes Insurer Financial Strength Ratings (has rated debt issues for over fifty years and insurance companies since 1971).

[4] Moody's Insurance Financial Strength Ratings are opinions of the ability of insurance companies to repay punctually senior policyholder claims and obligations (has rated bond issues since 1904 and insurers since the 1970s).

[5] Fitch, Inc. publishes National Insurer Financial Strength Ratings. Ratings below AAA and above CC may be appended with a "+"or "–" to indicate relative position within the rating category.

[6] Includes three levels of ratings (i.e., AA–, AA, AA+; A–, A, A+; BBB–, BBB, BBB+; BB–, BB, BB+; B–, B, B+; CCC–, CCC, CCC+; D–, D, D+; E–, E, E+).

[7] Includes three levels of ratings (i.e., Aa1, Aa2, Aa3; A1, A2, A3; Baa1, Baa2, Baa3; Ba1, Ba2, Ba3; B1, B2, B3; Caa1, Caa2, Caa3).

[8] Under regulatory supervision.

[9] In liquidation.

[10] Payment default on financial commitments.

(continued on next page)

LIFE INSURANCE RATINGS AGENCIES (continued)

TOP LIFE INSURER RATINGS PROFILE[1]

	A.M. Best	S&P	Moody's	Fitch
Northwestern Mutual	A++	AA+	Aaa	AAA
New York Life	A++	AA+	Aaa	AAA
Lincoln National Life Insurance Company	A+	AA−	A1	A+
Transamerica	A+	AA−	A1	AA−
State Farm Life	A++	AA	Aa1	
Pacific Life	A+	A+	A1	A+
Prudential Financial	A+	AA−	A1	A+
MassMutual Financial Group	A++	AA+	Aa2	AA+
MetLife Companies	A+	AA−	Aa3	AA−
John Hancock Life Insurance Company	A+	AA−	A1	AA−
Guardian Life Ins Co of America	A++	AA+	Aa2	AA+
American General Life Companies	A	A+	A2	A+
Zurich North America	A	A	A3	
Mutual of Omaha Companies	A+	A+	A1	
Nationwide Life	A+	A+	A1	
Primerica Life Insurance	A+	AA−	A2	
Minnesota Life	A+	A+	Aa3	AA−
Banner Life Insurance Company	A+	AA−		
AXA Equitable	A+	A+	Aa3	AA−
National Life Group	A	A	A2	
NACOLAH Life (Illinois)	A+	A+		
Bankers Life and Casualty (Illinois)	B++	BBB+	Baa2	BBB
Allianz Life of NA	A	AA	A2	
Protective Life	A+	AA−	A2	A
Allstate Life	A+	A+	A1	A−
RiverSource Life Insurance Company	A+	AA−	Aa3	
Penn Mutual	A+	A+	Aa3	
Principal Life Group	A+	A+	A1	AA−
Ohio National Life Companies	A+	AA−	A1	
Gerber Life Insurance Company	A	BBB		

[1] *Source:* Limra Research, 2Q 2014.

LIFE INSURANCE IN RETIREMENT PLANNING ("LIRP")

For many people, planning for retirement has become one of their biggest financial priorities and one of their greatest financial challenges. Many people fear that Social Security and company-sponsored pension plans will not provide sufficient income for their retirement goals. As a result, they recognize the need to save as much money as possible to supplement their retirement.

Ordinarily, qualified plans such as a 401(k) (see pages 268-271) or a 403(b) (see pages 272-275) are an excellent way to save for retirement, but these plans are only available if your employer offers one. And, if offered, these plans have contribution limitations which may not meet your full savings needs. IRAs (see page 405) and Roth IRAs (see page 527) both offer additional qualified savings opportunities, but they have their own limits (dollar amounts and income levels) to participate or deduct. Ultimately you may still need to put away more money.

Despite a small reduction in the top marginal individual income tax rate from 39.6 percent to 35 percent, ordinary income and capital gains tax rates remain relatively high. In fact, because of the elination of certain deductions (especially the deduction for state and local taxes) – the 2017 Tax Act resulted in a tax increase for a significant number of taxpayers. When combined with state taxes, it isn't unusual for taxpayers in high-tax states to have a marginal income tax rate approaching or exceeding 50 percent.

To avoid (or at least defer) these high marginal tax rates on monies intended for retirement, people are often looking for ways to help them supplement their retirement savings after they have fully funded their available qualified plans and IRAs. For these people, life insurance may be a solution. During your working years, the life insurance policy death benefit can protect your family and replace income that would otherwise be lost should something happen to you. At retirement, you can usually access the policy cash value via tax-favored loans and withdrawals.

Life Insurance in Retirement Planning, sometimes referred to as Life Insurance Retirement Plans, 401(k) Alternative or Supplement Income, is a simple means of self-funding your retirement needs. It is not a qualified plan and is not backed by the federal government. A LIRP arrangement simply requires the purchase of a permanent life insurance policy on your life on which you will pay the premiums with after-tax dollars.

The life insurance policy will provide a death benefit that will ordinarily be received by the beneficiary on an income tax-free basis. This can help protect a family during a client's working years. Because a permanent life insurance policy also has the potential to develop a cash value, which will grow on a tax-deferred basis, you may access any potential policy cash to supplement your retirement income via tax-favored loans and withdrawals. Life insurance offers many benefits, including the potential to increase the amount left to heirs. Because life insurance cash surrender values grow tax-deferred, the policy cash surrender values are not reduced by ordinary income or capital gains taxation.

(continued on next page)

LIFE INSURANCE IN RETIREMENT PLANNING ("LIRP") (continued)

For Example.

Jane Smith, Female, Preferred Non Smoker, Age 40, 28% Tax Bracket

Year	Approximate Annual Premium	Cumulative Amount Received from Policy	Approximate Cash Surrender Value	Approximate Death Benefit Net of Loans/ Withdrawals
1	$4,500	$0	$637	$153,650
10	$4,500	$0	$50,400	$200,500
20	$4,500	$0	$155,600	$305,600
26	$0	$20,000	$233,750	$350,650
30	$0	$100,000	$208,100	$270,650
40	$0	$300,000	$112,400	$128,300

The figures used in this case study are hypothetical, for discussion purposes only, are not guaranteed and may not be used to project or predict results. Actual results may be more or less favorable. Specific product and policy elements would be found in a policy illustration provided by an insurer. With any decision regarding the purchase of life insurance, a client would need to determine which type of life insurance product is most suitable for their specific needs.

LIFE INSURANCE AND STATE LAWS

ALABAMA

Death Benefit: Exempt from debts of owner and/or insured if payable to someone other than owner or insured whether or not the right to change the beneficiary has been reserved. [Ala. Code § 6-10-8]

Endowment and Surrender Proceeds: Cash surrender value is exempt from claim of creditors if spouse and/or children named as beneficiaries. Exempt proceeds includes death benefits, cash surrender and loan values, premiums waived and dividends. [Ala. Code § 27-14-29(c)]

Bankruptcy

Federal: Federal exemptions not available. [Ala. Code §6-10-11]

State: State exemptions same as non-bankruptcy context above. [Ala. Code §6-10-11]

ALASKA

Death Benefit: Proceeds payable to a spouse or dependent of the insured are considered "earnings" and are exempt to the extent that do not exceed $350 per week. (Amount is indexed annually for inflation) [Alaska Stat § 09.38.030(a) and (e)(4)]

Endowment and Surrender Proceeds: Unmatured annuity and life insurance contracts are exempt from creditors' claims up to $500,000. [Alaska Stat. §09.38.025]

Bankruptcy

Federal: Federal exemptions not allowed. [Alaska Stat. §09.38.055]

State: State exemptions same as non-bankruptcy context above. [Alaska Stat. §09.38.055]

ARIZONA

Death Benefit: Exempt from the debts of the owner if payable to a person other than the owner or owner's legal representatives. [Ariz. Rev. Stat. §20-1131] Proceeds made payable to a surviving spouse or child of the insured are exempt from creditors up to $20,000. [Ariz. Stat. §33-1126(a)(1)]

Endowment and Surrender Proceeds: Exempt if debtor has for a continuous unexpired period of two years, has named the insured's surviving spouse, child, parent, brother, sister or other dependent as beneficiary. [Ariz. Rev. Stat. §20-1131 and §33-1126(a)(6)]

Bankruptcy

Federal: Federal exemptions not available. [Ariz. Rev. Stat. §33-1133]

State: State exemptions same as non-bankruptcy context above. [Ariz. Rev. Stat. §33-1133]

(continued on next page)

LIFE INSURANCE AND STATE LAWS (continued)

ARKANSAS

Death Benefit: Proceeds of life insurance are exempt from claims of creditors of the insured or the beneficiary whether or not the right to change beneficiary has been reserved. [A.C.A. §23-79-131 and A.C.A. §16-66-209]

Endowment and Surrender Proceeds: Exempt but the courts have imposed a $500 exemption ceiling on life insurance benefits and policies' cash surrender value. *Federal Savings and Loan Ins. Co. v. Holt*, 894 F2d 1005 (8th Circuit 1990)

Bankruptcy

Federal: Federal exemptions are available. [A.C.A. §16-66-217]

State: State exemptions same as non-bankruptcy context which means subject to $975 limited exemption. [A.C.A. §16-66-217]

CALIFORNIA

Death Benefit: Exemption available to the extent necessary for the support of judgment debtor and spouse and dependents of debtor. [Cal. Code of Civ. Proc. §704.100(c)]

Endowment and Surrender Proceeds: Loan value of unmatured policies are exempt from debts of owner to the extent of $9,700. (if married, each spouse is entitled to a seperarte exemption) (adjusted every three years) [Cal. Code of Civ. Proc. §704.100(b) and §703.150]

Bankruptcy

Federal: Federal exemptions are not available. [Cal. Code of Civ. Proc. §703.130]

State: One of two options are available (1) Same state exemptions as in non-bankruptcy (2) Unmatured life insurance policy owned by debtor may be exempted up to $12,860 (adjusted every three years) of debtor's aggregate interest in any accrued dividend or interest under, or loan value of the policy if the debtor is the insured or a dependent of the insured. [Cal. Code of Civ. Proc. §703.140(b)(8)]

COLORADO

Death Benefit: Exempt from debts of insured when paid to beneficiary other than insured's estate. [C.R.S. §13-54-102]

Endowment and Surrender Proceeds: Exempt up to $250,000 from the debts of the insured except for increases contributed up to forty-eight months before writ of attachment or execution is issued. [Colo. Rev. Stats. §13-54-102(1)(I)(A)]

Bankruptcy

Federal: Federal exemptions not available. [C.R.S. §13-54-107]

State: State exemptions same as in non-bankruptcy context. [C.R.S. §13-54-107]

(continued on next page)

LIFE INSURANCE AND STATE LAWS (continued)

CONNECTICUT

Death Benefit: Exempts from debts of insured when paid to a beneficiary other than the insured's estate. [Conn. Gen. Stat. §38a-453]]

Endowment and Surrender Proceeds: Loan values of unmatured policies up to $4,000 are exempt if the insured is the person claiming the exemption or a dependent of the insured. [Conn. Gen. Stat. §52-352b(s)]

Bankruptcy

Federal: Federal exemptions are available.

State: State exemptions same as in non-bankruptcy. [Conn. Gen. Stat. 38a-453]

DELAWARE

Death Benefit: Exempt from claims of insured if payable to someone other than insured and exempt also from debts of the beneficiary. [Del. Code Ann. Title 18 §2725]

Endowment and Surrender Proceeds: No statutory provision.

Bankruptcy

Federal: Federal exemptions not available. [Del. Code Ann. Title 10 §4914]

State: State exemptions same as in non-bankruptcy context above. [Del. Code Ann. Title 10 §4914]

DISTRICT OF COLUMBIA

Death Benefit: Exempt from debts of insured if payable to someone other than insured. [DC ST §31-4716] Death benefits are exempt from debts of beneficiary if debtor was a dependent of the insured and is head of household or family. [DC ST §15-501(11)(C) In other situations, death benefit is exempt from debts of beneficiary up to $400 if beneficiary is providing support for family or $120 if not providing support. [DC ST §15-503]

Endowment and Surrender Proceeds: Unmatured policy is exempt from debts of owner other than a credit insurance contract. [DC ST 15-501(5)]

Bankruptcy

Federal: Federal exemptions are available.

State: State exemptions same as in non-bankruptcy context above.

(continued on next page)

LIFE INSURANCE AND STATE LAWS (continued)

FLORIDA

Death Benefit: Proceeds of life insurance paid to any named beneficiary (other than insured's estate) are exempt from the claims of the insured's creditors. [F.S.A. §222.13]

Endowment and Surrender Proceeds: Exempt from debts of the insured. [F.S.A. 222.14]

Bankruptcy

Federal: Federal exemptions not available except those listed at 11 U.S.C. §522(d)(10), F.S.A. §222-20 and §222.201.

State: State exemptions same as in non-bankruptcy context above.

GEORGIA

Death Benefit: Exempt from debts of insured if payable to someone other than insured or his estate. [Ga. Code Ann. §33-25-11]

Endowment and Surrender Proceeds: Exempt from the debts of the owner-insured. [Ga. Code Ann. §33-25-11]

Bankruptcy

Federal: Federal exemptions are not available. [Ga. Code Ann. §44-13-100(b)]

State: State exemptions same as non-bankruptcy context above except only $2,000 of cash surrender value is exempt. [Ga Code Ann. §44-13-100(a)(9). Debtor can also exempt proceeds of an insurance policy received on an insured of whom the debtor was a dependent, to the extent reasonably necessary for the support of the debtor and any dependents of debtor. [Ga. Code Ann. §44-13-100(a)(11)(C)]

HAWAII

Death Benefit: Exempt from the debts the owner and/or insured if payable to the insured's spouse, child, parent or other dependent, and from debts of beneficiaries under a settlement plan. [H.R.S. §431:10-232]

Endowment and Surrender Proceeds: Exempt when policy is payable to insured's spouse, child, parent or other dependent. [H.R.S. §431:10-232]

Bankruptcy

Federal: Federal exemptions are available.

State: State exemptions same as in non-bankruptcy context above. [H.R.S. 431:10-232]

(continued on next page)

LIFE INSURANCE AND STATE LAWS (continued)

IDAHO

Death Benefit: Exempt from debts of owner and/or insured as long as payable to someone other than owner and/or insured. Also exempt from debts of the beneficiary. [Idaho Code §41-1833]

Endowment and Surrender Proceeds: Unmatured policies are exempt. Dividends, interest and loan values are exempt up to $5,000. [Idaho Code § 11-605(9) and §11-605(10)]

Bankruptcy

Federal: Federal exemptions are not available. [Idaho Code §11-609]

State: State exemptions same as in non-bankruptcy context above. [Idaho Code §11-609]

ILLINOIS

Death Benefit: Exempt from debts of insured if payable to insured's spouse, child, parent, or other dependent. Death benefit exempt from debts of beneficiary to the extent reasonably necessary for the support of beneficiary and/or dependents if beneficiary was a dependent of the insured. [735 ILCS §5/12-1001(h) and 215 ILCS §5/238(a)]

Endowment and Surrender Proceeds: Exempt when policy is payable to insured's spouse, child, parent or other dependent. [735 ILCS §5/12-1001(f)]

Bankruptcy

Federal: Federal exemptions are not available. [735 ILCS §5/12-1201]

State: State exemptions same as in non-bankruptcy context above. [735 ILCS §5/12-1201]

INDIANA

Death Benefit: Exempt from debts of insured and spouse if payable to the spouse, child or any relative dependent of the insured. [I.C. §27-1-12-14] A policy naming as beneficiary, or assigned to, a spouse, child or dependent relative of the insured is exempt from the claims of creditors. This includes death proceeds, cash surrender and loan values, premiums waived and dividends. [I.C. §27-1-12-14]

Endowment and Surrender Proceeds: Exempt from creditors of the insured and the insured's spouse when policy is payable to insured's spouse, child, parent or other dependent. [I.C. §27-1-12-14]

Bankruptcy

Federal: Federal exemptions are not available. [I.C. §34-55-10-1]

State: State exemptions same as in non-bankruptcy context above. [I.C. §34-55-10-1]

(continued on next page)

LIFE INSURANCE AND STATE LAWS (continued)

IOWA

Death Benefit: Exempt from debts of the insured if payable to spouse, children, or other dependent of the insured. [Iowa Code Ann. §627.6(6) Death benefit also exempt from up to $15,000 from the debts of a beneficiary if beneficiary is a surviving spouse, child or dependent of the insured. [Iowa Code Ann. §627.6(6)]

Endowment and Surrender Proceeds: Exempt from execution any interest in dividend, interest, loan or cash surrender value if the beneficiary is a dependent but only to the amount of $10,000. [Iowa Code Ann. §627.6(6)]

Bankruptcy

Federal: Federal exemptions are not available. [Iowa Code Ann. §627.10]

State: State exemptions same as in non-bankruptcy context above. [Iowa Code Ann. §627.10]

KANSAS

Death Benefit: Exempt from debts of owner, insured and beneficiary to any person having an insurable interest in the insured. [Kan. Stat. Ann. §40-414]

Endowment and Surrender Proceeds: Exempt from creditors of the owner if policy payable to person has insurable interest in the insured and the policy was issued within the past year. [Kan. Stat. Ann. §40-414]

Bankruptcy

Federal: Only the exemptions provided by 11 U.S.C. 522(d)(10) are available. [Kan. Stat. Ann. §60-2312]

State: State exemptions same as in non-bankruptcy context above.

KENTUCKY

Death Benefit: Exempt from debts of the owner and/or insured if payable to someone other than the owner and/or insured and also exempt from debts of the beneficiary. [K.R.S. 304.14-300]

Endowment and Surrender Proceeds: Exempt from the debts of the owner. [K.R.S. §427.170]

Bankruptcy

Federal: Federal exemptions are available. [K.R.S. §427.170]

State: State exemptions same as in non-bankruptcy context above.

(continued on next page)

LIFE INSURANCE AND STATE LAWS (continued)

LOUISIANA

Death Benefit: Exempt from the debts of the insured, the owner or their estates and also from the debts of the beneficiary. [La. R.S. §22-912(A)(1)]

Endowment and Surrender Proceeds: Exempts but limited to $35,000 if the policy was issued within nine months of the policy being issued. [La. R.S. §22-912(A)(2)]

Bankruptcy

Federal: Federal exemptions are not available. [La. R.S. §13.3881(B)(1)]

State: State exemptions same as in non-bankruptcy context above.[La. R.S. 13.3881(B)(1)]

MAINE

Death Benefit: Exempt from debts of owner and/or insured if payable to someone other than owner and/or insured and also exempt from debts of the beneficiary. [24-A M.R.S.A. §2428]

Endowment and Surrender Proceeds: Unmatured life insurance owned by the debtor are exempt. Dividends, interest and loan values exempt from debts of debtor up to $4,000, provided insured is the debtor or debtor's dependent. [14 M.S.R. §4422(10) & (11)]

Bankruptcy

Federal: Only federal exemptions provided by 11 U.S.C. 522(b)(3)(A) and (B) are available. [14 M.S.R. §4426]

State: State exemptions same as in non-bankruptcy context above. [14 M.S.R. §4426]

MARYLAND

Death Benefit: Exempt from debts of insured if payable to spouse, child or dependent of the insured. [MD Insurance Code Ann. §16-111] Death benefits exempt from debts of beneficiary. [MD Court and Judicial Proc. Code Ann. §11-504(b)(2)]

Endowment and Surrender Proceeds: Exempt from debts of owner if beneficiary is spouse, child or dependent relative of the insured. [MD Insurance Code Ann. §16-111)]

Bankruptcy

Federal: Federal exemptions are not available [MD Court and Judicial Proc. Code Ann. §11-504(g)]

State: State exemptions same as in non-bankruptcy context above.

(continued on next page)

LIFE INSURANCE AND STATE LAWS (continued)

MASSACHUSETTS

Death Benefit: Exempt from debts of owner if policy payable to a beneficiary other than the owner. [M.G.L.A. ch. 175 §125] Death benefits exempt from debts of beneficiary. [M.G.L.A. ch. 175 §§119A and 126]

Endowment and Surrender Proceeds: Exempt from debts of owner if beneficiary has been unchanged since policy's issuance. [M.G.L. ch. 175 §125]

Bankruptcy

Federal: Federal exemptions are available.

State: State exemptions same as in non-bankruptcy context above.

MICHIGAN

Death Benefit: Exempt from the debts of owner and/or insured if payable to someone other than the owner and/or insured. [M.C.L.A. §500.2207]

Cash Value: Exempt from debts of the owner. [M.C.L.A. §500.2207]

Bankruptcy

Federal: Federal exemptions are available [M.C.L.A. 600.6023]

State: State exemptions same as in non-bankruptcy context above. [M.C.L.A. 600.6023]

MINNESOTA

Death Benefit: Exempt from the debts of the owner if payable to someone other than the owner [Minn. Stat. §61A.12] and up to $46,000 of death benefit exempt from the debts of beneficiary if a spouse or dependent child (increased by $11,500 for each additional dependent child) [Minn. Stat. §550.37(10)]

Cash Value: Up to $9,200 in any dividends, interest or loan value exempt from debts if owner is insured or dependent of the insured. [Minn. Stat. §550.37(23)

Bankruptcy

Federal: Federal exemptions are allowed. [Minn. Stat. §550.371]

State: State exemptions same as in non-bankruptcy context above.

(continued on next page)

LIFE INSURANCE AND STATE LAWS (continued)

MISSISSIPPI

Death Benefit: Exempt from debts of insured if payable to someone other than insured. [Miss. Code Ann. §85-3-11]

Cash Value: Exempt from debts of insured if payable to someone other than the insured; provided, that a maximum of $50,000 of cash value is exempt if purchased within twelve months of issuance. [Miss. Code Ann. §85-3-11]

Bankruptcy

Federal: Federal exemptions are not available. (Miss. Code Ann. §85-3-2)

State: State exemptions same as in non-bankruptcy context above. [Miss. Code Ann. §85-3-11]

MISSOURI

Death Benefit: Exempt from the debts of the owner and/or insured and also exempt from the debts of the beneficiary. [Mo. Rev. Stat. §§377.330 and 513.430(1)]

Cash Value: Wholly exempt from debts of owner. [Mo. Rev. Stat. §§377.330 and 513.430 (1)(7)]

Bankruptcy

Federal: Federal exemptions not available. [Mo. Rev. Stat. §513.427]

State: State exemptions same as in non-bankruptcy context above except that the cash value of an insurance policy is exempt only to a maximum of $150,000. No exemption for cash value of an insurance policy if purchased within one year prior to commencement of bankruptcy. [Mo. Rev. Stat. §513.430(1)(8)]

MONTANA

Death Benefit: Exemption from the debts of owner and/or the insured if payable to someone other than the owner and/or insured. [MT ST §33-15-511]

Endowment and Surrender Proceeds: Wholly exempt from debts of owner. [MT ST §25-13-608(k)]

Bankruptcy

Federal: Federal exemptions are not available. [MT ST §32-2-106]

State: State exemptions are available as provided in MT ST §32-2-106(1).

(continued on next page)

LIFE INSURANCE AND STATE LAWS (continued)

NEBRASKA

Death Benefit: Exemption from debts of insured if payable to someone other insured or insured's estate. Death benefit also exempt from debts of beneficiary is related to the insured by blood or marriage. [R.R.S. Neb. §44-371]

Endowment and Surrender Proceeds: Up to $100,000 are exempt from debts of owner provided that the cash value associated with contributions or premiums are not exempt if made within three years of bankruptcy. [R.R.S. Neb. §44-371(1)(b)]

Bankruptcy

Federal: Federal exemptions are not available. [R.R.S. Neb.§25-15,105]

State: State exemptions are available same as in non-bankruptcy context above. [R.R.S. Neb. §25-15.105]

NEVADA

Death Benefit: Exempt from the debts of owner and/or insured if payable to someone other than owner. Also exempt from the debts of the beneficiary. [NRS §687B.260]

Endowment and Surrender Proceeds: Exempt from debts of the owner. [NRS §21.090(1)(k)]

Bankruptcy

Federal: Federal exemptions are not available. [NRS 21.090(3)]

State: State exemptions are available same as in non-bankruptcy context above. [NRS 21.090(3)]

NEW HAMPSHIRE

Death Benefit: Exempt from debts of the owner and exempt from the debt of the beneficiary. [RSA §408:1]

Endowment and Surrender Proceeds: No exemption is available. [RSA §408:2]

Bankruptcy

Federal: Federal exemptions are available.

State: State exemptions are available same as in non-bankruptcy context above.

(continued on next page)

LIFE INSURANCE AND STATE LAWS (continued)

NEW JERSEY

Death Benefit: Exempt from debts of owner and/or insured if payable to someone other than owner and/or insured and from debts of beneficiary. [N.J.S.A. 17B:24-6]

Endowment and Surrender Proceeds: Exemption available if beneficiary is someone other than the owner and/or insured. [N.J.S.A. 17B:24-6]

Bankruptcy

Federal: Federal exemptions are available.

State: State exemptions are available same as in non-bankruptcy context above.

NEW MEXICO

Death Benefit: Exempt from debts of the insured except by special contract in writing. [N.M. Stat. Ann. §42-10-5]

Endowment and Surrender Proceeds: Exempt from debt of the owner. [N.M. Stat. Ann. §42-10-3]

Bankruptcy

Federal: Federal exemptions are available.

State: State exemptions are available same as in non-bankruptcy context above.

NEW YORK

Death Benefit: Exempt from debts of insured and/or owner if payable to someone other than insured and/or owner. Death benefit is exempt from debts of the owner who is a spouse of the insured. [NY Insurance Law §3212]

Endowment and Surrender Proceeds: Exempt from debts of owner and/or insured if payable to insured's spouse and/or children. [NY Insurance Law §3212(b)

Bankruptcy

Federal: Federal exemptions are not available. [NY Debtor and Creditor Law §284]

State: State exemptions are available same as in non-bankruptcy context above. [NY Debtor and Creditor Law §282]

(continued on next page)

LIFE INSURANCE AND STATE LAWS (continued)

NORTH CAROLINA

Death Benefit: Exempt from debts of insured and/or owner is payable to someone other than the owner and/or insured. [N.C. Gen. Stat. §1C-1601(a)(6)]

Endowment and Surrender Proceeds: Whole exempt from debts of owner and/or insured is payable to insured's spouse and/or children. [N.C. Gen. Stat. §58-58-95]

Bankruptcy

Federal: Federal exemptions are not available. [N.C. Gen. Stat. §1C-1601(f)]

State: State exemptions are available same as in non-bankruptcy context above. [N.C. Gen. Stat. §1C-160(f)]

NORTH DAKOTA

Death Benefit: Exempt from debts of the deceased even when payable to deceased as well as to wife, children or dependent relative. (ND C.C. §§26.1-33-40]

Endowment and Surrender Proceeds: Exempt absolutely from debts of owner and/or insured up to a maximum of $8,000. [ND C.C. §§26.1-33-36]

Bankruptcy

Federal: Federal exemptions are not available. [ND C.C. §28-22-17]

State: State exemptions are available same as in non-bankruptcy context above.

OHIO

Death Benefit: Exempt from debts of insured if payable to insured's spouse, children, dependent relative, charity or creditor. Also exempt if payable to trust for the benefit of any of the aforementioned. [Ohio Revised Code §3911.10,§2329.66(A)(6)(b)]

Endowment and Surrender Proceeds: Same as above.

Bankruptcy

Federal: Federal exemptions are not available. [Ohio Revised Code §2329.662]

State: State exemptions same as in non-bankruptcy context.

OKLAHOMA

Death Benefit: Exempt from the debts of both the insured and the beneficiary. [36 Okl. St.§3611]

Endowment and Surrender Proceeds: Exempt from debts of the insured. [36 Okl. St. §3631.1]

Bankruptcy

Federal: Federal exemptions are not allowed. [31 Okl. St. §1]

State: State exemptions available same as in non-bankruptcy context above.

(continued on next page)

LIFE INSURANCE AND STATE LAWS (continued)

OREGON

Death Benefit: Exempt from debts of owner if payable to someone other than owner. [ORS §743.046(1)]

Endowment and Surrender Proceeds: Cash surrender value of a life insurance policy payable to a beneficiary other than the estate of the insured is exempt from claims of creditors. [ORS §743.046(3)]

Bankruptcy

Federal: Federal exemptions are not allowed. [ORS §18.300]

State: State exemptions available same as in non-bankruptcy context above.

PENNSYLVANIA

Death Benefit: Exempt from debts of the insured if payable to spouse, child or dependent relative of insured. [42 Pa. Cons. Stat. §8124(c)]

Endowment and Surrender Proceeds: Cash value is exempt from debts of owner when spouse, child or other relative dependent of the insured is beneficiary. [42 Pa. Cons. Stat. §8124(c)(6)]. When insured is beneficiary, exempt up to the amount of $100 per month. [42 Pa. Cons. Stat. §8124(c)(3)]

Federal: Federal exemptions are available. [42 Pa Cons. Stat. §8124(a)]

State: State exemptions are available same as in non-bankruptcy context above.

RHODE ISLAND

Death Benefit: Exempt from debts of owner and/or insured if payable to someone other than insured. [R.I. Gen. Laws §27-4-11]

Endowment and Surrender Proceeds: Exempts "proceeds and avails"" when beneficiary is other than the owner/insured. An unpublished Rhode Island Superior Court decision held that cash surrender proceeds were included in "proceeds and avails" under R.I. Gen. Laws §27-4-11.

Bankruptcy

Federal: Federal exemptions are available.

State: State exemptions available same as in non-bankruptcy context above.

SOUTH CAROLINA

Death Benefit: Exempt from debts of insured if payable to a beneficiary where proceeds are for benefit of spouse, children or dependents. {S.C. Code §38-63-40(A)] If bankruptcy filed within two years, a maximum of $4,000 is exempt from debts of the owner. [S.C. Code §§38-63-40(A), 15-41-30]

Endowment and Surrender Proceeds: Exempt from debts of insured if payable to insured's spouse, children or dependents. [S.C. Code §38-63-40(A)] Otherwise, up to $4,000 exempt from debts of the owner if debtor is the insured or dependent. [S.C. Code §§15-41-30, 38-65-90]

(continued on next page)

LIFE INSURANCE AND STATE LAWS (continued)

Bankruptcy

Federal: Federal exemptions are not available. [S.C. Code §15-41-35]

State: State exemptions same as in non-bankruptcy context above. [S.C. Code §15-41-35]

SOUTH DAKOTA

Death Benefit: Up to $20,000 exempt from debts of insured and beneficiary if payable to insured's spouse and/or children. [SDCL §58-12-4] Up to $10,000 exempt from debts of insured and beneficiary-spouse and/or children if payable to the insured's estate. [SDCL § 43-45-6]

Endowment and Surrender Proceeds: Up to $20,000 exempt from debts of insured and/or owner. [SDCL §58-12-4]

Bankruptcy

Federal: Federal exemptions not available. [SDCL §43-31-30]

State: State exemptions same as in non-bankruptcy context. [SDCL §43-31-30]

TENNESSEE

Death Benefits: Exempt from debts if life insurance is payable to the surviving spouse, children or dependent unless it is payable to the decedent's estate and the will directs otherwise. [Tenn. Code Ann. §§ 56-7-201, 56-7-202 and 56-7-203]

Endowment and Surrender Proceeds: Cash surrender value is exempt if payable to insured's spouse, children or dependent. [Tenn. Code Ann. §56-7-203, *In re Olien*, 256 Bankr. 280 (E.D. Tenn. 2000, *In re Billington*, 376 Bankr. 239 (M.D. Tenn. 2007)]

Bankruptcy

Federal: Federal exemptions are not available. [Tenn. Code Ann. §26-2-112]

State: State exemptions same as in non-bankruptcy context. [Tenn. Code Ann. §26-2-112]

TEXAS

Death Benefits: Exempt from both debts of insured and the debts of the beneficiary. [Texas Ins. Code §1108:051, 1108:052 and 1108:53]

Endowment and Surrender Proceeds: Exempt from debts of insured. [Texas Ins. Code §1108:51]

Bankruptcy

Federal: Federal exemptions are available.

State: Insurance benefits are exempt for both insured and beneficiary in bankruptcy proceedings. [Texas Ins. Code §1108:051(b)(2)(C)]

(continued on next page)

LIFE INSURANCE AND STATE LAWS (continued)

UTAH

Death Benefits: Exempt from both the debts of the insured and the beneficiary if payable to the insured's spouse and/or children and provided the contract for insurance was in existence for at least one year. [Utah Code Ann. §78B-5-505(xi),(xii)]

Endowment and Surrender Proceeds: Exempt except that any payments made on the contract within one year preceding a creditor's levy or execution are not exempt. [Utah Code Ann. 78B-5-505(1)(a)(xii)]

Bankruptcy

Federal: Federal exemptions are not allowed unless the individual is a nonresident of the state and has been for the 180 days immediately preceding the filing for bankruptcy. [Utah Code Ann. §78B-5-513]

State: State exemptions available same as in non-bankruptcy context above. [Utah Code Ann. §78B-5-513]

VERMONT

Death Benefits: Exempt from debts of insured and/or owner if payable to someone other than insured and/or owner. Also exempt from debts of the beneficiary to the extent reasonably necessary for the support of debtor and any dependents. [8 Vermont Stat. Ann. §3706 and 12 Vermont Stat. Ann. §2740(19)(H)]

Endowment and Surrender Proceeds: Unmatured policy exempt from debts of owner and/or insured. [12 Vermont Stat. Ann. §2740(18)]

Bankruptcy

Federal: Federal exemptions are available.

State: State exemptions available same as in non-bankruptcy context above.

VIRGINIA

Death Benefits: Exempt from debts of insured and/or owner if payable to someone other than insured and/or owner. [Virginia Code Ann. §38.2.3122]

Endowment and Surrender Proceeds: Exempts cash value but not if the owner has reserved the right to change beneficiaries. [Virginia Code Ann. §38.2-3123]

Bankruptcy

Federal: Federal exemptions are not available. [Virginia Code Ann. §34-3.1]

State: State exemptions available same as in non-bankruptcy context above. [Virginia Code Ann. §34-3.1]

WASHINGTON

Death Benefits: Exempt from debts of insured and/or owner is payable to someone other than insured and/or owner. Also applies to debts of beneficiary. Exemptions do not apply if a claim is made against the proceeds either by the insured or the person effecting the insurance. [Rev. Code of Washington §48.18.410]

(continued on next page)

LIFE INSURANCE AND STATE LAWS (continued)

Endowment and Surrender Proceeds: Protects "proceeds and avails" on insurance contract when someone other than insured and/or owner. [Rev. Code of Washington §48.18.410] Appears to include cash surrender value of policy but not entirely clear. See *In re Elliot* 74 Wash. 2d 600, 446 P.2d 347 (1968)

Bankruptcy

Federal: Federal exemptions are allowed.

State: State exemptions available same as in non-bankruptcy context above.

WEST VIRGINIA

Death Benefits: Exempt from debts of insured if payable to someone other than insured. [W. Va. Code §33-6-27]

Endowment and Surrender Proceeds: Exempts "proceeds and avails" when beneficiary is someone other than the owner and/or insured. [W. Va. Code §33-6-27]

Bankruptcy

Federal: Federal exemptions are not available. [W. Va. Code §38-10-4]

State: Debtor exempt up to $8,000 of cash value on policy owned by debtor if debtor is insured or dependent of the insured. [W. Va. Code §38-10-4(g) and (h)]

WISCONSIN

Death Benefits: Exempt if insuring the life of an individual of whom the debtor was a dependent to the extent reasonably necessary for the support of the debtor. [Wis. Stat. §815.18(3)(i)(a)]

Endowment and Surrender Proceeds: Exempt up to $150,000 if policy insures debtor's dependents or individual of whom debtor is dependent. Exemption limited to $4,000 if policy issued within 24 hours of action being filed. [Wis. Stat. § 815.18(3)(f)]

Bankruptcy

Federal: Federal exemptions are available.

State: State exemptions same as in non-bankruptcy context above.

WYOMING

Death Benefits: Exempt from debts of insured and/or owner if payable to someone other than insured and/or owner as well as the beneficiary. [Wyo. Stat. §26-15-129]

Endowment and Surrender Proceeds: Exempt from debts of owner if someone other than debtor is beneficiary. [Wyo. Stat. § 26-15-129]

Bankruptcy

Federal: Federal exemptions are not available. [Wyo. Stat. §1-20-109]

State: State exemptions same as in non-bankruptcy context above. [Wyo. Stat. §1-20-109]

LIFE SETTLEMENTS

The term "life settlement" generally refers to the sale to an investor of a life insurance contract when the insured is age sixty-five or older and *is not* terminally or chronically ill (i.e., the insured is expected to live more than two years). In contrast, the term "viatical settlement" is used to describe the sale of life insurance contract when the insured *is* terminally or chronically ill and expected to die within two years (see below). However, these terms are not consistently used, particularly in state laws and regulations. Life settlements typically require that the policy have a minimum face value of between $100,000 and $250,000, be beyond the contestability period, and be fully renewable. Policies that can be sold include term life, whole life, universal life, variable life, and survivorship life insurance. The prices paid are more than the current cash values, but less than the net death benefit.

When an application for a settlement is taken many states require that a disclosure statement be presented to the viator. (A "viator" is the owner of a life insurance policy who enters into a contract to sell the policy to a third party, usually a viatical settlement provider.) These statements typically inform the policy owner that: other alternatives may be available, such as loans and accelerated death benefits (see page 291); sale proceeds may be subject to income taxes and claims of creditors; sale proceeds may adversely affect eligibility for Medicaid and other government benefits; and the contract contains a rescission provision. The owner of the policy does not have to be the insured (e.g., a trust owned policy or a policy owned by one spouse on the life of the other spouse). Insureds should also be informed that the sale of the policy could negatively affect their ability to obtain *future* life insurance coverage, since the outstanding investor-owned policy will likely be considered in the underwriting process (see the discussion of financial underwriting on page 379).

Before selling a life insurance policy the owner should give careful consideration to the impact that the loss of the death benefit will have upon family income requirements and existing estate plans. Life settlements are most appropriately considered when *changing circumstances* cause the owner to consider surrendering a policy for its cash value. (This should be distinguished from the regrettable practice of stranger-originated life insurance that is intended to evade the insurable interest laws, see discussion on page 558.) The following are examples of those changing circumstances which can lead to life settlements: (1) business is sold and policies purchased to fund buy/sell agreement are no longer needed; (2) executive leaves business or retires and there is no need for policy intended for key person insurance; (3) premiums are no longer affordable (due to change in financial condition or failure of policy to perform as originally projected); (4) changing family circumstances reduce or eliminate need for insurance coverage (e.g., death of spouse, divorce or newly acquired wealth); (5) desire to replace individual policy with last-to-die policy; and (6) decrease in size of estate or increase in tax credits or exemptions result in lowered estate taxes. But, it is important to realize the investor considers the policy a good investment – meaning that it is likely in the current owner's best interest to retain the policy if that is possible.

(continued on next page)

LIFE SETTLEMENTS (continued)

When the insured is expected to live twenty-four months or less the proceeds from the sale of a policy to a viatical settlement provider may be excluded from income. To obtain this favorable income tax treatment the viatical provider must be licensed in the state in which the insured resides. If the insured resides in a state not requiring such licensing, then there must be compliance with certain provisions of the Viatical Settlements Model Act (the Model Act) and requirements of the National Association of Insurance Commissioners (NAIC) relating to standards for evaluating the reasonableness of payments. To protect the viator (the individual selling the policy) the Model Act sets standards for evaluation of reasonable payments for terminally or chronically ill insureds. One alternative standard sets forth minimum percentages of the policy face that must be paid (ranging from 80 percent when the insured's life expectancy is less than six months, to 60 percent when the insured's life expectancy is at least eighteen but less than twenty five months).

Proceeds from a sale will be subject to income taxation. In Revenue Ruling 2009-13, the Service ruled that when a life insurance contract is *sold*, the cost of insurance protection must be subtracted from the net premiums paid in order to determine the owner's tax basis. The Service also ruled that a life insurance contract is a capital asset, and income recognized can qualify as long-term capital gain. (Basis is reduced by cost of insurance; the amount received in excess of basis up to cash surrender value is ordinary income; and the amount received in excess of cash surrender value is capital gain.) This ruling was not adversely applied to sales before August 26, 2009. However, in the 2017 Tax Act, Congress took it upon itself to reverse Rev. Rul. 2009-13 and specifically provide that basis is NOT reduced by cost of insurance and other reasonable expenses and charges. This change is retroactive to August 25, 2009.

In an effort to regulate the sale of life insurance policies, many states have enacted statutes based upon the Model Act. In keeping with the ongoing evolution of that Act, in 2004 the NAIC voted to not require a separate viatical broker's license for certain licensed insurance producers. However, in many states life and viatical settlements are considered *securities*, their sale is formally regulated and agents must be separately licensed. Further complicating the regulatory environment is the fact that states often do not distinguish between life settlements and viatical settlements. In view of these inconsistencies, and ongoing changes in state regulation, the agent should contact the appropriate state insurance or securities departments before engaging in the solicitation or sale of life and viatical settlements. In addition, agents need to be aware that some insurers do not permit agents associated with them to promote or otherwise engage in life settlements. In some instances, such restrictions may be included in the contractual agreement between agents and insurer.

In 2006, the NASD issued a notice to members reminding firms and associated persons that life settlements involving *variable* insurance policies are securities transactions subject to FINRA rules. In 2010, the Life Settlements Staff of the U.S. Securities and Exchange Commission submitted a report recommending that the definition of a security be amended by Congress to include life settlements. Their report also observed that with respect to state securities laws, most states now treat life settlements as securities under state laws, although some states exclude from the definition of security the original sale from the insured or the policy owner to the provider.

LIMITED LIABILITY COMPANY

The limited liability company (LLC) offers owners the limited liability of C corporations together with the tax and management advantages of partnerships, without the restrictions and complexities of S corporations. (However, in comparing a LLC to other business structures these advantages might be offset when state law is considered, because some states have a state corporate income tax or franchise tax which may apply to a LLC but not to an entity such as a limited partnership.) An LLC is created by filing articles of organization and complying with the relevant state law. The participants are called "members" and the rules governing the operation of an LLC are usually set forth in an "operating agreement."

The LLC form of business was first established by Wyoming in 1977 and has now been adopted by statute in all 50 states and the District of Columbia. However, the attractiveness of the LLC is often limited by the lack of uniformity between the various state statutes (e.g., some statutes contain no fiduciary duty provisions, some mirror those of partnerships, others mirror those of corporations, and still others mirror both).

The primary *advantages* of the LLC include: (1) no liability of owners for business debts (enjoyed by corporations and S corporations but not by general partnerships); (2) flow through of income and expenses to the individual owners (enjoyed by S corporations and partnerships but not by corporations); (3) the ability to allocate income and losses among members and include business liabilities in cost basis (enjoyed by partnerships but not by corporations and S corporations); and (4) freedom from the stringent requirements and restrictions of S corporations in the formation, operation and disposition of the business. For further discussions of partnerships and S corporations see the chart on page 211, 481-483, and 531-533. It has also been suggested that the LLC could serve as a viable alternative to the irrevocable life insurance trust, by affording the insured greater control and flexibility, in much the same way as the limited partnership. Members of an LLC that has elected to be taxed as a partnership are treated as partners for many (but not all) tax purposes, such as the transfer-for-value rule exception under IRC §101(a)(2)(B).

An LLC formed *after* December 31, 1996, will generally be taxed as a partnership if it has more than two owners, or as a sole proprietorship if it has only one owner, unless it elects to be taxed as a corporation. This election can be made under the "check the box" regulations by filing Form 8832 (Entity Classification Election). An LLC formed *before* January 1, 1997, will generally be treated as it was prior to January 1, 1997, unless it elects otherwise.

LIMITED LIABILITY COMPANY (LLC) V. ILIT AS LIFE INSURANCE OWNERSHIP STRUCTURE

The limited liability company (LLC) offers owners the limited personal liability of C corporations together with the tax and management advantages of partnerships, without the restrictions and complexities of S corporations (see summary of the LLC on page 449).

Because of the flexibilities of an LLC, they are often promoted as an alternative to an irrevocable life insurance trust (ILIT). While this may be a generally true analysis, the comparison of the LLC and ILIT is often not complete. Specifically, those comparing an LLC and an ILIT do not always consider the flexibilities that can be put into today's irrevocable trusts. Moreover, the law on LLCs funded exclusively or primarily with life insurance is not well developed – leaving significant uncertainties. Because LLCs are creations of state law, there is a lack of uniformity among the relevant statutes of the many jurisdictions, which necessarily makes the analysis, and potentially the choice, different in each state.

The common approach to ownership of life insurance by an LLC is usually to purchase the life insurance policy with cash provided by the insured to the LLC. The insured's contribution to the LLC is not a gift because the contribution is a contribution to the capital of the LLC as consideration for an ownership interest. The LLC organizational document ordinarily contains restrictions on distributions and transferability. These restrictions can have the dual benefit of restricting the value of the interest (i.e., creating valuation discounts) and protecting family members from creditors (much like an ILIT).

The insured can then transfer LLC interests to children or trusts for children (or Dynasty Trusts) through gift or by sale. The LLC interests are often transferred at a discount – sometimes in the 30 percent to 40 percent range. (See "Family Limited Partnerships" for a discussion of valuation discounts.) With the $5,600,000 lifetime gift tax exemption it is often easy to transfer most or all of the LLC interests shortly after issue. In some situations, the interests are transferred over time under the $15,000 annual gift tax exclusion. Unlike an ILIT, these annual exclusion gifts of LLC interests should not require Crummey notices (see Crummey Powers at page 332) or the associated holding period. However, gifts of LLC interests may require a professional appraisal. The insured retains management control in the LLC – usually with ownership of a small percentage of the LLC units.

(continued on next page)

LIMITED LIABILITY COMPANY (LLC) V. ILIT AS LIFE INSURANCE OWNERSHIP STRUCTURE (continued)

It is believed that the LLC is more flexible than the ILIT because the insured has retained management control of the LLC and can terminate the LLC or amend the LLC if the family situation changes. It is also believed that upon termination of the LLC that the insured can direct distribution of the LLC assets – thus determining who is in receipt of the life insurance policy. Any transfer of the policy to a member of the LLC should avoid the transfer for value rules because the LLC is treated as a partnership for income tax purposes. As a partnership, the transfer of the policy is treated as a transfer to a partner of the insured. (See Transfer for Value at pages 568-569).

It seems that in many instances, the biggest perceived advantage of an LLC over an ILIT is that the insured can retain control over the life insurance contact on his or her own life by having the right to make decisions for the policyholder – the LLC. So, it is believed, that the insured may only have 1 percent of the life insurance included in his or her estate (through the retained managing member LLC interest), yet the insured can make important insurance decisions. Some of the decisions that the policyholder can make (i.e., the insured as manager of the LLC) are: (1) maintain or surrender the policy, (2) investment of policy cash surrender values (with a variable type policy), (3) withdrawals and loans from a cash value policy, (4) conversion of a term policy, and (5) life settlements.

The possible disadvantages to an LLC ownership of life insurance, however, include unforeseen state income and franchise taxes. A number of states have income and franchise taxes that apply to an LLC that do not apply to an ILIT. Most importantly, however, some tax professionals remain unconvinced that an insured can enjoy all of the powers over the life insurance policy as manager of an LLC without estate tax inclusion of the policy. Clearly, IRC Section 2042 prohibits the retention of "incidents of ownership" in a life insurance contract. Because of Section 2042, it is known that an insured cannot ordinarily serve as the trustee of an ILIT that owns a policy on his or her own life. Some tax advisors continue to wonder if Section 2042 can really be avoided by having the policy owned in an LLC instead of a trust. Does the insured's right to surrender the policy, withdrawal cash, change investment strategies, direct distribution of the policy among LLC owners upon termination of the LLC really not cause estate tax inclusion because the policy is owned in an LLC? Those same powers, if held in a fiduciary capacity as trustee of an ILIT, would cause inclusion in the insured/trustee's estate. However, in *Estate of Knipp*, the Court held that the death benefit of a *partnership-owned* life insurance policy was not includible in the insured partner's life if the death benefit was payable to the partnership.

(continued on next page)

LIMITED LIABILITY COMPANY (LLC) V. ILIT AS LIFE INSURANCE OWNERSHIP STRUCTURE (continued)

In a corporate context the law seems well resolved that a minority shareholder does not have incidents of ownership just because the insured is the one actually managing the day to day affairs of the business. On the other hand, a controlling shareholder is treated as having any incidents of ownership over life insurance contracts owned by the corporation. Is the insured retaining a minority interest only in an LLC like a minority shareholder in an ordinary business situation? What if the LLC owns only the life insurance contact? Could the IRS make a form over substance argument (see Step Transaction Doctrine at page 555)? Some advisors feel that an LLC holding few assets other than a life insurance contact could be viewed differently than an active business which happens to own an insurance contact.

Many people, including advisors, view ILITs as inflexible. However, when comparing an ILIT to an LLC, the flexible provisions common today in ILITs should not be ignored. It is possible for the family (not the insured) to retain access to policy values through use of the so-called Spousal Access Trust (see page 554). Many states allow for liberal modification of irrevocable trust terms through a process known as "decanting" (see page 334). Trust protector powers can be used to check the powers of trustees and help insure that the trustee is acting in the best interest of the trust beneficiaries (see page 570). ILITs enjoy considerable creditor protection – in many states greater than protections afforded to LLC interests. An ILIT can give the trustee very flexible powers during the insured's lifetime to make distributions of policy cash values to trust beneficiaries. The right to make distributions can be spelled out in very creative ways. One of the ways in which trust distribution provisions is kept flexible is through the so-called "Incentive Trust" (see page 402).

In summary, the LLC is a popular and powerful planning tool. It provides flexibility, creditor protection, and possible valuation discounts. Although the LLC may have some advantages over the traditional ILIT when it comes to life insurance planning, it is important to consider the advantages and disadvantages carefully. Probably the biggest question being – does possible additional flexibility outweigh the seemingly yet unresolved estate tax issues? Today, ILITs need not be inflexible. State of the art trust drafting and liberal state trust laws make today's ILITs far more flexible than imagined not that many years ago.

LIVING WILL

The living will is a legal document that allows an individual to state in advance his or her unwillingness to be subjected to life-sustaining medical measures once there is no chance of recovery. Such a document relieves others of the legal and emotional burden of making such decisions.

For example, it can ease a doctor's fears of civil or criminal liability, since the doctor is abiding by the patient's wishes in withholding or withdrawing life-prolonging treatment. It can ease the stress and emotional pain for the family, which might otherwise be faced with having to make a most difficult decision as to what their loved one would have wanted. Further, it offers some hope of avoiding the legal battles that have occurred when a medical facility is unsure of its responsibility to the patient, and thus provides the family some protection from the financial devastation that a protracted death can cause.

Almost all of the states have some form of legislation governing living wills. Generally such a document must be in writing, dated, and witnessed by two persons who are not family members or possible heirs. The document must usually be notarized if a durable power of attorney is included giving another person the power to make medical treatment decisions (see discussion, page 351). In addition, language can be included providing for organ donation.

Copies of the living will should be given to close relatives, the family doctor and the family attorney. Both the living will and the durable power of attorney can be revoked at any time by either destroying all copies or by executing a signed and notarized statement revoking the prior document.

See also, Health Care Power Of Attorney, page 400.

LONG-TERM CARE HYBRID PRODUCTS

The risk of needing long-term care (LTC) is substantial and the costs of providing such care can be overwhelming (see chart on page 115).

Despite the need for long-term care insurance, sales of the stand-alone LTC insurance products have been negatively impacted by increasing product costs and the client's fears of paying premiums for a product from which they will never derive a benefit (i.e., the fear of "use it or lose it"). As a result, insurance companies are increasingly offering hybrid or so-called combination or living benefit products that combine the benefits of life insurance or annuities with the benefits of long-term care insurance. These products address both consumer fears of uncontrollable premium increases and paying for a product they will not use.

With a cash value life insurance policy the death benefits can be accelerated to make either per diem payments or expense reimbursements upon the insured's disability or chronic illness. A rider is often added to provide additional coverage in order to extend the LTC benefits once the contract cash values and death benefits have been exhausted. This effectively allows the consumer to purchase at an attractive cost one policy to insure against two risks. However, it must be recognized that LTC payments from the contract could reduce or even eliminate the life insurance death benefit. (The use of cash values and death benefits for LTC payments is considered a form of "self-funding.") The accelerated benefit, whether paid from the net amount at risk or from the rider providing separate LTC coverage, will be entitled to favorable tax treatment provided the contract is a "*qualified* long-term care insurance contract" (QLTCI). See discussion on page 509. Charges against policy cash values are not taxable even if there is gain in the contract. The cost of adding an LTC or chronic illness rider to a life insurance contact is often less than 10 percent of the life insurance only premium. The cost of the rider can be priced reasonably because the insurance company is already pricing for the death benefit – meaning that early payout for LTC or chronic illness costs is only a "timing difference."

Not all riders are equal, however. Some riders are structured as true LTC riders while others are structured as "chronic illness riders." LTC riders, with the classification of 7702B, require a physician to certify that the insured, for a period of at least ninety days, is unable to perform at least two Activities of Daily Living (ADLs) or suffers from severe cognitive impairment. This definition allows for certain temporary claims as well as permanent claims to be covered. True LTC riders are available for an additional charge and require underwriting. LTC underwriting focuses on morbidity risk rather than mortality risk meaning that not all people who can medically qualify for life insurance will qualify for the LTC rider.

(continued on next page)

LONG-TERM CARE HYBRID PRODUCTS (continued)

The main differentiator among 7702B LTC riders is whether the rider pays by an indemnity model or reimbursement model. Reimbursement plans, no matter what the stated maximum benefit is, will never pay more than the qualifying LTC expenses incurred but can exceed the IRS per diem limitations without adverse tax consequences. Reimbursement riders generally pay the benefits to the policy owner unless the owner elects to have the payments made directly to the caregiver. Qualifying expenses in reimbursement plans do not include the costs of home modification, medical equipment and other potential expenses that go along with LTC needs.

Indemnity plans pay the maximum benefit the policy allows, regardless of actual expenses. No bills or receipts are needed to justify the cost of care. Like the reimbursement plan, an indemnity plan generally pays benefits directly to the policy owner.

Some riders are classified as 101(g) only. These riders use the indemnity model of benefit payment. However, the term "long-term care" may *not* be used in marketing these products. These riders, usually referred to as "chronic illness riders," differ from LTC riders in that the physician must certify the chronic illness is likely to last the rest of the insured's life. For this reason, temporary conditions would not be eligible for claim. Although this seems like a significant difference, many LTC riders have "exclusionary periods" providing that benefits can only be accessed after a significant waiting period, thus, minimizing much of the benefit sometimes attributed to LTC type riders.

A main differentiator among chronic illness riders is whether the rider is paid for by an additional charge added to the policy (like a LTC rider) or is included as a policy feature with no underwriting. While a "free" chronic illness rider may sound like an advantage, these riders are essentially paid for at the time of claim making them often less efficient than LTC or chronic illness riders paid for by an additional charge.

Life insurance with LTC or chronic illness riders have become very popular products, largely because of increasing awareness of long-term care needs, the sky-rocketing cost of LTC care, and the uncertainty of stand-alone LTC product pricing. Carriers often promote their rider as "the best." In reality, "best" largely depends upon circumstances. It is important for advisors to understand the differences between true LTC riders and chronic illness riders. It is also important to understand the differences between indemnity and reimbursement type arrangements. In essence, like all life insurance decisions, it is simply important to understand the product features and costs in light of the insured and the family circumstances.

(continued on next page)

LONG-TERM CARE HYBRID PRODUCTS (continued)

With a **non-qualified annuity** LTC benefits can be paid from a tax-qualified LTC rider provided the rider complies with the requirements of a QLTCI. Benefits received after January 1, 2010 are entitled to favorable tax treatment (see page 509). Such coupling of a LTC rider with a non-qualified annuity provides a unique opportunity to use a non-qualified annuity for LTC needs since this favorable tax treatment is available even though the benefit payment reduces the annuity contract's cash values (i.e., untaxed inside buildup within the annuity may be paid out tax-free for LTC expenses).

Both life insurance and non-qualified annuities can be exchanged tax-free under Section 1035 for a QLTCI (see page 563). This would allow for an exchange of an existing life policy that has outlived its purpose into a combination life/LTC plan (i.e., gain in the policy would not be subject to current taxation). Likewise, one QLTCI can be exchanged for another QLTCI.

PLANNING WITH LONG-TERM CARE HYBRID PRODUCTS can add flexibility to a client's future financial options. Many clients prefer to own the product outright, to maintain control and facilitate the payment of benefits. Most products allow the owner to elect to have the benefits paid directly to the caregiver or to the owner. However, some clients choose to have the product insuring their lives owned by a third-party owner, such as a family member or a trust. If the product issuer allows third-party ownership, and also permits payment to the owner instead of directly to the caregiver, then such an arrangement can serve to accelerate the death benefit while reducing the taxable estate of the insured. However, careful tax consideration should be given to the specific product features to determine if the policy could cause incidents of ownership under IRC Section 2042 (see page 374). For instance, if the policy is a reimbursement type policy that contractually pays benefits to the insured rather than the policy owner - can ownership by an irrevocable trust or by another third-party keep the death benefit out of the insured's estate?

When the insured qualifies for benefits under the provisions of the product, the third-party owner of the product ordinarily receives the payment of the benefits, not the insured or the caregiver. In such cases, the insured will pay for the care from his or her own funds, thereby reducing the taxable estate. If no assets are available to the insured – it is ordinarily possible for the insured to indirectly get access to the benefits via gifts from children (if they are the beneficiary) or from trust loans (when the policy is trust owned). Different, and potentially more troubling, issues are raised in the rare product structure with contractual language that dictates payment of the lifetime benefit to the insured rather than the policy owner. Benefits received by a third-party owner are available for whatever use or investment the owner desires. It is well to note that the use of such arrangements is very new and not clearly anticipated by the laws governing the taxation of long-term care combination products. Some risk exists that the use of these products in such arrangements will not be found to enjoy the same tax benefits as more conventional ownership arrangements.

(continued on next page)

LONG-TERM CARE HYBRID PRODUCTS (continued)

Many advisors feel that a major impetus driving family-wide long-term care planning is the existence of so-called "filial laws" (also sometimes called "filial responsibility laws" or "filial piety laws"). While these laws take many forms across the many jurisdictions, they share a common aspect: the laws generally extend the responsibility for the care of an individual – and for the cost of such care – to other individuals, depending upon his or her relationship to the one cared for. Although a majority of states and Puerto Rico have one or more laws that extend some degree of responsibility for care (and sometimes liability for crimes) to family members, there has been very little development in the interplay between such laws and federal tax law. Most of the rare cases where such laws have been invoked by family members to show that a transfer was not a gift, but could have been required by filial law, have failed. At the same time, in many of the states where such laws exist, there are instances where the laws have been enforced against family members after a relative died insolvent with bills outstanding for care.

MANAGED CARE

Managed care is a comprehensive approach to health care with the intent of lowering costs by arranging for care at predetermined or discounted rates, specifying which doctors and hospitals the patient can use and overseeing physicians' treatments and referrals. The basic variations of managed care plans include:

1. **Health Maintenance Organization (HMO):** A health plan that combines coverages of health-care costs and delivery of health care for a prepaid premium. Members receive services from individuals employed by or under contract to the HMO. HMOs generally require patients to select a primary-care physician (PCP) who coordinates the patient's care. Patients usually need referrals from the PCP before going to a specialist or a hospital. The PCP is often referred to as a "gatekeeper." In return for accepting these restrictions, patients are relieved of deductible or coinsurance payments and copayments are typically only $10 to $20 per visit to the doctor. This is in contrast to the traditional major medical plan or fee-for-service plan under which patients can choose both their doctors and hospitals, but must pay 20 percent of the costs (subject to caps). In HMOs the direct relationship between the financing and delivery of health care has generated criticism of: (1) the existence of "gag rules" that prohibit physicians from discussing all possible treatment options with patients; (2) the denial of access to specialists; (3) the denial of reimbursements for emergency room charges in hospitals outside the plan; (4) limits placed on hospital stays for certain procedures; and (5) treatment decisions designed to save money and adverse to the patient's health.

2. **Point-Of-Service (POS):** A managed-care option that allows members to seek care outside the HMO network, but at a higher cost (usually in the form of higher premiums, co-payments, and deductibles).

3. **Preferred Provider Organization (PPO):** A network of independent physicians, hospitals, and other healthcare providers who contract with insurance companies to provide care at discounted rates. Members are given incentives to use the PPO physicians but for a higher cost are allowed to use doctors and hospitals outside the network. This is also referred to as a "managed indemnity" plan.

MARITAL DEDUCTION

By taking advantage of the marital deduction, unlimited amounts of property can be passed between spouses, during lifetime or at death, free of gift taxes and estate taxes. However, the marital deduction is generally not allowed if the property represents a terminable interest (i.e., an ownership right that will come to an end after a period of time or upon the occurrence of some specified event in the future).

The marital deduction can be obtained through the use of any of the following techniques:

1. **Outright transfer** – passes property directly to the surviving spouse. This can be accomplished in a variety of ways, including: joint ownership with rights of survivorship; beneficiary designation; bequest or devise; inheritance; and dower or curtesy (or under state intestate succession laws).

2. **Power of appointment trust** – gives the surviving spouse a right to all income for life and a general power of appointment over the trust assets (i.e., the unlimited right to withdraw property during lifetime or appoint property at death). In the chart on page 21, the "A" trust represents a power of appointment trust, which is also referred to as a "marital deduction trust." An expanded discussion of "general power of appointment" is contained on page 493.

3. **QTIP trust** – gives the surviving spouse a right to all income for life, with principal to children, or others, upon death of the surviving spouse. The primary advantage of the QTIP arrangement is that the *first* spouse to die controls who gets QTIP trust assets following the death of the surviving spouse while still qualifying the transfer to the QTIP trust for the unlimited marital deduction. Thus, QTIP trusts are an exception to the terminable interest rule. The executor or executrix must make the QTIP election. Property placed in a QTIP trust is subject to estate taxation in the surviving spouse's estate. See the discussion and chart on pages 30-33.

4. **Estate trust** – can accumulate income without payments to the surviving spouse, but must be paid to the estate of the surviving spouse (i.e., surviving spouse determines who eventually receives property placed in this trust, plus any accumulated income).

5. **Qualified domestic trust** – assures collection of the federal estate tax when the surviving spouse is a non-citizen. An expanded discussion is contained on page 509.

MEDICAID

This state-run public assistance program provides medical benefits to groups of low-income people, some who may have no medical insurance or inadequate medical insurance. Although the federal government establishes general guidelines for the program, the Medicaid program requirements are actually established by each State. A State is required to include certain types of individuals or eligibility groups under its Medicaid plan and the plan may include others. States' eligibility groups include: *categorically needy* such as Supplemental Security Income (SSI) recipients, *medically needy* such as blind persons, and *special groups* such as community Long Term Care services for individuals who are Medicaid eligible and qualify for institutional care.

Qualifying For Medicaid. Basic to qualifying for Medicaid assistance is the requirement that applicants do not have sufficient *income* to provide for their own care. Most states permit individuals with excess income to qualify for Medicaid, provided they "spend down" this income by incurring medical expenses (but some "income cap" states deny benefits whenever there is excess income). Medicaid qualification also requires that the applicant have very limited amounts of personal *resources* (spousal impoverishment rules allow a non-institutionalized spouse to maintain separate property). In 2018, the home equity that is exempt is limited to $750,000 in most states, although some states have elected the higher limit of $840,000.There is no limit for homes occupied by a stay-at-home spouse (referred to as a "community spouse"). To discourage applicants from making transfers for inadequate consideration, transfers during a "look-back" period can delay eligibility for a period equal to the amount of the transfers divided by the average costs to a private patient in a nursing facility in the state.

MEDICAID PLANNING

Households with incomes up to 138 percent of the federal poverty level ($16,394 a year for an individual or $33,534 for a family of four) qualify for medicaid health care coverage. Children up to age six and pregnant women qualify with an income up to 160 percent of the federal poverty level ($38,880 for a family of four).

Medicaid long-term care benefits require that an institutionalized individual can have countable assets of no more than $2,000. If married, the non-institutionalized spouse can retain countable assets within limits set by the Federal government (the specific amount varies from state to state, but was limited to a maximum of $120,900 in 2017). Countable assets include virtually all investments, savings, and real estate owned by the applicant and his or her spouse. See also, page 460.

Annuities. An immediate annuity can be used as a means of transforming "countable" assets into an income stream that does not affect Medicaid long-term care eligibility. To qualify the annuity must be: (1) irrevocable – periodic payments cannot be changed, (2) non-transferable – benefits cannot be changed to another beneficiary, (3) "actuarially sound" – a term certain annuity cannot be payable for longer than the annuitant's actuarial life expectancy; and (4) the state must be named the first remainder beneficiary up to the amount of Medicaid benefits paid on the annuitant's behalf (if a surviving spouse or blind or disabled child is named as the primary beneficiary, then the state may be named the secondary beneficiary).

Purchase of life estate. The purchase of a life estate is not considered a transfer of assets provided the purchaser resides in the home for a period of at least one year after the date of purchase (e.g., father living in son's home purchases from the son a life estate in the home, lives there for at least one year, and then enters a nursing home). This transforms a countable resource (cash) into a non-countable resource (the life estate), provided payment for the life estate does not exceed its fair market value as calculated in accordance with certain tables. Before entering into such an arrangement the capital gains tax consequences to both the parent and the child should be carefully considered (e.g., potential elimination of capital gains tax exemption upon a subsequent sale of the home).

Transfer in trust for disabled child. Transfers to a supplemental needs trust for the "sole benefit" of the applicant's permanently and totally disabled (or blind) child do not affect Medicaid eligibility (see page 551).

Planning for the home. The value of the applicant's home is important in determining eligibility for Medicaid benefits to pay the costs of long-term care. Home equity that is exempt was limited in 2017 to $750,000, although states could raise this to $840,000. However, this limitation on home equity does not apply if any of the following persons reside in the home: (1) the individual's spouse; (2) the individual's child under twenty-one; (3) the individual's blind or disabled child; (4) a sibling who has an ownership interest in the home and was residing in the home for a period of at least one year immediately before the individual became institutionalized; or (5) a caregiver child who resided in the home for a period of at least two years immediately before the individual became institutionalized and whose care permitted such individual to reside at home. Further, Medicaid eligibility is not compromised if the individual receiving Medicaid *transfers* the home to any of these same people (e.g., the home is given to the caregiver child). Once transferred, the home is no longer subject to a Medicare reimbursement claim, as such claim can only be asserted against the recipient's estate.

MEDICAL INFORMATION BUREAU

The Medical Information Bureau (MIB) is a nonprofit trade association of over 700 life insurance companies that was first organized in 1902 to conduct a confidential interchange of underwriting information among its members as an alert against fraud. This interchange enables MIB member companies to protect the interests of both insurance consumers and life and health insurance providers. MIB's basic purpose is to detect and deter fraud and misrepresentation in connection with the underwriting of life and health insurance and claims.

Upon receipt of an application accompanied by a suitable authorization, member companies conduct a search of MIB records as part of their usual underwriting procedure. Members are also required to report relevant results of their underwriting evaluation to the MIB; that is, of conditions that are significant to health or longevity. Both favorable and unfavorable medical information is reported. Certain nonmedical information of a very restricted nature regarding insurability is also reported (e.g., confirmed adverse driving record, hazardous sports activity and aviation activity). In order to help preserve confidentiality the information is reported and maintained in code symbols. Members may not report codes based on claim information.

MIB information is used only to alert member companies to the possible need for further information. It *may not* be used as a basis for establishing eligibility for insurance. An MIB report does not indicate the underwriting action of the reporting company or the amount of coverage applied for.

Only member companies have access to MIB information and then only after receiving written authorization from the proposed insured in the course of the application process. The proposed insured's spouse cannot give this authorization. MIB information is not released to nonmember companies, credit or consumer reporting agencies, or governmental agencies, except pursuant to court order or authorization from the consumer.

The consumer who applies for life, health, or disability insurance receives a brief written notice that describes MIB and its function. In addition, this notice tells how the consumer can access and correct his MIB record when needed. To obtain a copy of their MIB record, if one exists, or to seek correction of the MIB record, consumers can contact the MIB toll-free at 866-692-6901. Their web site is located at www.mib.com.

MEDICARE

Medicare is a federal health insurance program for persons sixty-five or older, persons of any age with permanent kidney failure, and certain disabled persons. The program is administered by the Centers for Medicare & Medicaid Services (CMS). Medicare claims are processed and paid by various commercial insurance companies under contract with CMS.

Part A – Hospital Insurance protection provides institutional care, including inpatient hospital care, skilled nursing home care, post-hospital home health care, and, under certain circumstances, hospice care.

(a) **Enrollment**. Any person eligible for Social Security monthly benefits is automatically eligible for Hospital Insurance protection, beginning with the first day of the month in which the person turns age sixty-five. An individual who is *already receiving* Social Security monthly benefits need not file again to receive Medicare Part A benefits. A person *eligible for, but not yet receiving*, Social Security monthly benefits may apply separately for Medicare Part A benefits. Most retired individuals pay no Part A premium (see premium summary on page 465).

(b) **Coverage**. For the first sixty days, all covered hospital expenses are paid in full except for an initial inpatient deductible ($1,316 in 2017). For the next thirty days, the patient must pay a daily coinsurance charge ($329 per day in 2017). Thereafter, the patient has available an additional lifetime reserve of 60 hospital days, during which the patient must pay a daily coinsurance charge ($658 per day in 2017). Skilled nursing facility care, home health care, and hospice care, are also covered, but intermediate and *custodial care* are not covered. Beyond 150 days there is no coverage. See benefits summary on page 466.

Part B – Medical Insurance protection is a voluntary program of health insurance, which covers physician services, outpatient hospital care, physical therapy, ambulance trips, medical equipment, prosthetics, and a number of other services not covered under Part A. This is also known as "Supplementary Medical Insurance (SMI)."

(a) **Enrollment**. Those who are receiving Social Security benefits are enrolled automatically at the time they become entitled to Hospital Insurance, unless they elect not to be covered for Medical Insurance. For persons born after 1938 normal retirement age is not age sixty-five (see page 637). These persons must enroll before the beginning of the month in which age sixty-five is reached, in order to obtain coverage at the earliest possible date (unless they have elected early retirement, in which case they are enrolled automatically). See premium summary on page 465.

(continued on next page)

MEDICARE (continued)

(b) **Coverage**. Medical Insurance helps pay for covered services received from a doctor in the doctor's office, in a hospital, in a skilled nursing facility, in the patient's home, or any other location. After the patient pays the first $134 of covered services in each calendar year, Medicare usually pays 80 percent of the approved charges for doctors' services and the cost of other services. See benefits summary on page 466. Medical Insurance under Medicare *does not cover*: (1) most routine physical examinations and tests directly related to such examinations; (2) most routine foot care and dental care; (3) examinations for prescribing or fitting eyeglasses or hearing aids, and most eyeglasses and hearing aids; (4) immunizations (except annual flu shots and limited vaccinations for certain persons at risk); (5) most cosmetic surgery; and (6) custodial care at home or in a nursing home. (Although Medicare does provide a limited benefit for home health care, it is the Medicaid system that provides for nursing home care.)

Part C – Medicare Advantage, previously known as Medicare+Choice, permits contracts between CMS and a variety of different managed care and fee-for-service organizations. These plans must provide all current Medicare-covered items and services, and they may incorporate extra benefits in a basic package, or they may offer supplemental benefits priced separately from the basic package. Most Medicare beneficiaries can choose to receive benefits through the original Medicare fee-for-service program, or through a coordinated care plan (including Health Maintenance Organizations (HMOs), Preferred Provider Organizations (PPOs), and Provider-Sponsored Organizations (PSOs)), or a private fee-for-service plan that reimburses providers on a fee-for-service basis.

Part D – Prescription drug plans, provides a comprehensive voluntary prescription drug benefit available to everyone with Medicare. The plans are provided by insurance companies and other private companies approved by Medicare. Coverage is available under stand-alone plans, or through Medicare Advantage plans that integrate with health care coverage provided under Part C of Medicare. In 2017 the average basic premium is about $34 a month.

(a) **Enrollment**. There is an opportunity to enroll when joining Medicare, or during an annual open enrollment period running from November 15th to December 31st. Although enrollment is optional, those who fail to enroll will pay a penalty of about 1 percent for each month of delay (e.g., delaying enrollment for fourteen months will result in a 14 percent lifetime increase in premiums). Persons who have prescription drug coverage "at least as good" as the basic plan (see next paragraph) will not incur a penalty. However, not all drugs are available in every plan.

In selecting a plan the enrollee must balance the three Cs of cost, coverage, and convenience. For example, plans may charge a higher monthly premium in return for enhanced coverage offering a greater selection of drugs (set out in a "formulary"), lower deductibles, lower co-pays, and greater geographic coverage. Plan selection has been made difficult by the sheer number and variety of plans offered. A drug finder program can be found at www.medicare.gov.

(continued on next page)

MEDICARE (continued)

(b) **Coverage**. All plans must provide coverage "at least as good" as the standard coverage set by Medicare. In 2017, under standard coverage, once the enrollee has paid a $400 annual deductible, the enrollee pays 25 percent and Medicare pays 75 percent of drugs costs on the next $3,700. The enrollee then pays 79 percent for generic drugs and 47.5 percent for brand name drugs on the next $4,950 (this represents the continued phase out of the donut hole coverage gap under The Patient Protection and Affordable Care Act of 2010). Thereafter, the enrollee pays 5 percent, and Medicare pays 95 percent of drug costs. Plans cover both generic and brand-name drugs. Low-income subsidies provide for no gap in coverage, and reduce, or eliminate, premiums, deductibles, and co-payments.

For those individuals who have retiree prescription drug benefits from their employers, substantial direct subsidies, and tax benefits, are offered to employers who maintain drug coverage for retired workers. The previous Medicare-approved drug discount cards have been phased out.

Premium Summary

2019

HOSPITAL (Part A)

Monthly Premium*	Quarters of Medicare-Covered Employment
$240	30 or more
$437	less than 30 (and not otherwise eligible for premium-free hospital insurance)

MEDICAL (Part B)

	Income of Beneficiaries Who File					
Monthly Premium	Married Filing Jointly		Married Filing Separately		Other Than Married	
	Over	To	Over	To	Over	To
$135.50	0	170,000	0	85,000	0	85,000
$189.60	170,000	214,000	-	-	85,000	107,000
$270.90	214,000	267,000	-	-	107,000	133,500
$352.20	267,000	320,000	-	-	133,500	160,000
$433.40	320,000	750,000	85,000	415,000	160,000	500,000
$460.50	750,000	-	415,000	-	500,000	-

* Most retired individuals pay no Part A premium.

(continued on next page)

MEDICARE (continued)

Benefits Summary
2019

HOSPITAL (Part A)

	Benefit	Individual Pays	Medicare Pays
Hospitalization	first 60 days	$1,364	balance
	61st to 90th day	$341 a day	balance
	91st to 150th day	$682 a day	balance
	beyond 150 days	all costs	nothing
Skilled Nursing Facility Care	first 20 days	nothing	all (as approved)
	next 80 days	$170.50 a day	balance
	beyond 100 days	all	nothing
Home Health Care	first 100 days in spell of illness	nothing for services 20% for durable medical equipment	all balance
Hospice Care	unlimited (doctor must certify)	outpatient drugs and inpatient respite care	balance

MEDICAL (Part B)

Medical Expenses	unlimited	$185 deductible plus 20% of remaining	balance
Clinical Laboratory Services	unlimited	nothing	all
Home Health Care	unlimited (but covers only what is not covered under Part A)	nothing for services 20% for equipment	all balance
Outpatient Hospital Treatment	unlimited	$185 deductible plus 20% of remaining	balance

Benefits must be medically necessary. Under Part A hospitalization benefits from 91st to 150th day are the 60 "reserve" days that may be used only once in a lifetime.

MINIMUM DEPOSIT INSURANCE

Minimum deposit insurance is not a particular type of life insurance contract. It is a method of paying premiums using policy loans. (In contrast, see the discussion of Premium Financing on page 494.)

Because consumer interest is not deductible, minimum deposit insurance is unattractive for most individual policy owners. Nevertheless, within strict limits a business (including a corporation, partnership, or sole proprietorship) can deduct interest payments that are reasonable business expenses on a policy that is "tax qualified." This deduction is limited to loan interest paid on policies insuring a "key person" for up to $50,000 of indebtedness. A key person is an officer or a 20-percent owner of the business. The number of individuals who may be treated as key persons is limited to the greater of: (1) five persons; or (2) the lesser of five percent of the total officers and employees or twenty individuals (i.e., no more than 20 persons can be treated as key persons).

In addition, interest in excess of an "applicable rate" cannot be deducted (referred to as an interest rate "cap"). The applicable rate is that rate described in Moody's Corporate Bond Yield Average - Monthly Average Corporates, as published by Moody's Investors Service.

Except for application of a modified interest rate cap, contracts issued prior to June 21, 1986, are "grandfathered" (e.g., they are not subject to the key person provisions described above). Loans taken on nongrandfathered policies before 1996 are subject to a phase-in of the disallowance of the interest deduction. No deduction is allowed for the part of the taxpayer's interest expense which is "allocable to unborrowed policy cash values," which are defined as the excess of the cash surrender values (determined without regard to surrender charges) over the amount of any policy loans. However, there is an exception which applies to policies and contracts owned by entities if the policy covers only one individual who, at the time first covered by the policy, is: (1) a 20-percent-owner of the entity; or (2) an individual who is an officer, director or employee of the trade or business. See **Q 31**, *Tax Facts on Insurance & Employee Benefits (2018)* for a more complete explanation of the above limits on policy loan interest.

Most plans of minimum deposit insurance can be best explained as follows: (1) cash values are borrowed at a relatively low rate of interest; (2) borrowed cash values are used to pay premiums; (3) if any 4 out of the first seven years' premiums are paid from unborrowed funds and borrowing in the other three years does not exceed the annual premiums, the policy is considered "tax qualified" and the interest paid on the borrowed cash values is deductible within the limits established under IRS regulations; (4) if the interest is deductible, after-tax cost is reduced; (5) if desired, beginning in the eighth year, both the premium and the after-tax cost of interest payments can be borrowed.

MINORS AND IRAs

IRA established for a minor. If a minor has earned income, the minor can have his or her own IRA (federal law has no age requirement). State law determines whether the financial institution is able to contract direct with a minor. If the minor cannot directly open an account, then the IRA can be established by a custodian under a custodial account (see Uniform Transfers/Uniform Gifts to Minors Acts, page 575). An IRA can also be established by a court appointed guardian, but this can be both timely and costly. When either a custodial account or guardianship is used, it must be accepted that the minor will have legal title to the IRA upon attaining the age of majority (this varies from eighteen to twenty-one years of age depending upon the state).

Typically this may not a major disadvantage, since the account is likely to have only modest value.

Minor as beneficiary of inherited IRA. A minor can also be named the primary or contingent beneficiary of another individual's IRA account (e.g., in the parent's IRA the spouse is named the primary beneficiary and a minor child is named the contingent beneficiary). As with an IRA established for the minor, either a custodial account or a guardianship arrangement can be used with an inherited IRA. However, the arrangement terminates once the beneficiary has reached the age of majority and there is no control as to how the funds are spent. This can be a major disadvantage, since inherited IRAs often have substantial value.

With a trust the grantor can prevent the minor from having access to the entire value of the IRA, until such time as determined by the grantor. However, the grantor cannot delay all distributions to the minor. Unlike the IRA account holder who can delay required minimum distributions (RMDs) until age 70½, minors who are IRA beneficiaries must take RMDs each year following the account holder's death. Because minors have relatively long life expectancies, the amounts of these yearly distributions are very low, with the result that the bulk of the account can continue to grow tax-deferred for many years (with the Roth IRA this growth is *tax-free*).

Keeping these distributions low requires that the RMD calculation be based upon the minor's life (or at least upon the life of a relatively young individual). To accomplish this it is important that the trust contain very specific language and the trust beneficiaries be limited, otherwise it is possible that the trust could be forced to make all distributions within as little as five years of the IRA owner's death (i.e. there would be no opportunity to make "stretch distributions" to the minor over his or her lifetime). See the discussion of See-Through Trust on page 541.

MINORS AND LIFE INSURANCE

Insurance companies will not knowingly accept a minor as the direct owner of a life insurance contract (for minor as insured, see page 312). Although trusts provide the most flexible way of managing policies and proceeds, establishing and administering them involves both time and expense. Policy ownership and beneficiary arrangements involving minors are governed by either the Uniform Transfers to Minors Act (UTMA) or the Uniform Gifts to Minors Act (UGMA) (see page 575). Other than South Carolina and Vermont, where the older and more restrictive UGMA is still in effect, all states have statutes based upon the UTMA. But, despite the general adoption of UTMA by most states, it is important to consult individual state laws, since states typically alter the text of the uniform versions.

If the beneficiary designation includes a custodial nomination, the proceeds can be transferred to a custodian without appointing a guardian. Any trust company or adult other than the insured can be nominated custodian (an adult under state UTMAs is usually age twenty-one). A designation paying a death benefit to a child of the insured might read: "[name of child], child of the insured; provided that if any proceeds become payable when [name of child] is a minor as defined in the [state] Uniform Transfers to Minors Act, such proceeds shall be paid to [name of adult] as custodian for [name of child] under the [state] Uniform Transfers to Minors Act." Note that this language covers the possibility that the child might become an adult by the time a death benefit is paid. A substitute custodian should be named in case the primary custodian cannot serve.

Without a custodial nomination, it is possible that the insurance company will require appointment of a guardian of the minor's property prior to making payment of death proceeds. The only exception allows for payment of small amounts, usually $10,000, to either a trust company or an adult member of the minor's family (a no-nomination transfer).

To give an *existing* policy to a minor, the owner signs a change of ownership form naming the custodian as owner. In the case of a *new* policy, the custodian is designated as owner on the application. In either case, the ownership designation reads: "[name of adult], as custodian for [name of child] under the [state] Uniform Transfers to Minors Act." In contrast, the purchase of a policy using custodial funds is a reinvestment of funds. If the minor is the insured then the minor's estate should be named beneficiary. If someone else is the insured then the beneficiary must be the minor, the minor's estate, or a custodian, and the designation must be irrevocable so long as the custodianship remains in effect. In this situation the beneficiary designation might read: "[name of child], child of the insured, if living, otherwise to the estate of [name of child]; provided that the proceeds shall be paid to [name of adult] as custodian for [name of child] under the [state] Uniform Transfers to Minors Act if the proceeds become payable while such custodianship remains in effect; without the right to change while such custodianship remains in effect."

MONEY PURCHASE PENSION PLAN

Under the money purchase pension plan each employee/participant has an individual account into which the employer makes annual contributions pursuant to the plan's contribution formula. These employer contributions are required and the employer is subject to a minimum funding penalty if they are not made. The formula used to determine contribution amounts must be nondiscriminatory and typically sets employer contributions at a specific percentage of the employee's annual compensation. Only the first $275,000 (as indexed in 2018) of each employee's compensation can be taken into consideration. The maximum annual addition that can be contributed to a money purchase plan is the lesser of 100 percent of the participant's compensation, or $55,000 (as indexed in 2018). In determining the level of employer contributions, integration with Social Security is allowed.

The maximum amount an employer may deduct for money purchase plan contributions is 25 percent of compensation (i.e., generally payroll, but subject to the $275,000 per participant limit in 2018). Prior to 2002 this 25 percent limit provided money purchase pension plans with an advantage over profit sharing plans, since the deduction for profit sharing contributions was limited to 15 percent of payroll. Without this advantage, employers have increasingly chosen to establish the more flexible profit sharing plan, rather than a money purchase pension plan that requires annual employer contributions.

Unlike the defined benefit pension plan, under a money purchase pension plan the employee bears the investment risk of the plan (i.e., the employer is obligated only to make the initial contribution, after that *the risk of poor investment performance is borne by the participant*). The employee also bears the risk that the amounts accumulated at retirement might be insufficient to fund retirement needs. Upon retirement the participant's account balance can be paid in a lump sum, paid in installments for a number of years, or used to purchase an annuity providing an income for life (this is the origin of the term "money purchase"). Of all qualified plans the money purchase pension plan is generally considered the simplest to design, explain, install and administer.

See also, the discussions of Qualified Retirement Plans on page 512 and Life Insurance in Qualified Plans on pages 419-420.

NET UNREALIZED APPRECIATION

With certain exceptions, distributions from qualified retirement plans are subject to taxation as ordinary income. To avoid current taxation, it is common for an individual receiving a lump sum distribution from a qualified retirement plan to make a tax-free rollover to a traditional IRA. However, if the rollover includes *appreciated employer stock*, then the employee should consider taking distribution of the stock (i.e., not rolling it over into an IRA). By doing this, the stock's net unrealized appreciation (NUA) will qualify for long-term capital gains rates whenever the stock is sold by the employee, by the employee's spouse, or by the employee's heirs. NUA is the stock's fair market value in excess of basis. Basis is generally the value of the stock at the time that it was acquired by the plan. Subsequent appreciation of the stock in excess of NUA is taxed as either short-term or long-term capital gains, depending upon how long the stock is held after it is distributed from the plan.

To take advantage of this favorable tax treatment, the employee must receive the stock as part of a "lump sum distribution" from a qualified retirement plan (i.e., payment within one year of the entire account balance as a result of the employee's separation from service, attaining age 59½, disability, or death). The employee must also pay ordinary income taxes on the cost basis of the stock distributed (i.e., the value of the stock at the time that it was acquired by the plan). The decision for the employee comes down to this: Is it worth paying current ordinary income taxes on the stock's basis in return for obtaining long-term capital gains treatment for the stock's NUA at some point in the future?

The employee may also make a tax-free rollover to a traditional IRA of some, but not all, of the employer stock. (The NUA within the stock rolled over to the IRA would end up being taxed as ordinary income.) Likewise, when a distribution consists of both employer stock and other assets, these other assets may be rolled into an IRA to avoid current taxation. All rollovers must be made within 60 days of the distribution.

For example, assume an employee receives a lump-sum distribution from his 401(k) plan of $600,000 in employer stock with a cost basis of $125,000, pays ordinary income taxes on the $125,000, and sells the stock six years later for $850,000. Of this amount, the cost basis of $125,000 is not taxed (it was taxed upon distribution), NUA of $475,000 is taxed as long-term capital gains, and the after-distribution gain of $250,000 is taxed as either short-term or long-term capital gains – depending upon the holding period (long-term in this example).

If the stock with NUA remains unsold at death, the NUA is treated as income in respect of a decedent and it is not entitled to a step-up in basis (but it is entitled to capital gains treatment when sold by the heirs). See income in respect of a decedent, page 403, and stepped-up basis, page 556.

NIMCRUT

The term NIMCRUT stands for Net Income with Make-up Charitable Remainder UniTrust. As a form of charitable remainder unitrust (CRUT), the trust assets are valued annually creating a unitrust amount (variable annuity payment) made at least annually to one or more trust beneficiaries. Distributions consist of the *lesser of*: (1) a fixed percentage (not less than 5 percent) of the value of the trust assets (valued annually); or (2) the net income of the trust for the current year. Unlike the CRUT (see page 309), a make-up account is created in any year that income earned is less than the fixed percentage allowed. The make-up account is then paid out in any future year in which the income earned exceeds the fixed percentage payout for that specific year (i.e., the NIMCRUT provides for "make-up" distributions). No adjustment for the time value of money is allowed for these make-up distributions. *Pre-contribution* capital gains are generally not available for distribution. *Post-contribution* capital gains may be classified as income, provided this does not conflict with state law (see the discussion of the Prudent Investor Rule on page 503).

A NIMCRUT provides a great deal of flexibility for the donor who wishes to defer income for retirement. Trust income can be deferred by having the trustee make appropriate investment selections (e.g., a deferred annuity), or by donating to the trust low-income or non-income producing assets (e.g., growth stocks, closely held stock, or real estate). Unlike the CRUT, if trust income is not adequate, the trustee has no obligation to pay out the full unitrust amount and the donor may be positioned to receive larger make-up payments after retirement. Also, as with the CRUT, a donor may make multiple gifts to the same NIMCRUT. However, before making gifts to any NIMCRUT, it is essential that the donor fully understand that payments are contingent upon the trust earning income.

For the donor who desires greater flexibility, a FLIP unitrust might be considered. This technique begins with a NIMCRUT, or a NICRUT (similar to a NIMCRUT but without the makeup provisions), that is converted to a standard CRUT upon the occurrence of an approved triggering event. Approved triggering events cannot be controlled by the donor, unitrust beneficiary, trustee, or any other person. For example, the beneficiary's 65th birthday is an approved triggering event, but not the beneficiary's retirement, as that event is controlled by the beneficiary. Unfortunately, when a NIMCRUT flips to a standard CRUT, any outstanding make-up amounts are forfeited.

See also, Charitable Remainder Trust chart on page 59.

NONCITIZEN ESTATE PLANNING

For the purpose of estate and gift tax planning, it is helpful to recognize three categories of individuals: (1) United States citizens; (2) resident aliens (i.e., non-citizens who are resident in the United States); and (3) nonresident aliens (i.e., non-citizens who are resident in another country).

Resident aliens. The property of a resident alien is subject to United States estate and gift tax laws, no matter where it is located. For estate and gift tax purposes, residency means that the person is actually "domiciled" in the United States. Generally, a person acquires a domicile by living in a place, even for a brief period of time, with no definite present intention of leaving and living elsewhere. This is a rather subjective determination that is influenced by where the individual's time is spent, as well as the location of other family members, business interests, social activities, driver's license, and financial and tax relationships. It is important to recognize that although a person can have more than one "residence," they can have only one domicile (i.e., do not confuse the terms "residence" and "residency"). See the expanded discussion of domicile on pages 136-137.

Although a resident alien is generally subject to the same estate and gift tax rules much the same as a United States citizen, the unlimited marital deduction is unavailable if the spouse is not a United States citizen (gifts to foreign spouses are limited to $152,000 in 2018, see page 509). Because of the unified gift and estate tax system, gifts made prior to becoming a resident may also be included in the resident alien's estate. However, resident aliens can take advantage of the full unified credit (page 14), annual exclusion gifts (page 50), split-gifts with spouses (page 42), and irrevocable life insurance trusts (page 54).

Nonresident aliens. Property located within the United States is subject to both gift and estate taxes (i.e., it has a "situs" within the United States and is therefore taxed). Only the first $60,000 of property is free of transfer taxes and the unlimited marital deduction is not available unless the spouse is a United States citizen (in 2018 gifts to foreign spouses are limited to $152,000, see page 509). Gifts of *tangible* property and *real estate* are subject to gift taxes (but gifts of *intangible* property are generally free of gift taxes). However, bank deposits and life insurance are specifically excluded from both gift and estate taxation (i.e., they are deemed not to have a "situs" within the United States). Thus, the proceeds of a life insurance policy on the life of a nonresident alien are not subject to estate taxes, even though the beneficiary is a resident or citizen of the United States.

A foreign death tax credit is available for estate taxes actually paid to a foreign country or United States possession in which the property is located (but there is no credit for foreign *gift* taxes). Foreign death and gift tax treaties can also offer relief from the double taxation often imposed upon both resident and nonresident aliens. However, such planning can be very complicated, and the advice of competent tax counsel should be sought.

NONQUALIFIED EXECUTIVE BENEFITS

With an aging workforce and an economic boom now nearing a decade since the global financial crisis of 2008, businesses are increasingly aware of the valuable role employee benefits play in retaining and recruiting key employees. Many employee benefits are offered to everyone in the organization. They consist of the more common or traditional types of benefits — such as 401(k) plans, health insurance, and paid vacation. While these benefits may include certain tax breaks and other advantages to employers, they are usually considered standard by employees in large organizations, and can be a determining factor in attracting employees to small businesses.

By contrast, Nonqualified Executive Benefits are designed primarily for highly compensated employees and key people. They can give key individuals an incentive to stay at an organization ("golden handcuffs") and can fill gaps where other benefits fall short. An example of the later may be a plan that supplements retirement income where caps on the employer's 401(k) plan may limit how much an executive can set aside to replace their income in retirement.

These plans fall under a category called Nonqualified Executive Benefits because they fall outside of the traditional qualified plans which must be offered to everyone and must comply with ERISA. These nonqualified plans can be discriminatory and offered to only a select group of employees. As such they can avoid certain aspects of ERISA such as participation requirements. However, the nature of the plan may pull them into certain other aspects of ERISA.

Employers should be careful as to how widely they offer these nonqualified benefits so as to be certain they remain limited, discriminatory plans. If they are offered too widely, they may be further pulled into full compliance under ERISA. As such, they should only be offered to a highly select group of executives, often called "Top-Hat" employees. Where possible an employer may want to offer customized terms to emphasize the selective nature of these plans. There are other times where the plan may need an outside administrator and some commonality may be incorporated to make it cost efficient to administer the plans. A good advisor can help balance these plans to keep them in a nonqualified category.

Nonqualified Plans fall under three broad categories:

- Executive Bonus
- Split Dollar, and
- Deferral Plans/Supplemental Executive Retirement Plans

(continued on next page)

NONQUALIFIED EXECUTIVE BENEFITS (continued)

Each is briefly discussed, below. When deciding between these plans there are contrasting considerations that need to be weighed. For example, certain arrangements afford the employer complete control at the expense of current deductibility. In other plans, the employer may receive a current tax deduction for funding the plan, but will generally retain less control over the plan. At times what an employer may value in a plan might conflict with what an employee might value as a benefit. Only after weighing and balancing these considerations is it possible to determine the appropriate plan for a particular employer and employee. Balancing the interests of both the employee and employer are critical in determining which plan will be mutually beneficial.

Executive Bonus plans are generally employer-paid life insurance where the policy is owned by the employee or a family member. These are often designed to offer death benefit protection, but are also often focused on additionally offering cash value with the potential for supplemental retirement income through policy withdrawals and loans.

Typically the employer will receive an immediate income tax deduction for the premium payments and the executive will pay taxes on the same amount. In some cases an employer may "gross-up" the executive's pay to cover the tax bill the executive might pay. This variation on Executive Bonus plans is often called a Double Bonus Plan. In other variations the employer might simply loan the tax amount to an Executive. However, they must be careful to not retain an interest or lien in the policy or they will jeopardize their income tax deduction.

With traditional Executive Bonus plans the policy is not controlled by the employer. Where an employer might wish some control a variation has developed that places an endorsement on the life insurance contract. The endorsement restricts the policyowner's rights in the contract until it is lifted by the employer. Generally the executive must meet certain requirements, such as years of service, at which point the restrictions are lifted. Although this is a limited control, it offers at least some element of control to the employer. This variation goes by several names such as Restricted Executive Bonus Arrangement (REBA) or Golden Handcuff Executive Bonus (GEBA). For a more detailed discussion on Restricted Bonus Plans see page 236.

Split Dollar plans are arrangements where the employer pays premiums for a life insurance policy and the policy's death benefit and cash values are split. The tax treatment of these plans is controlled by who owns the policy, the employer or employee.

Where the employer owns the contract, they generally own the cash value and have endorsed the death benefit over to the employee or a family member or trust. In these instances the employee, which retains an interest in the policy cannot deduct the premium payments. The Executive, who has no ownership in the policy, will recognize income taxation based on the death benefit they receive.

(continued on next page)

NONQUALIFIED EXECUTIVE BENEFITS (continued)

The amount of death benefit is net of the cash value owned by the employer. This is often called the risk portion of the policy. The amount of taxation is calculated based on this risk portion. A cost per each thousand dollars of death benefit is assessed as income to the employee each year. The amount is per thousand is generally controlled by Table 2001, established by the IRS in 2000 when it revamped guidelines for split dollar plans. Under certain circumstances a carrier's own term rates might be available as an alternative to Table 2001. For a more detailed discussion on Split Dollar see page 240.

There is different tax treatment where the employee (or an employee's trust or other third party) owns the policy. Under this other version of split dollar, the employer is treated as making a loan to the policy owner(s). Interest must be charge on the loan equal to the monthly federal rate, and relate to whether the loan is short term (under three years), mid-term (three to nine years) or long-term (nine years or longer). The loan might also be a demand loan in which case the short term rate is charged. Most split dollar loans fall under these interest rate categories. However, if the rate doesn't comply, it falls under the imputed income rules of Tax Code Section 7872 and certain additional interest might be recognized as early as the year of the loan. For a more detailed discussion of Interest-Free Loans, see page 410.

Deferral and Supplemental Plans – these are two different varieties of plans where the employer controls the benefit the most directly and the employee remains a general creditor of the employer until they receive receipt of the benefit.

With a deferral plan, the employee defers current compensation or foregoes bonuses. These are held by the employer and usually some type of earnings are accrued for the benefit of the employees. The earnings can be based on the performance of the employer, one or more stock indices or mutual funds or even a fixed crediting rate. The benefit payout can then be made after a preselected (prior to the deferral) period of years, as retirement income or as survivor death benefits. With a supplemental plan (often called a SERP, or Supplemental Employee Retirement Plan) the employer proactively sets aside additional (supplemental) funds for a select group of employees. In keeping with the earlier discussion, this must be for a select group of upper level employees.

To avoid falling under ERISA these plans must remain "unfunded." Employers cannot offer any indication that funds or other business assets are specifically allocated to these nonqualified benefit plans. If this were to occur the deferral or supplemental plan may fall under ERISA as a funded plan subject to more stringent ERISA reporting and participation requirements. However, employers may informally fund these plans with either mutual funds matched to the executive elections or with life insurance. In many instances life insurance may offer a tax advantage because funds can grow tax deferred. With variable life insurance policies an employer might be able to closely match changes executives make in their deferral elections. Because these plans are "unfunded" and the employee remains a general creditor of the employer, some executives use a Rabbi Trust to help offer some protection from creditors. These are discussed at page 514.

NONQUALIFIED STOCK OPTIONS

Nonqualified stock options (NQSOs), also referred to as "nonstatutory stock options," are rights to purchase a certain number of shares of stock at a fixed exercise price within a specified period of time. With NQSOs a corporation is able to provide selected employees with the opportunity to share in the future growth of the company, without having to make any current cash outlays for salary or bonuses. Because there are few regulatory restrictions on how they may be designed, NQSOs offer a great deal of flexibility in meeting specific corporate objectives.

The option's exercise price is often referred to as the grant price or strike price. It may be set at the full fair market value (FMV) of the stock as of the date of the grant, at a price below FMV (at a "discount"), or at a price above FMV (at a "premium"). Options may be exercised after the passage of a set period, upon the occurrence of a certain event, and may even be immediately exercisable, although this is not usual. They can also be subject to vesting rules (e.g., after three years of continuous employment).

At the time they are granted NQSOs are generally not taxed to the employee, provided they do not have a "readily ascertainable fair market value." In contrast to options for stock actively traded on an established market, an option to acquire closely held stock has no readily ascertainable fair market value. (Note that it is the option itself that must be tradeable, not the underlying stock.) When the option is exercised the difference between the exercise price and the market value, referred to as the bargain element, is taxed to the employee as ordinary income. At the time of exercise the employer is entitled to a corresponding compensation deduction.

NQSOs are referred to as "nonqualified" stock options because they do not meet the requirements of the Code to be qualified as "incentive" stock options (ISOs). Although ISOs offer income tax advantages that are not available to NQSOs, the Code imposes limitations and restrictions upon ISOs that are not applicable to NQSOs. For example, ISO gains may be taxed at favorable capital gains rates, but ISOs are not transferable during lifetime.

In contrast to ISOs, if permitted by the underlying stock option agreement or plan, NQSOs are transferable during the employee's lifetime. Provided the option is vested, its transfer to a child or other heir is treated as a completed gift (see chart, page 51). However, the donor-employee remains liable for any income taxes when the option is subsequently exercised by the donee-child (i.e., the income tax consequences cannot be transferred). This tax treatment is similar to that imposed upon the trust income of a Intentionally Defective Trust (see chart, page 75).

See also, the discussion of Incentive Stock Options on page 401.

OPPORTUNITY ZONES CREATED BY THE 2017 TAX ACT

The 2017 Tax Act created new rules governing the taxation of capital gains stemming from investments in certain designated low-income qualified opportunity zones. Opportunity zones were designated by the states themselves during a "determination period" which was a ninety-day period immediately after the date of enactment of the 2017 Tax Act. The number of opportunity zones cannot exceed 25 percent of the number of low-income communities in the state. Such a designation remains in effect for a ten-year period.

Generally, the new rules allow a taxpayer to elect to defer recognizing any gains from a sale or exchange of any property held by the taxpayer to the extent that the gains do not exceed the aggregate amount that the taxpayer has invested in a qualified opportunity fund during the 180-day period. Instead, the gain will be included in income in the year that includes the earlier of (1) the date the investment is sold or exchanged or (2) December 31, 2026. The amount included is the excess of (1) the lesser of the amount excluded or the fair market value of the investment as of the date of the sale or exchange or December 31, 2026 over (2) the taxpayer's basis in the investment.

The basis in the investment begins at zero and is increased as gain is recognized. If the investment is held for at least five years, the basis is increased by 10 percent of the gain deferred. If the investment is held for at least seven years, the basis is increased by an additional 5 percent of the gain deferred. If the taxpayer so elects and the investment is held for at least ten years, the basis is equal to the fair market value of the investment on the date the investment is sold or exchanged.

A "qualified opportunity fund" means an investment vehicle organized as a corporation or partnership for the purpose of investing in qualified opportunity zone property where at least 90 percent of its assets are qualified opportunity zone property.

Qualified opportunity zone property means property that is:

1. qualified opportunity zone stock (generally, stock in a qualified opportunity zone acquired for cash after December 31, 2017),

2. qualified opportunity zone partnership interests (generally, interests in a qualified opportunity zone partnership acquired for cash after December 31, 2017), and

3. qualified opportunity zone business property (tangible property used in a trade or business of the qualified opportunity fund where substantially all of the property's use is in a qualified opportunity zone, the property was acquired by purchase after December 31, 2017 and the original use begins with the qualified opportunity fund or the fund substantially improves the property.

(continued on next page)

OPPORTUNITY ZONES CREATED BY THE 2017 TAX ACT (continued)

Qualified opportunity zone business means a trade or business that meets the following requirements: (1) substantially all of the property owned by the business is qualified opportunity zone business property, (2) at least 50 percent of the gross income of the entity is derived from the active conduct of business, (3) a substantial portion of the intangible property of the entity is used in the active conduct of any such business, (4) less than 5 percent of the average of the aggregate unadjusted bases of the property of the entity is attributable to nonqualified financial property, (5) the business is not used to provide facilities such as a golf course, country club, massage parlor, sun tanning salon, racetrack or other gambling facility, or store that primarily sells alcohol.

If tangible property ceases to be qualified opportunity zone business property, it will continue to be treated as such for the lesser of (1) five years after the date it ceases to be qualified or (2) the date when the property is no longer held by a qualified opportunity zone business.

ORAL TRUSTS

Ordinarily, considerable care goes into drafting a trust document. The provisions of the trust are carefully considered to obtain the desired fiduciary standards and the desired tax results. But, in practice, the use of oral trusts is not uncommon. For example, it is not unusual at the end of the year for advisors to transfer property under an oral trust to take advantage of annual gift tax exclusions or to otherwise facilitate year-end planning. So, can you create an oral trust?

In most jurisdictions, establishing a trust does not require a written document. However, the difficulties with an oral trust are considerable. As between grantor and trustee, the existence of a trust might be clear, but for the trust to be respected by all other parties (e.g., the IRS or the courts), some evidence is necessary. For starters, the terms of the trust must be established. Without a written trust agreement, the conduct of the parties and other evidence must be examined to determine if a trust exists and what the terms of that trust are. Often, the dispute over trust terms will happen at the most inopportune time – after the death or disability of the purported grantor. Moreover, trusts are often used to move property out of the grantor's estate for estate planning purposes. Imagine the difficulty, without documentary evidence, of convincing the IRS that the transfer was irrevocable, immediate, and that the grantor retained no interests, rights, or powers over the property that would cause the property to be included in the transferor's estate.

In addition to practical considerations, local law must be considered when looking to the enforceability of a purported oral trust. This becomes particularly problematic when the property at issue is real property. Most (but not all) states specifically require a writing to create a trust of real property. This requirement dates back to the Statute of Frauds incorporated into English law in 1677. A number of states specifically prohibit oral trusts for other types of property as well.

In short, while it might be slightly over-stated, the old adage that "an oral trust is not worth the paper it's printed on" is solid advice. While the oral trust is sometimes discussed as a year-end or temporary solution – it is not usually a solution that is prudent. It is far better to engage a qualified attorney and create a written trust that complies with local law and protects the desired property and tax results. Careful planning at the time of the transfer in trust can avoid creating considerable problems down the road.

PARTNERSHIPS

Family Limited Partnership

A chart describing the family limited partnership (FLP) is on page 211. The following advantages, disadvantages, and requirements will help in better understanding this important planning technique.

The principal *advantages* of the FLP include:

1. **Retention of control** by the general partner, who has property which he is willing to transfer to family members but is reluctant to lose control over the property. A general partner operating under a well-drafted partnership agreement can maintain indirect control without adverse income and estate tax consequences.
2. **Shifting of income** within certain family partnership limits. The general partner often has the power to retain current profits for investment and reasonable business needs.
3. **Protection of partnership assets** from the creditors of limited partners by restricting the limited partners' abilities to dispose of their limited partnership interests. Because the general partner has the ability to retain profits, the flow-through nature of partnership income taxation gives him or her the ability to create a tax liability without making cash distributions for tax payments (i.e., an "ugly" asset).
4. **Reduction of value** through minority discounts and lack of marketability. The typical limited partnership gift represents a minority interest. Lack of marketability can be established by prohibitions against terminating the partnership without the concurrence of all partners. Valuation discounts ordinarily range from 30 to 70 percent.
5. **Facilitating gifts** of assets which otherwise are not easily divisible (e.g., the family farm). Often the ultimate goal is for the parent to eventually own only modest partnership interests, with the bulk of the FLP being held by other family members.

Some *disadvantages* of the FLP include:

1. The traditional partnership freeze is subject to the impact of the Chapter 14 valuation rules (see pages 371-372). However, most of the techniques used to reduce the effect of, or to avoid, these rules with respect to recapitalizations will also work with partnerships.
2. Much of the ability to reduce taxes by shifting income from parent to younger children has been curtailed by the "kiddie tax" (see discussion on page 575).

(continued on next page)

PARTNERSHIPS (continued)

3. There are additional expenses associated with establishing and accounting for an FLP (e.g., filing and annual fees, an information tax return must be filed).

4. Gifts do not receive a step-up in income tax basis.

5. Retained partnership interests continue to appreciate in the parent's estate until they are transferred during lifetime or at death.

The principal *requirements* for an FLP are:

1. Capital must be income-producing and requiring management. A personal service business where income consists primarily of fees or commissions would not qualify for operation as a family partnership (lawyer, doctor, photographer, plumber, etc.). The IRS has argued (with various degrees of success) that marketable securities or cash without other active assets cannot create a valid FLP.

2. If the partnership has been created by gift, the donor (parent) must be given a reasonable salary for services rendered to the partnership before profits can be allocated among the partners (the concept of "gift" also includes intra-family sales).

3. Profits of the partnership must be allocated, or divided, in proportion to each partner's capital investment.

4. All partners must actually own a "capital interest" (i.e., an interest in partnership assets which is distributable to the partner upon his withdrawal from the partnership or upon partnership liquidation).

5. In order to avoid inclusion under Code section 2036 (i.e., prohibition against retained life estates) of the underlying partnership assets (rather than the partnership itself) a donor or decedent should adhere to all partnership formalities and *should not*: (1) put virtually everything they own in the partnership; (2) retain complete control over the income of the partnership; and (3) use the partnership to pay personal expenses (see also, page 375).

(continued on next page)

PARTNERSHIPS (continued)

Partnership Used As Alternative To Irrevocable Life Insurance Trust

Partnerships are increasingly being used as a substitute for the irrevocable life insurance trust. When contrasted to the irrevocable life insurance trust the primary advantages of a partnership are the *control* that a general partner can exercise over the partnership, which is not available with a trust since the grantor cannot be a trustee, and the *flexibility* a partnership offers to adjust to changing circumstances, which is not available with the irrevocable life insurance trust. Implementation of the technique involves creation of either a general or limited partnership of which the insured is the managing or general partner. Limited partnership interests are obtained by family members either by having the insured make cash gifts to them, after which the funds are contributed to the partnership in return for partnership interests, or by having the insured contribute cash to the partnership in return for partnership interests which are then given to family members. Assuming the insured holds no incidents of ownership, and the death proceeds are paid to the partnership, only his proportionate partnership share, including the insurance proceeds, will be in his estate. See also comparison of Limited Liability Company v. ILIT at pages 450-452.

Partnership Created To Avoid Transfer For Value Problem

Until changed by the 2017 Tax Act, insurance death benefits paid to a C corporation to fund a stock redemption agreement were generally subject to the corporate alternative minimum tax (see pages 327-329). Even today with the corporate AMT repealed, corporate ownership in an entity buy-sell structure is probably not optimum tax planning – because the remaining shareholders do not receive a basis step-up when an entity buy-sell is used.

Therefore, it is common for shareholders to convert a corporate entity buy-sell to some form of cross-purchase arrangement (see pages 174-177) and Cross Endorsement Buy-Sell (see pages 182-185). Although the AMT is no longer a concern and basis step-up can be achieved by converting an entity buy-sell to a cross purchase agreement, transferring existing corporate owned policies to co-stockholders of an insured can run afoul of the transfer for value rules, meaning that the death benefits would be subject to ordinary income taxes (see pages 568-569). Transfers to a partnership of which the insured is a partner are exempt from the transfer for value rules. In a private letter ruling, the IRS has approved the creation of a partnership for the purpose of receiving corporate-owned policies. Although a partnership must be for a valid business purpose, and not just for avoiding taxes, this ruling appears to approve a partnership whose sole purpose is to "engage in the purchase and acquisition of life insurance policies on the lives of the partners." However, use of this technique might cause the proceeds received by the partnership to be taxed in the insured's estate, since the proceeds are not being retained by the partnership, but rather distributed to the surviving partners to fund a cross purchase agreement (i.e., as a partner the insured possesses an incident of ownership in the policy on his own life and there may be no double taxation issue since the value of the proceeds are not included in valuing the insured's partnership interest). It is probably advisable to avoid using such a "sole purpose" partnership until this estate taxation issue is resolved.

PENALTIES – ESTATE AND GIFT TAXES

Failure to file return. A 5 percent penalty if the failure is for not more than 1 month, with an additional 5 percent for each additional month, not to exceed a total of 25 percent; unless it is shown that the failure was due to reasonable cause and not due to willful neglect. If the failure to file is fraudulent then the monthly penalty is increased from 5 percent to 15 percent, and the total penalty from 25 percent to 75 percent. *Section 6651.*

Failure to pay tax. A 0.5 percent penalty if the failure is for not more than 1 month, with an additional 0.5 percent for each additional month, not to exceed a total of 25 percent; unless it is shown that the failure was due to reasonable cause and not due to willful neglect. *Section 6651.*

Fraud penalty. Penalty is 75 percent of the underpayment attributable to fraud. If the IRS establishes that any portion of an underpayment is attributable to fraud, the entire underpayment will be treated as such. The taxpayer must establish the part not attributable to fraud. *Section 6663.*

Accuracy related penalty. A 20 percent penalty is imposed on any underpayment attributable to negligence or a ***substantial*** valuation understatement. A substantial valuation understatement exists if the value of property on the return is 65 percent or less of the amount determined to be correct (penalty is 40 percent if property on return is 40 percent or less of correct amount). No penalty for a substantial valuation understatement is imposed if the underpayment is no more than $5,000. Also, no penalty is imposed if the taxpayer acts with reasonable cause and good faith. *Sections 6662 and 6664.*

Statute of limitations on assessment. Generally, three years after return filed. If the taxpayer omits items that exceed 25 percent of total amounts stated on return, statute of limitations is six years after date of return. There is no statute of limitations if no return is filed, or if return was false or fraudulent and filed with intent to evade tax. *Section 6501.*

False statement as crime. Any person who under the penalties of perjury willfully makes and subscribes a return, statement, or other document, and who does not believe it to be true and correct, is guilty of a felony, and will be fined not more than $100,000 or imprisoned not more than 3 years, or both, together with the costs of prosecution. *Section 7206.*

Removal or concealment as crime. Any person who removes or conceals any goods with intent to evade or defeat the assessment or collection of taxes is guilty of a felony, and will be fined not more than $100,000 or imprisoned not more than three years, or both, together with the costs of prosecution. *Section 7206.*

Statute of limitations on criminal prosecutions. If the taxpayer willfully attempts to evade any payment or willfully fails to make a return or pay a tax, the statute of limitations is six years. *Section 6531.*

PENSION BENEFIT GUARANTY CORPORATION (PBGC)

The PBGC is a federal agency created by the Employee Retirement Income Security Act of 1974 (ERISA) to protect defined benefit pension plans (defined contribution plans are not covered). Plans sponsored by churches, governmental bodies, and small professional employers with fewer than twenty-six employees are generally not covered by the PBGC. The PBGC guarantees "basic benefits" earned before a plan has been terminated, which include: (1) pension benefits at normal retirement age; (2) most early retirement benefits; (3) annuity benefits for survivors of plan participants; and (4) disability benefits for disabilities that occurred before the plan ended. Benefits are not adjusted for inflation (i.e., there are no cost-of-living increases). Health care, vacation pay, and severance pay are not guaranteed. More than 40 million American private sector pension plans are protected by the PBGC.

Although most people receive the full benefit they earn before the plan ends, there is a maximum benefit guaranteed by the PGBC according to the year the plan is terminated. For example, with pension plans ending in 2018, the maximum guaranteed amount is $5,420.45 per month ($65,045 per year) for workers who retire at age sixty-five. The maximum guaranteed amount is lower if the participant receives payments before age sixty-five, or if the pension includes benefits for a survivor or other beneficiary (e.g., a joint and survivor annuity).

PER STIRPES – PER CAPITA

These terms are used in making beneficiary designations in life insurance policies, wills, and trusts.

The term **per stirpes** is used when it is desired that the share of a deceased beneficiary go to the beneficiary's children (in Latin it means "by the trunk," "by right of representation," or "by roots or stocks"). For example, assume John Smith desires to name his wife primary beneficiary of his life insurance policy with his children as contingent beneficiaries. However, should one of his children predecease him, John wants the children of that child (i.e., his grandchildren) to share equally their deceased parent's share. The following beneficiary wording might be used: "Sally Smith, wife of the insured, if she survives the insured, otherwise in equal shares to the surviving children of the insured, and to the surviving children of any deceased children of the insured, per stirpes." If Sally died before John and upon his subsequent death John had two children who were alive (A and B) and one child who had previously died leaving two children (deceased child C who left John's grandchildren D and E), then A and B would each take one-third of the proceeds and D and E would each take one-sixth of the proceeds (i.e., they would share their deceased parents' one-third). In some jurisdictions the term "by representation" is used in lieu of "per stirpes."

The term **per capita** is used when it is desired that the children of a deceased beneficiary share equally with the surviving members of the original group of beneficiaries (in Latin it means "by the head," "according to the number of individuals," or "share and share alike"). Again, assume that John Smith desires to name his wife primary beneficiary of his life insurance policy with his children as contingent beneficiaries. However, should one of his children predecease him, John wants the children of that child (i.e., his grandchildren) to share equally with all other beneficiaries. The following beneficiary wording might be used: "Sally Smith, wife of the insured, if she survives the insured, otherwise in equal shares to the surviving children of the insured, and to the surviving children of any deceased children of the insured, per capita." Again, if Sally died before John and upon his subsequent death John had two children who were alive (A and B) and one child who had previously died leaving two children (deceased child C who left John's grandchildren D and E), then A, B, D, and E would each take one-fourth of the proceeds (i.e., all beneficiaries would share equally).

For an expended discussion of beneficiary designations involving minors, see page 469.

PERSONAL HOLDING COMPANY

A personal holding company exists when more than 50 percent of a corporation's outstanding stock is owned by five or fewer individuals, directly or indirectly, and 60 percent of the corporation's adjusted ordinary gross income is personal holding company income. Personal holding company income is essentially passive income such as dividends, rents, and royalties. If this income is not distributed during the year it will be subject to a 20 percent penalty tax (as increased from 15 percent by the American Taxpayer Relief Act of 2012). Laws pertaining to personal holding companies were not changed by the 2017 Tax Act, but as business owners consider possibly changing their business structure from S corporation to C corporation – the personal holding company rules need to be considered. See also Issues Pertaining to Change to C-Corp Status at page 326.

Because of the limited marketability of personal holding company stock, courts have often allowed substantial valuation discounts (i.e., the stock of the personal holding company is held to be worth less than the value of its underlying assets). Because of this, under some circumstances personal holding companies can function as a particularly effective means of transferring future appreciation to other family members.

For example, an individual with a large estate containing a portfolio of stock that is expected to appreciate substantially would form a corporation with both voting and nonvoting common stock. His or her portfolio of stock is transferred to the personal holding company in return for the voting and nonvoting common stock. Thereafter, the nonvoting common is transferred by gift, or by sale, to other family members, and all future appreciation of this stock is shifted outside the stockholder's estate. By retaining ownership of the voting common the stockholder maintains control of the personal holding company (and of the investment decisions).

In addition to the penalty tax on undistributed income, a personal holding company can result in double taxation if appreciated assets are sold and the proceeds distributed to stockholders. Also, it is important to avoid running afoul of the special valuation provisions of Chapter 14 (see discussion on pages 371-372).

The penalty tax can be avoided with regard to a personal service contract by having the corporation reserve to itself the right to designate the professional who is to render services rather than giving the client the right to make the choice. In that case the income from such a personal service contract is not treated as personal holding company income.

PET ESTATE PLANNING

The law treats a pet as tangible personal property. The simplest way of providing for a pet after the owner's death is to identify a relative or close friend to whom a testamentary transfer of both the pet and sufficient funds to care for the pet can be made. While this method may be the least expensive, it is subject to will challenges by disgruntled relatives, does not become effective until the will is probated, and is not legally enforceable.

Trusts. The vast majority of states have passed laws that enable pet owners to set up trusts providing funds for the care of pets after the owner has died. (See, *e.g.*, Texas Property Code § 112.037) While these statutes vary widely, they commonly recognize pet trusts as valid and enforceable and provide for termination of the trust upon the death of the pet (see www.professorbeyer.com/Articles/Animal_Statutes.html). Under most of these statutes, the courts are authorized to reduce the amount transferred in trust if it is determined that the trust property substantially exceeds the amount needed for pet care (e.g., Leona Helmsley's bequest of $12 million to her aptly named dog Trouble). Both inter vivos and testamentary pet trusts are used. An inter vivos trust offers the advantage that it becomes effective immediately and the trustee is empowered to use trust assets to care for a pet immediately upon the owner's disability or death. However, inter vivos trusts typically entail additional start-up costs and administration fees. Although pet trusts often have a separate trustee and caretaker, many pet trusts simply use a single caretaker-trustee.

Caretaker organizations. There are numerous organizations that have established formal programs for the care of pets after the death of the owner. Typically these charities and perpetual care programs involve payments or donations to the organization prior to or after the owner's death (see www.professorbeyer.com/Articles/Animals_More_Information.html).

Power of attorney. Language may be included in a pet owner's durable power of attorney that gives the owner's agent express authority to care for the pet (see page 351). Such authority should include permission to take possession of the pet and to further use the funds supplied to provide for the health, care, and welfare of the pet.

Living will. This document provides direction to the veterinarian and other pet care providers regarding the owner's feeling about end-of-life treatment and euthanasia.

Pet card. This is a card carried in the owner's wallet or purse for the purpose of providing information about the pet. The information provided includes the pet's name, location, breed, sex, and veterinarian. Availability of the card helps assure that the animal survives to the time when the owner's plans for the pet's care can take effect.

PHANTOM STOCK PLAN

Phantom stock plans are a form of nonqualified deferred compensation made available to select employees. They are also referred to as "shadow stock plans" or "as if" deferred compensation (i.e., the amount deferred is treated as if invested in a designated stock, most often that of the employer).

The advantage to the employee is that his or her efforts and loyalty are rewarded by having an economic interest or stake in the business similar to that of the owners. The advantage to the owners of a small and closely held family business is that they are able to retain a valued employee without diminishing their percentage of ownership. Phantom stock plans are used in both regular C corporations and S corporations, limited liability companies, partnerships, and sole proprietorships.

To implement a phantom stock plan, a bookkeeping account in the name of the employee is established. This account is then credited with hypothetical shares of stock (when used with a noncorporate employer, the business equity credited to the employee is referred to as a "participation unit"). Periodically, the account can be credited with additional stock, as well as with dividends and stock splits. The deferral period is usually set at a specific number of years or upon the employee's retirement. At the end of the deferral period, the employee is entitled to receive cash payments equal to the excess of the market value of the stock on that date over its value on the date awarded. If appropriate, a vesting schedule can be used that provides for nonforfeitable appreciation rights prior to the end of the deferral period.

The terms "stock appreciation right" and SAR have been used to describe a benefit under which the employee receives only the appreciation of the stock, but not the stock value itself. For example, assume that ten shares of stock are awarded to an employee, with a current value of $150 each. If, at the end of the deferral period, the stock has increased in value to $275 per share, the employee is entitled to a payment of $1,250 ($275 – $150 = $125 appreciation per share; $125 × 10 shares = $1,250). Alternatively, in addition to any appreciation, the plan could provide for the employee to receive the underlying value of the stock. Assuming such a design, the employee would be entitled to a payment of $2,750 ($1,500 initial stock value plus $1,250 appreciation).

As with other nonqualified deferred compensation plans, the employer's obligation to the employee is unsecured. Income is not recognized by the employee until the benefits are actually paid or made available. The employer then deducts the payment made to the employee (assuming compensation is reasonable, see page 575). Phantom stock plans are often informally funded with cash value life insurance. Life insurance also allows the employer to provide a preretirement death benefit payable to the employee's family (see chart entitled Deferred Compensation on page 127, and footnotes 6 and 7 on page 129).

PLANNED GIVING

The term "planned giving" can be defined in terms of the **sources of funds** which donors use to make charitable gifts. In contrast to the annual gifts made from the donor's *disposable income* in support of the operational needs of a charitable or religious organization, the concept of planned giving involves gifts of the donor's *accumulated assets* to ensure the organization's long-term financial viability. The process often requires that donors make decisions regarding the distribution of significant portions of their estates. In recognizing that planned gifts must be coordinated with the donor's overall financial and estate plans, one definition simply describes planned giving as involving "any charitable gift that requires assistance by a qualified professional to complete." The terms "deferred giving" and "charitable gift planning" are also used.

Planned giving can also be defined in terms of the **techniques and products** used when making charitable gifts. In addition to providing for a substantial charitable gift, the donor and his or her family also often enjoy both income and estate tax benefits and an ongoing income. These techniques and products include:

1. **Wills** that transfer assets by *outright* bequests of named assets (e.g., cash or real estate), *residuary* bequests of property remaining after payment of debts, estate costs, devises, bequests, and legacies, and *contingent* bequests (e.g., "I direct payment of $100,000 to XYZ Charity provided my spouse dies before me").

2. **Retirement plan assets** transferred at death from both IRAs and qualified retirement plans – see pages 310-311 and 512.

3. **Charitable gift** annuities providing income as a general obligation of the charity and **pooled income funds** providing income from co-mingled investments.

4. **Charitable trusts**, including:

    a. **Charitable remainder annuity trust** paying a fixed amount annually to the donor or other beneficiary – see pages 58 and 309.

    b. **Charitable remainder unitrust** paying a fixed percentage of the trust's value, as determined yearly. Variations of the unitrust include net income with makeup unitrusts (NIMCRUT), net income unitrusts (NICRUT), FLIP unitrusts, and charitable lead trusts (CLT) – see pages 58, 309, and 472.

5. **Life insurance** by transferring ownership directly or by irrevocably designating the charity as owner and beneficiary – see page 308.

6. **Private foundations** and **donor-advised funds** allowing for limited donor influence over fund disbursements – see page 497.

PORTABILITY

Historically, each individual had the right to leave to the next generation a specific amount of property free of the federal estate tax. This could be done during lifetime by gift, or upon death, but the right could not be passed to a surviving spouse (i.e., you either used it during lifetime or upon death, or you lost it). It required prior planning to take advantage of the exemption.

The 2010 Tax Relief Act introduced the concept of portability by allowing any unused exemption to be passed to a surviving spouse. There was no longer a need to re-title assets and establish complex wills and trusts (e.g., QTIP, credit shelter, by-pass, or family trusts) solely for this purpose. The unused exemption is called the "Deceased Spousal Unused Exclusion Amount," or DSUEA. In order to take advantage of this portability, the executor of the estate of the deceased spouse need only file an estate tax return and make a DSUEA election. Under The 2010 Tax Relief Act, the exemption was increased to $5,000,000 per person and indexed for inflation beginning in 2012. The American Taxpayer Relief Act of 2012 made permanent both portability and the $5,000,000 exemption with indexing (as indexed, the exemption was increased to $5,600,000 in 2018). The 2017 Tax Act temporarily doubled the exemption ($11.2 million in 2018) with sunsetting on January 1, 2026.

Assuming none of the $5,490,000 was used by a decedent during life, adding the $5,600,000 DSUEA to the surviving spouse's "basic exclusion amount" of $5,600,000 produces an "applicable exclusion amount" of $11,200,000 in 2017 (with temporary doubling from 2018 to 2026). This is the amount that can be passed during lifetime or at death by the surviving spouse free of federal gift or estate taxes. Despite the advent of portability, there remain many non-tax reasons to use trust wills in estate plans. Surviving families require asset management, parents require assurance that assets will pass to their children and not to subsequent spouses, professionals require asset protection from civil suits, blended and nontraditional families have special needs, business interests must be continued, and incapacity planning often can best be accomplished with trusts.

It may be ill-advised to rely solely on the portability of the federal estate tax exemption to plan an estate, as many states have their own *state death taxes* and virtually all states are continually seeking new sources of income in a financially challenging economy. See Summary of State Inheritance and Estate Taxes on page 138. Portability does not apply to generation-skipping transfers (i.e., a surviving spouse cannot receive the deceased spouse's unused GST exemption).

POST MORTEM PLANNING

Post mortem (after death) planning is not limited to merely "picking up the pieces" for the families of decedents who have failed to plan in advance. In fact, rather than being a substitute for good planning, post mortem planning is best used as a means of effectively implementing plans that had been set in motion during the decedent's life, or of adapting to changing circumstances prior to or after the decedent's death. No matter how well an estate is planned, changing family and business circumstances, not to mention estate tax laws that are ever mutating, make it essential to build flexibility into every estate plan (see page 5). Such flexibility anticipates the use of both tax and nontax post mortem planning options and elections. The following are examples of some of these techniques:

Disclaimers. The use of disclaimers in estate planning can often result in obtaining greater flexibility by providing the opportunity for post mortem decisions, when more facts are likely to be available regarding assets, taxes, and beneficiaries. Disclaimers can be used with respect to gifts, wills, or even life insurance proceeds. The disclaimant has no authority to direct the distribution of the property, and it passes as though the disclaimant had predeceased the decedent. See Disclaimer on page 346.

Section 6166 election. Estate taxes attributable to an interest in a closely held business may be paid in installments, provided certain conditions are met. See Deferral of Estate Tax on page 336.

QTIP election. Not only gives the executor the power to determine how much, if any, of the estate will be taxed at the first death, but also provides great flexibility for post death planning based upon changing circumstances. See the QTIP Trust chart on page 31.

Alternate valuation date. Electing to value the gross estate six months after death can lower estate taxes. See Fair Market Value on page 376.

Special use valuation. Lower valuations can help to minimize federal estate taxes, provided the estate qualifies and the required restrictions are acceptable to the heirs. See Reduced Valuation on pages 518-519.

Donation of conservation easements. Allowing for a donation to be made after the decedent's death, but before the estate tax return is filed, can significantly reduce estate taxes, while allowing a family to retain their lands. See Qualified Conservation Easement on page 507.

Section 303 redemptions. These after-death sales of partial stock interests to a corporation receive tax-favored treatment as capital transactions, rather than as dividends. See the Partial Stock Redemption chart on page 195.

POWER OF APPOINTMENT

A power of appointment is the delegation of authority from one individual (the donor) to another individual (the donee) to direct the transfer, use, benefit, or enjoyment of property, both real and personal. A power exercisable in favor of the power-holder, the estate, the creditors, or the creditors of the power-holder's estate is a *general* power of appointment. Any other power of appointment is a *special* power of appointment.

Whether a power of appointment is general or special is important, since a general power of appointment will cause the value of any assets subject to the power to be included in the power-holder's estate (even if the power is not exercised), whereas the value of any assets subject to a special power of appointment is generally excluded for estate tax purposes. The existence, release, or lapse of a general power of appointment all have the potential of causing the property subject to such power to be included in the estate of the power-holder.

With the exemption trust will, as shown in the chart on page 21, property placed in the marital trust ("A" trust) will qualify for the marital deduction only if the surviving spouse has a general power of appointment over the property (an exception to this statement would be a trust that qualified as a QTIP trust). This assures that even though the property was not taxed at the first death, it will eventually be subject to estate taxes upon the subsequent death of the surviving spouse.

If the power to consume, invade, or appropriate property from a trust is limited to *ascertainable standards* (e.g., for "health, education, maintenance, or support," but not for "comfort, welfare, or happiness"), it will not be considered to be a general power of appointment. Again referring to the chart on page 21, a surviving spouse can be given the right to invade the family or nonmarital trust ("B" trust) without causing the trust property to be included in the surviving spouse's estate (except to the limit of the standard), provided the power is limited to such ascertainable standards, and therefore not treated as a general power of appointment.

Even though it might be considered a general power of appointment, a noncumulative power of appointment that does not exceed the greater of $5,000 or 5 percent of the value of the assets subject to the power (such as a trust) will not cause the lapse of such a power to be treated as a gift or included in the power-holder's estate. However, such a power held at death would be included in the power-holder's estate. See also the expanded discussion of the Marital Deduction on page 459.

PREMIUM FINANCING

The term "premium financing" describes a method of purchasing large premium life insurance contracts using money borrowed from a commercial bank or lender.

Low market interest rates usually bring increased attention to premium financing as a means of funding the termination of split-dollar plans (see Split-Dollar Rollout, page 553). Premium financing is also used to fund company-owned life insurance (see discussion on page 319) and trust-owned life insurance. With an irrevocable life insurance trust, the loan is entered into between the trustee and the lender, and interest payments are often made from gifts to the trust by the trust grantor or others (see Life Insurance Trust chart, page 55).

Where a policy is purchased using premium financing the loan is typically collateralized by the underlying life insurance policy; however, additional collateral is usually required at least until such time as policy cash surrender value equals the outstanding loan balance. Because the policy cash value is typically used as collateral for the loan – security laws (such as the 50 percent limitation on margin loans) come into play making it unusual and difficult to use variable universal life (VUL) in premium financing. However, the cash value upside potential provided by indexed universal life (IUL) combined with the fact that it is not regulated by the SEC makes it the most popular product in premium financing.

In addition, it is important to recognize that there are no tax advantages to premium financing, since the interest paid will *not* be tax deductible. It is sometimes suggested that businesses can deduct the interest on premium financed corporate owned life insurance – but IRC Section 264(a) suggests otherwise. It is important to consult with competent independent tax professionals when considering any arrangement whereby the cost to acquire or maintain life insurance is suggested to be deductible.

The rate of interest is often based upon commercial loan rates using the one-year LIBOR (London Interbank Offered Rate), plus a spread and loan origination free totaling perhaps 1.5 to 2.0 percent. For example, the September, 2018, one-year LIBOR was 2.91 percent (up from 1.74 percent in September of 2017), meaning that the effective typical interest rate for premium financing would be approximately 5 percent. Although the spread is typically guaranteed for the loan's duration, because the underlying LIBOR rate is subject to annual adjustments the loan interest rate can increase substantially (e.g., in November, 2006, the one-year LIBOR was 5.24 percent). Also, unlike the loan provisions provided in most life insurance contracts, if the underlying insurance contract requires ongoing premium payments, commercial lenders are unlikely to guarantee rates to be charged on future loans. However, lenders may not provide assurance that future loans will be made.

In order for premium financing to make economic sense – it is essential that the rate of return on policy values (cash values and death benefit that are intended to repay the loan) exceed the interest rate paid on the loan or the interest rate remains less than the return on retained assets (ie, those assets which would have been otherwise liquided to purchase needed insurance).

When interest rates are low, premium financing is often shown with illustrated loan interest rates remaining at relatively low rates and policy crediting rates (usually indexed universal life) being significantly higher than the interest rate on the loan. This form of illustrated "free insurance" is not guaranteed and, in reality, unlikely to happen. It is important when considering premium financed life insurance that the need be real and that the policyholder has a strategy for repayment of the loan in the event that loan rates increase and arbitrage is reduced or illiminated.

PRENUPTIAL AGREEMENTS

A prenuptial agreement, sometimes referred to as an antenuptial agreement or premarital agreement, is a contract entered into prior to marriage. The agreement typically provides guidelines for division or property and spousal support in the event of divorce or separation. A prenuptial agreement can set the law to be applied upon termination of the marriage (rather than the state of divorce which is the norm). Some prenuptial agreements also address division of assets in the event of death. A postnuptial agreement is similar, except it is entered into during the marriage. Generally, a prenuptial agreement can be modified by a properly executed postnuptial agreement.

Although prenuptial agreements are generally enforceable, it is important that both parties have lawyers representing them to ensure enforceability. Although prenuptial agreements are generally recognized in all states and the District of Columbia, they can be attacked in court for a number of reasons including: failure to disclose assets and unconscionability.

The general requirements in most states for a valid prenuptial agreement are:

- Must be in writing (oral agreements are generally unenforceable but *Hall v. Hall*, 222 Cal. App. 3d 578, 1990 is a notable exception)
- Full and fair disclosure of property
- Must be executed voluntarily
- Cannot be unconscionable
- Acknowledged before a notary public

Generally, a prenuptial agreement CANNOT control issues related to children of the marriage. Child support payments cannot be set in advance. As a general rule, child custody cannot be addressed in a prenuptial because custody must be determined based on best interest of the child at the time the marriage ends.

In most states, a prenuptial agreement has no "sunset provision" and lasts for the life of the marriage unless a term is included in the agreement. However, some states do include a maximum number of years. In Maine, prenuptial agreements lapse after the birth of a child to the marriage.

Not surprisingly, prenuptial agreements are most common in marriages where one spouse brings disproportionate property, anticipated inheritance, or earnings potential to the marriage. And, probably also not surprisingly, courts are most cautious in enforcing agreements in such situations. Situations where one spouse has a considerable financial advantage dictate specific caution in drafting the agreement and a well-experienced family lawyer should be consulted. The financially advantaged spouse needs to take caution to fairly disclose assets and not make the agreement "unconscionable." A determination of unconscionability will be made by taking into consideration the financial situation of the couple (as opposed to community standards). In other words – a wealthy spouse should be cautious to be sure a divorced spouse is treated "fairly." And, it should be remembered that fair will be determined at the time of the divorce. Put another way – pigs get fat and hogs get slaughtered.

PRIVATE ANNUITY

The private annuity has been most effectively used in family situations where it is desired to make a transfer of a business interest, or other asset, from one generation to the next free of estate taxes (see chart, page 39). Under a typical private annuity transaction, a parent will sell part or all of the business interest, or other asset, to his child or children. In return, the children would promise to pay the parent an income for life (called a "straight life" annuity). While the annuity obligation cannot be secured, it does represent a contractual obligation that is legally enforceable. Since payments terminate at the parent's death, the annuity has generally been considered to have no value and to escape taxation in the parent's estate.

The amount of the annual payment is determined by use of annuity valuation factors. The entire amount of the gain or loss must be recognized at the time of the transaction. Annuity payments are made up of interest income and a nontaxable recovery of basis. If it is desired to provide an ongoing income to *both* surviving parents, a reduced income can be paid for as long as either parent is alive (called a "joint and survivor" annuity). Although the value of the survivorship benefit is includable in the estate of the first parent to die, it should escape taxation because of the unlimited marital deduction. At the time the annuity is established, the child receives a "temporary basis" equal to the value used in calculating the annuity. After the parent's death, this temporary basis is adjusted to reflect the amount actually paid.

It would be best to avoid stipulating lower annual payments than those calculated under the annuity tables. Such annuity payments result in a gift from the parent to the child (i.e., the child is not paying full value from his separate funds). If there is a gift element, then its value is the difference between the fair market value of the asset and the present value of the annuity payments.

Furthermore, if the child does not pay full value, the property transferred in exchange for the private annuity could be included in the parent's estate as a gift with a retained life estate. The courts have also found a gift with retained life estate (resulting in the full value being included in the grantor's estate) where a grantor transferred assets to her grantor trust in exchange for a private annuity for less than adequate consideration.

PRIVATE FOUNDATION

A private foundation is a not-for-profit organization established by an individual charitable donor that operates as either a trust or a corporation. (It is referred to by the IRS as a "private non-operating foundation.") The foundation is controlled by the foundation's board or trustees, who may be selected by the founder. Private foundations are particularly suited to those individuals who wish to make substantial donations while providing a lasting legacy in the family name. Unlike outright gifts to public charities, the founder and family are able to maintain control over assets given to the foundation and retain the flexibility to redirect charitable gifts with changing community needs. Active involvement of the founder's children and other family members as board members has the ancillary benefit of teaching others how to share the family wealth consistent with the founder's values and vision.

To assure that private foundations adequately serve a public purpose, there are very strict rules and regulations governing their operation. In particular, a prohibition against "self-dealing" prevents any transactions, with certain exceptions, between the foundation and "disqualified persons." Such disqualified persons include the founder, the founder's spouse, and lineal descendants, as well as the foundation managers and others involved in business relationships with a substantial contributor to the foundation. Compliance with these rules is essential and penalties for self-dealing are substantial. One exception to these rules allows disqualified persons to be paid by the foundation for reasonable and necessary work performed for the foundation, provided the compensation is reasonable.

Although the earnings on investments held by private foundations are not subject to income taxes, they are subject to an excise tax of 2 percent on investment income. Income on investments must be distributed to qualified charities each year. Regardless of income, approximately 5 percent of its "net investment assets" are required to be distributed within twelve months of the close of the fiscal year. Specific steps must be taken to verify the tax-exempt status of grant recipients. Added to these requirements are annual information tax returns, corporate filings, documentation of gifts received, and requirements for public inspection and disclosure.

The maximum amount a donor may deduct in one year for gifts to a private foundation is 30 percent of his contribution base, generally equal to adjusted gross income. This is reduced to 20 percent for appreciated capital gain property (see footnote 4, page 61). Private foundations cannot receive gifts of interests in a closely held or family-owned business stock under the rules governing "excess business holdings."

PRIVATE PLACEMENT LIFE INSURANCE

Private Placement Life Insurance ("PPLI") is a type of permanent life insurance offering a tax-efficient accumulation of cash value as well as a death benefit component. PPLI is structured similar to a retail variable life policy, but unlike a retail variable life product it can ordinarily be offered without a formal securities registration.

Death benefits are received income and estate tax free. Distributions in an amount up to cost basis are treated as a return of investment and not taxed. Like a retail cash value life insurance policy, cash value growth is ordinarily not taxed unless gains are accessed during life (taxation of the cash value received over the policy tax basis is taxed as ordinary income). However, even amounts received during life in excess of basis can avoid taxation if taken as a loan and not a withdrawal or policy surrender.

Among the common investments in PPLI are hedge funds. Because hedge funds typically involve frequent trading, the income from hedge funds is often taxed at ordinary rates. By "wrapping" the hedge fund in an insurance policy the taxation can be changed from that of the underlying hedge fund to that of a life insurance policy. In addition, PPLI allows wealthy investors to access funds and other investment strategies not regularly made available in commercial variable universal life insurance.

PPLI can be attained from domestic life insurance carriers, but is more commonly purchased from an offshore carrier. Offshore jurisdictions can offer advantages not available domestically. Common offshore jurisdictions include Bermuda, Luxembourg, Liechtenstein, and Singapore. Since the "mortality risk" (the amount of the death benefit over the premiums paid) is ordinarily provided by the same global reinsurance companies that reinsure much of the domestic insurance market there is little difference in the pure risk pricing. However, there are other policy costs that can be less offshore. For example, most domestic life insurance policies charge a U.S. state premium tax which ordinarily runs between 1 and 3 percent of the premium. In addition, a federal "DAC" tax is often charged which can exceed 1 percent of the premium. For large life insurance policies, the fee structure may also be lower offshore since offshore companies typically pay lower (or no) sales commissions and operate without large marketing and corporate overhead.

(continued on next page)

PRIVATE PLACEMENT LIFE INSURANCE (continued)

As previously mentioned, however, the greatest advantage of offshore PPLI is investment flexibility. Unlike domestic carriers, offshore carriers are not limited by SEC and state insurance and security law. In most offshore jurisdictions, local securities and insurance regulation are much less restrictive than in the U.S. However, flexibility over investment options is sometimes misunderstood – especially in offshore PPLI. Rules governing "investor control" still apply to PPLI – meaning that the insured CANNOT directly control the investment. The life insurance cash value must be an investment which is controlled by an investment manager other than the insured. The best example of this issue is probably Webber v. Commissioner, 144 T.C. No. 17 (June 30, 2015). The IRS position is set forth in Rev. Rul. 77-85 and Rev. Rul 2003-91.

But, despite potential advantages to offshore offerings, it's important to know who you are working with. While some offshore carriers are subsidiaries of large U.S. or international insurance companies – some are small carriers that are lightly capitalized. It's important to understand the capitalization and who, if anyone, is backing the carrier's claims paying ability. It's also important to consider the strength of the local government. Despite political disagreement in the U.S. between partisan groups – the stability of the U.S. dollar and legal system are generally considered the envy of the world. Consider that no U.S. death benefit has gone unpaid because of a carrier insolvency. Are the policyholders and beneficiaries satisfied that the foreign jurisdiction provides the stability and protection that the U.S. regulatory authorities and courts provide to U.S. policyholders?

PROBATE

Although the term is now often used in referring to the entire estate settlement process, "probate" originally referred to the act of proving a will before a court or other authorized person. Courts having jurisdiction over probate matters are called probate courts, surrogates courts, or orphans courts. The first step in settling an estate is to offer the will for probate. If the will is not likely to be contested, informal proceedings, usually called probate in *common form*, establish that the document offered is the valid last will of the decedent. However, if there is any doubt regarding validity, formal probate proceedings, usually known as probate in *solemn form*, are required.

After admission of the will to probate, the court appoints an executor (male) or executrix (female) and provides them with letters testamentary as evidence of their appointment. If there is no will, the court appoints an administrator (male) or adminstratrix (female) and provides them with letters of administration. The personal representative (a term including an executor, executrix, administrator and administratix) is then qualified to carry out his or her duties. Typically, the personal representative will hire an attorney to advise and assist in settling the estate.

The personal representative then collects, safeguards, and manages estate assets, has assets appraised, prepares lists of assets, converts personal property into cash, distributes assets as directed by the decedent (pursuant to specific bequests in the will), disposes of business interests, publishes notices giving creditors of the estate an opportunity to file their claims, and pays death taxes, income taxes, property taxes, court costs, appraisal fees, and fees and reimbursement expenses of the personal representative and the attorney. After a court accounting (called a judicial settlement of the account) is made and accepted by the court, the personal representative makes a distribution of the net estate to the heirs as required by either the will or the statute of intestate succession (see pages 586-594).

In recent years, much has been written about the benefits of "avoiding probate." The advantages cited include avoiding fees associated with the probate process, maintaining confidentiality, better control of assets, reduction in delays, and avoiding ancillary probate of property located in another state. However, there are some distinct advantages to having an estate go through probate. For example, protection is provided beneficiaries by having a court oversee the collection and distribution of assets. By giving creditors notice and the opportunity to make claims against the estate, beneficiaries are provided with clear title to estate assets. In addition, the Uniform Probate Code, as enacted by many states, simplifies and streamlines the probate process by providing for self-proved wills, proof of a will by affidavit of witnesses, waiver of bond, and unsupervised administration.

PROFESSIONAL CORPORATION

Professional corporations (sometimes referred to as Professional Service Corporations) are closely held corporations formed by doctors, dentists, optometrists, lawyers, and others. They may be established by an individual or by a group of professionals and are organized primarily to take advantage of the tax deductible benefits available to employees of corporations but not to sole proprietors or partners. Typically they are organized under state professional corporation and professional association acts.

A professional in a high personal tax bracket incorporates, becomes an employee of the corporation (as well as an owner-stockholder) and receives a salary from the corporation. The usual business deductions are allowed, including salaries for stockholder-employees, as well as special corporation deductions.

Professional corporations are taxed under the same rules as other corporations. Prior to the 2017 Tax Act, professional corporations in which substantially all of the activities involve the performance of services in the fields of health, law, engineering, architecture, accounting, actuarial science, performing arts, or consulting are considered qualified personal service corporations and corporate income were taxed at a flax rate of 35 percent. Now, like other C corporations, the income of a professional corporation is taxed at a flat 21 pecent rate.

A wide variety of employee benefits are available to the stockholder-employees of a professional corporation, including accident and health plans, group term life insurance, salary allotment, executive equity (page 232), split-dollar insurance (page 240), survivor income (page 122), deferred compensation (page 126), disability income plans (page 252), health reimbursement arrangements (page 256) and tax-favored retirement plans (page 264).

State laws generally restrict ownership of stock in professional corporations to qualified professionals (as a condition of continued authorization to provide professional services). Therefore, with professional corporations it is most important to implement buy-sell agreements that prevent the transfer of stock to anyone who is a nonprofessional. In addition to providing for the sale of stock upon death, such agreements should also contain provisions for sale in the event of retirement, permanent disability, and termination of employment or professional disqualification.

While the typical choice involves either an entity purchase agreement (page 170) or a cross purchase agreement (page 174), hybrid arrangements involving "wait and see" buy/sell agreements (page 186) and partial stock redemptions (page 194) are also used. Whichever method is chosen, adequate funding with life insurance will provide funds to meet the underlying obligations.

PROFIT SHARING PLAN

Profit sharing plans are often used by employers to distribute profits to their employees. Employer contributions to a profit sharing plan can be entirely discretionary, made according to a formula provision, or a combination of both. If on a discretionary basis, then the employer determines each year whether or not to make contributions to the plan (but a failure to make "recurring and substantial" contributions could result in disqualification of the plan). It is not necessary that the employer actually have current or accumulated profits. If on a formula basis, then contributions are made under a formula typically tied to employer profits (e.g., 5 percent of net profits after taxes, 10 percent of gross profits in excess of $100,000, or some other profit-driven formula). In either case, the employer can deduct up to 25 percent of total payroll of plan participants.

Once the amount of contribution is determined, it is then allocated among the participants' individual accounts under a nondiscriminatory formula that must be definite and predetermined. For example, each participant might receive an allocation of a percentage determined by comparing his compensation to the total compensation of all plan participants. If the employer's total contribution to the plan was $100,000, and the participant's $150,000 of compensation represented 15 percent of the $1,000,000 total payroll, then the allocation to his account would be $15,000 ($100,000 × .15 = $15,000). For 2018, the maximum compensation base for any participant is limited to $275,000. An overall "annual additions" limit for defined contribution plans limits each participant to the lesser of $54,000 or 100 percent of compensation. In determining this allocation formula integration with Social Security is allowed under most plans.

Upon the participant's termination or retirement, benefits under the plan consist of the participant's account value. This account value reflects total employer contributions, forfeitures from other plan participants, and returns on plan investments (i.e., interest, dividends and capital gains). As with a money purchase pension plan, the employee/participant bears the risks associated with investment performance. In addition, because employer contributions and profits are not assured, unlike defined benefit or money purchase pension plans, the employee is unable to project with any certainty his account values at retirement. In contrast to pension plans, certain profit sharing plans can offer participants the opportunity to take "in-service distributions" prior to retirement (subject to a 10-percent early withdrawal tax penalty prior to age 59½). In order to avoid this penalty, profit sharing plans sometimes allow participants access to account funds through plan loans at reasonable rates of interest and within specified limits.

See also, the discussion of Qualified Retirement Plans on page 512, and Life Insurance in Qualified Plans on pages 419-420.

PRUDENT INVESTOR RULE

Under the Uniform Prudent Investor Act of 1994, the prudent *investor* rule replaced the prudent *person* rule. A majority of states have now enacted some form of the prudent investor rule.

With its focus on minimizing risk, the prudent person rule forces trustees to adopt conservative fixed-income approaches to investing trust assets. Such a conservative approach may well be appropriate for the small-to-mid-size trust whose primary function is to provide support for the current beneficiary (e.g., a marital deduction trust for the support of a surviving spouse, as in the chart on page 21). However, with larger trusts, application of the rule often results in underperforming investments and dissatisfied life and remainder beneficiaries (amusingly referred to as the trustee's duty to "disappoint equally").

State Principal and Income Acts further compounded the problem. These statutes usually defined "income" to include dividends, interest, and rents, but not capital gains. As a result, investment decisions were often driven by the character of the return, rather then the rate of return (e.g., trustees could distribute to income beneficiaries interest from low-yield certificates of deposit, but were prohibited from using capital gain from highly appreciated stock). The Uniform Principal and Income Act of 1997 gives trustees the authority to allocate principal to income, but it has not been adopted in all states.

Under the prudent investor rule, a trustee is required to develop an overall investment strategy having risk and return objectives reasonably suited to the trust and its beneficiaries. The trustee is to be judged by considering the performance of the portfolio as a whole, rather than individual investments. Although the trustee may delegate investment functions, there remains a duty to review and monitor overall performance. Consistent with modern portfolio analysis, the trustee may invest for capital appreciation in a diversified portfolio of equity and growth stocks. A reduction in the risk of loss is achieved by a reasonable diversification of investments. Because the trustee has a positive duty to reduce investment costs, passive investment strategies are permitted (e.g., the purchase of indexed mutual funds). It is appropriate for the trustee to seek to maintain the beneficiaries' purchasing power, and the tax implications of trust investments and distributions may be considered. Clearly, the flexibility provided by the prudent investor rule enables a trustee to better serve all beneficiaries and sizes of trusts.

Some planners have suggested that a total return unitrust can take maximum advantage of this flexibility. As with the charitable remainder unitrust, the total return unitrust requires the trustee to pay a fixed percentage of the trust principal to the life beneficiary each year. See the discussion of the total return unitrust on page 566.

QUALIFIED BUSINESS INCOME DEDUCTIONS

The 2017 Tax Act made substantial changes to the treatment of pass-through business income, which, prior to reform, was typically simply "passed through" the entity and taxed at the business owners' individual ordinary income tax rates. Partnerships (and entities that elect partnership taxation, such as certain LLCs), S corporations and sole proprietorships are subject to the new pass-through taxation rules, which will apply for tax years beginning after December 31, 2017. As with other individual tax law changes made by the 2017 Tax Act, this provision is set to sunset for tax years beginning on or after January 1, 2026.

Under the 2017 Tax Act, a pass-through entity is entitled to deduct 20 percent of "qualified business income." Although the rules are complicated – understanding this provision is made easier if the underlying reason for it is remembered. The main purpose of the 2017 Tax Act was to reward active businesses – manufacturing and businesses that put people to work. As a result, income from nonservice businesses receive an unlimited 20 percent deduction where most service businesses have the deduction capped. Taxpayers who own service businesses and have income below the applicable threshold level plus $50,000 ($100,000 for joint returns) also qualify. The applicable threshold levels for 2018 are $315,500 (married filing jointly) or $157,500 (single filers), so taxpayers in service businesses where income exceeds $415,000 (married filing jointly) or $207,500 (single filers) will not receive the benefit of the new deduction.

The deduction is available regardless of whether the taxpayer itemizes, and is applied based on ownership interest (i.e., a partner who owns 25 percent of a partnership is entitled to apply the deduction to 25 percent of his or her qualified business income). The calculation is made on an entity-specific basis, meaning that the deduction must be applied separately to each entity rather than based upon the cumulative income of all entities owned by the taxpayer.

Qualified business income is generally the net amount of qualified items of income, gain, deduction and loss with respect to qualified trades or businesses of the taxpayer, excluding qualified REIT dividends, qualified cooperative dividends and qualified publicly traded partnership income. Income, gain, deduction and loss items are generally qualified if they are connected with a U.S. trade or business and are included or allowed in calculating taxable income. Amounts related to the following investment items are excluded: capital gains, qualified dividend income (or the equivalent), non-business interest income, foreign base company income taken into account under IRC Section 954(c), and non-business annuity distributions.

For alternative minimum tax purposes, qualified business income is calculated without regard to otherwise allowable adjustments.

(continued on next page)

QUALIFIED BUSINESS INCOME DEDUCTIONS (continued)

When the pass-through entity's income exceeds the $315,500/$157,500 threshold, the deduction is capped at the greater of (1) 50 percent of W-2 wage income or (2) the sum of 25 percent of the W-2 wages of the business plus 2.5 percent of the unadjusted basis, immediately after acquisition, of all "qualified property." There are additional rules for taxpayers whose income only exceeds the threshold by $50,000 ($100,000 for joint returns).

"Qualified property" generally includes depreciable property that is used in the taxpayer's trade or business for the production of income as of the end of the tax year, as long as the depreciation period has not expired before the end of that year. The depreciation period is a period that begins on the first day that the taxpayer places the property in service and ends the later of (1) ten years after that date or (2) the last day of the last full year in the applicable recovery period that would apply to the property under IRC Section 168 (without regard to Section 168(g)).

A "specified service business," where the 20 percent exclusion is not available, is a trade or business involving the performance of services in the fields of health, law, consulting, athletics, financial services, brokerage services or any trade or business where the principal asset of the business is the reputation or skill of one or more employees or workers, or one which involves the performance of services consisting of investing and investment management trading or dealing in securities, partnership interests or commodities.

To determine the "qualified business income" with respect to a specified service trade or business, the taxpayer takes into account only the applicable percentage of qualified items of income, gain, deduction, or loss, and of allocable W-2 wages. With respect to S corporations, qualified business income (QBI) does not include any amounts that are treated as reasonable compensation of the taxpayer. Similarly, qualified business income does not include guaranteed payments or amounts paid or incurred by a partnership to a partner, when the partner is providing services and is not acting in his or her capacity as a partner. There are existing "reasonable compensation" rules in the Tax Code which currently apply only to S corporations and C corporations. Currently, they have not been specifically extended into the partnership arena.

If the qualified business income for the year is a loss, it is carried forward as a loss for the next tax year. Any deduction allowed for that subsequent tax year is reduced by 20 percent of any carried forward business loss from the previous year.4

The deduction is allowed as a reduction that reduces taxable income, rather than as a deduction in computing adjusted gross income (i.e., the deduction does not impact limitations based on adjusted gross income). Further, trusts and estates are also eligible for the 20 percent deduction.

For partnerships and S corporations, these rules apply at the partner or shareholder level (each partner is treated as having W-2 wages for the year equal to that partner's allocable share of the partnership).

(continued on next page)

QUALIFIED BUSINESS INCOME DEDUCTIONS (continued)

Entities that are taxed under the rules governing pass-through taxation are generally entitled to a 20 percent deduction for qualified business

(a) the lesser of the combined QBI amount for the tax year or an amount equal to 20 percent of the excess of the taxpayer's taxable income over any net capital gain and cooperative dividends, plus

(b) the lesser of 20 percent of qualified cooperative dividends or taxable income (reduced by net capital gain).

The sum discussed above may not exceed the taxpayer's taxable income for the tax year (reduced by net capital gain). Further, the 20 percent deduction with respect to qualified cooperative dividends is limited to taxable income (reduced by net capital gain).

The deductible amount for each qualified trade or business is the lesser of:

(a) 20 percent of the QBI with respect to the trade or business, or

(b) the greater of (x) 50 percent of W-2 wage income or (y) the sum of 25 percent of the W-2 wages of the business plus 2.5 percent of the unadjusted basis, immediately after acquisition, of all qualified property (see **Q 27**, *Tax Facts on Insurance & Employee Benefits (2019)*).

If the taxable income is below the applicable threshold levels (in 2018, $157,500 for single filers and $315,000 for joint returns), the deduction is simply 20 percent.

If the taxable income exceeds the relevant threshold amount, but not by more than $50,000 ($100,000 for joint returns), and the amount determined under (b), above, is less than the amount under (a), above, then the deductible amount is determined without regard to the calculation required under (b). However, the deductible amount allowed under (a) is reduced by the amount that bears the same ratio to the "excess amount" as (1) the amount by which taxable income exceeds the threshold amount bears to (2) $50,000 ($100,000 for joint returns).

The "excess amount" means the excess of amount determined under (a), above, over the amount determined under (b), above, without regard to the reduction described immediately above.

Example: Marty (a taxpayer who is subject to the W-2 wages and capital limit) does business as a sole proprietorship conducting a widget-making business. The business buys a widget-making machine for $100,000 and places it in service in 2020. The business has no employees in 2020. The limitation in 2020 is the greater of (a) 50 percent of W-2 wages, or $0, or (b) the sum of 25 percent of W-2 wages ($0) plus 2.5 percent of the unadjusted basis of the machine immediately after its acquisition: $100,000 × .025 = $2,500. The amount of the limitation on Marty's deduction is $2,500.

QUALIFIED CONSERVATION EASEMENT

The executor of a decedent may elect on the estate tax return to exclude from the decedent's taxable estate up to 40 percent of the value of any land subject to a "qualified conservation easement." In addition to meeting the requirements of a "qualified conservation contribution," the land must be located within the United States or its possessions and must have been owned by the decedent or a member of his or her family for three years. The American Taxpayer Relief Act of 2012 permanently repealed geographic limitations within the United States that otherwise would have restricted the exclusion. The exclusion is generally not available when the property is debt-financed or the donor has retained development rights (i.e., the donor cannot retain the right to develop property for general recreational use by the public, such as a ski resort). The granting of the easement can be made by the decedent before death or by the decedent's executor.

The exclusion amount is limited to $500,000. The 40-percent exclusion percentage is reduced by 2 percent for each percentage point by which the value of the qualified conservation is less than 30 percent of the value of the land. For example, assume that property with a basis of $500,000 has a value of $1,000,000 before an easement is granted and the easement reduces the value of the property to $750,000, a reduction of 25 percent. This is 5 percent less than the minimum 30 percent threshold. Therefore, the 40 percent exclusion must be reduced by 10 percent to 30 percent (40 – (5 × 2)). The property is included in the estate at a reduced value of $525,000 ($750,000 × .30 = $225,000 reduction; $750,000 – $225,000 = $525,000 reduced value). The value of the property excluded from the decedent's estate under this provision does not receive a step-up in basis. This means the new basis is $675,000 ($525,000 stepped-up basis plus $150,000 carryover basis attributable to fact that 30 percent of the property was excluded from the gross estate; $500,000 × .30 = $150,000).

A "qualified conservation contribution" requires that the donor convey a qualified real property interest to a qualified organization exclusively for conservation purposes. A taxpayer who makes such a contribution may take a charitable income tax deduction equal to the difference in the value of the land immediately before and after the easement is placed on the property (i.e., the loss of value due to the placement of the easement). A portion of the income tax savings might be used to fund a wealth replacement trust for family members (as in the chart on page 59).

It is important to have competent tax advisors and solid appraisals when planning for a conservation easement. In recent years, the IRS has had success in Tax Court challenging conservation easements. Most recently, the case of *Wendall Falls Development, LLC v. Commissioner*, TC 2018-45 has received considerable attention among those active in promoting conservation easements.

Granting a conservation easement during lifetime can provide the property owner with an income tax deduction plus a potential estate tax savings attributable to both the easement's depressing the value of the property and to the partial exclusion of that reduced value from the gross estate. However, because the exclusion reduces the adjusted gross estate, it could affect qualification for a partial stock redemption (page 194), estate tax deferral (page 336), and special use valuation (page 518).

QUALIFIED DOMESTIC RELATIONS ORDER (QDRO)

ERISA and the Code generally do not permit retirement benefits under a qualified retirement plan to be assigned or transferred to another person. As an exception to this rule, in order to satisfy family support or marital property obligations, a qualified domestic relations order (QDRO) is allowed to create or recognize the existence of an alternate payee's right to receive benefits under a pension plan. An alternate payee can be a spouse, former spouse, child, or other dependent.

A QDRO must contain the following information: (1) the name and last known mailing address of the participant and each alternate payee; (2) the name of each plan to which the order applies; (3) the dollar amount or percentage (or the method of determining the amount or percentage) of the benefit to be paid to the alternate payee; and (4) the number of payments or time period to which the order applies. A QDRO may be included as part of a divorce decree or court-approved property settlement, or issued as a separate order. It cannot provide for benefits that are not otherwise available under the plan, nor can it increase benefits payable under the plan.

Pension plans are required to establish written procedures relating to QDROs. The administrator of the pension plan that provides the benefits affected by an order is initially responsible for determining whether a domestic relations order is a QDRO. Intervening events, such as a participant's retirement, remarriage, or death, or the death of a nonparticipant spouse, can complicate the division of property interests and even result in a loss of anticipated benefits. Therefore, it is very important that a QDRO be filed in a complete and timely manner.

Under the Code transfers "incident to a divorce" are generally not taxable to either spouse. Distributions made to an alternate payee under a QDRO are not subject to the 10-percent-penalty tax normally applied to *premature distributions* from qualified retirement plans (i.e., distributions before the participant reaches age 59½). For the purpose of determining required *minimum distributions*, if the nonparticipant spouse's share is segregated (i.e., accounted for separately), the required distributions will be calculated without regard to the participant's portion of the account, except that distributions must begin by the participant's required beginning date. See pages 411-413 and 535.

The Department of Labor is a very good resource for information and forms pertaining to QDROs. For example, see www.dol.gov/ebsa/Publications/qdros.html.

QUALIFIED DOMESTIC TRUST (QDOT)

The federal estate tax is imposed on the taxable estate of every resident of the United States, wherever the property is located, and whether the decedent is a citizen or a noncitizen. In order to prevent a noncitizen surviving spouse from leaving and removing property from the United States, the unlimited marital deduction is not available, unless: (1) the noncitizen surviving spouse becomes a citizen prior to the time for filing the deceased spouse's federal estate tax return; or (2) the property is passed to a qualified domestic trust (QDOT). In short, no federal estate tax marital deduction is available when the surviving spouse is a noncitizen, unless use is made of a QDOT.

Both probate and nonprobate property will qualify for QDOT treatment if transferred directly from the decedent to the QDOT, or irrevocably assigned to the QDOT prior to the time that the federal estate tax return is filed. However, it is not necessary that property be placed in the QDOT in any particular fashion or by any particular person.

The requirements for a QDOT are: (1) there must be an irrevocable election for QDOT treatment; (2) the trust must require that at least one trustee be a U.S. citizen and that no distribution can be made unless such trustee has the right to withhold any estate tax which may become due; (3) the transfer must otherwise qualify as one which would be eligible for the marital deduction; and (4) specific additional procedural requirements must be met in order to ensure collection of the estate tax.

Events that trigger an estate tax on assets placed in a QDOT include: (1) failure of the QDOT to meet any of the above requirements; (2) the surviving spouse's death; or (3) any payment to the surviving spouse other than income or a "hardship" distribution. The surviving spouse cannot be given a power to invade the trust corpus unless the U.S. trustee can withhold any estate tax from the distribution (compare chart on page 21).

When property previously placed in a QDOT becomes subject to estate taxes, it is taxed using the marginal estate tax rate of the deceased citizen spouse. This means that although the unified credit is available to the surviving noncitizen spouse, it cannot be used unless the surviving spouse dies in possession of a separate estate.

There is available a gift tax exclusion which allows for annual tax-free transfers of up to $152,000 (as indexed in 2018 for inflation) to a noncitizen spouse. Taking advantage of this annual exclusion will create a separate estate for the noncitizen spouse, part of which could be used to purchase life insurance on the citizen spouse. Provided the noncitizen spouse was both policy owner and beneficiary, the life insurance proceeds would not be included in the estate of the insured citizen spouse. This would diminish the need to fund a QDOT in order to provide support for the surviving noncitizen spouse.

See also, Noncitizen Estate Planning, page 473.

QUALIFIED LONG-TERM CARE INSURANCE

A "qualified" long-term care insurance contract: (1) must provide only coverage for "qualified long-term care services"; (2) cannot pay or reimburse for services covered under Medicare; (3) must be guaranteed renewable; (4) cannot provide a cash surrender value; (5) must apply premium refunds or dividends to either reduce future premiums or increase future benefits; and (6) must satisfy consumer protection provisions, disclosure and nonforfeitability requirements as set forth by the National Association of Insurance Commissioners (NAIC).

Qualified long-term care services are defined as necessary diagnostic, preventive, therapeutic, curing, treating, mitigating, and rehabilitative services, and maintenance or personal care services, which are required by a chronically ill individual and are provided under a plan of care set forth by a licensed health care practitioner. A person is considered "chronically ill" if certified by a health care professional as unable to perform for a period of at least 90 days, without substantial assistance, at least two activities of daily living (i.e., eating, toileting, transferring, bathing, dressing, and continence) or requires substantial supervision to protect himself or herself from threats to health and safety due to a "severe cognitive impairment" (i.e., a deterioration or loss of intellectual capacity that places the individual in jeopardy of harming self or others).

Premiums. *Individuals* can deduct premiums as medical expenses to the extent that they, along with other unreimbursed medical expenses (including Medicare premiums), exceed 10 percent of adjusted gross income. This deduction for premiums paid is further subject in 2018 to the following annual age-based limits: $420 if age forty or less; $780 if age 41 through fifty; $1,560 if age fifty-one through sixty; $4,160 if age sixty-one through seventy; and $5,200 if age seventy-one and over (these limits are indexed for inflation). Subject to these age-based limits, *self-employed individuals* can deduct 100 percent of premiums. Premiums paid by an *employer* for a nonowner employee are fully deductible by the employer and are not includable in the employee's income.

Benefits. Amounts received from a qualified long-term care contract in 2018 are generally not included in income up to the greater of $420 per day or the actual costs incurred. It is not necessary to prove a need for medical care in order to deduct unreimbursed long-term care expenses for nursing homes, assisted-living facilities, adult homes and home care. This is very much to the taxpayer's advantage.

QUALIFIED PERSONAL RESIDENCE TRUST (QPRT)

A qualified personal residence trust, also referred to as a "residence GRIT," is created by transferring a residence, or a second home, into a split interest trust for a specific period of time, typically between ten and twenty years. The principal advantages of such a trust include transfer of the property at a low gift tax value and shifting of future appreciation out of the grantor's estate, provided he or she lives to the end of the trust term. However, with the estate and gift tax exemption currently at $11.2 million per person – for most taxpayers it may be easier to simply gift the residence to heirs while the exemption remains high (it is scheduled to revert to $5.6 million in 2026).

At the time of the transfer, the value of the gift is determined by the value of the remainder interest in the residence calculated using actuarial tables (i.e., the value of the property is discounted for the fact that it will not be available to the remainderperson for many years). The grantor can also transfer limited amounts of cash to the trust in order to service debt and maintain the residence. The grantor can serve as trustee. Although a taxable gift is made when establishing a qualified personal residence trust, the value of the gift is minimized by the remainder interest calculations, and the grantor can avoid actually paying gift taxes by utilizing unused unified credit. However, because the gift is of a future interest, the annual exclusion is not available (see page 50).

Unlike other transfers with a retained interest, the grantor can continue to use the residence throughout the term of years established by the trust, yet the property will be removed from the grantor's estate provided he or she lives to the end of the term (the same as a GRIT, see page 394). Although death prior to the termination of the trust would cause the full date of death value to be brought back into the grantor's estate, purchase of life insurance on the grantor's life could provide for payment of any estate taxes. A desire to lengthen the trust term in order to lower gift tax exposure upon establishing the trust must be balanced against the loss of all estate tax benefits if the grantor dies before the end of the trust term.

The QPRT can also give the grantor a contingent reversionary interest, which will cause the residence to revert back into his or her estate in case of death before the end of the term. With such a provision, the grantor could utilize the marital deduction by passing the residence to a surviving spouse, thereby postponing estate taxes, while at the same time causing the trust to be classified a "grantor trust," which would allow the grantor to deduct property taxes and mortgage interest on the grantor's own tax return during the term of the trust. The existence of such a reversionary interest would also cause a further reduction in the value of the gift, measured by the probability that the grantor would not survive the term of the trust.

Upon the termination of the trust, the grantor may wish to continue living in the residence. To accomplish this, the grantor can either rent the residence from the remainderperson, or purchase the residence prior to the expiration of the trust term (for a fair rental rate or a fair market value). However, regulations prohibit a sale of the residence to the grantor or the grantor's spouse during the original term or while a grantor trust.

QUALIFIED RETIREMENT PLANS

A qualified retirement plan, also referred to as a "qualified plan," is a tax-favored retirement arrangement established by an employer that is designed to satisfy the requirements of Section 401 of the Internal Revenue Code. The employer may be a corporation, a partnership or a sole proprietorship. The "plan" is the document that sets forth in writing the rules by which the plan operates, such as how employees become participants and the method of calculating the benefits to which they become entitled. Contributions to the plan are transferred to a trustee or insurance company that holds and invests them until they are distributed upon the participant's termination of employment, retirement, or death. Assuming the necessary requirements are met, contributions are deductible to the employer (within limits) and are not currently taxable to the employee/participant. Earnings on plan investments grow tax-deferred and are not taxable to the employee until withdrawn or distributed.

Types Of Qualified Retirement Plans*		
	Defined Contribution	Defined Benefit
Pension	Money Purchase Pension Plan [470] Target Benefit Plan [562]	Defined Benefit Pension Plan [339] Cash Balance Pension Plan [306] 412 (e)(3) Plan [276]
Profit Sharing	Profit Sharing Plan [502] 401(k) Plan [268] Stock Bonus Plan [557] ESOP [360] Age-Weighted Profit Sharing Plan [296] Savings/Thrift Plan [534]	n/a
* Numbers in brackets [ ] indicate page numbers.		

Qualified retirement plans can be categorized in a number of ways. One method distinguishes between plans according to the nature of the employer's obligation. Under a **defined contribution** plan the employer makes specific contributions to the plan, after which the participant's retirement benefits are determined by the account value at retirement (i.e., the *employee* bears the investment risk). In contrast, under a **defined benefit** plan the employer is obligated to provide a specific retirement benefit to the participant (i.e., the *employer* bears the investment risk).

Another way of categorizing plans distinguishes between them according to whether employer contributions can be tied to employer profits. Under a **pension** plan the employer is obligated to provide a "definitely determinable benefit." However, under a **profit sharing** plan employer contributions can be completely discretionary and based on employer profits.

QUALIFIED SMALL BUSINESS STOCK

In order to raise capital, small businesses may designate certain stock as "qualified small business stock." Provided all statutory requirements are met, noncorporate investors may exclude from gross income 100 percent of their gain from the sale of stock that has been acquired after September 28, 2010 (the PATH Act made this temporary provision originally set to expire at the end of 2014 permanent). Gain that may be excluded from a single issuer of stock is limited to the greater of 10 times the stockholder's adjusted basis in the stock or $10 million (but reduced to $5 million for married couples filing separately). The benefits of the small business stock exclusion, sometimes referred to as Section 1202 Stock, can be passed by gift or inheritance.

In order to be eligible for this favorable tax treatment, the following qualifications must be met:

1. The stock must have been issued by a domestic C corporation after August 10, 1993. Because of the requirement that qualified small business stock has to be issued by a C corporation – the Section 1202 provisions were relatively infrequently utilized. However, with the 2017 Tax Act lowering the tax rate on C corporations to a flat 21 percent, Section 1202 should become a more popular planning strategy.
2. The stock must be acquired at its original issue and held for more than five years.
3. The issuing corporation must be engaged in a "qualified trade or business," which is defined to be *any trade or business other than* those involved in:
    a. the performance of services in the fields of health, law, engineering, architecture, accounting, actuarial science, performing arts, consulting, athletics, financial services, brokerage services, or any trade or business where the principal asset is the reputation or skill of one or more of its employees;
    b. banking, insurance, financing, leasing, investing, or similar business;
    c. farming (including the business of raising or harvesting trees);
    d. the production or extraction of products for which a percentage depletion deduction is allowed; or
    e. operating a hotel, motel, restaurant, or similar business.

If all requirements are met the corporation need not be a newly formed business. But stock is not eligible if the corporation, within certain periods of time, purchases stock from the stockholder, or persons related to the stockholder.

There is an active business requirement, meaning that the corporation must use at least 80 percent by value of its assets in the active conduct of one or more qualified trades or businesses. Also, there is a gross asset test requiring that, both before and immediately after the stock's issue date, the corporation's gross assets cannot exceed $50 million. The corporation must also agree to submit periodic reports documenting its status as a qualified small business.

RABBI TRUST

The term "rabbi" trust comes from an IRS private letter ruling involving a trust established by a religious organization for its rabbi. A rabbi trust is used to fund non-qualified deferred compensation arrangements and provide plan participants with some measure of security that promised future benefits will be paid. Because the funds placed in such a trust continue to be subject to claims of the employer's creditors, the security is in large measure psychological; generally, the employer's duty to pay the benefits to the employee at the designated time from whatever source is a binding legal obligation.

However, because the trust is generally made *irrevocable*, it does protect the employee from being denied payment of the funds by a change of management, as might occur under the conditions of a hostile takeover.

The rabbi trust has been a popular device for "informally" funding non-qualified deferred compensation. In fact, this popularity caused the Internal Revenue Service to publish a model trust instrument in Revenue Procedure 92-64. (See also IRS Notice 2000-56 for guidance on Rabbi Trusts). The model trust serves as a safe harbor for employers adopting rabbi trusts; used properly, the model trust will not cause current taxation of employees under either the constructive receipt or the economic benefit doctrines.

The law provides two specific prohibitions relative to the funding of non-qualified deferred compensation plans. The first rule prohibits the setting aside of assets in an off-shore trust for purposes of paying deferred compensation. (This prevents the use of offshore rabbi trusts but should not affect domestic rabbi trusts.) The second rule prohibits the use of triggers designed to protect assets set aside to pay deferred compensation upon a change in the employer's financial health. A properly drafted rabbi trust should not run afoul of this second rule, provided it protects the employee from his employer's refusal to honor the deferred compensation (i.e., offers protection from the *contract* risk, but not the *credit* risk). See also, the discussion of Section 409A on page 538.

Substantial penalties make it important not to violate these prohibitions when drafting, implementing, and funding deferred compensation plans. Violating them can result in an additional 20 percent tax and imposition of interest at a rate that is 1 percent higher than the normal underpayment rate. These rules apply to any amounts deferred after December 31, 2004, and to any plan that is "materially modified" after October 3, 2004.

RECESSIONARY ESTATE PLANNING

Although interest rates have begun to trend upward, they remain low by historical standards. Federal fiscal policy continues to encourage low rates in an effort to continue to push forward an economy which has struggled since 2008. This combination of depressed asset values and low interest rates created unique estate planning opportunities that many affluent families used to transfer considerable wealth over the past decade. These low interest rates are reflected in the "Section 7520 rate." (Section 7520 of the Internal Revenue Code requires the use of a set of actuarial tables for valuing many popular forms of asset transfers used in estate planning.) Although asset values have increased and interest rates have increased, many clients and advisors continue to believe that the economy will continue to grow – in part because of the reductions in business tax rates resulting from the 2017 Tax Act. For anyone who believes interest rates will continue to increase, it is important to discuss these planning techniques with clients sooner rather than later.

Things To Consider

Asset Valuations. Review current asset values. Low interest rate assumptions can negatively impact asset valuations.

Grantor Retained Annuity Trust (GRAT). Donor creates a trust and retains a right to receive fixed annual annuity payments. Upon trust termination, the remainder interest is paid to trust beneficiaries. The lower Section 7520 rate produces a higher value for the retained annuity interest (i.e., larger retained interest reduces value of gift) and a lower value for the remainder interest (i.e., uses less gift tax unified credit). However, the transfer tax benefits of the GRAT depend upon the transferred property producing a return in excess of the Section 7520 rate. See chart on page 63 and comparison with GRITs and GRUTs on page 394.

Charitable Lead Annuity Trust (CLAT). Donor creates a trust and a charity receives annual annuity payments. Upon trust termination, the principal is paid to individual beneficiaries. The lower Section 7520 rate produces a higher value for the annuity interest to the charity (i.e., higher charitable deduction) and a lower value for the remainder interest to the individual beneficiaries (i.e., uses less gift tax unified credit). Subsequent appreciation of the depressed property held in a CLAT is excluded from the donor's estate.

Self-Cancelling Installment Note (SCIN). The installment debt obligation involves both a risk premium and market interest. Both of these benefit from a low interest rate environment. See page 542.

Private Annuity. A decrease in the Section 7520 interest rate lowers the payments from child to parent, thereby increasing the efficacy of the private annuity as a wealth transfer technique. See footnote 1 on page 41 and page 496.

(continued on next page)

RECESSIONARY ESTATE PLANNING (continued)

Installment Sale To Intentionally Defective Grantor Trust. Grantor creates trust that is defective for income taxes purposes (i.e., grantor will be taxed on all trust income), but irrevocable for gift and estate tax purposes (i.e., growth of trust is excluded from grantor's estate). Once established, the grantor makes a gift to the trust, equal in value to 10 percent or more of the value of the property to be sold to the trust by the grantor in a subsequent installment sale. Property that is currently depressed in value with high appreciation potential is ideally suited for this purpose. For details see the chart on page 75 and discussion of grantor trust rules on page 393.

Things That Might Not Work

Qualified Personal Residence Trust (QPRT). Low interest rates increases the value of the gift to heirs (not good). An analysis is required to determine whether this technique is viable. See page 511.

Charitable Remainder Annuity Trust (CRAT). The CRAT is the mirror image of the CLAT. Donor creates a trust and retains an annuity for a period of years with a charity as remainder beneficiary. A decrease in the Section 7520 interest rate reduces the charitable deduction. See the chart on page 59 and comparison with other charitable trusts on page 309.

Charitable Gift Annuities. As with the CRAT, the lower Section 7520 rates reduce the value of the remainder interest available for the charity. This results in a lower charitable deduction. Also, in response to the economic downturn the American Council on Gift Annuities has lowered the suggested charitable gift annuity rates, meaning that the purchasers of charitable gift annuities will receive lower payout rates. Despite these negatives, many donors with strong charitable commitments will continue to purchase charitably gift annuities. See page 307.

RECIPROCAL TRUST DOCTRINE

Irrevocable trusts are powerful estate planning tools for protecting valuable assets for the benefit of loved ones. These trusts are typically created in pairs (such as when a married couple creates two life insurance trusts, each for the benefit of the other spouse and the children). These trusts are often created as so-called Spousal Access Trusts (see discussion, page 554).

The reciprocal trust doctrine is a means by which the IRS or a court can ignore trusts created by two grantors (such as a husband and wife) and hold that the economic substance of the transaction is the same as if each grantor had transferred the assets to a trust for his or her own benefit (e.g., the assets are still taxable in his or her estate). Simply stated, the reciprocal trust doctrine is applied to prevent tax avoidance.

The reciprocal trust doctrine is easily demonstrated by an example. Assume Andy and Brenda are husband and wife, and Andy wishes to use his $5 million estate and gift tax exemption to create an irrevocable trust for the benefit of Brenda (his wife) and their children. Likewise, Brenda wishes to use her $5 million exemption to create an identical (or very similar) trust for the benefit of Andy (her husband) and their children.

Based upon the holdings of a number of court cases (including: *Lehman v. Commissioner*, 2nd Cir. 1939 and *Sather v. Commissioner*, 8th Cir. 2001), the IRS could conclude that the economic substance of the transaction is the same as if Andy had created a trust for the benefit of himself and their children and that Brenda had created a trust for the benefit of herself and their children. In such a case, Andy and Brenda would be incorrect in believing that they had gotten the future appreciation on the $5 million transferred to each trust out of each of their estates for estate tax purposes. Imagine the possible tax impact of the application of this doctrine if the trusts were ignored and the assets in the trusts appreciated to fifteen or twenty million each during Andy and Brenda's lifetimes.

The reciprocal trust doctrine is most likely to be invoked when two trusts are identical. In attempting to avoid application of the doctrine, trusts are differentiated in a variety of ways (e.g., by time of creation, type of asset contributed, and dispositive terms). Unfortunately, no exact objective standard exists for determining when the reciprocal trust doctrine will or will not be applied.

REDUCED "SPECIAL" VALUATION

An executor of an estate may elect special methods for valuing real property used in a farm, trade, or business. When available, these methods allow the real property to be valued on the basis of current use, rather than on its fair market value.

To qualify, the following requirements must be met:

1. As of the decedent's death, the real property must have been involved in a "qualified use"; i.e., used as a farm for farming purposes, or in a trade or business.
2. The adjusted value of all business or farm property, *both real and personal*, must be at least 50 percent of the adjusted gross estate.
3. The adjusted value of the business or farm *real property* must be at least 25 percent of the adjusted gross estate. Under *Estate of Finfrock* (2012) the court held that 25 percent of the real estate need not be subject to the special valuation election (the requirement is that 25 percent is eligible for the election). Not all eligible real estate need to be adjusted on the return.
4. The decedent, or a member of his family, must have owned and been a "material participant" in the operation of the business or farm for at least five of the last eight years preceding the earliest of the decedent's death, disability, or retirement (rental property does not qualify).
5. The business or farm must pass to a "qualified heir," including, among others, his spouse and immediate family.

In determining current use value the following factors apply:

1. The capitalization of the *fair rental value* of the land for farmland or closely held business purposes.
2. The capitalization of *income* that the land can be expected to yield for farming or closely held business purposes.
3. Actual assessed land values if the state provides a use value assessment law for such land.
4. Comparable sales of other farm or closely held business land located in an area where nonagricultural use is not a significant factor in determining the sales price.
5. Any other factors that could be fairly used to determine the farm or closely held business value of the land.

(continued on next page)

REDUCED "SPECIAL" VALUATION (continued)

Alternatively, when farm land is to be valued, the executor can elect a formula utilizing the average annual Gross Cash Rental for comparable land, less the average annual State and Local Real Estate Taxes for comparable land, divided by the average annual effective Interest Rate For Federal Land Bank Loans in the farm credit bank district in which the property is located (from 5.15 percent to 6.19 percent in 2014). The formula reads:

$$\frac{\text{Gross Cash Rental} - \text{State and Local Real Estate Taxes}}{\text{Interest Rate for Federal Land Bank Loans}}$$

Before relying on the reduced valuation provisions, a business owner should give serious consideration to the following qualifications and restrictions that are imposed:

1. The special methods for valuation cannot decrease the estate by more than $1,140,000 (as adjusted in 2018 for inflation, rounded down to the next lowest multiple of $10,000).

2. The business or farm must be continuously operated by a qualified heir for ten years after the decedent's death (a two-year grace period immediately following death is available, but it extends the recapture date). It is permissible to make a cash lease to a member of the lineal descendant's family, who then continues to operate the business or farm.

3. If the property is sold or the use is discontinued within ten years, the taxes must be recomputed based upon the original fair market value (a sale to another qualified heir does not trigger recapture).

4. The qualified heir who receives the property must sign an agreement to be *personally liable* for the additional tax. It is due and payable within six months after the date of sale or cessation of the use.

REINSURANCE

In its simplest form, reinsurance is the sharing of a risk by a number of insurance companies so that the mortality and profits of any one company are not greatly impacted by its claims experience. A reinsurance agreement between companies is often referred to as a reinsurance "treaty." The three main elements involved in reinsurance are retention limits, automatic reinsurance and facultative reinsurance.

"Retention" is the face amount of coverage on one life that a company retains. The amount retained is influenced by numerous considerations, including capital, surplus, insurance in force, and average policy size.

Under an **automatic** agreement the primary or ceding company (i.e., the company sending the risk out for reinsurance) must offer – and the reinsurer must accept – all risks that fall within the terms of the reinsurance agreement. The primary company does not provide the reinsurer with underwriting information. For example, the automatic agreement might provide that the reinsurer will accept the lesser of $3,000,000 or four times the primary company's retention limit, provided the total amount of insurance in force and applied for in all companies is $12,000,000 or less. If the total amount of insurance exceeds these limits then the automatic agreement is not effective and the companies resort to facultative reinsurance.

Under a **facultative** agreement the primary carrier submits the application and underwriting information to the reinsurer for review. The reinsurer then makes an independent underwriting decision and communicates its offer to the primary carrier. With larger or special risks the reinsurer may itself have special reinsurance arrangements.

"Best offer" underwriting is often used in substandard cases and typically involves sending the case to a number of reinsurance companies for underwriting. The primary company then issues the case utilizing the best offer obtained.

Reinsurers may refuse to consider a case if they receive notice that multiple applications have been submitted to a number of primary insurance companies. Because of this it is most important not to submit applications on the same insured to multiple companies unless they are fully informed of the submissions.

See also the discussion of financial underwriting on page 379.

RETIRED LIVES RESERVES (RLR)

Retired lives reserves are funds that can be established to continue group term life insurance for retired employees. Contributions to the fund are generally tax deductible to the employer, yet not taxable income to the employee. Upon either retirement or permanent disability, the employee can continue to receive limited amounts of tax-free coverage.

If the illustrated interest rate assumptions are not achieved, or if the employees live beyond actuarial life expectancy, the employer must make additional payments to the fund in order to provide the anticipated death benefits for the retired employees.

Much of the attractiveness of RLR rested upon the tax deductibility of corporate contributions to fund large amounts of insurance for key employees. Because of this, the RLR concept lost favor with passage of the Deficit Reduction Act of 1984, which imposed the following restrictions on RLR plans:

1. Generally, no deduction can be taken for RLR funding for insurance in excess of $50,000.
2. A separate account must be established for each covered key employee and benefits paid only from that separate account.
3. The group term rate for excess coverage after retirement must be reported in income (i.e., coverage over $50,000).
4. In a discriminatory plan the higher of the Table I or the actual term cost of the coverage (including the first $50,000) is taxable to retired key employees.
5. There is a 100-percent excise tax on funds returned to the employer to the extent they are attributable to deductible contributions.

Because of these severe restrictions, this arrangement is rarely used today. Instead, it may be advisable to consider other alternatives for funding personal insurance for key employees. Executive Equity (chart, page 233), Restrictive Bonus Plan (chart, page 237) and Split-Dollar Insurance (chart, page 241) offer viable alternatives to RLR.

RETIREMENT INCOME PLANNING

Retirees are living longer, healthier, and more active lives. For example, according to the 2000 Annuity Mortality Tables, the life expectancy of a male age sixty-five is 20.4 years. This means that there is a 50 percent chance that a sixty-five-year-old male will live beyond age eighty-five. Under these same tables the life expectancy of a female age sixty-five is 23.0 years, meaning that there is a 50 percent chance that a sixty-five-year-old female will live to at least age eighty-eight. Further, with a couple who are both age sixty-five, there is a 50 percent chance that one or both of them will live beyond age ninety-two. Such long life expectancies make it essential that adequate retirement income planning take place.

Retirement income planning requires a shift of focus from performance and accumulation to withdrawal and sustainability. The basic objective is to assure that the retiree will receive an *inflation-adjusted stream of income that will not be outlived*. In retirement jargon ... a "sustainable withdrawal strategy" must be developed.

Determining resources. The first step involves identifying potential sources of retirement income. Sources of income, and assets that can be converted into income, include:

1. Government benefits such as Social Security and veteran benefits.
2. Tax-favored retirement plans including:
   a. Qualified retirement plans, both *defined contribution plans* (pension plans such as money purchase and target benefit plans, and profit sharing plans such as 401(k) plans and savings/thrift plans) and *defined benefit plans* (traditional defined benefit plans, cash balance plans, and 412(i) plans).
   b. Individual retirement arrangements, such as traditional IRAs, Roth IRAs, SIMPLE IRAs, and simplified employee pension plans (SEPs).
   c. 403(b) plans and 457 plans.
3. Cash reserves including checking accounts, money market accounts, regular savings, CDs, and life insurance cash values.
4. Income assets such as bonds, fixed annuities, installment payments, and nonqualified deferred compensation plans.
5. Equity assets including stocks, mutual funds, variable annuities, and business interests.
6. Tangible assets such as real estate investments (primary residence, second home and commercial rental property).
7. Anticipated inheritances and life insurance death benefits.

Establishing a plan. The planning process is significantly different and can be more complex than that needed when accumulating assets. However,

(continued on next page)

RETIREMENT INCOME PLANNING (continued)

having a well thought out plan can bring peace of mind to those who would otherwise be uneasy about beginning the drawdown of a lifetime's savings and investments. There are a lot of variables to be considered and tradeoffs to be made. For example, the process will likely include:

1. Determining *retirement income needs* using realistic inflation assumptions (typically between 2 and 4 percent per year, but increases in healthcare costs have been substantially higher). Life expectancies must be estimated. Lifestyle choices and increases in the years of healthy life during retirement will significantly impact income needs (see table on page 601). The spending lifecycle of persons during their retirement years must be anticipated. For example, in the early retirement years retirees typically spend more on travel and entertainment, whereas the latter years bring increased health care expenditures.

2. Projecting realistic *rates of return on investments*, taking into consideration the retirees' time horizons and tolerance for risk. For example, because investment returns are not linear, Monte Carlo simulations are used to determine the likelihood that a particular withdrawal rate can be sustained (typically between 4 and 6 percent annually). Asset allocation, rebalancing of investments and annual plan review are essential.

3. Determining income, if any, that will come from part-time *employment* (e.g., the trend toward "phased" retirement has led the IRS to issue regulations that permit workers who are near retirement age to reduce their working hours and make up lost wages by taking in-service distributions from defined benefit plans, see 72 FR 28604).

4. Avoiding *penalties* associated with tax-deferred savings (e.g., before age 59½ withdrawals and after age 70½ distributions) and determining the impact of early retirement on Social Security retirement benefits (see page 637).

5. Evaluating and using *techniques* and *products* that are effective in meeting retirement objectives. These include using systematic withdrawal plans with mutual funds and annuities, laddering of bonds, purchasing long-term care insurance, and using reverse mortgages to access home equity. Indexed annuities can mitigate not only the longevity and inflation risks, but can reduce the investment risk by providing a guaranteed minimum income benefit.

6. Determining the tax consequences of distributions, minimizing taxes, and selecting those accounts to be drawn down first.

7. Implementing estate *plans* involving powers of attorney, wills, trusts, gifts, and asset protection.

8. Establishing and monitoring a *retirement budget*.

REVERSE MORTGAGE

A reverse mortgage is a loan against a home that requires no repayment so long as the homeowner lives in the house. With a traditional mortgage, payments *made by* the homeowner increase home equity (rising equity, falling debt); whereas, with a reverse mortgage, payments *received by* the homeowner reduce home equity (falling equity, rising debt).

The most popular reverse motrtgage program is the Home Equity Conversion Mortgage (HECM). Each year, the Federal Housing Administration (FHA) sets the funding limits and guidelines for HECM loans. In 2016, reverse mortgage guidelines generally require: The qualifications to obtain a reverse mortgage generally include: (1) all of the homeowners must be at least sixty-two years old; (2) the home cannot be subject to a mortgage (or the mortgage must either be paid off prior to the loan or paid from loan proceeds); and (3) the home must be the homeowner's principal residence (single family house, two to four housing unit, federally approved condominium, or planned unit development). Note that there are no income qualifications. The 2017 lending limit is $636,150 (i.e., the maximum portion of the home value that can be borrowed against, no matter what the appraised value may be).

The mortgage is a "nonrecourse" loan, meaning that the amount owed can never be more than the net proceeds received from the eventual sale of the home. For example, assume that upon a homeowner's death the amount owed under the reverse mortgage is $76,000, but the amount realized from the home's sale is only $70,000. The estate is not liable for the $6,000 difference. On the other hand, if the net proceeds from the sale were $100,000, the estate would be entitled to the excess $24,000.

Although, the most widely available reverse mortgage program is the federally insured HECM. The amount obtained from a reverse mortgage *can vary substantially* depending upon the program selected, the interest rate, the homeowner's age, and the home's value. Funds can be paid as an immediate cash advance, a creditline account, a monthly cash advance (payable either for a specific number of years, as long as the homeowner lives in the home, or for life by purchasing a commercial annuity), or any combination of these methods. Creditline accounts can be either flat or increasing each year by a specified rate. A commercial annuity offers the advantage of ongoing income for life whether or not the home is sold, but the disadvantage of a high loan balance in case of early death (i.e., cash advance purchases annuity).

The National Center for Home Equity Conversion, an independent not-for-profit organization, is an excellent source for more information (see www.reverse.org). See also the information provided by the National Reverse Mortgage Lenders Association at www.reversemortgage.org.

RISKS – TYPES OF

There are many categories and types of risks, from physical risks to social risks, and ethical risks to monetary risks. The following risks are associated with risk management in financial and retirement planning.

1. **Market Risk** - the risk that unrelated factors will decrease the value of an investment (e.g., world events or legislation). Market risk can be lessened by diversification of investments and dollar cost averaging (see chart, page 641).

2. **Interest Rate Risk** - the risk that interest rates will rise, decreasing the value of bonds or other fixed interest rate investments.

3. **Concentration Risk** - the risk that concentration of investments in a particular stock, bond, or market segment could result in a large loss of portfolio value (e.g., investing 50 percent of a portfolio in a particular stock). This risk can be reduced by acquiring a combination of fixed and equity investments, including mutual funds.

4. **Economic Risk** - the risk that the economic environment will decrease the value of an investment or other source of income. For example, the increasing costs of the Social Security system might require a change in the amount or timing of benefits (see footnote 2, page 267).

5. **Political Risk** - the risk that the political climate will result in changes in regulations and laws that impact the economy, tax laws, and Social Security benefits.

6. **Tax Risk** - the risk that changes in the tax laws will result in greater taxes. For example, prior to 1984 Social Security benefits were free of income taxes, but under present law up to 85 percent of Social Security benefits may be subject to income taxes (see discussion, page 550). With federal deficits continuing to rise, many clients and tax advisors fear that income taxes will be higher in the future.

7. **Inflation Risk** - the risk that goods and services will cost more in future years and that inflation will erode the purchasing power of fixed income or investments.

8. **Longevity Risk** - the risk that a person's longevity will result in outliving his income or suffering a loss of purchasing power (see mortality table, pages 613-614). This risk can be reduced through the purchase of life annuities and equity investments. (see Life Insurance Ratings Agencies on pages 425-429).

9. **Security Risk** - the risk that there could be a failure of a financial institution (e.g., bank or insurance company).

10. **Currency Risk** - the risk that a decrease in the underlying value of a nation's currency will reduce the purchasing power of income or investments paid in that currency.

ROTH 401(k)

The Roth 401(k) feature combines the structure of a 401(k) plan with tax benefits similar to those of a Roth IRA. Under a Roth 401(k) feature employees who make after-tax contributions may take fully tax-free withdrawals in retirement (i.e., to the extent there is a "qualified distribution" the growth is never subject to federal income taxes). This is the reverse of the traditional 401(k) which allows employees to make before-tax contributions, but then fully taxes all retirement withdrawals (see chart, page 269).

Contributions are governed by the 401(k) rules, meaning that up to $18,500 may be contributed in 2018, plus an additional $6,000 as a "catch-up" contribution if the participant is at least fifty years old. These maximum elective deferrals apply to *total* contributions to both the pre-tax and Roth accounts. Participants in 401(k) plans that have adopted Roth provisions have three choices: (1) continue to contribute only to the pre-tax account; (2) divert all contributions to the after-tax Roth account; or (3) split contributions between the two. (Note that stand-alone Roth 401(k) plans are not allowed.) Plans must provide separate accounts for the designated Roth contributions and earnings on these contributions. Unlike the Roth IRA, there are no income limits beyond which contributions may not be made (e.g., in 2018 if taxable income exceeds $199,000, a married couple filing jointly cannot make a Roth IRA contribution, see page 633). Likewise, there are no maximum age limits for participants; they need only be working for an employer offering a 401(k) plan with a Roth feature. A similar "qualified Roth contribution program" known as a Roth 403(b) plan may be made available to participants in 403(b) plans. Participants in these programs are able to designate all or a portion of their elective deferrals as Roth contributions (see also the 403(b) Plans chart on page 43).

Distributions from a Roth 401(k) are generally treated very much like distributions from Roth IRAs. Once the participant is age 59½ tax-free "qualified distributions" may be made, provided the account is at least five years old (i.e., five years have passed since the first contribution). Tax-free distributions are also allowed after the participant's disability or death. Although subject to lifetime required minimum distributions, funds in a designated Roth contribution account may be rolled over into a Roth IRA that is not subject to these requirements (see pages 527 and 595). This makes the Roth 401(k) attractive for those wishing to leave their children an income-tax-free inheritance (i.e., no taxable "income in respect of a decedent," see page 403).

The Roth 401(k) feature is likely to be most attractive to younger employees in lower tax brackets who can take advantage of many years of tax-free growth. However, for many other individuals it will not be easy to determine whether the tax-free withdrawals in retirement years will be worth the upfront cost.

ROTH IRA

The Roth IRA permits individuals in 2018 to make nondeductible contributions to an IRA of up to the lesser of 100 percent of compensation or $5,500 per year. Husband and wife may each contribute $5,500 per year provided there is sufficient compensation. An additional "catch-up" contribution of $1,000 is allowed for individuals who attain age 50 before the close of the taxable year. Unlike traditional IRAs, contributions may be made after age 70½.

As with the traditional IRA, the Roth IRA accumulates tax-deferred. Provided the account has been held for at least five years, distributions are not subject to income taxes if: (1) the owner is at least age 59½; or (2) the distribution is made after the owner's death (e.g., to a surviving spouse or children); or (3) the distribution is attributable to the owner being disabled; or (4) the distribution is for qualified first-time home buyer expenses (limited to $10,000 for both the owner and specified family members). A 10-percent-penalty tax may apply to the taxable portion of withdrawals that are not qualified (but even if withdrawals are not qualified the owner can withdraw his original nondeductible plan contributions free of both income taxes and the 10-percent-penalty tax, only the earnings are subject to these taxes). Unlike traditional IRAs, there are no requirements that distributions be started or completed by any particular date, unless the owner dies.

The annual contribution limit is reduced (dollar-for-dollar) by all contributions to a traditional IRA. Also, in 2018 the maximum yearly contribution is subject to a pro rata phaseout for taxpayers filing jointly with modified adjusted gross incomes between $189,000 and $199,000 (for single taxpayers and heads of households with modified adjusted gross incomes between $120,000 and $135,000). In contrast, with a traditional IRA if the participant is an active participant in a qualified plan the deductible phaseout limits in 2018 are $101,000 to $121,000 for taxpayers filing jointly and $63,000 to $73,000 for single taxpayers. See also, pages 405 and 631-633.

A Roth IRA may generally accept a conversion from a traditional IRA (but for tax years beginning prior to 2010, modified adjusted gross income could exceed $100,000). Distributions in excess of basis from the traditional IRA are included in gross income (but not for purposes of determining modified adjusted gross income).

The following factors might be considered when determining whether for a particular taxpayer the Roth IRA is better than a traditional IRA, or whether to make a taxable rollover to a Roth IRA: (1) the current age of the taxpayer; (2) the taxpayer's current and anticipated future marginal income tax brackets; (3) the taxpayer's need for a current income tax deduction; (4) the availability of other funds to pay the taxes on Roth IRA contributions or rollovers; and (5) anticipated reduction of taxes on Social Security income caused by receiving untaxed IRA income.

See also Roth IRA Conversion on page 528.

ROTH IRA CONVERSION

The process of converting some or all of a traditional IRA into a Roth IRA is known as a "Roth IRA conversion." There is no longer any income limit on those taxpayers who can convert (in tax years beginning on or before December 31, 2009, only individuals or couples with modified adjusted gross income of $100,000 or less could convert).

Conversion to a Roth IRA provides many advantages. While both the traditional IRA and the Roth IRA provide for tax-deferred growth of retirement savings, only the Roth IRA enables the account holder, the account holder's surviving spouse, or even the account's holders surviving children, to receive distributions free of income taxes (but the account must be held at least five years and meet additional requirements, see page 527).

In addition, since Roth IRAs are not subject to the minimum distribution requirements, no distributions are required during the account holder's lifetime (see page 411). Nor will distributions be required during the surviving spouse's lifetime, provided the spouse is the sole designated beneficiary and elects to treat the Roth IRA as his or her own (but upon the spouse's death the account will be subject to the after-death requirements, see pages 412-413). With respect to inherited benefits: (1) a traditional IRA inherited by a spouse may be converted to a Roth IRA (but a nonspouse beneficiary may not convert a traditional IRA to a Roth IRA); and (2) a *qualified* plan benefit inherited by either a spouse or nonspouse beneficiary may be rolled over into an inherited Roth IRA (e.g., the nonspouse beneficiary of a 401(k) plan can either convert to an inherited Roth IRA or transfer the benefit to an inherited traditional IRA). See the types of Qualified Retirement Plans on page 512.

Potentially tax-free income, no minimum distributions, tax-deferred growth, and the flexibility to stretch out distributions years into the future among multiple beneficiaries all combine to offer the account holder a unique opportunity to create a permanent but flexible tax-free savings plan. With all these advantages, it might appear the decision should be relatively easy. But upon conversion, the account holder must pay *ordinary income taxes* on both the tax-deductible contributions previously made to the traditional IRA and the subsequent tax-free growth. The account holder's decision is influenced by two expectations: (1) that on any given amount distributed, less income taxes will be paid currently than in the future (e.g., as a result of higher future tax rates, fewer deductions, or more taxable income); and (2) that there will be adequate time and investment opportunity for growth within the Roth IRA to more than offset the cost of making an early payment of income taxes. Recognizing that a conversion is a taxable event, it is generally agreed that the best time for converting is before account values appreciate and tax rates increase. Because the 2017 Tax Act grandfathers the recent individual tax cuts (the top marginal rate was reduced from 39.6 percent to 37 percent for example) after 2025 – it is more likely than previously that taxpayers will be in a higher tax rate in retirement than today.

(continued on next page)

ROTH IRA CONVERSION (continued)

Prior to the 2017 Tax Act, a traditional IRA that had been converted into a Roth IRA could be recharacterized as a traditional IRA until the due date (including extensions) of the account holder's return for the year the conversion was made. This meant that the account holder had up until October 15th of the following year to decide whether to recharacterize. For example, assume that an account holding stock valued at $80,000 was converted to a Roth IRA in January of 2013. Now assume further, that by September of 2014 the stock's value fell to $65,000. By recharacterizing the conversion, the account holder could avoid having to report $80,000 of ordinary income on stock having a value of only $65,000. On the other hand, if the stock's value had increased, the account holder could have let the conversion stand, report taxes on the conversion, and enjoy his or her investment returns. The 2017 Tax Act eliminated this provision meaning that taxpayers doing a conversion take the risk of a decline in valuation.

Conversions may also be made from a traditional 401(k), a section 403(a) annuity plan, a section 403(b) tax-sheltered annuity, or an eligible Section 457 governmental plan. See the discussion of the Roth 401(k) on page 526.

There are no easy answers to the question of whether an individual should, or should not, make a Roth IRA conversion. Both tax and non-tax factors should be considered, as well as the account holder's individual circumstances. Some of the factors for and against conversion are set forth below.

Factors Favoring Conversion	Factors Against Conversion
Have other sources for paying income taxes due from conversion.	Must use IRA proceeds to pay income taxes (possible early withdrawal penalty).
Will not need funds within the next 5 years.	Might need funds within 5 years (exposed to 10 percent early distribution penalty).
Expect to be in a *higher* income tax bracket during retirement years (e.g., believe tax rates will likely increase in the future). 2017 Tax Act currently sunsets lower individual rates after 2025.	Expect to be in a *lower* income tax bracket during retirement years (e.g., expect to have less taxable income in retirement).
Have many years before retirement – opportunity for tax-free buildup of interest, dividends, and capital gains.	Close to or in retirement – limited opportunity for tax-free buildup and distribution of earnings.
Large amount in traditional IRA will be forced out by RMD rules.	Need income from traditional IRA and not concerned about RMD rules.
Desire to leave tax-free income to heirs (i.e., Roth IRA is not taxed as IRD, see page 403).	Not particularly concerned about leaving tax-free income to heirs.
Payment of income taxes will reduce large estate and exposure to estate taxes.	Estate is not large enough to be exposed to federal estate taxes or state death taxes.
Live in state that has extended IRA bankruptcy protection to Roth IRA.	Live in state that has not extended IRA bankruptcy protection to Roth IRA.
Estate is large enough to be subject to estate taxes and prepayment of income taxes reduces taxable estate.	Estate is relatively small and assets are needed to provide income in retirement.

RULE AGAINST PERPETUITIES

This is a common law principle that no interest in property is good unless it must vest, if at all, not later than twenty-one years after some life or lives in being at the time of creation of the interest. The reason for this rule is to prevent an individual from unreasonably attempting to control from the grave the disposition of his estate by creating property interests in succeeding unborn generations. In some states, a wait-and-see rule would permit the trust to function until it became clear the rule was violated, as opposed to an immediate termination of all interests.

EXAMPLE A

Testator leaves Blackacre to "my wife, W, for her lifetime, then to my son, S, for his lifetime, then to S's children who survive him for their lifetimes, and then in equal shares to such of my great grandchildren as are alive when the last of my son S's children dies."

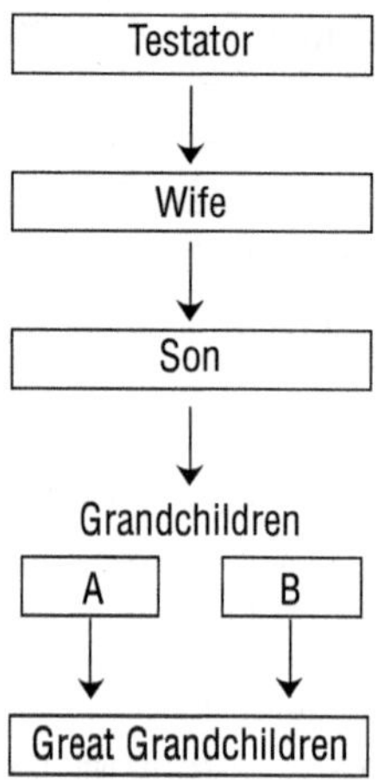

The gift over to great grandchildren fails because it is not possible to know in whom the title ultimately vests until the last of the grandchildren dies, and it is possible that one or more of these great grandchildren would not have been born (in being) within 21 years of the testator's death.

EXAMPLE B

Testator leaves Blackacre to "my wife, W, for her lifetime, then to my son, S, for his lifetime, then in equal shares to such of my grandchildren as are alive when S dies."

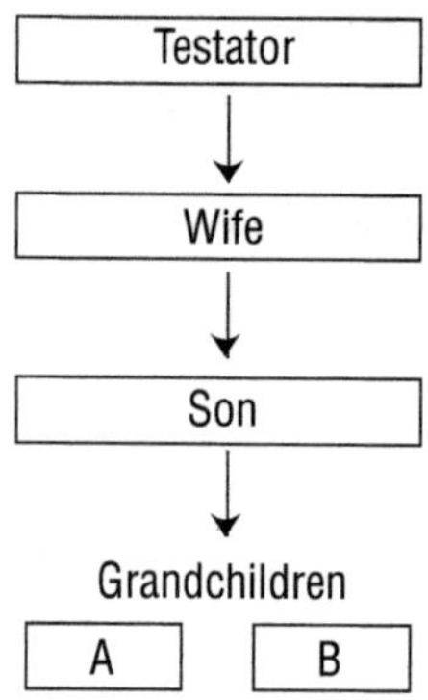

This devise is good, since there are no circumstances under which the interest would fail to vest within the required period. The gift over to the grandchildren is good since it is limited to grandchildren who are alive when son dies, son being either a life in being at testator's death or the gift to the grandchildren will vest immediately.

In recent years, a growing number of states and the District of Columbia have modified or effectively eliminated the rule against perpetuities for trusts in those states. These jurisdictions have apparently made this change in order to encourage trust business in their states. Thus, it now appears that a trust may be established to last in perpetuity for the benefit of infinite future generations, provided the trust has sufficient connection with one of these states (as specified by state statute) to be governed by the state's trust law. Attention should be paid when "decanting" a trust (see page 334) either under the protection of specific statutory provisions or otherwise to consider the potential consequences of the jurisdiction's rule against perpetuities.

S CORPORATION

This is a corporation that elects to have its income taxed to its stockholders, rather than to the corporation. The manner of taxation is very similar to a partnership, in that it avoids the double taxation that can occur when dividends are paid by a regular C corporation. The following conditions must exist for subchapter S status to be effective:

1. It must be a domestic corporation.
2. It must not have more than 100 stockholders, none of whom is a non-resident alien (a husband and wife are considered one stockholder, and a family can elect to be treated as one stockholder).
3. Only individuals, certain trusts and estates, and certain charitable organizations and qualified retirement plans (but not corporations or partnerships) may own stock.
4. It can have only one class of stock outstanding (but there may be variations in voting rights).
5. A proper election must be made (all stockholders must consent).

S corporations offer the following advantages: (1) they are not subject to the corporate alternative minimum tax adjusted current earnings adjustment (see pages 327-329); (2) provided the S corporation has no earnings and profits, the attribution rules are not a problem (see pages 218-223); (3) there is no double taxation of earnings; (4) under some circumstances they will generate passive income which can offset passive activity losses from tax shelters; and (5) the individual income tax rates are generally lower than the corporate tax rates (see Federal Income Tax Rates, page 581).

The 2017 Tax Act included a 20 percent deduction for qualified business income from certain pass-through busineses, including S corporations. However, this deduction is capped for most service businesses so it is important to fully understand these new provisions when considering business form. Even if all S corporation income can be reduced by 20 percent – that only reduces the top individual marginal tax rate from 37 percent to 29.6 percent. C corporations are taxed at a flat 21 percent rate. See discussion of Qualified Business Income(see pages 504-506 and analysis of Conversion to C Corporation.(see pages 325-326).

The tax-favored employee benefits that can be received by stockholder-employees are quite restricted. Only those benefits received by stockholder-employees owning *two percent or less* of the S corporation's stock will be deductible as a business expense by the corporation (e.g., amounts paid for certain accident and health plans, and the cost of up to $50,000 group term life insurance). Stockholder-employees owning *more than two percent* of the stock are treated in the same manner as partners in a partnership and the cost of their benefits is generally not deductible to the corporation. However, they can take advantage of the rules covering health insurance premiums and medical expenses (see footnote 1, page 259).

Tracking of basis is very important with S corporations, since a stockholder's basis in his stock shields the stockholder from taxation when he or she receives distributions of income (or sells his or her stock).

(continued on next page)

S CORPORATION (continued)

The higher the basis is, the higher is the untaxed distribution that can be received. A stockholder's basis increases when the corporation has income, either taxable or tax exempt. A stockholder's basis decreases: (1) when income is distributed; (2) when there is a loss; (3) when there is a nondeductible expenditure (e.g., a life insurance expense); and (4) when there is a capital distribution.

Example 1: How basis works - tax-free distribution of death benefit

A and B form S corporation, with A contributing $14,000 and B contributing $6,000. The corporation purchases a $500,000 term life insurance policy on key employee C. Ignore the Accumulated Adjustments Account (it is explained in Example 3).

Year 1: Corporate income of $35,000 and a $4,700 premium is paid for the $500,000 term insurance policy. Basis is increased for $35,000 of income taxed to stockholders, and reduced for the nondeductible $4,700 life insurance expense.

Year 2: Corporate income of $44,000 and a $5,100 premium is paid. Basis is increased for $44,000 of income taxed to stockholders and reduced for the nondeductible $5,100 life insurance expense.

Year 3: C dies and $500,000 death benefit is paid to corporation. Basis is increased for $37,000 of income taxed to stockholders and the $500,000 death benefit, which is tax-exempt income. Basis is decreased $500,000 for distributions to stockholders.

		Stock Basis			Accumulated Adjustments Account (AAA)
			A	B	
		Total	70% Owner	30% Owner	
Year 1:	Opening Basis	20,000	14,000	6,000	0
	Taxable Income	35,000	24,500	10,500	35,000
	Premium Expense	(4,700)	(3,290)	(1,410)	n/a
	Ending Basis	50,300	35,210	15,090	35,000
Year 2:	Opening Basis	50,300	35,210	15,090	35,000
	Taxable Income	44,000	30,800	13,200	44,000
	Premium Expense	(5,100)	(3,570)	(1,530)	n/a
	Ending Basis	89,200	62,440	26,760	79,000
Year 3:	Opening Basis	89,200	62,440	26,760	79,000
	Taxable Income	37,000	25,900	11,100	37,000
	Tax Exempt Income	500,000	350,000	150,000	n/a
	Total	626,200	438,340	187,860	116,000
	Distributions	(500,000)	(350,000)	(150,000)	
	Ending Basis	126,200	88,340	37,860	

Example 2: A reason to purchase permanent cash value insurance

Stockholder basis is not reduced for any expense "properly chargeable to capital account." The term "capital account" includes policy cash values. Therefore, with permanent insurance the basis reduction should be limited to the amount of the premium less the cash value increase (or cumulative premiums in excess of cumulative cash values). For example, if the $5,100 premium in year 2 of Example 1 was for permanent insurance, a cash value increase of $2,000 in that year would result in basis being reduced by only $3,100. A higher basis allows stockholders to receive increased tax-free distributions from the corporation.

(continued on next page)

S CORPORATION (continued)

Example 3: Dealing with earnings and profits

If an S corporation has earnings and profits (E&P) it maintains an Accumulated Adjustments Account (AAA) in order to prevent double taxation of stockholders, while at the same time assuring that distributed E&P will be taxed as a dividend. This account increases when the corporation earns taxable income and decreases when the income is distributed to stockholders. Referring to Example 1, a distribution of the $500,000 death benefit with prior E&P of $100,000 would be taxed as follows (steps 1 and 3 reduce basis, whereas step 2 does not reduce basis):

		Total	A 70% Owner	B 30% Owner
	Basis at End of Year 3	626,200	438,340	187,860
1.	Tax-free (up to AAA)	116,000	81,200	34,800
2.	Taxable (up to E&P)	100,000	70,000	30,000
3.	Tax-free (up to basis)	284,000	198,800	85,200
	Total Distribution	500,000	350,000	150,000

Example 4: Avoiding a wasted increase of basis

Now assume that stockholder B was insured by the $500,000 term life policy for the purpose of funding a purchase of B's stock by the corporation. B dies on May 10th of Year 3 and the death proceeds are received by the corporation prior to the sale of B's stock to the corporation on June 11th. Allocating the $500,000 of tax exempt insurance proceeds and the $37,000 of taxable income using the normal "per share, per day" method recognizes that B owns 30 percent of the stock for only 161 days out of 365 days, or 44.11 percent of the year. Therefore, multiplying this 44.11 percent by his 30 percent of ownership results in allocating 13.23 percent of all income to his stock's basis, or a total of $71,045 (.1323 × 37,000 = 4,895; .1323 × 500,000 = 66,150; 4,895 + 66,150 = 71,045). However, allocating the full $71,045 to B's stock is considered a "wasting" of the allocation, because his stock already received a full step-up in basis as a result of his death (page 556).

		Total	A 70% Owner	B 30% Owner
Year 3:	Opening Basis	89,200	62,440	26,760
	Taxable Income	37,000	32,105	4,895
	Tax Exempt Income	500,000	433,850	66,150
	Ending Basis	626,200	528,395	97,805

If the S corporation is a cash basis taxpayer, then an election can be made by *all* stockholders in their stock purchase agreement to terminate the taxable year whenever any stockholder terminates his interest in the corporation (e.g., by sale of all stock after death). This division of the taxable year into two short years is known as a "books and records" election. However, the redemption of stock must take place *prior* to the receipt of the insurance proceeds. Payment for B's stock could be made with a corporate note, which would be paid upon subsequent receipt of the death proceeds. This election would provide A with a basis increase equal to the full $500,000, which could be used to absorb subsequent tax-free distributions to A. The following assumes $20,000 of taxable income *before* the sale of B's stock and $17,000 of taxable income *after* the sale of B's stock:

		Total	A 70% Owner	B 30% Owner
Year 3:	Opening Basis	89,200	62,440	26,760
	Taxable Income	37,000	31,000	6,000
	Tax Exempt Income	500,000	500,000	0
	Ending Basis	626,200	593,440	32,760

SAVINGS/THRIFT PLAN

Savings and thrift plans are defined contribution plans in which employee contributions generally make up a relatively large part of total contributions. Employer contributions typically equal a percentage of at least some part of the employee contributions. Although the Code makes no specific provision for these plans, they may be tax qualified provided they meet the requirements for a pension, profit sharing, or stock bonus plan. Frequently they qualify as profit sharing plans by providing for employer contributions out of current or accumulated profits.

These employer contributions to a profit sharing plan can be entirely discretionary, made according to a formula provision, or a combination of both. If on a discretionary basis, then the employer determines each year whether or not to make contributions to the plan (but a failure to make "recurring and substantial" contributions could result in disqualification of the plan). It is not necessary that the employer actually have current or accumulated profits. If on a formula basis, then contributions are made under a formula typically tied to employer profits (e.g., 5 percent of net profits after taxes, 10 percent of gross profits in excess of $100,000, or some other profit-driven formula). In either case, the employer can deduct up to 25 percent of total payroll of plan participants.

To encourage employee savings, the employer will typically match a portion or all of the employees' contributions. Although employee contributions are not deductible, employer-matching contributions are typically excludable from the employee's taxable income. Earnings on employee and employer contributions are not taxed to the employee until withdrawn.

Convenient payroll deduction of employee contributions, together with income tax deferral on employer contributions and tax deferred growth of both employee and employer contributions made these plans an attractive way to save money. At one time they enjoyed widespread use but have now been largely replaced by 401(k) plans offering the opportunity for before-tax employee contributions (see chart, page 269).

See also, the discussion of qualified retirement plans on page 512.

SECTION 72(t) CALCULATION

In addition to ordinary income taxes, taxable distributions from an IRA prior to age 59½ are generally subject to an early distribution penalty tax equal to 10 percent of the portion of the distribution that is includible in gross income. Upon reaching age 59½, an individual can withdraw any amount at any time without being subject to this penalty tax. A periodic payment exception allows penalty-free distributions prior to age 59½, provided they are part of a series of "substantially equal periodic payments," made at least annually, and lasting a specified duration. Payments made under this exception are referred to as "72(t) payouts."

The **duration requirement** is met if payments are made for the life or life expectancy of the individual or the joint lives or joint life expectancy of the individual and a designated beneficiary. Payments must continue for the longer of five years or until the individual has reached age 59½ (e.g., payments started at age 57½ must continue for five years to age 62½). Payment changes resulting from death or disability do not trigger penalties or interest. Three IRS-approved **calculation methods** are available for calculating penalty-free distributions prior to age 59½:

(1) **Required minimum distribution (RMD) method** is calculated by dividing the account balance by the individual life or joint life expectancy. The annual payment is recalculated each year and varies depending upon the account balance. A one-time change to the RMD method from either of the following methods is allowed.

(2) **Fixed amortization method** is calculated by amortizing the initial account balance over a specified number of years equal to life expectancy (single, uniform, or joint and last survivor) and an interest rate that is not more than 120 percent of the federal mid-term rate. The annual payment remains fixed in subsequent years.

(3) **Fixed annuitization method** is calculated using a mortality table provided by the IRS and an interest rate that is not more than 120 percent of the federal mid-term rate. The annual payment remains fixed in subsequent years.

Comparison of IRA Early Payout Options IRA Owner Age 50 – $100,000 Account Balance			
Interest Rate	**RMD Method**	**Fixed Amortization Method**	**Fixed Annuitization Method**
2.5%	$2,151	$4,384	$4,524
3.5%	$2,151	$5,060	$5,255
4.5%	$2,151	$5,784	$6,029
Payouts shown are annual. RMD method shown uses uniform lifetime table. Fixed amortization method and fixed annuitization method shown are based upon a single life. See RMD tables in Appendix F of *Tax Facts On Insurance & Employee Benefits (2018)*.			

SECTION 303 AND THE UNLIMITED MARITAL DEDUCTION

Under Section 303 of the Internal Revenue Code, the partial redemption, or sale, of stock may be made between the corporation and only that party having liability for the federal and state death taxes, funeral, and administrative expenses (see discussion, page 194). Because of this restriction, the utility of a Section 303 redemption to a surviving spouse is limited since no federal estate taxes will be paid if the marital deduction is fully used. For this reason, there may be some *advantage* to incurring a federal estate tax by passing more than the unified credit equivalent in stock to a surviving child, trust, or beneficiary other than the surviving spouse. With the estate tax exemption currently at $11.2 million as a result of the temporary doubling provided by the 2017 Tax Act, passing property to children and grandchildren (rather than a surviving spouse) can be done more easily without estate tax ramifications. This could allow full advantage to be taken of a redemption under Section 303, but would also avoid subsequent appreciation of the stock in the surviving spouse's estate. For an explanation of the unlimited marital deduction, see the chart entitled Trust Will, on page 21.

ESTATE

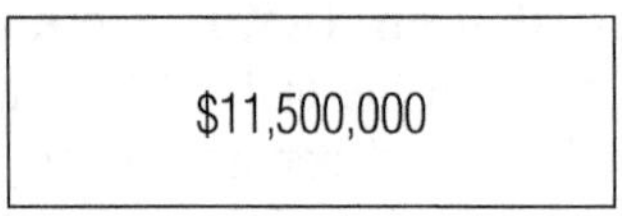

UPON THE FIRST DEATH

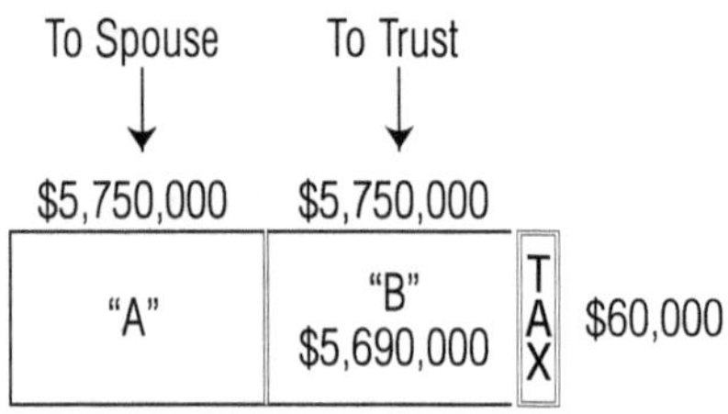

SECTION 306 STOCK

In a recapitalization, preferred stock issued as a dividend on outstanding common stock is generally considered Section 306 stock, to the extent that the issuing corporation has undistributed "earnings and profits." For this purpose, the term "earnings and profits" has a special meaning. Section 306 stock is said to be "tainted," in that a subsequent sale of the stock will produce ordinary income, not capital gain.

Upon the subsequent sale of Section 306 stock, such ordinary income treatment can cause adverse tax consequences beyond the loss of favorable capital gains treatment. If the sale is a capital transaction, the seller can subtract his or her basis in calculating any gain subject to taxation. If the sale is of Section 306 stock, the amount realized is first treated as a withdrawal of earnings and profits and the seller could be taxed on the full amount received.

Even in a "true" recapitalization (i.e., an exchange of *all* of a stockholder's stock for a different class of stock), the problem of tainted Section 306 stock cannot be avoided if, at the time of the recapitalization, other family members are, and continue to be, stockholders. The family attribution rules (as set forth on pages 218-223) have been extended to apply to such "true" recapitalizations. However, this whole problem can be avoided if the stock is not sold until *after* the death of the stockholder. If the stock is then sold at a price representing the fair market value on the date of death (or on the optional valuation date), the "stepped-up basis" at death will eliminate any taxable gain. In this regard, see the discussion of Stepped-Up Basis on page 556.

SECTION 409A

Section 409A was passed by Congress to eliminate perceived abuses in deferred compensation arrangements (e.g., triggers in Enron's plan provided accelerated payments to senior executives, while lower-level employees were left with 401(k) accounts containing worthless company stock). Virtually every nonqualified deferred compensation plan is covered by the very broad provisions of Section 409A. Included are severance payments, bonus deferral arrangements, supplemental executive retirement plans (page 474), phantom stock plans (page 489), stock appreciation rights (page 489), and nonqualified stock options (page 477). Qualified plans are not covered (see page 512).

Election. Plan participants must elect to defer *before* the beginning of the year in which they earn the compensation. (First time participants may make the election within thirty days after becoming eligible, but only for services performed after the election.) On the deferral date, participants must make a one-time election as to how, and when, they want to be paid (e.g., annual payments for ten years, beginning at age sixty). Provided it is permitted by the plan, participants who desire to further delay receipt of the money for at least an additional five years, may make a re-deferral election no later than twelve months before the payment is due.

Distribution. Participants can receive distributions under only six circumstances: separation from service, death, disability, plan-specified date, unforeseeable emergency, and upon change in ownership or control of the corporation. However, full distributions are not required immediately upon occurrence of these events (e.g., permissible alternatives include "one year after change of control," or "in equal installments over five years after disability"). Certain key employees of publicly traded corporations may not take distributions until six months after separation from service.

Acceleration. Except under circumstances specified by the IRS, a nonqualified deferred compensation plan may not permit the acceleration of payments under the plan. These limited circumstances include distributions made to fulfill domestic relations orders, and distributions to comply with conflict-of-interest rules (i.e., situations that are unanticipated and nonelective). Triggers may not be used to protect assets from a change in the employer's financial health (e.g., acceleration if profits fall below a certain level).

Funding limitation. In addition to prohibiting triggers, plans may not set aside assets in an off-shore trust for the purposes of paying deferred compensation (but onshore Rabbi Trusts are not affected, see page 514).

Penalties. There are stiff penalties for failing to comply with 409A. Retroactive constructive receipt is imposed, with the money being taxed as of the time of the intended deferral. A 20 percent tax must be paid, in addition to the normal income tax, and interest is charged on the late payment at 1 percent higher than the normal underpayment rate.

SECTION 529 PLANS

Section 529 plans, also called qualified tuition programs (QTPs), are state-sponsored or privately-sponsored programs, authorized by federal law, that allow a taxpayer to: (1) purchase tuition credits or certificates on behalf of a designated beneficiary under a prepaid educational arrangement (PEA); or (2) make contributions to an educational savings account (ESA) established to fund the "qualified higher education expenses" (QHEEs) of a designated beneficiary. However, private colleges and universities may establish PEAs, but not ESAs. QHEEs include tuition, fees, special-needs services, room and board, and the costs of books, supplies, and equipment, required by a designated beneficiary at an eligible educational institution (post secondary education to include graduate school). There is a large difference among individual programs, many of which are more restrictive than required by Section 529. Before selecting a plan, the investor would be well advised to carefully review the individual account agreement and research the past performance of the underlying investment options.

Federal law generally does not place any limits on who may participate as an account owner, contributor, or designated beneficiary (except that the beneficiary must be an individual). In order to avoid excess contributions, they are typically limited to the amount necessary to provide five years of education at more expensive schools (e.g., some programs allow for contributions of up to $250,000). Contributions must be in cash, are not tax deductible, and are treated as completed gifts eligible for the gift tax annual exclusion ($15,000 in 2018). This gift tax treatment is unusual, given the owner's power to withdraw funds from the account – subject to penalties and taxes – or to designate a new beneficiary. Gifts in excess of the annual exclusion may be "front-loaded," meaning that a donor may avoid using available unified credit by treating the gift as made over a period of five years (for a maximum of $70,000 per spouse, or $140,000 per couple, to each designated beneficiary).

State-sponsored ESAs may permit the owner to choose among different investment strategies offered by the plan: (1) when the account is opened, (2) once every twelve months, and (3) whenever the beneficiary designation is changed. Certain age-based plans automatically move to more conservative investments as the beneficiary ages. Separate accounting must be maintained for each designated beneficiary, with no pledging of the account assets by either the owner or the beneficiary. However, the account can be attached by the creditors of the owner, but not by the creditors of the beneficiary. In contrast, the value of the account is included in the estate of the designated beneficiary.

All account earnings are tax deferred. Distributions used to pay QHEEs are excluded from gross income. Distributions not used for QHEEs are subject to a 10-percent-penalty tax on the taxable portion of the distribution.

The 2017 Tax Act expanded 529 Plans by allowing for both private (including religious) and public costs for kindergarten through twelfth grade. Previously, distributions were only tax-free if used at certain colleges and universities. This is a major change in law and has caused considerable additional interest in using 519 plans as a savings strategy.

SECULAR TRUST

The "secular" trust (as distinguished from a "rabbi" trust) is used to formally fund and secure nonqualified deferred compensation. Funds placed in a secular trust are not subject to the claims of the employer's creditors. So, unlike the rabbi trust (see page 514), the secular trust can protect employees from both an employer's future *unwillingness* to pay promised benefits and an employer's future *inability* to pay promised benefits due to bankruptcy or other financial difficulties.

However, the security offered by the secular trust comes at a price to the executive, because the executive is generally subject to current taxation. To offset the executive's current tax liability, the employer will sometimes pay a bonus to the executive. Current taxation of the executive is attractive to the employer because it provides the employer with a current tax deduction. Of course, as with any deferred compensation arrangement, all deferrals and bonuses must be reasonable compensation (see page 576).

There are two principal types of secular trusts: the employer-funded trust and the employee-funded trust. Because of its negative tax treatment, the employer-funded trust has lost popularity.

In an *employer*-funded secular trust, it is the Service's position that highly compensated employees will generally be taxed each year, not just on vested contributions to the trust, but also on any vested earnings of the trust. And because the Service further believes that employer-funded trusts cannot be employer-grantor trusts, the trust itself would also be taxed on this same income! Funding the secular trust with life insurance might avoid this double taxation by eliminating trust taxation: the cash value increases should be tax-deferred to the trust. Unfortunately, life insurance funding might not relieve the executive from taxation on trust earnings, because the Service appears to believe that these cash value increases would be currently taxed to highly compensated executives. It has generally been thought that distributions from employer-funded secular trusts will be taxed under the rules relating to annuities. But the Service has questioned the applicability of those rules to distributions to highly compensated employees from most employer-funded secular trusts.

In an *employee*-funded secular trust, either the employee contributes cash to the trust *or* the employer contributes cash to the trust after giving the employee a choice between receiving cash (or some cash equivalent) or a trust contribution. The employee is currently taxed on either the cash the employee actually receives and contributes to the trust, or on the employer contributions to the trust (the executive is considered to have constructively received the money). The employee-funded trust is generally considered an employee-grantor trust and its income is taxed to the employee only. Because the employee is fully taxed on both trust contributions and income, distributions from the trust should be free of income taxes.

SEE-THROUGH TRUST

Increasingly, IRAs are the major asset in many estates. Given the size of these accumulations effective estate planning may involve the use of trusts to distribute proceeds and protect beneficiaries (e.g., to assure that IRA assets pass to beneficiaries chosen by IRA owner upon the death of a surviving spouse). However, unless the trust used qualifies as a "see-through" trust, it may not be possible to fully maximize the benefits of income tax deferral for the IRA beneficiaries (the see-through trust is also referred to as a "look-through" trust). Before the estate tax exemption was increased to $5 million – and then doubled by the 2017 Tax Act to what is now temporarily $11.2 million – use of "see-through trusts" had become rather standard practice. However, with the higher exemption and so few estates subject to estate taxation, the use of this strategy is less necessary than it was a few years ago.

The problem can be stated as follows: (1) distributions over the lifetime of the beneficiary, called "stretch distributions," may only be made to "designated beneficiaries"; (2) a trust cannot be a designated beneficiary, it has no life expectancy (only individuals may be "designated beneficiaries"); (3) an IRA with a nondesignated beneficiary must be distributed over a period of not less than five years; (4) if a trust is named beneficiary, then the IRA has no designated beneficiary and distributions must be made over a period of not less than five years. However, if a trust qualifies as a see-through trust, it is basically ignored and the individuals who are the trust beneficiaries are treated as the IRA beneficiaries.

The basic requirements for a see-through trust are: (1) the trust must be valid under state law; (2) the trust must be irrevocable, or become irrevocable upon the death of the IRA owner; (3) the trust beneficiaries must be identifiable from the trust instrument; and (4) relevant documentation must be provided to the IRA custodian in a timely manner (e.g. the current trust document). As beneficiary of an IRA, a see-through trust with multiple beneficiaries makes RMD withdrawals from an IRA account based upon the age of the oldest beneficiary of the trust (the older the age, the shorter the deferral period). This can be a problem when there is a substantial difference in age between the beneficiaries, as it will shorten the required distribution period for younger beneficiaries. For this purpose beneficiaries *include both residuary and contingent beneficiaries*.

To exclude both residuary and contingent beneficiaries from consideration, a "conduit" trust might be used (conduit trusts are also referred to as "flow-through" trusts). With a conduit trust the income beneficiaries are considered the sole beneficiaries and the ages of the residuary or contingent beneficiaries are not be considered in determining the age of the oldest designated beneficiary. To qualify as a conduit trust, the trustee must pay the RMD to the income beneficiaries as it is received from the IRA custodian. In contrast, the trustee of a see-through trust has the power to accumulate RMD for the benefit of trust beneficiaries.

For an expanded discussion, see **Q 3896**, *Tax Facts on Insurance & Employee Benefits (2019)*.

SELF-CANCELLING INSTALLMENT NOTES (SCINs)

A self-cancelling installment note (SCIN) is a sale of property in exchange for an interest-bearing promissory note which terminates on the earlier of the expiration of a fixed term or the seller's death. Although a hybrid of the installment sale and private annuity, SCINs retain most of the tax advantages of the installment sale. For example, unlike a private annuity (see page 496), SCINs may be secured without jeopardizing their installment sale status and gain is generally deferred (see chart, page 39).

Under the typical installment sale, deferred gain is eventually recognized by either the seller or the seller's heirs. If the balance of the note is unpaid at death, the present value of future payments is includable in the seller's estate. Cancellation of the installment sale note at death does not avoid inclusion of the fair market value of the note in the seller's estate. When the seller and buyer are related, the fair market value of the note is considered to be no less than its full face value (i.e., the unpaid principal of the note).

With a SCIN, nothing will be included in the seller's gross estate (similar to a private annuity). Generally having gain reported in the decedent's tax return offers far more advantages than requiring the estate to report the gain, because the income taxes may then be claimed as a deduction for estate tax purposes. To properly establish a SCIN, the installments should be for a term shorter than the seller's life expectancy (this avoids characterization of the arrangement as a private annuity). There is case law suggesting that the life expectancy should be reasonably adjusted for the seller's specific health conditions. In addition, the purchaser must pay a "risk premium" to the seller as consideration for the cancellation of the note at the seller's death. There is no specific statutory or regulatory guidance as to how this risk premium should be calculated. Apparently the premium can be reflected as an increase in the sales price, referred to as a SCIN-PRIN, or as an increase in the interest rate, referred to as a SCIN-INT. Despite these and other unresolved tax issues, the SCIN provides substantial flexibility in allocating income and deductions between seller and purchaser, while freezing the value of an asset through purchase by children or other family members. Under the right circumstances, the SCIN can be an attractive estate and income tax planning tool. The IRS has occasionally challenged SCINs on valuation issues, notably the value (as perceived by willing buyer/seller) of risks arising from the medical history of the seller.

A SCIN can produce estate and gift tax savings if the property sold produces an annual return in excess of the amounts needed to make all payments on the SCIN or if the seller dies prematurely.

SELF-EMPLOYED RETIREMENT PLANS

There is a great variety of retirement plans available for the self-employed. The following generally lists them in the order of amount of maximum annual contribution, costs to set up, complexity, and difficulty of administration.

1. **Roth IRA.** In 2018 the maximum *nondeductible* contribution is limited to the lesser of 100 percent of compensation or $5,500, subject to a phaseout for taxpayers filing jointly with adjusted gross incomes between $189,000 and $199,000 (phaseout for single taxpayers is between $120,000 and $135,000). If age 50 or over catch-up provisions allow an additional $1,000 (for a total of $6,500). Husband and wife may each contribute $5,500 per year provided there is sufficient compensation. Early withdrawals of contributions are tax-free and penalty-free. Loans are not permitted. Generally low administrative fees and responsibilities. See page 527.
2. SIMPLE IRA. SIMPLE stands for Savings Incentive Match Plan for Employees. In 2018 the maximum deductible contribution is $12,500. If age 50 or over catch-up provisions allow an additional $3,000 (for a total of $15,500). The employer is required to either contribute 2 percent of the entire payroll or match contributions of up to 3 percent of each employee's salary. Early withdrawals prior to age 59½ are subject to a penalty. Loans are not permitted. Generally low administrative fees and responsibilities. See page 548. There are also SIMPLE 401(k) Plans (see page 629).
3. SEP-IRA – Also referred to as a SEP or Simplified Employee Pension. In 2018 the maximum contribution is limited to the lesser of $55,000 or 25 percent of the first $275,000 of net earned income (with sole proprietorships and partnerships, owners are effectively limited to 20 percent). There are no catch-up provisions. No minimum funding standards are imposed. Early withdrawals prior to age 59½ are subject to a penalty. Loans are not permitted. Generally easy to set up and administer. See page 549.
4. Keogh Plan – Also referred to as a HR-10 Plan. The typical Keogh Plan is designed as a defined contribution plan without a fixed contribution formula (in 2018 participants can contribute up to 100 percent of income to a maximum of $55,000). Plans may also be designed as a defined benefit plans (see below). Early withdrawals prior to age 59½ are subject to a penalty but loans are permitted. Administrative responsibilities and fees are high. Used in organizations consisting of ten or fewer highly paid employees.
5. Individual 401(k) Plan – Also referred to as a Solo 401(k) Plan. In 2018 the maximum contribution is $55,000. If age 50 or over catch-up provisions allow an additional $6,000 (for a total of $61,000). No minimum funding standards are imposed. Early withdrawals prior to age 59½ are subject to a penalty but loans are permitted. Administrative responsibilities and fees are potentially high. See page 404.
6. Defined Benefit Plan. In 2018, depending upon age and projected income, the annual benefit at age 65 could be as high as $220,000. Nondiscrimination regulations restrict design for owner-employees of closely held businesses. Early withdrawals prior to age 59½ are subject to a penalty but loans are permitted. Administrative responsibilities and fees are high. See page 339.

SEQUENCING OF RETURNS WITH LIFE INSURANCE

All planners and clients are familiar with the maxim – Buy Low and Sell High. However, predicting these events is a challenge. Clients buying near the top of a market followed by a market drop may often wait years before an asset recovers its original starting point, or basis.

The same holds true in retirement. Prior to retirement a client may weather multiple market ups and downs. However, all those fluctuations become "moot" at retirement. At the point of retirement, clients have concluded their accumulation phase; they then begin a new phase of their planning, the decumulation phase. But market performance continues to be important. Clients who start retirement at a market peak may face market losses, possibly exacerbating the market decline in their retirement assets by being forced to sell into the loss to meet income needs. This issue is often referred to as the "Sequencing of Returns."

If clients had an alternative source of funds that they could draw on to relieve the pressure on their traditional retirement assets, their near- and long-term situation might then change. For the right client, a cash value life insurance policy can help mitigate the impact of a negative sequence of returns. During a client's working years life insurance offers a client's family protection against the loss of a breadwinner. During those years cash value life insurance can also provide a source of funds for emergencies or special planning goals. However, in retirement, life insurance cash values may act as an alternative source of funds for a client's retirement during market loss years. These are selective withdrawals, as opposed to the traditional way life insurance cash values are positioned for retirement. They are a potential cushion instead of a supplement. Rather than focus on the traditional maximum funding into a cash value life insurance policy, followed by maximum withdrawals and loans, Sequencing of Returns with Life Insurance simply requires reasonable funding into such a policy and then strategic withdrawals timed only around market losses in a client's retirement assets. By taking withdrawals and loans from the life insurance policy only after market loss years, a client may have the ability to refrain from taking funds from the traditional retirement accounts after market losses, allowing those funds time to recover.

Example – How Cash Value Life Insurance Can Stabilize Traditional Retirement Assets

Tom is a sixty-five-year-old who has accumulated $1,000,000 towards his retirement. He knew he had to build a retirement pool of his own and could not rely on government or employer retirement options; these only make a small piece of his retirement funding. Tom needs $100,000 a year in retirement to maintain his lifestyle and there is little coming in from other sources:

- Social Security - $20,000
- Pension - $10,000
- Tom's Savings – need to make up the other $70,000

(continued on next page)

SEQUENCING OF RETURNS WITH LIFE INSURANCE (continued)

Tom knows he needs to draw down on his $1,000,000 retirement fund at $70,000/year. He is risk tolerant and believes this is a reasonable rate. However, he's concerned that if the stock market is unstable in his early retirement, he may not have sufficient funds. He works with his advisors and they look at a twenty-year return for the market, long enough to carry him to age eighty-five, comfortably beyond life expectancy for a sixty-five-year-old. (See Life Expectancy on page 601). In doing the modeling, Tom's advisors don't look to the 1980s and 1990s, where the market increased in most years. Instead, they look at what the market experienced in the 1970s and 1980s, when there was a bigger mix of gains and losses. In their planning they assume 1 percent average annual inflation.

In examining models using a mix of market gains and losses, retiring in years with early market losses severely erodes Tom's retirement assets even at just 1 percent inflation. Using a snapshot of S&P market performance from 1973-1993 (a period with two early market losses although only five negative years over the twenty-year period), Tom is projected to erode his assets by 56 percent. However, by accessing his policy cash surrender values in the years following a market loss, preserving his traditional retirement funds so that they might recover, the effect of adding life insurance policy cash surrender values to his retirement asset mix is that Tom can avoid selling in down years and locking in those losses. The combination might even enhance Tom's retirement.

A summary of how the approach might enhance Tom's overall retirement, and ease his concerns is illustrated in the chart on the next page.

How the Numbers Work for Tom – With and Without Sequencing of Returns with Life Insurance

Concerns about market losses eroding retirement funds are legitimate. Since 1950, every twenty year period in the market has contained from four to six years of losses by the S&P 500®. In the planning for Tom, modeling using the twenty-year period from 1973-1993 showed a middle ground of five years of losses. The impact and erosion on retirement assets can be particularly severe when these losses occur early in retirement as was the case in 1973 and 1974, the first two years of the model period used for Tom. If Tom withdraws the $70,000 he needs to meet his living expenses, with the sequence of returns shown below, his retirement assets will be eroded away, even with modest inflation. Based on this sequence of returns, his retirement funds will decrease by over 56 percent.

By taking strategically timed withdrawals and loans from life insurance policy cash values – in years following market losses – a client has the ability to potentially change the performance of his retirement assets, while still preserving a death benefit. This can be seen in this example where Tom stops withdrawals in selected years. In that approach, turning off withdrawals in just five selected years, Tom can increase his retirement assets, possibly substantially. In this example, with this sequence of returns, he might see an increase from $1,000,000 to $3,587,396. In fact, by alternating between traditional retirement sources and life insurance cash values following negative market years, Tom can increase his retirement fund withdrawals to $100,000. At age eighty-five, and using the same sequence of returns, Tom would have $1,679,551.

The Sequence of Returns Can Have a Substantial Effect

The performance of a client's assets in the years following retirement makes a significant difference in the long-term stability and longevity of assets during retirement. In Tom's example, above, using the time period from 1973-1993, a $1,000,000 retirement portfolio was eroded by nearly 56 percent to $444,971. This example used only an average annual 1 percent inflation rate. The major reason is that two of the first three years in retirement were showed negative returns.

(continued on next page)

SEQUENCING OF RETURNS WITH LIFE INSURANCE (continued)

However, no client or Financial Professional can predict market performance. A client fortunate enough to retire into an "up" market might have very different results. If you modeled the same $1,000,000 using the S&P 500 results recorded from 1990-2010, also with five years of market losses, you get a radically different result. The 1990s were one of the strongest-performing decades in the stock market. Although they were followed by the 2000s, arguably one of the weakest decades in the market, the early years made a significant difference. In this instance, the strong performance of the first decade provided a cushion against the poor performance of the second ten-year period. Even without life insurance, taking the same $70,000 a year in withdrawals, you would have nearly $2.2 million in the retirement fund balance at age eighty-five. Clearly, the performance of each client's retirement portfolio will greatly vary.

However, a client will not know what retirement performance they will see in retirement. If they are fortunate enough to see a repeat of market performance in the 1990s they would not have needed an alternative asset source in retirement, such as that offered by a cash-value-rich life insurance policy. However, a life insurance policy can offer a client both the alternative options of cash value, but also offer the client family death benefit protection during the client's working years.

Many clients will have some or all of their retirement funds in qualified retirement plans, 401(k)s, 403(b)s or IRAs that mandate RMDs – usually beginning the year following a client's 70½ birthday. (See IRA Distribution Planning on page 411.) As a result, a client won't be able to cease all withdrawals from his or her retirement accounts. Every client's own situation will be different. Some may have all of their assets in accounts that mandate RMDs. Other clients may have little or no assets in these accounts. Moreover, how much clients will have in these qualified accounts will vary widely, particularly with the advent of Roth IRAs and Roth 401k accounts. This approach, using life insurance to smooth the effect of sequencing of returns can help a client eliminate the need to draw down on assets at the time of a loss.

Retirees have a new set of challenges as they leave their accumulation years and begin years of "decumulation" of their retirement assets. There are many ways to address concerns about risks of market loss in retirement, but one means may be to have a pool of alternative assets on hand to help supplement retirement income. Life insurance may offer such an alternative source of funds, given the potential tax free accumulation and the ability to withdraw life insurance cash values tax free via withdrawals and loans. The traditional way to show life insurance as an accumulation asset (a maximum funded policy) remains viable, but selective withdrawals timed to years following market losses in traditional retirement assets can provide a relatively low-cost means of protecting a non-correlated investment portfolio. By turning off access to traditional retirement assets following down market years a client is able to allow these assets to recover rather than selling into the losses and exacerbating the erosion of retirement funds.

SIMPLE CAFETERIA PLANS

SIMPLE cafeteria plans can be established by employers who have employed an average of 100 or fewer employees for either of the prior two years (the concept is similar to the SIMPLE 401(k) and SIMPLE-IRA). A small employer that establishes a plan and later exceeds the 100-employee limit may continue the plan until the year after a year in which it employs an average of 200 or more employees. When a plan qualifies as a SIMPLE cafeteria plan for any given year it is treated as meeting any applicable nondiscrimination requirements for that year (i.e., non-discrimination testing is not required). In general, employer contributions are deductible, not subject to Social Security tax, and employee deferrals are not taxable income, so the available benefits can be purchased with pre-tax dollars. A SIMPLE cafeteria plan must satisfy certain eligibility and participation requirements.

Employees with at least 1,000 hours of service during the preceding plan year must be eligible to participate. However, employees that may be excluded include those who: (1) have not attained age twenty-one before the end of the plan year (the plan may provide a younger age); (2) have less than one year of service as of any day during the plan year; (3) are covered under a collective bargaining agreement; or (4) are nonresident aliens. An employer may have a shorter age and service requirement but only if such shorter service or younger age applies to all employees.

A SIMPLE cafeteria plan must provide for employer nonelective contributions on behalf of every non-highly compensated and non-key employee. This requirement can be meet by contributing: (1) a uniform percentage of at least 2 percent of each qualified employee's compensation; or (2) at least the lesser of; (a) 6 percent of the qualified employee's compensation for the plan year; or (b) twice the amount of each employee's contribution. As noted above, these employer contributions are deductible, not subject to Social Security tax, and any employee deferrals are not taxable income. Highly compensated employees (per Code section 414(q)) and key employees (per Code section 416(i)) may participate, so long as they really are "employees" and do not receive disproportionate employer nonelective or matching contributions.

Available benefits may include health and dental insurance, reimbursement for health and dental expenses not covered by insurance, dependent care, group term life insurance, and disability insurance.

SIMPLE IRA PLANS

SIMPLE IRA plans ("SIMPLE" stands for Savings Incentive Match Plan for Employees) are easier to install and administer than a qualified plan. The SIMPLE IRA is considered a replacement for the SAR-SEP IRA and must be established by an employer for employees using either Form 5304-SIMPLE or Form 5305-SIMPLE.

In order to set up a SIMPLE IRA plan, the employer must not maintain another employer-sponsored retirement plan (including qualified plans, tax-sheltered annuities, and SEPs) and in the preceding year must have employed 100 or fewer employees earning at least $5,000. The plan must cover any employee who has earned at least $5,000 in any two preceding years and is reasonably expected to earn at least $5,000 in the current year. However, the employer may establish less restrictive eligibility requirements. Self-employed individuals may establish and participate in a SIMPLE IRA plan.

The employee is allowed to contribute up to $12,500 per year (in 2018). Although the deferral amount is expressed as a percentage of compensation, there is no limit on this percentage (e.g., in order to defer the maximum $12,500 per year, an employee earning $12,500 could elect to defer 100 percent of compensation). The $5,500 limit for traditional IRAs does not apply to a SIMPLE IRA. In addition, if the plan so provides, an individual age fifty or over may make catch-up contributions of up to $3,000 in 2018.

The employer is required to either contribute 2 percent of the entire payroll (under a nonelective contributions formula) or match contributions of up to 3 percent of each employee's salary (under a matching formula). However, a special rule permits the employer to elect a lower percentage under the matching formula, but not less than 1 percent, and it cannot be used for more than two out of any five years.

A SIMPLE IRA plan is not subject to nondiscrimination testing or top-heavy rules, and the reporting requirements are simplified. All contributions are excludable from the employee's income and must be fully vested. The penalty for early withdrawal prior to age 59½ is 25 percent during the first two years of participation and 10 percent thereafter (unless one of the exceptions applies).

A SIMPLE 401(k) plan is a 401(k) plan that satisfies the non-discrimination requirement by adopting certain SIMPLE 401(k) provisions that are similar to the above requirements. Such a plan is not subject to nondiscrimination tests and the top-heavy rules, but it will be subject to other qualified plan requirements. For details, see **Q 3770**, *Tax Facts on Insurance & Employee Benefits (2019)*.

SIMPLIFIED EMPLOYEE PENSION (SEP)

A simplified employee pension (SEP) is an employee's individual retirement account that may accept an expanded rate of contribution from his employer. Because payments are made into an IRA established for each employee, they are also referred to as SEP-IRAs. SEPs can be established with sole proprietorships, partnerships, or corporations, and are particularly attractive for the self-employed who has no employees or the individual who has additional income from outside employment. Generally, all employees must be included in a SEP except for: (1) employees who have not worked for the employer three out of the last five years; (2) employees who earn less than $600 (as indexed in 2018 for inflation); (3) employees who have not reached age 21; (4) employees covered by a collective bargaining agreement; and (5) non-resident aliens. They are generally easy to set up and require little administration.

SEPs can be established and funded as late as the due date (plus extensions) of the employer's (or self-employed's) tax return. In 2018 pre-tax contributions are limited to the lesser of $55,000 or 25 percent of the first $275,000 of net earned income (with sole proprietorships and partnerships the owners are effectively limited to 20 percent). No minimum funding standards are imposed. These limits compare very favorably to other opportunities available for small business owners – such as the 401(k) which has a limit of $18,500 (or $24,500 for taxpayers over age fifty-five).

Contributions are not subject to income tax withholding, FICA or FUTA. Typically these plans are self-directed, in that the individual participant decides how funds will be invested. All earnings within the plan accumulate on a tax-deferred basis. The employer may not prohibit withdrawals from the plan, although they may be subject to a penalty tax if made before age 59½. Essentially, there are four types of SEP plans with varying degrees of complexity:

5305-SEP is very easy to implement, requiring only the completion of five questions on IRS Form 5305-SEP. However, this may not be used by employers who maintain other qualified retirement plans, use leased employees, or have had a defined benefit plan.

SEP prototype plans are provided by financial institutions (with or without a fee). Prototype plans are particularly useful if the employer wants to integrate the SEP contributions with Social Security (i.e., provide increased contributions for highly paid employees).

Individually designed plans are typically drafted by an attorney. They tend to be more expensive and complicated, therefore less often used.

SAR-SEP plans are salary reduction SEPs that allow employees to make pretax contributions to their IRAs. The provisions permitting the establishment of these plans were terminated at the end of 1996. SAR-SEPs already in existence prior to 1997 may continue to operate under preexisting law, receive contributions, and add new employees, but new SAR-SEPs may not be established. In their place, individuals may wish to consider the SIMPLE IRA (see discussion on page 548).

SOCIAL SECURITY - TAXATION OF BENEFITS

Approximately 67 million Americans receive a Social Security benefit. The average monthly benefit for retired workers is about $1,400 (or $17,000 annually). Under a two-tier system, up to 85 percent of that Social Security benefit may be subject to income taxation. Under the **first tier**, if modified adjusted gross income (adjusted gross income plus tax-exempt income, or MAGI) plus one-half of Social Security income exceeds a base amount, an individual must include in gross income the *lesser* of: (1) 50 percent of the benefit; or (2) 50 percent of such excess over the base amount ($32,000 for married couples filing joint returns, zero for married couples filing separately who lived together during any portion of the year, and $25,000 for all other taxpayers). Under the **second tier**, if a taxpayer's MAGI plus one-half his or her Social Security benefit exceeds an "adjusted" base amount, the taxpayer must include the *lesser* of: (1) 85 percent of the Social Security benefit, or (2) the sum of (a) 85 percent of such excess over the adjusted base amount, plus (b) the smaller of the amount includable under the first tier of taxation (see above), or $4,500 (single taxpayers) or $6,000 (married taxpayers filing jointly). The "adjusted" base amount is $44,000 for married couples filing joint returns, zero for married couples filing separately that lived together during any portion of the year, and $34,000 for all other taxpayers.

For example, the taxable benefit would equal $8,550 for a married couple filing jointly who had Social Security benefits of $14,000, adjusted gross income of $37,000 and tax-exempt interest of $3,000:

		The Lesser Of
85% of Social Security benefit (85% × $14,000)		$11,900
		or
Modified adjusted gross income	$40,000	
One-half the Social Security benefit	+ 7,000	
Total	47,000	
Adjusted base amount	(44,000)	
The excess multiplied by 85% ($3,000 × .85)	2,550	
Lesser of amount includable under first tier ($7,000) or $6,000	+ 6,000	
Sum of 85% of excess plus smaller of amount includable under first tier, or $6,000		$8,550

There is no longer any reduction in benefits once an individual reaches *normal retirement* age (i.e., earnings during and after the month the individual reaches normal retirement age will not reduce benefits). However, *early retirement* benefits will be reduced by: (1) $1.00 for every $2.00 of earnings over $15,120 during the years *before* reaching normal retirement age; and (2) $1.00 for every $3.00 of earnings over $40,080 during the calendar year before the month the individual reaches normal retirement age (e.g., there would be a reduction of $973 if an individual who reaches normal retirement age in April of 2017 had earned $43,000 in January thru March ($43,000 – $40,080 = $2,920 ÷ 3 = $973).

SPECIAL NEEDS PLANNING

Special needs planning involves providing for a physically or mentally disabled member of the family. Most often the disabled individual is a minor or adult child, but special needs planning also involves planning for dependent parents or other relatives. With a disabled adult child such planning should provide for the child once his or her parents orthe caregivers become disabled or die. The ability of the disabled child to function will determine the required level and cost of care. Although caring for a person with a mental illness is generally considered more difficult and complicated than caring for a person with a developmental or physical disability, each situation is unique and must be planned for on an individual basis. Planning for adults with substance abuse problems include many of the same issues faced in special needs planning.

Even when other members of the family, such as siblings, are willing to assume the duties of caregiver, it is still important to provide for the management of assets. Either a testamentary or living trust can be used for these purposes (see chart on page 25). Such a trust, sometimes called a "supplemental needs trust," should: (1) appoint someone to take care of the child's property and money; (2) select a guardian for the child; (3) set out instructions on how the child is to be cared for; (4) ensure, to the extent possible, that the child will not lose payments or benefits from government agencies; and (5) integrate the trust with the remainder of the parent's estate plan. Survivorship life insurance on both parents would provide a cost-efficient means of funding this trust upon the deaths of both parents (see discussion, page 561). However, family dynamics should be considered when one or the other parent is the primary caregiver. Individual insurance on the primary care provider may be more appropriate when one parent provides most of the care. Disability income insurance on a working parent should also be considered.

At one time or another during his or her lifetime a disabled person could receive benefits from Social Security Disability Income (SSDI), Supplemental Security Income (SSI), Medicare and Medicaid. With a special needs trust the objective is to have the child's inheritance supplement, not replace, these government programs.

Eligibility for government assistance can be negatively affected by the *disabled child's assets* (e.g., for purposes of the SSI benefit a single disabled person cannot own more than $2,000 in cash and liquid assets). Even when a trust consists of *third party assets*, if the discretionary powers of the trustee are not carefully limited, state laws may cause trust assets to be "available" to the beneficiary. However, under the federal Medicaid statute a trust established with the assets of a third party, such as a parent, is not considered "available" to the trust beneficiary.

Special needs planning may also affect other estate planning techniques. For example, under federal law a Medicaid recipient cannot refuse a gift. This means that a disabled child should not be given Crummey withdrawal powers, since his failure to make a withdrawal could jeopardize his Medicaid eligibility (see discussion, page 332).

(continued on next page)

SPECIAL NEEDS PLANNING (continued)

Local laws governing special needs trust are in constant development, and recent state court cases have held that a trustee of such a trust may have an affirmative duty to determine the needs of a beneficiary with a disability, despite the grant of "discretion" by the trust provisions. Client's counsel should examine the relevant state statutes governing the conduct of such trustees, especially where the use of a lay trustee is contemplated.

The Achieving a Better Life Experience Act of 2014 (ABLE) was enacted by Congress to help families with special needs individuals. In effect, it shields private assets from jeopardizing the special needs individual's access to public funds, within certain limits.

ABLE, effective for tax years 2015 and beyond, allows for the creation of a tax-free account that can be used to save for disability-related expenses.

ABLE is administered as a state-level program, similar to a Section 529 plan. Accounts can be created by individuals to support themselves or by families to support their dependents. Assets in these accounts can be invested, accumulated and distributed free from federal taxes. Contributions to the accounts are not income tax deductible.

In order to establish an ABLE account, an individual must show that he/she was afflicted with blindness or otherwise severely disabled before the age of 26. Receipt of benefits under SSI or Social Security Disability Insurance automatically qualifies an individual to open an ABLE account. Each disabled person is limited to one ABLE account, and total annual contributions by all individuals to any one ABLE account can be made up to the gift tax exclusion amount ($15,000 in 2018, adjusted annually for inflation). Aggregate contributions are subject to the state limit for education-related Section 529 accounts. Assets can generally be rolled over only into another ABLE account.

Money in an ABLE account can be withdrawn tax free for disability-related expenses, including education, housing, transportation, employment support, health, prevention, and wellness costs, assistive technology and personal support services, and other expenses. Distributions used for nonqualified expenses are subject to income tax on the earnings portion of the distribution, plus a 10 percent penalty on those earnings.

In general, ABLE accounts have no impact on Medicaid, but are subject to Medicaid reimbursement at death. The first $100,000 in ABLE account balances is exempt from SSI's $2,000 individual resource limit. However, account distributions for housing expenses count as income for SSI purposes. If the balance of an individual's ABLE account exceeds $100,000, the individual is suspended, but not terminated, from eligibility for SSI benefits but remains eligible for Medicaid. Finally, contributions by family member for a child, stepchild, grandchild or step grandchild are protected in bankruptcy, if they are made more than 365 days prior to the donor's bankruptcy filing.

SPLIT-DOLLAR ROLLOUT

This term refers to the termination of a split-dollar agreement when an employer-owned policy is transferred, or "rolled out," to the employee, or the cash values of an employee-owned policy are used to pay off the employer. The rollout can be at any time, but is usually timed to occur once the employee reaches normal retirement age.

As an insured grows older the endorsement and nonequity collateral assignment split-dollar plans taxed under the economic benefit regime can become very costly to maintain (see footnote 3, page 121). Likewise, the nondeductible loan interest due under an equity collateral assignment plan can become burdensome. When there is a permanent need for life insurance, such as to pay estate taxes, it is important to establish some means of maintaining the policy (often described as an "exit strategy").

Under a split-dollar plan taxed under the *loan regime* the employer is generally reimbursed for all cumulative premiums paid under the split-dollar agreement (i.e., employer releases assignment of cash values in employee-owned policy upon repayment of loans). Under a split-dollar plan taxed under the *economic benefit regime* when the employer-owned policy is transferred to the employee, or others (e.g., a trust), either the employer is paid for the policy or the employee is taxed on the value of the policy (as reasonable compensation). This value is determined without regard to surrender charges that would apply if the policy was terminated.

These exit strategies also include transferring the policy as a dividend distribution, distribution of the policy at capital gains rates in liquidation of the company, or funding purchase of the policy by a grantor trust using income from assets transferred into the trust at discounted values (see Intentionally Defective Trust chart, page 75).

SPOUSAL ACCESS TRUST (SLAT)

A Spousal Access Trust (also known as a Spousal Lifetime Access Trust or SLAT) is simply a type of irrevocable trust. These trusts are often funded with property which can include life insurance on the life of the grantor (non-beneficiary) spouse. With a Spousal Access Trust, unlike many traditional irrevocable trusts, *the grantor's spouse can be a beneficiary of the trust*. By permitting the spouse to be a trust beneficiary, flexibility is retained while still removing property (including life insurance proceeds) from the taxable estate of both spouses.

A Spousal Access Trust may be best explained by an example. Assume that Andy and Brenda are husband and wife. Andy creates a trust (as grantor) and names Brenda as Trustee. Brenda and their children are named permissible beneficiaries during the term of the trust and the children are the remainder beneficiaries upon termination of the trust. Brenda's rights to receive distributions during her lifetime are limited to needs for her health, education, maintenance, and support. At the death of Andy and Brenda, the trust will terminate and property will pass to their children. The Spousal Access Trust can be created in such a way as to be out of the estates of both Andy and Brenda.

Note that Brenda as the non-grantor (and non-insured spouse) can serve as the trustee of a Spousal Access Trust funded with a single life insurance policy on the grantor spouse (Andy) if the non-grantor spouse's (Brenda's) distribution rights are limited to the health, education, maintenance, and support ascertainable standard. If someone other than the non-grantor spouse (Brenda) is named as trustee, it may be possible to give the trustee greater flexibility over distributions. Neither spouse can be a trustee if a Spousal Access Trust is funded with a second-to-die life insurance policy, since the trust should not own a policy on the life of the trustee.

Because of today's relatively high income tax rates, cash value life insurance is an increasingly popular means of providing protection against early death while allowing accumulation of cash for lifetime needs. By utilizing a Spousal Access Trust, husband and wife (through the beneficiary spouse) can maintain access to the policy's cash surrender value (as well as any other property used to fund the trust) for such things as supplemental retirement and uninsured medical treatment. In contrast, with the less flexible irrevocable life insurance trust the insured's spouse does not have access to the cash surrender values. In community property states it is important to fund the Spousal Access Trust with separate property (i.e., do not fund with community property). If Spousal Access Trusts are created for each spouse the Reciprocal Trust Doctrine must be avoided (see discussion, page 517).

As with other irrevocable trusts, the advice of qualified counsel should be sought when considering a Spousal Access Trust.

STEP TRANSACTION DOCTRINE

In construing tax statutes, the step transaction doctrine requires that interrelated steps of an integrated transaction be taken as a whole rather then treated separately. The doctrine is used by both the IRS and the courts to link several prearranged steps or contemplated steps, even though there is no contractual obligation or financial compulsion to follow through. The following are examples of circumstances that could attract application of the doctrine:

1. Parent gives money to a child who then purchases an annuity naming the parent as the annuitant, and the child as both owner and beneficiary. If the child subsequently and consistently gives the annuity proceeds to the parent, the step transaction doctrine might be applied to collapse the parent-to-child and child-to-parent gifts.

2. Borrower places a second mortgage on his house and uses the funds to purchase a single premium annuity. Normally, interest paid on a second mortgage is deductible (within limitations). But no deduction is allowed for loans taken to purchase a single premium annuity. The step transaction doctrine could be applied to collapse the borrowing-on-mortgage and purchase-of-annuity transactions.

Related tax doctrines include: (1) the tax avoidance doctrine (transaction primarily intended to reduce taxes rather than to achieve nontax business or personal objectives); (2) the substance-over-form doctrine (transaction has minimal, if any, nontax consequences); and (3) the business purpose doctrine (transaction has no business purpose). It is suggested that one way of recognizing when a proposed transaction might run afoul of one or more of these doctrines, is to apply the "if it is too good to be true, it probably is" test. It is also wise to be cautious of any arrangement promising "tax deductible life insurance."

STEPPED-UP BASIS

In Years 2001-2009, 2011 And Later

At death, the income tax basis of appreciated property in an estate is increased, or "stepped-up," to its fair market value as of the date of death. For this reason, when property is subsequently sold, there is no taxable gain if the sales price, or amount realized, is the same as the value on the date of death. However, when property has decreased in value, the basis will be "stepped-down" under the same rules as govern the determination of a step-up in basis.

The step-up in basis applies only to property that is included in the decedent's estate for federal estate tax purposes. This value can sometimes be influenced by the personal representative of the estate by filing an election to have the gross estate, including stock in a closely held corporation, valued on an alternate valuation date, usually six months after death. If this is done, the stepped-up basis equals the fair market value as of the alternate valuation date. Note, however, that use of the alternate valuation date is permitted only if its use would result in a reduction in the value of the gross estate and a reduction in the sum of the estate tax and generation-skipping transfer tax payable.

Because of the increased estate tax exemption (temporarily set at $11.2 million per person by the 2017 Tax Act), the vast majority of decedents will not be impacted by estate taxes. For this reason, it is very important that advisors give proper consideration to basis planning. Making gifts to avoid estate taxation on appreciation was previously standard planning – but today it may make more sense for older clients to hold assets until death to get a basis step-up and allow heirs to avoid capital gain taxation on a potential or planned sale.

With property owned jointly between husband and wife, the stepped-up basis applies to only one-half of the property, since only one-half the value of such property is included in the estate of the first to die.

Special rules apply in order to prevent the transfer of property in anticipation of the donee's death. Therefore, there is no step-up in basis when property is acquired by a decedent (the donee) within one year of death and this same property is then at death passed back to the original donor or the donor's spouse.

In Year 2010

The 2010 Tax Relief Act repealed the modified carryover basis provisions of EGTRRA 2001 and restored the stepped-up basis. However, in the case of decedents dying after December 31, 2009, and before January 1, 2011, the excutor was given the option of electing back into a modified carryover basis. Electing back meant that the estate would not be subject to estate taxes, but would receive a limited step-up in basis. This is essentially a *carryover basis*, but modified to allow: (1) an aggregate step-up of $1,300,000; plus (2) a spousal step-up of $3,000,000 for assets passed to a surviving spouse; plus (3) the decedent's unused losses. To be entitled to the $3 million spousal step-up, the property must have been "qualified spousal property" (i.e., the interest could not be a terminable interest).

STOCK BONUS PLAN

A qualified stock bonus plan is similar to a profit sharing plan (see page 502). However, in contrast to a profit sharing plan, the account values are often fully invested in the employer's stock. (A profit sharing plan may not invest more than 10 percent of its holdings in employer stock unless it meets the requirements for an "individual account plan.") Separate accounts are established for each participant and allocation of contributions and distributions of benefits are generally subject to the same requirements as a profit sharing plan.

Contributions are made either in cash (which is then used to purchase the stock of the employer) or in the stock of the employer. If made in stock, the amount of the employer's deduction for the contribution is determined by the fair market value of the stock when it is contributed. Unless the stock is publicly traded, some or all of the voting rights must be passed through to participants. Employer contributions are not fixed or required, may vary from year to year, and may or may not come from employer profits.

Distributions are generally in the form of employer stock, but a stock bonus plan may provide for payment of benefits in cash if certain conditions are met. [If employer securities are not readily tradable on an established market, the participant has a right to require the employer (not the plan) to repurchase employer securities under a fair valuation formula. This is referred to as a "put option."] When stock is received in a lump sum distribution any net unrealized appreciation of the stock while held in the plan is not taxed until it is subsequently sold (i.e., taxation of gain is deferred). For example, assume a stock bonus plan purchased stock for $1,000 and it appreciated in value to $5,000. The stock is then distributed to a participant in a lump sum distribution, at which time the participant pays taxes on $1,000, but would not be currently taxed on the $4,000 of unrealized appreciation.

An employee stock ownership plan (ESOP) must meet the requirements for a stock bonus plan, as well as certain additional requirements (see pages 349-350).

See also, the discussion of qualified retirement plans on page 512.

STRANGER-ORIGINATED LIFE INSURANCE (STOLI)

Stranger-originated life insurance (STOLI), also known as investor-owned, investor-initiated and investor-originated life insurance, includes a variety of plans, or "schemes," to purchase large amounts of life insurance with the present intention of benefiting outside investors who have no independent insurable interest in the life of the insured. Althoug it isn't accurate to say that STOLI is dead, in recent years courts have rescinded numeroius STOLI policies and some producers promoting abusive arrangements have been sanctioned and even imprisoned. And, when sued by insureds and insurance companies-these promoters have often discovered that their errors and omissions (E&O) insurance would not cover legal fees or damages. So, despite the lessons learned from STOLI, the allure of selling "free insurance" will continue to drivee the next great gimmick. Don't forget that if something seems too good to be true-it probably is.

Charitable variation. This is a complex arrangement which seeks to utilize the insurable interests of a charity to provide investment gains to outside investors. A typical arrangement involves the establishment of a trust by a charity. The trust then borrows funds from outside investors with the promise that the investors will be paid a fixed income. These borrowed funds are used to purchase single premium immediate annuities on the lives of a select group of charitable donors (i.e., wealthy and older donors). Life insurance is purchased on these same individual donors – under state laws that give a trust created by a charity an insurable interest in a donor's life. The annuity income is used to pay the life insurance premiums and to make the fixed income payments to the investor group. As the life insurance death benefits are received, the investor group is repaid its investment and the charity receives any remaining proceeds.

Individual variation. A typical arrangement may involve an individual purchasing a life insurance policy on his life using funds from a nonrecourse loan obtained from outside investors. (If a nonrecourse loan is not repaid, the lender has no recourse against the borrower, only a right to seize the policy pledged as security.) Typically, after two years, the insured can choose to repay the loan with interest, sell the policy to a life settlement company, or transfer the policy to the lenders in full satisfaction of the loan. From their inception, these arrangements are structured in anticipation that the outside investors will take over ownership of the policy; it is not intended that the insured will retain the life insurance. In fact, these arrangements are marketed on one side to potential insureds as providing "free insurance" (albeit for only two years), and on the other side to "sophisticated" investors as a way of reaping enhanced returns on "portfolios" of life insurance policies.

There is something inherently disturbing about STOLI. These arrangements are suspect for many reasons: (1) the "renting" of an insurable interest to third-party investors is likely to be against public policy (see page 407); (2) investment returns are problematic (i.e., projections are dependent upon the timing of death proceeds from a small group of insureds); (3) participating charities are subjecting themselves to loss of their tax-exempt status; (4) large outstanding policies could negatively affect the insured's ability to obtain future life insurance coverage (see page 379); (5) these arrangements often include misrepresentation and/or fraud pertaining to health or finances by the insured or the agent; and (6) turning life insurance into a commoditized investment could ultimately jeopardize its tax-favored status.

STRUCTURED SETTLEMENT

Structured settlements are used to provide long-term financial security in physical injury cases, by providing the injured party with periodic payments tailored to meet medical expenses and the needs of basic living. Whereas lump sum payments often result in the proceeds being poorly invested or squandered, structured settlements provide a stream of tax-free income from a reliable financial institution.

Situations appropriate for structured settlements involve: (1) wrongful death where a surviving spouse and/or children require ongoing income; (2) worker's compensation; (3) guardianship involving minors or incompetents; and (4) disabled or severely injured individuals.

To initiate a structured settlement, an agreement is reached between the plaintiff and the defendant regarding the benefits due to the injured party. This agreement can be reached before, during, or after a lawsuit. It may be agreed to privately, or it may be by order of the court (e.g., in situations involving the support of a minor child). Calculations on the costs of providing for the injured party's long-term needs are made by a structured settlement specialist, or structured settlement broker. There is great flexibility in designing the terms of a structured settlement. For example, periodic payments can be provided for a specific number of years, or made for the lifetime of the injured party with a guaranteed minimum number of years.

Once a settlement has been reached, the defendant, or its insurer, generally transfers the obligation to a financially secure and experienced life insurance company. This assignment relieves the defendant of any further obligation to make payments to the injured party. The life insurance company will typically use an immediate annuity to make the required payments. To assure that payments are received free of federal income taxes, the injured party, or annuitant, does not own the annuity contract; it is owned by the defendant, or its insurer.

Under Federal law the benefits under a structured settlement may not be assigned as collateral for a loan. However, in recent years there is a growing market involved in the purchase of existing structured settlements. In response, some states have enacted consumer protection statutes strictly regulating these transactions. Some structured settlement purchasers have taken to purchasing life insurance on annuitants to protect their investment against early death (most structured settlements end at the annuitant's death). The existence of insurable interest in such cases is not universally accepted among insurance companies (see Insurable Interest on page 407).

SUPPLEMENTAL EXECUTIVE RETIREMENT PLAN (SERP)

A Supplemental Executive Retirement Plan (SERP) is an agreement between an employer and a selected key employee in which the employer agrees to provide a specified benefit at retirement, or upon termination, disability, or death prior to retirement.

SERPs are funded entirely by the employer with no contribution by the employee. In this sense, SERPs are unlike nonqualified deferred compensation plans in which the employee is, at least in theory, *deferring* compensation that otherwise could be taken currently (see chart, page 127). Unfortunately, SERPs are often described as "deferred" compensation agreements. In any case, SERPs are exactly what their name implies, they provide retirement benefits that *supplement* all other retirement plans such as IRAs, 401(k) plans, or qualified defined benefit pension plans.

The retirement benefits to be provided are generally determined using either a defined benefit or a defined contribution approach. A *defined benefit* agreement specifies an exact dollar amount to be paid (in a lump sum or otherwise) upon retirement, or upon termination, disability, or death prior to retirement. In recruiting high level executives, this type of SERP is often used to replace retirement benefits that will be forfeited when leaving another company. Rather than a fixed dollar amount, benefits under a defined benefit approach are more likely to be determined using a formula that considers the employee's years of service and pay (e.g., 70 percent of final five years average pay). When a *defined contribution* approach is used, individual accounts are established into which either discretionary or results-tied contributions are made based on company performance (e.g., 20 percent of salary if profitability exceeds a pre-determined target). Vesting schedules are often used to provide for a graded benefit should the employee terminate employment prior to retirement.

Payments under the SERP are taxed as ordinary income to the employee in the year received and are deductible to the employer in the year paid. Should the employee die, payments to the surviving beneficiaries are also taxed as ordinary income (i.e., the life insurance death benefit is paid to the employer, not to the employee's beneficiary).

When life insurance is used to informally fund the employer's obligations under a SERP, the employer purchases cash value life insurance on the employee's life (see notice and consent requirements, page 320). The employer owns the policy, pays the premiums, and is the policy beneficiary. If the employee dies prior to retirement, the policy death benefit is payable to the employer. These funds can then be used to provide survivor benefits to the employee's beneficiary under the terms of the agreement. Upon the employee's retirement, the employer can use policy cash values to assist in meeting its obligations under the agreement, maintain the policy until the insured's death, or otherwise sell or dispose of the policy (see Transfer for Value, pages 568-569).

SURVIVORSHIP LIFE INSURANCE

Survivorship life insurance, also known as last-to-die insurance or second-to-die insurance, insures two lives, and pays a death benefit after the death of both insureds. Generally, the premium required is less than that for comparable insurance on either individual life, since the odds of two individuals dying during any given year are substantially less than of one individual dying.

While the many potential uses of survivorship life include charitable gifts (chart, page 59, and discussion, page 309), family income for surviving children, key person insurance (chart, page 203), and funding installment sales within a family (chart, page 39); survivorship life is most often used to fund the payment of estate taxes, when the marital deduction defers taxes until the death of both spouses (chart, page 21). Survivorship life offers the advantage of simplicity by paying a death benefit exactly when taxes are due – upon the second death. With a rated or uninsurable client, coverage can usually be obtained, provided the spouse is insurable at standard rates. Despite much higher estate tax exemptions and, therefore, fewer estates subject to estate taxes, second to die insurance has remained popular as a means of leveraging family wealth to leave a significant inheritance upon the second death of mom and dad.

There are some disadvantages to relying solely upon survivorship life insurance to fund the payment of estate taxes. For example, when the marital deduction is used to defer all estate taxes until the second death, appreciation of assets in the surviving spouse's estate can substantially increase total estate taxes. The flexibility provided by the use of disclaimers may be severely limited when there are no funds for payment of estate taxes at the first spouse's death (see discussion, page 346). After divorce the unlimited marital deduction is no longer available, unless the bulk of the estate is left to a new spouse.

Split-dollar is often used to pay premiums on a survivorship policy funding a life insurance trust (see Split-Dollar Funding Life Insurance Trust chart, page 119). The value of the gift to the trust can be substantially reduced by using the very low joint life rates that measure the probability of *two* deaths in one year. Use of low joint life rates allows substantial coverage to be purchased within the "present interest" limits (see Gifts & Split-Gifts chart, page 51; and footnote 4, page 57). But it must be recognized that no death benefit will be paid until *both* insureds have died. This means that a survivorship policy must generally be funded for longer periods then a policy insuring just one individual. Also, after the first death, the value of the gift to the trust will be measured using higher single life rates (currently Table 2001, see page 596). This amount could exceed the $15,000 (as indexed in 2018) annual exclusion limit for present interest gifts.

TARGET BENEFIT PLAN

Under the target benefit plan, calculation of the employer's contribution takes into consideration not only the participant's compensation but also the participant's age when first entering the plan. By using age as a factor in allocating contributions employers are able to allocate more of their contributions towards older employees. In fact, when compared to a money purchase plan, a target benefit plan can substantially increase the annual contributions for older employees who have higher levels of compensation (see discussion of Money Purchase Pension Plan on page 470).

The target benefit plan is essentially a hybrid plan. Although the target benefit plan is a type of money purchase plan, it initially uses a defined benefit approach to determine a theoretical or "targeted" benefit that is expressed as a defined benefit formula (e.g., 50 percent of average compensation payable at a normal retirement age of sixty-five). Actuarial assumptions involving investment rates of return and mortality are used to develop a table of contribution percentages (called a target benefit table) that is incorporated into the plan. A defined contribution approach is then used and the employer is required to make fixed annual contributions to the separate account of each participant according to the percentages contained in the target benefit table (the table typically sets the annual employer contribution as a percentage of compensation). Because the target benefit plan is a defined contribution plan, the annual additions are limited per participant to the lesser of 100 percent of compensation, or $55,000 (in 2018). Any increase in employee compensation will produce an additional benefit under the target benefit table (i.e., the increase in compensation produces a separate benefit that is funded with an additional annual contribution).

The employer does not guarantee the ultimate retirement benefit and the employee/participant bears the entire investment risk. If the earnings are lower than assumed, the actual benefit will be lower than the targeted benefit. Conversely, if the fund's earnings are greater than the actuary has assumed, the participant's actual benefit will be higher than the targeted benefit.

See also, the discussion of qualified retirement plans on page 512.

TAX-FREE EXCHANGE

Tax-free exchanges recognize that when property is exchanged by a taxpayer for "like kind" property, gain or loss need not be recognized and the transaction should not be subject to current taxation, since the taxpayer is in essentially the same position after the transaction as he was before the transaction. Under Section 1031 of the Code real estate transactions are frequently structured as tax-free exchanges. The 2017 Tax Act put additional limits on Section 1031 exchanges – essentially limiting them to domestic real estate exchanges.

Life insurance and annuity contracts can also benefit from the provisions for tax-free exchanges. These are often referred to as "Section 1035 exchanges" after the governing Code provision. In an exchange situation, life insurance policies are the most flexible, since they may be exchanged for another life insurance policy, an endowment contract or an annuity. Although an endowment contract cannot be exchanged for a life insurance policy, it can be exchanged for either an annuity or another endowment contract (provided the maturity date of the new contract is not later than the maturity date of the original contract). An annuity contract is the least flexible contract as it can be exchanged only for another annuity contract.

For purposes of a Section 1035 exchange, an endowment contract is considered a contract "which depends in part on the life expectancy of the insured, but which may be payable in full in a single payment during his life." The exchange of an endowment contract must be made *prior* to its maturity date.

In an exchange involving life policies, the policies must be on the life of the *same* insured and the new policy must be issued to the same person owning the old policy.

Tax-free exchanges can be particularly useful when it is desired to avoid taxation of cash values in excess of the policy owner's basis in the contract (net premiums paid, or generally total premiums paid less dividends, if any), or when it is desired to preserve the old contract's basis (substantial premiums have been paid in excess of available cash values). The old policy need not have been issued by the same company issuing the new policy. Some companies will accept assignment of policies containing an outstanding loan.

If there is a loan against the policy given in exchange, and no loan (or a lower loan) against the policy received in the exchange, the difference is treated as cash ("boot") received. The lesser of this amount or any gain in the policy given is taxable income. There is gain if total cash values, including loans, exceed total premiums paid, less dividends, if any. If there is no gain, then there is no tax (the amount simply reduces basis). Likewise, a withdrawal of policy values shortly before or after the exchange may be characterized by the IRS as a step transaction resulting in taxable boot. (See page 555.)

TAX LAW – SOURCES

Because many sources are cited as tax authority, it is important to understand the differences in the weight given them by the courts and their reliability as precedent. The citation at the end of each paragraph provides an example of how each source is cited.

Legislative and Administrative Sources

Internal Revenue Code. Congressional legislation that is the primary source of our federal tax law. [*IRC Sec. 417(a)(6)*]

Treasury Regulations. Amplify, supplement and interpret the Code. Given substantial weight by the courts and may generally be relied upon by taxpayers. Proposed regulations usually are not considered binding. [*Reg. §1.401(a)-20*]

Revenue Rulings. Issued by the National Office of the IRS. Although not as authoritative as regulations, they are given varying weight by the courts. Can generally be relied upon by taxpayers. Although revenue rulings can be revoked by the IRS, revocation is rarely retroactive. [*Rev. Rul. 72-25*]

Revenue Procedures. Reflect the internal management and state procedures the IRS will follow in specific situations. [*Rev. Proc. 95-3*]

Private Letter Rulings. Issued to a particular taxpayer by the National Office of the IRS. Although letter rulings are only uncertain indications of one line of reasoning by the Service and are not binding precedents, courts have considered them in reaching decisions. [*Let. Rul. 9212024*]

Technical Advice Memoranda. Issued to IRS personnel by the National Office of the IRS to assist with application of the Code, regulations and other precedents. Generally have the same effect as private letter rulings. [*TAM 9050006*]

Field Service Advice. Non-binding opinion written by IRS attorneys for internal use. Provides some insight into the thinking of the IRS at the time written. [*FSA 1998-252*]

Judicial Sources

Supreme Court. All courts follow Supreme Court decisions. The few tax cases it hears are accepted as a matter of discretion (certiorari). [*Gregory v. Helvering*, 293 U.S. 465 (1935)]

U.S. Courts of Appeals. Organized in thirteen circuits. Decisions of a court of appeals bind those lower courts within its appellate jurisdiction. [*Crummey v. Comm.*, 397 F.2d 82 (9th Cir. 1968)]

Tax Court. The majority of tax cases are litigated in this court (it was formerly the Board of Tax Appeals). Taxes need not be paid before initiating a suit and there is no jury. Decisions reviewed by the entire Tax Court take precedence over unreviewed decisions (either regular or memorandum); unreviewed "regular" decisions take precedence over unreviewed "memorandum" decisions. The Tax Court has said that unreviewed memorandum decisions are not precedents, but this policy may be changing. Appeals (where available) are made to the appropriate U.S. court of appeals. Other federal courts and the Service are not bound by Tax Court decisions in future cases. [*Estate of Vandenhoeck*, 4 T.C. 125 (1944)]

Federal District Courts. Taxes must be paid before initiating suit, but a jury may be requested (jury decides facts, judge decides law). A district court is expected to follow its decisions, but its decisions do not bind other federal courts or the Service in future cases. Appeals are made to the appropriate U.S. court of appeals. [*Silberman v. U.S.*, 333 F. Supp. 1120 (W.D. Pa. 1971)]

U.S. Court of Federal Claims. Taxes must be paid before initiating suit and there is no jury. The court (previously, the U.S. Claims Court) is expected to follow its decisions, but does not bind other federal courts or the Service in future cases. Appeals are made to the Court of Appeals for the Federal Circuit. [*Arkla, Inc. v. U.S.*, 27 Fed. Cl. 226 (1992)]

TOP-HAT PLAN

A top-hat plan is an unfunded nonqualified deferred compensation plan established by an employer to benefit a select group of management or highly compensated employees. It is generally assumed that top-hat plans cover individuals who are in a position to negotiate for their own benefits and typically function as tax deferral devices rather than as an essential source of post-retirement income. Because of this such plans are generally exempt from ERISA's participation, funding, vesting, and fiduciary requirements (i.e., they are exempt from any meaningful regulation under ERISA). See the discussion of ERISA on page 368. Whether a particular plan is a top-hat plan, and thus exempt from ERISA, depends upon the facts and circumstances of each individual plan.

Although the term "top-hat" is not defined under ERISA, the exemption is available provided the plan is both (1) unfunded and (2) primarily for the purpose of providing deferred compensation for a select group of employees.

As with other nonqualified plans, determining compliance with the first requirement for a top-hat plan is relatively straightforward. To be *unfunded* plan benefits must be paid out of the employer's general assets and any vehicle used to informally fund the benefits must remain subject to the claims of the employer's general creditors.

Secondly, the plan must be maintained primarily for the purposes of providing deferred compensation to a *select group* of management or highly compensated employees. Satisfying the "purpose" requirement is typically not difficult given that the plan need only be maintained primarily, but not exclusively, for the purpose of providing deferred compensation. Satisfying the "select group" requirement can often be troublesome, since the Department of Labor has not provided definitive guidance regarding the term "select group."

The select group requirement includes both quantative elements and qualitative elements. For example, from a *quantitative* perspective a court has considered that a group constituting 18.7 percent of the total workforce of a company was too large to be select, whereas numerous other cases have determined that plans benefiting 10 percent or less of the workforce met the quantitative requirement to be a top-hat plan. To meet this requirement it is probably best to limit plans to 15 percent or less of the total work force. With respect to the *qualitative* elements, a select group must include either highly compensated or management-level employees. The "highly compensated" test is met provided there is a significant disparity between the average compensation of the top-hat group and the average compensation of all other employees. To be considered a "management-level employee" requires that the employer have established a basis for designating the employee as performing management functions. The mere fact that the employer considers the employee "key" does not meet this requirement.

TOTAL RETURN UNITRUST

The total return unitrust is an attempt to reconcile the conflicting interests of the income and remainder beneficiaries by allowing the trustee to invest trust assets for total return (i.e., for capital appreciation as well as income).

The traditional "income and principal" trust directs that the trustee pay all trust income to the income beneficiary, with corpus distributed to the remainder beneficiaries upon the death of the income beneficiary (e.g., "income to my wife for life, then payment of the corpus in equal shares to my children"). In order to provide for the income beneficiary, trust assets were typically invested in fixed *income* investments (e.g., bonds). However, failing to take advantage of strong stock market performance creates disgruntled *remainder beneficiaries* (e.g., the children). To remedy this situation, a majority of states have enacted some form of the prudent investor rule (see discussion, page 503). Under this rule, trustees can utilize modern portfolio theory and invest for capital appreciation in a diversified portfolio of equity and growth stocks. However, foregoing trust income in order to attain greater trust appreciation creates disgruntled *income beneficiaries* (e.g., surviving spouses).

Caught in the middle is the trustee – who has a duty of fairness to both the income and remainder beneficiaries. The "total return unitrust" is an attempt to balance the competing interests of the income and remainder beneficiaries while obtaining greater trust appreciation.

Rather than focusing on income producing investments, under the "total return" approach a trustee, governed by the prudent investor rules, can invest in equities in order to obtain greater long-term growth of trust assets. With a "total return unitrust," the trustee is required to pay out a fixed percentage of the fair market value of the trust assets each year; thereby *enabling the income beneficiary to enjoy the benefits of trust appreciation*. A "smoothing" formula is used to cushion rapid year-to-year changes in trust value (e.g., using a three-year rolling average to determine fair market value).

The IRS has issued regulations intended to accommodate state law changes to the concepts of income and principal. Under the regulations, allocations between income and principal will be respected by the Service if state law provides for a "reasonable apportionment" between the income and remainder beneficiaries of the total return of the trust, to include ordinary income, capital gains, and unrealized appreciation (e.g., a unitrust amount of three to five percent would be considered reasonable).

Transfers in trust avoid current gift and estate taxes provided a spouse, as income beneficiary, is entitled to all trust income for life (i.e., the trust qualifies for the unlimited marital deduction, as in the "A" trust on page 21). Under the proposed regulations, this "all income to spouse" requirement is met – and the marital deduction is preserved – when a unitrust makes such a "reasonable apportionment" of the total return of the trust.

TRADITIONAL IRA

This is another name for the original (regular) individual retirement arrangement that was first made available in 1974 under the Employee Retirement Income Security Act (ERISA). Under this Act, the primary purpose of the Individual Retirement Account, or IRA, was to give those individuals not covered by an employer's retirement plan the opportunity to save for retirement on their own by establishing tax-deferred accounts with private financial institutions. Additionally, the IRA was also intended to provide a place for transferring, or rolling over, balances from employer-sponsored retirement plans; thus giving both retiring workers and individuals who were changing jobs a way to preserve their employer-sponsored retirement plan assets.

In Publication 590 (Individual Retirement Arrangements (IRAs)), the Internal Revenue Service defines a traditional IRA as "any IRA that is not a Roth IRA or a SIMPLE IRA" (i.e., the term is used to distinguish the original IRA from the Roth IRA and the SIMPLE IRA). See the expanded discussion of the traditional IRA on page 405.

In contrast to the traditional IRA, the SIMPLE IRA must be established for employees by an employer. It is not limited to the traditional IRAs $5,500 per year contribution limit. In 2018, with a SIMPLE IRA an employee may contribute up to $12,500 per year, plus age fifty and over catch-up contributions. See the expanded discussion of the SIMPLE IRA on page 548.

Likewise, in contrast to the traditional IRA, the Roth IRA permits an individual to make *non-deductible* contributions to a tax-deferred account up to the same dollar limits. Provided certain requirements are met, distributions from the Roth IRA are not subject to income taxes. See the expanded discussion of the Roth IRA on page 527.

TRANSFER FOR VALUE

The transfer for value of a life insurance contract jeopardizes the income tax-free payment of its proceeds. Under the transfer for value rule, if a policy is transferred for a valuable consideration, the death proceeds will be taxable as ordinary income, except to the extent of the consideration, the net premiums and certain other amounts paid by the transferee.

The transfer for value rules extend far beyond outright sales of policies (see **Q 280**, *Tax Facts on Insurance & Employee Benefits (2019)*). The naming of a beneficiary in exchange for any kind of valuable consideration would constitute a transfer for value. Consideration does not have to be in money, but could be an exchange of policies or a promise to perform some act or service. However, the mere pledging or assignment of a policy as collateral security is not a transfer for value.

Specific *exceptions* to this rule allow a transfer for consideration to be made to the following, without jeopardizing the income tax-free nature of the death benefit:

1. Transfers to the insured.
2. Transfers to a partner of the insured.
3. Transfers to a partnership in which the insured is a partner.
4. Transfers to a corporation in which the insured is a stockholder or officer (but there is no exception for transfer to a co-stockholder).
5. Transfer in which the recipient's cost basis in the policy is calculated in reference to the cost basis of the transferor (usually meaning a transfer between corporations in a tax-free reorganization if certain conditions exist).

A *bona fide gift* is not considered to be a transfer for value and subsequent payment of the proceeds to the grantee (donee) will be income tax-free. (Part sale/part gift transactions are also protected under the so-called "transferor's basis exception" that provides that the transfer for value rule does not apply where the transferee's basis in the policy is determined in whole or in part by reference to its basis in the hands of the transferor.)

The transfer for value problem does not exist with a partnership, because a transfer to a partner of the insured is one of the exceptions to the rule. Thus, it is possible to convert from an entity purchase agreement to a cross purchase agreement and use the same policies to fund the new agreement.

With respect to a corporation, once a stock redemption agreement (i.e., entity purchase agreement) has been funded with life insurance, it is *not* possible to change to a cross purchase agreement and use the *same* policies to fund the new agreement. Transfer by the corporation of an existing policy on the life of one stockholder to another stockholder would be a violation of the transfer for value rule (but transfer to a partner or a bona fide partnership of which the stockholder was a partner would fall within exceptions to the transfer for value rule). However, this problem does not exist in changing from a cross purchase agreement to a stock redemption agreement: the transfer to a corporation in which the insured is a stockholder is an exception to the rule (see 4 above).

(continued on next page)

TRANSFER FOR VALUE (continued)

Some planners have suggested the use of a trusteed cross purchase agreement to avoid a problem of multiple policies when there are more than just two or three stockholders. Under this arrangement, a trustee would be both owner and beneficiary of just one policy on each of the stockholders. However, it is likely that there is a prohibited transfer for value when one of the stockholders dies and the surviving stockholders then receive a greater proportional interest in the outstanding policies that continue to insure the survivors.

For example, assume A, B, C and D are equal stockholders in a corporation with a funded trusteed cross purchase agreement. Under the arrangement each stockholder is the beneficial owner of a one-third interest in the policies insuring the other three stockholders. Now assume D dies. A prohibited transfer for value could occur if D's proportional interests in the outstanding policies insuring A, B and C pass to the surviving stockholders upon D's death. However, the problem can be avoided by having the corporation purchase D's interests in the policies insuring A, B and C, with the intention of funding a combined cross purchase and entity purchase agreement (see chart entitled, "Wait And See" Buy/Sell Agreement, on page 187). Alternatively, the problem could also be avoided by simply using a stock redemption agreement, as shown in Entity Purchase Agreement chart on page 171. See page 178, for an expanded discussion of the Trusteed Cross Purchase Agreement.

The transfer-for-value rule does not apply to the transfer of a life insurance policy to a grantor trust, when the policy insures the life of the grantor of the trust (e.g. the policy is sold to the trust). For tax purposes the trust and the insured grantor are one and the same, and thus the sale is considered a transfer to the insured. See Grantor Trust Rules on page 393.

Transfer for value problems can occur in rather unexpected circumstances. For example, the transfer of existing life insurance policies insuring stockholders to the trustee of a trusteed cross purchase agreement does not fall within one of the exceptions to the transfer for value rule. To avoid this initial ownership problem the trustee should be the original applicant, owner and beneficiary of the policies.

The sale of a life insurance policy in a viatical settlement (or similar commercial arrangement) is obviously a transfer for value. Previously, promoters and their tax council had made arguments as to why the arrangement was an exception – hence attempting to exempt the death benefit received by the investor(s). The 2017 Tax Act contains new provisions addressing what is referred to as "reportable policy sales." These new provisions contain information reporting requirements, as well as specific language making it clear that any such "reportable policy sale" is NOT covered by an exception to the transfer for value.

A prohibited transfer for value can also occur when a split-dollar agreement involving a trustee is terminated pursuant to a "rollout" (see page 553). When the agreement is between the employer and the trustee of an irrevocable trust, using endorsement split-dollar with the policy owned by the employer would require a transfer of the policy to a trustee who does not fall within any of the exceptions to the transfer for value rules. However, using collateral assignment split-dollar established under the "loan regime" will avoid this transfer for value problem. See the discussion of Equity Split-Dollar on pages 362-365.

TRUST PROTECTOR

The concept of a "trust protector" owes its origin to the foreign (offshore) asset protection trust (see page 299). In an effort to protect assets from the claims of creditors, the grantor of a foreign asset protection trust will typically transfer substantial amounts of property to a trust that cannot be directly amended or revoked by the grantor. Using a trusted party to act as the trust protector gives the grantor a degree of *influence over*, or even de facto control of, the foreign trust. (Some asset protection trusts name the grantor as the initial trust protector, but the grantor *should not* be named the trust protector of a domestic trust.)

With a domestic trust, such as an irrevocable life insurance trust (chart, page 55), utilization of a trust protector provides a means of *monitoring* the trustee's performance in order to assure that the grantor's original intentions are carried out. Additionally, the trust protector provides *flexibility* in adapting the trust to changing family circumstances and evolving tax laws.

The trust protector powers are ordinarily *limited* to: (1) correct any drafting errors in the original trust instrument; (2) modify or amend the trust instrument to achieve favorable tax status, or to adjust to changes in the Internal Revenue Code, state laws, rulings, and regulations; (3) remove or replace the trustee; (4) increase or decrease the interests of trust beneficiaries (e.g., limiting a beneficiary's right of withdrawal or power of appointment); (5) appoint trust assets to another trust created by the same grantor; (6) regulate trust investments; and (7) change the situs of the trust (if possible under state law).

The trust protector is often someone whom the grantor knows and has confidence in, such as a close family friend or a professional advisor. It is important that this person be independent of both the trustee and the beneficiaries. Therefore, the trust protector should not be the grantor, the spouse of the grantor, a person who has either a present or future beneficial interest in either the trust income or principal, a person who has ever made a transfer to the trust, or the spouse of any such person.

With domestic trusts, use of a trust protector is a relatively new practice. Although there is currently little, if any, case law and legislative direction relative to the functioning of a domestic trust protector, the concept appears sound and can be expected to gain in acceptance.

TRUSTS FOR MINORS

In order for a gift to qualify for the annual exclusion, the donee must have the right to immediate use and enjoyment of the property (chart, page 51). As a matter of principle, many donors will object to placing title to property in the name of a minor, and it can create problems in dealing with the property. Fortunately, for those who intend to make substantial gifts over a number of years, the Code authorizes two types of trusts that can be used to obtain the annual exclusion:

Section 2503(c) Trust. Under this trust, both income and principal may be expended by or on behalf of the beneficiary prior to age twenty-one, and the unexpended income and principal *must* be paid to the beneficiary upon attaining age twenty-one or sooner. If the minor beneficiary dies before age twenty-one, the trust corpus passes to the minor's estate or is subject to a general power of appointment by the minor. It is permissible for the trustee to purchase life insurance on the minor's life and pay premiums from trust income (if the trust authorizes purchase of insurance on the grantor's life, or on the life of the grantor's spouse, there will be a violation of the grantor trust rules, and all income will be taxable to the grantor). Distributed income is taxable to the minor, and accumulated income is taxable to the trust. The donor should not be named trustee, as that will cause the trust assets to be included in his estate if he dies prior to the minor's reaching age twenty-one.

Section 2503(b) Trust. This trust should be considered by the donor who does not want trust corpus and unexpended income to be distributed at age twenty-one or sooner. The principal can be paid to the beneficiary at whatever dates or times are established by the donor, and need not ever be paid to the beneficiary, but rather paid to another person specified by the donor or the trust beneficiary. However, such a trust must provide for a *mandatory distribution of income* to the beneficiary, at least annually, or more frequently (but could be deposited to a custodial account). Making the gift requires a calculation that involves dividing the gift into an income portion (that which qualifies for the annual exclusion) and a principal or remainder portion (that which is considered a gift of a future interest).

Because establishment of both types of trusts can be expensive and time consuming, many donors may find it more convenient to make gifts under the Uniform Transfers to Minors Act or the Uniform Gifts to Minors Act (page 575).

UNDERWRITING: MARIJUANA AND e-CIGARETTES

An increasingly discussed area in life insurance circles is the manner in which marijuana and e-cigarettes are addressed by life insurance carriers. There are ramifications for both relative to medical underwriting and there are financial underwriting issues surrounding marijuana.

Background

E-cigarettes are plastic and metal devices that heat a liquid nicotine solution in a disposable cartridge creating vapor that the user inhales. Surprisingly, the first e-cigarette was patented as early as 1963, but it only became popular after a 2003 patent.[1] Tobacco use remains high. Although it has dropped significantly in the US since the 1964 Surgeon's General Report (a drop among adults from 43 percent in 1965 to 19 percent in 2014) usage remains high. Nearly 50 million Americans still use some form of tobacco with 443,000 smoking attributed death each year (10 percent attributed to second hand smoke). Worldwide there is an estimated 1.2 billion tobacco users with 6 million tobacco-related deaths annually. E-cigarette usage is only a small fraction of sales compared to traditional cigarettes (about 20 percent have tried e-cigarettes). Sales approached $2 billion in the US in 2013, but are forecast to rise to $10 billion in the next several years.

There are significant differences between traditional tobacco and e-cigarettes. There are over 7,000 know toxins and carcinogens in tobacco. By contrast, the toxic substances in e-cigarettes are lower. An analysis of 12 different types of e-cigarettes show toxic substances at levels 9 to 450 times lower; nicotine concentrations range from 7.4 to > 18mg/e-cig cartridge.[2] Still, there is no long term analysis of the effects of e-cigarettes. Nor is there any regulation or oversight of their manufacture; and no guidelines relative to sterile manufacturing. There are currently (2014) over 200 manufacturers each using widely different standards. Currently only e-cigarettes that are marketed for therapeutic purposes are regulated by the Food & Drug Administration (FDA). However, the FDA is expected to treat e-cigarettes akin to tobacco.

Marijuana is the most common illicit drug used in the United States accounting for over 75 percent of all current illicit drug use. In the US, about 5 million use it frequently (at least 51 days per year). The Federal government considers marijuana a Schedule I substance (having no medicinal uses and high risk for abuse). That aside, indivdual states are increasingly legalizing marijuana (or decriminalizing its use) for adult recreational use and additional states have passed laws allowing its use as a treatment for certain medical conditions. Among the possible benefits are autoimmune disease (inflammation and pain), seizures and substance abuse). These continue to be tested in National Institute for Health (NIH) studies.

(continued on next page)

[1] Many of the statistics quoted here are from a presentation, Vapor and Herb in the Breeze, by Dr. Bruce Hendricks on March 29, 2014 at the Risk Appraisal Forum.

[2] The highest concentrations approach the same concentration as a nicotine patch.

UNDERWRITING: MARIJUANA AND e-CIGARETTES (continued)

Medical Underwriting

From a medical perspective, e-Cigarettes have not been fully studied so consumers and insurers currently don't know the potential risks of e-cigarettes when used as intended and how much nicotine or other potentially harmful chemicals are being inhaled during use. Although the harmful effects of traditional cigarette smoking lies in the tobacco leaf and other chemicals, most carriers have limits on both cigarette smoking and tobacco in any other form, such as chew.

For many carriers e-cigarette use falls into the "other form of tobacco product." Typically nicotine is detected through tests of a proposed insured's urine. If the nicotine content in urine is negative then a no-tobacco rating is often available. However, If the nicotine is present in one's urine (positive) the some form of tobacco rates will usually be offered. It will be difficult for an underwriter to determine if an individual is using e-cigarettes or traditional tobacco products. As such, from a medical underwriting perspective there is little advantage to use e-cigarettes.

There is some speculation that in the future carriers may be able to offer rates for e-cigarette use that would be better than tobacco use rates, but higher than no-tobacco use rates.[1] However, that is likely to be some years away, requiring long-term controlled studies of e-cigarette users compared to control populations.

Unlike e-cigarettes, for marijuana there is a wide understanding of its medical underwriting implications. Marijuana contains a number of Tetrahydrocannabinol (THC) like intoxicants that are immediately taken up by fat cells, stored and then released slowly over time. THC may be detectable anywhere from 3 days to a month later. By contrast, alcohol contains only one intoxicant, ethanol, that is not stored in the body and is metabolized in a linear, predictable, fashion. As a result, there is no reliable method to quantify marijuana impairment, although plasma levels are being tested in Colorado. It's worth noting that THC levels in marijuana today are close to 15 percent (compared to 4 percent in the 1980s).

From a medical underwriting standpoint it is difficult to distinguish between inhaled and ingested forms. As a result, both forms are generally treated the same for underwriting purposes. Among the concerns associated with marijuana use are 1) altered perceptions and mood, 2) impaired and difficulty with thinking and problem solving, 3) impaired motor skills and 4) when used heavily by young people its effects on cognitive skills and memory may be long-term or permanent as well as having an addiction potential. Related to mental impairment judgment and motor coordination is the increased risk of injury and death while driving. Chronic marijuana use is also linked to mental illness. Additionally, marijuana users have an increased risk of heart attack in the first hour after taking the drug. In its inhaled form, marijuana remains an irritant to the lungs, can have many of the same respiratory effects as experienced by tobacco smokers. Use in pregnancy can trigger issues in fetal neurological development as well as post-partum neurological issues.

(continued on next page)

1 Ibid, note one.

UNDERWRITING: MARIJUANA AND e-CIGARETTES (continued)

As far as underwriting, most carriers will treat marijuana the same for both illicit and prescription use. Most will treat users as some form of smoker rate (because of the inability to distinguish between ingested and inhaled forms). For many carriers marijuana that is less than once per month should be able to obtain a smoker rate, possible preferred. As use increases to 2 joints per week the underwriting category may be reduced to Standard smoker. At more than 2 per week that rate may slide to mild substandard rate.

Financial Underwriting Considerations

Financial Underwriting where marijuana is involved can be problematic. Because marijuana remains a controlled substance under Federal law, transacting business involving marijuana is considered illegal. In June 2011, the U.S. Department of Justice issued a memo conveying the consequences of those individuals caught cultivating, selling or distributing marijuana, and those who engage in transactions involving the proceeds of such activity may also be in violation of federal money laundering statutes and other federal financial laws. Subsequently, most financial institutions have chosen to deny access to financial services for marijuana dispensaries. As a result, legal marijuana dispensary businesses are often conducted as cash-based business, as they have difficulty opening and/or maintaining bank and investment accounts. Similarly, American Express, MasterCard and Visa have all opted not to accept credit cards for the payment of marijuana purchases. This topic is currently under discussion with the Department of the Treasury, Department of Justice and various financial regulators. It is anticipated that official government guidance will be rendered on this topic in the future.

This presents a current dilemma relative to financial underwriting any business or individuals involved in transacting marijuana related businesses. It becomes difficult to determine what assets an entity or individual in these activities hold, even if legal at the state level. Some carriers will not consider cases involving marijuana and others will reconsider cases in the event facts involving the marijuana trade become known after policy issue. At least one carrier will insure owners of a state-legal marijuana business – so long as the premium is NOT made from a bank account created or otherwise directly tied to the marijuana business. However, it seems that no carrier will allow a policy to be owned directly by a business in the state legal marijuana industry.

UNIFORM TRANSFERS/UNIFORM GIFTS TO MINORS ACTS

Gifts can be made to a minor by transferring property to a custodian under the Uniform Transfers to Minors Act (UTMA) or the Uniform Gifts to Minors Act (UGMA). Because the UGMA places restrictions on the types of property that can be the subject of a custodial gift, most states have now adopted the UTMA. It appears that life insurance policies may be the subject of a gift in all states. However, in most states there are restrictions on who may be named insured; there may also be restrictions on who may be named beneficiary (see discussion of Minors and Life Insurance, page 469).

Gifts made under either act can qualify for the annual exclusion (see chart, page 51). All income from the gift will be taxable to the minor (unless it is used to discharge the legal obligation of another person, in which case the income would be taxable to that person). Unlike a minor's trust, the custodian does not file a separate tax return and all income is reported by the minor on his own tax return. The minor has the right to receive possession of the property upon attaining the age specified in the relevant state's statute (age varies from state to state, and may depend upon the instructions of the donor or the nature of the transaction that created the custodianship).

If the donor appoints himself as custodian, the property will be included in his taxable estate if he dies while serving as custodian. There can be only one beneficiary per custodial account, and therefore separate accounts must be established for multiple beneficiaries. Likewise, each account can only have one custodian and successor custodians are usually the minor's guardians.

In 2018 the unearned income of a child that exceeds $2,100 generally is taxed to the child at the parent's maximum rate (known as the "kiddie tax"). For this purpose a child is considered an individual who is: (1) under age eighteen; (2) under age nineteen whose earned income does not exceed half of his or her own support; or (3) under age twenty-four, if a full-time student, whose earned income does not exceed half of his or her own support.

However, in 2018 a parent can elect to claim the unearned income of a child on the parent's return if: (1) the child's income is solely from interest and dividends; and (2) the income is more than $1,050 but less than $10,500; and (3) there has been no backup withholding or estimated tax payments under the child's taxpayer identification number. For this purpose the child must be either: (1) under age eighteen; (2) under age nineteen whose earned income does not exceed half of his or her own support; or (3) under age twenty-four, if a full-time student, whose earned income does not exceed half of his or her own support. If the election is made, the parent includes as income taxable at the parent's rate any gross income of the child in excess of $2,100. With respect to the first $2100 for each child to whom the election applies, there is a tax of 10 percent of the lesser of (1) $1,050 or (2) the excess of the gross income of the child over $1,050. Under the American Taxpayer Relief Act of 2012 the 10 percent rate of tax is made permanent (it had been scheduled to increase to 15 percent in 2013).

UNREASONABLE COMPENSATION

The payment of an "excessive" amount to an employee for services rendered is considered to be unreasonable compensation. Whether compensation is excessive, and therefore unreasonable, is often determined by reference to payments by similar corporations to employees performing like services. The problem is most often encountered with regard to employee-stockholders, where a *salary* would be a deductible business expense to the businesses, but a *dividend* would be nondeductible.

Underlying any discussion of employee benefits is the assumption that, if challenged by the Internal Revenue Service, the increased compensation could be shown to be reasonable. Compensation includes not only money, but also payments "in kind." For example, all of the following are considered compensation: the personal use of an automobile, lodging for the employee's family while on vacation, premiums for group term insurance, medical expense reimbursements, premiums paid under an executive equity plan, and the value of life insurance protection under an endorsement split-dollar plan. It should be noted that no deduction is allowed for compensation that is paid to certain highly compensated officers of publicly-held corporations in excess of $1,000,000. See discussion on page 392.

However, it appears to be the experience of many accountants and tax advisors that the threat of a successful challenge by the Service is more imagined than real. This may often be due to a belated recognition by the courts, as well as the Service, that the business owner spent many years being underpaid while the business grew, and now has the "right" to compensation for those earlier services. After all, it was the owner who made the small closely-held business a success, and sooner or later he should be paid for his efforts. It is probably also recognition that individual income tax rates can exceed corporate rates-limiting the incentive to pay high rates of compensation to owner-employees. In the end, the determination of reasonable compensation depends on the circumstances of each situation.

VALUATION OF LIFE INSUANCE

Over the years it has been generally accepted among financial service professionals that, as a general rule, "unused premiums" were used for valuing a term life insurance policy and "net surrender values" were used for valuing a permanent life insurance policy. Although at one time these values were probably a fair approximation, today life insurance contracts are far more complex and these outdated rules do not always create reasonable approximations of fair market value. These general guidelines were developed during a time when life insurance policies were basically either whole life or annual renewable term. For these specific types of policies, in the absence of some serious health issue, the "net cash value" of a whole life contract is probably close to fair market value and the "unused premiums" on an annual renewable term is also a reasonable approach to determining fair market value.

In addition to whole life and renewable term, today's life insurance market includes a variety of level term, universal life, variable life, and equity index life products. Many of these universal life products come with long term or even lifetime guarantees. In many of them the guaranteed death benefit and not the cash value drives the policy values.

For tax purposes many tax professionals use an adjusted version of the "interpolated terminal reserve," or ITR, as the appropriate value of a life insurance policy (in fact, interpolated terminal reserve is specifically mentioned on IRS Form 712). In disagreement, many actuaries believe that ITR is actually a whole life term and not really applicable to a universal life or level term chassis product. The IRS has provided "safe harbor" calculations for valuation of policies transferred from qualified plans or transferred in compensation for services in employment scenarios.

When valuing a product other than whole life or annual renewable term most carriers today report a "reserve" value of some type, and many report an ITR value for term contracts as well. Some carriers use their statutory "book" reserve, while others use the tax reserve that they are required to hold. In the case of a product with a long-term guaranty, these reserve numbers (for both universal life and long-term level term) can create valuation numbers that are well in excess of premiums paid.

Unfortunately, valuation of today's life insurance products is very unsettled. The IRS has not provided clear guidance and carriers report using inconsistent methodology. When contemplating the transfer of a life insurance policy the carrier should be consulted about the policy's value *before* the transfer. With larger policies, if the carrier's valuation appears to exceed fair market value, consideration should be given to employing an independent valuation firm to appraise the policy before the transfer.

VARIABLE ANNUITIES

With a variable annuity the annuity owner has the opportunity to allocate his premiums among a number of subaccounts. In return for the opportunity to benefit from any appreciation in underlying investments, the owner assumes the risk that his investments may decrease in value, thereby resulting in lower accumulation values or a lower monthly income. The variable annuity is considered a "security" under federal law and anyone selling a variable annuity must have the required securities licenses and the purchaser must be given a prospectus (see footnote 3, page 45). The purchase can be made with either a single premium or a series of premiums (see Annuity Matrix, page 287).

In addition to a fixed or general account, the typical variable annuity might offer the following investment options: (1) growth or common stock fund; (2) balanced fund; (3) index fund; (4) global fund; (5) bond fund; (6) government securities fund; and (7) money market fund. Asset management or investment fees will vary depending upon the type of fund. In addition to an annual administration fee, an annual mortality charge is made for a guaranteed "death benefit" (e.g., provided the owner dies prior to age eighty his beneficiary is guaranteed to receive the greater of his original investment or the policy's value at the time of death, less withdrawals). Some contracts offer "stepped up" death benefits that lock in investment gains at a given point in time.

During the *accumulation* phase premium payments are applied toward the purchase of accumulation units. The value of an accumulation unit is determined by dividing the market value of the underlying investments by the total number of units outstanding. Dividends and capital appreciation or depreciation are reflected in the value of the accumulation units. The owner also has the option to transfer funds between investment subaccounts, subject to certain dollar amounts and timing limitations. Unlike mutual funds, all accumulations are tax deferred and transfers of assets between accounts are free of current income taxes. A decreasing surrender charge is generally applied if the annuity is surrendered within a given period (see chart, page 43).

During the *distribution* phase the annuity owner can cash in the contract, take periodic withdrawals, or annuitize the contract. All gains are taxed as ordinary income when distributed. Annuity payments can be received on a fixed or variable basis, or a combination of both, and can be paid as a single life annuity or joint and survivor annuity. If variable benefits are to be received the accumulation units are first exchanged for annuity units. Unlike accumulation units, the number of annuity units then remains constant. Variable benefit payments will differ from month to month, or from year to year, depending upon the value of the annuity units. A new living benefit feature currently being developed offers a guaranteed minimum account value, or minimum payout amount, regardless of the actual performance of the subaccounts. See also, the discussion of the Guaranteed Lifetime Withdrawal Benefit on page 396.

WELFARE BENEFIT FUND

A welfare benefit fund (WBF) is a fund (which is either taxable or a tax-exempt entity, as with a VEBA trust) into which employer(s) make deposits to provide specific benefits to their employees. Typical benefits include severance pay and preretirement death benefits. A WBF is not a qualified plan, nor is it a plan of deferred compensation (which would result in the employer losing his current tax deduction). To avoid classification as deferred compensation, plans are designed to: (1) include a broad group of employees; (2) cover businesses with more than one employee; (3) base funding on actuarial determinations; and (4) avoid any reversion of assets to employers.

Although strict limits are placed on an employer's deductions for contributions to a WBF, these limits do not apply to contributions made to a "ten-or-more employer plan." By requiring the pooling of funds in a ten-or-more employer plan, it was expected that the plan would be "self-policing" (e.g., an employer would not be tempted to make excess contributions beyond that needed to pay promised benefits to its own employees since these contributions might benefit the employees of *another* employer).

Regulations have halted what the IRS considers abusive ten-or-more plans (e.g., plans purporting to guarantee payments based upon contributions for specific employees). Under these regulations a ten-or-more employer plan is a single plan: (1) to which more than one employer contributes; (2) to which no employer normally contributes more than 10 percent of the total contributions by all employers; (3) that does not maintain "experience-rating arrangements" with respect to any individual employer; and (4) that satisfies compliance rules (i.e., written plan document, record keeping, and right of inspection by the IRS and participating employers). A prohibited experience-rating occurs if an *employer's costs* or an *employee's benefits* are based upon the employer's overall experience (e.g., claims or expense experience, investment results, or over or underfunding). Although the regulations do not prohibit the use of cash value life insurance, they do express concern that any pass-through of premiums associated with an employer's employees may result in a prohibited experience-rating arrangement. Likewise, these regulations seem to provide no deduction for funding with cash value life insurance.

The single-employer welfare benefit plan to prefund post-retirement medical benefits appears to offer an attractive supplemental employee benefit. However, it would be prudent to seek guidance from qualified counsel on plan design and any unresolved tax questions. See in general, IRS Notice 2007-65, IRS Notice 2007-83 and IRS Notice 2007-84.

FEDERAL INCOME TAX RATES

(Tax Years Beginning in 2019)

MARRIED FILING JOINTLY

Taxable Income Over	To	Tax Equals	Plus %	Of Excess Over
0	19,400	0	10	0
19,400	78,950	1,940.00	12	19,400
78,950	168,400	9,086.00	22	78,950
168,400	321,450	28,765.00	24	168,400
321,450	408,200	65,497.00	32	321,450
408,200	612,350	93,257.00	35	408,200
612,350		164,709.50	37	612,350

HEAD OF HOUSEHOLD

Taxable Income Over	To	Tax Equals	Plus %	Of Excess Over
0	13,850	0	10	0
13,850	52,850	1,385.00	12	13,850
52,850	84,200	6,065.00	22	52,850
84,200	160,700	12,962.00	24	84,200
160,700	204,100	31,322.00	32	160,700
204,100	510,300	45,210.00	35	204,100
510,300		152,380.00	37	510,300

SINGLE

Taxable Income Over	To	Tax Equals	Plus %	Of Excess Over
0	9,700	0	10	0
9,700	39,475	970.00	12	9,700
39,475	84,200	4,543.00	22	39,475
84,200	160,725	14,382.50	24	84,200
160,725	204,100	32,748.50	32	160,725
204,100	510,300	46,628.50	35	204,100
510,300		153,798.50	37	510,300

MARRIED FILING SEPARATE

Taxable Income Over	To	Tax Equals	Plus %	Of Excess Over
0	9,700	0	10	0
9,700	39,475	970.00	12	9,700
39,475	84,200	4,543.00	22	39,475
84,200	160,725	14,382.50	24	84,200
160,725	204,100	32,748.50	32	160,725
204,100	306,175	46,628.50	35	204,100
306,175		82,354.75	37	306,175

ESTATES AND TRUSTS

Taxable Income Over	To	Tax Equals	Plus %	Of Excess Over
0	2,600	0	10	0
2,600	9,300	260.00	24	2,600
9,300	12,750	1,868.00	35	9,300
12,750		3,075.50	37	12,750

CORPORATIONS

Taxable Income Over	To	Tax Equals	Plus %	Of Excess Over
0	50,000	0	15	0
50,000	75,000	7,500	25	50,000
75,000	100,000	13,750	34	75,000
100,000	335,000	22,250	39	100,000
335,000	10,000,000	113,900	34	335,000
10,000,000	15,000,000	3,400,000	35	10,000,000
15,000,000	18,333,333	5,150,000	38	15,000,000
18,333,333		6,416,667	35	18,333,333

Note: **Personal service corporations** are subject to a flat rate of 35 percent; and they include corporations in which substantially all of the activities involve the performance of services in the fields of health, law, engineering, architecture, accounting, actuarial science, performing arts, or consulting, and substantially all of the stock of which is held by employees, retired employees, or their estates.

FEDERAL ESTATE & GIFT TAX RATES

Unified Rate Schedule

TAXABLE ESTATE/GIFT OVER	TO	TAX EQUALS	PLUS %	OF EXCESS OVER
0	10,000	0	18	0
10,000	20,000	1,800	20	10,000
20,000	40,000	3,800	22	20,000
40,000	60,000	8,200	24	40,000
60,000	80,000	13,000	26	60,000
80,000	100,000	18,200	28	80,000
100,000	150,000	23,800	30	100,000
150,000	250,000	38,800	32	150,000
250,000	500,000	70,800	34	250,000
500,000	750,000	155,800	37	500,000
750,000	1,000,000	248,300	39	750,000
1,000,000		345,800	40	1,000,000

Under the American Taxpayer Relief Act of 2012 the above rates, the basic exclusion amount of $5,000,000, and the indexing of the basic exclusion have been made permanent, and the 2017 tax reform legislation made changes to the transfer tax exemption amount. As indexed in 2019 the basic exclusion is $11,400,000 (projected). The credit is $4,505,800 (projected) in 2019. The basic exclusion is also referred to as the "tax-free amount." The gift and estate tax systems have been reunified since 2011.

See page 584 for calculation steps.

CHECKLIST OF DOCUMENTS

	Check As Obtained
1. Wills – client	❑
– spouse	❑
2. Trust Agreements	❑
3. Life Insurance Policies – client	❑
– spouse	❑
4. Medical Insurance Policies	❑
5. Disability Income Policies	❑
6. Personal Balance Sheet (or similar listing of cash, securities, real estate, personal effects, mortgages and other liabilities)	❑
7. Business Balance Sheets	❑
8. Business Profit and Loss Statements	❑
9. Business Disposition Agreements (buy/sell agreements, partnership agreements, etc.)	❑
10. Employee Benefits (retirement plans, stock options, deferred compensation, etc.)	❑
11. Income Tax Return (most recent)	❑
12. Gift Tax returns	❑
13. Dates of Birth (of family members)	❑

14. Other: ______________________________
____
____
____
____

Date of Meeting: ______________________________
Time: ______________________________
Place: ______________________________

GIFT TAX CALCULATION STEPS

Gross Value of Current Gift(s)	$________
Less: 50% of Gift if Split-Gift(s)	(________)
Annual Exclusion[1]	(________)
Marital Deduction[2]	(________)
Charitable Deduction[2]	(________)
Current Taxable Gift(s)	$________
Plus: Sum of All Prior Taxable Gifts	________
Total Cumulative Taxable Gifts	$________
Tax on Total Cumulative Taxable Gifts[3]	$________
Less: Taxes Paid on Prior Taxable Gifts	(________)
Tentative Tax	$________
Less: Unified Credit	(________)
Gift Tax Payable[4]	$________

ESTATE TAX CALCULATION STEPS

Gross Estate	$________
Less: Debts of Decedent	(________)
Administration Expenses	(________)
Losses during Administration	(________)
Adjusted Gross Estate	$________
Less: Marital Deduction[2]	(________)
Charitable Deduction[2]	(________)
State Death Tax Deduction	(________)
Taxable Estate	$________
Plus: Adjusted Taxable Gifts	________
Computation Base	$________
Tentative Tax[3]	$________
Less: Post-1976 Gift Taxes Payable	(________)
Unified Credit	(________)
Pre-1977 Gift Tax Credit	(________)
Foreign Death Tax Credit	(________)
Credit for Tax on Prior Transfers	(________)
Estate Tax Payable[5]	$________

[1] See page 42 for details regarding the gift tax annual exclusion.

[2] Full value of property passed to spouse or charity may be taken as a deduction.

[3] See page 582 for estate and gift tax rates.

[4] Transfer taxes payable during life may also include the generation-skipping transfer tax.

[5] Transfer taxes payable at death may also include the generation-skipping transfer tax (see chart, page 35).

INTESTATE'S "WILL"

Being of sound mind and memory, I ________________________________, do hereby publish this as my Last Will and Testament:

First

I give my wife [husband] only one-third of my possessions, and I give my children the remaining two-thirds.

I appoint my wife [husband] as guardian of my children, but as a safeguard I require that she [he] report to the Probate Court each year and render an accounting of how, why, and where she [he] spent the money necessary for the proper care of my children.

As a further safeguard, I direct my wife [husband] to produce to the Probate Court, a performance bond to guarantee that she [he] guarantee that she [he] exercises proper judgment in the handling, investing, and spending of my children's money. As a final safeguard, my children shall have the right to demand and receive a complete accounting from their mother [father] of all her [his] financial actions with their money as soon as they reach legal age.

When my children reach age 18, they shall have full rights to withdraw and spend their share of my estate. No one shall have any right to question my children's actions on how they decide to spend their respective shares.

Second

Should my wife [husband] remarry, her [his] second husband [wife] shall be entitled to one-third of everything my wife [husband] possesses. Should my children need some of this share for their support, the second husband [wife] shall not be bound to spend any part of his [her] share on my children's behalf.

Such second husband [wife] shall have sole right to decide who is to get his [her] share, even to the exclusion of my children.

Third

Should my wife [husband] predecease me or die while any of my children are minors, I do not wish to exercise my right to nominate the guardian of my children. Rather than nominating a guardian of my preference, I direct my relatives and friends to get together and select a guardian by mutual agreement. In the event that they fail to agree on a guardian, I direct the Probate Court to make the selection. If the court wishes, it may appoint a stranger acceptable to it.

Fourth

Under existing tax law, there are certain legitimate techniques open to me to lower death taxes. Since I prefer to have my money used for government purposes rather than for the benefit of my wife [husband] and children, I direct that no effort be made to lower taxes.

IN WITNESS WHEREOF, I have set my hand to this my LAST WILL AND TESTAMENT this ________ day of ____________________, 20________.

____

STATE LAWS ON INTESTATE SUCCESSION

When someone dies without a will, state law effectively provides a "one-size-fits-all" will through intestate succession statutes. It is important to remember, though, that just as a will may not control all of a decedent's property, state intestate succession statutes may not determine how all of a decedent's property is distributed at his death. Determining how the law will divide the property of a decedent who dies without a will can be complex. Property may pass by title (e.g., joint ownership with rights of survivorship), by contract (e.g., a life insurance beneficiary designation), or by some state statute other than the intestate succession statute.

These "other" statutes include dower and curtesy statutes, homestead statutes, right of election statutes, family allowance and support statutes, and statutes in common law states preserving the community property nature of property previously acquired by a married couple in a community property state. These statutes can be significant in determining the ultimate disposition of an intestate decedent's property.

Nonetheless, the statutes of intestate succession are quite important. The following briefly summarizes the shares into which the various states' intestate succession statutes divide the intestate estate when a decedent dies without a will and *leaves a surviving spouse and child(ren) but no other issue* (i.e., no grandchildren, no great grandchildren, etc.). Special rules may determine whether certain individuals – such as adopted, step or illegitimate children of the decedent – will qualify as "children" of the decedent for purposes of intestate succession.

Unless separately stated, community property includes "quasi-community property" (generally defined as property acquired in another state that would have been considered community property had it been acquired within the community property state). See discussion of community property on pages 317-318. Unless otherwise noted, property passing to the decedent's children is divided equally among them.

One final note of caution! Because state laws can change, the reader should consult local counsel for current law.

Alabama

If all children are issue of the surviving spouse also: spouse gets first $50,000, plus ½ of balance; remainder to child(ren).

If any child is not issue of surviving spouse: ½ to spouse; ½ to child(ren). Ala. Code §43—8-41

Alaska

If all children are issue of the surviving spouse and the decedent leaves no other surviving descendants or parents: all to spouse.

If all children are issue of the surviving spouse also, but the surviving spouse has one or more surviving issue who are not also issue of the decedent: the first $150,000 plus ½ of balance; remainder to the decedent's child(ren).

If any child is not issue of the surviving spouse: spouse gets first $100,000 plus ½ of balance; remainder to child(ren). Alaska Stat. Ann. §13.12.102

Arizona

If all children are issue of the surviving spouse also, spouse gets entire estate.

If any child is not issue of surviving spouse: spouse gets ½ of decedent's *separate* property, and none of decedent's share of *community* property; remainder to child(ren). Ariz. Rev. Stat. Ann. §14-2102

Arkansas

All property to child(ren). Ark. Code Ann §28-9-214

California

Community property: all to spouse or domestic partner.

Separate property: if one child, then ½ to spouse or domestic partner and ½ to child; if more than one child, then ⅓ to spouse or domestic partner and ⅓ to children. Cal. Prob. Code §6401

Colorado

If all children are issue of the surviving spouse also and there are no other issue of the surviving spouse: all to the spouse.

If all of the children are issue of the surviving spouse also but the surviving spouse has one or more surviving issue who are not also issue of the decedent: first $225,000 plus ½ of any balance to the spouse; the rest to the decedent's child(ren).

If one or more of the children is not also issue of the surviving spouse: the first $150,000 plus ½ of any balance to the spouse; the rest to the decedent's child(ren). Colo. Rev. Stat. Ann. §15-11-102

Connecticut

If all children are issue of the surviving spouse also: spouse gets first $100,000, plus ½ of balance; remainder to child(ren).

If any child is not issue of surviving spouse: ½ to spouse; ½ to child(ren). Conn. Gen. Stat. Ann §45a-437

Delaware

If all children are issue of the surviving spouse also: spouse gets first $50,000 of the *personal* estate, plus ½ of balance of the personal estate, plus a life estate in the *real* estate; rest to child(ren).

If any child is not issue of surviving spouse: spouse gets ½ of *personal* estate, plus a life estate in the *real* estate; rest to child(ren). Del. Code Ann. Tit 12, §502

District of Columbia

If all children are issue of the surviving spouse or domestic partner and the surviving spouse or domestic partner has no other descendants, ⅔ to spouse or domestic partner.

If surviving spouse or domestic partner has one or more surviving descendants who are not descendants of the decedent or if the decedent has one or more surviving descendants who are not descendants of the surviving spouse or domestic partner, spouse or domestic partner takes ½. D.C. Code §19-302

Florida

If all children are issue of the surviving spouse also: all to spouse.

If any child is not issue of surviving spouse, or if all children are issue of the surviving spouse also, but the surviving spouse has one or more surviving issue who are not also the issue of the decedent: ½ to spouse; ½ to decedent's child(ren). Fla. Stat. Ann. §732.102

Georgia

Spouse shares equally with child(ren); but spouse entitled to at least ⅓. Ga. Code Ann. §53-2-1

Hawaii

If all children are issue of the surviving spouse also and there are no other issue of the surviving spouse: all to spouse.

If all children are issue of the surviving spouse also but the surviving spouse has one or more surviving issue who are not the issue of the decedent: first $150,000 plus ½ of balance to spouse; the rest to the decedent's child(ren).

If one or more of the children is not also issue of the surviving spouse: the first $100,000 plus ½ of balance to surviving spouse; the remainder to the decedent's child(ren). Haw. Rev. Stat. §560:2-102

Idaho

Community property: all to spouse.

Separate property: spouse gets ½ of estate and ½ goes to child(ren). Idaho Code Ann. §15-2-102

Illinois

½ to spouse; ½ to child(ren). 755 Ill. Comp. Stat. Ann 5/2-1

Indiana

½ to spouse; ½ to child(ren). If no child is a child of the surviving spouse, such spouse takes ½ of personal property, remainder of personal property to child(ren); spouse takes ¼ of fair market value of decedent's lands minus the value of the liens and encumbrances on the lands; ¾ to child(ren). Ind. Code Ann §29-1-2-1

Iowa

If all children are issue of the surviving spouse also: spouse gets all of *real* property, plus all *personal* property that was exempt from execution in hands of decedent as head of family at death, plus all of remainder not necessary for payment of debts and charges. Iowa Code Ann §633.211

If any child is not issue of surviving spouse: spouse gets ½ of *real* property, plus all *personal* property that was exempt from execution in hands of decedent as head of family at death, plus ½ of remaining *personal* property not necessary for payment of debts and charges; remainder to child(ren) (but spouse entitled to minimum of $50,000 in value from entire net estate). Iowa Code Ann §633.212

Kansas

½ to spouse; ½ to child(ren). Kan. Stat. Ann. §59-504

Kentucky

All to child(ren). Ky. Rev. Stat. Ann. §391.010

Louisiana

Community property: decedent's share to children, but subject to usufruct in favor of surviving spouse (beneficial use until death or remarriage, unless decedent spouse specifies such use shall be for life or a shorter period).

Separate property: all to children. La. Civ. Code Ann. Art. 889-890,894-895

Maine

If all children are issue of the surviving spouse or surviving registered domestic partner also: spouse or surviving registered domestic partner gets first $50,000, plus ½ of balance; remainder to child(ren).

If any child is not issue of surviving spouse or surviving registered domestic partner: ½ to spouse; ½ to child(ren). Me. Rev. Stat. Title 18-A §2-102

Maryland

If a surviving minor child: ½ to spouse; ½ to child(ren).

If no surviving minor child but there is surviving issue: spouse gets first $15,000, plus ½ of balance; remainder to child(ren). Md. Code Ann., Est. & Trusts §3-102

Massachusetts

If all issue are children of the surviving spouse and no other surviving children of the surviving spouse: spouse takes entire estate.

If all issue are not children of the surviving spouse, or surviving spouse has surviving child(ren) not issue of decedent: spouse takes first $100,000, then half of balance; remainder to child(ren). Mass. Gen. Laws Ann. 190B §2-102

Michigan

If all children are issue of the surviving spouse also: spouse gets first $150,000 plus ½ of balance; remainder to child(ren).

If at least one, but not all, child(ren) are not issue of surviving spouse, or if the surviving spouse has at least one, but not all child(ren) who are not issue of decedent: the first $150,000 plus ½ of balance to spouse; remainder to children.

If none of decedent's surviving children are issue of the surviving spouse: the first $100,000 plus ½ to the spouse. Mich. Comp. Laws Ann. §700.2102

Minnesota

If all children are also children of the surviving spouse: spouse takes entire estate.

If one or more surviving children are not also issue of the surviving spouse, or surviving spouse has children not issue of decedent: first $150,000 plus ½ balance of estate to spouse, remainder to children. Minn. Stat. Ann. §524.2-102

Mississippi

Spouse shares equally with each child, but is entitled to only ½ of the real and personal estate even if there are no surviving issue. Miss. Code Ann. §§ 91-1-7; 91-5-25

Missouri

If all children are issue of the surviving spouse also: spouse gets first $20,000, plus ½ of balance; remainder to child(ren).

If any child is not issue of surviving spouse: ½ to spouse; ½ to child(ren). Mo. Ann. Stat. §474.010

Montana

If all children are issue of the surviving spouse also and the surviving spouse has no other surviving issue: all to spouse.

If all children are issue of the surviving spouse but the surviving spouse has any surviving issue who is not also issue of the decedent: the spouse gets first $150,000, plus ½ of any balance; the rest to decedent's child(ren).

If any child is not also issue of the surviving spouse: spouse gets first $100,000, plus ½ of balance; the rest to the decedent's child(ren). Mont. Code Ann. §72-2-112

Nebraska

If all children are also issue of the surviving spouse: spouse gets first $100,000, plus ½ of balance; remainder to child(ren).

If any child is not issue of surviving spouse: ½ to spouse; ½ to child(ren). Neb. Rev. Stat. §30-2302

Nevada

Community property: all to spouse. Nev. Rev. Stat. Ann. §123.250.

Separate property: if one child, then ½ to spouse and ½ to child; if more than one child, then ⅓ to spouse and remainder to child(ren) equally. Nev. Rev. Stat. Ann. §134.040

New Hampshire

If all children are also issue of the surviving spouse: spouse gets first $250,000, plus ½ of balance; remainder to child(ren).

If any child is not also issue of surviving spouse: the first $100,000 + ½ to spouse; remainder to child(ren). If surviving spouse has issue that are not also issue of decedent, first $150,000 + ½ to surviving spouse; remainder to child(ren). N.H. Rev. Stat. Ann. §561:1

New Jersey

If all children are issue of the surviving spouse also and the surviving spouse has no other surviving issue who are not also issue of the decedent: spouse gets entire estate.

If all children are issue of the surviving spouse but the surviving spouse has one or more surviving issue who are not issue of the decedent: the first 25% of the intestate estate, but not less than $50,000.00 nor more than $200,000.00, plus one-half of the balance of the intestate estate.

If there are children who are not also issue of the surviving spouse: the first 25% of the intestate estate, but not less than $50,000.00 nor more than $200,000.00, plus one-half of the balance of the intestate estate. N.J. Stat. Ann. §3B:5-3

New Mexico

Community property: all to spouse.

Separate property: ¼ to spouse; ¾ to child(ren). N.M. Stat. Ann. §45-2-102

New York

$50,000 plus ½ of the balance to spouse; the rest to child(ren). N.Y. Est. Powers & Trusts Law §4-1.1

North Carolina

If only one child: *real* property goes ½ to spouse and balance to child; with respect to *personal* property, spouse gets first $60,000 plus ½ of balance, and remainder to child.

If two or more children: *real* property goes ⅓ to spouse and balance to children; with respect to *personal* property, spouse gets first $60,000 plus ⅓ of balance, and remainder to children. N.C. Gen. Stat. Ann. §29-14

North Dakota

If all children are issue of the surviving spouse also and the surviving spouse has no other surviving issue: all to spouse.

If all children are issue of the surviving spouse also but the surviving spouse has one or more surviving issue who are not issue of the decedent: the first $225,000 plus ½ of any balance to the spouse; the rest to the decedent's child(ren).

If any child is not issue of the surviving spouse also: the first $150,000 plus ½ of any balance to the spouse; the rest to the decedent's child(ren). N.D. Cent. Code Ann. §30.1-04-02

Ohio

If spouse is natural or adoptive parent of all child(ren): spouse takes entire estate.

If there is only one child, and the surviving spouse is not the natural or adoptive parent: spouse takes first $20,000, plus ½ of balance, remainder to child.

If there is more than one surviving child, and the spouse is the natural or adoptive parent of one, but not all: spouse takes first $60,000, or $20,000 if the spouse is the parent to none, and 1/3 of balance, remainder to children. Ohio Rev. Code Ann. §2105.06

Oklahoma

If all children are issue of the surviving spouse also: an undivided ½ interest in the property of the estate to spouse; the balance in undivided equal shares to child(ren).

If any child is not issue of surviving spouse: an undivided ½ interest in property acquired by joint industry of husband and wife during marriage to spouse; the spouse and the child(ren) take equal undivided shares in the property of the decedent not acquired by the joint industry of the husband and wife during marriage; the remainder of estate in undivided equal shares to the child(ren). Okla. Stat. Ann. Title 84, §213

Oregon

If all children are issue of the surviving spouse also, spouse gets entire estate.

If any child is not issue of surviving spouse: ½ to spouse; ½ to child(ren). Or. Rev. Stat. Ann. §112.025

Pennsylvania

If all children are issue of the surviving spouse also: spouse gets first $30,000, plus ½ of balance; remainder to child(ren).

If any child is not issue of surviving spouse: ½ to spouse; ½ to child(ren). 20 Pa. Cons. Stat. Ann. §2102

Rhode Island

Real property: Estate descends to the surviving spouse for their natural life, then all to child(ren). R.I. Gen. Laws Ann. §§ 33-1-1; 33-1-5

Personal property: ½ to spouse; ½ to child(ren).R.I. Gen. Laws Ann. §33-1-10

South Carolina

½ to spouse; ½ to child(ren). S.C. Code Ann. §62-2-102

South Dakota

If all children are also issue of the surviving spouse, spouse gets entire estate.

If any child is not also issue of the surviving spouse: spouse gets first $100,000 plus ½ of any balance, remainder to child(ren). S.D. Codified Laws §29A-2-102

Tennessee

Spouse gets either ½ or a child's share of the entire inestate estate, whichever is greater. Tenn. Code Ann. §31-2-104

Texas

Community property: if all children are also issue of the surviving spouse, then all to the surviving spouse; if any child is not also issue of the surviving spouse, then ½ of the community estate is retained by the surviving spouse and ½ passes to child(ren). Tex. Estates Code Ann. §201.003

Separate property: with respect to *personal* property, ⅓ to spouse and balance to child(ren); with respect to *real* property, spouse takes life estate in ⅓, remainder to child(ren) [Presumably by "remainder" the statute means the remainder interest in the spouse's life estate *and* the fee interest in the remaining ⅔ of the real estate] Tex. Estates Code Ann. §201.002

Utah

If all children are issue of the surviving spouse also, spouse gets entire estate.

If any child is not issue of surviving spouse: spouse gets first $75,000 plus ½ of any remaining balance. Utah Code Ann. §75-2-102

Vermont

If all of the decedent's surviving issue are also issue of the surviving spouse, spouse gets entire estate.

If one or more of the decedent's issue are not also issue of the surviving spouse; ½ to spouse. Vt. Stat Ann Title 14, §311

Virginia

If all children are issue of the surviving spouse also, spouse gets entire estate.

If any child is not issue of surviving spouse: ⅓ to spouse; remainder to child(ren). VA Code Ann. §64.2-200

Washington

Community property: all to spouse or state registered domestic partner.

Separate property: ½ to spouse or state registered domestic partner. Wash. Rev. Code Ann. §11.04.015

West Virginia

If all children are issue of the surviving spouse also and the surviving spouse has no other surviving issue, spouse gets entire estate.

If all children are issue of the surviving spouse also but the surviving spouse has any surviving issue who is not also issue of the decedent: 3/5 to spouse; 2/5 to decedent's child(ren).

If any child is not issue of the surviving spouse: ½ to spouse; ½ to decedent's child(ren). W. Va Code Ann. §42-1-3

Wisconsin

If all children are issue of the surviving spouse also, spouse gets entire net intestate estate.

If any child is not issue of surviving spouse: spouse gets ½ of net intestate estate consisting of decedent's property other than marital property (i.e., property acquired during marriage) or property that the decedent and the surviving spouse held as tenants in common; remainder to child(ren). Wis. Stat. Ann. § 852.01

Wyoming

½ to spouse; ½ to child(ren). Wyo. Stat. Ann. §2-4-101

LIFETIME REQUIRED MINIMUM DISTRIBUTIONS

(Uniform Lifetime)

Age	Distribution Period	Age	Distribution Period	Age	Distribution Period	Age	Distribution Period	Age	Distribution Period
70	27.4	80	18.7	90	11.4	100	6.3	110	3.1
71	26.5	81	17.9	91	10.8	101	5.9	111	2.9
72	25.6	82	17.1	92	10.2	102	5.5	112	2.6
73	24.7	83	16.3	93	9.6	103	5.2	113	2.4
74	23.8	84	15.5	94	9.1	104	4.9	114	2.1
75	22.9	85	14.8	95	8.6	105	4.5	115 & Over	1.9
76	22.0	86	14.1	96	8.1	106	4.2		
77	21.2	87	13.4	97	7.6	107	3.9		
78	20.3	88	12.7	98	7.1	108	3.7		
79	19.5	89	12.0	99	6.7	109	3.4		

Application: Used in calculating lifetime required minimum distributions from IRAs, qualified plans, and TSAs. For example, assume an individual turned age 74 in 2017, and on the previous December 31, 2016, his account balance was $325,000. Using this table, his life expectancy is 23.8 years. He must receive a distribution of $13,655 ($325,000 ÷ 23.8 = $13,655) for the 2017 year, no later than December 31, 2017. See the discussion on pages 521-523.

Source: Treasury Reg. §1.40(a)(9)-9, A-2

TABLE I RATES

Value Per $1,000 Of Life Insurance Protection For One Year

Ages	Value	Ages	Value	Ages	Value
Under 25	.60	40 to 44	1.20	60 to 64.	7.92
25 to 29	.72	45 to 49	1.80	65 to 69	15.24
30 to 34	.96	50 to 54	2.76	70 & Over	24.72
35 to 39	1.08	55 to 59	5.16		

Application: As a measure of the value of excess group term insurance.

Source: Treas. Reg. §1.79-3(d)(2) – the rates as set forth in the regulation are given in costs per $1,000 of protection for 1-month periods (i.e., the cost at age 42 is 10 cents per $1,000 per month).

TABLE 2001 RATES
&
P.S. No. 58 RATES

One Year Term Premiums For $1,000 Of Life Insurance Protection

Age	Table 2001	P.S. 58	Age	Table 2001	P.S. 58	Age	Table 2001	P.S. 58	Age	Table 2001	P.S. 58
15	.38	1.27	32	.93	2.70	49	2.13	8.53	66	13.51	34.28
16	.52	1.38	33	.96	2.86	50	2.30	9.22	67	15.20	37.31
17	.57	1.48	34	.98	3.02	51	2.52	9.97	68	16.92	40.59
18	.59	1.52	35	.99	3.21	52	2.81	10.79	69	18.70	44.17
19	.61	1.56	36	1.01	3.41	53	3.20	11.69	70	20.62	48.06
20	.62	1.61	37	1.04	3.63	54	3.65	12.67	71	22.72	52.29
21	.62	1.67	38	1.06	3.87	55	4.15	13.74	72	25.07	56.89
22	.64	1.73	39	1.07	4.14	56	4.68	14.91	73	27.57	61.89
23	.66	1.79	40	1.10	4.42	57	5.20	16.18	74	30.18	67.33
24	.68	1.86	41	1.13	4.73	58	5.66	17.56	75	33.05	73.23
25	.71	1.93	42	1.20	5.07	59	6.06	19.08	76	36.33	79.63
26	.73	2.02	43	1.29	5.44	60	6.51	20.73	77	40.17	86.57
27	.76	2.11	44	1.40	5.85	61	7.11	22.53	78	44.33	94.09
28	.80	2.20	45	1.53	6.30	62	7.96	24.50	79	49.23	102.23
29	.83	2.31	46	1.67	6.78	63	9.08	26.63	80	54.56	111.04
30	.87	2.43	47	1.83	7.32	64	10.41	28.98	81	60.51	120.57
31	.90	2.57	48	1.98	7.89	65	11.90	31.51			

Application: As a measure of the value of insurance protection provided under; (1) split-dollar plans, (2) qualified pension and profit sharing plans, and (3) tax sheltered annuities.

Source: Notice 2002-8, 2002-4 CB 398; Revenue Ruling 55-747, 1955-2 CB 228; and Revenue Ruling 66-110, 1966-1 CB 12. Notice 2002-8 provides Table 2001 rates for below age 15 and above age 81 (Appendix C, *Tax Facts on Insurance & Employee Benefits (2019)* contains the full table).

NOTE: For plans entered into *on or after* January 28, 2002, until further IRS guidance is received, only Table 2001, or the insurer's published premium rates, may generally be used; with the qualification that for periods after December 31, 2003, if the insurer's published premium rates are used, the insurer must actually make known and sell term insurance at these rates (see Notice 2002-8 regarding limitations on using an insurer's published premium rates for periods after December 31, 2003). For split-dollar plans entered into *before* January 28, 2002, Table 2001 rates, P.S. 58 rates (if specified by the split-dollar agreement), or the insurer's published premium rates may generally be used.

TABLE 38

Probability Of Dying In Each Year Of Age

Age	Probability (q)	Age	Probability (q)	Age	Probability (q)
20	.00165	49	.00874	78	.09644
21	.00171	50	.00945	79	.10479
22	.00177	51	.01022	80	.11382
23	.00183	52	.01106	81	.12358
24	.00191	53	.01198	82	.13413
25	.00198	54	.01299	83	.14550
26	.00207	55	.01408	84	.15776
27	.00216	56	.01528	85	.17094
28	.00226	57	.01658	86	.18511
29	.00237	58	.01800	87	.20032
30	.00249	59	.01956	88	.21661
31	.00263	60	.02125	89	.23402
32	.00277	61	.02309	90	.25261
33	.00293	62	.02511	91	.27239
34	.00310	63	.02730	92	.29341
35	.00329	64	.02970	93	.31568
36	.00350	65	.03230	94	.33921
37	.00372	66	.03514	95	.36399
38	.00397	67	.03824	96	.39001
39	.00424	68	.04160	97	.41721
40	.00453	69	.04527	98	.44555
41	.00485	70	.04926	99	.47493
42	.00520	71	.05360	100	.50525
43	.00558	72	.05831	101	.53638
44	.00600	73	.06344	102	.56816
45	.00646	74	.06901	103	.60039
46	.00695	75	.07506	104	.63286
47	.00750	76	.08162	105	1.00000
48	.00809	77	.08873		

Explanation of Table. Table 38 has been used as a measure of the value to the employee of insurance protection provided under split-dollar plans involving survivorship life policies. Although based on the underlying actuarial assumptions of the P.S. 58 rates, the only authority for use of the Table 38 rates is an unofficial letter from the General Actuarial Branch of the IRS. In this letter it was suggested that: "it is acceptable to apply the formula for the one year term rate on an insurance of two lives, payable on the second death, as expressed by the symbols v q_x q_y where v is 1/1.025 and q_x q_y are the annual mortality rates for ages x and y computed from values in U.S. Life Table 38." The probability of two individuals dying in the same year can be calculated by multiplying their individual probabilities. For example, the probability of two individuals ages 65 and 70 dying in any one year is .0015911 (.03230 x .04926 = .0015911). The value per year per thousand of death benefit is $1.55 (1/1.025 × .03230 × .04926 × 1,000 = 1.55).

Limitations on Application: In Notice 2002-8 the IRS announced that the P.S. 58 rates can no longer be used for split-dollar plans entered into *on or after* January 28, 2002. Until further guidance is received, an argument could be made for using Table 38 rates in split-dollar plans entered into *before* January 28, 2002. As to plans entered on or after January 28, 2002, it is clear from Notice 2002-8 that the rates used should reflect "appropriate adjustments" to the Table 2001 rates set forth on page 596. Actuarial guidance should be requested from the issuing life insurance company. See also, treatment of Employer/Employee Split-Dollar Plans, on pages 284-286, and the discussion of Survivorship Life Insurance, on page 561.

COMMISSIONERS
1980 STANDARD ORDINARY MORTALITY TABLE

	Male		Female	
Age	deaths per 1,000	average future lifetime	deaths per 1,000	average future lifetime
0	4.18	70.83	2.89	75.83
1	1.07	70.13	.87	75.04
2	.99	69.20	.81	74.11
3	.98	68.27	.79	73.17
4	.95	67.34	.77	72.23
5	.90	66.40	.76	71.28
6	.85	65.46	.73	70.34
7	.80	64.52	.72	69.39
8	.76	63.57	.70	68.44
9	.74	62.62	.69	67.48
10	.73	61.66	.68	66.53
11	.77	60.71	.69	65.58
12	.85	59.75	.72	64.62
13	.99	58.80	.75	63.67
14	1.15	57.86	.80	62.71
15	1.33	56.93	.85	61.76
16	1.51	56.00	.90	60.82
17	1.67	55.09	.95	59.87
18	1.78	54.18	.98	58.93
19	1.86	53.27	1.02	57.98
20	1.90	52.37	1.05	57.04
21	1.91	51.47	1.07	56.10
22	1.89	50.57	1.09	55.16
23	1.86	49.66	1.11	54.22
24	1.82	48.75	1.14	53.28
25	1.77	47.84	1.16	52.34
26	1.73	46.93	1.19	51.40
27	1.71	46.01	1.22	50.46
28	1.70	45.09	1.26	49.52
29	1.71	44.16	1.30	48.59
30	1.73	43.24	1.35	47.65
31	1.78	42.31	1.40	46.71
32	1.83	41.38	1.45	45.78
33	1.91	40.46	1.50	44.84
34	2.00	39.54	1.58	43.91
35	2.11	38.61	1.65	42.98
36	2.24	37.69	1.76	42.05
37	2.40	36.78	1.89	41.12
38	2.58	35.87	2.04	40.20
39	2.79	34.96	2.22	39.28
40	3.02	34.05	2.42	38.36
41	3.29	33.16	2.64	37.46
42	3.56	32.26	2.87	36.55
43	3.87	31.38	3.09	35.66
44	4.19	30.50	3.32	34.77
45	4.55	29.62	3.56	33.88
46	4.92	28.76	3.80	33.00
47	5.32	27.90	4.05	32.12
48	5.74	27.04	4.33	31.25
49	6.21	26.20	4.63	30.39
50	6.71	25.36	4.96	29.53
51	7.30	24.52	5.31	28.67
52	7.96	23.70	5.70	27.82
53	8.71	22.89	6.15	26.98
54	9.56	22.08	6.61	26.14
55	10.47	21.29	7.09	25.31
56	11.46	20.51	7.57	24.49
57	12.49	19.74	8.03	23.67
58	13.59	18.99	8.47	22.86
59	14.77	18.24	8.94	22.05
60	16.08	17.51	9.47	21.25
61	17.54	16.79	10.13	20.44
62	19.19	16.08	10.96	19.65
63	21.06	15.38	12.02	18.86
64	23.14	14.70	13.25	18.08
65	25.42	14.04	14.59	17.32
66	27.85	13.39	16.00	16.57
67	30.44	12.76	17.43	15.83
68	33.19	12.14	18.84	15.10
69	36.17	11.54	20.36	14.38
70	39.51	10.96	22.11	13.67
71	43.30	10.39	24.23	12.97
72	47.65	9.84	26.87	12.28
73	52.64	9.30	30.11	11.60
74	58.19	8.79	33.93	10.95
75	64.19	8.31	38.24	10.32
76	70.53	7.84	42.97	9.71
77	77.12	7.40	48.04	9.12
78	83.90	6.97	53.45	8.55
79	91.05	6.57	59.35	8.01
80	98.84	6.18	65.99	7.48
81	107.48	5.80	73.60	6.98
82	117.25	5.44	82.40	6.49
83	128.26	5.09	92.53	6.03
84	140.25	4.77	103.81	5.59
85	152.95	4.46	116.10	5.18
86	166.09	4.18	129.29	4.80
87	179.55	3.91	143.32	4.43
88	193.27	3.66	158.18	4.09
89	207.29	3.41	173.94	3.77
90	221.77	3.18	190.75	3.45
91	236.98	2.94	208.87	3.15
92	253.45	2.70	228.81	2.85
93	272.11	2.44	251.51	2.55
94	295.90	2.17	279.31	2.24
95	329.96	1.87	317.32	1.91
96	384.55	1.54	375.74	1.56
97	480.20	1.20	474.97	1.21
98	657.98	.84	655.85	.84
99	1000.00	.50	1000.00	.50

Source: Selected figures from published table. Age is given as nearest birthday.

COMMISSIONERS
2001 STANDARD ORDINARY MORTALITY TABLE

	Male		Female	
Age	deaths per 1,000	average future lifetime	deaths per 1,000	average future lifetime
0	.97	76.62	.48	80.84
1	.56	75.69	.35	79.88
2	.39	74.74	.26	78.91
3	.27	73.76	.20	77.93
4	.21	72.78	.19	76.95
5	.21	71.80	.18	75.96
6	.22	70.81	.18	74.97
7	.22	69.83	.21	73.99
8	.22	68.84	.21	73.00
9	.23	67.86	.21	72.02
10	.23	66.88	.22	71.03
11	.27	65.89	.23	70.05
12	.33	64.91	.27	69.07
13	.39	63.93	.30	68.08
14	.47	62.95	.33	67.10
15	.61	61.98	.35	66.13
16	.74	61.02	.39	65.15
17	.87	60.07	.41	64.17
18	.94	59.12	.43	63.20
19	.98	58.17	.46	62.23
20	1.00	57.23	.47	61.26
21	1.00	56.29	.48	60.28
22	1.02	55.34	.50	59.31
23	1.03	54.40	.50	58.34
24	1.05	53.45	.52	57.37
25	1.07	52.51	.54	56.40
26	1.12	51.57	.56	55.43
27	1.17	50.62	.60	54.46
28	1.17	49.68	.63	53.49
29	1.15	48.74	.66	52.53
30	1.14	47.79	.68	51.56
31	1.13	46.85	.73	50.60
32	1.13	45.90	.77	49.63
33	1.15	44.95	.82	48.67
34	1.18	44.00	.88	47.71
35	1.21	43.05	.97	46.75
36	1.28	42.11	1.03	45.80
37	1.34	41.16	1.11	44.84
38	1.44	40.21	1.17	43.89
39	1.54	39.27	1.23	42.94
40	1.65	38.33	1.30	42.00
41	1.79	37.39	1.38	41.05
42	1.96	36.46	1.48	40.11
43	2.15	35.53	1.59	39.17
44	2.39	34.61	1.72	38.23
45	2.65	33.69	1.87	37.29
46	2.90	32.78	2.05	36.36
47	3.17	31.87	2.27	35.43
48	3.33	30.97	2.50	34.51
49	3.52	30.07	2.78	33.60
50	3.76	29.18	3.08	32.69
51	4.06	28.28	3.41	31.79
52	4.47	27.40	3.79	30.90
53	4.93	26.52	4.20	30.01
54	5.50	25.65	4.63	29.14
55	6.17	24.79	5.10	28.27
56	6.88	23.94	5.63	27.41
57	7.64	23.10	6.19	26.57
58	8.27	22.27	6.80	25.73
59	8.99	21.45	7.39	24.90
60	9.86	20.64	8.01	24.08
61	10.94	19.85	8.68	23.27
62	12.25	19.06	9.39	22.47
63	13.71	18.29	10.14	21.68
64	15.24	17.54	10.96	20.90
65	16.85	16.80	11.85	20.12
66	18.47	16.08	12.82	19.36
67	20.09	15.37	13.89	18.60
68	21.85	14.68	15.07	17.86
69	23.64	13.99	16.36	17.12
70	25.77	13.32	17.81	16.40
71	28.15	12.66	19.47	15.69
72	31.32	12.01	21.30	14.99
73	34.62	11.39	23.30	14.31
74	38.08	10.78	25.50	13.64
75	41.91	10.18	27.90	12.98
76	46.08	9.61	30.53	12.34
77	50.92	9.05	33.41	11.71
78	56.56	8.50	36.58	11.10
79	63.06	7.98	40.05	10.50

Source: Composite figures from 2001 CSO published table (ultimate only). Age is given as nearest birthday. Death is assumed to occur at age plus six months. See next page for selected nonsmoker and smoker figures.

COMMISSIONERS
2001 STANDARD ORDINARY MORTALITY TABLE (continued)

Age	Male deaths per 1,000	Male average future lifetime	Female deaths per 1,000	Female average future lifetime
80	70.14	7.49	43.86	9.92
81	78.19	7.01	49.11	9.35
82	86.54	6.57	54.95	8.81
83	95.51	6.14	60.81	8.29
84	105.43	5.74	67.27	7.79
85	116.57	5.36	74.45	7.32
86	128.91	5.00	80.99	6.87
87	142.35	4.66	90.79	6.43
88	156.73	4.35	101.07	6.02
89	171.88	4.07	112.02	5.64
90	187.66	3.81	121.92	5.29
91	202.44	3.57	126.85	4.96
92	217.83	3.35	136.88	4.61
93	234.04	3.15	151.64	4.26
94	251.14	2.96	170.31	3.93
95	269.17	2.78	193.66	3.63
96	285.64	2.62	215.66	3.38
97	303.18	2.47	238.48	3.18
98	321.88	2.32	242.16	3.02
99	341.85	2.19	255.23	2.82
100	363.19	2.07	275.73	2.61
101	380.08	1.96	297.84	2.42
102	398.06	1.86	322.21	2.23
103	417.20	1.76	349.06	2.06
104	437.56	1.66	378.61	1.89
105	459.21	1.57	410.57	1.74
106	482.22	1.48	443.33	1.60
107	506.69	1.39	476.89	1.47
108	532.69	1.30	510.65	1.36
109	560.31	1.22	545.81	1.25
110	589.64	1.14	581.77	1.16
111	620.79	1.07	616.33	1.08
112	653.84	.99	649.85	1.00
113	688.94	.92	680.37	.93
114	726.18	.85	723.39	.86
115	765.70	.79	763.41	.79
116	807.61	.72	804.93	.73
117	852.07	.66	850.44	.67
118	899.23	.61	892.44	.61
119	949.22	.55	935.11	.56
120	1000.00	.50	1000.00	.50

Source: Composite figures from 2001 CSO published table (ultimate only). Age is given as nearest birthday. Death is assumed to occur at age plus six months. See below for selected nonsmoker and smoker figures.

NonSmoker vs. Smoker

Male

Age	Nonsmoker deaths per 1,000	Nonsmoker average future lifetime	Smoker deaths per 1,000	Smoker average future lifetime
20	.95	57.95	1.27	52.86
25	.98	53.22	1.63	48.22
30	1.02	48.48	1.80	43.62
35	1.09	43.72	2.00	39.00
40	1.46	38.97	2.77	34.42
45	2.33	34.29	4.57	29.96
50	3.32	29.73	6.45	25.70
55	5.50	25.28	10.56	21.62
60	8.92	21.06	16.29	17.88
65	15.47	17.13	26.63	14.51

Female

Age	Nonsmoker deaths per 1,000	Nonsmoker average future lifetime	Smoker deaths per 1,000	Smoker average future lifetime
20	.45	61.79	.58	56.07
25	.50	56.93	.77	51.24
30	.64	52.09	1.03	46.45
35	.89	47.27	1.53	41.72
40	1.20	42.49	2.12	37.07
45	1.71	37.77	3.13	32.49
50	2.81	33.14	5.39	28.08
55	4.68	28.68	9.08	23.96
60	7.40	24.43	13.97	20.16
65	11.05	20.41	20.34	16.67

Source: Selected smoker and nonsmoker figures are calculated from the 2001 CSO published table (ultimate only). Age is given as nearest birthday.

HEALTHY LIFE EXPECTANCY

	Expected Years						
	of life	in excellent health	in good or better health	without any activity limitation	without major activity limitation	without work limitation	without ADL assistance*
Male							
At Birth	72.8	27.1	64.6	60.5	68.5	-	-
20 years	54.0	17.2	46.2	43.0	49.8	47.9	52.9
30 years	44.9	13.0	37.3	34.4	40.8	39.2	43.7
45 years	31.5	7.4	24.6	22.5	27.9	26.9	30.4
65 years	15.9	2.4	11.2	9.9	14.1	14.4	14.9
70 years	12.8	1.7	8.8	8.0	11.8	-	11.8
75 years	10.1	1.2	6.7	5.9	9.1	-	9.1
80 years	7.7	0.8	4.9	4.3	6.8	-	6.8
Female							
At Birth	78.8	25.7	68.4	64.6	74.7	-	-
20 years	59.8	15.8	49.8	46.3	55.7	53.5	58.1
30 years	50.1	12.3	40.6	37.3	46.1	44.3	48.4
45 years	35.9	7.3	27.6	24.6	32.4	31.2	34.3
65 years	18.8	2.8	13.4	11.4	16.8	17.6	17.3
70 years	15.1	2.1	10.6	8.9	13.7	-	13.7
75 years	11.7	1.6	8.0	6.3	10.3	-	10.3
80 years	8.7	1.2	5.7	4.0	7.2	-	7.2

*ADL refers to activities of daily living (see discussion of Qualified Long-Term Care Insurance on page 510).

Source: U.S. Department of Health and Human Services & National Center for Health Statistics, *Healthy People 2010 - Summary Measures of Population Health*, 2003, Tables 3.1- 3.4 (1995 data) on pages 30-33 (http://www.cdc.gov/nchs/healthy_people.htm).

SURVIVOR CHECKLIST

		Check As Accomplished
1.	Request 10 copies of death certificate (funeral director will assist). Deceased's date of birth: ______________________________ .	❏
2.	Contact employer regarding group insurance and other benefits.	❏
3.	Contact insurance companies (auto, life, and health). Have policy numbers available.	❏
4.	If deceased was a government retiree or employee, contact Civil Service Personal Management Office (1-888-767-6738: www.opm.gov).	❏
5.	If deceased was retired from the military, contact Defense Finance and Accounting Service (1-800-321-1080: www.dfas.mil).	❏
6.	If deceased was a veteran, contact Veterans Administration (1-800-827-1000: www.va.gov/survivors).	❏
7.	Notify Social Security Administration (1-800-772-1213: www.ssa.gov). Deceased's Social Security number: ______________________ . Spouse's Social Security number: ______________________ .	❏
8.	Check items in safe deposit box.	❏
9.	Locate Last Will and Testament and Trust documents.	❏
10.	Notify banks and stock brokerage companies.	❏
11.	Contact credit card companies and other charge accounts.	❏
12.	Check on credit life insurance with all creditors.	❏
13.	Locate personal balance sheet (or similar listing of cash, securities, real estate, personal effects, mortgages, and other liabilities).	❏
14.	Locate business disposition agreements (buy/sell agreements, partnership agreements, etc.).	❏
15.	Call attorney and arrange for meeting to discuss probate and other matters: ______________________________ .	❏
16.	As time for filing tax return approaches – call accountant, CPA, or tax preparer.	❏
17.	Other: ______________________________________ ______________________________________	❏

EVALUATING THE RISK OF DEATH

One Individual

The following tables provide the odds of death within the next 10 and 20 years for an individual according to age and sex. For example, a male age 38 has a 2.1 percent chance of dying within the next 10 years and a 7.0 percent chance of dying within the next 20 years; whereas a female age 38 has a 1.6 percent chance of dying within the next 10 years and a 5.6 percent chance of dying within the next 20 years.

Odds Of Death Within 10 Years

Age	Male	Female	Age	Male	Female	Age	Male	Female
21	1.1	0.6	36	1.8	1.4	51	6.5	5.4
22	1.1	0.6	37	2.0	1.5	52	7.1	5.9
23	1.1	0.6	38	2.1	1.6	53	7.9	6.4
24	1.1	0.6	39	2.3	1.7	54	8.7	7.0
25	1.1	0.7	40	2.5	1.9	55	9.6	7.6
26	1.1	0.7	41	2.7	2.1	56	10.5	8.2
27	1.2	0.8	42	2.9	2.3	57	11.6	8.9
28	1.2	0.8	43	3.2	2.5	58	12.7	9.6
29	1.2	0.9	44	3.5	2.7	59	13.9	10.3
30	1.2	0.9	45	3.8	3.0	60	15.2	11.1
31	1.3	1.0	46	4.1	3.3	61	16.5	12.0
32	1.4	1.1	47	4.5	3.7	62	18.0	13.0
33	1.4	1.1	48	4.9	4.1	63	19.6	14.0
34	1.5	1.2	49	5.4	4.5	64	21.3	15.1
35	1.7	1.3	50	5.9	4.9	65	23.1	16.4

Odds Of Death Within 20 Years

Age	Male	Female	Age	Male	Female	Age	Male	Female
21	2.4	1.6	36	5.8	4.7	51	21.9	16.7
22	2.4	1.6	37	6.4	5.1	52	23.8	18.1
23	2.5	1.7	38	7.0	5.6	53	25.9	19.5
24	2.6	1.8	39	7.6	6.1	54	28.1	21.1
25	2.8	2.0	40	8.3	6.7	55	30.4	22.7
26	2.9	2.1	41	9.0	7.3	56	32.9	24.5
27	3.1	2.2	42	9.9	8.0	57	35.6	26.4
28	3.3	2.4	43	10.8	8.7	58	38.4	28.4
29	3.5	2.6	44	11.8	9.5	59	41.4	30.5
30	3.7	2.8	45	13.0	10.3	60	44.6	32.8
31	4.0	3.0	46	14.2	11.2	61	48.0	35.3
32	4.3	3.3	47	15.5	12.2	62	51.5	37.9
33	4.6	3.6	48	17.0	13.2	63	55.2	40.8
34	5.0	3.9	49	18.5	14.3	64	58.9	43.8
35	5.4	4.3	50	20.2	15.5	65	62.6	47.0

Source: Calculations are based upon the Commissioners 2001 Standard Ordinary Mortality Table.

(continued on next page)

EVALUATING THE RISK OF DEATH (continued)

Two Individuals

The risk of *at least one of two individuals* dying is substantially greater than the risk of one individual dying. For example, within the next 10 years the risk of a male age 50 dying is 5.9 percent and the risk of a female age 45 dying is 3.0 percent (see page 603, Evaluating The Risk Of Death - One Individual); but the risk of at least one of them dying within the next 10 years is 8.7 percent. And this risk increases considerably with time (i.e., for a male age 50 and a female age 45 the risk of at least one of them dying within the next 20 years increases to 28.4 percent).

Odds Of At Least One Death Within 10 Years

	Male Age									
	20	**25**	**30**	**35**	**40**	**45**	**50**	**55**	**60**	**65**
20	1.6	1.7	1.8	2.2	3.1	4.3	6.4	10.1	15.6	23.5
25	1.8	1.8	1.9	2.3	3.2	4.4	6.5	10.2	15.7	23.6
30	2.0	2.1	2.2	2.6	3.4	4.7	6.8	10.4	15.9	23.8
35	2.3	2.4	2.5	2.9	3.8	5.0	7.1	10.7	16.2	24.1
40	2.9	3.0	3.1	3.5	4.4	5.6	7.7	11.3	16.7	24.5
45	4.1	4.1	4.2	4.6	5.5	6.7	8.7	12.3	17.7	25.4
50	5.9	6.0	6.1	6.5	7.3	8.5	10.5	14.0	19.3	26.9
55	8.6	8.6	8.7	9.1	9.9	11.0	13.0	16.4	21.6	28.9
60	12.1	12.1	12.2	12.6	13.4	14.5	16.4	19.6	24.6	31.6
65	17.3	17.3	17.4	17.8	18.5	19.5	21.3	24.4	29.1	35.7

Odds Of At Least One Death Within 20 Years

	Male Age									
	20	**25**	**30**	**35**	**40**	**45**	**50**	**55**	**60**	**65**
20	3.7	4.2	5.2	6.8	9.6	14.2	21.3	31.5	45.4	63.2
25	4.2	4.7	5.6	7.2	10.1	14.7	21.7	31.8	45.7	63.4
30	5.0	5.5	6.4	8.0	10.8	15.4	22.4	32.4	46.1	63.7
35	6.5	6.9	7.8	9.4	12.2	16.7	23.6	33.4	47.0	64.2
40	8.8	9.3	10.2	11.7	14.4	18.8	25.5	35.1	48.3	65.1
45	12.4	12.8	13.7	15.2	17.8	22.0	28.4	37.6	50.3	66.5
50	17.4	17.8	18.6	20.0	22.5	26.4	32.5	41.2	53.2	68.4
55	24.5	24.9	25.6	26.9	29.1	32.7	38.3	46.2	57.2	71.1
60	34.4	34.7	35.3	36.4	38.4	41.5	46.4	53.3	62.8	74.9
65	48.2	48.5	49.0	49.8	51.4	53.9	57.7	63.1	70.6	80.2

Source: Calculations are based upon the Commissioners 2001 Standard Ordinary Mortality Table.

FACTS ABOUT ...

Facts About Fathers

Father's Age When Child Is Born	Fathers Who Will Die Before Child Enters College	Fathers Who Will Die Before Child Graduates
25	1 in 43	1 in 30
30	1 in 33	1 in 22
35	1 in 23	1 in 15
40	1 in 15	1 in 10

Facts About Mothers

Mother's Age When Child Is Born	Mothers Who Will Die Before Child Enters College	Mothers Who Will Die Before Child Graduates
25	1 in 61	1 in 43
30	1 in 44	1 in 29
35	1 in 29	1 in 19
40	1 in 19	1 in 12

Facts About Children

The Cost of Raising a Child to Age 18

Family Income	Costs
less than $61,530	$176,550
$61,530 – $106,540	245,340
more than $106,540	407,820

The Annual Costs of a College Education

Year	Amount
2015	$39,879
2020	50,897
2025	64,958
2030	82,905

Source of facts about fathers and mothers: Calculations based upon the Commissioners 2001 Standard Ordinary Mortality Table (see pages 599-600), and assume that the child enters a 4-year college at age 18.

Source of costs of raising a child to age 18: U.S. Department of Agriculture, Expenditures on Children by Families, 2013, Table 1, Calculations based upon data from the 2005-06 Consumer Expenditure Survey updated to 2013 using the Consumer Price Index table. College costs are not included.

Source of the annual costs of a college education: Author research of college Internet sites during the month of December 2014, supplemented by direct inquiry when required. College costs are for the 2014-2015 year, and are based upon a representative sampling of 42 state and private colleges in 39 states. Projections are based upon cost increases of 5 percent per year. In recent years actual college costs have increased more than 5 percent.

(continued on next page)

FACTS ABOUT ... (continued)

Facts About The Value Of An Education

Having an education will often determine the economic opportunities available over a lifetime. Persons with a bachelor's degree or more on the average earn 3 times more than those who have completed less than 9th grade, and 2 times more than those who have completed only high school.

	Median Annual Income		
	Less than 9th grade	High school graduate	Bachelor's degree or more
Men	$32,385	$44,803	$81,066
Women	21,644	34,951	57,242

Facts About Funerals

According to the last available survey conducted by the National Funeral Directors Association, in 2001 the average adult funeral cost $6,130. Updated by the consumer price index this would cost $7,944 in 2014. However, the ultimate costs will depend upon the specific items and services.

Item/Service	Cost
Professional service charges	$1,213
Embalming	420
Other preparations (Cosmetology, hair, etc.)	150
Visitation/Viewing	275
Funeral at Funeral Home	350
Transfer of remains to funeral home	154
Hearse (local)	185
Service Car/Van	85
Acknowledgement cards	18
Casket	2,330
Vault	950
Total	$6,130

Source of Facts About The Value Of An Education: U.S. Census Bureau, Current Population Survey, 2014 Annual Social and Economic Supplement Table PINC-04, Educational Attainment-People 18 Years Old and Over, by Total Money Earnings in 2013, Age, Race, Hispanic Origin, and Sex (at www.census.gov/hhhes/www/cpstables/032014/perinc/pinc04_000.htm).

Source of Facts About Funerals: The National Funeral Directors Association. These costs do not include cemetery charges, such as a grave space, opening and closing grave, crypts and mausoleum, monument or marker.

FACTS ABOUT ... (continued)

Facts About The Cost Of Child Care

According to the U.S. Census Bureau weekly child care expenses in the year 1999 averaged $94 per week ($4,888 per year) for children under age 5 and $75 per week ($3,900 per year) for children age 5 to 14. As adjusted in 2014 for inflation, this would be $131 per week ($6,834 per year) for children under age 5 and $105 per week ($6,834 per year) for children age 5 to 14.

According to the Children's Defense Fund in the year 2000 for a 4-year-old child:

(1) In *rural* child care centers annual costs ranged from $3,574 in Nebraska to $9,997 in Alaska (from $3,574 to $9,997 in 2014 as adjusted for inflation).

(2) In *urban* child care centers annual costs ranged from $3,640 in Arkansas to $8,121 in Massachusetts (from $5,089 to $9,997 in 2014 as adjusted for inflation). In all states but Vermont, the cost of child care in an urban area center was more than the cost of public college tuition (in over one-quarter of states the average cost of child care was more than *twice* the cost of public college tuition).

Facts About The Value Of A Homemaker

In valuing a homemaker's services two basic methods are used. The "opportunity cost" method seeks to determine the wages that homemakers might have demanded had they opted to follow an alternate career (e.g., a full-time homemaker who is a trained nurse has foregone a nurse's salary). Under the "replacement cost" method, also called the "market alternative" method, valuation is based upon the prevailing wage rates for similar services, taking into consideration the time spent on each task and the wage rates paid for similar jobs in the marketplace, such as:

	Hourly Wage		Hourly Wage
Maid	$ 10.64	Private Household Cook	$ 13.15
Dishwasher	9.22	Lodging Manager	26.83
Child Care Worker	10.33	Concierge	14.39
Interior Designer	26.06	Taxi Driver	12.12
Teacher's Assistant	14.05	Licensed Practical Nurse	20.63
Recreation Worker	12.29	Nonfarm Animal Caretaker	10.82

Source of Facts About The Cost Of Child Care: U.S. Census Bureau, PPL Table 6 (Average Weekly Child Care Expenditures by Employed Mothers), revised to January 2014; and *The High Cost of Child Care Puts Quality Care Out of Reach for Many Families*, Children's Defense Fund, 2000, revised to January 2014.

Source of Facts About The Value Of A Homemaker: Bureau of Labor Statistics, Washington, D.C., National Occupational Employment and Wage Estimates using Standard Occupational Classification (SOC) system, May 2013. See http://www.bls.gov/oes/current/oes_nat.htm. Hourly wage of a teacher's assistant is estimated by dividing average annual wage of $25,570 by assumed 1,820 annual hours.

FACTS ABOUT ... (continued)

Facts About Human Life Value in the Courtroom

A study of wrongful death case files selected at random revealed the following:

- The average amount of loss was $1,290,000 but the amount of life insurance was only $302,308.
- The average percent of the families' losses covered by life insurance was only 28 percent.
- Only 15.3 percent of the families had more than 50 percent of their loss covered by life insurance.
- Only 53.8 percent of families had more than 25 percent of their loss covered by life insurance.
- The largest percentage of any one family's loss covered by life insurance was 65 percent.

Note: Those cases which contained no life insurance were excluded from the study. The life insurance amounts are net of accidental death benefits and credit card related benefits.

Source of *Facts About Human Life Value in the Courtroom*: Study conducted in 1996 by Litigation Analytics Inc. of Ridgefield, Connecticut, as reported by John E. Scarbrough, PhD, in "Measuring Human Life Value From the Courtroom to the Living Room," *Journal of the American Society of CLU and ChFC* (January 1998), page 68.

HUMAN LIFE VALUE

The value of $10,000 in annual earnings, discounted by 5 percent, according to the number of "working years to retirement" and rates of projected growth.

Working Years To Retirement	Projected Growth In Earnings 4%	5%	6%	7%	8%
1	10,000	10,000	10,000	10,000	10,000
2	19,905	20,000	20,095	20,191	20,286
3	29,719	30,000	30,290	30,576	30,862
4	39,436	40,000	40,578	41,157	41,745
5	49,062	50,000	50,960	51,943	52,935
6	58,597	60,000	61,444	62,935	64,444
7	68,037	70,000	72,032	74,136	76,286
8	77,389	80,000	82,721	85,550	88,467
9	86,655	90,000	93,509	97,177	100,995
10	95,828	100,000	104,397	109,025	113,880
11	104,913	110,000	115,392	121,100	127,135
12	113,912	120,000	126,489	133,408	140,770
13	122,826	130,000	137,692	145,947	154,790
14	131,656	140,000	149,003	158,728	169,214
15	140,404	150,000	160,424	171,754	184,049
16	149,067	160,000	171,953	185,025	199,306
17	157,647	170,000	183,589	198,548	215,001
18	166,146	180,000	195,339	212,331	231,144
19	174,564	190,000	207,197	226,375	247,747
20	182,902	200,000	219,171	240,687	264,826
21	191,159	210,000	231,258	255,273	282,393
22	199,339	220,000	243,461	270,135	300,460
23	207,449	230,000	255,779	285,277	319,044
24	215,465	240,000	268,217	300,714	338,160
25	223,413	250,000	280,773	316,442	357,823
26	231,286	260,000	293,447	332,468	378,045
27	239,081	270,000	306,239	348,797	398,843
28	246,802	280,000	319,152	365,438	420,235
29	254,452	290,000	332,193	382,400	442,242
30	262,028	300,000	345,353	399,680	464,873
31	269,532	310,000	358,643	417,294	488,159
32	276,966	320,000	372,061	435,246	512,112
33	284,330	330,000	385,605	453,538	536,748
34	291,622	340,000	399,281	472,179	562,087
35	298,846	350,000	413,086	491,177	588,153
36	306,000	360,000	427,021	510,535	614,958
37	313,088	370,000	441,091	530,264	642,535
38	320,104	380,000	455,289	550,360	670,887
39	327,056	390,000	469,624	570,842	700,054
40	333,938	400,000	484,092	591,708	730,046

TRUSTS AND THEIR USES

TYPE	CHARACTERISTICS	TAX IMPLICATIONS Income	Gift	Estate
Revocable	Created during grantor's life. If unfunded, acts as a will substitute. If funded, can manage property for benefit of grantor, spouse, and other beneficiaries. See chart, page 25.	Trust income taxable to grantor.	No gifts, since grantor retains control of property.	No estate tax advantages, but payment of insurance proceeds to trust can provide greater flexibility than settlement options.
Irrevocable	Created during grantor's life. Grantor gives up all control over assets in order to gain estate tax advantages (chart, page 55). Also, see Dynasty Trust, page 356.	Trust pays tax if income accumulated in trust. Beneficiaries pay taxes if income distributed. Income taxed to grantor if certain strings retained.	When property placed in trust there is a gift. With "Crummey powers," gifts are considered present interest gifts that qualify for the annual exclusion (chart, page 51).	Generally not included in estate, except proceeds of life insurance given to trust within 3 years of death (pages 374-375), or if grantor retains interest in trust.
Testamentary	Created upon death pursuant to a will (chart, page 21, and page 459).	None, trust created at death.	None, trust created at death.	Taxable in testator's estate.
Minor's Trust (Section 2503(c))	Created during grantor's life. Trust's accumulated income and principal must be paid to beneficiary upon attaining age 21 (further discussion, page 571).	Trust pays taxes if income accumulated in trust. Beneficiaries pay taxes if income is distributed.	When property placed in trust there is a gift that qualifies for the annual exclusion.	Not included in grantor's estate, except life insurance given within 3 years of death.
Income Trust (Section 2503(b))	Created during grantor's life. Trust must distribute income annually, but principal need not be paid to beneficiary (further discussion, page 571).	Beneficiaries pay taxes when income is distributed.	When property placed in trust there is a gift that qualifies for the annual exclusion.	Not included in grantor's estate, except life insurance given within 3 years of death.

ODDS OF DEATH BEFORE AGE 65

When a business has two or more owners, the odds of at least one death before age 65 increase dramatically. *The risk is not remote.* Proper planning calls for making provisions for the continuation of the business as well as providing support for the surviving family.

One-Owner Business

Ages	Odds of Death Male	Odds of Death Female	Ages	Odds of Death Male	Odds of Death Female
30	14.9%	11.8%	45	13.0%	10.3%
35	14.4	11.5	50	11.6	9.3
40	13.8	11.0	55	9.6	7.6

Two-Owner Business

Ages	Odds Of One Death Male	Odds Of One Death Female	Ages	Odds Of One Death Male	Odds Of One Death Female
30-30	27.6%	22.3%	45-45	24.2%	19.6%
30-35	27.2	22.0	45-50	23.1	18.7
30-40	26.7	21.6	45-55	21.3	17.1
35-35	26.7	21.7	50-50	21.8	17.8
35-40	26.2	21.3	50-55	20.0	16.2
35-45	25.5	20.7	50-60	16.9	13.5
40-40	25.7	20.8	55-55	18.2	14.5
40-45	25.0	20.2	55-60	15.0	11.8
40-50	23.8	19.3	60-60	11.7	9.0

Three-Owner Business

Ages	Odds Of One Death Male	Odds Of One Death Female	Ages	Odds Of One Death Male	Odds Of One Death Female
30-30-30	38.4%	31.5%	40-45-50	33.7%	27.7%
30-35-40	37.2	30.6	40-50-60	28.4	23.0
30-40-50	35.2	28.9	45-45-45	34.1	27.9
35-35-35	37.3	30.7	45-50-55	30.4	24.8
35-40-45	35.8	29.4	50-50-50	30.9	25.4
35-45-55	32.6	26.7	50-55-60	24.9	20.1
40-40-40	36.0	29.5	55-55-55	26.0	21.0

Using the following percentages, it is possible to calculate the odds of at least one death before age 65 for any particular group of owners. After multiplying the percent for each owner by the percent for each other owner, subtract the results from 1. For example, the calculations for the odds of at least one death for three male owners, ages 40, 45, and 50: $1 - (.8617 \times .8703 \times .8840) = 1 - .6630 = 33.7\%$.

Age	Living To Age 65 Male	Living To Age 65 Female	Age	Living To Age 65 Male	Living To Age 65 Female	Age	Living To Age 65 Male	Living To Age 65 Female	Age	Living To Age 65 Male	Living To Age 65 Female
30	85.10%	88.15%	38	85.92%	88.77%	46	87.27%	89.82%	54	89.94%	92.01%
31	85.20	88.21	39	86.04	88.87	47	87.52	90.00	55	90.44	92.44
32	85.29	88.28	40	86.17	88.98	48	87.80	90.21	56	91.00	92.91
33	85.39	88.34	41	86.32	89.10	49	88.09	90.43	57	91.63	93.44
34	85.49	88.42	42	86.47	89.22	50	88.40	90.69	58	92.34	94.02
35	85.59	88.49	43	86.64	89.35	51	88.74	90.97	59	93.11	94.67
36	85.69	88.58	44	86.83	89.50	52	89.10	91.28	60	93.95	95.37
37	85.80	88.67	45	87.03	89.65	53	89.50	91.63			

Source: Commissioners 2001 Standard Ordinary Mortality Table.

ODDS OF DEATH WITHIN 10 AND 20 YEARS

When a business has two or more owners, the odds of at least one death within any given period of time increase dramatically. *The risk is not remote*. Proper planning calls for making provisions for the continuation of the business.

One-Owner Business – MALE

	Odds Of Death Within	
Age	10 Years	20 Years
30	1.2%	3.7%
35	1.7	5.4
40	2.5	8.3
45	3.8	13.0
50	5.9	20.2
55	9.6	30.4

One-Owner Business – FEMALE

	Odds Of Death Within	
Age	10 Years	20 Years
30	0.9%	2.8%
35	1.3	4.3
40	1.9	6.7
45	3.0	10.3
50	4.9	15.5
55	7.6	22.7

Two-Owner Business – MALE

	Odds Of One Death Within	
Ages	10 Years	20 Years
30-30	2.5%	7.3%
30-35	2.9	8.9
30-40	3.7	11.7
35-35	3.3	10.4
35-40	4.1	13.2
35-45	5.4	17.6
40-40	5.0	15.9
40-45	6.2	20.2
40-50	8.3	26.8
45-45	7.4	24.2
45-50	9.4	30.5
45-55	13.0	39.5
50-50	11.5	36.3
50-55	14.9	44.5
50-60	20.2	55.8
55-55	18.2	51.6
55-60	23.3	61.5
55-65	30.4	74.0

Two-Owner Business – FEMALE

	Odds Of One Death Within	
Ages	10 Years	20 Years
30-30	1.9%	5.5%
30-35	2.2	6.9
30-40	2.8	9.3
35-35	2.6	8.4
35-40	3.1	10.7
35-45	4.3	14.2
40-40	3.7	12.9
40-45	4.8	16.4
40-50	6.7	21.1
45-45	5.9	19.6
45-50	7.8	24.2
45-55	10.3	30.7
50-50	9.6	28.6
50-55	12.1	34.7
50-60	15.5	43.2
55-55	14.5	40.3
55-60	17.8	48.1
55-65	22.7	59.0

Three-Owner Business – MALE

	Odds Of One Death Within	
Ages	10 Years	20 Years
30-30-30	3.7%	10.8%
30-35-40	5.3	16.4
30-40-50	9.4	29.5
35-35-35	4.9	15.2
35-40-45	7.8	24.5
35-45-55	14.4	42.7
40-40-40	7.4	22.8
40-45-50	11.7	36.3
40-50-60	22.2	59.4
45-45-45	10.9	34.1
45-50-55	18.1	51.7
50-50-50	16.7	49.1
50-55-60	27.8	69.2
55-55-55	26.0	66.3
50-60-70	47.9	91.6

Three-Owner Business – FEMALE

	Odds Of One Death Within	
Ages	10 Years	20 Years
30-30-30	2.8%	8.2%
30-35-40	4.0	13.2
30-40-50	7.6	23.4
35-35-35	3.8	12.3
35-40-45	6.1	19.9
35-45-55	11.5	33.7
40-40-40	5.5	18.8
40-45-50	9.5	29.3
40-50-60	17.1	47.0
45-45-45	8.8	27.9
45-50-55	14.8	41.4
50-50-50	14.0	39.6
50-55-60	21.9	56.1
55-55-55	21.0	53.8
50-60-70	36.1	80.1

Source: Commissioners 2001 Standard Ordinary Mortality Table.

LONGEVITY IN RETIREMENT – Male

Current Age	Chances of Living to Age										
	70	71	72	73	74	75	76	77	78	79	80
60	82.8	80.3	77.7	74.9	72.0	68.9	65.7	62.4	59.0	55.4	51.7
61	83.8	81.3	78.6	75.8	72.8	69.8	66.5	63.2	59.7	56.1	52.3
62	84.9	82.4	79.7	76.8	73.8	70.7	67.4	64.0	60.5	56.8	53.0
63	86.1	83.6	80.8	77.9	74.9	71.7	68.4	65.0	61.4	57.6	53.8
64	87.5	84.9	82.1	79.2	76.1	72.9	69.5	66.0	62.4	58.6	54.7
65	89.1	86.4	83.6	80.6	77.4	74.2	70.7	67.2	63.5	59.6	55.6
66	90.8	88.1	85.2	82.1	78.9	75.6	72.1	68.5	64.7	60.8	56.7
67	92.7	89.9	87.0	83.9	80.6	77.2	73.6	69.9	66.1	62.0	57.9
68	94.9	92.0	89.0	85.8	82.5	79.0	75.4	71.6	67.6	63.5	59.3
69	97.3	94.4	91.3	88.0	84.6	81.0	77.3	73.4	69.3	65.1	60.8
70		97.0	93.8	90.5	87.0	83.3	79.4	75.4	71.3	66.9	62.5
71			96.7	93.3	89.6	85.8	81.9	77.8	73.4	69.0	64.4
72				96.4	92.7	88.8	84.7	80.4	75.9	71.3	66.6
73					96.1	92.0	87.8	83.4	78.8	74.0	69.0
74						95.8	91.4	86.7	81.9	77.0	71.8
75							95.4	90.6	85.6	80.4	75.0
76								95.0	89.7	84.2	78.6
77									94.5	88.7	82.8
78										93.9	87.7
79											93.3

Current Age	Chances of Living to Age										
	81	82	83	84	85	86	87	88	89	90	95
60	47.9	44.0	40.1	36.1	32.2	28.3	24.5	20.9	17.5	14.4	3.9
61	48.5	44.6	40.6	36.6	32.6	28.6	24.8	21.2	17.7	14.6	3.9
62	49.1	45.2	41.1	37.0	33.0	29.0	25.1	21.4	18.0	14.8	4.0
63	49.9	45.8	41.7	37.6	33.5	29.4	25.5	21.8	18.2	15.0	4.0
64	50.7	46.5	42.4	38.2	34.0	29.9	25.9	22.1	18.5	15.3	4.1
65	51.5	47.4	43.1	38.9	34.6	30.4	26.4	22.5	18.9	15.5	4.2
66	52.5	48.3	44.0	39.6	35.3	31.0	26.9	22.9	19.2	15.8	4.2
67	53.7	49.3	44.9	40.5	36.0	31.7	27.5	23.4	19.6	16.2	4.3
68	54.9	50.5	45.9	41.4	36.9	32.4	28.1	24.0	20.1	16.5	4.4
69	56.3	51.7	47.1	42.5	37.8	33.2	28.8	24.6	20.6	17.0	4.5
70	57.9	53.2	48.4	43.6	38.9	34.2	29.6	25.3	21.2	17.4	4.7
71	59.7	54.8	49.9	45.0	40.1	35.2	30.5	26.0	21.8	18.0	4.8
72	61.7	56.7	51.6	46.5	41.4	36.4	31.6	26.9	22.6	18.6	5.0
73	64.0	58.8	53.5	48.2	43.0	37.8	32.7	27.9	23.4	19.3	5.2
74	66.6	61.2	55.7	50.2	44.7	39.3	34.1	29.1	24.4	20.0	5.4
75	69.5	63.9	58.2	52.4	46.7	41.0	35.6	30.3	25.4	20.9	5.6
76	72.9	67.0	61.0	54.9	48.9	43.0	37.3	31.8	26.7	21.9	5.9
77	76.7	70.5	64.2	57.9	51.5	45.3	39.3	33.5	28.1	23.1	6.2
78	81.2	74.6	68.0	61.3	54.6	48.0	41.6	35.5	29.7	24.5	6.6
79	86.5	79.5	72.4	65.2	58.1	51.1	44.2	37.7	31.7	26.1	7.0

Application: Used for estimating years in retirement. For example, a male age 65 stands a 55.6% chance of living to age 80 (i.e., 556 out of 1,000 males age 65 will live to age 80).

Source: Calculations are based upon the longevity data contained in the 2008 Valuation Basic Table developed by the Society of Actuaries.

LONGEVITY IN RETIREMENT – Female

Current Age	Chances of Living to Age										
	70	71	72	73	74	75	76	77	78	79	80
60	88.4	86.7	84.8	82.8	80.7	78.5	76.0	73.5	70.7	67.8	64.7
61	89.1	87.4	85.5	83.5	81.3	79.1	76.6	74.0	71.3	68.3	65.2
62	89.9	88.1	86.2	84.2	82.0	79.7	77.3	74.7	71.9	68.9	65.8
63	90.7	89.0	87.1	85.0	82.8	80.5	78.0	75.4	72.6	69.6	66.4
64	91.7	89.9	88.0	85.9	83.7	81.3	78.8	76.2	73.3	70.3	67.1
65	92.7	90.9	89.0	86.9	84.6	82.3	79.7	77.0	74.2	71.1	67.9
66	93.9	92.0	90.1	87.9	85.7	83.3	80.7	78.0	75.1	72.0	68.7
67	95.2	93.3	91.3	89.2	86.9	84.4	81.8	79.1	76.1	73.0	69.7
68	96.6	94.7	92.7	90.5	88.2	85.7	83.1	80.3	77.3	74.1	70.7
69	98.2	96.3	94.2	92.0	89.6	87.1	84.5	81.6	78.6	75.3	71.9
70		98.0	95.9	93.7	91.3	88.7	86.0	83.1	80.0	76.7	73.2
71			97.9	95.5	93.1	90.5	87.7	84.7	81.6	78.2	74.6
72				97.6	95.1	92.5	89.6	86.6	83.4	79.9	76.3
73					97.4	94.7	91.8	88.7	85.4	81.9	78.1
74						97.2	94.2	91.0	87.6	84.0	80.2
75							96.9	93.7	90.2	86.4	82.5
76								96.6	93.0	89.2	85.1
77									96.3	92.3	88.1
78										95.9	91.5
79											95.4

Current Age	Chances of Living to Age										
	81	82	83	84	85	86	87	88	89	90	95
60	61.4	57.9	54.3	50.5	46.5	42.4	38.3	34.2	30.0	26.0	9.4
61	61.9	58.4	54.7	50.9	46.9	42.8	38.6	34.4	30.3	26.2	9.4
62	62.4	58.9	55.2	51.3	47.3	43.1	38.9	34.7	30.5	26.4	9.5
63	63.0	59.5	55.7	51.8	47.7	43.5	39.3	35.0	30.8	26.7	9.6
64	63.7	60.1	56.3	52.3	48.2	44.0	39.7	35.4	31.1	26.9	9.7
65	64.4	60.8	56.9	52.9	48.8	44.5	40.2	35.8	31.5	27.2	9.8
66	65.2	61.5	57.6	53.6	49.4	45.1	40.7	36.3	31.9	27.6	9.9
67	66.1	62.4	58.4	54.3	50.1	45.7	41.2	36.8	32.3	28.0	10.1
68	67.1	63.3	59.3	55.1	50.8	46.4	41.9	37.3	32.8	28.4	10.2
69	68.2	64.4	60.3	56.0	51.7	47.1	42.6	37.9	33.3	28.8	10.4
70	69.5	65.5	61.4	57.1	52.6	48.0	43.3	38.6	33.9	29.4	10.6
71	70.8	66.8	62.6	58.2	53.6	49.0	44.2	39.4	34.6	30.0	10.8
72	72.4	68.3	64.0	59.5	54.8	50.0	45.2	40.3	35.4	30.6	11.0
73	74.1	69.9	65.5	60.9	56.1	51.2	46.2	41.2	36.2	31.4	11.3
74	76.1	71.8	67.2	62.5	57.6	52.6	47.5	42.3	37.2	32.2	11.6
75	78.3	73.9	69.2	64.3	59.3	54.1	48.8	43.5	38.3	33.1	11.9
76	80.8	76.2	71.4	66.4	61.2	55.8	50.4	44.9	39.5	34.2	12.3
77	83.6	78.9	73.9	68.7	63.3	57.8	52.1	46.5	40.9	35.4	12.7
78	86.8	81.9	76.7	71.3	65.7	60.0	54.2	48.3	42.4	36.7	13.2
79	90.6	85.4	80.0	74.4	68.6	62.6	56.5	50.4	44.3	38.3	13.8

Application: Used for estimating years in retirement. For example, a female age 65 stands a 67.9% chance of living to age 80 (i.e., 679 out of 1,000 females age 65 will live to age 80).

Source: Calculations are based upon the longevity data contained in the 2008 Valuation Basic Table developed by the Society of Actuaries.

COMPOUND INTEREST & FUTURE VALUE OF MONEY

Given the choice of being paid \$1.00 today,
or \$1.00 four years from now,
you would choose to be paid \$1.00 today.

AND

Given the choice of being paid \$1.00 today,
or \$16.00 four years from now,
you would choose to be paid \$16.00 four years from now.

HOWEVER

Given the choice of being paid \$1.00 today,
or \$1.50 four years from now,
your decision would require you to carefully consider the

FUTURE VALUE OF MONEY

The future value of money is a very important concept in estate and business planning and can be best understood by referring to the Future Value Table on page 617. If you took the \$1.00 today and could invest it at 8 percent, you would have \$1.36 in four years (read down the 8 percent rate column until year 4). By waiting four years, you could receive \$1.50, which is 14 cents more than you would get by taking the money and investing it at 8 percent.

However, if you believed that you could invest your funds at 18 percent, you would expect to have \$1.94 in four years (\$1.00 × 1.939 = \$1.939). In this case you would probably take the \$1.00 today rather than the \$1.50 in four years.

But what if your choice was as follows:

Being paid \$1.00 each year for the next 4 years,
or being paid \$5.50 4 years from now.

The Future Value Table on page 618, will help you make the decision, since it shows the sum to which one dollar per year will grow if placed in accounts at varying rates of interest. If you took the \$1.00 each year and were able to invest it at 8 percent, you would have \$4.87 in four years (\$1.00 × 4.867 = \$4.867). By waiting four years, you could receive \$5.50, which is 63 cents more than you would have by taking the money and investing it at 8 percent.

However, if you believed that you could invest your funds at 15 percent, you would expect to have \$5.74 in four years (\$1.00 × 5.742 = \$5.74). In this case you would probably take the \$1.00 each year for the next four years.

COMPOUND INTEREST & PRESENT VALUE OF MONEY

Given the choice of being paid $1.00 three years from now,
or $1.00 four years from now,
you would choose to be paid $1.00 three years from now.

AND

Given the choice of being paid $1.00 three years from now,
or $2.00 four years from now,
you would choose to be paid $2.00 four years from now.

HOWEVER

Given the choice of being paid $1.00 three years from now,
or $1.15 four years from now,
your decision would require you to carefully consider the

PRESENT VALUE OF MONEY

The present value of money can be calculated by referring to the Present Value Table on page 619. If you viewed money as having a time value of 8 percent, the present value of that $1.00 payment due in three years from now is 79 cents ($1.00 × .7938 = $.7938). The present value of a $1.15 payment four years from now is 84 cents ($1.15 × .7350 = $.84525). You would accept payment of $1.15 four years from now.

However, if you viewed money as having a time value of 18 percent, the present value of that $1.00 payment due in three years from now is 61 cents ($1.00 × .6086 = $.6086). The present value of a $1.15 payment four years from now is only 59 cents ($1.15 × .5158 = $.59317). You would not accept the offer to pay $1.15 four years from now, but would rather demand payment of $1.00 three years from now.

But what if your choice was as follows:

Being paid $1.25 at the end of each year for the next 3 years,
or being paid $1.00 at the end of each year for the next 4 years.

The Present Value Table on page 620, will help you make the decision. If you viewed money as having a time value of 8 percent, the present value of that $1.25 payment at the end of each year for the next three years is $3.22 ($1.25 × 2.577 = $3.22125). The present value of a $1.00 payment each year for four years is $3.31 ($1.00 × 3.312 = $3.312). You would accept payment of $1.00 per year for the next four years.

However, if you viewed money as having a time value of 18 percent, the present value of that $1.25 payment at the end of each year for the next three years is $2.72 ($1.25 × 2.174 = $2.7175). The present value of a $1.00 payment each year for four years is $2.69 ($1.00 × 2.690 = $2.690). You would not accept payment of $1.00 per year for four years, but would rather demand payment of $1.25 per year for the next three years.

FUTURE VALUE TABLE

The Sum To Which One Dollar Principal Will Increase

	Rate					
	1%	2%	3%	4%	5%	10%
Years						
1	1.010	1.020	1.030	1.040	1.050	1.100
2	1.020	1.040	1.061	1.082	1.103	1.210
3	1.030	1.061	1.093	1.125	1.158	1.331
4	1.041	1.082	1.126	1.170	1.216	1.464
5	1.051	1.104	1.159	1.217	1.276	1.611
6	1.062	1.126	1.194	1.265	1.340	1.772
7	1.072	1.149	1.230	1.316	1.407	1.949
8	1.083	1.172	1.267	1.369	1.477	2.144
9	1.094	1.195	1.305	1.423	1.551	2.358
10	1.105	1.219	1.344	1.480	1.629	2.594
11	1.116	1.243	1.384	1.539	1.710	2.853
12	1.127	1.268	1.426	1.601	1.796	3.138
13	1.138	1.294	1.469	1.665	1.886	3.452
14	1.149	1.319	1.513	1.732	1.980	3.797
15	1.161	1.346	1.558	1.801	2.079	4.177
16	1.173	1.373	1.605	1.873	2.183	4.595
17	1.184	1.400	1.653	1.948	2.292	5.054
18	1.196	1.428	1.702	2.026	2.407	5.560
19	1.208	1.457	1.754	2.107	2.527	6.116
20	1.220	1.486	1.806	2.191	2.653	6.727
21	1.232	1.516	1.860	2.279	2.786	7.400
22	1.245	1.546	1.916	2.370	2.925	8.140
23	1.257	1.577	1.974	2.465	3.072	8.954
24	1.270	1.608	2.033	2.563	3.225	9.850
25	1.282	1.641	2.094	2.666	3.386	10.835
26	1.295	1.673	2.157	2.772	3.556	11.918
27	1.308	1.707	2.221	2.883	3.733	13.110
28	1.321	1.741	2.288	2.999	3.920	14.421
29	1.335	1.776	2.357	3.119	4.116	15.863
30	1.348	1.811	2.427	3.243	4.322	17.449
31	1.361	1.848	2.500	3.373	4.538	19.194
32	1.375	1.895	2.575	3.508	4.765	21.114
33	1.389	1.922	2.652	3.648	5.003	23.225
34	1.403	1.961	2.732	3.794	5.253	25.548
35	1.417	2.000	2.814	3.946	5.516	28.102
36	1.431	2.040	2.898	4.104	5.792	30.913
37	1.445	2.081	2.985	4.268	6.081	34.004
38	1.460	2.122	3.075	4.439	6.385	37.404
39	1.474	2.165	3.167	4.616	6.705	41.145
40	1.489	2.208	3.262	4.801	7.040	45.259

FUTURE VALUE TABLE

The Sum To Which One Dollar Per Annum,
Paid At The *Beginning* Of Each Year, Will Increase

Years	1%	2%	3%	4%	5%	10%
1	1.010	1.020	1.030	1.040	1.050	1.100
2	2.030	2.060	2.091	2.122	2.152	2.310
3	3.060	3.122	3.184	3.246	3.310	3.641
4	4.101	4.204	4.309	4.416	4.526	5.105
5	5.152	5.308	5.468	5.633	5.802	6.716
6	6.214	6.434	6.662	6.898	7.142	8.487
7	7.286	7.583	7.892	8.214	8.549	10.436
8	8.369	8.755	9.159	9.583	10.027	12.579
9	9.462	9.950	10.464	11.006	11.578	14.937
10	10.567	11.169	11.808	12.486	13.207	17.531
11	11.683	12.412	13.192	14.026	14.917	20.384
12	12.809	13.680	14.618	15.627	16.713	23.523
13	13.947	14.974	16.086	17.292	18.599	26.975
14	15.097	16.293	17.599	19.024	20.579	30.772
15	16.258	17.639	19.157	20.825	22.657	34.950
16	17.430	19.012	20.762	22.698	24.840	39.545
17	18.615	20.412	22.414	24.645	27.132	44.599
18	19.811	21.841	24.117	26.671	29.539	50.159
19	21.019	23.297	25.870	28.778	32.066	56.275
20	22.239	24.783	27.676	30.969	34.719	63.002
21	23.472	26.299	29.537	33.248	37.505	70.403
22	24.716	27.845	31.453	35.618	40.430	78.543
23	25.973	29.422	33.426	38.083	43.502	87.497
24	27.243	31.030	35.459	40.646	46.727	97.347
25	28.526	32.671	37.563	43.312	50.113	108.182
26	29.821	34.344	39.710	46.084	53.669	120.100
27	31.129	36.051	41.931	48.968	57.403	133.210
28	32.450	37.792	44.219	51.966	61.323	147.631
29	33.785	39.568	46.575	55.085	65.439	163.494
30	35.133	41.379	49.003	58.328	69.761	180.943
31	36.494	43.227	51.503	61.701	74.299	200.138
32	37.869	45.112	54.078	65.210	79.064	221.252
33	39.258	47.034	56.730	68.858	84.067	244.477
34	40.660	48.994	59.462	72.652	89.320	270.024
35	42.077	50.994	62.276	76.598	94.836	298.127
36	43.508	53.034	65.174	80.702	100.628	329.039
37	44.953	55.115	68.159	84.970	106.710	363.043
38	46.412	57.237	71.234	89.409	113.095	400.448
39	47.886	59.402	74.401	94.026	119.800	441.593
40	49.375	61.610	77.663	98.827	126.840	486.852

PRESENT VALUE TABLE

The Worth Today of One Dollar Due In The Future

	Rate					
	1%	2%	3%	4%	5%	10%
Years						
1	0.9901	0.9804	0.9709	0.9615	0.9524	0.9091
2	0.9803	0.9612	0.9426	0.9246	0.9070	0.8264
3	0.9706	0.9423	0.9151	0.8890	0.8638	0.7513
4	0.9610	0.9238	0.8885	0.8548	0.8227	0.6830
5	0.9515	0.9057	0.8626	0.8219	0.7835	0.6209
6	0.9420	0.8880	0.8375	0.7903	0.7462	0.5645
7	0.9327	0.8706	0.8131	0.7599	0.7107	0.5132
8	0.9235	0.8535	0.7894	0.7307	0.6768	0.4665
9	0.9143	0.8368	0.7664	0.7026	0.6446	0.4241
10	0.9053	0.8203	0.7441	0.6756	0.6139	0.3855
11	0.8963	0.8043	0.7224	0.6496	0.5847	0.3505
12	0.8874	0.7885	0.7014	0.6246	0.5568	0.3186
13	0.8787	0.7730	0.6810	0.6006	0.5303	0.2897
14	0.8700	0.7579	0.6611	0.5775	0.5051	0.2633
15	0.8613	0.7430	0.6419	0.5553	0.4810	0.2394
16	0.8528	0.7284	0.6232	0.5339	0.4581	0.2176
17	0.8444	0.7142	0.6050	0.5134	0.4363	0.1978
18	0.8360	0.7002	0.5874	0.4936	0.4155	0.1799
19	0.8277	0.6864	0.5703	0.4746	0.3957	0.1635
20	0.8195	0.6730	0.5537	0.4564	0.3769	0.1486
21	0.8114	0.6598	0.5375	0.4388	0.3589	0.1351
22	0.8034	0.6468	0.5219	0.4220	0.3419	0.1228
23	0.7954	0.6342	0.5067	0.4057	0.3256	0.1117
24	0.7876	0.6217	0.4919	0.3901	0.3101	0.1015
25	0.7798	0.6095	0.4776	0.3751	0.2953	0.0923
26	0.7720	0.5976	0.4637	0.3607	0.2812	0.0839
27	0.7644	0.5859	0.4502	0.3468	0.2678	0.0763
28	0.7568	0.5744	0.4371	0.3335	0.2551	0.0693
29	0.7493	0.5631	0.4243	0.3207	0.2429	0.0630
30	0.7419	0.5521	0.4120	0.3083	0.2314	0.0573
31	0.7346	0.5412	0.4000	0.2965	0.2204	0.0521
32	0.7273	0.5306	0.3883	0.2851	0.2099	0.0474
33	0.7201	0.5202	0.3770	0.2741	0.1999	0.0431
34	0.7130	0.5100	0.3660	0.2636	0.1904	0.0391
35	0.7059	0.5000	0.3554	0.2534	0.1813	0.0356
36	0.6989	0.4902	0.3450	0.2437	0.1727	0.0323
37	0.6920	0.4806	0.3350	0.2343	0.1644	0.0294
38	0.6852	0.4712	0.3252	0.2253	0.1566	0.0267
39	0.6784	0.4619	0.3158	0.2166	0.1491	0.0243
40	0.6717	0.4529	0.3066	0.2083	0.1420	0.0221

PRESENT VALUE TABLE

The Worth Today of One Dollar Per Annum
Paid At The *End* of Each Year

	Rate					
	1%	2%	3%	4%	5%	10%
Years						
1	0.990	0.980	0.971	0.962	0.952	0.909
2	1.970	1.942	1.913	1.886	1.859	1.736
3	2.941	2.884	2.829	2.775	2.723	2.487
4	3.902	3.808	3.717	3.630	3.546	3.170
5	4.853	4.713	4.580	4.452	4.329	3.791
6	5.795	5.601	5.417	5.242	5.076	4.355
7	6.728	6.472	6.230	6.002	5.786	4.868
8	7.652	7.325	7.020	6.733	6.463	5.335
9	8.566	8.162	7.786	7.435	7.108	5.759
10	9.471	8.983	8.530	8.111	7.722	6.145
11	10.368	9.787	9.253	8.760	8.306	6.495
12	11.255	10.575	9.954	9.385	8.863	6.814
13	12.134	11.348	10.635	9.986	9.394	7.103
14	13.004	12.106	11.296	10.563	9.899	7.367
15	13.865	12.849	11.938	11.118	10.380	7.606
16	14.718	13.578	12.561	11.652	10.838	7.824
17	15.562	14.292	13.166	12.166	11.274	8.022
18	16.398	14.992	13.754	12.659	11.690	8.201
19	17.226	15.678	14.324	13.134	12.085	8.365
20	18.046	16.351	14.877	13.590	12.462	8.514
21	18.857	17.011	15.415	14.029	12.821	8.649
22	19.660	17.658	15.937	14.451	13.163	8.772
23	20.456	18.292	16.444	14.857	13.489	8.883
24	21.243	18.914	16.936	15.247	13.799	8.985
25	22.023	19.523	17.413	15.622	14.094	9.077
26	22.795	20.121	17.877	15.983	14.375	9.161
27	23.560	20.707	18.327	16.330	14.643	9.237
28	24.316	21.281	18.764	16.663	14.898	9.307
29	25.066	21.844	19.188	16.984	15.141	9.370
30	25.808	22.396	19.600	17.292	15.372	9.427
31	26.542	22.938	20.000	17.588	15.593	9.479
32	27.270	23.468	20.389	17.874	15.803	9.526
33	27.990	23.989	20.766	18.148	16.003	9.569
34	28.703	24.499	21.132	18.411	16.193	9.609
35	29.409	24.999	21.487	18.665	16.374	9.644
36	30.108	25.489	21.832	18.908	16.547	9.677
37	30.800	25.969	22.167	19.143	16.711	9.706
38	31.485	26.441	22.492	19.368	16.868	9.733
39	32.163	26.903	22.808	19.584	17.017	9.757
40	32.835	27.355	23.115	19.793	17.159	9.779

AMORTIZATION TABLE

Annual Payment Necessary To Amortize A Loan Of $1,000

	Rate					
	1%	2%	3%	4%	5%	10%
Years						
1	1,010.00	1,020.00	1,030.00	1,040.00	1,050.00	1,100.00
2	507.51	515.05	522.61	530.20	537.80	576.19
3	340.02	346.75	363.53	360.35	367.21	402.11
4	256.28	262.62	269.03	275.49	282.01	315.47
5	206.04	212.16	218.35	224.63	230.97	263.80
6	172.55	178.53	194.60	190.76	197.02	229.61
7	148.63	154.51	160.51	166.61	172.82	205.41
8	130.69	136.51	142.46	148.53	154.72	187.44
9	116.74	22.52	128.43	134.49	140.69	173.64
10	105.58	111.33	117.23	123.29	129.50	162.75
11	96.45	102.18	108.08	114.15	120.39	153.96
12	88.85	94.56	100.46	106.55	112.83	146.76
13	82.41	88.12	94.03	100.14	106.46	140.78
14	76.90	82.60	88.53	94.67	101.02	135.75
15	72.12	77.83	83.77	89.94	96.34	131.47
16	67.94	73.65	79.61	85.82	92.27	127.82
17	64.26	69.97	75.95	82.20	88.70	124.66
18	60.98	66.70	72.71	78.99	85.55	121.94
19	56.05	63.78	69.81	76.14	82.75	119.55
20	55.42	61.16	67.22	73.58	80.24	117.46
21	53.03	58.78	64.87	71.28	78.00	115.62
22	50.86	56.63	62.75	69.20	75.97	114.01
23	48.89	54.67	60.81	67.31	74.14	112.57
24	47.07	52.87	59.05	66.59	72.47	111.30
25	45.41	51.22	57.43	64.01	70.95	110.17
26	43.87	49.70	55.94	62.57	69.56	109.16
27	42.45	48.29	54.56	61.24	68.29	108.26
28	41.12	46.99	53.29	60.01	67.12	107.45
29	39.90	45.78	52.11	58.88	66.05	106.73
30	38.75	44.65	51.02	57.83	65.05	106.08
31	37.68	43.60	50.00	56.86	64.13	105.50
32	36.67	42.61	49.05	55.95	63.28	104.97
33	35.73	41.69	48.16	55.10	62.49	104.50
34	34.84	40.82	47.32	54.31	61.76	104.07
35	34.00	40.00	46.54	53.58	61.07	103.69
36	33.21	39.23	45.80	52.89	60.43	103.34
37	32.47	38.51	45.11	52.24	59.84	103.03
38	31.76	37.82	44.46	51.63	59.28	102.75
39	31.09	37.17	43.84	51.06	58.76	102.49
40	30.46	36.56	43.26	50.52	58.28	102.26

BUSINESS COMPARISON

Question	Unincorporated	Incorporated
What is the extent of liability for:		
Contract?	To all business and personal assets of each individual owner.	Usually limited to business assets in most states.
Negligence of owner-employees?	To all business and personal assets of each individual owner.	Generally limited to business assets except professional liability.
Negligence of employees?	To all business and personal assets of each individual owner.	Limited to business assets.
Business debts?	To all business and personal assets of each individual owner (but see discussion of Limited Liability Company, page 449).	Limited to business assets except where owners have personally guaranteed loan by endorsement or otherwise.
To whom are profits taxed?	Individual owners.	To the corporation if retained as earnings. To owner-employees if paid out as reasonable compensation or dividends (page 576).
Can a small portion of the ownership interest have full control?	Not in any practical way (but see Family Limited Partnership chart, page 211).	Yes – by use of voting preferred and non-voting stock (page 214).
Can the business interest be easily transferred to one or more purchasers or recipients?	No – transfer of individual assets or creation of new entity can result in complications.	Yes – stock may be easily transferred to either the corporation, other stockholders, key persons, or outsiders (pages 170, 174, and 190)
Who pays income taxes on dollars used to pay for life insurance funding a buy/sell agreement?	Individual owners.	Choice of corporation or stockholder-employee.
Can the business purchase a portion of a deceased owner's interest on a tax-favored basis?	No	Yes – under Code section 303 the corporation can purchase some stock, while allowing the surviving family to retain an ownership interest (page 194).
Does the business entity enjoy any tax-favored investment advantages?	No	Yes – under Code section 243 a corporation can deduct from 70% to 100% of the dividends received from domestic corporations.

Note: "Unincorporated" refers to sole proprietorships and partnerships, but not to limited partners; "incorporated" refers to C corporations, but not to S corporations.

Question	Unincorporated	Incorporated
Can the business have a different fiscal year than the owners?	Not in any practical way.	Yes
What is the annual cost of Social Security for each owner-employee?	In 2019 12.40% OASDI tax on first $132,900 of self-employment income and 2.90% hospital insurance tax without limit, all paid by the individual owner.	In 2019 6.20% OASDI tax on first $132,900 of income and 1.45% hospital insurance tax without limit, paid by the owner-employee. Equal amounts of tax are also paid by the corporation, but deductible as a business expense.
What is the cost of unemployment taxes for each owner-employee?	None	In 2019 both state and federal (FUTA) taxes will be a maximum $42 per employee, i.e., 6.2% of first $7,000 in wages.
What is the cost of worker's compensation?	None	If set by state law, can often be exempt from coverage. If paid, it is considered a deductible business expense.
Is there any extra cost for franchise fees and bookkeeping?	–	A small annual franchise fee is usually payable. Corporate minutes must be kept on an annual basis. Bookkeeping costs may be somewhat higher.
Is there any extra cost to prepare a corporate tax return?	–	Preparation of corporate return can cost more, but usually not much greater than Schedule C (Profit or Loss From Business or Profession) or Form 1065 (U.S. Partnership Return of Income).
Could there be a problem with unreasonable compensation to owner-employees?	No	Yes – under Code section 162 only a reasonable allowance for compensation can be deducted. This is usually not a serious problem, but should be considered (page 576).
Is there a potential for double taxation?	No	Yes – if not properly planned there could be a corporate income tax, plus a personal income tax on dividends received.
Could a personal holding company penalty tax of 15% be levied?	No	Yes – a penalty tax could be applied if 60% of income is essentially passive, such as dividends, rents and royalties.

Note: "Unincorporated" refers to sole proprietorships and partnerships, but not to limited partners; "incorporated" refers to C corporations, but not to S corporations.

Question	Unincorporated	Incorporated
Can individual owner-employees have deferred compensation?	No	Yes – Income may be deferred (Deferred Compensation, page 126).
Can the business pay premiums for personal life insurance, and have the premiums paid tax-free for owner-employees?	No	Yes – up to $50,000 of group insurance is available under Code section 79.
Are tax-favored personal life insurance programs available to owner-employees?	No	Yes – individual plans can be established (Executive Equity, page 232, and Split-Dollar Insurance, page 240).
Is a qualified retirement program available?	Yes – HR-10 permits sole proprietors and partners to be covered under qualified plans.	Yes – under qualified plan rules (Qualified Retirement Plans, pages 264, 306, 339, 534, 548, 557, and 562).
Are other tax-deductible benefits available to owner-employees, such as:		
Disability income plans?	No	Yes – under Code sections 105 and 106 (Disability Income Plan, page 252).
Medical and dental expense reimburse-ment arrangements?	Not generally, but limited deduction available (footnote 2, page 259).	Yes – under Code sections 105 and 106 (Health Reimbursement Arrangements, page 256).
Survivor income plans?	No	Yes – as a form of salary continuation death benefit (Survivor Income, page 122).

Note: "Unincorporated" refers to sole proprietorships and partnerships, but not to limited partners; "incorporated" refers to C corporations, but not to S corporations.

COMPARISON
CROSS PURCHASE & ENTITY PURCHASE

	Cross Purchase	Entity Purchase
Purchaser	Surviving stockholders (see charts, pages 175, 179, and 187).	Corporation (see charts, pages 171 and 187).
Seller	Deceased stockholder's estate.	Deceased stockholder's estate.
Policy Owner	Individual stockholders (or trustee, see chart page 189).	Corporation.
Number of Policies Required	Multiple policies depending upon number of stockholders (unless trusteed cross purchase, or funded with first-to-die insurance, see chart page 189 and page 380).	One policy on each stockholder.
Premiums	Paid by individual stockholders and not deductible (but could use split-dollar, see chart, page 245).	Paid by corporation and not deductible.
Taxation of Life Insurance Death Benefits	Received tax-free by surviving stockholders (but may be subject to notice and consent requirements, see pages 319-321).	Received tax-free provided notice and consent requirements have been met (see pages 319-321). Could be subject to corporate alternative minimum tax (see page 327).
Effect on Surviving Stockholders	Stockholder's basis increases in an amount equal to price paid for deceased's stock.	Value of stock owned by survivors increases if corporation retires stock (but no increase in stockholder's basis).
Impact of Attribution	No effect.	Redemption is subject to attribution rules (see pages 218-223).
Taxation of Deceased Stockholder's Heirs	Basis is stepped-up at death and no gain recognized (see page 556).	Basis is stepped-up at death and no gain recognized, provided redemption meets either Code section 302(b)(3) or Code section 303 requirements. (see footnote 1, page 197 and page 556).
Legality of Arrangement	No problem, unless professional corporation and state law restricts sale to other professionals.	Must meet state laws regarding corporate purchase of own stock.
Flexibility to Change Plans	Transfer of existing policies to corporation could be an exception to transfer for value rules (see page 568).	Transfer of corporate owned policies to co-stockholder violates transfer for value rules, unless co-stockholder is also a partner of the insured (see page 568).

COMPARISON
CROSS PURCHASE & TRUSTEED CROSS PURCHASE

	Cross Purchase	Trusteed Cross Purchase
Purchaser	Surviving stockholders (see chart, page 175).	Trustee as escrow agent for surviving stockholders (see chart, page 179).
Seller	Deceased stockholder's estate.	Deceased stockholder's estate. Stock certificates held in escrow by trustee are transferred to surviving stockholders.
Policy Owner	Individual stockholders.	Trustee as agent for stockholders.
Policy Beneficiary	Individual stockholders.	Trustee as agent for surviving stockholders. Trustee transfers funds to deceased's estate in return for deceased's stock interest.
Number of Policies Required	Multiple policies depending upon number of stockholders (see footnote 3, page 177).	One policy on each stockholder (see footnote 7, page 181).
Premiums	Paid by individual stockholders.	Paid by trustee from funds obtained from stockholders (see footnote 5, page 181).
Taxation of Life Insurance Death Benefits	Received tax-free by surviving stockholders (but may be subject to notice and consent requirements, see pages 319-321).	Received tax-free by trustee as agent for surviving stockholders (but may be subject to notice and consent requirements, see pages 319-321).
Effect on Surviving Stockholders	Surviving stockholder's basis in stock increases in an amount equal to price paid for deceased's interest.	Surviving stockholder's basis in stock increases in an amount equal to price paid for deceased's interest.
Taxation of Deceased Stockholder's Heirs	Basis is stepped-up at death and no gain recognized (see page 556).	Basis is stepped-up at death and no gain recognized (see page 556).
Flexibility to Change Plans	Transfer of existing policies to corporation could be an exception to transfer for value rules (see pages 568-569).	Transfer of existing policies to corporation could be an exception to transfer for value rules. However, there is a potential transfer-for-value problem after the first death (see footnote 8, page 181 and pages 568-569).

Note: A trusteed cross purchase agreement can also be used with a partnership (see footnote 1, page 181).

QUALIFIED PLANS CHECKLIST

Element	**Limitation**
Maximum limits.	**Defined Benefit Plan:** Benefits are limited to the lesser of 100% of pay, or $225,000 (as indexed for 2019). **Defined Contribution Plan:** The annual additions limit is the lesser of 100% of salary, or $56,000 (as indexed for 2019). In a profit sharing plan the total annual employer deduction is 25% of total compensation of plan participants. **401(k) Plans (traditional or safe harbor):** During calendar year 2019, the allowable employee deferral is $19,000 (during 2019 participants who are age 50 or over may be permitted to make additional catch-up contributions of $6,000). SIMPLE 401(k) plans are limited in 2019 to $13,000 elective deferrals and $3,000 catch-up.
Eligibility to participate.	Exclusions are permitted for age and years of service (maximum of age 21 and one year of service).
Integration with Social Security.	A plan integrated with Social Security will often permit significantly higher benefits for higher paid employees within certain limits. Defined *contribution* plans may provide additional contributions of up to 5.7% of pay in excess of current Social Security wage base ($132,900 in 2019). Defined *benefit* plans may provide additional monthly benefits of up to the lesser of .75% of earnings, or the base benefit percentage for the plan year. In either type of plan the percentage of total contributions/benefits for those above the "integration level" may not be more than two times the percentage of contributions/benefits below that level. In addition, the disparity between the two percentages must be uniform with respect to all participants. If additional requirements are met, the "integration level" may be lower than the Social Security wage base.
Employee vesting.	Employer contributions need not become immediately and irrevocably vested, but may be contingent upon continued employment. Thus, costs to the employer may be reduced or benefits increased for employees who continue their employment. "Top-heavy" plans, and certain employer match contributions, are subject to special rapid vesting rules.

Element	Limitation
Definition of a "top heavy" plan.	A plan is top heavy if for "key employees" the present value of accrued benefits in a defined *benefit* plan or account balances in a defined *contribution* plan exceeds 60% of accrued benefits or account balances for all employees. Key employees include: (1) officers earning more than $180,000 (as indexed for 2019), (2) any 5% owner of the employer, and (3) any 1% owner who earns more than $150,000 per year.
For top-heavy plan purposes, definition of the term "officer."	The term "officer" has a very special meaning. Officers of any employer include no more than either: (1) 50 employees; or, if *less*, (2) the greater of 3 employees or 10% of the employee group. In other words, the maximum number of employees considered officers is 10% of the employee group, up to 50.
Fund investment flexibility.	Trustee may direct the investments into nearly any type of investment media. Strict fiduciary standards apply.
Distributions.	Generally, distributions to a non-5%-owner must be started by April 1 of the year following the year the individual attains age 70½ or retires, whichever is later. Distributions to a 5%-owner cannot be delayed until retirement.
Premature distributions.	Distributions prior to age 59½ will be subject to a 10% penalty tax (25% during first two years with SIMPLE IRA) unless distribution is due to death, disability, separation from service after age 55, or in the event of certain specified hardships. The penalty tax is also waived if the distribution is annuitized or to the extent needed to pay family medical expenses in excess of 7½% of adjusted gross income.
Federal estate tax status of death benefits.	Fully included in estate.
Availability of $6,000 IRA deduction (in 2019).	*Not* available if covered by pension, profit sharing or stock bonus plan, a 403(b) plan, a SIMPLE IRA, a SEP, or a government plan and adjusted gross income in 2019 exceeds: (1) $74,000 – individual return (2) $123,000 – joint return *Partially* deductible if covered by plan (listed above) and adjusted gross income ranges from: (1) $64,000-$74,000 – individual return. (2) $103,000-$123,000 – joint return *Fully* available if not covered by listed plan. See discussions on page 397 and page 521.

401(k) PLAN DESIGNS

Traditional 401(k) Plan

Maximum salary deferral is $19,000 in 2019, plus $6,000 if age 50 or over.

Employer can sponsor other qualified retirement plans.

Employer contribution is not required. Overall maximum contribution per employee limited to 100% of compensation and not to exceed $56,000 in 2019.

Graduated vesting allowed on employer contributions, but immediate vesting required on employee contributions.

Subject to both ADP/ACP tests and top heavy rules.

See also, chart on page 271.

Safe Harbor 401(k) Plan

Maximum salary deferral is $19,000 in 2019, plus $6,000 if age 50 or over.

Employer can sponsor other qualified retirement plans.

Employer contribution is required, either:

- 100% on first 3% of employee deferral, plus 50% of next 2% of employee deferral (total of 4%), or
- 3% of compensation to all eligible employees (i.e., nonelective).

Immediate vesting is required.

Deemed to satisfy ADP/ACP tests and generally not subject to top heavy rules.

SIMPLE 401(k) Plan

Maximum salary deferral is $13,000 in 2019, plus $3,000 if age 50 or over.

Employer cannot sponsor other qualified retirement plans. Employer limited to 100 or fewer eligible employees.

Employer contribution is required, either:

- 100% on up to 3% of employee's compensation, or
- 2% of compensation to all eligible employees (i.e., nonelective).

Immediate vesting is required.

Deemed to satisfy ADP/ACP tests and not subject to top heavy rules.

Automatic Enrollment Safe Harbor 401(k) Plan

(available for plan years beginning on or after January 1, 2008)

Default elective deferral must be at least 3% the 1st year, 4% the 2nd year, 5% the 3rd year, and 6% the 4th year (not to exceed 10% in any year).

Employer contribution is required, either:

- 100% on first 1% of compensation, plus 50% on next 5% (maximum of 3½%), or
- 3% of compensation to all eligible employees (i.e., nonelective).

Vesting after two years of service is allowed on employer contributions.

Deemed to satisfy ADP/ACP tests and not subject to top-heavy rules.

- **Roth 401(k) Feature**
  1. This is a separate account to which after-tax contributions may be designated.
  2. Distributions are potentially tax-free, if certain requirements are met.
  3. Subject to the same salary deferral limit as overall plan.
  4. See also, discussion on page 526.
- **Individual 401(k) Plan**
  1. Also referred to as a solo or mini-401(k) plan.
  2. This is a single-participant profit sharing plan with 401(k) features (the name itself has been created by the marketplace, it is not found in the Code).
  3. Requirements depend on which of the four designs above is used.
  4. See also, discussion on page 404.

EMPLOYEE BENEFIT LIMITS

Type of Limit	Year				
	2015	2016	2017	2018	2019
Defined Benefit Section 415	210,000[1]	210,000	215,000	220,000	225,000
Defined Contribution Section 415	53,000[2] or 100% of salary	53,000 or 100% of salary	54,000 or 100% of salary	55,000 or 100% of salary	56,000 or 100% of salary
Elective Deferral for traditional and safe harbor 401(k) Plans, 403(b) Plans (TDAs), & SEPs	18,000[3]	18,000	18,000	18,500	19,000
Catch-Up for traditional and safe harbor 401(k) Plans (age 50 and over)[4]	6,000[3]	6,000	6,000	6,000	6,000
Catch-Up for 403(b) Plans (TDAs)[4]					
age 50 and over	6,000[3]	6,000	6,000	6,000	6,000
15 years of service	3,000	3,000	3,000	3,000	6,000
Elective Deferral Limit for Section 457	18,000[4]	18,000	18,000	18,500	19,000
Catch-Up for Section 457 Plans - age 50 and over[4]					
other than last 3 year before retirement[5]	6,000[3]	6,000	6,000	6,000	6,000
during last 3 years before retirement	18,000[3]	18,000	18,000	18,500	19,000
Elective Deferral Limit for SIMPLE IRAs and SIMPLE 401(k) Plans	12,500	12,500	12,000	12,500	13,000
Catch-Up for SIMPLE IRAs and SIMPLE 401(k) Plans[4]	3,000[3]	3,000	3,000	3,000	3,000
Highly Compensated Employee Definitional Limit	120,000[1]	120,000	120,000	120,000	125,000
Maximum Compensation for Qualified Plans, SEPs, TSAs, & VEBAs	265,000[1]	265,000	270,000	275,000	280,000

[1] Subject to indexing in $5,000 increments.

[2] Subject to indexing in $1,000 increments.

[3] Subject to indexing in $500 increments.

[4] Catch-up amounts are in addition to the elective deferral limit.

[5] Use the participant's compensation, reduced by any other elective deferrals made that year, if less than the applicable dollar amount shown in the table.

THE IRA SPECTRUM

Type	Eligibility for Plan	Limits on Contributions[1]	Deductible	Tax Advantages	Withdrawals/Distributions
Roth (page 527)	Individual: In 2019 AGI[2] less than $137,000 (phase-out $122,000-$137,000) Married filing jointly: In 2019 AGI[2] less than $203,000 (phase-out $193,000-$203,000)	Individual: $6,000. Married filing jointly: $12,000. Contributions allowed after age 70½. Catch-up for individuals who have reached age 50 is $1,000.	No	Tax-free earnings. Early withdrawals of contributions tax-free and penalty-free.	Tax-free if after 5 years and: after age 59½, for first home, disability, or upon death. Distribution *not* required at age 70½.
Traditional – deductible (page 405)	Not active participant in employer-sponsored retirement plan, or Individual: In 2019 AGI[2] less than $74,000 (phase-out $64,000-$74,000). Married filing jointly: In 2019 AGI[2] less than $123,000 (phase-out $103,000-$123,000).	Individual: $6,000. Married filing jointly: $12,000. Contributions *not* allowed after age 70½. Catch-up for individuals who have reached age 50 is $1,000.	Yes	Tax-deferred earnings, but taxable upon withdrawal.	Penalty-free if after age 59½, for first home, higher education, or upon death. Distribution required at age 70½.
SIMPLE (page 548)	Self-employed or employed by company with 100 employees or less.	Employer: 3% matching or 2% non-elective. Employee: $13,000. Catch-up for individuals who have reached age 50 is $3,000.	Contributions are before taxes.	Tax-deferred earnings, but withdrawals taxable.	Distribution required at age 70½.
SEP (page 549)	Self-employed or employed by sponsoring employer.	Up to 25% of employees salary or $56,000 maximum. See also SEP-IRA, page 549.	Contributions are before taxes.	Tax-deferred earnings, but withdrawals taxable.	Distribution required at age 70½.

[1]Combined annual contributions to both Roth IRA and Traditional IRA are limited to $6,000 (effectively, $12,000 for a married couple).

[2]AGI stands for adjusted gross income.

WHICH IRA — ROTH OR TRADITIONAL?

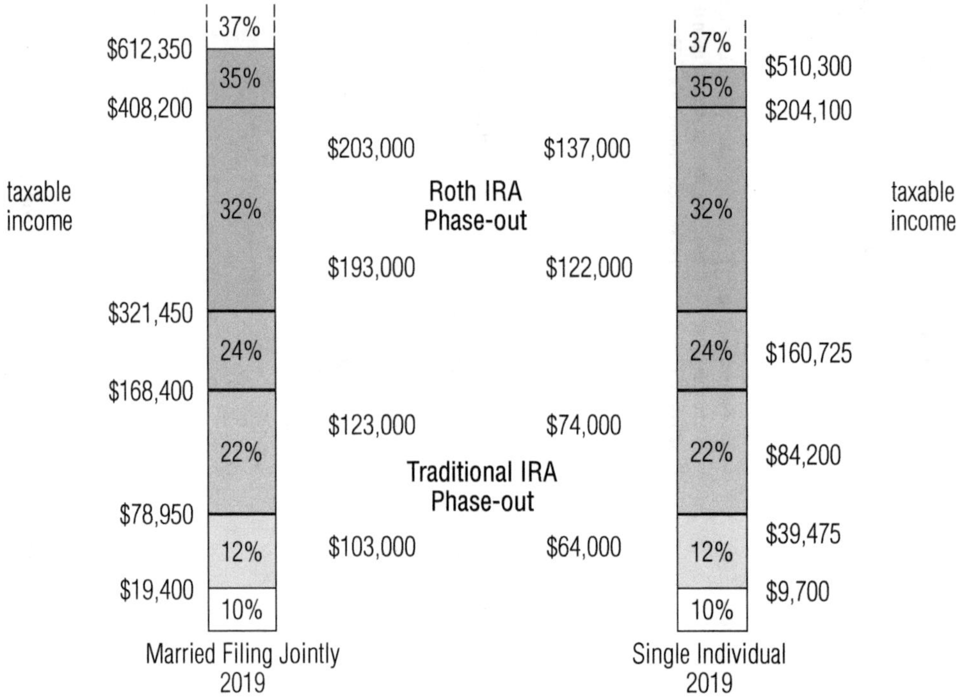

A Roth IRA offers the following potential advantages: (1) distributions are not required at age 70½; (2) contributions may continue after reaching age 70½; (3) phaseout limits are higher than those for deductible contributions to a Traditional IRA; and (4) tax-free retirement distributions will not push modified adjusted gross income above the threshold that triggers taxation of Social Security benefits (see page 550). This analysis focuses on after-tax accumulations and requires assumptions regarding tax rates prior to and after retirement (the above chart may help).

Assuming the **same** tax rate prior to and after retirement: (1) there is no difference between the after-tax distributions from a Roth IRA and a Traditional IRA if all funds can be deposited in a Traditional IRA, or other tax deductible fund (see Table A, page 633); (2) the Roth IRA offers the advantage of larger after-tax distributions if before-tax funds exceed the $6,000 limit that can be deposited in a Traditional IRA and the excess must be placed in a nondeductible side fund (see Table B, page 633). Further, the Roth IRA advantage increases if the side fund earnings are currently taxed.

Assuming a **lower** tax rate after retirement, the Traditional IRA generally provides larger after-tax distributions (i.e., 25 percent prior to retirement and 15 percent after retirement). For active participants, no comparison need be made assuming a tax rate higher than 22 percent since deductible contributions to a Traditional IRA are phased out before reaching the 24 percent tax rate (i.e., no deduction is allowed in 2019 for "married filing jointly" once modified adjusted gross income exceeds $123,000 and for a "single individual" once modified adjusted gross income exceeds $74,000). Note that marginal tax rates in the above chart vary according to *taxable income*, whereas IRA contributions are phased out according to *modified adjusted gross income* (see pages 405, 527, 628, and 631). Taxable income is equal to adjusted gross income less deductions and personal exemptions.

Assuming a **higher** tax rate after retirement, the Roth IRA provides larger after-tax distributions (e.g., 25 percent prior to retirement and 28 percent after retirement).

WHICH IRA — ROTH OR TRADITIONAL? (continued)

Table A – This table assumes an 8 percent interest rate and 25 percent tax rate. The nondeductible Roth IRA deposit requires $1,333 before taxes (1,000/(1 - .25) = 1,333). This is the same as making a deductible deposit of $1,333 to a Traditional IRA. There is no Roth IRA advantage.

	Roth IRA			Traditional IRA		
Year	Deposit	Plus Interest	Value	Deposit	Plus Interest	Value
1	1,000	80	1,080	1,333	107	1,440
2	1,000	166	2,246	1,333	222	2,995
3	1,000	260	3,506	1,333	346	4,675
4	1,000	360	4,867	1,333	481	6,489
5	1,000	469	6,336	1,333	626	8,448
6	1,000	587	7,923	1,333	782	10,564
7	1,000	714	9,637	1,333	952	12,849
8	1,000	851	11,488	1,333	1,135	15,317
9	1,000	999	13,487	1,333	1,332	17,982
10	1,000	1,159	15,645	1,333	1,545	20,861
11	1,000	1,332	17,977	1,333	1,776	23,970
12	1,000	1,518	20,495	1,333	2,024	27,327
13	1,000	1,720	23,215	1,333	2,293	30,953
14	1,000	1,937	26,152	1,333	2,583	34,869
15	1,000	2,172	29,324	1,333	2,896	39,099
16	1,000	2,426	32,750	1,333	3,235	43,667
17	1,000	2,700	36,450	1,333	3,600	48,600
18	1,000	2,996	40,446	1,333	3,995	53,928
19	1,000	3,316	44,762	1,333	4,421	59,683
20	1,000	3,661	49,423	1,333	4,881	65,897
Less Taxes			0			16,474
Net Distribution			49,423			49,423

Table B – This table assumes an 8 percent interest rate and 25 percent tax rate. The nondeductible Roth IRA deposit requires $7,333 before taxes (5,500/(1 – .25) = 7,333). This is the same as making a deductible deposit of $5,500 to a Traditional IRA *plus* a nondeductible deposit of $1,375 to a Side Fund (5,500 + 1,375/(1 – .25) = 7,333). The Roth IRA advantage is $6,364 when compared to a currently taxed side fund (190,956 – 143,217 – 41,395 = 6,364) and $5,060 when compared to a tax deferred side fund (190,956 – 143,217 – 42,679 = 5,060).

	Roth IRA		Traditional IRA		Side Fund		
Year	Deposit	Value	Deposit	Value	Deposit	Currently Taxed	Tax Deferred
1	5,500	5,775	5,500	5,775	1,375	1,427	1,444
2	5,500	11,839	5,500	11,839	1,375	2,907	2,960
3	5,500	18,206	5,500	18,206	1,375	4,442	4,551
4	5,500	24,891	5,500	24,891	1,375	6,035	6,223
5	5,500	31,911	5,500	31,911	1,375	7,688	7,978
6	5,500	39,281	5,500	39,281	1,375	9,403	9,820
7	5,500	47,020	5,500	47,202	1,375	11,182	11,755
8	5,500	55,146	5,500	55,146	1,375	13,028	13,787
9	5,500	63,678	5,500	63,678	1,375	14,943	15,920
10	5,500	72,637	5,500	72,637	1,375	16,930	18,159
11	5,500	82044	5,500	82,044	1,375	18,992	20,511
12	5,500	91,921	5,500	91,921	1,375	21,130	22,980
13	5,500	102,292	5,500	102,292	1,375	23,349	25,573
14	5,500	113,182	5,500	113,182	1,375	25,652	28,296
15	5,500	124,616	5,500	124,616	1,375	28,040	31,154
16	5,500	136,622	5,500	136,622	1,375	30,518	34,156
17	5,500	149,228	5,500	149,228	1,375	33,089	37,307
18	5,500	162,465	5,500	162,465	1,375	35,756	40,616
19	5,500	176,363	5,500	176,363	1,375	38,524	44,091
20	5,500	190,956	5,500	190,956	1,375	41,395	47,739
Less Taxes				47,739		0	5,060
Net Distribution		190,956		143,217		41,395	42,679

EDUCATIONAL TAX INCENTIVES

Contributions, Benefits, & Offsets

Incentive	Limit	Tax Nature	Covers	AGI Phaseout[1]	Note
American Opportunity Credit (§25A)	2,500	Credit against taxes (refundable in part).	First *four* years of post-secondary education.	S: 80,000-90,000 J: 160,000-180,000	ABC
Lifetime Learning Credit (§25A)	2,000	Credit against taxes.	Unlimited number of years.	S: 55,000-65,000 J: 110,000-130,000	ABC
Trade or Business Expense (§162)	None.	Below-line deduction (must itemize).	Employee expenses in maintaining or improving skills.	None.	n/a
Employer Tuition Reimbursement (§127)	5,250	Not included in income.	Covers both undergraduate and graduate programs.	None.	A
Coverdell Education Savings Account (§530)	2,000	Contributions not deductible; but earnings are tax-free.	Qualified education expenses.[2]	S: 95,000-110,000 J: 190,000-220,000	B
Student Loans (§221)	2,500	Above-line deduction for interest (need not itemize).	Student loan interest.	S: 65,000-80,000 J: 135,000-165,000	n/a
Section 529 Plans	Varies.	Contributions not deductible; but distributions are tax-free.	Tuition, fees, special-needs services, room, board, books, supplies, and equipment[2].	None.	C
Educational Savings Bonds (§135)	Varies.	Interest tax-free.	Qualified educational expenses.	S: 79,700-94,700 J: 119,550-149,550	n/a

A – American Opportunity and Lifetime Learning Credits are not available for the same expense excluded as an Employer Tuition Reimbursement.

B – Earnings on Coverdell Education Savings Account are not tax-free if used for same expenses as American Opportunity and Lifetime Learning Credits.

C – Section 529 qualifying expenses are reduced to the extent they are used in determining American Opportunity and Lifetime Learning Credits.

[1] S – single taxpayer; J – married filing joint return.

[2] Includes elementary and secondary education (K-12) at private, public, or religious institutions, and post secondary education at accredited public, nonprofit, and proprietary institutions (college and graduate programs).

HISTORICAL INCREASES OF SOCIAL SECURITY TAXES

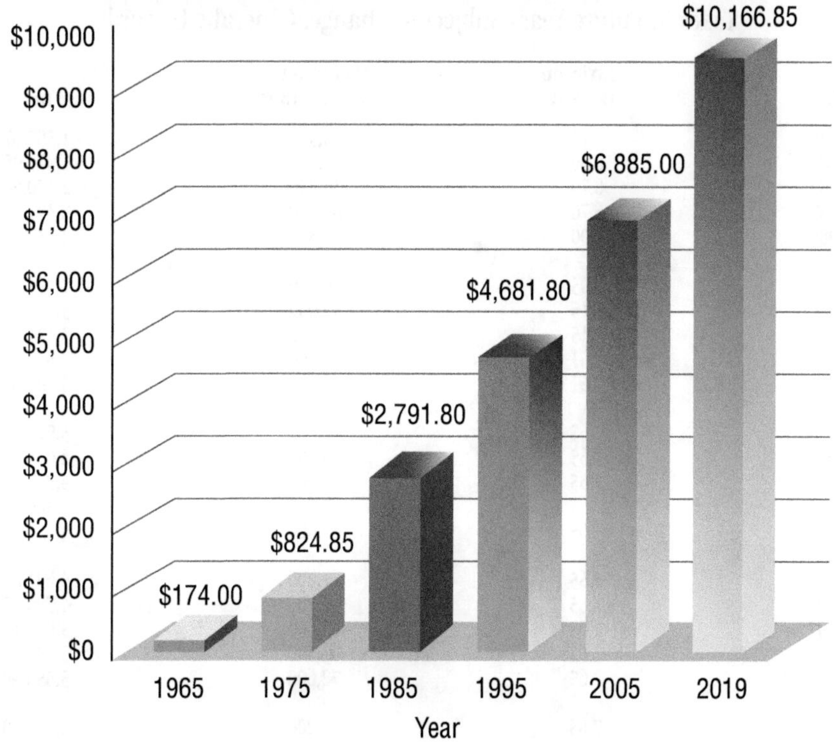

Social Security Tax. The Social Security Tax (FICA) is paid by both the employer and the employee. For example, in 2019 an employer who pays an employee wages of $132,900 per year will pay an additional $10,166.85 (Social Security Taxes equal to 7.65% of $132,900). The employee must also pay $10,166.85 (6.2% OASDI plus 1.45% hospital insurance tax). (The OASDI rate reduction of 2% that was available in 2012 was not extended by Congress.)

Federal Unemployment Tax. In addition to these Social Security Taxes, Unemployment Taxes may have to be paid. In 2019, the Federal Unemployment Tax (FUTA) is 6.0% of the first $7,000 of wages paid to each employee, or $420 (credit is given to employers for contributions to state unemployment funds).

Self-Employment Tax. An individual who is self-employed must pay a Self-Employment Tax on net earnings from self-employment when these earnings are $400 or more. The tax is equal to the combined employer-employee Social Security tax and is 12.40% OASDI tax on the first $132,900 of self-employment income in 2019, or a maximum tax of $16,479.60, plus 2.90% hospital insurance tax on all self-employment income in 2019. (The OASDI rate reduction of 2% that was available in 2012 was not extended by Congress.) For self-employed individuals with earnings in excess of certain filing status thresholds (e.g., $250,000 if married filing jointly and $200,000 if filing single) the Medicare portion of the self-employment tax is increased by 0.9 percent – from 2.90% to 3.80%.

Tax on Investment Income. Effective January 1, 2013, the 2010 Health Care Tax Act imposes a 3.80% Medicare tax on investment income on the lesser of (a) net investment income or (b) the excess of modified adjusted gross income in excess of $250,000 in the case of married taxpayers filing a joint return, $125,000 for married taxpayers filing a separate return, and $200,000 for all other taxpayers.

SOCIAL SECURITY PAYROLL TAXES

Taxes in Future Years Subject to Change, Generally Upward!

Year	Maximum Tax Rate	Maximum Taxable Earnings	Tax
1980	6.13	25,900	1,587.67
1981	6.65	29,700	1,975.05
1982	6.70	32,400	2,170.80
1983	6.70	35,700	2,391.90
1984	7.00	37,800	2,532.60
1985	7.05	39,600	2,791.80
1986	7.15	42,000	3,003.00
1987	7.15	43,800	3,131.70
1988	7.51	45,000	3,379.50
1989	7.51	48,000	3,604.80
1990	7.65	51,300	3,924.45
1991	7.65	53,400	4,085.10
1992	7.65	55,500	4,245.75
1993	7.65	57,600	4,406.40
1994	7.65	60,600	4,635.90
1995	7.65	61,200	4,681.80
1996	7.65	62,700	4,796.55
1997	7.65	65,400	5,003.10
1998	7.65	68,400	5,232.60
1999	7.65	72,600	5,553.90
2000	7.65	76,200	5,829.30
2001	7.65	80,400	6,150.60
2002	7.65	84,900	6,494.85
2003	7.65	87,000	6,655.50
2004	7.65	87,900	6,724.35
2005	7.65	90,000	6,885.00
2006	7.65	94,200	7,206.30
2007	7.65	97,500	7,458.75
2008	7.65	102,000	7,803.00
2009	7.65	106,800	8,170.20
2010	7.65	106,800	8,170.20
2011	5.65	106,800	6,034.20
2012	5.65	110,100	6,220.65
2013	7.65	113,700	8,823.12
2014	7.65	117,000	8,950.50
2015	7.65	118,500	9,027.00
2016	7.65	118,500	9,065.25
2017	7.65	127,200	9,730.80
2018	7.65	128,400	9,822.60
2019	7.65	132,900	10,166.85

Note: All earnings above $132,900 are subject to an additional 1.45% hospital insurance tax (see page 635).

SOCIAL SECURITY RETIREMENT BENEFITS

When To Take

Social Security retirement benefits are based upon the worker's primary insurance amount (PIA). The PIA is the monthly amount that would be paid to a worker who receives benefits at normal retirement age. The normal retirement age differs, depending upon the worker's year of birth.

Year of birth	Normal Retirement Age	Year of birth	Normal Retirement Age
Before 1938	65 years	1955	66 years, 2 months
1939	65 years, 2 months	1956	66 years, 4 months
1940	65 years, 6 months	1957	66 years, 6 months
1941	65 years, 8 months	1958	66 years, 8 months
1942	65 years, 10 months	1959	66 years, 10 months
1943-1954	66 years	1960 and after	67 years

A worker can take retirement benefits as early as age 62, but the amount received is calculated by *reducing* the PIA by 5/9 of 1 percent per month for the first 36 months, plus 5/12 of 1 percent for any additional months. For example, a worker taking payments three years prior to normal retirement age will receive only 80 percent of his PIA (i.e., $100 - (5/9 \times 36) = 80$). In addition, a worker who no longer pays social security taxes fails to *increase* his PIA.

Many authorities agree that, for the average worker, it is best to wait until normal retirement age in order to take full (unreduced) retirement benefits. Despite this, Social Security records indicate that well over 50 percent of retiring workers take early (reduced) benefits. Clearly, if life expectancy is less than average, then taking an early benefit is indicated. However, if an individual is in good health, and does not require the money to provide for retirement, the following table may assist in making the decision:

Cross-Over Point Based Upon Life Expectancy*			
Discount Rate	When Reached	Discount Rate	When Reached
0%	13 years, 3 months	6%	19 years, 9 months
2%	14 years, 8 months	8%	26 years, 1 month
4%	16 years, 8 months	10%	Never

This table compares the present values of the income streams produced by reduced (early) and unreduced (normal) retirement benefits. For example, using a discount rate of 4%, for the first 16 years and 8 months the present value of reduced retirement payments are greater than the present value of unreduced retirement payments (assuming retirement three years prior to normal retirement age, and 2.5% annual increases in retirement benefits); when the cross-over point is reached at 16 years and 8 months, the present value of the unreduced benefits will finally exceed the present value of the reduced benefits. Absent other considerations, a person who views the time value of money at 4% should consider early retirement if he expects to live *less than* 16 years and 8 months. On the other hand, if he expects to live *at least* 16 years and 8 months, he should wait until normal retirement. See also, Compound Interest & Present Value of Money, page 616.

* Assumes payments begin 36 months prior to normal retirement age, and Social Security benefit increases of 2.5% per year (the average increase during the 10-year period 2007-2016).

PROJECTED EARNINGS

5% Annual Increase In Earnings

Present Earnings	Yearly Earnings In: 5 Years	10 Years	15 Years	20 Years	Total Earning Over Next: 10 Years	20 Years
10,000	12,763	16,289	20,789	26,533	125,779	330,660
12,000	15,315	19,547	24,947	31,840	150,935	396,791
14,000	17,868	22,805	29,105	37,146	176,090	462,923
16,000	20,421	26,062	33,263	42,453	201,246	529,055
18,000	22,973	29,320	37,421	47,759	226,402	595,187
20,000	25,526	32,578	41,579	53,066	251,558	661,319
25,000	31,907	40,722	51,973	66,332	314,447	826,649
30,000	38,288	48,867	62,368	79,599	377,337	991,979
35,000	44,670	57,011	72,762	92,865	440,226	1,157,308
40,000	51,051	65,156	83,157	106,132	503,116	1,322,638
45,000	57,433	73,300	93,552	119,398	566,005	1,487,968
50,000	63,814	81,445	103,946	132,665	628,895	1,653,298
60,000	76,577	97,734	124,736	159,198	754,674	1,983,957
70,000	89,340	114,023	145,525	185,731	880,452	2,314,617
80,000	102,103	130,312	166,314	212,264	1,006,231	2,645,276
90,000	114,865	146,601	187,104	238,797	1,132,010	2,975,936
100,000	127,628	162,889	207,893	265,330	1,257,789	3,306,595

8% Annual Increase In Earnings

Present Earnings	Yearly Earnings In: 5 Years	10 Years	15 Years	20 Years	Total Earnings Over Next: 10 Years	20 Years
10,000	14,693	21,589	31,722	46,610	144,866	457,620
12,000	17,632	25,907	38,066	55,931	173,839	549,144
14,000	20,571	30,225	44,410	65,253	202,812	640,667
16,000	23,509	34,543	50,755	74,575	231,785	732,191
18,000	26,448	38,861	57,099	83,897	260,758	823,715
20,000	29,387	43,178	63,443	93,219	289,731	915,239
25,000	36,733	53,973	79,304	116,524	362,164	1,144,049
30,000	44,080	64,768	95,165	139,829	434,597	1,372,859
35,000	51,426	75,562	111,026	163,133	507,030	1,601,669
40,000	58,773	86,357	126,887	186,438	579,462	1,830,479
45,000	66,120	97,152	142,748	209,743	651,895	2,059,288
50,000	73,466	107,946	158,608	233,048	724,328	2,288,098
60,000	88,160	129,535	190,330	279,657	869,194	2,745,718
70,000	102,853	151,125	222,052	326,267	1,014,059	3,203,337
80,000	117,546	172,714	253,774	372,877	1,158,925	3,660,957
90,000	132,240	194,303	285,495	419,486	1,303,791	4,118,577
100,000	146,933	215,892	317,217	466,096	1,448,656	4,576,196

Explanation of Tables. These tables assume that earnings increase at an annual rate of either 5 or 8 percent. For example, at annual increases of 5 percent an individual earning $50,000 today would be earning $81,445 in 10 Years, and total earnings over 10 Years would be $628,895.

PENALTY OF WAITING

What It Takes To Save $100,000 By Age 65
Assuming 6% Interest

Current Age	Monthly Deposit	Total Deposits	Penalty of Waiting 1 Year	Penalty of Waiting 5 Years
21	40.42	21,342	877	4,707
22	43.06	22,219	905	4,867
23	45.88	23,124	945	5,043
24	48.92	24,069	973	5,208
25	52.17	25,042	1,007	5,387
26	55.66	26,049	1,037	5,567
27	59.40	27,086	1,081	5,758
28	63.44	28,167	1,110	5,944
29	67.77	29,277	1,152	6,137
30	72.45	30,429	1,187	6,334
31	77.49	31,616	1,228	6,535
32	82.94	32,844	1,267	6,740
33	88.83	34,111	1,303	6,950
34	95.20	35,414	1,349	7,168
35	102.12	36,763	1,388	7,382
36	109.63	38,151	1,433	7,604
37	117.81	39,584	1,477	7,830
38	126.73	41,061	1,521	8,059
39	136.48	42,582	1,563	8,289
40	147.15	44,145	1,610	8,528
41	158.87	45,755	1,659	8,769
42	171.79	47,414	1,706	9,010
43	186.06	49,120	1,751	9,257
44	201.87	50,871	1,802	9,507
45	219.47	52,673	1,851	9,760
46	239.14	54,524	1,900	10,017
47	261.22	56,424	1,953	10,277
48	286.16	58,377	2,001	10,536
49	314.47	60,378	2,055	10,800
50	346.85	62,433	2,108	11,067
51	384.17	64,541	2,160	11,338
52	427.57	66,701	2,212	11,610
53	478.56	68,913	2,265	11,878
54	539.23	71,178	2,322	12,160
55	612.50	73,500	2,379	12,433
56	702.58	75,879	2,432	12,697
57	815.74	78,311	2,480	12,971
58	961.80	80,791	2,547	13,268
59	1,157.47	83,338	2,595	13,542
60	1,432.21	85,933	2,643	14,067

Explanation of Table: This table shows the amount of money which must be deposited at the beginning of each month in order to accumulate $100,000 by age 65. Interest is credited at a 6 percent net annual rate and is compounded monthly (i.e., it is credited at the end of each month assuming a 6 percent annual after tax or untaxed growth). The Penalty Of Waiting 1 Year is calculated by subtracting total deposits at the current age from total deposits one year later (e.g., at age 45 the penalty of waiting one year is $54,524 - $52,673, or $1,851). The Penalty Of Waiting 5 Years is calculated by subtracting total deposits at the current age from total deposits five years later (e.g., at age 45 the penalty of waiting five years is $62,433 - $52,673, or $9,760).

EARLY SAVER vs. LATE SAVER

The Advantage Of Saving Early For Retirement
Assuming 8% Interest

	Age	Early Saver	Late Saver	Age	Early Saver	Late Saver	Age	Early Saver	Late Saver
	30	$2,000	0						
	31	2,000	0						
	32	2,000	0						
	33	2,000	0						
	34	2,000	0						
	35	2,000	0						
	36	2,000	0						
	37	2,000	0						
	38	2,000	0						
	39	2,000	0						
	40	0	$2,000	40	$2,000	0			
	41	0	2,000	41	2,000	0			
	42	0	2,000	42	2,000	0			
	43	0	2,000	43	2,000	0			
	44	0	2,000	44	2,000	0			
	45	0	2,000	45	2,000	0			
	46	0	2,000	46	2,000	0			
	47	0	2,000	47	2,000	0			
	48	0	2,000	48	0	$2,000			
	49	0	2,000	49	0	2,000			
	50	0	2,000	50	0	2,000	50	$2,000	0
	51	0	2,000	51	0	2,000	51	2,000	0
	52	0	2,000	52	0	2,000	52	2,000	0
	53	0	2,000	53	0	2,000	53	2,000	0
	54	0	2,000	54	0	2,000	54	2,000	0
	55	0	2,000	55	0	2,000	55	2,000	0
	56	0	2,000	56	0	2,000	56	0	$2,000
	57	0	2,000	57	0	2,000	57	0	2,000
	58	0	2,000	58	0	2,000	58	0	2,000
	59	0	2,000	59	0	2,000	59	0	2,000
	60	0	2,000	60	0	2,000	60	0	2,000
	61	0	2,000	61	0	2,000	61	0	2,000
	62	0	2,000	62	0	2,000	62	0	2,000
	63	0	2,000	63	0	2,000	63	0	2,000
	64	0	2,000	64	0	2,000	64	0	2,000
Total Invested		$20,000	$50,000		$16,000	$34,000		$12,000	$18,00
Amount at Age 65		$214,296	$157,909		$85,008	$72,900		$31,676	$26,973

Explanation of Table: This table demonstrates the advantage of beginning to save early for retirement. For example, a 40-year-old Early Saver who saves $2,000 per year for eight years, and earns 8 percent per year on his savings, will accumulate $85,008 by age 65. In comparison, a 48-year-old Late Saver who saves $2,000 per year until age 65, will accumulate only $72,900. Whereas the Late Saver has invested $18,000 more than the Early Saver, he has accumulated $12,108 less than the Early Saver ($34,000 - $16,000 = $18,000; $85,008 - $72,900 = $12,108). If savings had been placed in a tax deferred investment, then the Amount At Age 65 will likely be reduced by income taxes.

DOLLAR COST AVERAGING

Investing A Fixed Sum At Regular Intervals
means that
More Shares Are Bought At Low Prices Than High Prices
and
Average Cost Is Lower Than Average Share Price

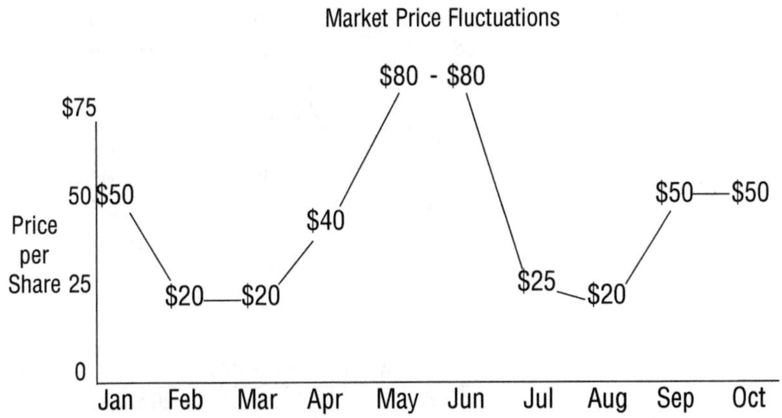

INVESTING FIXED SUM - DOLLAR COST AVERAGING

											Totals
Cost	$100	$100	$100	$100	$100	$100	$100	$100	$100	$100	$1,000
Shares	2	5	5	2.5	1.25	1.25	4	5	2	2	30

Average Cost Per Share $33.33

↑ end up with same number of shares ↓

BUYING FIXED NUMBER OF SHARES

Shares	3	3	3	3	3	3	3	3	3	3	30
Cost	$150	$60	$60	$120	$240	$240	$75	$60	$150	$150	$1,305

Average Cost Per Share $43.50

Note. Dollar cost averaging neither guarantees a profit nor protects against a loss.

HOW MONEY GROWS

How Much Monthly Savings Will Accumulate To

	Accumulated at 5%		
Save Per Month	5 Years	10 Years	20 Years
50	3,414	7,796	20,637
100	6,829	15,593	41,275
250	17,072	38,982	103,187
500	34,145	77,965	206,373
1,000	68,289	155,929	412,746

	Accumulated at 8%		
Save Per Month	5 Years	10 Years	20 Years
50	3,698	9,208	29,647
100	7,397	18,417	59,295
250	18,492	46,041	148,237
500	36,983	92,083	296,474
1,000	73,967	184,166	592,947

	Accumulated at 10%		
Save Per Month	5 Years	10 Years	20 Years
50	3,904	10,328	38,285
100	7,808	20,655	76,570
250	19,521	51,638	191,424
500	39,041	103,276	382,848
1,000	78,082	206,552	765,697

Explanation of Table. All accumulations assume monthly contributions are made on the first day of the month with interest compounded monthly. All results are rounded to the nearest whole dollar. Accumulated amounts assume the funds are invested at a rate of 5, 8, or 10 percent before taxes (i.e., during the accumulation phase appreciation is not subject to current income taxation). For example, if an individual invested $100 per month and earned 8 percent compounded monthly, at the end of 10 years the funds would accumulate to $18,417. Referring to the table How Money Goes on page 643, if this $18,417 were invested at 5 percent per year compounded monthly, it would provide $195 per month for 10 years or $121 per month for 20 years. Withdrawing interest only, without invading principal, would provide $77 per month. All withdrawal amounts are before taxes.

HOW MONEY GOES

How Much Can Be Withdrawn Monthly From A Given Accumulation

Amount	At 5% Interest			At 8% Interest		
Accumulated	10 years	20 Years	Forever	10 Years	20 Years	Forever
3,414	36	22	14	41	28	23
3,698	39	24	15	45	31	25
3,904	41	26	16	47	32	26
6,829	72	45	28	82	57	46
7,397	78	49	31	89	61	49
7,796	82	51	32	94	65	52
7,808	82	51	33	94	65	52
9,208	97	61	38	111	77	61
10,328	109	68	43	124	86	69
15,593	165	102	65	188	130	104
17,072	180	112	71	206	142	114
18,417	195	121	77	222	153	123
18,492	195	122	77	223	154	123
19,521	206	128	81	235	162	130
20,637	218	136	86	249	171	138
20,655	218	136	86	249	172	138
29,647	313	195	124	357	246	198
34,145	361	224	142	412	284	228
36,983	391	243	154	446	307	247
38,285	404	252	160	461	318	255
38,982	412	256	162	470	324	260
39,041	412	257	163	471	324	260
41,275	436	271	172	497	343	275
46,041	486	303	192	555	383	307
51,638	545	339	215	622	429	344
59,295	626	390	247	715	493	395
68,289	721	449	285	823	567	455
73,967	781	486	308	891	615	493
76,570	809	503	319	923	636	510
77,965	824	512	325	940	648	520
78,082	825	513	325	941	649	521
92,083	973	605	384	1,110	765	614
103,187	1,090	678	430	1,244	857	688
103,276	1,091	679	430	1,245	858	689
148,237	1,566	974	618	1,787	1,232	988
155,929	1,647	1,025	650	1,879	1,296	1,040
184,166	1,945	1,210	767	2,220	1,530	1,228
191,424	2,022	1,258	798	2,307	1,591	1,276
206,373	2,180	1,356	860	2,487	1,715	1,376
206,552	2,182	1,357	861	2,489	1,716	1,377
296,474	3,132	1,948	1,235	3,573	2,463	1,976
382,848	4,044	2,516	1,595	4,614	3,181	2,552
412,746	4,360	2,713	1,720	4,975	3,430	2,752
592,947	6,263	3,897	2,471	7,146	4,927	3,953
765,697	8,088	5,032	3,190	9,228	6,362	5,105

Explanation of Table. Withdrawals are assumed to be made at the beginning of each month with interest compounded monthly on the remaining funds invested at either 5 or 8 percent interest. Results are rounded to the nearest whole dollar. All calculations and amounts are before taxes. It is intended that this table be used with the table How Money Grows on page 642 (i.e., first obtain the amount accumulated from How Money Grows, then enter this table). See explanation at the bottom of page 642.

MEDICAL EXPENSE PROGRAMS

A variety of medical expense programs are available, each with unique features, benefits and tax implications. This chart provides an overview of their essential characteristics.

Health Reimbursement Arrangement HRA

This is an "arrangement"; it is not an account. Allows tax-free reimbursement to employees for qualified health care expenses, including the employee's purchase of health insurance (e.g., long-term care premiums). Plans are either insured or self-insured. Governed by IRC Section 105, it is funded and owned by the employer.

Formal guidance from the IRS allows a carryover of unused amounts to later years. Not available to the self-employed.

See Health Reimbursements Arrangements chart, page 257.

Flexible Spending Account FSA

A health FSA allows employees to make pre-tax contributions to an account to pay for health care expenses or their share of health insurance premiums (dependent care FSAs allow payment of qualifying child care expenses). Reimbursement for over-the-counter drugs is not allowed. Governed by IRC Section 125.

Can only be set up by employers (not available to the self-employed). Typically included under cafeteria plans, but may stand-alone. Any unused balance is forfeited at the end of the year (the infamous use-it-or-lose-it provision).

See Cafeteria Plans, page 303.

Health Savings Account HSA

The HSA is similar to the now outdated Medical Savings Account (MSA), but without the restrictions or limits on participation. Any "eligible individual" with a "high deductible health plan" can contribute. Generally allows reimbursement for "qualified medical expenses," to include long-term care insurance premiums but not over-the-counter drugs. May be included under cafeteria plans. Governed by new IRC Section 223. Contributions may be invested like IRAs (e.g., in stocks and bonds). Undistributed amounts may be carried forward.

See Health Savings Accounts chart, page 261.

Consumer-Directed Health Plan

Also referred to as a "Consumer-Driven" Health Plan, this is a catch-all term that can include Health Reimbursement Arrangement (HRAs), Flexible Spending Accounts (FSAs), and Health Savings Accounts (HSAs).

DISABILITY STATISTICS

Odds This Year For Different Risks Covered By Insurance

1 out of 5 that your auto will be damaged in an accident (National Safety Council).

1 out of 21 that you will have a disabling accident (National Safety Council).

1 out of 96 that you will have a fire (National Safety Council).

1 out of 114 that you will die (World Almanac).

Income Lost Through Disability Is

2 times as great as *auto* accident losses.

3 times as great as *fire* losses.

Risk of Disability Is Substantially Greater Than Risk Of Death (Male)

At age 30, long-term disability is 4.0 times more likely than death.

At age 40, long-term disability is 2.9 times more likely than death.

At age 50, long-term disability is 2.3 times more likely than death.

Risk Of Disability Within Groups Of People

The following chart indicates the odds of at least one long-term (90-day) disability occurring before age 65 to any one person out of one, two, or three persons.

	Chances out of 1,000 of Disability Occurring Prior to Age 65		
Age of Each Person	To Any One Person	To Any One Person out of Any Two People	To Any One Person out of Any Three People
30	467	716	849
35	451	699	835
40	430	675	815
45	401	641	785
50	360	590	738

From the chart we can conclude, for example, that 43 percent of all people age 40 will have a long-term disability prior to age 65.

Long-Term Disabilities

If a long-term (90-day) disability has lasted two years, it will probably continue longer – even for life.

Age When Disabled For 90 Days	Percentage Of People Still Disabled At End Of 2 Years And 90 Days	Percentage Of People Still Disabled At End Of 5 Years And 90 Days
25	63.5%	44.2%
35	69.7	52.6
45	73.6	58.0
55	77.6	59.6

Source: Figures based upon Commissioners Disability Table and Commissioners 1980 Standard Ordinary Mortality Table.

DISABILITY INCOME - TAX CONSIDERATIONS

	PREMIUM PAYMENTS Income Tax Effects As To		PROCEEDS Income Tax Effects As To	
	Employer	Insured	Employer	Insured
NONCONTRIBUTORY PLANS				
Employer pays premium	deductible IRC §162(a)		no effect	
Insured owns policy receives benefit		not taxable IRC §106(a)		taxable
Employer pays premium owns policy receives benefit	not deductible IRC §265		proceeds subject to corporate AMT (see pages 327-329) but deductible when paid to employee	
Insured receives benefit		not taxable IRC §106(a)		taxable when received from employer
CONTRIBUTORY PLAN				
Employer pays part of each premium	deductible IRC §162(a)		no effect	
Insured owns policy pays balance of premium receives benefit		not taxable on employer's contribution		taxable on amount attributable to employer contribution but not taxable on amount attributable to own contribution
NO PLAN NECESSARY				
Employer pays bonus to insured	deductible IRC §162(a)		no effect	
Insured pays premium owns policy receives benefit		taxable as salary IRC §61		not taxable IRC§104(a)(3)

Note: Insured is assumed to be an employee (not partner or sole proprietor).

CODE CRIB SHEET

A Listing of Selected Code Provisions

Code Section	Description	2019 Field Guide Page	2019 Tax Facts Question
22	Credits for the permanently disabled.	344	757
25A	Hope and lifetime learning credit.	314-315, 634	759
55	Alternative minimum tax (Section 56 provides for ACE adjustment).	327	767
61	Gross income defined.	232, 646	654, 717
72	Annuities; living proceeds of endowment and life insurance contracts - income tax treatment.	42, 102, 518	8, 29, 65, 495-649
83	Taxation of property transferred in connection with performance of services – substantial risk of forfeiture.	126, 280, 477, 518, 540, 553	295, 3536, 3562, 3608, 4015
101	Certain death benefits - exclusion of life insurance death benefits from income (includes transfer for value rules). Includes the treatment of employer-owned life insurance under Code section 101(j).	98, 291, 319, 321, 423, 447-448, 568	54, 57, 63, 65, 77, 79, 153, 276, 282, 285, 289, 299, 307, 315
102	Gifts and inheritances - exclusion from income.	18, 20, 50	654
104	Compensation for injuries or sickness.	252, 256, 342, 646	226-228, 387
105	Amounts received under accident and health plans.	252, 256, 342, 646	332-345
106	Contributions by employer to accident and health plans.	252, 256, 646	332, 347-348
125	Cafeteria plans.	303, 644	3501-3515
127	Educational assistance programs.	634	693
135	Income from United States bonds used to pay higher education tuition and fees.	633	7685
162	Trade or business expenses - deductibility.	232, 576, 634, 646	262, 264, 272
163	Interest - deductibility.	409, 494	30, 731, 734
170	Charitable contributions and gifts - deductibility.	58, 308, 309	120-125, 739, 8091
221	Interest on education loans.	314, 634	734

Note: This table contains selected citations to *Tax Facts on Insurance & Employee Benefits (2019)* and *Tax Facts on Investments (2019)*. A complete listing of citations to IRC Sections is contained on pages 771 and 625 of those publications, respectively.

Code Section	Description	2019 Field Guide Page	2019 Tax Facts Question
222	Qualified tuition and related expenses.	634	689, 8040
223	Health and Medical Savings Accounts.	260	397-429
264	Business life insurance - premiums not deductible but policy loan interest deductible within strict limits.	467	3, 30, 129-130, 262, 264, 274, 437
265	Expenses and interest relating to tax-exempt income.	342, 646	385, 387
302	Distributions in redemption of stock.	170, 186, 197	300-301
303	Distributions in redemption of stock to pay death taxes - partial stock redemptions.	194, 198, 536	303, 308
306	Dispositions of certain stock - tax treatment of stock received as a dividend pursuant to a recapitalization.	214, 537	303
318	Constructive ownership of stock -attribution.	170, 218	300, 303
368	Definitions relating to corporate reorganizations - recapitalizations.	214, 369	290
401	Qualified pension, profit sharing and stock bonus plans - including Section 401(k) plans.	264, 268, 296, 306, 339, 360, 470, 502, 513, 534, 562	140, 3717, 3720, 3726, 3733-3734, 3736-3742, 3749, 3752-3798, 3810, 3820, 3827-3882, 3901-3906, 3916, 3934
402(b)	Taxability of beneficiary of nonexempt trust.	540	3530-3532, 3537
402(e)(4)	Net unrealized appreciation.	471	3960
402A	Elective deferrals as Roth contributions in 401(k) plans.	526	3771-3779
403(b)	Taxation of annuities purchased by Section 501(c)(3) organizations and public schools.	272, 275	3994, 4019, 4021-4030, 4039-4040, 4044, 4062, 4075-4077
408	Individual retirement accounts and annuities.	264, 405, 411, 548-549, 567, 628, 631, 632	3638, 3649, 3653, 3666, 3668, 3679, 3697, 3702
408(q)	Deemed IRA.	-	3642, 3771, 3779
408A	Roth IRAs.	527, 528, 61-632	3651-3662, 3670

Note: This table contains selected citations to *Tax Facts on Insurance & Employee Benefits (2019)* and *Tax Facts on Investments (2019)*. A complete listing of citations to IRC Sections is contained on pages 771 and 665 of those publications, respectively.

Code Section	Description	2019 Field Guide Page	2019 Tax Facts Question
409A	Nonqualified deferred compensation plans deferral and distribution rules.	322, 514, 538	3539, 3562, 3565
410-412	Minimum participation, vesting, and funding standards - qualified plans.	264, 268, 276, 627	3724, 3726-3731, 3742-3747, 3753, 3831-3838, 3853
415	Limitations on benefits and contributions under qualified plans.	264, 627	3652, 3742, 3820, 3853, 3922, 4025
419	Treatment of funded welfare benefit plans.	569	4075-4077
453	Installment method of reporting income.	38, 406, 542	670
457	Deferred compensation plans of state and local governments and tax-exempt organizations.	280	3579-3600
483	Interest on certain deferred payments.	406	670, 903
501	Exemption from tax on corporations, certain trusts, etc. – includes religious, charitable, scientific and educational organizations.	272, 275	3530, 3579, 4020
529	Qualified tuition programs.	313, 539, 634	689-691, 854, 913
530	Coverdell Education Savings Accounts.	330, 634	683, 689
531	Accumulated earnings tax.	294	787
541	Personal holding company tax.	487	787
664	Charitable remainder trusts.	58, 299	8073-8075
671-677	Grantor trust rules.	393	119
691	Income in respect of decedents.	17, 403	748, 3962-3964
701-761	Partnerships.	210, 481	311, 318, 320, 322, 802-803, 945
1001	Determination of amount and recognition of gain or loss.	563	387, 573
1014	Basis of property acquired from a decedent (stepped-up).	556	305, 694
1015	Basis of property acquired by gifts and transfers in trust.	50	694, 696
1035	Certain exchanges of insurance policies – tax-free exchange of life insurance and annuity contracts.	563	573

Note: This table contains selected citations to *Tax Facts on Insurance & Employee Benefits (2019)* and *Tax Facts on Investments (2019)*. A complete listing of citations to IRC Sections is contained on pages 771 and 665 of those publications, respectively.

Code Section	Description	2019 Field Guide Page	2019 Tax Facts Question
1041	Transfer of property incident to divorce.	347	79, 106, 599
1202	Gain from small business stock.	-	654, 7522
1361	S corporation defined.	531	794
2001	Imposition and rate of estate tax.	14, 582	-
2002	Executor's liability for payment of estate tax.	336	164
2010	Unified credit against estate tax.	14, 582	871
2014	Foreign death tax credit.	473	871
2032	Alternate valuation - six months after death.	372, 556	322, 927
2032A	Valuation of certain farms and other real property.	518	322, 926
2033	Property in which the decedent had an interest - transfers at death.	14	623, 834
2035	Adjustments for gifts made within 3 years of decedent's death - transfers of life insurance.	54, 98, 374	81, 96, 99, 224
2036	Transfers with retained life estate - power to designate possession or enjoyment of property.	375, 493	183, 834
2037	Transfers taking effect at death.	375	99, 834
2038	Revocable transfers - retention of power to revoke interest in property includes value in the estate.	375, 610	178, 834
2039	Annuities - taxation of surviving beneficiary's interest.	42	100, 627, 629, 635, 857, 3502, 3709
2040	Joint interests - including co-tenancies with right of survivorship.	10	842
2041	Powers of appointment - general power of appointment.	459, 493	181, 201, 204, 206, 834
2042	Proceeds of life insurance - payable to estate or in which decedent had incidents of ownership.	99, 374	81-82, 85-92, 96, 175, 318-321, 325, 834
2044	Certain property for which marital deduction was previously allowed - qualified terminable interest.	30, 459	181, 202, 857
2053	Expenses, indebtedness, and taxes – allowable deductions for claims against the estate.	10, 14, 584	857-861
2054	Losses - those deductible from taxable estate	584	860

Note: This table contains selected citations to *Tax Facts on Insurance & Employee Benefits (2019)* and *Tax Facts on Investments (2019)*. A complete listing of citations to IRC Sections is contained on pages 771 and 665 of those publications, respectively.

Code Section	Description	2019 Field Guide Page	2019 Tax Facts Question
2055	Transfers for public, charitable, and religious uses - estate tax charitable deduction.	57, 308-309	126, 857
2056	Bequests to surviving spouse - estate tax marital deduction.	18, 20, 459	191-192, 857
2056A	Qualified domestic trust.	509	857
2206	Recovery by executor of estate taxes on life insurance proceeds.	17	94
2207A	Recovery by decedent's estate of estate taxes on certain marital deduction property.	17	-
2503	Present interest gifts - including gifts in trust for minors.	50, 332, 571, 610	160, 222, 903, 915
2514	Powers of appointment (including lapse of Crummey power).	57, 332	159-162, 915
2518	Disclaimers.	346	850, 905
2522	Charitable and similar gifts.	58, 308-309	127, 923
2523	Gift tax marital deduction.	459	587, 903, 922
2601-2604	Generation-skipping transfers.	34	884-901
2701-2704	Also known as Chapter 14.		
2701	Special valuation rules in case of transfers of certain interests in corporations or partnerships.	166, 214, 371	944-948, 954
2702	Special valuation rules in case of transfers of interest in trusts.	65, 371, 394, 511	948
2703	Special valuation rules (e.g., with regard to buy/sell agreements certain rights and restrictions disregarded).	371	953-954
2704	Treatment of certain lapsing rights and restrictions.	371	834, 954
6018	Estate tax returns - generally must be filed if gross estate exceeds applicable exclusion amount.	14	877-879
6075	Time for filing estate and gift tax returns.	14	877, 925
6166	Extension of time for payment of estate tax where estate consists largely of interest in closely held business (14 2/3 years).	336	877

Note: This table contains selected citations to *Tax Facts on Insurance & Employee Benefits (2019)* and *Tax Facts on Investments (2019)*. A complete listing of citations to IRC Sections is contained on pages 771 and 665 of those publications, respectively.

Code Section	Description	2019 Field Guide Page	2019 Tax Facts Question
6324	Special liens for estate and gift taxes.	14, 336	164, 210
6531	Statute of limitations on criminal prosecutions.	484	-
6651	Failure to file return or pay tax.	484	-
6663	Penalty for fraud.	484	-
7206	Concealment of goods to evade taxes, including false statement, is a felony.	299, 484	-
7520	Valuation tables for valuing life estates, remainder interests, and private annuities.	65, 496	932
7702	Life insurance contract defined – guideline premium requirements.	424	10-20, 63, 69, 153
7702A	Modified endowment contract defined.	423	10-20, 69, 143
7702B	Long-term care.	114, 510	477-494
7872	Treatment of loans with below-market interest rates.	410	666, 903

Note: This table contains selected citations to *Tax Facts on Insurance & Employee Benefits (2019)* and *Tax Facts on Investments (2019)*. A complete listing of citations to IRC Sections is contained on pages 771 and 665 of those publications, respectively.

INDEX

(References in parentheses are to footnotes. All other references are to page numbers)

(References in parentheses are to footnotes. All other references are to page numbers)

(References in parentheses are to footnotes. All other references are to page numbers)

(References in parentheses are to footnotes. All other references are to page numbers)

(References in parentheses are to footnotes. All other references are to page numbers)

(References in parentheses are to footnotes. All other references are to page numbers)

(References in parentheses are to footnotes. All other references are to page numbers)

(References in parentheses are to footnotes. All other references are to page numbers)

(References in parentheses are to footnotes. All other references are to page numbers)

(References in parentheses are to footnotes. All other references are to page numbers)

(References in parentheses are to footnotes. All other references are to page numbers)

(References in parentheses are to footnotes. All other references are to page numbers)

(References in parentheses are to footnotes. All other references are to page numbers)

(References in parentheses are to footnotes. All other references are to page numbers)

(References in parentheses are to footnotes. All other references are to page numbers)

(References in parentheses are to footnotes. All other references are to page numbers)

(References in parentheses are to footnotes. All other references are to page numbers)

(References in parentheses are to footnotes. All other references are to page numbers)

(References in parentheses are to footnotes. All other references are to page numbers)

(References in parentheses are to footnotes. All other references are to page numbers)

(References in parentheses are to footnotes. All other references are to page numbers)

(References in parentheses are to footnotes. All other references are to page numbers)

(References in parentheses are to footnotes. All other references are to page numbers)

(References in parentheses are to footnotes. All other references are to page numbers)

(References in parentheses are to footnotes. All other references are to page numbers)

(References in parentheses are to footnotes. All other references are to page numbers)

(References in parentheses are to footnotes. All other references are to page numbers)

(References in parentheses are to footnotes. All other references are to page numbers)

(References in parentheses are to footnotes. All other references are to page numbers)

(References in parentheses are to footnotes. All other references are to page numbers)

(References in parentheses are to footnotes. All other references are to page numbers)

(References in parentheses are to footnotes. All other references are to page numbers)

(References in parentheses are to footnotes. All other references are to page numbers)

(References in parentheses are to footnotes. All other references are to page numbers)

(References in parentheses are to footnotes. All other references are to page numbers)

(References in parentheses are to footnotes. All other references are to page numbers)

(References in parentheses are to footnotes. All other references are to page numbers)

(References in parentheses are to footnotes. All other references are to page numbers)

(References in parentheses are to footnotes. All other references are to page numbers)

(References in parentheses are to footnotes. All other references are to page numbers)

(References in parentheses are to footnotes. All other references are to page numbers)

(References in parentheses are to footnotes. All other references are to page numbers)

(References in parentheses are to footnotes. All other references are to page numbers)

(References in parentheses are to footnotes. All other references are to page numbers)

(References in parentheses are to footnotes. All other references are to page numbers)

(References in parentheses are to footnotes. All other references are to page numbers)

(References in parentheses are to footnotes. All other references are to page numbers)

(References in parentheses are to footnotes. All other references are to page numbers)

(References in parentheses are to footnotes. All other references are to page numbers)

(References in parentheses are to footnotes. All other references are to page numbers)

(References in parentheses are to footnotes. All other references are to page numbers)

(References in parentheses are to footnotes. All other references are to page numbers)

(References in parentheses are to footnotes. All other references are to page numbers)

(References in parentheses are to footnotes. All other references are to page numbers)

(References in parentheses are to footnotes. All other references are to page numbers)

(References in parentheses are to footnotes. All other references are to page numbers)

(References in parentheses are to footnotes. All other references are to page numbers)

(References in parentheses are to footnotes. All other references are to page numbers)

(References in parentheses are to footnotes. All other references are to page numbers)

(References in parentheses are to footnotes. All other references are to page numbers)

(References in parentheses are to footnotes. All other references are to page numbers)

(References in parentheses are to footnotes. All other references are to page numbers)

(References in parentheses are to footnotes. All other references are to page numbers)

(References in parentheses are to footnotes. All other references are to page numbers)